System Requirements

- ■ IBM PC or compatible Intel 80386SX machine or higher.

- ■ 3.5MB of hard disk space.

- ■ A 3.5-inch floppy disk drive.

- ■ MS-DOS 5 or higher and 640K of RAM memory for Dual Module Player and DMP Companion.

- ■ Microsoft Windows 3.1 and 4MB of RAM memory for the Windows programs.

- ■ Sound Blaster, Sound Blaster Pro, Sound Blaster 16, or 100% compatible sound card.

- ■ A mouse is necessary for the Windows programs.

- ■ For VoiceAssist, a microphone is required.

WARNING: BEFORE OPENING THE DISK PACKAGE PROVIDED WITH THIS BOOK, CAREFULLY READ THE TERMS AND CONDITIONS OF THE DISK WARRANTY THAT FOLLOWS.

Disk Warranty

This software is protected by both United States copyright law and international copyright treaty provision. You must treat this software just like a book, except that you may copy it into a computer to be used and you may make archival copies of the software for the sole purpose of backing up our software and protecting your investment from loss. By saying, "just like a book," Osborne/McGraw-Hill means, for example, that this software may be used by any number of people and may be freely moved from one computer location to another, so long as there is no possibility of its being used at one location or on one computer while it is being used at another. Just as a book cannot be read by two different people in two different places at the same time, neither can the software be used by two different people in two different places at the same time (unless, of course, Osborne's copyright is being violated).

Limited Warranty

Osborne/McGraw-Hill warrants the physical diskette(s) enclosed herein to be free of defects in materials and workmanship for a period of sixty days from the purchase date. If Osborne/McGraw-Hill receives written notification within the warranty period of defects in materials or workmanship, and such notification is determined by Osborne/McGraw-Hill to be correct, Osborne/McGraw-Hill will replace the defective diskette(s).

The entire and exclusive liability and remedy for breach of this Limited Warranty shall be limited to replacement of defective diskettes(s) and shall not include or extend to any claim for or right to cover any other damages, including but not limited to, loss of profit, data, or use of the software, or special, incidental, or consequential damages or other similar claims, even if Osborne/McGraw-Hill has been specifically advised of the possibility of such damages. In no event will Osborne/McGraw-Hill's liability for any damages to you or any other person ever exceed the lower of the suggested list price or actual price paid for the license to use the software, regardless of any form of the claim.

OSBORNE, A DIVISION OF McGRAW-HILL, INC., SPECIFICALLY DISCLAIMS ALL OTHER WARRANTIES, EXPRESS OR IMPLIED, INCLUDING BUT NOT LIMITED TO, ANY IMPLIED WARRANTY OF MERCHANTABILITY OR FITNESS FOR A PARTICULAR PURPOSE. Specifically, Osborne/McGraw-Hill makes no representation or warranty that the software is fit for any particular purpose, and any implied warranty of merchantability is limited to the sixty-day duration of the Limited Warranty covering the physical diskette(s) only (and not the software), and is otherwise expressly and specifically disclaimed.

This limited warranty gives you specific legal rights; you may have others which may vary from state to state. Some states do not allow the exclusion of incidental or consequential damages, or the limitation on how long an implied warranty lasts, so some of the above may not apply to you.

Sound Blaster:
The Official Book,
Second Edition

Peter M. Ridge, David M. Golden,
Ivan Luk, and Scott Sindorf

Osborne **McGraw-Hill**

Berkeley New York St. Louis San Francisco Auckland Bogotá Hamburg London Madrid Mexico City
Milan Montreal New Delhi Panama City Paris São Paulo Singapore Sydney Tokyo Toronto

Osborne **McGraw-Hill**
2600 Tenth Street
Berkeley, California 94710
U.S.A.

For information on software, translations, or book distributors
outside of the U.S.A., please write to Osborne McGraw-Hill at the
above address.

Sound Blaster: The Official Book, Second Edition

1234567890 DOC 9987654

ISBN 0-07-882000-6

Series Design: Seventeenth Street Studios

CONTENTS AT A GLANCE

HARDWARE AND
SOFTWARE
ENHANCEMENTS

SOUND BLASTER
PROGRAMMING

CONTENTS

**SOUND BLASTER
SOFTWARE**

5   Windows Applications   **111**

HARDWARE AND
SOFTWARE
ENHANCEMENTS

SOUND BLASTER PROGRAMMING

IV

Acknowledgments

It's commonly believed that the first edition of a book is the hardest to produce and that subsequent editions are simple add-ons. In the case of *Sound Blaster: The Official Book, Second Edition*, it was quite the opposite. Since sound technology is constantly changing, this book required a lot of work to ensure that it contained all of the latest information.

However, we could not accomplish this feat alone and would like to take this opportunity to give special thanks to the people that helped make this book possible.

From the various departments at Creative Labs:

- Deane Rettig, for bringing his knowledge of MIDI music composition to the chapter on Cakewalk Apprentice for Windows and Steve Ouimette for letting us include one of his cool .WRK files.

- Tom Bouril, Dave Hubbard, and Douglas Kaden, for their hard work to bring source code examples to all you programmers out there.

- Craig Lemas, for gathering the invaluable advice and tips from Creative's technical support group.

- Theresa Pulido, Steffanee White, and Gail Pomerantz, for providing photographs, product information, and support from the Marketing Department.

And at Osborne/McGraw-Hill:

- Cindy Brown, Bill Pollock, and Bob Myren for pulling the book together. Wasn't it fun?

- Sally Zahner, Carl Wikander, and Linda Medoff for making sure that everything ended up on the page correctly and that we crossed our t's, dotted our i's, and used proper English.

Introduction

After the success of the first edition of *Sound Blaster: The Official Book*, we sought to improve upon it based on feedback from readers like you. With this second edition, we reorganized the book and added many valuable chapters and information not found in other books. Since computer technology changes and improves rapidly, we've expanded our coverage to include the latest offerings from Creative Labs. But unlike other books, we didn't remove coverage of earlier Sound Blaster versions because we know that many of you still have your original Sound Blaster. As a result, this is by far the most up-to-date and comprehensive book available on the Sound Blaster family of sound cards.

This book is very different from the all-too-typical computer book that rewrites the manufacturer's manual, providing little more than extra pictures, fancy formatting, and a few tips, not to mention sparse and often inaccurate diagrams of the hardware. Since this is the only book specifically endorsed by Creative Labs, we have been privileged to have worked very closely with them to ensure technical accuracy. In fact, two of the authors of this book are Creative Labs engineers.

This second edition of *Sound Blaster: The Official Book* is loaded with valuable hints, tips, and information for every Sound Blaster user—whether you're a game enthusiast, a business person interested in multimedia, or a programmer who wishes to program the Sound Blaster. We've plugged the gaps in your *Sound Blaster User Reference Manual* by delivering a wealth of information not found in your manual, including previously unavailable information about the Sound Blaster and its software—information that you won't find anywhere else.

In this introduction, we'll look at the short history of sound on the PC and the emergence of Creative Labs as a strong leader in this field. We'll then continue with the organization of this book, followed by descriptions of the carefully selected programs included on the disk that accompanies *Sound Blaster: The Official Book*.

A SHORT HISTORY LESSON

Even prior to the recent burst of interest in sound cards, the PC wasn't silent. The first IBM PC could produce clicks and beeps out of its 50-cent speaker, and it could generate enough tones to play simple melodies. However, this early sound can hardly be called music, nor could it produce intelligible speech or decent sound effects.

Soon after the PC was introduced in 1981, various musicians and PC enthusiasts noted this poverty of sound. A personal computer should be able to make better sounds—after all, other computers, including the Atari, Apple, and Commodore, could play a decent tune. In these early years, a few sound cards for musicians and very simple speech synthesizers did appear, but none became particularly popular.

Games Galore

Sound card sales accelerated in the late 1980s and began to really take off in 1990, driven by skyrocketing sales of game software. Once PCs with color graphics became affordable and started becoming commonplace in the home, computer games would inevitably catch on. Multimedia is hyped as the next wave in business computing, and sound cards are frequently purchased for this reason, but most people buy sound cards for "edutainment"—education and entertainment—reasons. An estimated 90 percent of sound cards are used primarily for adding sound to games.

Computerized Music and MIDI

Electronic music and computer-based score production had existed for decades, and blossomed in the 1970s, but the equipment was so expensive that only academics and crazed artists could experience it. At that time, a lack of standards created anarchy. If you bought a keyboard synthesizer from one company, you couldn't connect it to the drum module of a second company, or the keyboard synthesizer from a third. This incompatibility had a chilling effect on instrument sales, because once you started buying equipment from one company, you were locked into that company. In 1981, a group of musical instrument companies came together to bring coherence to the industry.

By 1982, the Musical Instrument Digital Interface (MIDI, pronouced "middy") standard for musical instruments was published by the International MIDI Association (IMA). This standard ensured that all instruments and sequencers, whether manufactured by Korg, Roland, Yamaha, or some other company, could all talk to each other. Consumer acceptance was so strong that in a few years MIDI became an unchallenged music industry standard.

Along with this acceptance came the need for MIDI interface cards to turn the PC into the control center for an entire studio. Musicians discovered that blending computer technology and MIDI music technology revealed a wonderful new musical universe. With a computer that "talks MIDI" they could play MIDI instruments such as a keyboard synthesizer or drum machine, record the notes, modify the composition, and then replay and even print the score on paper.

The Emergence of AdLib

The card that truly began to blast sound from the PC (at least in the Western World) was the AdLib card. When the relatively inexpensive AdLib sound card was launched in August 1987, this novelty was greeted with skeptical curiosity by the still nascent PC game software industry. A few software games made use of the AdLib card even though hardly anyone possessed one of these cards. A turning point came when Taito of America, a major software publisher at that time, decided to put its support behind the AdLib card. People playing the Taito games were amazed at how much more fun a computer game could be with the special effects and music provided by the FM synthesizer on the AdLib card. Soon the word spread near and far that anyone who took games seriously absolutely had to buy one of these AdLib cards. The software game industry was revolutionized, and the sound card industry followed in quick pursuit.

AdLib, a Canadian company, held a virtual monopoly on the game card market from 1987 to 1989. AdLib wasn't the sole source of these sound cards. Competitors hoping to cash in on this new market showed up from all over, but they all made the same mistake: No one wanted to "share" this burgeoning market with AdLib. Since engineers have a very difficult time restraining their creative juices, a lot of "new and improved" sound cards appeared on the market. They were interesting products but were incompatible with the games already published for the AdLib card.

Game developers showed little interest in these new products. Each new card required laborious customization of the game software on the part of the game developers. This expensive programming effort scarcely seemed worthwhile, since AdLib sold many cards while the other manufacturers collectively sold a relative few. This situation changed dramatically in November 1989, when Creative Labs released its Sound Blaster card. Not just another competitor, Sound Blaster was different: It was fully AdLib-compatible—and more.

In Steps Creative

Creative isn't exactly a new kid on the block. The mother company, Creative Technology, founded by then-26-year-old Sim Wong Hoo in 1981, has become one of Singapore's biggest success stories. He is the Bill Gates of Singapore and one of the richest and most famous young entrepreneurs in his country.

Sim began with a dream of designing and producing the first computer in his native country, Singapore. An electrical engineering graduate from the local Ngee Ann Polytechnic University, his first encounter with a computer was on a TRS-80. He was hooked, and started building add-ons for the TRS-80 after purchasing a set of manuals. It took some effort, but by 1984, Sim raised enough capital to release the Cubic 99 personal computer. It was not only a computer that was compatible with both CP/M and Apple (which in itself was a notable achievement), but one with a sound card—capable of speaking Chinese. By 1986, Creative Technology had finished work on a more advanced computer, the Cubic CT. Few realize now, or knew back then, but Sim had actually created the first multimedia computer before anyone had any idea what "multimedia" meant.

The computers from Creative Technology, while technologically advanced, were a marketing failure. Computer salesmen couldn't effectively explain or sell the Cubic 99 nor the Cubic CT. The IBM PC was by then the predominant standard—and selling another IBM PC clone in a crowded market was not an attractive alternative for Creative. Then a light bulb came on, and Sim correctly deduced that what he needed to do was to sell the element of advanced technology that was found in his computers to millions of IBM PC users—the sound card. The Creative Music System (CMS) was the product of this idea, and was first introduced in Singapore. CMS was an add-on card for IBM PCs and compatibles which synthesized, or emulated, the sound of 12 different musical instruments. Ironically, the CMS was actually released at about the same time (albeit in Singapore) that the AdLib was released in the United States. After much success in Singapore and other parts of the world, Sim left Creative Technology in the hands of his partners and headed stateside.

Coming to America

From a small office in South San Francisco, Sim formed what is known today as Creative Labs, Inc. Creative Labs launched the Creative Music System in the U.S. in August 1988 under the name Game Blaster. After talking with distributors and trying the mail order/direct mail route, he hit the gold mine when he convinced the leading game software companies at that time, Broderbund Software and Activision, to support the use of music via the Game Blaster. However, the AdLib card was already well on its way to market dominance after having beat the Game Blaster to the U.S. market by about a year.

On the surface, the Game Blaster seemed able to compete with AdLib. It could play 12 instruments simultaneously in stereo, while AdLib could play just 11 instruments in monaural, single-speaker sound. The crucial factor proved to be competing music technologies. Game Blaster used an old synthesis method to simulate musical instruments, while AdLib used newer technology, pioneered at Stanford University and quickly picked up by Yamaha and other musical instrument manufacturers, called FM (frequency modulation) synthesis. You're already familiar with FM, the technique used to broadcast FM radio signals. FM creates better instrument sounds than the older synthesis technique used by the Game Blaster. As a result, the Game Blaster, even in stereo, didn't sound as good as the AdLib in mono, and the Game Blaster quickly became a footnote in sound card history.

After the Game Blaster fiasco, Sim began work on a new project, code-named the Killer Card, that went on to become Sound Blaster. Sim went back to the drawing board after first interviewing the leaders in the game industry to find out what they wanted. This time, he decided to design a sound card that could be used with all the software designed for AdLib. Sim reasoned that just building a compatible card wouldn't be enough to take on AdLib, so he endowed the new card with extra features. He added a joystick port, a MIDI interface, and circuitry for digital audio. The card's digital audio circuitry both recorded and played speech, music, and sound effects from disk. The Killer Card provided not just music, but added sounds like "man overboard," explosions, and all the booms, bangs, and zaps we now take for granted in arcade and computer games.

Blasting the Competition

The Sound Blaster was introduced at the Fall 1989 COMDEX computer show in Las Vegas. Sim did not expect the 600 orders he would receive the week of the show. By February of 1990, Creative had begun shipping the Sound Blaster; and in another short six months, sales increased to over

10,000 units a month. The same venture capitalists who denied Sim the capital for his first computer project were now begging him to go public. When he did, it was a daring move and a big gamble, but he listed in NASDAQ instead of the Singapore or Hong Kong stock exchange favored by Asian investors. With nearly $500 million from market capitalization, Creative was set to remain the dominant force in the PC sound market for some time to come.

Building an AdLib-compatible card was a relatively easy task, since AdLib used the Yamaha 3812 integrated circuit, procured from Yamaha. Sound Blaster attracted many game players because of its built-in joystick port—the AdLib required the second purchase of a joystick card and the hassle of installing it in your PC. And Sound Blaster became the musician's choice for its built-in MIDI controller. As you can see, the Sound Blaster had all the ingredients for a commercial success. Compatible with the leading hardware and the installed base of game and music software, it offered more features and a better value, and—soon to become very important—it had proprietary digital audio technology that took some effort to copy.

You're probably wondering what happened to AdLib. They entered the sound card market at the perfect time and made a ton of money because of it. At first, AdLib wasn't very concerned about Creative Labs because AdLib had already designed their next generation sound card. Stereo sound and 12-bit digital audio, made it clearly superior over the new kid on the block, Sound Blaster. AdLib ran a very expensive advertising campaign, which stimulated considerable interest. Unfortunately for AdLib, there was one "minor" complication. They had nothing to sell. AdLib designed their sound card around the latest-and-greatest integrated circuits for sound, to be manufactured by a well-known semiconductor company. For over a year AdLib ran full-page advertisements in leading magazines, expecting to receive these crucial integrated circuits in the near future. As it turned out, by the time manufacture of these new circuits had been perfected, AdLib had run out of money.

THE EMERGENCE OF MULTIMEDIA

Creative Labs' success didn't go unnoticed, and both opportunities and storm clouds were on the horizon. The opportunities took the form of an effort by Microsoft, Tandy, Creative Labs, and others to define software and hardware standards for supporting multimedia on the PC. This effort culminated in November 1990 when the Microsoft Multimedia Conference published the specifications for the Multimedia PC (MPC). This standard is now known as the MPC Level 1 specification. The MPC Level 1 standards for a sound card were actually heavily based on the capabilities of the Sound Blaster card.

MPC Standards

The Multimedia Personal Computer (MPC) standard was created by the MPC Marketing Council. The council consists of, and was formed by, a number of hardware and software vendors including Microsoft and Creative Labs. The goal was to establish and license a standard that specifies the minimum requirements for an IBM PC-compatible computer to be considered multimedia-ready. To upgrade a typical PC to an MPC running Microsoft Windows 3 on a multimedia platform, the following must be added: a sound card, a CD-ROM drive, speakers, and Microsoft Windows software. The MPC council also specifies the minimum expected requirements for the computer's central processing unit (CPU), random access memory (RAM), video display, and disk storage.

The MPC logo is licensed only to hardware companies that sell complete multimedia PCs, to companies that provide upgrade kits that include both a sound card and CD-ROM drive, and to software companies whose software requires an MPC-compliant computer to run on. You most likely won't see the MPC logo on a CD-ROM drive alone. However, a CD-ROM drive does have to meet certain minimum criteria to qualify as an MPC-compliant drive.

There are currently two levels, or minimum performance standards, that have been established by the council: MPC Level 1, established in November 1990, and MPC Level 2, adopted in May 1993. The main difference between the two is performance—the Level 2 specifications require faster and improved hardware as compared to Level 1.

When Level 1 was first adopted, the standard specified a minimum of an 80286/12MHz computer. The council, finally acknowledging that this computer platform was inadequate, increased the minimum requirements for Level 1 to a more realistic 80386SX/16MHz computer. The current MPC specifications are summarized in Table 1-1. Feel free to buy better hardware than the minimum recommended for MPC Level 1 or 2. For example, a computer with an 80386 running at 40MHz is faster than either the 80386SX/16MHz or 80486SX/25MHz.

MPC Level 2 was introduced to keep up with the growth in hardware capabilities. This specification defines the hardware platform for the next generation of multimedia PCs designed to play back a video clip in a

320-by-240 window on your screen at 15 frames (images) per second. The key difference between Level 1 and Level 2 is the performance expected from the CD-ROM drive. While Level 1 requires a sustained data transfer rate of 150KB/sec (150 kilobytes or about 150,000 bytes per second), Level 2 requires at least a double speed drive with a sustained transfer rate of 300KB/sec. This means an MPC Level 2 CD-ROM drive can transfer information—such as screen images—into your computer twice as fast as an MPC Level 1 drive. You'll definitely notice this speed difference when you're using a multimedia application. MPC Level 2 is fully backward-compatible with MPC Level 1, which means you can use all MPC Level 1 CD-ROM disks and multimedia software with an MPC Level 2 multimedia system.

You should be aware that the MPC Council did not actually test products. Originally, the manufacturer simply paid a fixed fee for the right to use the logo and claim MPC compatibility. This changed when the Level 2 specification was approved. Now, all members are issued a set of test programs which they self-administer to ensure compatibility. The MPC standard has become a stamp of certification, which makes it more valuable than before.

CREATIVE LABS TODAY

Creative Labs did not rest on their laurels. Recognizing the imminent acceptance of CD-ROM as a storage device, the Sound Blaster Pro was created with a CD-ROM drive interface which the original Sound Blaster lacked. The Pro card also featured stereo music capability, an improvement from the monophonic Sound Blaster. Creative also started bundling CD-ROM drives with their sound cards. These multimedia upgrade kits are one of the most economical ways of upgrading your computer for multimedia.

Toward the end of 1992, Creative Labs introduced the Sound Blaster 16. This new card is the mainstay and technological tour-de-force from Creative Labs. It improves on the Sound Blaster Pro in many ways, including multiple versions that support various CD-ROM drives, the ability to record and play back 16-bit sound (as opposed to 8-bit), and the option of adding a high quality daughterboard (Wave Blaster) to further improve upon the music that can be produced with just the Sound Blaster card alone. A programmable on-board processor, the Advanced Signal Processor, allows the card to perform various sound enhancements not possible with the earlier Sound Blaster cards.

THE FUTURE

Visitors to the November 1993 Comdex computer show in Las Vegas were given a glimpse into the next generation of audio technology: the EMU8000 integrated audio digital signal processing chip from E-Mu Systems, Inc (E-Mu). E-Mu, founded in 1972 and now a wholly owned subsidiary of Creative Labs, is a leading manufacturer of digital sample-based musical instruments. E-Mu is regarded as a leader in the recording, musical instrument, and file/video post production industries. Based on their extensive experience with professional equipment, they have created a high-quality, low-cost chipset that combines the most important functions for music synthesis: wave-sample synthesis, full MIDI support, audio mixing, 32-voice polyphony, built-in audio filtering, and digital effects such as reverberation, chorus, digital equalization, panning, sample rate conversion, and pitch change.

This technology will appear as the state of the art in PC sound cards. Imagine all the things that make the Sound Blaster 16 a technological wonder: CD-quality digital audio, MPU-401 compatible MIDI port, built-in joystick port, and built-in CD-ROM interface (now with SCSI-2 support). Now, add the E-Mu EMU8000 with 1MB of sampled instruments sounds in read-only memory (ROM) and 512KB of random access memory (RAM), upgradable to 32MB, and you get great quality General MIDI support with the ability to add your own samples.

Also around the corner is the latest in speech synthesis (text-to-speech conversion) technology licensed exclusively from Digital Equipment Corporation (DEC). The DECtalk *speech engine*, a tightly written software module that's been optimized for speech synthesis, is regarded as the most natural-sounding text-to-speech engine created to date.

The new speech package, called TextAssist, not only sounds more natural than Monologue for Windows, but also offers many additional features including nine pre-defined voices, male and female, child and adult, all with excellent voice quality. You'll be able to add your own voices to match your personal tastes by adjusting parameters such as the pitch, phoneme duration, speed, and volume settings, as well as the physical characteristics of the voices.

For more in-depth discussion on these advances in audio technology, see Appendix A, "Advanced Sound Topics."

HOW THIS BOOK IS ORGANIZED

This book is divided into five parts so that you can easily dive into the material you are most interested in.

Part I provides an overview of the Sound Blaster family of cards, including both a history and a description of the newest member of the family: the Sound Blaster 16.

- Chapter 1 gives you a good foundation on the basics of sound with explanations of MIDI, General MIDI, FM synthesis, digital audio sampling, analog-to-digital and digital-to-analog conversion, and a host of other technical topics.

Part II, "The Sound Blaster Family," takes you inside the Sound Blaster cards for a little anatomy lesson so you will understand what's going on in your fancy piece of hardware. We explain and compare every member of the Sound Blaster family, down to a description of the jumpers, connectors, and most significant electronic circuitry.

- Chapter 2 covers the Sound Blaster 2.0 and the Sound Blaster Deluxe packages.

- Chapter 3 describes the Sound Blaster Pro, Sound Blaster Pro 2, and the Sound Blaster Pro Deluxe.

- Chapter 4 details the new features and capabilities of the Sound Blaster 16, Sound Blaster 16 SCSI-2, and Sound Blaster 16 MCD. There is also coverage of the Advanced Signal Processor and Wave Blaster upgrades.

Part III, "Sound Blaster Software," is everything you need to know to fully exploit the software programs provided with your sound card.

- Chapter 5 covers all the Windows software that comes with all the Sound Blaster cards.

- Chapter 6 follows up with descriptions of all the DOS-based applications and utilities.

- Chapter 7 is devoted to the two speech technologies supported by the Sound Blaster family: speech recognition and speech synthesis. Descriptions, highlights and invaluable tips on VoiceAssist and Monologue will help you make the most of these tools.

- Chapter 8 is a tutorial on the popular Cakewalk Apprentice for Windows, a full-featured MIDI sequencer. Learn all the tricks to making music files that incorporate synthesized and digitally recorded audio.

- Chapter 9 dives into facets of Sequencer Plus Pro, the MIDI sequencer software package that comes with the Creative Labs MIDI Kit. We have tried to cover the most common stumbling blocks for users of this MIDI music composition package.

Part IV, "Hardware and Software Enhancements," presents a concise summary of many leading software and hardware products that can be used with your Sound Blaster. This section should give you the background to ensure that you are satisfied with any speakers or additional software you have purchased for your sound card.

- Chapter 10 provides short descriptions of well-known third-party software programs that work with the Sound Blaster family. Both commercial products and less expensive shareware programs are described, and addresses and phone numbers are given so you can contact these companies.

- Chapter 11 presents a clear discussion of CD-ROM technology including topics such as MPC compliance, seek time, transfer rate, interface, etc. Using diagrams, you will learn the advantages and disadvantages of different CD-ROM drives that are compatible with the Panasonic or SCSI interface on the various Sound Blaster cards. The chapter will equip you with the knowledge required to make a good CD-ROM drive purchase.

- Chapter 12 provides tips on selecting the right speakers for use with the Sound Blaster cards. Topics such as frequency response and shielding are discussed thoroughly. The chapter includes mini-reviews of some of the more readily available speakers on the market designed for PC use.

- Chapter 13 provides information regarding some of the innovative peripheral products that can be used with the Sound Blaster cards. We will cover everything from steering wheels and flight control yokes to advanced joysticks featuring multiple buttons and a five-way switch hat.

Part V, "Sound Blaster Programming" and its accompanying chapter "Programming the Sound Blaster Family," provides clear instructions on how to write your own applications using the SBSIM programming interface. Source code examples are included that show you exactly how to do specific tasks such as playing and recording digital audio. The chapter also provides more experienced programmers with discussions on bypassing SBSIM and accessing Creative's drivers directly.

The Appendixes that follow Part V contain a wealth of reference information, including descriptions on earlier members of the Sound Blaster family and Technical Support from Creative Labs.

- Appendix A takes Chapter 1, "PC Sound Fundamentals," one step further and explores the more technical side of computer sound technologies, including the next generation sound card from Creative.

- Appendix B contains information on the Sound Blaster 1.0/1.5, Sound Blaster MCV, and Sound Blaster Pro MCV. This appendix serves as the library for information on older Sound Blaster cards that other books have dropped altogether.

- Appendix C supplements the installation chapter of the Sound Blaster User Reference Manual, providing a complete step-by-step guide for installing the sound card. If you have any problems with the card installation—or problems later on, when using your card—either Appendix C or Appendix D, the troubleshooting section, will come to your rescue.

- Appendix D covers the most common problems encountered with Sound Blaster ... and provides solutions, direct from the technical support staff at Creative Labs.

- Appendix E is your handbook to the most popular online services such as CompuServe and America Online. Learn about the resources available to Sound Blaster owners and how to join an online service.

- Appendix F provides a buyer's guide to other products offered by Creative Labs including speakers, MIDI kits, the Video Blaster, and Video Spigot.

- Appendix G describes the software and files included with this book. Get a taste of all the things your Sound Blaster can do with these applications and utilities.

TERMINOLOGY USED IN THIS BOOK

Some of the abbreviations and terms used in this book are also commonly used among Sound Blaster users. To alleviate confusion when encountering these terms, they are listed below with appropriate definitions. Please refer to this list if at any time you are unsure of the meaning of a term used in this book.

- Advanced Signal Processor: The chip upgrade for the Sound Blaster that allows the card to do computation-intensive work such as real-time compression/decompression and specialized sound processing.

- Digital Signal Processor: A chip that specializes in performing complex tasks on digital data such as digital audio. The Advanced Signal Processor is a digital signal processor.

- Digital Sound Processor: The chip on Sound Blaster cards that interprets all commands sent to the sound card.

- Creative: The Creative family of companies consisting of Creative Technology, Ltd. in Singapore and all its subsidiaries—Creative Labs, Inc. in California, E-Mu Systems, Inc. in California, ShareVision Technology, Inc. in California, Creative Labs U.K. in England, Creative Labs S.A. in France, Creative Labs GmbH in Germany, Avidtek Co., Ltd. in Taiwan, Beijing Newstone Multimedia Computer, Ltd. in Beijing, and Creative Multimedia K.K. in Japan.

- Creative Labs: Creative Labs, Inc. in Milpitas, California, a subsidiary of Creative Technology, Ltd.

- Creative Technology: The mother company Creative Technology, Ltd. located in Singapore. Creative Techology is listed on the NASDAQ stock market under the symbol CREAF.

- Sound Blaster: Sound Blaster 1.0, 1.5, 2.0. Also used generically in reference to any sound card in the Sound Blaster family.

- Sound Blaster Pro: Model CT1330. Also used generically in reference to both versions of the Sound Blaster Pro (CT1330 and CT1600).

- Sound Blaster Pro 2: Unofficial name for model CT1600 of the Sound Blaster Pro.

Abbreviations and Acronyms

- CSP: Creative Signal Processor. Acronym substitued for the Advanced Signal Processor chip. All drivers for the Advanced Signal Processor begin with CSP (e.g. CSP.SYS and CSPMAN.DLL) The obvious acronym ASP has been dropped due to a naming conflict between Creative and ASP Computers.

- DSP: In the case of Sound Blaster cards, this is the Digital Sound Processor. The industry-standard definition is Digital Signal Processor. (*See also* Digital Signal Processor and Digital Sound Processor.)

- IMA: International MIDI Association.

- MIDI: Musical Instrument Digital Interface.

- MPC: Multimedia PC.

- SB: Sound Blaster.

- SBP: Sound Blaster Pro.

- SBP2: Sound Blaster Pro 2.

- SB16: Sound Blaster 16.

- SB16CSP: Sound Blaster 16 with Advanced Signal Processing.

- SB16 Basic: Sound Blaster 16 without the software bundles of the SB16, SB16CSP, SB16MCD, and SB16SCSI packages.

- SB16MCD: Sound Blaster 16 MultiCD.

- SB16SCSI: Sound Blaster 16 SCSI-2.

- SBMCV: Sound Blaster Microchannel Version.

- SBPMCV: Sound Blaster Pro Microchannel Version.

- UART: Universal Asynchronous Receiver/Transmitter. A chip that sends and receives digital data. The serial port in the PC uses a UART as does the Sound Blaster MIDI port.

REACHING THE AUTHORS

We wouldn't put our name on something we don't believe in—and we believe that this is the best book for anyone looking to take full advantage of their Sound Blaster card. In our continuing efforts toward this objective, we invite your comments and suggestions. You can reach us by sending your letters to:

Osborne/McGraw-Hill
2600 Tenth Street
Berkeley, CA 94710
U.S.A.
Attn: Sound Blaster: The Official Book

Your feedback is very important to us. We want to provide you with the most useful and valuable book for your Sound Blaster card—you can help us do that. We look forward to hearing from you.

I

Fundamentals

1

Basics of Sound and the Sound Blaster

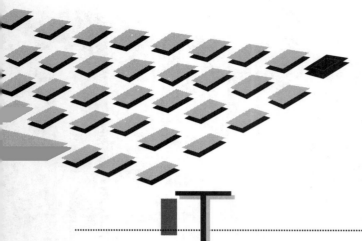

THIS chapter is designed to provide a quick but essential foundation for understanding the concepts and technologies underlying sound in your sound card. The first section, "Science of Sound," presents an introduction to the principles underlying sound and its perception (we'll spare you from dealing with formulas and math). We'll touch upon audio engineering, describing how the performance of audio equipment such as your sound card is measured. This background is not only interesting, but it's also useful for fully understanding the PC audio technology section that follows later in this chapter. Once you've got these concepts under your belt, you'll march into your computer or audio store with a new level of confidence.

The next major section in this chapter, "PC Audio Technologies," takes a different tack toward sound. It first talks about the audio technologies used to synthesize sounds created by musical instruments, such as a piano or flute. By knowing what's really going on when you're enjoying your Creative Labs sound card, you'll be in complete control of your software. Second, that section compares two technologies for synthesizing music: FM synthesis and sampled-wave synthesis. The discussion then dives into the technology of digital audio, which doesn't create musical or special effects but rather records and plays back sound. You'll get the information you need to make the best recordings possible.

The section "Using Your Sound Blaster Software" dives into the practical details of running your DOS programs, working with software drivers, and editing ASCII files needed by these programs.

The "Sound File Formats" section summarizes the types of audio files you're likely to encounter, providing you with a valuable reference for one of the most confusing areas in audio software.

Appendix A builds on the introduction to sound presented here. It's designed for anyone who wants to know more about the technological nitty-gritty of sound cards and their software.

THE SCIENCE OF SOUND

Musicians have their own terminology for describing the contrasts in the quality of sound, such as brightness and flatness. Similarly, there are a few key technical measurements that are used by audio engineers and audio enthusiasts to describe the quality of a sound or, equivalently, the ability of an instrument or device such as the sound card to reproduce a performance. Some of these key terms are bandwidth, dynamic range, distortion, and noise level, all of which are discussed in this section.

The Nature of Sound

Sound is a vibration that is propelled through air, courtesy of air molecules that pass the vibration along, to our ears. The same principle applies when you toss a rock into a pond: the disturbance from the rock causes the water to fan out in all directions until the waves are so small in amplitude (or wave height), they can no longer be seen. Figure 1-1 illustrates the physical vibrations of a tuning fork that has been struck. The tuning fork vibrations force the air molecules to clump into regions of greater and lesser density, causing the air pressure to momentarily increase and decrease. The tuning fork is an excellent example of a sound source for two reasons. First, you can see the back-and-forth motion of its arms while hearing the results of this vibration. Second, the tuning fork vibrates at a constant *frequency* (vibrations per second) until all its energy has been dissipated as sound.

Figure 1-1 illustrates the disturbance of air molecules, which are represented by small circles. The region with very few circles is a momentary rarefaction, where the air pressure is below normal and there are fewer air molecules; the area crowded with circles represents an area with more air molecules than normal and a higher-than-average air pressure. A disturbance traveling through air is called a *wave,* and the shape of the wave is called the *waveform.*

Characterizing Simple Waves

The tuning fork waveform is the simplest of all waveforms, called a *sine wave.* You may have seen waveforms like this on the screen of an electronic instrument called an *oscilloscope.* Such simple waves are characterized by their frequency and *amplitude,* the maximum amount of disturbance as seen by the peaks of the wave.

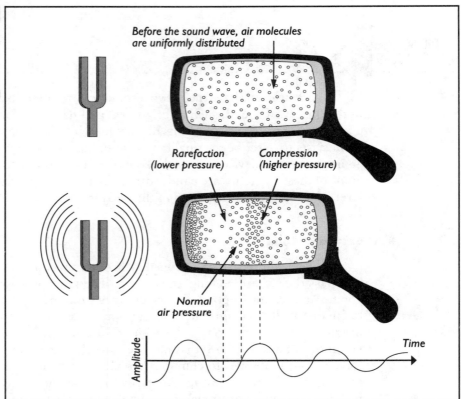

FIGURE 1-1

Simple sine wave emanating from a tuning fork

Before the sound wave, air molecules are uniformly distributed

Rarefaction (lower pressure)

Compression (higher pressure)

Normal air pressure

Amplitude

Time

The frequency of sound is measured in units called hertz (Hz). A sound that vibrates once per second measures 1 Hz. Frequencies are often written in kilohertz (kHz), the unit representing 1,000 Hz. A young person with healthy ears can hear sounds in the range of 20 Hz to 20,000 Hz (20 kHz).

In Figure 1-1, note how the amplitude of the wave diminishes as the sound travels away from its source, spreading in all directions. (The figure exaggerates how quickly the wave diminishes in air.)

Your ear and a microphone plugged into your sound card are remarkably similar. Both convert small variations in air pressure into an electrical signal that can be understood and stored by their respective "brains" (either the human one or the CPU in your computer). A *signal* is the term for information, such as a sound, when it's been transformed from its original form—molecules bumping into each other in the air—into an electrical version that can be saved, manipulated, and played back. Later, when we talk about digital audio, we'll use the term signal frequently because we'll be dealing not with sound but rather with a computer representation of it.

How Pitch Differs from Frequency

There is a subtle but important distinction between frequency and pitch. *Frequency* refers to a scientific measurement of the number of vibrations per second. *Pitch* refers to our perception of how vibrations compare. We typically speak of pitch as "low" or "high." For instance, a triangle or cymbal has a high pitch, whereas a bass guitar or a bass drum has a low pitch. In sound recording and playback, the lower range of frequencies, such as 20 Hz, is referred to as bass; while the upper range, 15 kHz, is referred to as treble. You may also hear the term *midrange* in the context of speakers, which refers to frequencies between 300 Hz and 5,000 Hz.

Amplitude

Measuring the amplitude of a wave is important because it tells us the *strength,* or amount of energy, in a wave, which in turn translates into the loudness we hear. If you've ever pumped your legs on a playground swing or been hit by one accidentally, you have already experienced the importance of amplitude. As you increase the amplitude of the swing, you can't help but notice how much more energy it takes to get just a bit more height. And clearly a child swinging six feet into the air packs a much bigger wallop than a child swinging only half that height.

We promised no formulas, so we'll only talk about decibels and not burden you with the formula. A *decibel,* abbreviated as dB, is a unit measuring signal strength and is useful when comparing the loudness of two sounds. The sensitivity of human hearing is extraordinary, with a very large *dynamic range,* or variation in loudness. Most human ears can pick up the sound of a leaf rustling yet can still function after being subjected to the blast of a jet engine. What's amazing is that the strength of a jet engine blast is at least 10 million times that of a leaf rustling in a breeze.

The ear requires large-percentage jumps in sound strength before a change in loudness is sensed, meaning that the ear's sensitivity to sound strength is *logarithmic.* The ear works as a logarithmic device, so the decibel, a logarithmic measurement unit, is the sensible choice to measure sound strength. The practical side of amplitude is that it increases by only 3dB when the loudness of a sound doubles. For example, a sound at 86dB has twice the strength of a sound at 83dB and four times the strength of a sound at 80dB. From the standpoint of our perception of loudness, a 3dB increase, which doubles the strength, is perceived as only slightly louder. It takes a full 10dB increase to make a sound appear twice as loud to our ears. Table 1-1 illustrates a range of sounds and how they compare in strength, as measured in the logarithmic decibel system.

Sound	Sound Strength (pressure in dB)
In front of 12" cannon	220
	210
	200
Rocket engine	190
	180
	170
	160
Jet engine	150
Threshold of pain	140
Airport runway	130
Threshold of feeling	120
Orchestra climax	110
Rock band	100
Heavy truck traffic	90
Someone shouting	80
Noise office/busy street	70
Normal speech	60
Quiet office	50
Quiet home	40
	30
Recording studio	20
Whisper	10
Threshold of hearing	0

TABLE 1-1   *Comparing sound levels* ■

Dynamic Range

No matter how good recorded music sounds, it never compares to the real thing. Much of the reason is that stereo equipment cannot duplicate the full dynamic range of an orchestra or rock concert. An orchestra can reach about 110dB at its climax, and drop to as low as 30dB at its softest, giving a dynamic range of 80dB. This is beyond the dynamic range of a typical stereo system and, in fact, beyond the recording ability of media such as vinyl records and audiotape.

Bandwidth

Now we'll dive into practical stuff like the frequency range of a CD player and our voice. Table 1-2 shows the *bandwidth,* the range of frequencies within which electronics like our sound card and musical instruments—as well as our ears and voice—are capable of hearing or producing sound. Bandwidth is clearly important to our enjoyment of music (as evidenced by our complaint of how "tinny" a pocket radio sounds), and it is an important criterion when you're selecting audio equipment to use with your sound card. What's important is not the exact numbers, which will vary according to who is taking the measurement and other external factors, but rather the magnitude of the difference. For example, the theoretical bandwidth of FM radio is approximately three times that of AM radio.

An interesting fact is that the bandwidth of our ear is superior to that of most consumer electronics. You can see from Table 1-2 one of the reasons why FM radio stations are more pleasing to listen to than AM broadcast channels: FM stations transmit more of the high-frequency components of music than do AM stations. You can also tell, by comparing the bandwidths for the telephone and the human voice, why we sometimes mistake a person's voice over the telephone—we simply don't have all the information we normally receive to recognize the voice.

Sound Source or Detector	Bandwidth
FM radio (theoretical best)	50 Hz to 15 kHz
AM radio (theoretical best)	80 Hz to 5 kHz
CD player	20 Hz to 20 kHz
Sound Blaster 16 sound card	30 Hz to 20 kHz
Inexpensive microphone	80 Hz to 12 kHz
Trumpet	180 Hz to 8 kHz
Telephone	300 Hz to 3 kHz
Children's ears (prerock music)	20 Hz to 20 kHz
Older ears (and rock concert enthusiasts)	50 Hz to 10 kHz
Male voice	120 Hz to 7 kHz
Female voice	200 Hz to 9 kHz

TABLE 1-2   *Audible frequency range (bandwidth)* ◼

NOTE: *The bandwidth is often abbreviated to a single number when the low frequency is reasonably close to zero. For example, the bandwidth of a woman's voice is said to be 9 kHz even though it really spans from about 200 Hz to 9 kHz.*

When comparing the bandwidths of two similar pieces of equipment, such as sound cards or microphones, be certain to compare apples with apples by looking at how the bandwidth is defined. Different manufacturers may take these measurements using different methods, making comparisons between products from two different makers difficult. Fortunately, a fairly standard measurement exists for defining the bandwidth: the range of frequencies over which the signal amplitude doesn't depart from average by more than 3dB. The frequency at which the 3dB drop occurs is known as the *roll-off* frequency. A value of 3dB is used for the roll-off point, because 3dB is the minimum change in signal strength that can be definitively perceived as a change in loudness by the average set of ears.

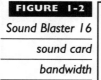

TIP: *Don't get carried away with bandwidth measurements—the ultimate arbiter is your own set of ears.*

Sound Card Bandwidth

The sound card has a surprisingly wide bandwidth, effectively covering the entire range of human hearing. As the idealized plot in Figure 1-2 illustrates, the Sound Blaster 16 sound card bandwidth extends from about 20 Hz to 20 kHz. Strictly speaking, this is the bandwidth for digital audio playback.

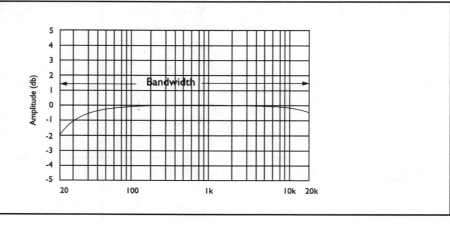

FIGURE 1-2

Sound Blaster 16 sound card bandwidth

System Bandwidth

It's important to note that the overall bandwidth of your sound system is dependent on the weakest link in the chain, which is almost certainly not your Sound Blaster sound card. The quality of sound heard from your computer system reflects the combined effort of many players, and the outcome will be no better than the performance of the least skillful member of the team. In the case of your computer's sound system, a signal must pass through many stages of audio transformation and a variety of devices. For example, consider sound that is recorded from a microphone and then played back. The sound picked up by the microphone is converted to an electrical signal by the sound card, which then converts it to digital audio and stores it to disk. The digital audio on disk is later converted back to an electrical signal and played through the headphones or speakers. The effective bandwidth of your sound system is limited by the narrowest bandwidth among the devices that process your sound.

Assume you're using the Sound Blaster 16's highest *sample rate* (the number of samples taken per second) of 44.1 kHz and 16-bit samples. The weak link when recording is likely to be the microphone, which probably has a 3dB roll-off in response at about 12 kHz. When playing back, the weak link is most likely to be your PC speakers, unless you really splurged on speakers.

Noise and Distortion

Just as you can be troubled by noise and echoes in a room, you can get noise and distortion from your sound card, speakers, and microphone. *Noise*—random sounds that surreptitiously slip in and mask the desired sound—is measured in decibels. Because it's no more possible to have a perfectly quiet digital audio recording environment than it is to have a perfectly quiet library, what's important is how much noise is introduced by your sound equipment, especially your sound card, relative to the signal. The strength of the music, speech, or other desired sound as compared to the average strength of noise, is referred to as the *signal-to-noise (s/n) ratio*. The higher the s/n ratio, the better the job done by the recording setup. For example, the low-noise Sound Blaster 16's electronic circuitry that records and plays back digital audio is rated at a very respectable 85dB s/n. This means that the strength of the signal is 85dB stronger than the strength of the noise. A 70dB s/n ratio is considered OK for music purposes, and 65dB is borderline. The 8-bit Sound Blaster and Sound Blaster Pro have a theoretical best s/n ratio of approximately 48dB based on their 8-bit sample size, which is fine for game sounds, educational software, and having fun, but not adequate for making recordings for multimedia presentations or for satisfying an audiophile.

In addition to noise, the other pollutant of high-fidelity sound is *distortion,* the subtle change in frequency of components of a signal as it passes through the sound card and other audio equipment. Distortion is measured as percentage, and a popular measurement is called *total harmonic distortion* (THD). Contrary to the s/n ratio, the lower the THD the better the sound. Generally speaking, a THD of .5 percent or less is considered to be adequate, and .1 percent should satisfy the most demanding audiophiles. The Sound Blaster 16's digital audio playback circuitry is rated at a superior .07 percent THD.

PC AUDIO TECHNOLOGIES

Creative Labs sound cards are packed full of features and technology, some of which overlap in their capabilities. The key technologies include *FM synthesis,* the most common technology for creating musical sounds on PC sound cards, and *sampled-wave synthesis,* a better-sounding but more expensive technology. We'll also discuss the digital audio circuitry of your sound card that turns your PC into a digital tape recorder.

The Variety of Sound Types

Your Sound Blaster sound card has a rich variety of sound types to choose from. Synthesized music is created by the FM synthesizer and, in the case of the Sound Blaster 16's optional Wave Blaster, by a sampled-wave synthesizer as well. Digital audio can be used to record and play back music, speech, and other sounds. If you have a CD-ROM player you can also add audio CD sound, provided by either an audio CD disc or a CD-ROM disc, to your inventory of audio sources.

NOTE: *You may encounter sound of varying quality coming from your CD-ROM drive. A CD-ROM stores audio CD sound (also known as Redbook audio), the same as a CD player. A CD-ROM disc may contain MIDI music files and other types of sound as well. If the sound from your CD-ROM lacks the fidelity you've grown accustomed to for audio CDs, then it's probably not Redbook digital audio.*

Creating Music and Sound Effects

Here we introduce the audio technologies for creating musical-instrument sounds: FM synthesis and sampled-wave synthesis. There remains a large gulf between playing an instrument note and playing a musical composition. This gulf is filled by the MIDI music language, which is discussed later in the chapter.

FM Synthesis

The remarkably simple frequency modulation (FM) technique for synthesis of music was invented by John Chowning of Stanford University in 1971. *Frequency modulation* refers to the subtle variation in frequency of one wave by another. Chowning discovered that by using one sine wave to modulate another, a third wave rich in musical *timbre* (musical complexity or richness) could be created. The third wave consists of the two original waves, their sum and difference, and harmonics. These *harmonics,* waves with a frequency that is a multiple of the two original waves, give all types of sound—including FM synthesized instruments—their unique timbre.

The FM synthesizer is the most popular electronic technology for creating musical sounds. All Creative Labs sound cards have an FM synthesizer, and it works just like the one in a Yamaha keyboard synthesizer. The FM synthesizer (which musicians abbreviate to "synth") produces a wide range of sounds, including both music and special effects. In recent years, Yamaha has reduced FM synthesis technology to a single chip smaller than a fingernail. Chances are that the electronic music heard from your PC comes from the FM synthesizer.

FM SYNTHESIZER ON YOUR SOUND CARD   The Sound Blaster Pro Deluxe, the Sound Blaster Pro 2 (model CT1600), and the Sound Blaster 16 are built with the newer Yamaha YMF262 (OPL3) FM synthesis chip that produces FM-synthesized sound in stereo using either two-operator or four-operator synthesis. In two-operator mode, the FM synthesizer can generate up to 16 melody sounds and 6 percussion sounds, including a tom-tom or snare drum. The *melody sounds* are instrument sounds set up by software, probably a software driver; these sounds can be changed by music software programs that send new instructions to the FM synthesizer chip. The *percussion sounds* are programmed into the chip when it is made in the factory, so your music software has limited control over them. In four-operator mode, the FM synthesizer can support up to 6 melody sounds and 5 percussion sounds. The earlier Sound Blaster Pro (model CT1330) was designed before the

YMF262 was available and consequently uses two of the earlier, monaural Yamaha 3812 (OPL2) FM synthesis chips in tandem to create 22 stereo sounds. The Sound Blaster Deluxe and earlier Sound Blaster cards, which are monaural, contain a single Yamaha 3812 (OPL2) chip.

Figure 1-3 illustrates two-operator FM synthesis and shows how the Yamaha chip's modulator cell modulates the second cell, called the carrier cell. The *carrier cell* determines the base frequency of the tone, while the *modulator cell* determines the overtones that give the tone its unique timbre. In four-operator mode, two pairs of cells are connected in a series, resulting in timbre that's richer than with two-operator mode.

By carefully programming the parameters of the FM synthesizer, a wide variety of musical-instrument and special-effect sounds can be created. A particularly valuable feature of the Yamaha FM synthesis chip—its ability to handle the work involved in creating musical sound, thereby saving your CPU from the burden—has led to its adoption by most sound cards.

NOTE: *See Appendix A for more details on how both two-operator and four-operator synthesis make a wide range of instrument and special-effect sounds.*

DRAWBACKS TO FM SYNTHESIS   FM synthesis has two drawbacks. The most serious is that the music sounds, at best, just OK. You recognize a flute sound as that of a woodwind instrument, but even a five-year-old child listening to it might think, "Isn't that a weird flute?" A second drawback is that it's difficult to faithfully recreate the sound of familiar instruments. This is because the physics of FM synthesis bear little direct relationship to the physics of how most musical instruments produce sound, so creating sounds that resemble familiar instruments is a trial-and-error process. In other words, FM synthesis is more of a black art than a science.

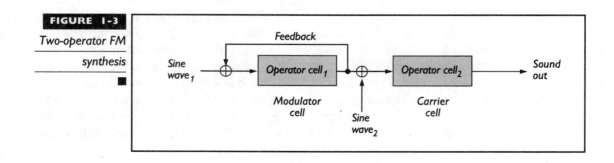

FIGURE 1-3

Two-operator FM synthesis

Sampled-Wave Synthesis

To date, the most common technique for synthesizing the sound of musical instruments has been FM synthesis. However, another technology called sampled-wave synthesis is on the march and will ultimately take over when its cost drops.

Sampled-wave synthesis, which is also referred to as *wave-table synthesis,* works by digitally manipulating a representative sound sample to create the complete range of notes. These notes are digitally processed to adjust their pitch as well as to add keyboard velocity or bowing intensity and other performance effects like *tremolo,* a slow, subtle variation in the strength of a note as it's played.

NOTE: *You may have already experienced sampled-wave technology if you've played one of those electronic pianos that sound remarkably similar to the real thing. Many of these electronic marvels have switches on them, so by flipping a switch and closing your eyes, you can be playing a harpsichord or grand piano instead.*

Sound Blaster 16 with the Wave Blaster is the first Creative Labs sound card to sport this new technology. A Sound Blaster 16 with the Wave Blaster *daughterboard* (a little card that plugs into the sound card) attached turns the PC into a professional-caliber music studio. The wave-table daughterboard contains 4MB of read-only memory (ROM) that contains digital samples of genuine instruments. These samples provide much more realistic instrument sound than is possible with four-operator—or even eight-operator—FM-synthesized sound. The wave-table instrument samples are 16-bit, CD-quality audio samples.

Playing Musical Compositions with MIDI

The *Musical Instrument Digital Interface* (MIDI, pronounced "middy") has completely reshaped the music world by delivering sophisticated music recording and performing capabilities to amateur musicians. Since MIDI was introduced ten years ago, it has become a worldwide standard for electronic music. It is the standard by which synthesizers, keyboards, *sound modules* (synthesizers without a keyboard), computers, and other MIDI devices talk to each other. While FM synthesis and wave-table synthesis are technologies for playing instrument sounds, MIDI is the technology that plays a musical composition comprising hundreds of notes as well as other details of a musical performance.

Anything you play on a MIDI keyboard or other MIDI instrument can be recorded by your computer and saved as a MIDI file. Likewise, a MIDI file stored in your computer can be played back on your sound card's own synthesizer or on an external MIDI keyboard synthesizer or MIDI instrument.

MIDI Music Data

A *sequencer* software package directs MIDI instruments to play music by playing a sequence of notes and other music instructions that are stored as a MIDI file. A MIDI file (which usually has an extension like .MID or .MFF) contains the same information that you see on an actual musical score: a list of notes of varying duration and pitch, with tempo, phrasing, and much more. This sequence of MIDI instructions specifies which instrument to play, what key to press, and when to press it and with how much strength. The beauty of sequencer software is that it can recreate a musical *performance*, not just replay a recording of a past performance. Unlike with a recording, you can change the instruments and even the melody itself. For this reason, MIDI music has become an essential part of the recording studio, serving as a tireless backup band.

MIDI files are signficantly different from digital audio files such as VOC and WAV files. Digital audio files contain actual sound, recorded in digital form by taking thousands of samples each second. MIDI music, on the other hand, contains only instructions on how to play an instrument. Digital audio files may require millions of bytes of data to play just a few minutes of music, but just a few thousand bytes of MIDI data can play hours of music.

A MIDI file is not only more compact than a digitized audio file, it is also completely editable. An appropriate analogy of these two types of files might be a fax document and a word processing file. The fax document can be read, and the digitized audio file can be played, but you can't modify either one much except for cutting and pasting to move the pieces around. A MIDI file, on the other hand, is like a word processing file; you can modify it endlessly.

MIDI Interface

Many keyboards and electronic pianos today have a MIDI interface built in. When you install a Creative Labs sound card, you automatically add a MIDI interface to your computer. The MIDI interface cable that comes with Creative Labs' optional MIDI upgrade kits has a connector on one end that plugs into the MIDI/joystick port of your sound card. The other end plugs into a MIDI device, most frequently a keyboard synthesizer. With the right software—probably a MIDI sequencer program—you can use your computer to control an entire network of MIDI devices including the omnipresent keyboard synthesizer. This interface is bidirectional, accepting MIDI data from a MIDI keyboard or other *controllers* (devices that control synthesizers and sound modules) as well as transmitting MIDI data to external MIDI instruments.

MIDI Upgrade Kits

Creative Labs offers several MIDI upgrade kits. The most frequently purchased MIDI kit includes both MIDI sequencer software and an interface cable. These kits now include a Microsoft Windows sequencer program called Cakewalk Apprentice for Windows by Twelve Tone Systems. Previously, the MIDI kit included a DOS sequencer program called Sequencer Plus Pro (SP Pro) by Voyetra Technologies. See Appendix F for more detail on the variety of MIDI upgrade kits offered by Creative Labs.

MIDI and Software Drivers

Software drivers are the bridge between the hardware that creates the sound of the note and the software programs that play MIDI music, such as a sequencer program like Cakewalk Apprentice, and MIDI players such as Creative JukeBox and Microsoft Media Player. The hardware is a synthesizer on the sound card, the FM synthesizer that's on all Creative Labs sound cards, or the Wave Blaster sampled-wave synthesizer that's available for the Sound Blaster 16. Alternatively, MIDI data can pass between your computer and MIDI equipment through the sound cards' MIDI interface. See Appendix C for more details on the Windows drivers for MIDI.

Recording and Playing Audio: The Basics of Digital Audio

Before your computer can record, manipulate, and play back sound, the sound must be transformed from an audible analog form to a computer-friendly digital form by a process called *analog-to-digital conversion* (ADC). Once sound data is stored as computer bytes, you can tap the power of your computer's CPU to massage this sound in a thousand ways. With the right software, for example, you can add a reverberation, or echo, to music or speech. You can eliminate pieces of speech, like the "not" in a recorded statement. You can mix sound files together, adjust the pitch so the voice can't be recognized, and so forth. Finally, when you're ready to hear your masterpiece, the *digital-to-analog conversion* (DAC) process converts the sound bytes back into an analog electrical signal that comes out of the speakers. The pulse code modulation (PCM) circuitry in your sound card that handles ADC and DAC is excellent, almost comparable to that in CD players, so you're more likely to be limited by your imagination than by your sound card's performance ability.

Sampling: Analog-to-Digital Conversion and Back

Let's begin with capturing sound using the microphone. When sound waves reach the microphone, the mechanical motion is translated into an electrical signal. This signal is called an *analog signal* because it is a continuously changing signal, analogous to the original sound.

ANALOG-TO-DIGITAL CONVERSION (ADC)   The ADC process converts this continuous analog signal into a series of discrete digital values by *sampling,* taking measurements of the instantaneous amplitude of the signal, at a constant rate. If the measurements are done at a sufficiently high sample rate, such that the signal waveform doesn't change much between samples, the ADC process can do a good job of approximating the analog sound wave. Figure 1-4 shows how analog-to-digital conversion works. Notice that the continuous wave is approximated by a series of 8-bit point values, varying in value from +128 to –127, which will be stored as bytes in a disk file. By using a larger, 16-bit sample size, you can create a more faithful replica of your sound.

DIGITAL-TO-ANALOG CONVERSION (DAC)   The DAC process converts the dis-

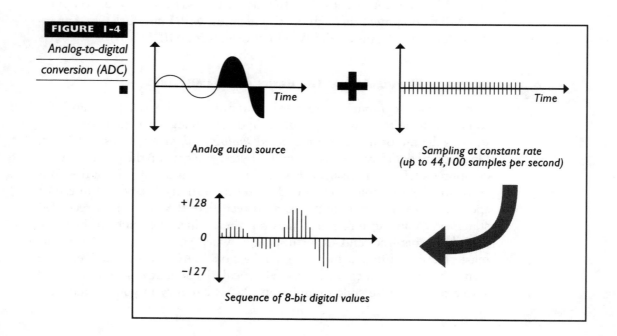

FIGURE 1-4

Analog-to-digital conversion (ADC)

Time

Time

Analog audio source

Sampling at constant rate
(up to 44,100 samples per second)

+128

0

–127

Sequence of 8-bit digital values

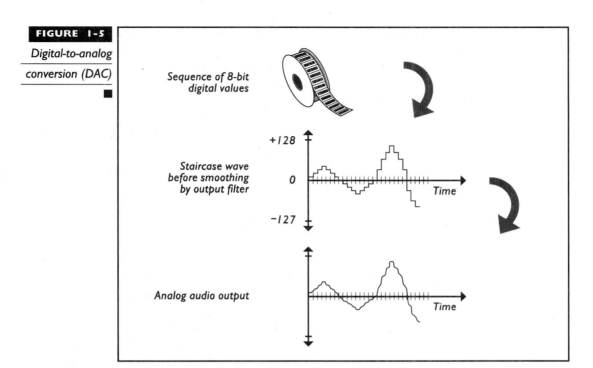

FIGURE 1-5

Digital-to-analog conversion (DAC)

crete digital values representing the sound into a continuous analog signal by using a smoothing filter to round out the rough edges, as shown in Figure 1-5. Digital audio stored on disk is represented in Figure 1-5 by a tape reel with data bytes. The roughness of the reconstructed analog signal waveform has been exaggerated to emphasize the analog-to-digital conversion technique.

Sample Rate and Sample Size

The *fidelity*—audiophile terminology for the faithfulness in replication of the original music—of digital audio sound depends on the judicious selection of the correct sample rate and *sample size,* the number of bytes used to store each sample.

SAMPLE RATE   The sample rate (also referred to as *sampling rate*) must be high enough that high-frequency sounds, such as the ringing of a crystal wine glass or the bowing of a violin, can be captured accurately. According to the *Nyquist theorem* (it's got to be a real theorem with a name like that), you can faithfully replicate a waveform only if the sample rate is at least twice the frequency of the highest-frequency component. The highest frequency that the human ear can perceive is slightly over 20 kHz, so the Sound Blaster

16's and Sound Blaster Pro's top sampling rate of 44.1 kHz should be more than adequate. This is the same rate used by today's audio CD players.

Digital audio files can be recorded with your choice of sampling rate. The higher the sampling rate, the better the sound quality. For example, 6,000 Hz (6,000 samples per second) is fine for a typical man's voice, but not good enough for the typical woman's voice, which has higher frequency components. A sampling rate of 8,000 Hz would provide a higher-quality recording of a woman's voice. The highest sampling rate you can use depends on which sound card you have. The following table lists some sound cards and their sampling rates:

Card	Max Record Rate	Max Playback Rate
Sound Blaster 16	44,100 (mono or stereo)	44,100 (mono or stereo)
Sound Blaster Pro	22,050 (stereo) or 44,100 (mono)	22,050 (stereo) or 44,100 (mono)
Sound Blaster 2.0	15,000 (mono)	44,100 (mono)
Sound Blaster 1.0, 1.5	13,000 (mono)	23,000 (mono)

The Sound Blaster 16 can record in stereo, recording up to 44,100 samples per second with both a left and a right channel sample for a combined sample rate of 88,200 samples per second. The Sound Blaster Pro and Sound Blaster 16 cards are also capable of stereo with a top playback rate of 22,050. Both the Sound Blaster and Sound Blaster Pro take 8-bit (1-byte) sound samples; each measurement consumes 1 byte of storage in your computer's memory or on disk. The Sound Blaster 16 handles 16-bit (2-byte) samples, delivering speech and music with fidelity equivalent to today's CD players.

You may not be able to use the highest sampling rates for several reasons. First, high sample rates require a lot of storage capacity. Each 8-bit sample (Sound Blaster and Sound Blaster Pro) consumes 1 byte of memory or disk space. At a sample rate of 6,000 Hz, one minute of recording will fill a 360K disk. The Sound Blaster 16 is a disk drive vendor's dream come true. At the peak Sound Blaster 16 sample rate of 44,100 Hz (in stereo actually 88,200 samples per second), over 10MB of storage will be consumed in just one minute! You will be even more constrained if you record to memory rather than to disk. For example, when you use VEDIT2 (the Sound Blaster Pro's DOS sound recorder and editor) on a typical PC with 640K, you can record only about six seconds of stereo at 22,050 Hz before filling up conventional memory.

NOTE: *There are additional sample-rate restrictions for the Sound Blaster 1.x and 2.0 cards that are imposed by the sound cards' hardware. These restrictions will be discussed in detail for each utility program. The key restriction is that you cannot use too high a sample rate if you plan to pack (compress) your files.*

Recording Studio Sampling Rate

According to many audiophiles, CD audio lacks a certain richness in sound. This is partly because the sample rate is just a tad too slow to accurately reconstruct the highest frequency components. The complication is that an input filter, circuitry used to block high-frequency noise from infiltrating the recording, is an imperfect device; it can't block all frequencies above a certain frequency while perfectly passing all other frequencies below. Because the input filter has its own roll-off, which adds to the roll-off of the digital circuitry, the sound card's effective bandwidth is reduced slightly from the theoretical maximum. While 44.1 kHz sampling can, in theory, record frequencies as high as 22.05 kHz, in practical implementation the bandwidth is more like 20 kHz, which just barely matches that of the human ear. In fact, commercial recording studio equipment uses a sample rate of 48 kHz for this very reason.

SAMPLE SIZE   The sample size is the other major influence upon the fidelity of digital audio. The 16-bit Sound Blaster 16 cards offer a choice of either an 8-bit (1-byte) or a 16-bit (2-byte) digital audio sample size. The Sound Blaster and Sound Blaster Pro handle only 8-bit samples. While the MPC Level 1 specification requires 8-bit samples, the MPC Level 2 specification dictates 16-bit samples. (See the Introduction for MPC specifications.)

The sample size controls the dynamic range that can be recorded. For example, 8-bit samples limit the dynamic range to 256 steps (50dB range). In contrast, a 16-bit sample has a dynamic range of 65,536 steps (90dB range)—a major improvement. The human ear perceives a world of difference between these two sample sizes. Your ears are more sensitive to detecting differences in pitch than differences in loudness, but they are still remarkably sensitive to sound strength. Human ears, which are accustomed to detecting sounds that vary in strength by orders of magnitude, perceive 8-bit sound as dull or flat in tone when compared to 16-bit digital audio sound.

TRADE-OFFS IN SAMPLING   The motto "There is no such thing as a free lunch" clearly applies to digital audio. So far, based on what you've read, you might assume that all you have to do to get great sound is to record at the top speed of 44.1 kHz with 16-bit (2-byte) samples. The only problem with this recipe—assuming you've got a Sound Blaster 16 capable of this—is the cost in disk space. Assuming you're recording in stereo, with left and right channel samples taking place simultaneously at 44.1 kHz, a one-minute sound sample requires a mere 10.58MB (you read it correctly—10.5 million bytes!) of storage. If you've already bought a system with 20MB of memory to run Windows NT, you can store almost two minutes of digital audio in your system's RAM before your computer flashes an out-to-lunch message at you. The rest of us have no choice but to send that data directly to disk, but at over 10MB a minute you're likely to run out of disk space before you have time to put a sandwich together.

The bottom line regarding digital audio is that you must adhere to the following guidelines to conserve on storage:

- Record in monaural rather than stereo.

- Use the lowest sample rate practical.

- Use 8-bit samples rather than 16-bit samples for speech and sound effects whenever possible.

NOTE: *Sound Blaster 1.x/2.0 and Sound Blaster Deluxe owners need be concerned only with the sample rate since these cards are monaural and 8-bit only. The Sound Blaster Pro and Sound Blaster Pro Deluxe packages include a stereo 8-bit card so the advice on recording in monaural and using the lowest practical sample rate applies to this card.*

A sure method to save disk space is to record sound in monaural instead of stereo. With monaural you take only one sample at a time, while with stereo two samples are taken for each point of time, one for the left channel and one for the right. If you're recording from the microphone, you don't have a choice because the microphone input is only monaural, even on the Sound Blaster 16.

Use the lowest possible sample rate. For example, suppose you're planning to record a telephone conversation. The bandwidth of a telephone, as listed in Table 1.2, is only 3 kHz. According to the Nyquist theorem, you'll do an adequate job of recording by using a sample rate of 6 kHz or better.

When selecting the sample rate, also consider the overall bandwidth of your system. For example, there's not much point in recording digital audio at 44.1 kHz if your microphone performance drops off at 12 kHz and the sound source is a gravelly male voice that doesn't go much beyond 7 kHz.

While you'll want 16-bit samples for faithful reproduction of music, you can get by with 8-bit samples for special effects and for speech. Special effects are almost always a little noisy, so they're an especially good match for 8-bit samples and a slow sample rate. In the case of speech, try recording the sound with 8-bit samples; if it sounds OK, you've just saved 50 percent in storage.

Digital Audio Compression

Sound files are particular about compression, so you may not gain much by using a familiar compression utility program like LHA or PKZIP or even a disk-doubler utility. What audio files need are compression utilities containing software *algorithms,* or mathematical techniques, that understand what sound "looks like." Only if the software understands the format of sound can it do a decent job of compressing sound without losing much fidelity. Compression is done when saving to disk, after a recording has been made by the DOS Sound Blaster Voice Edit (VEDIT2) program that comes with Sound Blaster Pro. Creative Soundo'LE, which runs under Microsoft Windows and now ships with all Creative Labs sound cards, can optionally compress *while* you record if you're running a Sound Blaster 16. The compression techniques used by Soundo'LE and VEDIT2 are described in Appendix A.

USING YOUR SOUND BLASTER SOFTWARE

This section provides general information on how to locate and set up the programs that make your Sound Blaster card come alive.

Locating the Programs

If you follow the installation procedures found in your Creative Labs Sound Blaster User Reference Manual and in Appendix C of this book, your programs will be in a directory named \SB or \SBPRO or \SB16. (Appendix C tells you what directories the various Sound Blaster versions are stored in.) The instructions in this chapter assume you are using these directories names. Occasionally you'll read instructions for switching to another directory.

Command Syntax

To use your sound card and software effectively, you enter commands instructing the software to take action. Usually these commands are entered on the DOS command line. There are syntax rules for commands and their parameters, but you needn't be concerned with capitalization within the

commands—Sound Blaster software is not case-sensitive. For example, all of the following commands will work:

```
VPLAY CONGA.VOC
vplay conga.voc
```

```
VP1Ay CoNGA.voc
vplay conga.voc /T:5 /Q
vplay conga.voc  /q /T:5
```

Notice that in the last two commands in the previous list, the two command switches following the command (/q and /T:5) are reversed, yet they work the same way. Though command options may be typed in any order, you do need to be careful to type the complete filename correctly, such as CONGA.VOC, using the appropriate filename extension (such as .VOC) when you know it. You should always use the extension, although most programs will correctly guess the appropriate file extension. Do not type spaces between the filename and its extension. Also do not type spaces between a command switch and its parameter, as in /T:5.

Editing ASCII Files

To use a particular Sound Blaster program, you may need to create or modify a plain text file, which is frequently called an *ASCII* file. For example, the Sound Blaster has a software program called MMPLAY, which is used to create audio/visual presentations. When using MMPLAY, you create an ASCII script file that includes instructions for playing specific music and animation files.

Text files are called ASCII files because they use only the printable ASCII characters. ASCII files are different from the files that most word processing programs work with. Most word processors, such as Microsoft Word or WordPerfect or Ami Pro, embed special characters in their document files to specify formatting information. These formatting codes are likely to interfere with the ability of other programs to read these files.

NOTE: *A file with a .TXT extension is almost always an ASCII file. Many of your PC files that contain configuration information for the PC or its programs, such as AUTOEXEC.BAT, CONFIG.SYS, and the Microsoft Windows .INI files, are ASCII files.*

Recognizing the need to create or edit ASCII text files, most word processing applications offer command options that allow you to work with files without embedding the special formatting characters. For example, in WordPerfect 5.*x* these commands are the Text-in and Text-out commands. In Microsoft Word you can use the Save As Text option. And in Windows 3.1, the Write application allows you to save work as an ASCII file by selecting the File Save As Word for DOS/Txt Only menu option.

In addition to using your word processor to work with ASCII files, you can use a simple text editor such as the one that comes with DOS. In your

DOS directory you may have EDLIN, a programmer's tool, and EDIT or EDITOR, designed for everyone to use. If you're running Microsoft Windows, the Notepad application, found in your Accessories group, is designed specifically to work with ASCII files. You can use these tools to directly create or edit an ASCII file. You can verify that your word processor or text editor is really creating an ASCII file by peeking at the file using the DOS TYPE command. For example, suppose you want to see what's in your CONFIG.SYS file that helps define how your computer works. Type **C:>TYPE C:\CONFIG.SYS** and press ENTER(the \ is placed before the filename CONFIG. SYS to indicate that this file is located in the root directory of your C: drive). If your file is truly in ASCII format—which CONFIG.SYS must be—you will see the file contents scroll by on the screen. If the file is non-ASCII, and has embedded control characters, you will see unrecognizable symbols on the screen and the file display will probably terminate prematurely.

Managing Your Driver Software

Drivers are small software programs that shield an application program, such as the FM Intelligent Organ, from having to know the specifics of the hardware it runs on, such as the differences between Sound Blaster 1.5 and Sound Blaster Pro 2. A software driver is like a limousine driver—just tell it where to go, and it handles all the details. Your Sound Blaster driver handles all the details of communicating with the sound card. Having the correct driver—one that works well for the hardware—is just as important as having a smoothly running transmission. Small problems with either one can completely disable your machine.

An application usually loads drivers automatically when it needs them. For example, when you first install a word processing program, it asks you to pick from a list of printers. Later, when you print a file, the driver for the printer you've selected will be loaded automatically by the word processing program. The word processing program doesn't need to know much about the printer because the printer driver, as the intermediary, figures out how to print italic, underlining, strikeover, and other similar tasks.

Microsoft Windows drivers are manipulated through the Control Panel application found in the Main program group. For more information about Windows drivers, see Appendix C. The discussion that follows focuses on the drivers for DOS programs. Readers who run Microsoft Windows applications exclusively can skip ahead to the section titled "Sound File Formats."

How the Sound Blaster Programs Use DOS Drivers

The DOS software that comes with your Creative Labs card, as well as the programs included with this book, relies on drivers to communicate with the sound card. You will sometimes need to load a driver explicitly (that is, by typing its name at the DOS prompt); at other times drivers will be loaded automatically. For example, when you use the DOS program PLAYCMF, you must first load the driver called SBFMDRV, which controls the FM synthesizer part of the sound card. On the other hand, the FM Intelligent Organ automatically loads a driver called ORGAN.DRV.

Creative Labs does not recommend loading drivers into high memory. You may discover that some drivers, such as SBFMDRV, do work correctly in high memory, but there is little to gain in loading such a small driver into that part of your system.

Unloading DOS Drivers

If you load a DOS driver explicitly, by typing its name at the DOS prompt, you're also responsible for removing it from memory. Creative Labs DOS software drivers consume from 30K to 110K of conventional memory. If you forget to unload the driver, it will occupy conventional memory that may be needed by your other programs, affecting their performance or even preventing them from running at all.

The DOS drivers described in this book are typically unloaded by typing the driver name followed by the /U command option. For example, typing **SBFMDRV /U** will unload the SBFMDRV driver used by your SBSIM multimedia presentation software. If a software program loads a driver automatically, it will typically unload it automatically when you quit that program.

 TIP: *Should a program crash, a driver may be left in memory. You will have to reboot your computer to remove it from memory.*

Running Sound Blaster DOS Programs Under Windows 3.1

You should be aware of some of the issues and difficulties of running Sound Blaster DOS programs in the DOS compatibility box. The DOS compatibility box is provided in the Windows 3.1 environment so that you can continue using your favorite DOS applications for which you don't have a Windows counterpart. With the advent of the Deluxe packages, which provide a full suite of Windows software for all Sound Blaster cards, the DOS compatibility box is diminished in importance. This section is most beneficial to sound card owners who bought their Sound Blaster prior to the introduction of the Deluxe packages.

Sound card–related utility programs such as VOC-HDR and JOINTVOC that manipulate files only—not needing to interact with the sound card—should work fine in the DOS compatibility box. On the other hand, programs that generate music or other sound must do so in *real time*, meaning the sound must flow without interruption to properly simulate speech or the normal playing of an instrument. Game, music, and speech software may not work correctly in the DOS compatibility box since Windows can't guarantee that these programs will get the exclusive control over the PC necessary to ensure real-time operation. Examples of real-time applications that may suffer in performance include Sound Blaster's PARROT, SBTALKER, Dr. Sbaitso, and VEDIT2 programs since they all play and/or record digital audio.

To attempt to run DOS speech and music programs in the DOS compatibility box, you must run Windows 3.1 in 386 Enhanced mode at a minimum. It's also a good idea to provide these real-time applications with exclusive use of resources. See your Windows User's Guide for more information on how set up a PIF (program information file) to accomplish this.

NOTE: *If you have a 386SX or better CPU, and 4MB or more of memory, you're almost certainly already running in 386 Enhanced mode.*

Real-time DOS programs do not operate reliably in the Windows 3.1 DOS compatibility box because Windows 3.1 is a *time-slice multitasking operating environment*. This means Windows 3.1 permits each application that is running concurrently (multitasking) to intermittently take control (a time slice) of the PC. This interrupted access poses a problem for real-time applications with audio or video output if they can only intermittently gain control of the PC to utter the next sound or display the next frame. Sound output will sound cracked and video output will appear jerky.

NOTE: *With most applications you can't detect this rapid switching from program to program that happens with time-slice multitasking; but you will notice timing problems with real-time audio and video, because your ears and eyes are sensitive to breaks in sound or jerkiness in video.*

Collision of Windows and DOS Programs

You cannot run real-time Creative Labs DOS programs that produce sound or music in the DOS compatibility box if you're already running a

Windows program that vies for attention from the same sound card. For example, if the Sound Blaster 16's Windows mixer program is running, and you attempt to run the FM Intelligent Organ in the DOS compatibility box, you'll get the error message "Sound Blaster 16 is not accessible," indicating that the two programs have collided.

Though running Sound Blaster real-time DOS applications in the Windows 3.1 DOS compatibility box is not recommended, you needn't be too concerned. Creative Labs has provided owners of the newer Deluxe packages with several excellent Windows-based programs that take full advantage of the Windows graphical environment. In fact, you'll probably have more fun using the Soundo'LE and Creative WaveStudio than you will their DOS equivalents, VOXKIT and VEDIT2.

SOUND FILE FORMATS

ave you wondered whether an exotic shareware sound file on a bulletin board—TARZAN.YEL, for example—is worth downloading to your computer? Sound on the modern IBM PC–compatible computer has flowed from many tributaries, resulting in many different types of sound file formats, different ways in which sound is stored on disk, and different file extensions to distinguish among these formats. Each software program can usually read only a few file formats, so you should know a little bit about who uses what format before racking up a big telephone bill on CompuServe or buying a stack of useless shareware disks. Hardware platforms featuring their own unique brand of sound and sound files include the Commodore Amiga, Apple Macintosh, and of course the original IBM PC. With the arrival of Microsoft Windows, computer sound on the PC has been given additional file formats.

TIP: *You can convert between these different file formats by reading a file into a program and then saving it into another format. For example, Cakewalk Apprentice works best when you store your MIDI music composition in its proprietary Cakewalk workfile (WRK) file format since some information can't be stored in a MIDI file. At a later time you can create a copy of your MIDI composition for distribution by saving your work as a Standard MIDI (MID) file.*

The file formats you're most likely to see for personal computing are described in the following list. The list is ordered by file format name (the usual extension is in parentheses) and includes a short description of how each file format is used.

NOTE: *The term* block *is sometimes used in describing the internal architecture of a file format. A block is a subdivision of a file, similar to a block as a subdivision of a city. Each block, or "chunk," of information contains data of the same type, such as 16-bit digital audio or 8-bit digital audio or MIDI music.*

AUDIO INTERCHANGE FILE FORMAT (IFF)   The Audio Interchange File Format (IFF) is used by the Apple Macintosh for storing digitized audio sound samples. It supports a variety of sample rates and sample sizes, up to 32 bits per sample. A nice feature of this file format is that it supports loops, the repetitive play of a block or group of blocks. This file format traces its lineage to Elecronic Arts, which years ago tried to develop industry-standard file formats for graphics, text, and sound samples. This file format is also used on the Commodore Amiga. It's unlikely you'll see this file format for run-of-the-mill IBM PC sound applications.

CREATIVE MUSIC FORMAT (CMF)   The Creative Music Format (CMF) is one of two file formats promoted by Creative Labs for storing music. The CMF file is designed to work with the industry-standard Yamaha chip used for synthesizing FM music. A CMF file includes an instrument block, which in turn contains the parameters for programming the FM synthesizer on the sound card with the desired instrument sounds. The musical notes are stored in a music block, which adheres to the Standard MIDI File Format. A related file format is Creative Labs' Sound Blaster Instrument (SBI) format, which, like the instrument block of the CMF file, stores the parameters for creating instrument sounds. Up to 128 instrument voice parameters are stored together in a Sound Blaster instrument bank (IBK) file.

MIDI (MID OR MFF)   Should you need to share a MIDI file with a friend, save the file in Standard MIDI, the universal language of the MIDI music world, both amateur and professional. You'll most likely be exposed to two variations of "standard" MIDI with MIDI software. The standard MIDI Type 1 is the more modern variant of MIDI, which faithfully preserves your composition as a multitrack score. The older version, Type 0 format, is provided for compatibility with early sequencers. Type 0 isn't recommended, because it supports one track only.

MOD (MOD)   The MOD (pronounced "mod," as in "module") file format is inherited from the Commodore Amiga, where it's probably the most popular music file format. The unique characteristic of MOD files is that they contain digitized audio samples of actual musical instruments. When

MOD files are played back, each note is played by taking the sample instrument sound for that note and playing it slower or faster to give the correct musical pitch. MOD files generally contain four channels of music, and each channel is devoted to a single instrument sound.

MOD files have several nifty features. They can contain up to 31 instrument voices (typically only 4 or 8 are played at one time), each of which can be set to its own volume. Also, an instrument sound can be repeated indefinitely to create an echo or reverberation effect. Each note can be assigned special effects such as *vibrato,* a slow flutter in amplitude, and *pitch bend,* an upward or downward slide in the pitch. All of these features combine to produce great-sounding music.

MOD files have several advantages and disadvantages. MOD files are larger than MIDI, CMF, and ROL files. Although this may seem like a disadvantage, MOD files provide the quality and flexibility of digital audio without consuming the disk space of a full digital recording. A more serious disadvantage—and one that you should watch out for—is that MOD files exist in many varieties, so not all MOD files will play properly on all MOD players. Most MOD files have a .MOD file extension and contain four channels of music, but there's a trend toward eight-channel MOD players and music. Other available formats are NoiseTracker NST (four channels), ScreamTracker STM (four channels), ScreamTracker S3M (up to ten channels), and 669 (eight channels).

Dual Module Player, an especially popular MOD player from Finland, plays a wide range of MOD file variants (MOD, NST, STM, S3M, 669), supporting from four- to ten-channel MOD-type audio files.

RIFF (RMI) The Microsoft Resource Interchange File Format (RIFF) is designed to be the ultimate file format for Windows multimedia, capable of embedding "chunks" (Microsoft's term for blocks) of many different data formats. These formats include Wave (WAV) digital audio and MIDI chunks. The beauty of RIFF is that it can accommodate block types that haven't yet been invented. So far RIFF hasn't become wildly popular. See the description of Wave (WAV) files (a file type that can also be a RIFF chunk).

ROLL (ROL) Roll files originated with the Visual Composer, a software program provided by AdLib, Inc., for use with its AdLib sound card. The ROL file format was designed to support music on the AdLib card's Yamaha FM synthesizer chip. Because all Sound Blaster sound cards contain that same Yamaha chip, ROL files can be played on your Sound Blaster sound card if you have a suitable music utility program. Similar to the CMF file, the ROL file contains a list of notes, tempos, and instrument changes, although they are organized less efficiently than with CMF.

SOUND (SND)   The Sound Resource (SND) file format is a compact digital audio file format—only 8 bits per sample—supported by Apple. It's used for uttering short sounds, such as an alert sound on the Macintosh built-in speaker, and for use by Macintosh applications such as HyperCard for simple sound requirements.

SUN AUDIO (AU)   Sun Microsystems' workstations use 16-bit A-law and Π-law compressed audio files. This type of sound file is common on the Internet. Sun .AU files can be read and converted to another file type by a number of digital audio editors such as Goldware (a shareware editor) and Sound Forge by Sonic Foundry, and can be converted by utility programs such as SOX, available on the Internet. See Appendix E for more information about the Internet.

TURTLE SMP (SMP)   Turtle Beach Systems, writers of great music software, has its own 16-bit digital audio file format called SMP that applies only to its sound card.

VOICE (VOC)   Creative Labs popularized the Voice (VOC) file format for digital audio. Until recently VOC files were 8-bit only (file format version 1.10). With the introduction of the Sound Blaster 16, the Voice file format was extended to accommodate 16-bit samples (file format version 1.20). These 16-bit VOC files can be created and played with voice utility programs shipped with the Sound Blaster 16.

Voice file digital audio samples can be recorded in a wide range of sample rates. The data can be stored either as uncompressed samples or in a compressed form. The 8-bit samples can be compressed into one of three formats: 2-, 2.6-, or 4-bit per 8-bit sample, providing 4:1, 3:1, and 2:1 compression, respectively. The 16-bit samples can be compressed into two formats only: 4-bit, which results in 4:1 compression, and 8-bit, which yields 2:1 compression. Special features of the Voice file format include special markers that repeat a block, synchronization markers that multimedia presentation programs can use to synchronize the playing of VOC files with sound, graphics, and video; and silence markers, which replace stretches of silence with a small marker. Voice files are new to the Windows environment but are catching on, as evidenced by the appearance of sound editors and utilities supporting the format. At this time Microsoft's Wave file format is still the dominant format for digital audio in the Windows environment.

NOTE: *You're unlikely to encounter compressed VOC files unless you create them yourself. Few commercial products incorporate compressed VOC sound files because the compression scheme isn't compatible with many non–Sound Blaster sound cards.*

WAVE (WAV)   Microsoft adopted the Wave (WAV) file format for use with multimedia extensions to Windows. It stores either 8-bit or 16-bit digital audio samples, handles monaural as well as stereo data, and supports three sample rates: 11.025 kHz, 22.05 kHz, and 44.1 kHz. This file format is supported by virtually all Windows-based multimedia applications and sound cards. The raw sound data, stripped of the headers and other descriptive information, is identical to the digital audio found on CD-ROM discs. One drawback to Wave is that it doesn't support the looping of sound blocks.

WORK (WRK)   Twelve Tone Systems' Cakewalk Apprentice for Windows, a MIDI sequencer program, has its own format called a "work" file that has a .WRK file extension. This file format is the best choice while working with Cakewalk Apprentice, because it preserves information that can't be recorded in a MIDI (MID) file, like wave trigger data and Wave files. All versions of Cakewalk, including Cakewalk for DOS, Cakewalk for Windows, and Cakewalk Apprentice for Windows, read and write the same .WRK files.

II

The Sound Blaster Family

2

Sound Blaster 2.0 Deluxe

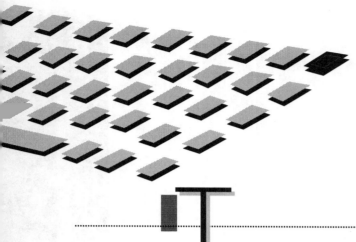

T H E Sound Blaster has become the sound card of choice for hundreds of thousands of game players worldwide. Creative Labs has continually refined this card, ensuring that it's the best value for anyone looking for an affordable sound card guaranteed to be compatible with virtually every game and educational software package. This chapter describes the two most recent incarnations of the Sound Blaster—the Sound Blaster 2.0 and the Sound Blaster Deluxe package that recently replaced the Sound Blaster 2.0. The sound card is actually the same—the Sound Blaster 2.0; however, the software has been enhanced to support Microsoft Windows 3.1 as well as DOS. Creative Labs added the "Deluxe" label when a value-packed suite of Microsoft Windows compatible software, such as Talking Scheduler and Soundo'LE, was added to complement the DOS software already included with the package. Prior versions of the Sound Blaster, 1.0 and 1.5, are described in Appendix B.

This chapter starts by describing the anatomy of your Sound Blaster 2.0 card, pointing out the chips, connectors, and jumpers that are the flesh and bones of your sound card. The Windows software that accompanies the Deluxe package—the same software now offered with the Sound Blaster Pro Deluxe and the Sound Blaster 16—is described in Chapter 5. The DOS application software provided with both the Sound Blaster 2.0 and the Sound Blaster Deluxe, such as The Talking Parrot, the VOXKIT sound editor, and various sound utility programs, are described in Chapter 6.

ANATOMY OF THE SOUND BLASTER 2.0

Creative Labs has released three versions of the original Sound Blaster, models 1.0, 1.5, and 2.0. These three Sound Blaster cards can be used on an IBM PC XT, AT, 386, 486, PS/2 (models 25/30), Tandy (except the 1000 EX/HX), and compatible computers. This chapter describes the currently shipping version, Sound Blaster 2.0.

The Sound Blaster 2.0, shown in Figure 2-1, is quite different from the earlier 1.0 and 1.5 models. It makes use of *surface mount* technology—state of the art in circuit board technology; as a result, the Sound Blaster 2.0 is smaller and more reliable than its predecessors. It plays back digital files at sampling rates as high as 44.1 kHz, as opposed to the 1.0 and 1.5 models' limit of 23 kHz; and it records at sampling rates as high as 15 kHz, as opposed to the limit of 12 kHz for the 1.0 and 1.5 models. Thus the sound quality of digital recordings with the 2.0 is quite a bit better than with the earlier models. (See Chapter 1 for more information on sampling.)

Beginning with version 2.0, the Sound Blaster has a line-level input connector in addition to the microphone input. The line-in connector is right above the microphone connector; see Figure 2-1 for its location.

NOTE: *The best way to distinguish between the different Sound Blaster models is to use the test program TEST-SBC.EXE. See Appendix C for more detailed information on running TEST-SBC and determining the version of your sound card.*

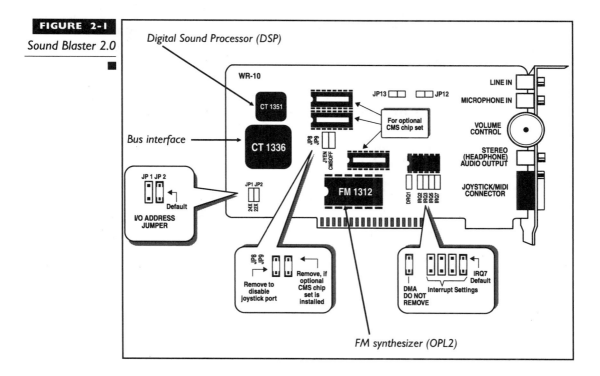

FIGURE 2-1

Sound Blaster 2.0

Digital Sound Processor (DSP)

WR-10

CT 1351

Bus interface

CT 1336

JP13 ☐☐   ☐☐ JP12

For optional
CMS chip set

JP8
JP9

JYEN
CMSOFF

FM 1312

DRQ1

IRQ2
IRQ3
IRQ5
IRQ7

LINE IN

MICROPHONE IN

VOLUME
CONTROL

STEREO
(HEADPHONE)
AUDIO OUTPUT

JOYSTICK/MIDI
CONNECTOR

JP 1 JP 2

Default

I/O ADDRESS
JUMPER

JP1 JP2

24X
22X

JP8
JP9

Remove, if
optional
CMS chip
set is
installed

Remove to
disable
joystick port

DMA
DO NOT
REMOVE

Interrupt Settings

IRQ7
Default

FM synthesizer (OPL2)

The Chips for Sound Blaster 2.0

The chips used on the Sound Blaster 2.0 are what bring all of its extraordinary features to life. These chips include the FM synthesizer, the Digital Sound Processor, and the bus interface.

Digital Sound Processor (DSP) Chip

The most versatile chip on the Sound Blaster 2.0 is the DSP chip; it processes all the commands that come from an application. The DSP chip must also instruct all the other sound chips on your Sound Blaster 2.0 in order to produce the sounds you hear. As shown in Figure 2-1, the DSP chip is labeled CT 1351.

When a music or multimedia program wants to play notes through the FM synthesizer, the DSP must accept the data from the computer and tell the FM chip how to play the music. When a game wants to surprise you with a digitally recorded explosion, the DSP accepts the sound data from the computer and converts it from digital to analog form so that you can hear the sound.

The DSP is responsible for sending and receiving the MIDI data used by electronic keyboards and synthesizers. The DSP also performs the analog-to-digital and digital-to-analog functions that allow you to do digital recording and playback of music, sound effects, and speech. Some digital sound files are stored in a compressed format to save disk space and must be decompressed. The DSP can play these sound files by decompressing the data as it arrives from the computer. By performing the decompression in the chip, your computer can spend its time doing more important things, such as keeping track of your game opponents on the screen.

The FM Synthesizer Chip

The FM synthesizer chip, labeled FM 1312 (and also known as the Yamaha 3812 OPL2), is visible in Figure 2-1. The FM chip is responsible for synthesizing the sounds of musical instruments. This chip can play up to 11 instruments simultaneously. It does this by manipulating sine waves to approximate the waveforms created by real instruments. Chapter 1 and Appendix A go into more detail on FM synthesis.

Other Chips on Your Sound Blaster 2.0

The rest of the chips on the Sound Blaster 2.0 card are support chips, including gates, buffers, and amplifiers that help the main chips communicate with your speakers, microphone, joystick, and computer. On Sound Blaster 2.0, the many chips used to communicate with the computer in earlier Sound Blaster cards have been replaced by the CT 1336 bus interface chip, as shown in Figure 2-1. This integration not only reduces the cost and size of the card but also greatly increases its reliability.

The Connectors for Sound Blaster 2.0

Figure 2-1 points out the various connectors on the Sound Blaster 2.0 card. These connectors provide a means for passing sound from the card to speakers, stereos, and headphones, and for receiving sound from a microphone, tape player, or stereo. There are four connectors on the 2.0 card.

- The topmost connector on the 2.0 card is a line-in connector for hooking up to the line-out from a tape deck, stereo, or CD player. It is a 1/8-inch stereo minijack.

- The microphone jack is the second connector on the 2.0. It is a 1/8-inch monaural minijack.

- The connector just below the volume knob is the speaker output. It too is a 1/8-inch stereo minijack. The speaker-out connector has a built-in amplifier that can output up to four watts of power per channel, so be sure to turn down the volume before connecting anything to it. Also, do not connect a mono 1/8-inch miniplug to the speaker output, as this can short-circuit and damage the amplifier.

- The last connector is a 15-pin, D-sub connector used for joystick input and MIDI input/output. The joystick/MIDI port can support one or two joysticks. Using two requires a Y-adapter from Creative Labs; generic Y-adapters from other vendors may not work properly. Two pins on the joystick/MIDI connector (pins 12 and 15) are used for MIDI Out and MIDI In, respectively. This allows you to connect MIDI keyboards and synthesizers to Sound Blaster 2.0 with the optional MIDI cable. See Appendix F for information about the MIDI cables that are available.

The Jumpers for Sound Blaster 2.0

The jumpers are used to configure the card so that it doesn't conflict with other cards in your computer. These jumpers set the card's configuration when you install your sound card. Their labels and locations can be seen in Figure 2-1.

- Jumper JP8 on the Sound Blaster 2.0 allows you to turn the built-in joystick on or off. The only time you will need to remove the jumper is if you have another joystick port in your computer. Many combination I/O cards have a joystick port that is turned on by default. If you have such a card, check the card's documentation to see if the joystick is enabled. If it is, disable the port on either the I/O card or Sound Blaster 2.0, but not on both.

- The DRQ1 jumper enables the direct memory access (DMA) channel on the sound card for digital sound recording and playback. Do not remove this jumper, as the sound card cannot perform digital sound functions correctly without it.

- The IRQ jumpers select the hardware interrupt number of the card, which is also known as its IRQ. These interrupts are compatible with XTs, ATs, and later machines. The interrupts are used for digital sound recording and playback, as well as for MIDI input.

- Jumpers JP1 and JP2 select the base I/O address of the 2.0 card. The I/O address is the location of the communications channel that the computer uses to send and receive data from Sound Blaster 2.0. Notice that Sound Blaster 2.0 only allows selection of ports 220H or 240H, as shown in Figure 2-1 (22X and 24X).

MIXING SOUND SOURCES

The Sound Blaster 2.0 doesn't have a mixer, so it will record whatever is detected from the microphone and line-in sources. You have to physically turn off or disconnect one of these two sources to record the other without interference. Sound Blaster Pro and Sound Blaster 16 come with mixer software, for both DOS and Windows, that lets you select the sources and their volume.

APPLICATION SOFTWARE

The Sound Blaster 2.0 includes a plethora of software applications and utilities. Below is a list of the standard software bundled with the Sound Blaster. Full descriptions and instructions on their use is found in Chapter 5 and Chapter 6.

SPEECH TOYS

- *The Talking Parrot* An onscreen, interactive parrot that repeats what you say to it.

- *SBTALKER* A speech synthesis utility for making the Sound Blaster read text out loud.

- *Dr. Sbaitso* "An onscreen "psychiatrist" discusses your problems in this application that uses artificial intelligence and speech synthesis technologies.

- *FM Intelligent organ* Play the organ on your PC keyboard with intelligent accompaniment.

DOS PLAY-AND-RECORD UTILITIES

- *VPLAY* VOC file playback utility.

- *VREC* VOC file recording utility.

- *PLAYCMF* Creative Music File playback utility.

WINDOWS APPLICATIONS

- *Microsoft Media Player* Play WAV files, MIDI files, and CD Audio from Windows.

- *Microsoft Sound Recorder* Simple recording-and-playback application.

- *Creative JukeBox* Cue up multiple MIDI files and enjoy music while you work.

DIGITAL AUDIO EDITING AND MANIPULATION

- *VEDIT2* Full-screen DOS editor for digital audio. Supports Creative Labs' VOC file format.

- *JOINTVOC* DOS utility to combine several VOC files for a medley of sounds.

- *VOC-HDR* DOS utility for putting the correct VOC header onto raw digital audio files.

- *VSR* DOS utility to change the sampling rate of your VOC files.

DELUXE SOFTWARE

- *MMPLAY* Multimedia scripting language for making presentations with sound and video.

- *PLAYMIDI* MIDI file playback utility for DOS.

- *SBSIM* Sound Blaster Simplified Interface Module. Provides programming-like control of the Sound Blaster using script files.

- *VOC2WAV* DOS utility to convert VOC files to WAV format.

- *WAV2VOC* DOS utility to convert WAV files to VOC format.

- *Mosaic* Sliding tile game for Windows with outrageous sound effects.

- *Soundo'LE* Sound recording and playback utility for Windows. Supports OLE for embedding wave files into documents.

- *Talking Scheduler* Keep track of your appointments with this handy Windows application that talks to you.

3

Sound Blaster Pro Deluxe

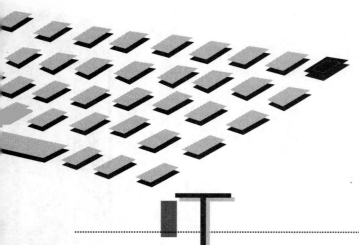

THE Sound Blaster's FM-synthesized music, 8-bit digitized sound recording and playback, and built-in joystick and MIDI ports are fine for some people. But these features represent only the most basic capabilities of the Creative Labs Sound Blaster family. Sound Blaster's big brother, the Sound Blaster Pro, shares these family traits but in addition adds three major capabilities: stereo sound, a sound source mixer, and a CD-ROM interface. In this chapter we'll focus on all the members of the Sound Blaster Pro family.

The latest member is the Sound Blaster Pro Deluxe, which is compatible with DOS, Windows 3.1 (MPC Level 1), and OS/2 2.*x*. "Deluxe" was tacked onto the Sound Blaster Pro name when Creative added a value-packed suite of Microsoft Windows compatible software to the Sound Blaster Pro package. The sound card is the same, only there are a lot more goodies, like The Software Toolworks Multimedia Encyclopedia on CD-ROM, First Byte's Monologue text-to-speech software, Creative Talking Scheduler and the Creative Soundo'LE wave editor, not to mention game and multimedia authoring software.

This chapter will demystify your Sound Blaster Pro. You'll discover the purpose of the various chips, connectors, and jumpers that populate your sound card. The anatomy lesson is followed by an exhaustive review of the mixer software that—in conjunction with the mixer chip—puts you in charge of your sound sources. You'll be able to combine different sound sources and individually select the volume levels for line-in (probably stereo input), FM synthesizer sound, CD-ROM audio, digital audio playback, microphone input, and of course the master volume. This chapter winds up with a quick tour of the wealth of software bundled with the Sound Blaster Pro 2 or Sound Blaster Pro Deluxe.

First we'll trace the evolution of the Sound Blaster Pro. The first version of the Sound Blaster Pro was the Sound Blaster Pro (CT 1330) package, which included the CT 1330 version of the sound card, a MIDI adapter box, and MIDI sequencing software for connecting the Sound Blaster Pro to a

MIDI keyboard or MIDI instruments. This package was phased out in favor of a refined version, the Sound Blaster Pro 2 (CT 1600), that sports evolutionary enhancements to the sound card. The most prominent of these changes is the use of the Yamaha OPL3 FM chip in place of the two Yamaha OPL2 FM chips. The OPL3's four-operator FM synthesis provides higher-quality sound generation than the two operators used in the OPL2.

NOTE: *The Sound Blaster Pro CT 1600 was affectionately dubbed the Sound Blaster Pro 2 by its customers because that was easier to remember. Nevertheless, it is an unofficial name and may not be recognized by everyone.*

As sales of Sound Blaster Pro boomed and the market expanded, fewer and fewer of the potential consumers were musicians or audiophiles interested in MIDI. As a result, Creative brought out a less expensive version of the Sound Blaster Pro 2, the Sound Blaster Pro Basic, to complement the Sound Blaster Pro 2 packages. The sound card is the same in the two packages. The only difference is that the Basic version lacks the MIDI adapter and sequencer software, making for a more affordable package.

ANATOMY OF THE SOUND BLASTER PRO

here have been two models of the Pro: the CT 1330 and the CT 1600 (also known as the Pro 2). The Sound Blaster Pro (CT 1330) is shown in Figure 3-1. The Sound Blaster Pro 2 (CT 1600) is shown in Figure 3-2. The Pro Basic is exactly the same as the Pro 2 except that it is packaged without a MIDI adapter and sequencing software.

As can be partially seen by comparing the chips and connectors against a picture of the Sound Blaster 1.*x*/2.0 card, the SB Pro sports 22-channel stereo FM music, and the SB Pro 2 has 20-channel stereo. Each Pro also offers stereo digital sound recording and playback, built-in joystick and MIDI ports, a built-in mixer, and an onboard CD-ROM interface for compatible CD-ROM drives.

The SB Pro card can be used on an IBM AT, 386, 486, PS/2 (models 25 and 30), Tandy AT, and compatible computers. With some limitations, it can also be used on an IBM PC XT, Tandy (except 1000 EX/HX), and compatible computers with 8-bit slots. See Appendix C for more information on limitations with use on 8-bit machines.

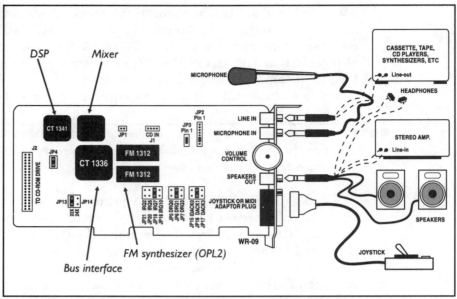

Sound Blaster Pro (CT 1330)

DSP · Mixer · FM synthesizer (OPL2) · Bus interface

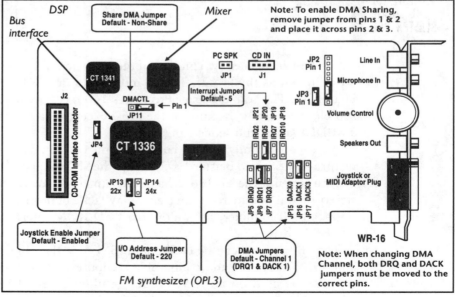

Sound Blaster Pro 2 (CT 1600)

FM synthesizer (OPL3)

NOTE: *It's more difficult to differentiate between Sound Blaster Pro and Sound Blaster Pro 2. See Appendix C for information on telling these Pro cards apart; the process is a bit more complex than simply running the test program TEST-SBC.*

The Chips for Sound Blaster Pro/Pro 2/Pro Basic

The chips used on the Pro, Pro 2, and Pro Basic bring to life all of the card's extraordinary features. These chips include the Digital Sound Processor (DSP), the FM synthesizer, the mixer, and the bus interface.

The Digital Sound Processor (DSP) Chip

The Sound Blaster Pro DSP chip, labeled CT 1341 in both Figures 3-1 and 3-2, is superior to the simpler monaural Sound Blaster. This chip can digitally record and play back in mono or stereo. It also has a high-speed mode that allows it to record and play back at sampling rates up to 44.1 kHz (44,100 cycles per second) in mono, or 22.05 kHz in stereo. The CT 1341 can decompress digital sound files as they are played back; thus no processor time is needed from the computer when playing compressed files. The DSP also handles all the MIDI input and output functions, and controls all the other sound chips on the card.

The FM Synthesizer Chip

The Sound Blaster Pro model CT 1330 has two FM chips. On the board in Figure 3-1 you will see two chips labeled FM 1312; these are also known as Yamaha OPL2 FM chips. Each one produces 11 FM instruments, and since the Pro card has two of them, it is capable of 22 FM instruments.

The Sound Blaster Pro 2 model CT 1600, on the other hand, does not have dual OPL2 chips. Instead, it has the newer stereo OPL3 FM chip (the Yamaha YMF-262-M) as seen in Figure 3-2. This chip is backward compatible with the older chips that use two-operator FM synthesis, but it also has a new four-operator mode that produces better-sounding instruments.

NOTE: *While in four-operator mode, the Pro 2 card cannot play as many instruments as in two-operator mode. The maximum number of instruments that can be used in four-operator mode depends on the arrangement and complexity of the instruments. Contact Yamaha for the OPL3 FM chip specifications.*

The Mixer

Another new chip introduced on the Pro cards is the CT 1345 mixer. This chip allows you to adjust and mix the sounds from the microphone, line-in, CD input, and the digital sound output. This way you can hear a blend of sounds, such as your voice from the microphone while FM music, digital sound, and CD audio play in the background. On the Sound Blaster 1.*x*/2.0, you can only hear FM and digital sound at the same time. You cannot, however, digitally record from multiple sources simultaneously. Only one recording source can be selected by the mixer. If you want to record from the microphone and a tape player, for example, you will need an external mixer.

With this built-in mixer to control volume, you may be wondering what the purpose of the manual volume control on the Sound Blaster Pro is. The manual volume control sets the final volume of the output. With this manual volume control, you know that when you turn down the volume, there's no way that the computer can override your setting.

The Bus Interface

The CT 1336 bus interface chip, shown in both Figures 3-1 and 3-2, passes messages between the Sound Blaster Pro and the computer. It is the same chip used on the Sound Blaster 2.0.

The Connectors for Sound Blaster Pro/Pro 2/Basic/Deluxe

Figures 3-1 and 3-2 point out the various connectors on the Pro cards. Connectors are used for passing sound from the card to speakers, stereos, and headphones, and for receiving sound from a microphone, tape player, or stereo. Four connectors are accessible from the outside of the computer:

- The line-in jack is shown at the very top of the card in Figures 3-1 and 3-2. It is a 1/8-inch stereo minijack and is used to hook in the line-out from a tape deck, stereo, or CD player.

- The next connector on the card is the microphone connector; it is a 1/8-inch mono minijack.

- The connector just below the volume knob is the speaker output. It is a 1/8-inch stereo minijack. The speaker-out connector has a built-in amplifier that can output up to four watts of power per channel, so be sure to turn down the volume before connecting anything to it. Also, do not connect a mono 1/8-inch miniplug to the speaker output, as this can short-circuit and damage the amplifier.

■ The 15-pin D-sub connector is used for joystick input and MIDI input/output. The joystick/MIDI port can support one or two joysticks. Using two requires a Y-adapter available from Creative Labs; generic Y-adapters from other vendors may not work properly. Two pins on the joystick/MIDI connector (pins 12 and 15) are used for MIDI Out and MIDI In, respectively. This allows you to connect MIDI keyboards and synthesizers to the Sound Blaster with the included MIDI cable.

NOTE: *The Sound Blaster Pro Basic does not include the MIDI cable.*

Three connectors on the card are accessible only from the inside of the computer: JP1, J1, and J2, all shown in Figures 3-1 and 3-2.

■ The JP1 connector allows you to connect the motherboard speaker output to the Sound Blaster Pro. The pin configuration for this connector is given in Table 3-1.

CAUTION: *If you connect JP1 to your motherboard, be prepared for the resulting loud volume level of the computer's beeps. The input on JP1 is not connected to the Sound Blaster Pro's mixer and can only be adjusted with the manual volume control.*

■ The J1 connector is a Molex-type (plastic) connector for the CD-ROM drive. It passes stereo audio from the CD-ROM drive to the Pro card. The pin configuration for this connector is shown in Table 3-2 for both the Pro and the Pro 2.

■ The J2 connector is the CD-ROM data cable connector. The data cable that runs between J2 and the CD-ROM drive allows the Sound Blaster Pro to directly control the CD-ROM drive. It is a proprietary interface connection for Creative Labs CD-ROM drives and some Panasonic/Matsushita drives. Contact Creative Labs for exact model information. J2 cannot be used by just any CD-ROM drive, and it is not a SCSI (Small Computer Standard Interface) or a subset of a SCSI-type interface.

Pin	Signal	I/O
1	+5V	IN
2	SPK	IN

TABLE 3-1   *PC Speaker Connector (JP1)* ■

Pin	Signal	I/O
1	Ground	IN
2	CD left channel	IN
3	Ground	IN
4	CD right channel	IN

TABLE 3-2 *CD IN Connector (J1)* ■

The Jumpers for Sound Blaster Pro/Pro 2/Basic/Deluxe

The jumpers are used to configure a card so that it doesn't conflict with other cards in your computer. These jumpers are set in the card's configuration when you install it. Their labels and locations can be seen in Figures 3-1 and 3-2.

■ Jumper JP4 lets you turn the built-in joystick on or off. The only time you will need to remove the jumper is when you have another joystick port in your computer. Many combination I/O cards have a joystick port that is turned on by default. If you have such a card, check the card's documentation to see if the joystick is enabled. If it is, disable the port either on the I/O card or on the Sound Blaster Pro, but not on both.

■ Jumpers JP5 through JP7 and JP15 through JP17 select the DMA channel of the sound card. The DMA channel is used when playing and recording digital sound. Choose from channels 0, 1, or 3. Channel 0 will only work on ATs and higher.

■ Jumper JP11 is available on the CT 1600 to allow the Pro 2 to share its DMA channel with another device that is using the same DMA channel. The only time you will need to use this function is when all the DMA channel selections in your computer are being used. This jumper will work only if the other device is also designed to share its DMA, so leave it disabled unless you are absolutely certain that this is the case. Otherwise, data could be lost, or one or both cards could be damaged.

■ Jumpers JP13 and JP14 select the base I/O address of the card. The I/O address is the location of the communications channel that the computer uses to send and receive data from the Sound Blaster Pro. You can choose between addresses 220H and 240H.

- Jumpers JP18 through JP21 select the hardware interrupt number (IRQ) of the card. The interrupts are used for digital sound recording and playback, as well as MIDI input. Choose from 2, 5, 7, and 10. IRQ 2, 5, and 7 are compatible with XTs, ATs, and higher machines. IRQ 10 only works on ATs and higher machines.

- Jumpers JP2 and JP3 are different from all the other jumpers on the board. They do not change the configuration of the board. Instead, JP2 and JP3 are an extension to the audio connectors on the board, making signal lines for the microphone and speaker accessible from within the computer. Their pin configurations are shown in Tables 3-3 and 3-4.

In Figures 3-1 and 3-2, notice that there is a jumper on pins 6 and 7 of JP2 and pins 1 and 2 of JP3. Removing these jumpers will prevent sound from coming out of the Speaker Out connector on the board.

WARNING: *Do not experiment with the Audio Extension jumpers unless you are experienced with audio electronics. A mistake in making connections here can damage the sound card.*

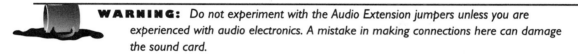

MIXING SOUND SOURCES

ound Blaster Pro owners quickly fall in love with the built-in *mixer,* a new feature of the Pro version cards. The major advantage of the mixer is

Pin	Description
1	MICR (microphone input, right channel). Input range 0.004 to 0.7 volt rms.
2	MICGEN (microphone input ground).
3	MICL (microphone input, left channel). Input range 0.004 to 0.7 volt rms.
4	SPKGND (speaker output ground).
5	SPKR (speaker output, right channel). Maximum output voltage 3 volt rms at 4 ohms.
6	SPKL (speaker output, left channel). Maximum output voltage 3 volt rms at 4 ohms.
7	SPKRL (speaker output return signal, left channel).
8	SPKRR (speaker output return signal, right channel).

TABLE 3-3   *Connector JP2 Pin Configuration* ■

Pin	Description
1	SPKR (speaker output, right channel). Maximum output voltage 3 volt rms at 4 ohms.
2	SPKRR (speaker output return signal, right channel).

TABLE 3-4   *Connector JP3 Pin Configuration* ■

that you can control the volume level of your individual sound sources. For example, your CD can provide subdued background music while you listen to louder voice annotations in a Windows document. In addition, you can control the overall volume level with a master volume control. The various mixer software programs also let you select which source to use for recording: microphone, line-in, or CD.

The following mixer software is discussed in this section:

- SBP-MIX
- SBP-SET
- Sound Blaster Pro Mixer

SBP-MIX is a pop-up, memory-resident program that makes it easy to adjust the mixer on your Sound Blaster Pro card—even when other programs are running. You can control the source levels, master volume, and other features of the mixer. Whenever you want to change the settings, you press a hot-key combination and your mixer program will appear.

SBP-SET is the nonresident, DOS command-line equivalent of SBP-MIX. It is ideal for inclusion in your AUTOEXEC.BAT file, so you can set up your Sound Blaster Pro whenever you start your computer.

The Sound Blaster Pro Mixer is an application that is installed in your Windows 3.1 Accessories group. It is the Windows mixer program that is functionally equivalent to the DOS mixer program, SBP-MIX, though it is not as feature rich.

SBP-MIX

SBP-MIX is a pop-up, memory-resident program supplied with the Sound Blaster Pro cards. One of the key advantages of Sound Blaster Pro versions over Sound Blaster 1.*x*/2.0 versions is the mixer (see Figures 3-1 and 3-2) that's built in to the sound card. The mixer lets you set the master volume level as well as the volume levels for all the audio inputs: microphone, line-in,

CD, voice (digitized audio), and FM synthesizer. The Intelligent Organ, as well as the PLAYCMF and PLAYMIDI utilities, all play through the FM Synthesizer, so SBP-MIX gives you control over these programs, too. With the pop-up mixer (Figure 3-3), you can adjust the mixer while simultaneously running your favorite software programs.

NOTE: *SBP-MIX updates settings on the Sound Blaster Pro board, so your settings will remain in effect even if you unload the pop-up mixer. As an alternative to SBP-MIX, you can run the SBP-SET utility at the DOS prompt. SBP-SET is described later in this chapter.*

Loading SBP-MIX

When you run SBP-MIX it is loaded as a memory-resident program (also known as a terminate-and-stay-resident program, or TSR). It will then appear when you press the assigned hot-key combination. To load the mixer program:

1. Switch to the \SBPRO directory, type **SBP-MIX** and press ENTER. Notice the message on the screen saying that ALT-1 will activate SBP-MIX. ALT-1 is your hot key for the pop-up mixer.

2. Now hold down the ALT key and press the 1 key (the one located at the top of your keyboard), and the pop-up mixer program will appear.

The mixer program stays in memory even after you select Exit from the mixer program's main menu and return to your computer's DOS prompt.

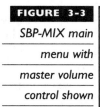

FIGURE 3-3

SBP-MIX main menu with master volume control shown

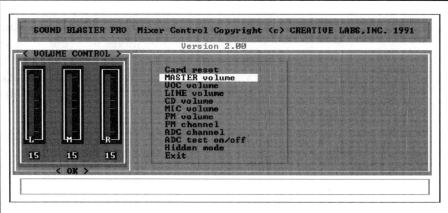

NOTE: *About Conflicting TSR IDs: If you get a message that SBP-MIX is already loaded, though you know it's not, you have a conflict with another TSR program that uses the same TSR ID as SBP-MIX, so the mixer program thinks it's already loaded. To solve this conflict, remove the other TSR (this may require rebooting). Or you can get an updated SBP-MIX program from Creative Labs that will load without any hitches; this updated version checks to see if the same TSR ID is already used before trying to load with that ID. Look for an updated mixer program on the Creative Labs bulletin board (BBS) or call their technical support line.*

NOTE TO WINDOWS USERS   When running Windows, you will use the Sound Blaster Pro Mixer for Windows, described later in this chapter. If you previously used your sound card in the DOS environment and used SBP-MIX, you must unload SBP-MIX before running Windows applications that access your Sound Blaster card.

SELECTING ANOTHER HOT KEY FOR SBP-MIX   To select another hot key, run SBP-MIX /K and add one of the SHIFT keys: CTRL, ALT, SHIFT-L for left shift or SHIFT-R for right shift. Add a number from 1 to 9 after the SHIFT key names. For example, to change the hot key to ALT-5 you should type **SBP–MIX /KALT-5.**

UNLOADING SBP-MIX   You will usually want to keep SBP-MIX loaded, so you can pop it up while running other programs, but there are situations where you will need to unload it. (Bear in mind that by unloading it, you free up 75K for use by other programs.)

To unload the pop-up mixer, type **SBP–MIX /U** and then press ENTER.

Popping Up the Mixer Program

You can pop up the mixer program when working with other software programs, such as your favorite word processor, by pressing ALT-1, or whatever hot key you have selected. Some software programs, however, take over the keyboard and prevent the mixer program from seeing the hot-key combination. For example, the FM Intelligent Organ will let you pop up the mixer program from the Organ's main screen, the one that shows function keys F1 through F8, but not after you press F2 and go to the Play screen.

POPPING UP THE MIXER PROGRAM IN GRAPHICS MODE   Many software programs run in graphics mode. To avoid causing display problems in the graphics environment, SBP-MIX will appear only as a single command line at the bottom of your screen. You can see this by invoking SBP-MIX during a multimedia presentation, such as the MMDEMO multimedia demonstration. At the bottom of your screen you will see this:

```
SBP-MIX function: Exit
```

To work within this line and access the available SBP-MIX functions, press UP ARROW. Just imagine you are viewing the full-screen mixer program main menu and moving the cursor from the bottom choice (Exit) to the top choice (Card Reset). To adjust volume, for instance, once the desired volume function is displayed, use LEFT ARROW to reduce the volume and RIGHT ARROW to increase the volume. You can also use the LEFT ARROW and RIGHT ARROW keys to toggle on and off the choices offered by other functions, such as FM Channel.

In some circumstances, depending on the current graphics mode or the combination of foreground and background screen colors, you may be unable to see the value assigned to a mixer function. For example, you might be able to see the function name FM Volume but not the value indicating the current setting. Indeed, the function names themselves might not be clearly visible. You will then have to visualize what the mixer program control looks like while making adjustments. Try to avoid selecting Card Reset accidentally!

When you're done making adjustments, press DOWN ARROW until Exit reappears, and then press ENTER.

USING HIDDEN MODE   The recommended method for adjusting the mixer while in the midst of a multimedia presentation is to use SBP-MIX's Hidden mode. You can turn on Hidden mode by selecting the Hidden mode menu and then selecting On. Hidden mode lets you control all the mixer volume settings from the keyboard without popping up the mixer program and interrupting your presentation.

Once Hidden mode is turned on, select the volume you want to control by pressing one of the following key combinations:

Master volume	CTRL-ALT-M
Line-in	CTRL-ALT-L
FM	CTRL-ALT-F
CD	CTRL-ALT-C
VOC	CTRL-ALT-V
Microphone	CTRL-ALT-I

To control the volume, use the following key combinations:

Increase volume	CTRL-ALT-U
Decrease volume	CTRL-ALT-D

You can also toggle sound output on and off with CTRL-ALT-Q

Using the Features of SBP-MIX

Many new features of the mixer program SBP-MIX, as discussed in this section, are not yet described in the Sound Blaster Pro User Reference Manual as this book goes to press. The SBP-SET program is better documented in the manual. The Windows Mixer program is also accurately portrayed in the most recent manual.

Card Reset

One of the most valuable features of SBP-MIX is the ability to reset your sound card from within SBP-MIX. The SBP-MIX Card Reset menu selection restores the mixer settings, such as the source and master volume levels, to the default values. This is convenient because some software programs—games in particular—don't always return your sound card to its original state when they end, and may leave the controls at unnatural settings. By using the SBP-MIX Card Reset command, you can silence your audio card without having to press your computer's reset button or turn the power off. Note that CTRL-ALT-DEL will not reset your audio card.

Controlling the Master Volume and the Individual Source Volume Levels

SBP-MIX provides many useful controls, including those for setting the master volume and the volume for each source. For stereo sources and the master volume control, you can adjust both channels simultaneously, or the left and right channels independently.

You access all these controls from a menu that appears when you press the hot key. For example, when you first select the master volume control, a marker appears at the top of the middle slide showing the average sound level. Press the RIGHT ARROW key to move this marker to the slide on the right, and adjust the right channel volume up or down by using the UP ARROW and DOWN ARROW keys, respectively.

When the ADC Test On/Off menu item is selected, it displays a horizontal sound-level meter (similar in concept to an analog "VU" meter) near the bottom of your screen. Before turning this meter on, select the input you wish to check from the ADC Channel menu item: microphone, CD, or line-in. The extent to which the bar spreads dynamically from the center shows the instantaneous sound level of the selected source. Note how the color of the bar changes with each measurement, helping your eye compare instantaneous changes in volume.

The ADC Channel menu item also lets you toggle between the low- and high-frequency settings for the input filter. This filter is useful for minimizing noise, especially the aliasing (a high-frequency ringing noise) that results from the analog-to-digital conversion process inherent to recording voice files.

Controlling FM Steering

SBP-MIX also lets you control FM steering, a feature not available with SBP-SET or with the Windows 3.1 Sound Blaster Pro Mixer. The FM channel settings are as follows:

- *No Steering.* The left channel FM synthesizer output is fed to the left speaker, and the right channel output is fed to the right speaker. This is the default setting.

- *Steer to Left.* Left and right FM synthesizer channel output is combined and fed to the left speaker; nothing goes to the right speaker.

- *Steer to Right.* Left and right FM channels are combined and fed to the right speaker; nothing goes to the left speaker.

- *Mute.* Neither FM channel is fed to the speakers.

TIP: *Game software will sometimes direct both FM channels to one speaker and, when the game is ended, will leave your sound card in that state. If you hear sound coming out of one speaker only, try correcting the problem by selecting No Steering.*

SBP-SET

SBP-SET is similar to the pop-up SBP-MIX program—both programs control the mixer on your Sound Blaster Pro card. But SBP-SET does not load into and stay in memory, as does the pop-up mixer. You run SBP-SET, with a series of command switches, by typing a line at the DOS prompt.

SBP-SET is ideal for setting up your mixer before doing routine procedures, such as preparing for a recording session, because it can be executed from a batch file and doesn't take up valuable conventional memory. It is typically run from AUTOEXEC.BAT to set up the sound card every time the computer is turned on.

SBP-SET's Control of Mixer Features

The following mixer features can be controlled by SBP-SET using the switches listed in the table when you enter the command to start the program. The default values for the settings are shown in square brackets.

Switch	Function	Values [Default]
/R	Reset mixer	
/LINE	Input line volume control	0-15 [0]
/FM	Input FM synthesizer volume control	0-15 [9]
/CD	Input CD-ROM player volume control	0-15 [0]
/X	Input microphone volume control	0-7 [0]
/M	Master (output) volume control	0-15 [9]
/ADCS	Recording source selection	MIC/CD/LINE [MIC]
/ADCF	Input (recording) filter	LOW/HIGH [LOW]
/ANFI	Input filter switch	ON/OFF [ON]
/DNFI	Output filter switch	ON/OFF [ON]
/Q	Quiet mode (suppress message output)	

An important use of SBP-SET is to reset the sound output and mixer settings of your sound board to their defaults. Type **SBP-SET /R** at the DOS prompt and then press ENTER.

NOTE: *SBP-SET has been improved. If you bought your Sound Blaster more than a year ago, what you read here may not match the description in your manual. To get a screen of help information indicating the capabilities of your mixer program, type* **SBP-SET /H** *at the DOS command-line prompt and then press ENTER.*

Running SBP-SET

To run SBP-SET, first switch to the \SBPRO directory. Then type the start-up command followed by any optional command switches you want to use, and press ENTER. The command syntax is

SBP-SET /*setting1* /*setting2* /*setting3* ...

The following command example shows how to set up the mixer for listening to your CD player:

SBP-SET /M:6,8 /X:0 /ANFI:OFF /DNFI:OFF /Q /CD:12

The switches in the above example establish the following controls:

- Master volume (/M) is set to a comfortable level, with a little extra boost to the right speaker.

- Microphone input (/X) is turned off to avoid picking up ambient noise (or perhaps the on/off switch is broken).

- Input filter (/ANFI) and output filter (/DNFI) are disabled, so that you can hear CD sound at its richest.

- Unnecessary messages are suppressed (/Q is present).

- CD input level (/CD) is set to a suitable level.

You can accomplish these same controls (except for control over the filters) from the pop-up mixer program SBP-MIX; but by placing these settings in a batch file, you can easily restore your mixer settings.

Mastering SBP-SET

You don't have to specify all your mixer settings with one SBP-SET command. SBP-SET changes only the mixer settings you specify, so you may find it more convenient to first specify the master volume level, and then the individual sources' volume levels, and so forth.

Only the settings you specify are revised from their previous settings. For instance, the SBP-SET example just described for listening to your CD player does not include a command switch for setting the FM Synthesizer volume level. As a result, SBP-SET will not change the FM Synthesizer volume from its previous level.

NOTE: *Since SBP-SET doesn't restore settings to their defaults, you should always set the volume control to 0 for all sources you don't use.*

The Input Filter

For the input filter (the /ADCF switch), the LOW setting is intended for voice recording through the microphone input, and the HIGH setting is recommended for high-quality speech and music. The default is ON for /ANFI and LOW for /ADCF.

The Output Filter

The output filter (the /DNFI switch) is also a low-pass filter, similar in characteristics to the input filter in a HIGH setting. The purpose of the output filter is to suppress noise found in poor recordings. When playing your CD player, you will get the best fidelity by turning this filter off. When playing digital audio files, it is best to enable this filter. The default setting is ON.

Volume Settings

SBP-SET volume settings range from 0 to 15. The master volume control and all input sources except the microphone have 16 steps. The microphone has 8 steps only. This means, for example, that microphone settings of either 14 or 15 will result in the same volume, the highest volume level.

Sound Blaster Pro Mixer (Windows)

The Sound Blaster Pro Mixer (SB Pro Mixer) is a Windows mixer provided by Creative Labs. This easy-to-use mixer program, as shown in Figure 3-4, controls both the source and master volume levels, and the input filter as well.

At this time, the two DOS mixer programs, SBP-MIX and SBP-SET, have more features than the Windows Sound Blaster Pro mixer. For example, controls available in SBP-MIX but not the Windows mixer program include FM channel steering and board reset.

FIGURE 3-4

The Sound Blaster Pro Mixer screen

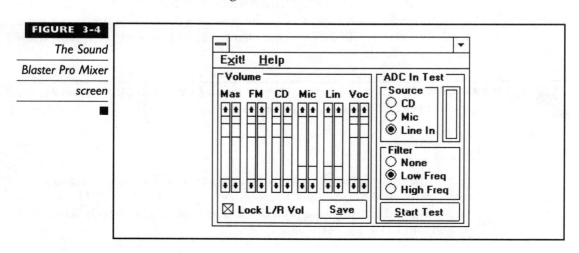

Loading and Running Sound Blaster Pro Mixer

To load the Sound Blaster Pro Mixer program, first start Windows 3.1. Double-click the Accessories group, and then double-click the Sound Blaster Pro Mixer icon. (This assumes you followed the installation recommendation to place the Sound Blaster Pro Mixer into the Accessories group; see Appendix C.

TIP: *Take advantage of Windows 3.1's ability to assign a shortcut to an icon. Assign a convenient hot key, such as* CTRL-ALT-1, *to your SB Pro Mixer program so you can easily access it.*

VOLUME CONTROL   When the SB Pro Mixer program is first launched, both the left and right channels of the stereo volume controls are locked together. Remove the X from the Lock L/R Vol control to adjust the channels independently. Note that the leftmost volume control, titled Mas, is the master volume control.

INPUT FILTER   With the Sound Blaster Pro Mixer program you have three choices for input filtering. Just click your choice to select it.

Setting	Function
None	Disables the input filter. Select this for listening to CD and high-fidelity line-in music.
Low Freq	Select this for speech and noise reduction.
High Freq	Select this for music.

SAVING THE SETTINGS   To save your current settings so that they will be automatically restored whenever you start Windows, click the Save button.

The ADC Test

The SB Pro Mixer's ADC Test feature is like an analog "VU meter." The height of the bar indicates the intensity of the selected source. If the bar reaches the top, the source volume level is excessive and distortion is occurring. Click the source you wish to monitor, and then click the Start Test button. When done, click the Stop Test button.

APPLICATION SOFTWARE

The Sound Blaster Pro includes a plethora of software applications and utilities. Below is a list of the standard software bundled with the Sound Blaster Pro. Full descriptions and instructions on their use are found in Chapter 5 and Chapter 6.

SPEECH TOYS

- *The Talking Parrot* An interactive, onscreen parrot that repeats what you say to it.

- *SBTALKER* Speech synthesis utility for making the Sound Blaster read text out loud.

- *Dr. Sbaitso* An onscreen psychiatrist diagnoses your problem in this application that uses artificial intelligence and speech synthesis technologies.

- *Pro FM Intelligent Organ* Play the organ on your PC keyboard with intelligent accompaniment.

MULTIMEDIA PRESENTATION

- *MMPlay* Multimedia scripting language for making presentations with sound and video.

DOS PLAY AND RECORD UTILITIES

- *VPLAY* VOC file playback utility.

- *VREC* VOC file recording utility.

- *WPLAY* WAV file playback utility.

- *WREC* WAV file recording utility.

- *PLAYCMF* Creative Music File playback utility.

- *PLAYMIDI* MIDI file playback utility.

- *SBSIM* Sound Blaster Simplified Interface Module. Provides programming-like control of the Sound Blaster using script files.

WINDOWS APPLICATIONS

- *Microsoft Media Player* Play WAV files, MIDI files, and CD Audio from Windows.

- *Microsoft Sound Recorder* Simple recording and playback application.

- *Creative JukeBox* Cue up multiple MIDI files and enjoy music while you work.

DIGITAL AUDIO EDITING AND MANIPULATION

- *VEdit2* Full-screen DOS editor for digital audio. Supports Creative's VOC file format.

- *Jointvoc* DOS utility to combine several VOC files together for a medley of sounds.

- *VOC-HDR* DOS utility for putting the correct VOC header onto raw digital audio files.

DELUXE SOFTWARE

- *VOC2WAV* DOS utility to convert VOC files to WAV format.

- *WAV2VOC* DOS utility to convert WAV files to VOC format.

- *Mosaic* Sliding tile game for Windows that has outrageous sound effects.

- *SoundoLE* Sound recording and playback utility for Windows. Supports OLE for embedding WAV files into documents.

- *Talking Scheduler* Keep track of your appointments with this handy Windows application that talks to you.

4

The Sound Blaster 16/SCSI-2/MCD

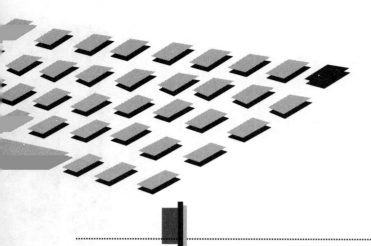

N this chapter, we'll describe the features common to all members of the Sound Blaster 16 (SB16) family. The Advanced Signal Processor is one of the new, exciting capabilities that is only available on the SB16, so we'll spend some time discussing its first advanced application—QSound—as well as its future potential. Next, we'll talk about the Wave Blaster (WB), which is an optional card that attaches directly to the SB16, improving the latter's capabilities significantly. We'll also discuss the software mixer enhancement for the SB16. Then we'll briefly describe some of the programs that are included with the various SB16 sound cards.

NOTE: *Creative's use of the acronym ASP has been dropped due to a naming conflict with ASP Computer Products Inc. As a result, the chip is referred to as the Advanced Signal Processor—or shortened to CSP (Creative Signal Processor). Currently, all SB16 cards that include the Advanced Signal Processor are identified by the phrase "with Advanced Signal Processing." This is quite confusing, but all is fair in love and lawsuits. We will use either the acronym CSP or the full name Advanced Signal Processor in this book.*

The manuals provided with your SB16 contain all the necessary instructions for installing and operating your SB16—read them carefully. You'll still want to check out our General Tips and Hints section later in this chapter for additional help on installing your SB16.

NOTE: *Throughout this chapter, we will refer to all versions of the Sound Blaster 16 family as SB16. Specific models will be addressed accordingly; for example, Sound Blaster 16 with Advanced Signal Processing will be SB16 CSP.*

ANATOMY OF
THE SOUND
BLASTER 16

he SB16 family is the latest and best offering from Creative Labs. The family comprises several versions: The SB16 Basic Edition (Basic), SB16 SCSI-2 (Small Computer Systems Interface), and the SB16 MultiCD (MCD). Both the SB16 SCSI-2 and SB16 MCD are also optionally available with the CSP chip installed, and are labeled accordingly; for example, SB16 SCSI-2 CSP. Table 4-1 shows the available configurations of SB16.

	Sound Blaster 16 Basic Edition	**Sound Blaster 16 MultiCD**	**Sound Blaster 16 SCSI-2**
Format	16-bit stereo	16-bit stereo	16-bit stereo
Advanced signal processing upgradability	Yes	Yes	Yes
Wave Blaster upgradability	Yes	Yes	Yes
CD-ROM compatibility	Creative Labs, Panasonic	Sony, Mitsumi, Creative Labs, Panasonic	Any SCSI or SCSI-2
Bundled microphone	No	Yes	Yes
Bundled software	Monologue for Windows	Monologue for Windows	Monologue for Windows
	Creative WaveStudio	Creative WaveStudio	Creative WaveStudio
	Creative Soundo'LE	Creative Soundo'LE	Creative Soundo'LE
	Creative Talking Scheduler	Creative Talking Scheduler	Creative Talking Scheduler
	Creative Mosaic	Creative Mosaic	Creative Mosaic
		Creative VoiceAssist	Creative VoiceAssist
		PC Animate Plus	PC Animate Plus
Suggested retail price	$199.95	$249.95	$279.95
With CSP upgrade	Not applicable	$299.95	$329.95
	(CSP available separately)		

TABLE 4-1   *The Various Configurations of SB16* ■

The differences between the various SB16s (whether with or without CSP) lie mainly in the CD-ROM interface. The regular SB16 has the standard proprietary Panasonic CD-ROM interface as carried over from the Sound Blaster Pro series. The SB16 SCSI-2 has a more flexible SCSI-2 interface, which allows you to hook up not only the latest and best CD-ROM drives, but also other SCSI devices such as hard drives. The SCSI interface uses an Adaptec chipset—one that is identical to the ones found on the Adaptec AHA-1510/1520/1522 SCSI host adapter series. The SB16 MCD on the other hand, not only includes the Panasonic CD-ROM interface (as with the regular SB16), but also an interface for proprietary Mitsumi CD-ROM drives as well as one for a proprietary Sony CD-ROM drive.

 TIP: Look in Chapter 11 for information and purchasing tips about the various CD-ROM drives you can connect to the various versions of the SB16. You will also find a table there showing which CD-ROM drives are compatible with each version of the SB16.

As with any evolutionary product, the SB16 is compatible with both the Sound Blaster and Sound Blaster Pro, and shares much in common with each. The MIDI/joystick port and the CD-ROM interface are unchanged. All software that supports the Sound Blaster MIDI port will work correctly with the SB16, and the Sound Blaster Pro's CD-ROM drive and drivers will also work fine on the SB16 Basic. The SB16 SCSI-2 and the SB16 MCD provide alternative CD-ROM interfaces for those of you who may want to use a CD-ROM drive other than the ones sold by Creative Labs.

The original Sound Blaster's joystick port is carried over to the SB16, so you may encounter calibration problems with some fast 386 or 486 PCs. If you do, you can purchase a separate joystick interface card that will adjust to high-speed computers. From the outside of the PC, the volume control wheel and input and output jacks on the back of the board are identical to the current crop of Sound Blasters.

The Chips for the Sound Blaster 16

There are many new chips used on the Sound Blaster 16. The fundamental operation of most of them has not changed, but the new chips offer more features and better performance. The chips used on the SB16 include the Digital Sound Processor (DSP), the FM synthesizer, the mixer, the bus interface, the Advanced Signal Processor, and on the SCSI-2 version, the Adaptec SCSI controller chip.

The Digital Sound Processor (DSP) Chip

The Sound Blaster 16 DSP chip, labeled CT 1741 in Figure 4-1, is the control center of the SB16. The DSP interprets all the commands sent to the SB16 and maintains compatibility with earlier Sound Blaster cards. It also interprets all the MIDI input and output functions, and controls all the other sound chips on the card.

The FM Synthesizer Chip

The Yamaha OPL3 FM synthesizer chip is used on the SB16. First used in the Sound Blaster Pro 2, this chip generates four-operator, 20-voice stereo FM sounds. This improves on the older two-operator, 11-voice mono Yamaha OPL2 (3812) FM chip still used on the Sound Blaster. The OPL3 can generate 15 melodies and 5 percussion sounds in two-operator mode, but only 6 melodies and 5 percussion sounds in full four-operator mode.

 TIP: *You can learn more about FM synthesis in Chapter 1 and in Appendix A.*

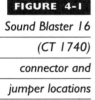

FIGURE 4-1

Sound Blaster 16

(CT 1740)

connector and

jumper locations

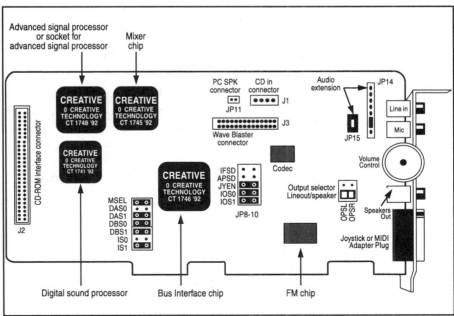

The Mixer

Another new chip introduced on the SB16 cards is the CT 1745 mixer. This chip allows you to adjust and mix the sounds from the microphone, line-in, CD audio, digital audio, MIDI (either FM or Wave Blaster), and the PC speaker. This way you can hear a blend of sounds, such as your voice from the microphone while FM music, digital sound, and CD audio play in the background. With this new mixer chip, you can even perform digital recording from multiple sources simultaneously. The Sound Blaster Pro, in contrast, can only record from one source at a time.

The mixer chip also provides bass and treble tone controls so that you can tailor the sound to suit your taste. If you are using small speakers on your SB16, try turning up the bass. It makes a difference with games, although it can't substitute for a pair of good powered speakers. If you get a lot of hiss from games that use 8-bit sound, try turning down the treble.

Another welcome feature of the 1745 mixer chip is the addition of a volume control for the PC speaker. On the Sound Blaster Pro, there was no way to adjust the volume of the PC speaker beeps relative to the other outputs. But on the SB16, you have full control over how loud the PC beeps through your speakers.

NOTE: *The PC speaker will only beep through the SB16 if a cable is connected between the PC motherboard and the PC_SPK connector on the SB16.*

Last, the new mixer allows you to adjust the gain of the inputs and outputs. If you have trouble getting an input level loud enough for a satisfactory recording, the SB16 lets you boost the signal up to eight times louder than the incoming signal. Similarly, if the output from the card seems too low, you can also boost the level by as much as eight times.

With a built-in mixer to control volume levels, you may be wondering what the purpose of the manual volume control on the Sound Blaster 16 is. The manual volume control sets the final volume of the output. With this manual volume control, you know that when you turn down the volume, there's no way the computer can override your setting.

The Bus Interface

The CT 1746 bus interface chip, shown in Figure 4-1, passes messages between the Sound Blaster 16 and the computer. All data, both commands and digital audio, must pass through the bus interface chip to communicate with the PC motherboard. The bus interface chip also provides the configuration settings for the card namely, the I/O port address, interrupt and DMA channel settings. Finally, the CT 1746 has a built-in buffer so that high sampling rates can be used even on slower 386 computers.

The CODEC

The CT 1701 CODEC performs analog-to-digital conversion when recording digital audio and digital-to-analog conversion when playing back digital audio. It can sample 8- or 16-bit audio at up to 44.1 kHz in full stereo. This is comparable to the sound quality available on compact discs (CDs) and digital audio tape (DAT). The CODEC also supplies dynamic filtering to eliminate aliasing noise. See Chapter 1 and Appendix A, for discussions on sampling and aliasing.

The Advanced Signal Processor

The Advanced Signal Processor CT 1748 is a programmable digital signal processor. Try not to confuse this with the Digital Sound Processor. The Advanced Signal Processor processes digital audio data based on a set of commands stored in its memory called CSP (Creative Signal Processor) code.

This chip can be programmed to perform a number of functions, including adding special effects to digital audio and providing advanced compression and decompression of audio. The operation of the Advanced Signal Processor and its related management software is covered later in this chapter in a section titled "Advanced Signal Processing Technology."

NOTE: *If you do not have an Advanced Signal Processor onboard your SB16, you will have an empty socket where the CT 1748 chip can be installed.*

The Connectors for Sound Blaster 16

Figures 4-1, 4-2, and 4-3 point out the various connectors on the SB16 cards. The connectors discussed in this section are common to all Sound Blaster 16 cards except where noted. For connectors specific to the SB16 SCSI-2 and SB16 MCD, see "The Connectors for Sound Blaster 16 SCSI-2" and "The Connectors for Sound Blaster 16 MCD" immediately following this section.

Connectors are used for passing sound from the card to speakers, stereos, and headphones, and for receiving sound from a microphone, tape player, or stereo.

Four connectors are accessible from the outside of the computer:

FIGURE 4-2

Sound Blaster 16 SCSI -2(CT 1770) connector and jumper locations ■

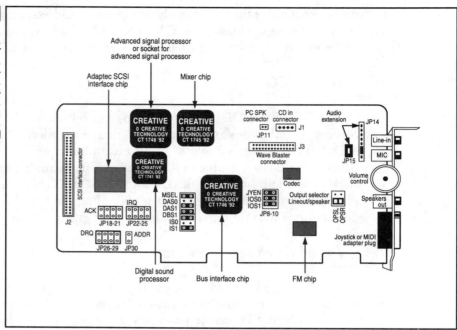

FIGURE 4-3

Sound Blaster 16 MCD (CT 1750) connector and jumper locations ■

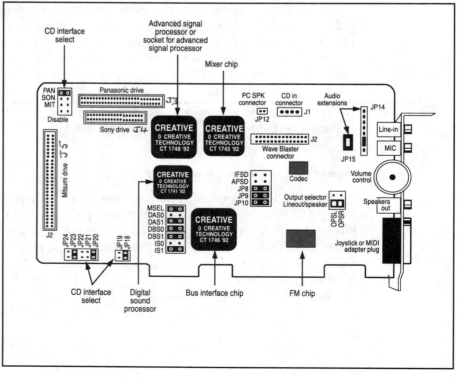

■ The line-in jack is shown at the very top of the card in Figure 4-1. It is a 1/8-inch stereo minijack, and is used to hook in the line-out from a tape deck, stereo, or CD player.

■ The next connector on the card is the microphone connector; it is a 1/8-inch mono minijack.

■ The connector just below the volume knob is the speaker output. It is a 1/8-inch stereo minijack. The speaker-out connector has a built-in amplifier that can output up to four watts of power per channel, so be sure to turn down the volume before connecting anything to it. Also, do not connect a mono 1/8-inch miniplug to the speaker output, as this can short-circuit and damage the amplifier.

■ The 15-pin D-sub connector is used for joystick input and MIDI input/output. The joystick/MIDI port supports one or two joysticks. Using two requires a Y-adapter available from Creative Labs; generic Y-adapters from other vendors may not work properly. Two pins on the joystick/MIDI connector (pins 12 and 15) are used for MIDI Out and MIDI In, respectively. This allows you to connect MIDI keyboards and synthesizers to the Sound Blaster with a Creative MIDI cable.

There are also three connectors on the card that are accessible only from the inside of the computer: PC_SPK, J1, and J2, all shown in Figure 4-1.

■ The PC_SPK connector allows you to connect the motherboard speaker output to the SB16. The pin configuration for this connector is given in Table 4-2.

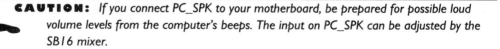

CAUTION: *If you connect PC_SPK to your motherboard, be prepared for possible loud volume levels from the computer's beeps. The input on PC_SPK can be adjusted by the SB16 mixer.*

■ The J1 connector is a Molex-type (plastic) connector for the CD-ROM drive. It passes stereo audio from the CD-ROM drive to the Pro card.

Pin	Signal	I/O
I	+5V	IN
2	SPK	IN

TABLE 4-2 *PC Speaker Connector (PC_SPK)* ■

The pin configuration for this connector is shown in Table 4-3.

- The J2 connector is the CD-ROM data cable connector, except on the SB16 MCD (see the following note). The data cable that runs between J2 and the CD-ROM drive allows the Sound Blaster 16 to directly control the CD-ROM drive. It is a proprietary interface connection for Creative Labs CD-ROM drives and some Panasonic/Matsushita drives. Contact Creative Labs for exact model information. J2 cannot be used by just any CD-ROM drive, and it is not a SCSI, or subset of a SCSI-type, interface.

NOTE: See "The Connectors for Sound Blaster 16 SCSI-2" and "The Connectors for Sound Blaster 16 MCD" later in this chapter for information on the CD-ROM connectors for those cards.

- Connector J3, located just below J1, is for the Wave Blaster daughterboard upgrade, except on the SB16 MCD, where it's labeled J2. When installing the Wave Blaster, be sure to line up all the pins correctly. A Wave Blaster that doesn't play is usually the result of a misaligned connection. Table 4-4 summarizes the pin configuration of the Wave Blaster connector.

WARNING: The pin configuration of the Wave Blaster connector is supplied here for informational purposes only. Incorrect use of these pins can permanently damage your Sound Blaster 16, Wave Blaster, or both.

The Connectors for Sound Blaster 16 SCSI-2

This section lists connectors that are specific to the SCSI version of the Sound Blaster 16 shown in Figure 4-2. All other connectors are the same on all Sound Blaster cards.

- J2 is the CD-ROM data cable connector on the SB16 SCSI. The data cable that runs between J2 and the CD-ROM drive allows the

Pin	Signal	I/O
1	Ground	IN
2	CD left channel	IN
3	Ground	IN
4	CD right channel	IN

TABLE 4-3 *CD IN Connector (J1)* ∎

Pin	Signal	Pin	Signal
1	Digital ground	2	No connection (NC)
3	No connection (NC)	4	MIDI Output
5	Digital ground	6	+5 volts
7	MIDI output	8	NC
9	Digital ground	10	+5 volts
11	Digital ground	12	NC
13	NC	14	+5 volts
15	Analog ground	16	NC
17	Analog ground	18	+12 volts
19	Analog ground	20	Line in: left channel
21	Analog ground	22	−12 volts
23	Analog ground	24	Line in: right channel
25	Analog ground	26	RESET

TABLE 4-4   *Wave Blaster Connector (J3 on SB16 and SB16 SCSI, J2 on MCD)* ■

Sound Blaster 16 to directly control the CD-ROM drive. This CD-ROM interface adheres to the SCSI-2 standard and is faster than most sound cards that only use SCSI-1. The SCSI interface also allows you to connect any other SCSI device such as hard disks, tape backups, and scanners.

The Connectors for Sound Blaster 16 MCD

This section lists connectors that are specific to the MCD version of the Sound Blaster 16 shown in Figure 4-3. All other connectors are the same on all Sound Blaster 16 cards.

- J3 is the CD-ROM data cable connector for CD-ROM drives that use the Panasonic proprietary interface. This is the same connector used on the regular Sound Blaster 16 and the SB16 Basic. It supports the Panasonic CD521, CR523 and CR563 drives.

- J4 is the CD-ROM data cable connector for CD-ROM drives that use the Sony proprietary interface. It supports the Sony CDU31A-02 drive.

- J5 is the CD-ROM data cable connector for CD-ROM drives that use the Mitsumi proprietary interface. It supports the Mitsumi CRMC LU005S and CRMC FX001/FX001d drives.

The Jumpers for Sound Blaster 16

Figures 4-1, 4-2, and 4-3 point out the various jumpers on the SB16 cards. The jumpers discussed in this section are common to all Sound Blaster 16 cards except where noted. For jumpers that are specific to the SB16 SCSI-2 and SB16 MCD, see "The Jumpers for Sound Blaster 16 SCSI-2" and "The Jumpers for Sound Blaster 16 MCD" immediately following this section.

The jumpers are used to configure the SB16 card so that it doesn't conflict with other cards in your computer. These jumpers are set into the card's configuration when you install your card.

- Jumper MSEL selects the I/O address for the MPU-40–compatible MIDI port. You can select 300H or 330H.

    300H: No jumper installed on MSEL
    330H: Jumper on MSEL (default)

TIP: *Many games and sequencers that use General MIDI or MT-32 will expect the MPU-401 MIDI port to be at address 330H since this is the default for the original Roland MPU-401. If you are having trouble with MIDI music in a game or sequencer, make sure you are using port 330H.*

- Jumpers DAS0 and DAS1 select the 8-bit DMA channel of the sound card. The 8-bit DMA channel is used when playing and recording 8-bit digital sound; 16-bit digital sound can also be played through the 8-bit DMA channel. See the 16-bit DMA channel jumper description below for more information.

    Channel 0: Jumpers on DAS0 and DAS1
    Channel 1: Jumper on DAS1 only (default)
    Channel 3: Jumper on DAS0 only

- Jumpers DBS0 and DBS1 select the 16-bit DMA channel of the sound card. The 16-bit DMA channel is used when playing and recording 16-bit digital sound. Choose from channels 5, 6, and 7.

Channel 5: Jumpers on DBS0 and DBS1 (default)
Channel 6: Jumper on DBS1 only
Channel 7: Jumper on DBS0 only

The default setting may conflict with some SCSI controller cards such as the Adaptec 15*xx* series. If you have a SCSI card installed, check this before installing the SB16. Try changing the DMA setting on the SCSI card if you have a conflict.

TIP: *If you are using DMA channel 6 or 7 and are having a problem running some games, try using DMA channel 5 instead. Many older games don't understand the 16-bit DMA setting and will only work at the default setting.*

NOTE: *Some motherboards have a faulty DMA controller and cannot reliably perform 16-bit DMA recording and playback. As a result, the SB16 has been designed to allow use of the 8-bit DMA channel for playing and recording 16-bit digital sound. Run TESTSB16.EXE in the SB16 directory to see if your motherboard has this problem. If it does, run SBCONFIG.EXE in the SB16 directory and follow the onscreen instructions to reconfigure your board for 8-bit DMA only.*

■ Jumpers IS0 and IS1 select the hardware interrupt number (IRQ) of the card. The interrupts are used for digital sound recording and playback, as well as MIDI input. Choose from 2, 5, 7, and 10.

IRQ2: Jumpers on IS0 and IS1
IRQ5: Jumper on IS1 only (default)
IRQ7: Jumper on IS0 only
IRQ10: No jumpers installed on IS0 and IS1

■ Jumpers IFSD and AFSD indicate to the SB16 whether or not an Advanced Signal Processor is installed. If you bought the SB16 with the chip, there will not be any jumpers here. If you do not have the chip, DO NOT remove these jumpers, or the SB16 will expect the Advanced Signal Processor to be on the card.

■ Jumper JYEN lets you turn the built-in joystick on and off. The only time you will need to remove the jumper is when you have another joystick port in your computer. Many combination I/O cards have a joystick port that is turned on by default. If you have such a card, check the documentation for the card to see if the joystick is enabled. If it is, disable the port either on the I/O card or the Sound Blaster 16, but not on both.

■ Jumpers IOS0 and IOS1 select the base I/O address of the card. The I/O address is the location of the communications channel that the computer uses to send and receive data from the Sound Blaster 16. You can choose from addresses 220H, 240H, 260H, and 280H.

    220H: Jumpers on IOS0 and IOS1 (default)
    240H: Jumper on IOS1 only
    260H: Jumper on IOS0 only
    280H: No jumpers installed on IOS0 and IOS1

■ Jumpers JP14 and JP15 (JP1 and JP2, respectively, on the MCD) are different from all the other jumpers on the board. They do not change the configuration of the board. Instead, JP14 and JP15 are an extension to the audio connectors on the board, making signal lines for the microphone and speaker accessible from within the computer. Their pin configurations are shown in Tables 4-5 and 4-6.

In Figure 4-1, notice that there is a jumper on pins 6 and 7 of JP14 and on pins 1 and 2 of JP15. Removing these jumpers will prevent sound from coming out of the Speaker Out connector on the board.

WARNING: *Do not experiment with the Audio Extension jumpers unless you are experienced with audio electronics. A mistake in connections here can damage the sound card.*

Pin	Description
1	MICGND (microphone input ground)
2	MICGND (microphone input ground)
3	MIC IN (microphone input) Input range 0.004 to 0.7 volt rms
4	SPKGND (speaker output ground)
5	SPKR (speaker output, right channel). Maximum output voltage 3 volt rms at 4 ohms, powered; 0.8 volt rms at 10 Kohms, line out.
6	SPKL (speaker output, left channel). Maximum output voltage 3 volt rms at 4 ohms, powered; 0.8 volt rms at 10 Kohms, line out.
7	SPKRL (speaker output return signal, left channel)
8	SPKRR (speaker output return signal, right channel)

TABLE 4-5 *Connector JP14 (JP1 on SB16 MCD) Pin Configuration* ■

Pin	Description
1	SPKR (speaker output, right channel). Maximum output voltage 3 volt rms at 4 ohms, powered; 0.8 volt rms at 10 Kohms, line out.
2	SPKRR (speaker output return signal, right channel). Maximum output voltage 3 volt rms at 4 ohms, powered; 0.8 volt rms at 10 Kohms, line out.

TABLE 4-6   *Connector JP15 (JP2 on SB16 MCD) Pin Configuration* ■

■ Jumpers OPSL and OPSR, just below jumpers JP14 and JP15, select the type of output for the Speaker Out connector. You have a choice of powered output or line-level output. Powered output is required if you are using speakers that don't have their own source of power or headphones. Select line-level output when connecting the SB16 to powered speakers or a stereo system for cleaner sound.

Powered speaker output: Jumpers on lower two pins (default)
Line-level speaker output: Jumpers on upper two pins

The Jumpers for Sound Blaster 16 SCSI-2

This section lists jumpers that are specific to the SCSI version of the Sound Blaster 16 shown in Figure 4-2. All other jumpers are the same on all Sound Blaster 16 cards.

■ JP30 selects the SCSI base I/O port address. Choose from 140H and 340H.

140H: No jumper installed on JP30 (default)
340H: Jumper on JP30

■ Jumpers JP22 through JP25 select the interrupt (IRQ) for the SCSI interface. Choose from IRQ9, IRQ10, IRQ11, and IRQ12.

IRQ9:   Jumper on JP22 only (the leftmost jumper in the group)
IRQ10: Jumper on JP23 only
IRQ11: Jumper on JP24 only (default)
IRQ12: Jumper on JP25 only (the rightmost jumper in the group)

■ Jumpers JP18 through JP21 and JP26 through JP29 select the DMA channel for the SCSI interface. Since the drivers for this model of the

Adaptec SCSI-2 interface chip use a 32-bit programmed I/O mode, there is no need to use any jumpers. 32-bit programmed I/O mode has two advantages over DMA mode. It is up to 20 percent faster and will not produce clicking noises caused by interrupts from the sound card.

The Jumpers for Sound Blaster 16 MCD

This section lists jumpers that are specific to the MCD version of the Sound Blaster 16 shown in Figure 4-3. All other jumpers are the same on all Sound Blaster 16 cards.

- Jumpers CD0 (JP18) and CD1 (JP19) select the base I/O address for the Mitsumi CD-ROM interface. Choose from 310H, 320H, 340H, and 350H.

  310H: Jumpers on CD0 and CD1
  320H: Jumper on CD1 only
  340H: Jumper on CD0 only (default)
  350H: No jumpers installed on CD0 and CD1

NOTE: *There are no jumpers for configuring the Panasonic or Sony interfaces. Both interfaces use the SB16 MCD base I/O address for the CD-ROM port.*

- JP20, JP21, and JP22 select the interrupt (IRQ) setting for the Mitsumi CD-ROM interface. Choose from IRQ3, IRQ10, and IRQ11.

  IRQ3:   Jumper on JP22 only
  IRQ10: Jumper on JP21 only
  IRQ11: Jumper on JP20 only (default)

- JP23 and JP24 set the DMA channel of the Mitsumi CD-ROM interface. Choose from DRQ6 and DRQ7.

  DRQ6: Jumper on JP24 only
  DRQ7: Jumper on JP23 only (default)

- JP25, JP26, JP27, and JP28 select the CD-ROM drive that you have connected to the SB16 MCD. You can also disable the CD-ROM interfaces by putting a jumper on JP28.

Panasonic: Jumper on JP25 only (default)
Sony: Jumper on JP26 only
Mitsumi: Jumper on JP27 only
Disable: Jumper on JP28 only

TIP: *You can use multiple CD-ROM drives on the MCD. You can make the Panasonic and Mitsumi interfaces active at the same time by putting a jumper on JP25 and a jumper on JP27. You can make the Sony and Mitsumi interfaces active at the same time by putting a jumper on JP26 and a jumper on JP27.*

NOTE: *You cannot use all three interfaces at the same time. The Panasonic and Sony interfaces also cannot be used at the same time. Both the Panasonic and Sony interfaces use the same I/O port and will conflict with each other.*

WHAT'S IN A NAME?

The "16" in Sound Blaster 16 denotes one of the new features of the board, namely the ability to record and play back 16-bit sound files (Chapter 1 takes a look at the differences and advantages of 16-bit versus 8-bit sounds, higher sampling rates, and other related topics). The 16-bit CODEC chip used in the SB16 is the same high-quality variety found in some professional DAT (Digital Audio Tape) machines. With the additional horsepower, the recording sample rate has also been fully extended to 44.1 kHz in stereo.

When sampling an audio signal at 44.1 kHz (44,100 samples per second) in 16-bit resolution and in stereo, a minute of recording requires the processing and storage of over 10MB. At this rate, you could gobble up 100MB in under 10 minutes!

Many applications, especially older games, will not yet take advantage of the higher-quality sound capability of the SB16. However, this situation is changing almost daily as new games are introduced and more SB16's are sold. The storage requirements for 16-bit sound are immense, but fortunately, CD-ROM provides a way to store these large 16-bit sound files at relatively low cost. Therefore, many new CD-ROM–based games designed for Windows feature high-quality 16-bit sound.

Be aware that the higher-quality circuitry of the SB16 may make some bad 8-bit recordings sound even worse. A dusty dress on a mannequin that may not seem so bad through a dirty window would look terrible through a clean one. The same principle applies with sound—the better the equipment, the more revealing it is of faults in the original material.

The SB16 will ruthlessly reveal the bad recording equipment and techniques used on many applications when playing 8-bit sounds, which are especially prevalent in older games. As all Sound Blasters prior to the SB16 are 8-bit cards, filters were used in the older cards to filter noise out of the 8-bit sound. However, the SB16 does not use as much high-frequency filtering as the 8-bit cards because such a large amount of filtering is detrimental to 16-bit sound. The most common anomaly you'll hear when the SB16 is playing an 8-bit sound is hiss.

TIP: *If you're experiencing a large amount of hiss, especially in many games, reduce the treble on the SB16 mixer.*

The implications of the new 16-bit capability of the SB16 are exciting. Once you've heard 16-bit sound versus 8-bit sound, you'll wonder why you ever put up with the mediocre 8-bit sounds. The higher quality afforded by the 16-bit recording and playback capability of the SB16 will bring CD quality sound to your PC. With 16-bit technology, games and other applications can use well-recorded sound effects to bring us a step closer to reality by enveloping our senses with sound that is virtually indistinguishable from the real thing.

Because 16-bit technology has such heavy storage requirements, data compression is almost a prerequisite to using it. That's where the Advanced Signal Processor chip comes in. In the following sections, we'll talk about other exciting possibilities of the SB16, including the Advanced Signal Processing chip and the Wave Blaster add-on.

ADVANCED SIGNAL PROCESSING TECHNOLOGY

The DSP (Digital Sound Processor), similar to the one found in previous Sound Blasters, is primarily responsible for interpreting, processing, and dispatching sound commands to the SB16. The Advanced Signal Processor is a new hardware add-on that is available on the SB16 SCSI-2 and SB16 MCD, or it can be purchased later as an upgrade to any SB16. A socket found on all SB16s provides the home for this easily installed chip.

The CSP (Creative Signal Processor) is used primarily to handle all digital audio data. Since this processor is fully programmable, you can change its function by simply downloading a new program to the CSP chip. Therefore, just like a math coprocessor processes complicated math calculations while your computer does something else, a variety of digital processing tasks can be handled at the same time by the CSP chip while your computer proceeds with other jobs. This is known as *multitasking*.

This multitasking feature is important because even a fast 386 computer will be bogged down with the processing requirements of data from stereo 44.1-kHz 16-bit sounds. The MPC (Multimedia PC) standards (as discussed in Chapter 1) specify that audio playback at 44.1 kHz in 8-bit sound should not consume more than 15 percent CPU (Central Processing Unit) utilization. Even the fastest 386 CPU may have problems adhering to that specification if it is also required to decompress the sound file at the same time. If the CPU is preoccupied with processing the digital audio, other tasks requiring its attention will be slowed or held up indefinitely. For example, if you have a presentation containing recorded music and accompanying animation, the frame rate (number of video frames that can be displayed per second) may suffer considerably since the CPU has little time to spend on loading the next frame of animation.

NOTE: *If you have a regular SB16 without the Advanced Signal Processor chip, you can upgrade to full Advanced Signal Processing capability at nominal cost by calling Creative Labs at (800) 998-5227. The Advanced Signal Processor Upgrade Kit will turn any regular SB16 into an SB16 with Advanced Signal Processing.*

As time and technology advance, the CPU will increase in speed until the simultaneous processing of high-quality digital audio and video becomes a nonissue. But for CPU-driven compression and decompression to be effective today, a more efficient plan is needed. The SB16's answer to minimizing the overhead of real-time compression and decompression is the use of hardware—the CSP. The CSP behaves in your computer like a specialized digital audio CPU, much like what a math coprocessor does for computer-aided design and spreadsheet applications. By taking care of the audio tasks, the CSP frees your computer to handle the video portion of any presentation, resulting in better sound and smoother animation.

How the CSP Works

Let's examine how the CSP works with the recording process. As shown in Figure 4-4, before starting the recording a program containing the data-compression algorithm is downloaded into the SB16's CSP. This is

FIGURE 4-4

Recording

compressed data

with the CSP

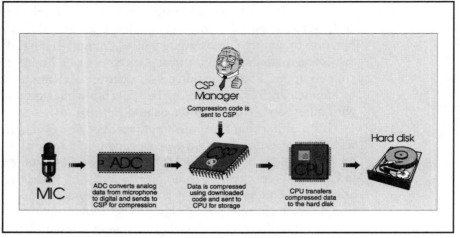

FIGURE 4-5

Playing back

compressed data

with the CSP

accomplished by the CSP manager (described later in this chapter). The DSP, via any digital sound recording software such as the Windows Recorder, then informs the ADC (analog-to-digital converter, explained in Chapter 1) to start converting analog data from an input device—a microphone in this instance—at a given sample rate and number of bits. The analog data is converted into digital data by the ADC and passed on to the CSP. The CSP compresses the digital data using the previously downloaded algorithm and sends the data to the PC for storage on your hard disk.

This process is reversed when playing back a previously saved recording. As shown in Figure 4-5, a special decompression program is first downloaded via the CSP manager to the CSP. The data from the storage device is

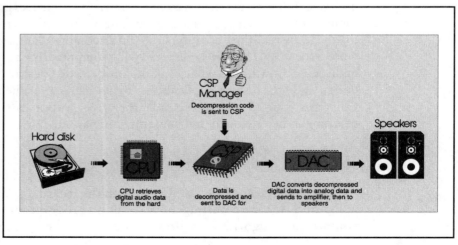

retrieved and sent to the CSP for processing. The CSP executes the program in its memory, decompresses the data, and sends it to the DAC. The DAC converts the decompressed digital data to analog data and hands it to the onboard amplifier, which in turn sends it to the speakers.

The CSP Manager

During installation, the DOS CSP manager is automatically added to your CONFIG.SYS. This TSR (terminate-and-stay-resident) program is merely 2.4K in size and is required by Windows and some DOS programs. You can conserve base memory by loading this driver into high memory.

TIP: *The SB16 manuals provide detailed instructions on how to load the CSP manager. Refer to the manual for step-by-step instructions.*

While all of the features of CSP may seem to require a lot of programming on the software developer's part, in fact the opposite is true. The CSP manager actually takes care of tracking the code in the CSP. When applications require the CSP for any application, the CSP manager automatically loads the appropriate code into the CSP.

This code-balancing act occurs transparently—neither user nor developer has to worry about it. For example, developers do not need to write the routines that compress or decompress a sound file; they simply have to have the CSP manager load the appropriate CSP routine. Even programs such as Microsoft Windows' Media Player, which knows nothing about sound decompression techniques, can work with fully compressed sounds. In the case of playback of compressed data, the CSP manager will place the proper code into the CSP when it sees a compressed wave identification number in the wave file. The operation is completely transparent to the user.

Creative Labs has pledged to make new CSP programs readily available to both developers and end-users alike. While SB16s will always ship with all the latest CSP programs available at the time, updated CSP drivers and programs can be downloaded via modem, or on disk by request. If a new 10:1 compression/decompression algorithm is discovered tomorrow, it can be translated into CSP code and made available rather quickly. These new CSP programs can then be copied to a hard disk and will be loaded transparently by the CSP manager when required. Currently, programs for the CSP chip are supplied only by Creative Labs; you cannot program the CSP chip yourself.

DOS and Windows versions of the CSP managers are included with the SB16. The SB16 is more than adequately equipped to handle current MPC requirements. Because of the CSP's programmable nature, it will handle new sound technologies with ease.

CSP Applications

Since the CSP is programmable, Creative can provide the SB16 with more than just compression and decompression routines. The flexible CSP can be programmed for many other digital audio tasks. Below are some of the many applications that can use the CSP chip to its fullest extent.

NOTE: *You can download the latest Creative Labs CSP programs (such as QSound) from CompuServe in the PACVEND forum. Alternatively, you can obtain them directly from Creative Labs.*

QSound

QSound is one of the first applications that utilize CSP technology. QSound allows programmers to project sounds not only from the left and right speakers, but from any location within a 180-degree soundscape (see Figure 4-6). The patented QSound algorithms are licensed by Creative Labs from QSound Labs, Inc. (formerly referred to as Archer Communications) of Alberta, Canada.

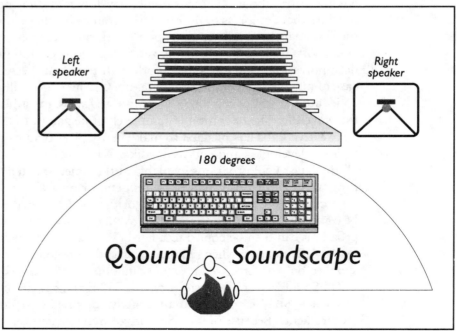

FIGURE 4-6

The QSound soundscape

Though surround sound has been around for years, its success has been diminished by the need for special equipment and additional speakers. This required users to devote much time and money to install these systems properly, and is certainly impractical for almost all computer setups at home. QSound is a system that successfully creates a similar soundscape or effect, but with only two speakers.

QSound Labs overcame substantial obstacles in developing QSound. The results are based on tests conducted with human test subjects—over 500,000 responses were gathered. This research led to the development of special filters that can be used during the recording or on playback to produce the QSound effect. QSound on the SB16 allows the sound to seemingly emanate from up to 33 locations. However, speaker placement is critical to QSound. You have to sit at least 20 inches away from the speakers, which must be separated by at least 16 inches. Moreover, the speakers have to placed at the same height, plane, and angle with equal volume for the optimum QSound effect. If you need to sit farther away, you'll have to increase the separation between the left and right speakers. This is a small price to pay, however, to elevate your aural experience to new levels.

NOTE: *The SB16's CSP handles all the additional processing required to produce QSound effects, so you will not experience any performance degradation when using QSound.*

QSound boasts an impressive list of users in the music recording, movie, television, and radio industries. Recording artists such as Sting, Kiss, Madonna, Paula Abdul, and Joe Cocker are among the many users. QSound was used in some famous movies including *Robin Hood: Prince of Thieves, Bill & Ted's Bogus Journey,* and *The Super.* Even large companies use them in their commercials, including McDonald's, General Motors, Jeep, and Budweiser. Sega of America also has begun using QSound in its latest CD-ROM games.

Creative Labs, together with QSound Labs, has made QSound technology available to all software developers. An Application Programmer's Interface (API) is available free to any developers interested in incorporating QSound into their software. Sample programs are provided together with separate DOS and Windows versions.

Continuous Speech Recognition

One of the most exciting applications of CSP is in speech recognition. There probably isn't a soul who has seen *Star Trek: The Next Generation* who wouldn't want to be able to say, "Computer, what is the current location of Captain Picard?" and then have the computer understand and process the request.

While Star Trek–like voice recognition remains far in the future, advanced voice recognition systems have made significant headway in recent years. There are PC programs today such as Creative's VoiceAssist that will translate short verbal commands fairly accurately (see Chapter 7). Continuous-speech recognition, however, places even greater demands on a processor than a compression/decompression algorithm. With the CSP, the SB16 can be used to process, or *off-load,* some of the processing required for future speech-recognition products. Voice-to-text dictation of word processing documents may not be as far off as it seems.

Speech Synthesis

The complement to speech recognition is speech synthesis, also known as text-to-speech. Speech synthesis enables the PC to read text out loud. In the past, text-to-speech applications sounded extremely mechanical. This was because complex algorithms required too much CPU power to be implemented on the PC. Now, by means of the CSP, Creative has brought the latest in speech synthesis technology to the PC platform. This new technology is 98 percent intelligible, and can even sing to you! See Appendix A for more information.

Special Effects

Special effects, such as echo and reverb, can also be performed in real-time with the CSP. Since the CSP acts like a separate, optimized computer, adding these effects will not affect the performance of the main CPU much. Spatial and surround sound effects (such as QSound) are also possible.

THE MPU-401 COMPATIBLE MIDI PORT

The Roland MPU-401 MIDI card has been the standard for MIDI cards on the PC for several years. At the time the original Sound Blaster was introduced, MPU-401 compatibility was important because it was the standard supported by all MIDI software.

The popularity of the Sound Blaster cards has brought about support for its proprietary MIDI port specification. In fact, since the coming of age of the Sound Blaster family, most MIDI software has been rewritten to support the Sound Blaster MIDI port.

Nevertheless, the SB16 is still the first Sound Blaster to fully support the MPU-401 UART standard. The port is full duplex, buffered, and will automatically switch between Sound Blaster MIDI and MPU-401 UART modes.

NOTE: *The Roland MPU-401 has two modes of operation: Smart mode and UART mode. Smart mode was designed for slow computers such as the IBM XT, Atari 800 and Commodore 64, that had trouble processing a lot of MIDI commands in a short period of time. As computers became faster, Smart mode was abandoned for UART mode. This mode simply passes MIDI data into and out of the computer. It doesn't do any processing of MIDI commands. The Sound Blaster 16 only supports MPU-401 UART mode. Software written for MPU-401 Smart mode will not work on the SB16. Some programs also claim to use UART mode while trying to sneak in Smart mode commands and can cause problems.*

SB16 MIXER SOFTWARE AND CONTROLS

Enhanced software usually means new software, and the SB16 is no exception to the rule. All the SB16 cards include a number of enhanced programs, including new Windows programs that take advantage of the added capabilities of the hardware. Also, new mixer software is provided to control the various functions of all the members of the SB16 family.

The SB16 DOS and Windows Mixers

A new mixer for both DOS and Windows (see Figure 4-7) is included with the SB16. Both mixers include new tone controls and input and output level controls. We'll describe the new controls available on the SB16 from either DOS or Windows mixers and then discuss the mixers themselves.

Treble and Bass Controls

The left and right channel treble and bass levels can be set independently in 15 levels from −14 dB (decibels) to +14 dB in 2-dB steps.

FIGURE 4-7

Sound Blaster 16

Windows mixer

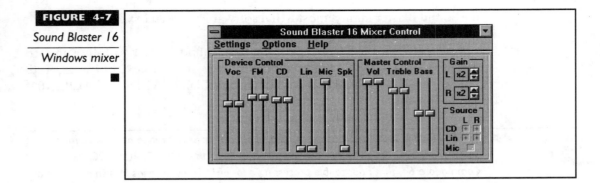

Volume Controls

Volume controls for the Master Volume, Digital Audio (DAC), CD Audio, FM Music, and Line In have been improved over the Sound Blaster Pro's 8 levels of stereo volume control to 32 levels of volume control in 2-dB steps on the SB16. This finer level of volume control should permit smoother panning of sounds from left to right and vice versa.

Microphone Input

The Microphone input has also been increased from mono 4-level attenuation to mono 32-level attenuation in 2-dB steps. As for the PC speaker input, it is adjustable in 6-dB steps with 4-level attenuation in mono.

A microphone is actually included with the SB16. It is of adequate quality for voice recording, but you'll have to purchase a better one if you're after 16-bit 44.1-kHz microphone recording quality.

Gain Control

Also new on the SB16 is the gain control, which allows the overall input and/or output levels to be increased by two, four, or eight times. The Automatic Gain Control, which can wreak havoc when you're recording from a microphone, can be disabled on the SB16 from either mixer.

Recording from More Than One Source Simultaneously

A useful enhancement to the new SB16 is the ability to record from more than one source at a time. On the Sound Blaster Pro, you get to select only one source for recording. The SB16 mixer allows you to selectively choose discrete left and/or right channels of all inputs to record from. You can record from the microphone while recording only the left channel from the line input, the right channel from the CD input, and both channels from the FM synthesizer (see Figure 4-8). You can even record yourself singing to a tune with musical accompaniment from a CD if you please!

The additional flexibility of the SB16 mixer also allows you to record the left channel of any input to the right channel or vice versa. Or you can record both channels from any input to the left or right channel only. The combinations are manifold, providing you with the most adaptable mixer yet for a Sound Blaster.

The DOS Mixer: SB16MIX

The DOS mixer, SB16MIX.EXE, is actually a large TSR program that eats up about 64K of memory. Once loaded in memory, it is activated by a hot key (ALT-1 by default, but you can change that).

When the screen is in text mode, a window will pop onto the screen (see Figure 4-9) when the hot key is pressed. When the mixer control panel is onscreen, it can be operated either with a mouse or with the keyboard. If you're running a graphics program like a VGA game for instance, the hot key will use the line at the bottom of the screen, as shown in Figure 4-10, and will only accept input from a keyboard.

Unlike the Sound Blaster Pro mixer (SBP-MIX.EXE), as long as the SB16 mixer (SB16MIX.EXE) is in memory, several key combinations can be used to control the various volume levels without necessarily bringing up the mixer panel. For example, you can press CTRL-ALT-M to enable the "master" volume control, followed by CTRL-ALT-U to "up," or increase, the setting and CTRL-ALT-D to "down," or decrease, the setting.

The DOS Interactive and Command-Line Mixer: SB16SET

Recognizing that SB16MIX.EXE may take memory away from programs that require the additional 64K to run, the traditional command-line utility

FIGURE 4-8

Windows mixer recording input selector

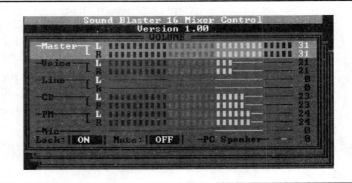

to set all the volume levels and tone controls is also included. SB16SET.EXE works with the SB16 as SBP-SET.EXE does with the Sound Blaster Pro. Of course, the additional features found in the SB16 can be controlled using new command-line switches for SB16SET.EXE.

SB16SET.EXE also includes a mouse-compatible interactive graphical interface for setting the various mixer levels. This is far more convenient than having to memorize the command-line switches. It is a good idea to include the subdirectory in which SB16SET.EXE resides in your PATH= statement to gain access to this handy non–memory-resident mixer wherever you are in DOS. Alternatively, you could move SB16SET.EXE to a directory that is already in the DOS path.

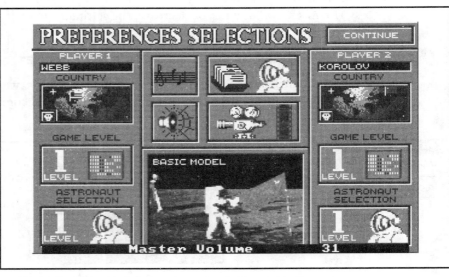

For those of you who are not using an external amplifier, it is more convenient to use the mixer volume control than it is to reach behind the computer to adjust the volume control on the back of the Sound Blaster. Create some batch files with preset volume settings so that you can quickly change volumes by simply executing the batch command. Here are examples of some batch files you could create:

Batch File Name	Contents
SOFT.BAT	C:\SB16\SB16SET /M:130
MED.BAT	C:\SB16\SB16SET /M:180
LOUD.BAT	C:\SB16\SB16SET /M:240

The Windows Mixer: SB16WMIX

The Windows mixer provides the same functionality as the DOS mixers described above. Since Windows alleviates most memory concerns, you can safely load SB16WMIX.EXE whenever you start Windows by adding it to the Program Manager StartUp Group or by adding it to the RUN= or LOAD= line in the WIN.INI file. If you add it to the Program Manager StartUp Group, you may select the "Run Minimized" check box in the Program Item Properties dialog box so that the mixer will show up as an icon at the bottom of your screen.

After adjusting the levels using the Windows Mixer, save the settings. The next time you start Windows and the mixer is loaded, your levels will revert to those that you had previously saved.

DOS SOFTWARE FOR SB16

The traditional lineup of DOS programs, some enhanced versions of the Sound Blaster Pro counterparts, can be found in the SB16 box. The following ones remain unchanged and are discussed elsewhere in this book:

- SBTALKER, which works with Dr. Sbaitso

- FM Intelligent Organ

- SBSIM, the Sound Blaster Standard Interface Module

- MMPLAY multimedia player

- PLAYMIDI and PLAYCMF music utilities

The voice utilities like VPLAY.EXE and VREC.EXE have been updated to support the new stereo 16-bit 44.1-kHz recording capability of the SB16. This new Voice file format is version 1.20; utilities to convert from the previous version 1.10 to the new version are also included. Since the Wave file format already handles the new recording and playback capabilities of the SB16, only small changes to allow this capability were made to the other programs such as VOC2WAV.EXE, WAV2VOC.EXE, WPLAY.EXE, and WREC.EXE.

NOTE: *All the above-mentioned DOS programs are described in Chapter 6.*

NEW WINDOWS 3.1 SOFTWARE

Besides the mixers and DOS programs, Creative Labs has included a whole slew of Windows applications for the SB16. First and most important are the Windows 3.1 drivers.

An automatic setup program makes the installation of these drivers a breeze. To install the drivers, you need only run WINSETUP.EXE while in Windows. When you run this program, the drivers are copied to the right directory, the SB16 program group (with icons) is added to Program Manager, and all the changes take effect after Windows is restarted (see Figure 4-11).

Windows provides an attractive and functional interface for the following programs that are bundled with the SB16. They are generally easier to learn and use than their cryptic DOS counterparts.

VoiceAssist

VoiceAssist is a speech recognition program that operates in Windows. It allows you to use the microphone attached to your SB16 to control your computer with your voice. Amazing as it seems, with VoiceAssist you can

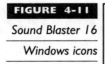

FIGURE 4-11

Sound Blaster 16

Windows icons

start up your calendar or electronic calculator program by simply saying "calendar" or "calculator." Refer to Chapter 7 for more insight into voice recognition and VoiceAssist.

NOTE: *If you purchased an SB16 without VoiceAssist, you can purchase it separately for a nominal fee by calling Creative Labs.*

WaveStudio

WaveStudio is a recording, playback, and editing program for WAV format files. It has the ability to work with several of these files at one time, allowing for cut and paste between them (see Figure 4-12). Special effects such as echo, fade, amplification, reverse, and merge can be easily performed on any Wave file.

There is a button on WaveStudio's toolbar to run the mixer for adjusting input levels prior to the start of any recording. Working with the SB16, it will record from multiple sources at one time in 16-bit stereo, at a 44.1-kHz sampling rate. WaveStudio supports the drag-and-drop Windows interface, which allows you to simply drag a file from the Windows File Manager onto a window or icon and have WaveStudio load the Wave file for editing.

WaveStudio eliminates the frustration and complexity of working with the DOS voice utilities when recording on the SB16. This program is so

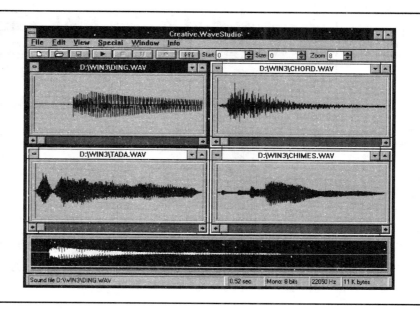

FIGURE 4-12

WaveStudio with four open WAV files

superior that even if you need files in the Creative Labs Voice format, it's best to record using WaveStudio and then the DOS Wave-to-Voice translation utility (WAV2VOC.EXE) to convert the recording to the desired Voice format.

Talking Scheduler

Talking Scheduler is a scheduling program that reminds you of your appointments verbally. Using a text-to-speech engine and one of three animated characters—Simon, Perkins, or Igor—Talking Scheduler will actually call you by name and announce your upcoming appointment (see Figure 4-13).

This multimedia program can even record your voice message and play it back as a reminder. OLE (Object Linking and Embedding), a Windows 3.1 feature, is fully supported by Talking Scheduler. By using OLE, you can easily attach a multimedia movie or spreadsheet, for instance, to an appointment—which can then be automatically retrieved when the reminder pops up on the screen. Imagine this: You can set a reminder for your wedding anniversary, have Igor tell you to go get a gift, have an animation clip showing Larry slapping Moe (from *The Three Stooges*) with the famous "woob woob" sound, and bring up your checkbook balance automatically. Is Talking Scheduler fun? You bet it is!

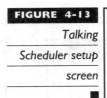

FIGURE 4-13

Talking Scheduler setup screen

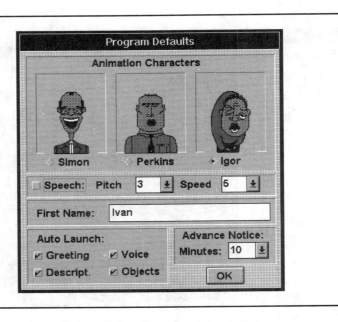

NOTE: *Refer to your Microsoft Windows manuals for a discussion of OLE technology.*

Soundo'LE

Soundo'LE is an OLE-compliant program that you can use to record and play back any Wave sound file in other Windows applications that support OLE (see Figure 4-14). It is not significantly better than the Windows Recorder if you're only going to do basic voice annotation. However, Soundo'LE does support the full capabilities of the SB16. The Windows Recorder, on the other hand, makes selecting sample rates and other parameters difficult and does not support real-time compression using the CSP manager.

Mosaic

Mosaic is a tile game with three levels of difficulty and can be configured up to an 8-by-8 grid. Like Windows' own Solitaire game, it is a very basic game, but it's good for when you're on a coffee break. Creative Labs enhanced the game by adding sound and colorful pictures (see Figure 4-15).

MM Jukebox

MM Jukebox is a program that allows you to queue MIDI files and play them in the background while you're working on something else. The new version 2.2 actually allows you to insert a MIDI file as an OLE object into any OLE client program. It will also play MIDI files in full stereo. Use JukeBox with the WB to provide CD-quality background music while you work in Windows.

FIGURE 4-14

Soundo'LE screen

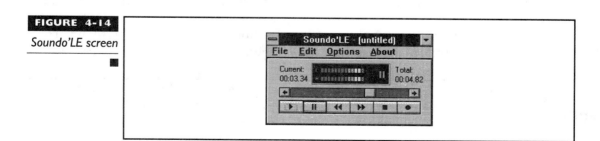

FIGURE 4-15

A Mosaic screen

OTHER VALUABLE SOFTWARE

Creative Labs aims to please with the SB16. Not only did the company include the wealth of programs described previously, they made arrangements with third-party companies to provide even more advanced applications. These programs would cost hundreds of dollars by themselves.

The Software Toolworks Multimedia Encyclopedia CD-ROM

This multimedia encyclopedia CD-ROM from Software Toolworks is the electronic version of *Grolier's Academic American Encyclopedia*. All 21 volumes are contained in this CD-ROM edition, which means you'll need a CD-ROM drive to use this program. It features more than 33,000 articles, 3,000 pictures, 250 maps, 30 animations, and 30 minutes of sound. You'll find the articles fully indexed by titles, words, pictures, and maps.

NOTE: *The Multimedia Encyclopedia program was not included when SB16 was first introduced, so you may not have this if you purchased the very first SB16 cards.*

HSC InterActive SE

HSC InterActive SE from HSC Software is an interactive multimedia presentation authoring system. The description may be daunting, but what HSCIA allows you to do is integrate sound, pictures, and animation in a variety of ways. HSCIA is a multimedia programming environment. Just as you would use Lotus 1-2-3 to create a spreadsheet, you would use HSCIA to create applications that require multimedia elements like sound. These applications can then be used for presentations, tutorials, and the like. If you're adventurous, you could even use HSCIA to create a computer tour of your home.

Unlike traditional programming methods, HSCIA uses an icon-driven interface for authoring. Using a flowchart metaphor, you create an HSCIA application by simply building the flowchart using different icons that represent different actions.

HSCIA is a Windows program. An animation editor, graphics editor, and an image-enhancement editor are all part of the HSCIA package.

PC Animate Plus

PC Animate Plus from Presidio Software is an animation studio. Much like the popular Autodesk Animator, you can use Animate Plus to create PC movies. A special effects generator and a paint program are included. If you have a compatible super-VGA video board, you can create animation with pictures of up to 32,000 colors.

Monologue for Windows

Monologue for Windows may not sound as natural as Hal from the movie *2001: A Space Odyssey,* or the computer on *Star Trek: The Next Generation,* but it does a credible job of verbalizing text. This program permits other Windows programs to speak their mind! Using a patented text-to-speech utility, Monologue will read any text copied onto the Windows Clipboard. Using the DDE (Dynamic Data Exchange) or DLL (Dynamic Link Libraries) interface, you can write to your own speech-enabled application if you're so inclined. In fact, the Talking Scheduler program uses this engine to create Igor's speech.

Speech synthesis has not been perfected yet—for many reasons. Monologue attacks some of the anomalies of spoken English with an "exception" dictionary. Here, you can use phonetics to force Monologue to pronounce a word more accurately. Also, you can vary the pitch and speed at which Monologue speaks.

At the very least, Monologue sounds better than Joshua, the talking computer from the movie *War Games*.

WAVE BLASTER UPGRADE OPTION

ne of the most significant additions to the SB16 is the MIDI Extension Connector, designed to be attached to the Wave Blaster (WB). While the CSP chip is designed to improve the digital signal processing capability of the SB16 (used for most sound effects), the WB improves the SB16's MIDI music capability. We believe the WB to be the most significant upgrade (besides a CD-ROM drive) you can make to your SB16. A WB can be added to any SB16—the CSP chip is not required for the WB to work.

The WB Upgrade is a daughterboard that uses a patented wave-table synthesis technology to generate 32-voice, multitimbral stereo music. The technology used in the WB originates from E-Mu Systems, a subsidiary of Creative Labs. E-Mu Systems has been providing this and other technologies to music keyboard synthesizer manufacturers for many years. By incorporating wave-table-synthesis technology into the WB, you'll be able to obtain professional-quality sound from your SB16. We'll explain the technology of the WB and describe its advantages in the following sections.

Wave-Table Synthesis

Wave-table synthesis technology accounts for some of the best and most realistically reproduced sounds you hear on the radio. This certainly is the next revolution in sound boards. Creative Labs has provided some obsolescence protection by offering the WB Upgrade for the SB16.

Here's how wave-table synthesis on the WB works: High-quality 16-bit recordings of actual instruments are stored in 4MB of ROM on the WB. These recordings are then manipulated digitally in real-time to produce the different notes on playback. A seven-point interpolation formula is used to perform the necessary calculations on sampled waveforms of musical instruments to achieve virtually perfect reproduction of these instrument sounds.

TIP: *Refer to Chapter 1 and Appendix A for more information on wave-table synthesis and other MIDI technology.*

The difference between wave-table synthesis sound and FM (frequency modulation) synthesized sound is like night and day. An FM-synthesized acoustic guitar sounds pathetic when compared to a real acoustic guitar. Acoustic instruments produce the most difficult sound waves to reproduce with the simplistic FM algorithms. That's why the piano and guitar sounds are clearly the most improved sounds on the WB versus the stock Sound Blaster. Instruments sound like the real ones played by professional musicians. And wait until you hear the drums—the difference is astonishing. The tinny sounds that used to emanate from the speakers are transformed into CD-quality music. Over 200 sounds are included.

A key advantage to having a quality synthesizer like the WB is that you can use MIDI files (described in Chapter 1) for playing professional-quality music in multimedia presentations. Since the quality of the sound produced from the WB can rival that of 16-bit CD sound, you can use the smaller and more efficient MIDI file format to store and play music. Quality recorded digital audio files in wave format, as we know, require a lot of processing and disk space. Instead of needing megabytes of storage for a short 20-second wave file, a 20K MIDI file could play for several minutes.

General MIDI Compatibility

The WB is General MIDI (GM) compatible. This is good news for programmers and musicians alike. In operating a MIDI instrument, if you want a piano sound, you have to figure out which *patch* (a predefined collection of sounds from various musical instruments) the instrument on that MIDI device is at and then send the MIDI messages to it via an appropriate channel. Different sounds in different synthesizers may be recalled using a different patch. For instance, violins may be patch 32 for synthesizer A and patch 18 for synthesizer B. This, of course, means lots of work for programmers and musicians to support every single synthesizer on the market.

The General MIDI specification was created to alleviate this confusion. In General MIDI, for example, patch 1 is always a piano sound, patch 41 always points to a violin sound, and patch 106 is a banjo sound. Different General MIDI–compatible synthesizers may have a different sounding violin, but it is always recalled as patch 41. This one feature of the WB Upgrade will make the WB Upgrade compatible with most of the MIDI, music, and gaming software on the market today—right out of the box.

NOTE: *Many newer games and applications support the General MIDI standard. Since the Wave Blaster is fully General MIDI compatible, use the General MIDI selection rather than the regular Sound Blaster selection whenever possible if you have a Wave Blaster attached to your SB16.*

Windows Software Included with Wave Blaster

The SB16 comes with a variety of Windows software, most of which cannot be bought separately. The software is briefly described here. You may want to check Chapters 5, 7, 8, and 9 for hints and tips on using some of the software described in this section.

WBPANEL

WBPanel, shown in Figure 4-16, can be used to change the mappings and download different instrument banks to the WB. Whenever you start WBPANEL, it automatically resets the WB to its start-up General MIDI–compatible bank list.

To get the full stereo effect, you may want to turn the pan sliders on and play with them. This will allow you to position the instrument sounds from left to right. You can also change parameters like velocity curves or tune the WB to another instrument.

WBMODE and the MT-32–Compatible Instrument Map

The Roland MT-32, CM-64 MIDI modules, and the LAPC-1 MIDI board (replaced recently with the Sound Canvas General MIDI series)

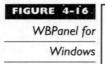

FIGURE 4-16

WBPanel for

Windows

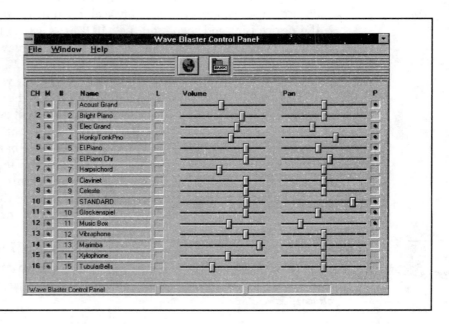

have dominated PC MIDI add-ons. It is no wonder then that the WB comes with a MT-32 bank–compatible setting. Keep in mind that the extended programming features and other advanced commands of the MT-32 are not supported. Many games will try to use these commands to set up the MT-32 and may hang up your computer if you specify that you have an MT-32 or compatible device. The MT-32–compatible bank mode of the WB simply consists of alternate patches that contain mappings of its instruments to match those of the MT-32. These patches are included with the WB and are described in the WB manual.

You can find out which games or applications support MT-32 and/or GM by referring to the game or application's manual. There is no harm in trying to get better sound from applications that support the MT-32 but not General MIDI or the WB directly. Use WBMODE to download the MT-32 compatible bank settings to the WB by typing the following command:

WBMODE MT32

Now try reconfiguring your application to use an MT-32. If the program hangs, or will not continue when you try to start it, just reboot your machine and reset the sound selection back to the Sound Blaster mode. Even if it does work, you may get some funny-sounding machine guns, for instance, since the program thinks it has downloaded a new sound to the MT-32 that the WB has not accepted. When everything works and sounds correct, you're in for a treat.

To return the Wave Blaster to General MIDI mode, simply reset it with the following command:

WBMODE /R

TIP: *You can obtain a file from the Creative Labs BBS that may make the WB work in MT-32 mode with some stubborn games. The filename is SBMPU401.EXE. It is also available on the PACVEND forum on CompuServe; the name of the file is MPU401.ZIP. Instructions are included in the file.*

Cakewalk Apprentice for Windows

Cakewalk Apprentice will get you started in the right direction for creating your musical masterpiece. It is a scaled-down version of its older sibling, Cakewalk Professional. This MIDI sequencer allows you to create MIDI music files from scratch or to modify an existing MIDI file. Remember to send in your registration card and also grab the excellent Romeo Music

Cakewalk Series. It contains over 60 top-notch MIDI sequences—serving as inspiration for budding musical prodigies. For a full tutorial on Cakewalk Apprentice for Windows, see Chapter 8.

GENERAL TIPS AND HINTS

Since the SB16 has excellent installation manuals, you'll want to read them thoroughly before attempting to install your SB16. The SB16 Getting Started manual contain diagrams and settings for all the available options, which we refer to later in the chapter. Have the manual handy to help decipher some of the tips we'll talk about.

Problems with 16-Bit Audio Playback

To smooth the transfer of large amounts of digital data inherent in 16-bit recordings, the SB16 actually uses a 16-bit DMA channel in addition to an 8-bit DMA channel. Using a 16-bit DMA channel speeds up data transfer from the memory on the SB16 to the PC bus, and then to the PC memory by freeing the CPU from having to move the data. Some computers may have problems with these 16-bit DMA transfers, but thankfully the SB16 allows the use of an 8-bit DMA channel as a substitute (albeit at the cost of speed and processor cycles).

TIP: *Many games will not work correctly with the new 16-bit DMA channels, nor the 16-bit IRQs on the SB16. If at all possible, stick to the default settings as the SB16 manual recommends.*

Using Powered Speakers

For users of powered speakers, the SB16 has a jumper to disable the internal 4W per channel amplifier. Bypassing the amplifier circuit should reduce hiss and interference. Since the bypass is post fader, all the input level and tone controls will still work fine. Try to locate the card as far away as possible from your video card, which is a major contributor of noise and interference.

TIP: *If you have powered speakers, disable the SB16's internal amplifier by moving jumpers OPSL and OPSR to pins 1 and 2, the upper two pins.*

Wave Blaster Installation Tips

For those of you lucky enough to have purchased both the SB16 and the WB together, consider installing the SB16 by itself first before adding the WB. Some of the jumpers for changing interrupts, DMAs, and port addresses cannot be reached once the WB is connected to the board. Since you may have to change the settings to avoid conflicts at first, avoid installing the WB until you've successfully installed the SB16. If you must install them at the same time, at least avoid using the plastic mounting posts until you find a setup that works correctly.

When adding the WB, it is easier to first insert the three plastic posts into the WB than to the SB16. After putting on the posts, lay the SB16 on a flat, hard surface like a desk or tile floor. Align the header pins and push down on the WB at the four corners, starting with the side where the header pins are. You need to exert some force when pushing the posts through the eyelets on the SB16.

Playing the Wave Blaster with a MIDI Keyboard

You may have wondered how you can "play" the WB the way you would a synthesizer keyboard. If you have a MIDI keyboard and the MIDI kit for the Sound Blaster, you can do this quite easily. Just attach your keyboard to the MIDI cable and use the special audition mode of WBPANEL by typing the following:

    WBMODE /A

If you got those bargain-basement speakers when you purchased your SB16, consider new speakers when upgrading to the WB. Better speakers will reveal the true glory of the WB's sound. The sound of its bass guitar and drums can really rattle any window with the right setup, and the WB can produce incredibly deep bass notes.

Using the MPU-401 MIDI Port in Windows

Certain software will only work with a MIDI device via a Roland MPU-401 MIDI port. This is not a problem since the SB16 and the WB will operate in that mode. However, in Windows, some applications may change some settings in the SYSTEM.INI file to point to the MPU-401 driver, which is not loaded by default when installing Windows. If that is the case, you may get an error that says "Failed to load MPU-401 driver," or "Cannot initialize MIDI device" when you try to start Windows or load any software that uses the WB. At this point, you can do one of two things. Keep in mind that the first method is the permanent fix, whereas the second fix may be undone the next time you run the program that changed your setup in the first place:

- Use the Windows Control Panel, select Drivers, click on Add, and double-click on Roland MPU-401. Windows will ask for a specific numbered disk. Insert the required disk and click OK. Windows will copy the required driver onto your hard disk. Follow the onscreen instructions and restart Windows. Your setup should work correctly from this point on.

- Use the Windows Control Panel, select Drivers, select the three SB16 drivers in sequence, and delete them. The drivers names are Creative SB16 Auxiliary Audio, Creative SB16 MIDI Synthesizer, and Creative SB16 Wave and MIDI. Now reinstall the drivers by selecting Add, and click on Unlisted or Updated Driver, and type in the path to the latest SB16 driver location (typically C:\SB16\WINDRV), selecting each one of the aforementioned drivers. Restart Windows, and everything should be back to normal.

IN SUMMARY

The SB16 is undoubtedly a much improved card that is worthy of upgrade consideration—especially if you have one of the original Sound Blasters. If nothing else, the WB Upgrade and additional software included with the SB16 at only a slight cost increase over the Sound Blaster Pro should help sway you toward upgrading to the SB16.

The potential usefulness of the CSP cannot be fully gauged at this moment. As new algorithms and programs are written for it, only then will we begin to see the capacity of the CSP. QSound is promising in this regard, and we should see new applications supporting this in the near future. The CSP chip does increase the stability and usability of multitasking operating systems such as Windows and OS/2 today. By offloading traditionally processor-intensive digital signal processing from the CPU, the CSP in the SB16 permits these operating systems more free time for running other programs concurrently—in other words, more breathing room.

Has the future of PC sound arrived? The answer from users of the SB16 with Advanced Signal Processing and the Wave Blaster is a resounding yes.

III

Sound Blaster Software

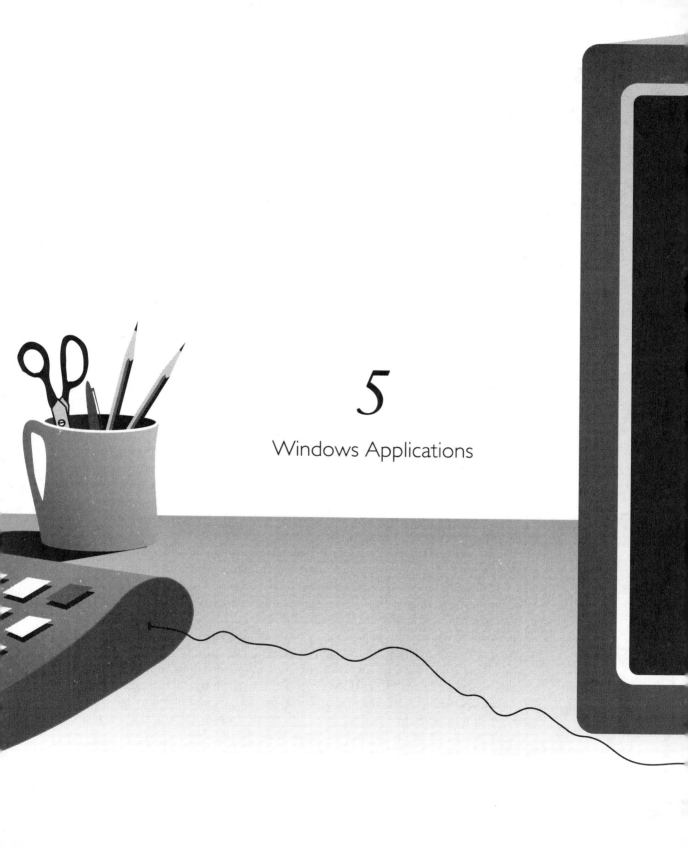

5

Windows Applications

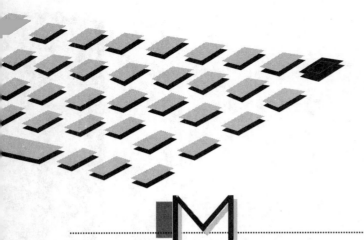

M I C R O S O F T Windows users are certain to gravitate toward the software programs described in this chapter. The Creative Labs Windows programs described here are, in order of their description, Creative Mosaic, Creative Soundo'LE, Creative Talking Scheduler, Creative JukeBox, Creative QuickCD, and Creative WaveStudio. These programs are included with the Deluxe version of Sound Blaster and Sound Blaster Pro, as well as with all versions of Sound Blaster 16. They demonstrate how the power of the computer is made readily accessible through elegant software design that combines good graphical user interface (GUI) design with sound.

Creative Mosaic is a fun tile game. Creative Soundo'LE is a digital audio recording tool, equally suitable for adding voice annotations to documents, preparing a voice-over for a multimedia presentation, or just having fun. Creative Talking Scheduler is an intriguing appointment book that provides verbal reminders. Creative JukeBox is a MIDI music JukeBox player ideal for enlivening an otherwise dreary session balancing your computer check book or reviewing a long report. The Creative QuickCD plays audio CDs placed into your computer's CD-ROM drive. Creative WaveStudio is an editor for digital audio files that can do amazing transformations to recordings.

Microsoft delivers a suite of useful software with Microsoft Windows 3.1, including several programs of special value to Sound Blaster owners. These include Microsoft Windows Media Player and Microsoft Windows Sound Recorder, which are the last two programs described in this chapter. Both programs are found in the Windows Accessories group. Media Player takes on a new role once a CD-ROM drive is installed: it'll play audio CDs loaded into your computer's CD-ROM drive. Prior to the introduction of the Deluxe packages, Sound Recorder was essential for making and playing digital audio recordings. Since then you receive, with the purchase of a Sound Blaster card, the Creative Soundo'LE and Creative WaveStudio, both of which are more powerful than Sound Recorder. You're likely to select one of these two rather than Sound Recorder as your recording partner.

NOTE: *This chapter does not go into detail on the Windows mixer programs that accompany the Sound Blaster Pro Deluxe and the Sound Blaster 16. Refer to Chapter 3 for details on the SB Pro mixer software, and refer to Chapter 4 for more information on the SB16 mixer software.*

Creative Mosaic is intended to be fun, a computer version of the tile game that has brought joy and frustration to millions of kids (and more than a few adults, too). Talking Scheduler looks and sounds like a toy, but it's really a useful appointment reminder that's been dressed up like a toy. Creative Soundo'LE is the Swiss army knife of Windows recording programs. This is the tool of choice for making digital audio recordings of your voice, audio CD sound, FM or Wave Blaster synthesizer music, or another source of sound you've hooked up to your sound card's Line In. From Soundo'LE you can record and play sound, access the mixer to fine-tune your recording session, and even embed sound into other Windows programs, such as your word processor or spreadsheet.

CREATIVE MOSAIC

Creative Mosaic is the computer version of the classic tile game in which you move the tiles about with your finger until they form a picture. Creative Mosaic is even more fun than the original game. This computer simulation shuffles the tiles for you, so you can start anew. You can choose the level of difficulty, in terms of both the number of rows and columns and how wickedly shuffled the tiles are when you begin. Best of all, you can customize the game by choosing a picture to arrange. When the game starts, you see a 3×3 arrangement of numbered tiles. By selecting Options,Picture, you pick among the four pictures available. If you pick the picture file titled JAPAN.BMP, for example, you see a tantalizing assortment of tiles (see Figure 5-1). Note that when you select this picture you're *not* likely to see the arrangement of tiles shown in the figure since Creative Mosaic starts each game with a random shuffle of the tiles.

You can now drag the tiles with your mouse and, courtesy of the 4-digit counter at the top right, see how many moves it took to solve the puzzle. If you're a hard-core puzzle solver, you've probably already selected Skill,Advanced and Size,8X8. When you restart the game by selecting the Key icon, the Advanced selection will give you the most difficult possible shuffling of the tiles. If you're not a maniac puzzle solver, you should stick to the default settings for Size and Skill and select Hints from the Help menu (Figure 5-1)

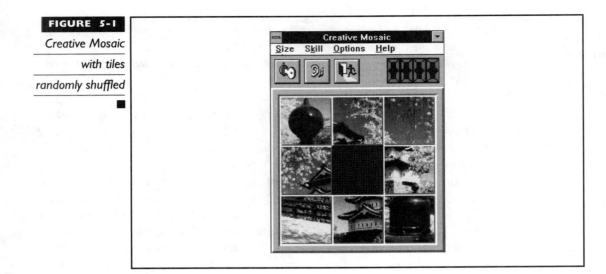

to see what the underlying picture looks like (Figure 5-2) before proceeding. To quit the game, select the icon featuring a person running for the door.

Create Your Own Puzzle

The Sound Blaster User Reference Manual doesn't mention the game's nicest feature: you can create your own puzzles. Creative Mosaic uses bitmap picture (BMP) files; you can create these files in the Microsoft Windows Paintbrush program, a Windows application that's found in your Accessory group. Figure 5-3 shows the puzzle picture (JAPAN.BMP is the filename) loaded into Paintbrush.

FIGURE 5-3

Viewing

JAPAN.BMP in

Windows

Paintbrush

■

You might want to surprise family members by using their picture as the puzzle! A scanner is ideal for adding your own pictures. If you don't have a scanner but you do have a fax/modem, you can ask a friend to fax a picture to your computer. First check whether your fax software can save a picture as a BMP file. If not, many graphics programs convert between file types, so you should be able to convert your fax file to a standard Microsoft Windows BMP file. In a pinch, you can use a service bureau or photo lab to convert a photograph or slide to a BMP file.

TIP: *Anything you can see on screen you can pull into Windows Paintbrush and then use for the puzzle picture. When you press the Windows* PRINTSCRN *key, a copy of the screen is copied to the Windows Clipboard and can be viewed by running the Clipboard application found in the Microsoft Windows Accessories\group. Once you place an image in the Clipboard, you can also bring it into the Paintbrush program by selecting Paste from the Paintbrush Edit menu.*

OBJECT LINKING AND EMBEDDING

Several of the Windows programs provided by Creative Labs support Object Linking and Embedding (OLE), a powerful feature made possible by Microsoft Windows 3.1. With OLE you can embed an object, such as sound (probably a WAV file), music (probably a MID file) or a picture (probably a Paintbrush BMP file) into an encompassing object such as a word processing document. An even more powerful feature of OLE is the ability to link an object rather than embed it. When you *embed* an object, you create a duplicate of the object. When you *link* an object, you're inserting just the name and address of your object, so only the original object exists—pretty important when audio and video files can easily exceed a million bytes each. Programs that provide objects for OLE are referred to as *OLE servers,* while programs that accept OLE objects are referred to as *OLE clients.*

Creative Labs Talking Scheduler and Soundo'LE programs, which are described in the next two major sections, support OLE. Talking Scheduler can act as an OLE client, while Soundo'LE can serve as an OLE server. You'll get the hang of what a client and server are when you experiment with the tutorials for these two programs. But to give you a feeling for what OLE delivers, here's an example of OLE in action. Soundo'LE is an OLE server, and the Microsoft Write word processor, found in the Accessories group, can serve as an OLE client. You can record your voice with Soundo'LE and stick the recording into a Write document. In this situation, Soundo'LE is the server, because in the midst of reading a Write document you can double-click on the Soundo'LE icon (which indicates that a sound sample is stored there), and Soundo'LE will immediately play a digital audio sound file.

NOTE: *If you follow the computer press closely, you've probably heard about OLE 2.0. The version of OLE currently being used, although powerful, hasn't proven an overwhelming success, since few people take advantage of it. The newer version, OLE 2.0, is much more successful at achieving OLE's goal of unifying application programs from different vendors seamlessly—at least from the user's perspective. It will appear some day in your favorite applications, but expect it to be slow in coming. OLE 2.0 represents a major technical challenge for even the most capable of Windows programmers.*

TALKING SCHEDULER

Creative Labs Talking Scheduler delivers an appointment book to you in a most entertaining form. At the scheduled time a window appears on your screen, and Simon, Perkins, or Igor reads aloud the details of your appointment. Figure 5-4 shows Simon reminding you that it's party time and to print the instructions for finding the party location.

After Simon finishes talking, you'll hear the voice memo that you recorded from the speaker phone, with the hostess rattling off the names of family and friends who will be at the party. To be on the safe side, you typed the

FIGURE 5-4

Simon

announcing that

it's party time!

■

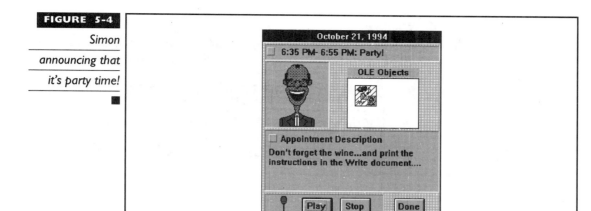

address and the rather lengthy directions (too long to fit into the appointment description) to the party, creating a Microsoft Write document called PARTY.WRI (Figure 5-5). Shortly after the voice memo finishes, your typed instructions appear on the screen.

The OLE object, the hatched icon seen in the OLE Objects box, is responsible for making Write and your written instructions appear. The tutorials that follow show you how to do all this and more.

NOTE: *For background on OLE, read the section entitled "Object Linking and Embedding," which follows the description of Creative Mosaic.*

Running Talking Scheduler

For all Talking Scheduler's flash, its initial screen is pretty boring. From the Main menu option you select SetUp to control how it operates; Clock to

FIGURE 5-5

An OLE object, in

this case a

document, as

part of an

appointment

reminder

■

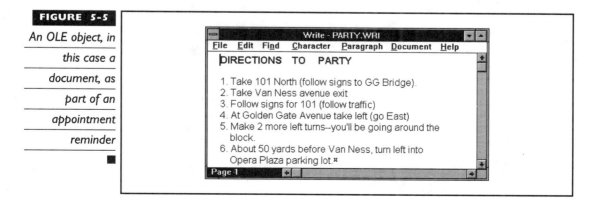

display the Windows clock; Run to minimize Talking Scheduler so it'll operate in the background, notifying you of appointments while you work on other tasks; or Quit to close this application and turn off the appointment notification.

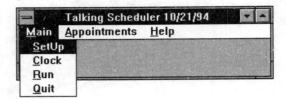

Setting Up Talking Scheduler

When you first start Talking Scheduler, you should select Main,SetUp to customize Talking Scheduler to your tastes. From the Program Defaults dialog box (Figure 5-6), you can pick a narrator, such as Igor or Simon, to read your appointment description. You can also modify the narrator's voice by selecting a pitch and speed.

A handy feature is Advance Notice. Since the number 5 has been selected, as shown in Figure 5-6, Talking Scheduler will remind you of your appointment five minutes before the scheduled time. Simon has been selected as narrator, and since the Auto Launch boxes are enabled, Talking Scheduler will automatically launch a greeting (announcing the appointment time), a Description (using speech synthesis to read aloud the short descriptor you typed as the appointment description), and a voice memo if you chose to

FIGURE 5-6

Setting up Talking Scheduler defaults

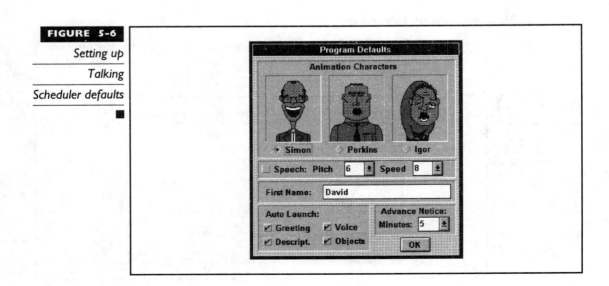

record one. The OLE box is checked too, which means that if you've attached a MIDI music file, a Paintbrush picture, or another OLE object to your appointment, it will also appear at the appointed time.

Talking Scheduler Tutorial

This section will run you through a fast-paced tutorial of Talking Scheduler that demonstrates the major features. For everyday use of Talking Scheduler, you'll select Appointments from the main menu as shown here.

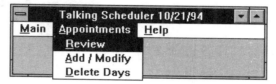

Add/Modify Appointments

When the Make Appointments screen appears (Figure 5-7), you see marked in red the days for which appointments have already been made: October 17, October 21 (circled because that's the current day), and October 25. The buttons on the bottom left flip the calendar to another month, while those on the right move to another year.

Click on a date to see the Appointments screen for that day, as shown for October 21 in Figure 5-8. Three appointments have been entered. The mouse cursor points to the 6:35-to-6:50 early evening appointment, the last one of the day. You select an appointment by clicking the pie slice that corresponds to the time of the appointment (appointments can't overlap). Once clicked, the pie slice turns from light blue to red and the appointment information appears on the screen, as shown in Figure 5-8. You will see the start and end times, the name of the person (or party in this case), and an appointment description of up to 127 characters. You can record a voice annotation (voice memo) of up to 30 seconds by clicking the Record button, or you can listen to an existing voice annotation by clicking the Play button. The tiny square icon in the OLE Objects box at the bottom indicates that something else—perhaps a MIDI music song or a picture or a word processing document—has been attached to this appointment.

ADD AN APPOINTMENT   The trickiest part of Talking Scheduler is specifying the appointment time. The trick is to place the tip of the mouse cursor slightly *outside* the clock dial, at the clock position for the *start* time, before holding down the left mouse button. Next, move *clockwise*, keeping the tip of the mouse cursor outside the clock dial until you've highlighted the appointment

FIGURE 5-7

Add/Modify

appointments

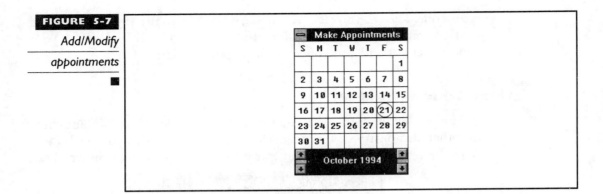

period in red. Then release the mouse button. You needn't be overly concerned with selecting the precise start and end times with the mouse since these times are easily adjusted by clicking the buttons to the right of Start Time and End Time. Appointments must be at least 15 minutes long. Once you've entered the precise appointment times, you have the option of adding a short textual description, a voice annotation, or OLE objects (you'll see how to do this in a step below). Then click the Done button to save the appointment information and return to the Make Appointments screen.

DELETE AN APPOINTMENT   Highlight the appointment you wish to delete by clicking that pie slice, then click the Delete button. Return to the Make Appointments screen by clicking the Done button.

FIGURE 5-8

Appointments for

October 21

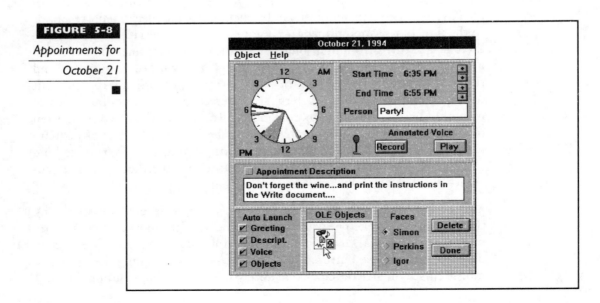

Review Appointments

To review existing appointments, select Appointments,Review from the Talking Scheduler main menu. When you click a date, the individual appointments for that day appear, as shown in Figure 5-9 for October 21. To review appointment details, click and highlight that appointment, as shown here for the 6:35 PM- 6:55 PM: Party! reminder. When you click the Review button, you immediately trigger the appointment reminder. Your friendly narrator then appears, as depicted previously in Figure 5-4.

DELETE FROM THE REVIEW APPOINTMENTS SCREEN   To eliminate an individual appointment, click and highlight that appointment and then click the Delete button. Click the Done button to quit the Review Appointments activity.

Delete All Appointments for a Day

You'll need to clean up your appointment calendar from time to time. To quickly delete all the appointments on a given day, select Appointments,Delete Days from the Talking Scheduler main menu. You now see a list of the days that contain appointments.

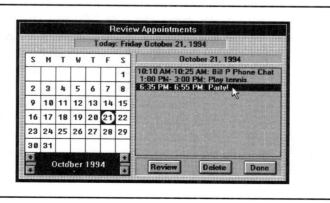

Click and highlight a day, then click the Delete button to eliminate that day's appointments.

Advanced Tutorial: Adding OLE Objects

Your Creative Labs User Reference Manual gives several examples of OLE and talks about dragging an OLE object, but it really doesn't demonstrate the full power of OLE. This tutorial shows you how to attach *any* type of OLE object to your appointment using an advanced OLE technique called *object packaging*. This advanced tutorial shows how to make a Microsoft Write document—perhaps containing birthday congratulations for someone in the office—appear at the designated time.

NOTE: *Selecting Object,Embed from the Add/Modify menu under Talking Scheduler's Appointments menu limits you to a small group of OLE objects. This restriction is removed when you use the Microsoft Windows drag-and-drop technique described in this tutorial to package an OLE object.*

First display the Appointments Add/Modify screen, as shown earlier in Figure 5-8, by selecting Appointments,Add/Modify from the Talking Scheduler main menu and then clicking on a date. Next, rearrange the layout of windows on your screen so that the appointments screen and Windows File Manager can appear side by side. To do so, load the File Manager if it's not already running. Then reduce the File Manager window to the shape and position shown in Figure 5-10.

Next you'll need to display the Talking Scheduler Appointments screen. If it's already running but not visible, you can use ALT-TAB to switch to it. You'll almost certainly have to adjust the Talking Scheduler's Appointment screen position so that the OLE Objects box is near the bottom of the screen yet accessible, as shown in this figure. The final step is to drag a copy of the object, in this case the Microsoft Write word processing file called PARTY.WRI, from the File Manager to the OLE Objects box in the Appointments screen. The mouse cursor in Figure 5-10 points to the PARTY.WRI file in File Manager. Position the cursor on this file, hold down the left mouse button, and drag the file to the OLE Objects box. When you release the button, the OLE icon for a Write file will appear, as shown in Figure 5-10. If you now double-click the Write icon here, or the icon in the appointment (Figure 5-4), the document will appear as seen previously in Figure 5-5. When this appointment reminder is triggered, the document will appear on screen after you hear your voice annotation.

FIGURE 5-10

Creating an OLE

object icon via

drag-and-drop

from the File

Manager

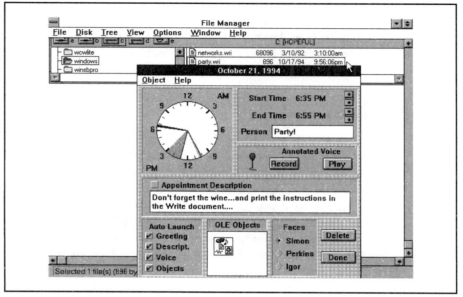

CREATIVE SOUNDO'LE

Soundo'LE is like a digital audio tape recorder except that it records to your computer's hard disk instead of to magnetic tape. It records and plays digital audio sound files that can be used by other Microsoft Windows applications that use Wave (WAV) files. When you start Soundo'LE, you'll see a screen representation of a tape recorder with buttons labeled with international symbols (Figure 5-11).

FIGURE 5-11

Soundo'LE

program that

records and plays

digital audio

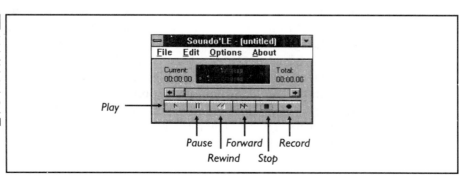

NOTE: If you're wondering about the catchy name Soundo'LE, it doesn't come from a Creative Labs Mexico City software development center. This is a concatenation of Sound and OLE, which is an acronym for Object Linking and Embedding, introduced earlier and described in greater detail later in this chapter.

Recording Tutorial

You'll now go through a quick tutorial explaining how to record and play back a digital audio file. Before you get to the fun stuff, you'll have to spend a little effort in setting up your mixer and recording environment. It's worth the effort to go through this process methodically, as described below, because once you learn how to control your recording environment, you'll be able to push your sound card to its full potential.

This tutorial features the mixer and recording control panels for the Sound Blaster 16; however, Sound Blaster Pro Deluxe and Sound Blaster Deluxe owners shouldn't feel left out. The SB Pro Deluxe mixer is similar to the Sound Blaster 16 mixer. Although Sound Blaster Deluxe cards lack mixer hardware, owners of the SB Deluxe will easily be able to follow and complete the tutorial. The sections specific to the SB16 have been marked as such. Even if you don't have an SB16 you'll probably find the discussion of SB16 compression and other features to be quite interesting.

NOTE: This tutorial can't go into all the nuances of the mixer software, since the mixer programs for the Sound Blaster Pro and Sound Blaster 16 are covered in Chapters 3 and 4, respectively. If you have questions about the mixer that aren't answered here, please refer to these chapters.

Setting Up the Mixer

The first step before recording is to ready your audio source, perhaps by loading a CD into the CD-ROM player or by selecting a MIDI file to play on your sound card's synthesizer. Next, you need to set up the mixer so it records from this source. To quickly access the mixer, select Mixer Settings from the Soundo'LE Options menu as shown in Figure 5-12.

Once you select Options,Mixer, the Mixer control panel appears. Figure 5-13 shows the author's Sound Blaster 16 mixer setup for recording from a microphone (if you own another sound card, such as the Sound Blaster Pro Deluxe, your mixer panel will look slightly different). Note how the mixer has been configured. The microphone slider (Mic) and the master volume slider (Vol) were pushed up to boost the Mic input signal strength. This is

FIGURE 5-12

Options menu

for setting up the

recording

environment

■

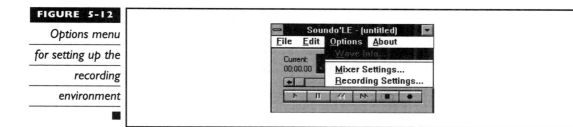

necessary so that the sound from the microphone will be strong relative to the noise latent in recordings.

NOTE: *It's fine to use another audio source, such as a CD-ROM player, for this tutorial. As you follow the tutorial, simply substitute your audio source for the microphone. Microphone input was selected for this tutorial because the authors were testing the fidelity of the Sound Blaster 16 card, UDM-328 microphone, and Sound Blaster CT-38 speakers. The test methodology was to see if a recording of a can of tuna being opened by a hand-held can opener elicits the same response from felines that the actual event does.*

SB16 only: When recording from the microphone it's a good idea to change the Gain setting to x2 or higher, giving the microphone input the extra boost it needs. The default Gain setting, 1X, is really intended for the other sources, such as the MIDI file (played via FM or Wave Table synthesizer) and CD, which have a stronger signal level than the microphone and don't require a boost.

The Mic Output box was clicked once (removing the green dot from the box) to exclude the microphone from the sound output to your headphones or speakers. This is done to avoid *feedback*, a phenomenon in which what you say to the microphone is broadcast by the speaker and picked up again by the microphone. This leads to an out-of-control spiral that results in an ear-splitting blast of noise that can damage speakers, headphones, and ears.

FIGURE 5-13

Mixer control for

recording from a

microphone

■

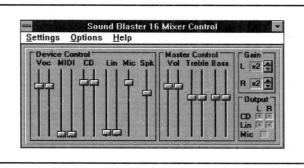

Setting Up the SB16 Recording Control

The second major step before recording, for owners of the Sound Blaster 16, is to select the appropriate Recording Control settings. With the mixer appearing, as shown earlier in Figure 5-13, select Settings,Recordings from the mixer's main menu. Doing this displays the SB16 Recording Control dialog box, as shown in Figure 5-14. As you can see in the figure, the Recording Control has been configured to restrict this recording to just one source, the microphone. It's a good idea when recording from the microphone to keep the automatic gain control (AGC) active, as shown here by the dot for AGC. Note how red dots and red labels are used for the settings that control recordings.

Selecting the Recording Options

The final step in the preparation for recording is to select the recording options. A good combination for microphone recording is displayed in Figure 5-15.

Microphone input is the only source that's monaural (note that there is only one box to choose for it in the Recording Control dialog box shown in Figure 5-14), so you should click the Mono choice. Selecting stereo will create a file twice as big as necessary with no advantages. The selected sample size is 8 bits rather than 16 bits—a nice move to conserve disk space. If you're recording music, you'll want the extra dynamic range (variation in loudness) provided by 16 bits, but for a quick voice memo it's better to stick to 8 bits. The sample rate selected is 11 kHz, one of the three choices available for Microsoft Wave files. It's fine to use 11 kHz for recording a person's voice. Music, however is best recorded at 22 or even 44 kHz.

SB16 Compression

If you own a Sound Blaster 16, the last choice you must make among the recording options is whether to compress or not. Digital audio recordings

---

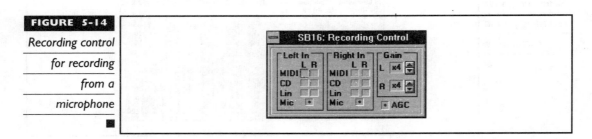

FIGURE 5-14

Recording control for recording from a microphone

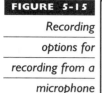

FIGURE 5-15

Recording

options for

recording from a

microphone

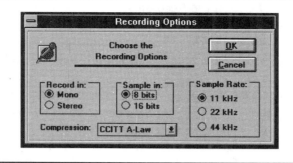

can eat up disk space at an alarming rate, so it's always tempting to compress your recordings. This is fine for a *voice annotation*, a voice memo, and sound effects, but it's inappropriate for other situations.

NOTE: *You shouldn't compress in the following situations. If you'd like to have the option to edit your digital audio file using WaveStudio or another digital audio editor, you shouldn't compress the audio since WaveStudio and many other editors can't revise compressed files. In fact, most Windows programs that play Wave files can't deal with compressed Wave files. In addition, if you're recording music or making special recordings that you'll treasure, you shouldn't compress since compression using ADPCM techniques results in a loss of fidelity, or sound quality (see Appendix A for more on ADPCM).*

The Recording Options dialog box gives you three choices for compression (in addition to "None" for no compression). Soundo'LE has an impressive capability: it can compress *while* it records, assuming your computer has enough horsepower. The choice made by the authors, as shown in the figure, is CCITT A-Law, an international telephony standard that does a good job of compression without demanding too much effort from your computer (see the discussion of compression in Appendix A for more detail). Click the OK button to close the Recording Options dialog box once you've chosen your recording options.

NOTE: *If you have a Sound Blaster 16 with Advanced Signal Processing, compression is performed by the digital signal processor chip on your sound card, relieving your computer of the computational burden. A Sound Blaster 16 without this DSP chip can compress too, but the computer's CPU must take up the slack. A 486SX/20 or less powerful system may not have enough horsepower to perform compression at the highest sample rates, such as 44,100 Hz in stereo.*

Perform the Recording

Once the recording environment is set up, it's a snap to make recordings. Just click the Soundo'LE Record button shown previously in Figure 5-11.

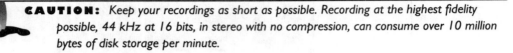

CAUTION: *Keep your recordings as short as possible. Recording at the highest fidelity possible, 44 kHz at 16 bits, in stereo with no compression, can consume over 10 million bytes of disk storage per minute.*

1. Click the Record button, the one with the red dot, to begin recording. Be ready to begin speaking as soon as the Recording status dialog box appears. You'll discover in short order that recording actually begins about 1/4 second *before* this dialog box appears.

2. Click the Stop button or press ENTER to terminate the recording.

3. Review your audio recording by clicking the Play button (the furthest left button).

4. Save your file to disk so you don't accidentally overwrite it with your next recording. Select File,Save, enter a DOS filename of your choice (but use the WAV file extension), and click OK.

5. Once sound has been captured to memory by Soundo'LE, or has been loaded from disk by selecting File,Open, you can check the audio recording settings. Select Options,Wave Info (the mouse cursor is pointing to this menu item in Figure 5-12), and you'll see a dialog box like this:

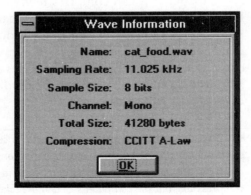

Soundo'LE and Object Linking and Embedding

OLE is a powerful tool for creating compound documents that include sound, pictures, and even video. If you're wondering what a really fun application for OLE and Soundo'LE would be, consider the following. Your printer, modem, computer, or whatever is making a strange noise. Use Soundo'LE to make a recording of this noise, embed the digital audio file into a Microsoft Write document (since everyone with Microsoft Windows can read and, if they have a sound card, listen to an embedded sound file), and send the file to your repair person! If you're on a computer network, you can follow up your trouble report with electronic mail (E-mail) messages begging—in your voice of course—for help.

NOTE: *For background on OLE, read the section entitled "Object Linking and Embedding," which follows the description of Creative Mosaic.*

OLE Tutorial

Let's try an OLE example. Go to the Windows Accessories program group and double-click on Write to bring up the word processor (Figure 5-16). Add text similar to that shown in Figure 5-16 and press ENTER; then select Insert Object from the Edit menu. Select Soundo'LE from the list of object types (the Creative Labs installation program automatically registered this with Windows when your sound card was installed). Now Soundo'LE will appear with the title bar "Soundo'LE - [Untitled]". Make a one- or two-second recording of your voice. Select the Play button to ensure the recording is OK. Next, select File,Exit & Return to Write. When prompted with the message "This object has been changed. Update Write before proceeding?" respond by selecting Yes. The Soundo'LE icon appears, serving as a place marker for the Soundo'LE sound file. Click the icon and you'll hear your voice.

If you save the Write word processing file and look for it with your File Manager (it's probably in your Windows directory), you can tell from the file size that your voice has been embedded in (rather than linked to) this file. Since the sound is embedded, you can copy the Write document to a disk or send the Write document across a network or across the world by E-mail, and your sound recording will hitch a ride.

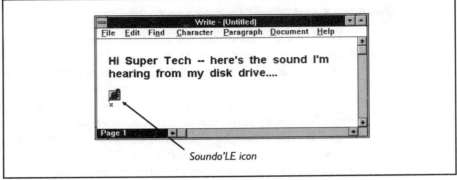

FIGURE 5-16

FIGURE 5-16

An OLE sound object embedded in a word processing file

CREATIVE JUKEBOX

The Creative Labs JukeBox (Figure 5-17), shipped with all Creative Labs sound cards since the introduction of Microsoft Windows 3.0, is designed specifically to play MIDI files. Like a real jukebox, you can load a single song or a "stack" of songs.

Running JukeBox

To load the Creative Labs JukeBox, switch to your Sound Blaster program group and double-click the Juke Box icon. Once this is loaded, you'll need to select MIDI files to play.

You'll find a collection of MIDI files in the PLAYMIDI subdirectory that's within your Sound Blaster directory (\SB or \SBPRO or \SB16 depending on

FIGURE 5-17

Creative JukeBox

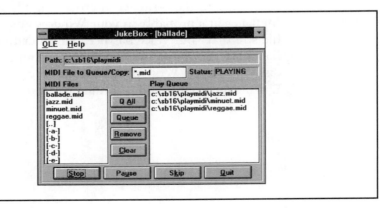

whether you own the Sound Blaster Deluxe, Sound Blaster Pro Deluxe, or the SB16, respectively). With earlier Sound Blaster packages, look for a \SB\MIDI directory. You can also use the CANYON.MID file located in your Windows directory (probably C:\WINDOWS).

The only tricky step in running JukeBox is navigating to the directory with sound files. The key is to double-click the Up Directory [..] item in the MIDI Files list to navigate to another, higher-level directory.

To select a single MIDI file among those visible in MIDI Files list, highlight that file and click the Queue button. To pick all the MIDI files present, click Q All. To remove the current Play Queue (the list of MIDI files stacked up for play), click Clear. Further instructions are available in the User Reference Manual provided to you by Creative Labs.

OLE Support

The most recent version of Creative JukeBox is shown in Figure 5-17. Note that the first menu item is OLE; previous versions sported the Help menu item only. By selecting the OLE menu item, you can copy the MIDI file to the clipboard in preparation for a copy to another sound application.

TIP: *If you're having problems with an earlier version of JukeBox, or you need the OLE capability, see Appendix D and contact Creative Labs support. Appendix D also provides other troubleshooting assistance.*

QUICKCD

Creative Labs QuickCD (look for the QCD icon in your Sound Blaster program group) makes it a snap to play audio CDs in your computer's CD-ROM drive. QuickCD resembles the front panel of an audio CD player, so it's easy to become acclimated to QuickCD. QuickCD has a few more bells and whistles than the usual CD player, as you can see in Figure 5-18. The track slider is dragged by the mouse cursor to a position within a track. The off switch at the bottom-left corner is unusual for a Windows application, but it's an intuitively obvious switch for exiting QuickCD. The control menu button at the top left opens the control menu (see Figure 5-19), providing the usual Microsoft Windows control menu options, such as Minimize and Move, plus a host of QuickCD–specific ones. Play, Pause, Stop, and Skip aren't necessary since there are buttons for these, but Always on Top and Preferences are only accessible from the control menu.

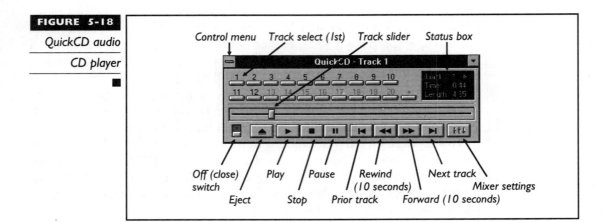

FIGURE 5-18

QuickCD audio

CD player

Always on Top does exactly what it says—keeps the QuickCD control panel visible on the screen regardless of what else is running. Select Preferences to access the dialog box (see Figure 5-20) for customizing QuickCD. By default, QuickCD is set up to play as soon as a CD is popped into the CD-ROM drive. In addition, it's set to play continuously, from the first track to the last track and back again to the first, until you give the command to stop.

CREATIVE WAVESTUDIO

reative WaveStudio makes child's play of recording and editing digital audio. WaveStudio and Creative Soundo'LE overlap in what they can

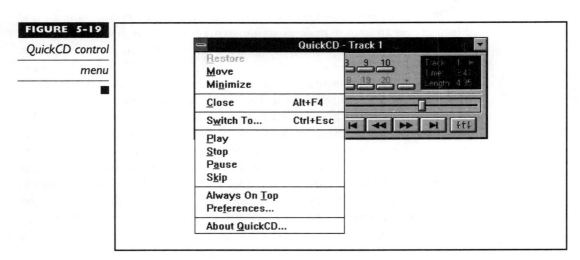

FIGURE 5-19

QuickCD control

menu

FIGURE 5-20

QuickCD

preferences

■

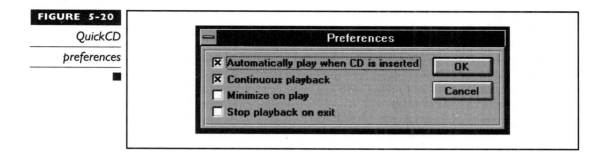

accomplish. Soundo'LE is ideal for quick and simple recordings, especially from the microphone. WaveStudio can record as well, but in addition it excels at delivering digital audio editing effects, such as echoes, fades, and waveform mixing, that go beyond the power of Creative Soundo'LE and the Microsoft Sound Recorder. WaveStudio is graceful and robust; the authors were unable to crash it after many concerted efforts under low memory conditions.

This section has the flow of a tutorial that illustrates WaveStudio's most outstanding features. It's much more than a tutorial, however, since it's sprinkled throughout with tips on how to make you the master of this product. You'll see how and—just as important—why to use special effects such as a fade-in or fade-out. You'll see the techniques you'll need to create amazing special effects and you'll discover the shortcuts that make working with WaveStudio a breeze. Don't feel limited to the examples that follow; feel free to experiment as you go along.

Starting WaveStudio

To run WaveStudio, double-click the Wave Studio icon in your Sound Blaster program group. Rather than begin the tutorial with an empty screen titled "Untitled - 1," Figure 5-21 shows what the fruits of your labor will look like.

No two digital audio recordings are ever the same, but this tutorial will walk you through the steps to create a transformation similar to that shown in Figure 5-21. The waveform (a sound wave) shown in Figure 5-21 makes for an incredibly dynamic echo. The left channel (the upper waveform) begins the echo, and then the right channel (the lower waveform) pours forth with the same echo 1/2 second later. This gives the impression of an echo that's first reflected from the nearby walls of a great canyon and then, 1/2 second later, is returned from the far reaches of the same canyon. You'll learn how to create a similar sound in the course of this tutorial, but first an

FIGURE 5-21

Waveform that

simulates a

Grand Canyon

echo

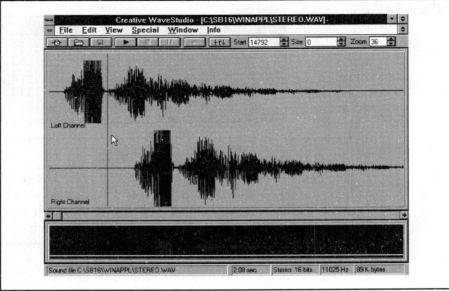

introduction into the parts of the WaveStudio window and the controls is necessary.

Status Bar

At the bottom of the screen is the status bar, shown in Figure 5-22 (broken in half in the figure). Each element of the status bar will be described, beginning from the left.

In Figure 5-21 you can see that a stereo recording was made, and this file was given the overused filename of STEREO.WAV, as shown by the status bar. When the sound card plays a stereo sound file, it simultaneously

FIGURE 5-22

Status bar

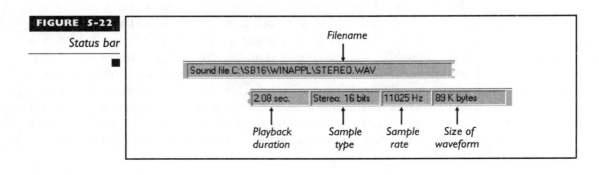

converts left and right channel sound bytes into left and right channel analog electrical signals that are sent to the left and right speakers. Looking at the status bar shown in Figure 5-22, you can see that the digital audio file is 2.08 seconds in length. Recording in stereo with 16 bits (2 bytes) at a sample rate of 11,025 stereo samples per second (Hz) results in a file with approximately 89,000 bytes (2.08×2×11,025×2). A file recorded in monaural (one channel only) or with 8-bit samples will be half this size, and a file recorded in both monaural and 8-bits will be one-quarter this size—which happens to be the recommended combination for voice memos since this combination conserves space.

NOTE: *Sound Blaster Deluxe doesn't support stereo. When working with Creative WaveStudio, Sound Blaster Deluxe users will see just one channel that's called the Master Channel. Sound Blaster Pro and Sound Blaster 16 owners will also see the Master Channel instead of Left and Right channels when recording in monaural.*

Edit Window

The large, middle section of the window is the edit window. This is where you select and manipulate segments of the waveform and see the results of edit operations. Selection in the context of WaveStudio means that you either pick a cursor position, by a click of the mouse button, or select a segment of the waveform. To select a segment, hold down the mouse button and drag. A segment may include a few tens of sound samples or several hundred thousand. Once a selection is made, an Edit command such as Cut, Copy, Delete, or Paste can be performed. The mouse cursor, the small arrow visible in Figure 5-21, points to the WaveStudio sound cursor, the much larger vertical bar. You can place the sound cursor in the desired position by clicking the mouse at that location in the edit window.

Preview Window

Between the edit window and the status bar at the bottom is the preview window, a picture of the entire waveform that's always visible. When you move the mouse cursor over the preview window, the mouse cursor turns into a miniature magnifying glass. To jump to a position in the waveform, click on the location in the preview window. The edit window will change to reflect the new location. What you see in the edit window will probably look unfamiliar; it's probably just a slice from the waveform, unless the waveform has been zoomed to hide the detail.

Button Bar

The button bar appears at the top of the WaveStudio screen. The button bar from the screen shown in Figure 5-21 is expanded in Figure 5-23 so you can recognize the buttons and see the status boxes. Several of the buttons are still difficult to see; buttons are dimmed when they're not appropriate for the current context. In short order you'll initiate a recording by clicking the Record button on the button bar. You'll then click the Stop, Play, and Pause/resume buttons to review your work. These buttons are explained in more depth in this section. First, you'll read about the status boxes on the right side of the button bar.

START AND SIZE BOXES   The Start box gives the precise WaveStudio sound cursor position. The value, 14792, indicates that the sound cursor is offset 14792 bytes into the waveform. If a rectangular region is selected, the size in bytes will appear in the Size box.

ZOOM BOX   The Zoom box shows the magnification of the waveform in the edit window, compared to that for the complete waveform as seen in the preview window. In order to view the entire waveform in the edit window, matching that in the preview window, a zoom of 36 is required. This value can be seen in the Zoom box of Figures 5-21 and 5-23. A zoom of 36 means that for every 36 samples of sound data, only one dot is shown in the edit window. Change the Zoom setting to 1, or select View,Actual Size to display the individual waveform samples in the edit window.

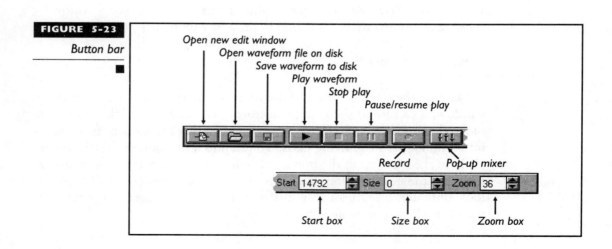

FIGURE 5-23

Button bar

TIP: *You can change the values in these boxes by clicking the scroll arrows or by typing a value. To enter a new value, click within the desired box, to the right of the existing value, press* BACKSPACE *until the box is cleared, and then type the new value.*

NEW WINDOW   Click this to create a new edit window.

OPEN FILE   This leads to a dialog box for opening a disk file.

PLAY   Plays the waveform visible in the current edit window. If you select a region, only that region will be played.

STOP   Stop waveform play.

PAUSE/RESUME   Pauses or resumes waveform play.

RECORD   Select this button to initiate a recording.

MIXER ACCESS   Click this button to access the Creative Labs Windows mixer program and, once started, click Settings,Recordings to access the Recording Control dialog box.

Recording

Although many of the examples assume that you're recording from the microphone, any sound source will do. For example, you can play audio CDs in your CD-ROM drive courtesy of Creative QCD CD player software. If you lack both a CD-ROM drive and a microphone, you can always record music from the Juke Box program that plays tunes on your sound card's FM synthesizer. If you're unfamiliar with these programs, QCD and Juke Box are documented in this chapter.

Prepare Your Audio Source

To follow along with the next steps, crank up your audio CD or Juke Box or switch that microphone to "on." You'll be recording shortly.

Prepare the Mixer and Recording Controls

Sound Blaster 16 and Sound Blaster Pro Deluxe owners must establish the correct mixer and recording settings before proceeding (Sound Blaster Deluxe owners don't have to worry about this step). The quickest way to access the mixer and recording controls is to click the Mixer button in the button bar as shown in the "Button Bar" section and then select Settings,Recording. The Recording Control window appears (see Figure 5-24).

FIGURE 5-24

Recording

Control window

■

It's especially important to select the correct button boxes in the Recording Control window. Figure 5-24 shows the SB16 Recording Control window with the CD-ROM button boxes selected. If you're going to record from the microphone, click on the Mic buttons to select the microphone source. Deselect other sources, the CD-ROM in this case, by clicking on them to remove the red dot.

NOTE: *The mixer and recording options are described in more detail in Chapter 3, Chapter 4, and in the discussion of Creative Soundo'LE in this chapter.*

Open New Edit Window

If the edit window looks blank and the Play button is dim, you're looking at an empty edit window that's ready for use. If you'd like to open a new edit window select File,New. WaveStudio supports the Windows MCI (multiple child interface) standard, which means that the WaveStudio application supports many child windows, each one potentially harboring a distinct waveform. This fosters real-world editing tasks like cleaning up a speech by cutting and pasting sentences from window to window. You switch between Windows in the usual Microsoft Windows fashion by selecting the Windows menu item.

Make a Recording

When you're ready to record, click the Record button. You now see the Record dialog box (Figure 5-25).

NOTE: *When the edit window is empty, a red dot appears on the Record button indicating that it's permissible to record. If the dot isn't apparent, you must save or erase the current contents of the window before proceeding. To erase the contents, select Edit,Select All and then press DEL. To save, click the disc button in the button bar.*

FIGURE 5-25

Record dialog box

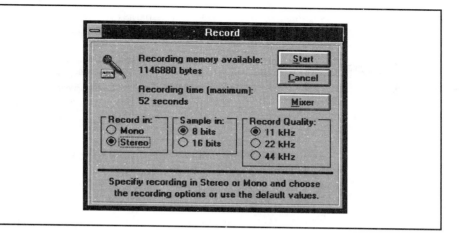

NOTE: *Sound Blaster Deluxe is a monaural, 8-bit sound card, so if you're using this card you won't be given the chance to record in stereo or select the 16-bit sample size.*

You need to make one last set of choices in the Record dialog box before starting: monaural or stereo, sample size, and sample rate. Here's a rule of thumb if you're recording from the microphone (which is only monaural) or short on disk storage or RAM memory: select Mono, 8 bits, and 11 kHz. If you're recording music and you have the stereo SB Pro or SB16 card, select Stereo, 16 bits, and 22 kHz. If you've got sufficient disk space and computer horsepower, try specifing 44 kHz. Remember that going for the gusto at 44 kHz chews up approximately 10.6MB of RAM memory for every minute of recording. If you forget to set up the mixer and recording settings, you can click the Mixer button here for quick access. If you're not comfortable with making these choices, review Chapter 1. Trade-offs in sampling rate and sample size are discussed in that chapter.

To begin recording, click the Start button. You now see the Recording status box:

Click Stop when you have finished recording. Should RAM memory run low, WaveStudio will automatically terminate recording.

> **CAUTION:** *Try to avoid consuming all available memory. This can lead to very slow execution of WaveStudio and the other Windows applications that are running. When Microsoft Windows gets low on memory, it'll continually swap programs to disk—a relatively slow operation—as it tries to free up enough elbow room to continue working.*

If you discover that you can't record for the desired duration, try a lower sample rate. If that's not acceptable, jump ahead to the discussion of memory management in the "WaveStudio Limitations" section at the end of the WaveStudio part of this chapter.

Once a recording has been made, WaveStudio's Save Sound File dialog box, shown in Figure 5-26, prompts you to save the digital audio to disk. Press the Cancel button to skip this step, the usual course of action when you're just experimenting, or enter a filename and click OK to save your work to disk. In the example shown in Figure 5-26, the digital audio recording will be saved as BLONDIE8.WAV.

Viewing the Entire Waveform

When you finish recording, or have just opened a sound file on disk, you won't see much of anything in the edit window. You'll see the entire waveform in the preview window but, since the default Zoom setting is 1 (see Figure 5-27), you'll see nothing or only an unrecognizable sliver of sound bytes in the edit window. To force the entire waveform to appear within the

FIGURE 5-26

Save Sound File

dialog box

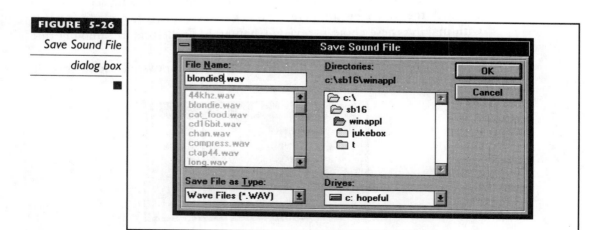

edit window, a recommended starting point for working with a sound file, select View,Fit Wave in Window.

TIP: *If you still see a flat line in the edit window—indicating silence—you failed to select the correct sound source in the Recording Control window shown in Figure 5-24.*

Playing the Waveform

Click the Play button or press ALT-P to hear the waveform. If you have a stereo recording and you'd like to listen to either the left or right channel in isolation, click the Mixer button and set the mixer accordingly.

To select a segment of the waveform to play, place the mouse cursor into either the edit window or the preview window. Hold down the left mouse button and drag the mouse cursor until you've selected a region. The selected region appears in yellow in the edit window.

TIP: *If you click the Play button and see the Stop and Pause buttons momentarily flash but you can't hear anything, here's what went wrong. You accidentally selected a very small segment of the sound file, too short to hear and too small to see as a selected region in yellow. If you don't hear anything, examine the Size box in the button bar. You'll probably see a small number there. To hear the entire waveform, change the Size to zero so WaveStudio will play the entire waveform rather than just your accidental selection.*

FIGURE 5-27

Fitting the entire waveform into the edit window

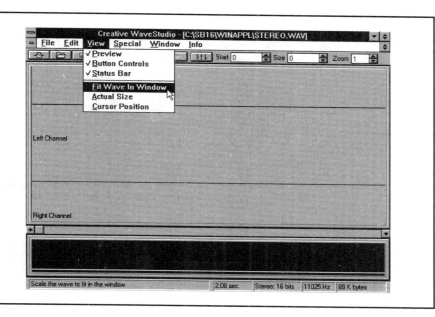

Quick Access Menu

When working in the edit window, you can access the most frequently needed commands by clicking the right mouse button. You'll see a special menu (Figure 5-28) with commands for playing, stopping play, accessing the mixer, and other important actions.

Waveform Edit Command

You can select all or a piece of the waveform to play or edit as described earlier in "Edit Window." When a selection is made, and you select an edit command from the Edit menu, you'll manipulate that one piece only. The edit commands are the familar Microsoft Windows commands like Cut, Copy and Paste, but with a few twists appropriate for a digital audio editor. Some of the commands you'll find under the Edit menu selection are described here.

PASTE   With Paste you can copy sound from one window to another via WaveStudio's own clipboard. Paste's behavior depends on whether you've marked a selection or simply selected a sound cursor position. If you've marked a selection, a Paste operation will replace that section. If you've simply placed the sound cursor, the Paste operation will insert the sound bytes at that location and push aside the waveform to the right.

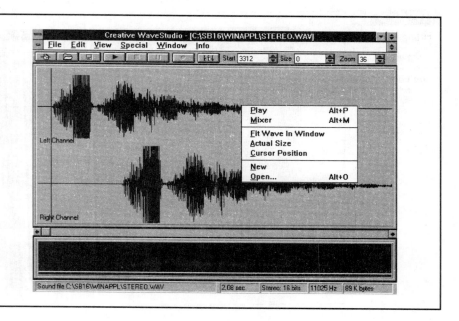

FIGURE 5-28

Click right mouse button while in the edit window to display quick access menu

PASTE MIX   Paste Mix combines sound from WaveStudio's clipboard with that in the destination window.

DELETE   Delete removes the selected portion of the waveform.

CROP TO SELECTION   This command deletes everything but the selected portion of the waveform.

SELECT ALL   This will select everything in the window. The fastest way to empty a window is to select Edit,Select All and then press ESC.

Selection and Crop Example

As an example of the edit commands, consider the following situation. You've recorded your favorite music. Now you'd like to capture just your favorite bars (perhaps you're going to place WPLAY into your AUTO-EXEC.BAT file in order to play this sound segment every time you start your computer). Figure 5-29 shows how a segment from the middle of a waveform (which you first saw in Figure 5-21) has been selected.

To locate such a segment, play the waveform and note the position on the preview window where you first hear the sound you'd like to capture. As you play the sound file, a yellow bar will snake across the preview window, showing you where you're at in the waveform. Take advantage of this to

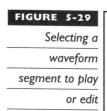

FIGURE 5-29

Selecting a waveform segment to play or edit

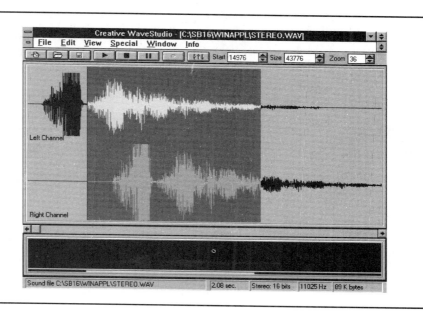

click at the location where the desired bars of music are heard and then drag the mouse to the right.

Now fine-tune your selection. Repeatedly adjust the position of the selection region and audition it by clicking the Play button. To make the selection longer (moving the right border of the selection), increase the Size in the button bar. To change the starting location of the selection (moving the left border of the selection) click the up scroll arrow for the Start box. Using these positioning controls, you'll be able to precisely position the selection.

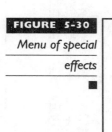

TIP: *If you'd like to extend the highlighted section all the way to the beginning or end of the file, you can do so quickly by entering a number directly into the appropriate box. To extend the selection to the beginning of the waveform, enter* **0** *in the Start box. To position to the end of the waveform, enter an impossibly large number such as* **999999** *into the Size box.*

Once you've isolated the music bars, select Edit,Crop to Selection to erase the extraneous part of the waveform—that is, everything outside the selected region.

Special Effects Commands

The best part of WaveStudio is the special effects. Select the Special menu item to see WaveStudio's bag of tricks (Figure 5-30). Many of these menu options are dimmed and unavailable until you select a segment of the waveform (or select Edit,Select All). Several of these effects will be illustrated in detail. Many of these effects, including Fade In, Fade Out, Amplitude, and Add Echo, are computationally intensive. Don't be surprised that your computer takes a little while to complete these operations. Here's the list of special effects available.

REVERSE   The sound data at the beginning is put at the end so you'll hear the recording played backward. There really isn't any practical business application for this but it's lots of fun.

ADD ECHO   You can add an echo or reverberation effect with this command. This is described in more detail in examples that follow.

RAP!   This repeats the selected portion of the waveform, placing it to the immediate right of the selection. It was given it's cute name since the command is ideal for creating your own "rap" music.

INSERT SILENCE   This inserts stretches of silence that are useful for separating words or other segments of your recording.

FORCE TO SILENCE   Select this to smother noise or other undesirable sounds in your recording. When working with stereo data, you can silence both channels or just the left or right channel.

FADE IN   This gradually increases the sound volume (amplitude) from the specified percent of full amplitude until full amplitude is reached.

FADE OUT   This gradually reduces the volume of sound from full amplitude to the specified percent of full amplitude.

AMPLIFY VOLUME   The Amplify Volume feature, shown here, changes the volume of the waveform:

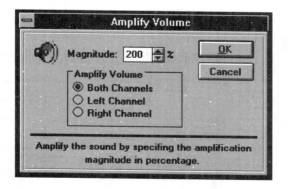

The default value, 200%, doubles the amplitude. A value of 50% halves the amplitude. Be careful to avoid excessive amplification, which causes clipping, a flattening of the top of the waveform. A small amount of clipping can be seen in Figure 5-21 (look at how the peaks have been flattened in the initial burst for each channel). Due to the background noise and special effects (an echo) the clipping in this recording isn't noticeable. However, clipping a music recording is rated a sin among audio enthusiasts.

Special Effect Example: Fades

Figure 5-31 shows a waveform that screams for a fade. You can see that Blondie is really belting out this song. To avoid subjecting your ears to the shock of suddenly hearing Blondie at full volume, there needs to be a fade in at the beginning of the recording and a fade out at the end.

Select the right half of the waveform. Then select Special, Fade Out from the menu. The Fade Out dialog box appears, prompting you for the degree to which the sound should be reduced. The default, 0%, means that through the course of the selected region the sound will gradually diminish from full (100%) volume to silence (0%). Figure 5-32 shows the results of a fade-out at the end and a fade-in at the beginning. Listening to this you would hear the music build up to a peak and then gently diminish before disappearing. With a longer recording, most of the music would play at full volume. You'd fade in the first few seconds and fade out the last few seconds.

Fades are absolutely essential for creating smooth segues (transitions) between audio segments. This is necessary to shield the listener from sudden transitions that draw their attention away from the underlying message in the advertisement or multimedia presentation. To give a practical example, imagine that you'd like to join audio segments in two edit windows. In one edit window you have some engaging music—the bait—while in another edit window you have the spoken message you'd like to convey. Before joining these two sound waveforms with the Paste command, you'd fade out the

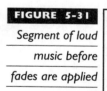

FIGURE 5-31

Segment of loud music before fades are applied

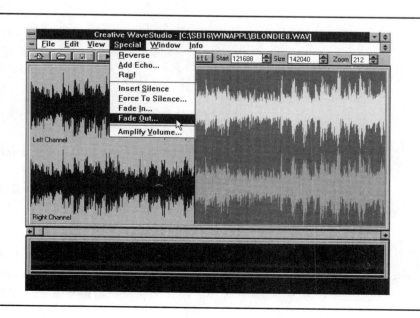

Fade-in followed

by a fade-out

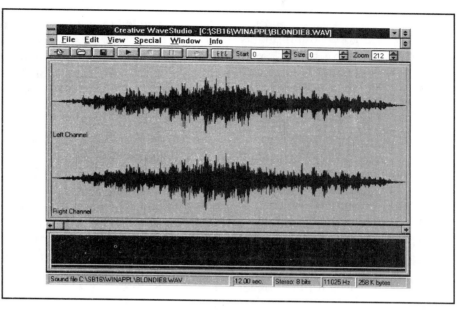

music and fade in the spoken words. The glue is applied by an Edit,Paste Mix that overlays the two.

Frequently an initial music segment will fade to a soft background serenade, perhaps at 10% to 20% of the initial volume, before the spoken words commence. In order to maintain the mood, you'll want the music to continue in the background. To do so, you can use the Special,Amplify Volume command to reduce the strength of the music once the fade is complete.

Special Effect Example: Add Echo

This example combines several special effect commands to create a grandiose echo. The goal is to illustrate the key steps involved in creating the waveform shown in Figure 5-21.

First make a short recording of one or two words. As a suggestion record a slowly spoken "Let's...." (this was used for Figure 5-21). Record in stereo, with 16-bit samples and an 11-kHz sample rate. The reason for stereo is that it offers more flexibility in manipulating the sound. In this case, the plan is to delay the sound from one channel relative to the other. This creates the impression of an echo in a deep canyon, where a reflection is heard from both nearby and distant parts of the canyon.

A 16-bit sample size is recommended over an 8-bit sample. This ensures good sound quality even after the sound data is repeatedly massaged by WaveStudio. Every time the audio data is transformed in form, a little bit of quality is lost, and this is potentially more noticeable with 8-bit samples. Since we're working with voice, an 11.025-kHz sample rate is more than adequate.

Before adding an echo, you should add a long silence period at the end of the waveform to set the stage for a long echo. Without this silence, the sound waveform will suddenly terminate at the end of this relatively short recording, and only the initial part of the echo will be heard. A quick way to add silence is to position the mouse cursor at the far right end of the preview window, hold the mouse button down, and drag the mouse cursor left a few inches. Now select Effects,Insert Silence. A segment of silence, matching the length of the segment just highlighted, will be inserted to the right. Select Special,Rap! to add another, identical segment of silence to the right. Repeatedly select Effects,Rap! until you've created a silence region that's several times longer than the original waveform, which will be the non-silence region that contains the sound that you'll echo.

NOTE: *You'll probably want to experiment with various echo effects. If you haven't already made a copy of your most recent recording, do so now. Click the disk icon in the button bar to accomplish this. When you need to recall this digital audio file for another experiment, select the File menu choice. Until you save another waveform, you'll see this audio sample as the first file in the list of most recently accessed sound files.*

Now select Edit,Select All to select the entire waveform, including the silent portion at the end. Then select Effects,Add Echo. You'll see the Add Echo dialog box, as shown in Figure 5-33.

Look carefully at Figure 5-33. You'll notice that the Echo Delay is 500 milliseconds (one-half second), five times that of the default value of 100 milliseconds. A long delay, several hundred or more milliseconds, provides for a strong echo. If you haven't already entered 50% for the magnitude and 500 for the millisecond delay, do so now and click OK. Give the computer a little time to perform this transformation for you (this would be almost instantaneous if the calculations were done on a digital signal processing chip) and then click the Play button. Select View,Fit Wave in Window to better see how the echo has propagated through the silent period.

MAGNITUDE AND ECHO DELAY   The Echo Delay is the time delay before an earlier sound is repeated. The Magnitude parameter is the strength of the sound when it's echoed after the delay. A magnitude of 50% means that each time a sound is echoed it will have 50% of its previous strength. A lower

FIGURE 5-33

Add Echo dialog

box set for 1/2

second echo delay

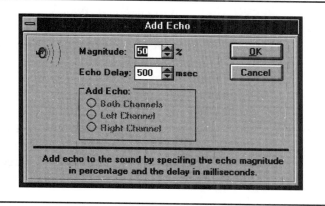

percentage for Magnitude will cause the echo to decay more quickly. A shorter Echo Delay will also accelerate how quickly the echo diminishes.

REVERBERATION   A delay of around 50 to 100 milliseconds creates what is known as a reverberation effect. This imparts a perception of richness to sound. A bathroom shower stall has proportions that lends itself to a nice reverberation effect, luring even hopelessly off-key singers into an occasional outburst of song. The reverberation effect is also an important consideration in the design of a concert hall, and concert recordings are best made with a capacity crowd to ensure the correct acoustics (this assumes that the acousticians were optimists who designed the hall to sound its best with a capacity crowd).

NOTE: *Karaoke lovers will delight to hear that Creative Labs' next generation sound technology will have a reverberation capability built into the sound card. See Appendix A for more details.*

CHORUS EFFECT   It's only natural for a group of musicians, such as the violin section, to play almost—but not quite—precisely in synchronization. To the ear, there's a slight but perceptible difference when notes are very slightly out of synchronization. By adding a slight reverberation, less than the 50 or so milliseconds that's typical for a reverbation, this effect can be simulated. The "chorus" effect gives instruments an extra richness, and this effect is frequently built into music synthesizers. Please note that this effect is very subtle, and you may not be able to simulate it effectively using Creative WaveStudio.

Special Effect Example: Paste Mix

Figure 5-21 was created by following these steps. The first three were presented in the previous section:

1. Make the initial recording.

   If you have an SB Pro or SB16, select the stereo button in the Recording Control window (Figure 5-24). If you have the monaural Sound Blaster Deluxe, there's nothing to set. You'll create one channel of echo only. Now record "Let's..." with the microphone.

2. Insert silence at the end.

3. Select the entire waveform and apply an echo with a delay of 500 milliseconds.

   The following steps will complete the effect by shifting the right channel echo so it lingers behind that heard from the left channel. This can be done only if you're running a stereo Sound Blaster card such as the Sound Blaster Pro Deluxe or SB16.

4. Select Edit,Copy to save a copy of the echo to the WaveStudio clipboard.

5. Select Special,Force to Silence and select the right channel button box. Click OK to erase that channel.

6. Click in the edit window such that the sound cursor is placed as shown in Figure 5-21, just after the first burst of sound from the left channel.

7. Select Edit,Paste Mix, select the right channel buttons, and click OK. The Waveform should now resemble Figure 5-21. Select the entire waveform (Edit,Select All) and click the Play button to hear the effect.

WaveStudio Limitations

WaveStudio is a joy to use, fast and intuitive, and is well suited for most digital audio editing needs. However, it does have the limitations discussed here.

Memory Management

WaveStudio performs its digital miracles at a snappy pace, since all of the sound data is stored in memory rather than sloshed back and forth from RAM to disk. This snappiness comes with a cost: you're limited to digital audio snippets that fit within available RAM memory. To maximize available memory, close all Windows applications that you don't need. To squeeze every last bit of memory out of your computer, close Microsoft Windows and restart Windows with only the essential applications running.

Compressed Sound

The current version of WaveStudio can't read or save compressed sound files, even with the top-of-the-line SB16 Advanced Signal Processing installed.

Sound File Types

WaveStudio creates only Microsoft Wave files. Future versions of WaveStudio are likely to support Creative's 16-bit VOC sound files. See Chapter 10 for information on other digital audio editors that support both WAV and 16-bit VOC.

Sample Rate Changes

Unfortunately there is no easy way to change WAV file sample rates. Be careful to select the most appropriate sample rate—11, 22, or 44 kHz—before making the recording.

There is a somewhat convoluted way to change the sample rate. Convert a file to VOC with the DOS utility WAV2VOC. Then convert back to a WAV file with VOC2WAV with the /S switch setting for the sample rate you desire. Fortunately, only the header information is changed when converting between VOC and WAV and therefore, there is no loss of sound fidelity.

Paste Limitations

Since WaveStudio can't change sample size (from 8-bit to 16-bit or vice-versa), you can't paste 8-bit data from one edit window into another edit window with 16-bit data. You can paste sound bytes with different sample rates, but, since the sample rate isn't converted the inserted sound bytes will play at the wrong speed.

Selecting a Digital Editor

To edit audio files too long for RAM, you'll need to acquire a disk-oriented digital audio editor. Chapter 10 describes popular editors including potent shareware editors.

MICROSOFT MEDIA PLAYER

The Microsoft Windows Media Player is an easy-to-use player for the entire gamut of sound and video files. This single program can play audio CD, MIDI music (MID), Wave (WAV) digital audio, and even motion video sequences. Media Player, as seen in Figure 5-34, is simple to operate once the media has been selected—just click the Play, Pause, Stop and Eject buttons to control play.

For the typical Sound Blaster owner, Media Player's most valuable feature by far is the ability to be a jack-of-all-trades: it plays WAV digital audio files, MIDI music files, and audio CDs. All of these tasks can also be performed by software provided by Creative Labs, beginning with the introduction of Creative Labs' Windows software for the SB16 and the Deluxe versions of Sound Blaster and Sound Blaster Pro. The Creative Labs software includes Soundo'LE and WaveStudio utilities for digital audio. Soundo'LE is more flexible than Media Player yet is just as easy to use, while WaveStudio is much more powerful than Media Player. Creative JukeBox is designed specifically for playing MIDI files, while Creative QuickCD is crafted specifically for playing audio CDs.

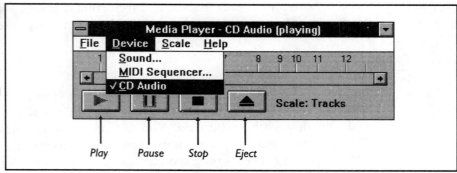

FIGURE 5-34

Microsoft Windows Media Player

Loading Media Player

To load the Microsoft Windows Media Player, switch to the Accessories program group and double-click the Media Player icon.

Selecting Media

Once Media Player is loaded, it's easy to play sound files. Microsoft makes a distinction between simple and compound media hardware. Examples of *compound* media are MIDI and digital audio, in which you must pick not just the type of sound to play, such as MIDI or digital audio, but also a specific file. The most prominent example of a *simple* media is an audio CD or CD-ROM disk, in which you specify only the device; there's no choice of media since the disk is already loaded.

Playing Audio CD Tracks

To play an audio CD inserted in the CD-ROM drive, select Device,CD Audio and then click the Play button.

To switch CD tracks, place the mouse cursor within the horizontal scroll bar, reasonably close to the track number desired. Repeatedly click until the scroll box reaches the desired track.

TIP: *Some CD-ROM disks contain audio CD tracks. The first CD-ROM track always contains data, so you can't play that one, but you may be able to play other tracks. Using Media Player to identify the audio tracks, you can find out which tracks of your multimedia CD-ROM disks can be played on your portable or car audio CD player!*

Once you've started play of a CD disk, click the Minimize button at the top right of Media Player. Media Player disappears from the screen but continues to play in the background until it has finished the disk.

Playing Digital Audio Files

To play a WAV digital audio file, select Device,Sound... and navigate to your WAV files. If you're looking for a sound file to play with, you'll find familiar sounding ones in your Windows directory (probably C:\WINDOWS). Look for TADA.WAV, DING.WAV, CHORD.WAV and CHIMES.WAV.

Microsoft Windows Media Player is useful for the quick audition of digital audio files. The Microsoft Windows User's Guide doesn't mention this, but

Media Player can play back most any digital audio file recorded by Soundo'LE, even those compressed in Creative Labs' proprietary ADPCM format.

TIP: *If you have Creative VOC digital audio files that you'd like to use with Media Player or other Windows programs, use the VOC2WAV utility to convert from VOC to WAV, the only type of digital audio file that Media Player can play.*

Playing MIDI Files

To play a MID file, select Device,MIDI Sequencer... and navigate to your MID files. In the latest packages from Creative Labs, you'll find a collection of MIDI files in the PLAYMIDI subdirectory that's within your Sound Blaster directory (\SB or \SBPRO or \SB16 depending on whether you own the Sound Blaster Deluxe, Sound Blaster Pro Deluxe, or the SB16, respectively). With Sound Blaster cards prior to the Sound Blaster Deluxe, look for a \SB\MIDI directory.

Troubleshooting

If you've selected the media to play, and the scroll box is advancing but you can't hear anything, you probably need to adjust the mixer. Make certain that for the media type you've selected the volume slider is at least half-way up. For more help with the Media Player, see your Microsoft Windows User's Guide. For more troubleshooting help see Appendix D.

Video and Other Media

The Device,Video for Windows menu option for playing video appears only if video drivers are loaded. Don't be surprised if the Video option suddenly appears one day. Media Player will automatically recognize drivers added to your PC. For example, the first time you install a CD-ROM title that involves video, such as the Mayo Clinic Family Health Book, the installation program will install video drivers (you don't need special hardware to run Microsoft Video for Windows video clips) and update your Windows SYSTEM.INI file. The next time you load Media Player, the video menu option will appear.

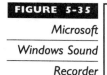

MICROSOFT SOUND RECORDER

The Microsoft Windows Sound Recorder (Figure 5-35), provided by Microsoft as part of Windows 3.1, is an extremely easy-to-use tool for recording. Although the Record button shows a picture of a microphone, when this button is selected Sound Recorder will record from all sources. This potentially includes microphone, CD-ROM, MIDI synthesizer, and line-in. The sources captured depend on what's hooked up to your sound card and, in the case of the Sound Blaster 16 and Sound Blaster Pro, on the mixer setup as well.

Sound Recorder is fun to use, despite certain limitations, for editing and special effects. Its biggest limitation is that it can record only as much sound as can be captured to available RAM memory; probably less than a minute on a 4MB computer. If you own a Sound Blaster 16, Sound Blaster Pro Deluxe, or Sound Blaster Deluxe, you have Creative's latest Windows software, including Creative Soundo'LE and Creative WaveStudio. If you have these two packages, you're unlikely to need Sound Recorder. If your sound card was purchased earlier, Sound Recorder is your primary tool for recording and playing digital audio.

FIGURE 5-35

Microsoft Windows Sound Recorder

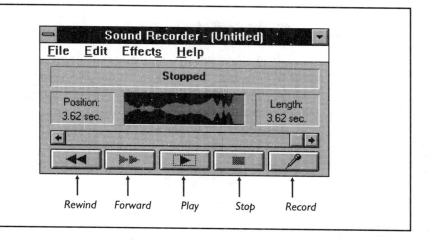

Creative Soundo'LE and the more powerful WaveStudio do everything that Sound Recorder does—with one exception. Sound Recorder lets you append a recording to the end of a sound file. With Soundo'LE and WaveStudio, the last recording is automatically erased when you next record.

Prepare for Recording

Before loading and running Sound Recorder, you need to set up your recording environment. If you have a Sound Blaster 16 or Sound Blaster Pro, check your mixer control panel. Be certain to select the source you wish to record, from the recording settings, and make certain that the volume slider is set to at least half of maximum volume. If you have a Sound Blaster Deluxe, you don't have mixer software but you should check whether your microphone is turned on or off and, if anything is attached to line-in, check that the line-in device is either ready or off.

Loading Sound Recorder

To load Sound Recorder, switch to your Accessories program group and double-click the Sound Recorder icon (the Recorder icon is for the macro recording program).

TIP: *For Sound Blaster 16 and Sound Blaster Pro, arrange your Windows desktop to have the Sound Recorder and the mixer software windows visible in adjacent, non-overlapping windows.*

Running Sound Recorder

Follow these steps to make a recording:

1. Select File,New to prepare for a new recording.

2. Select the Record button, the one with the microphone button (the other buttons will be disabled). The mouse cursor will change into an hourglass while Sound Recorder gets ready to record. Once it changes back to the normal mouse pointer, you'll also see the message "Recording - Maximum Length XX.XX seconds" in the status area centered under the menu items.

TIP: *If you're using the microphone, begin speaking as soon as the hourglass changes shape back to the pointer; otherwise there will be a noticeable pause at the beginning of the*

recording. A waveform in the green area in the middle of Sound Recorder will indicate recording activity. If you see a horizontal green line only, Sound Recorder can't hear anything. Check your mixer settings. It's likely that the audio source is shut off or at a very low volume setting. If you're using a microphone, check the microphone on/off switch and speak louder.

3. Click the Stop button as soon as you've finished speaking.

4. Reduce or shut off your sound source so you can review your recording. If recording from the microphone, switch the microphone off.

TIP: *Sound Recorder doesn't communicate with the Sound Blaster Pro Deluxe or Sound Blaster 16 mixer, so the recording sources are not shut off automatically when you play back a recording. Since the source volume is always louder than the playback volume, your recording may not be audible if your CD-ROM or line-in source is still playing.*

5. Click the Rewind button (the double triangle pointing to the left). Then click the Play button (the single triangle pointing to the right) to hear your recording.

Mastering Sound Recorder

You'll want to explore Sound Recorder's special effects, such as sound reversal (playing backward), speed changes, and echo. This program is handicapped by its rudimentary control over amplification and speed, but the capability to mix (overlay) one sound file over another and to insert one file within another is very useful. Here are a few hints on using the effects provided by Sound Recorder:

■ Volume. Decrease Volume complements the Increase Volume menu choice. If you increase the volume by 25 percent and then select Decrease Volume, the original volume is restored.

■ Speed. Decrease Speed complements the Increase Speed menu choice. If you increase the speed by 100 percent and then select Decrease Speed, the original speed is restored.

RECORDING SETTINGS   Sound Recorder does not give you the luxury of selecting the recording settings. The settings depend on which sound card you possess. For example, the default (and only) recording settings for the Sound Blaster 16 are 22,050 Hz sample rate, 16-bit samples, and monaural.

Sound Recorder is really tailored for making quick recordings from the microphone, for which these settings are appropriate. To check the recording settings for your sound card, select Help, About Sound Recorder after you've made a recording. The settings will appear immediately below the copyright notice.

6

DOS Applications

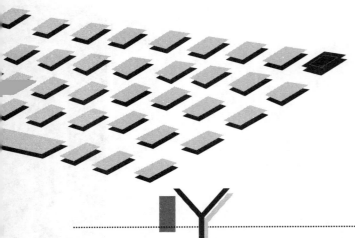

Y O U ' L L find a gold mine of information on the DOS programs for your Sound Blaster card in this chapter. Tips and hints the manual missed and everything you need to know to make your software work the way you want. This chapter is divided into several major sections. It starts off with Sound Blaster Toys, like The Talking Parrot that comes with Sound Blaster and Sound Blaster Pro. The FM Intelligent Organ, common to all Creative cards, follows in its own section. The chapter then rolls into the Play and Record *utilities,* small, specific-purpose programs such as VPLAY and VREC, which turn your computer into a digital tape recorder, and PLAYCMF and PLAYMIDI that play music files. Digital audio utilities are then revisited in a section titled Digital Audio Editing Utilities. With these you can edit digital audio files, chopping out the "um, um, um" from a recording of your voice or converting that great VOC file to WAV format for use with Microsoft Windows programs. Sound Blaster Pro owners who have a CD-ROM drive shouldn't waste a minute before checking out CDPLYR, the DOS CD player program.

Please note that even if you buy the top-of-the-line Sound Blaster 16, you won't see all the programs listed here. Some programs, such as VOXKIT and VSR, were shipped only with the early Sound Blasters, having been replaced with more powerful programs in the newer packages. Many programs were added when the Deluxe version of Sound Blaster and Sound Blaster Pro were introduced. To minimize confusion, underneath the title for each software program, we've listed the sound card packages that contain that program. You'll see a few abbreviations here, like SB for Sound Blaster and SB Pro for Sound Blaster Pro.

RUNNING DOS PROGRAMS UNDER WINDOWS

The programs described in this chapter are run from the DOS command prompt. The comments in this section are targeted toward those readers whose primary habitat is the Microsoft Windows graphical user interface.

From the Windows environment you can reach the DOS command prompt (the familiar C:> prompt) in two ways. By selecting File,Exit you will quit Windows and return to DOS. This is the sure-fire way to run all your DOS programs. When you're ready to return to Windows, simple type **WIN**.

The alternative way to reach the DOS command prompt is to bring up a special window called the DOS compatibility box. To do so switch to Program Manager, go to the Main program group, and select the MS-DOS Prompt icon. When you have finished working in the DOS environment type **EXIT** and press ENTER to return to Windows. You've never actually left Windows—if you press CTRL-ESC you see the list of tasks running—one of which is the MS-DOS Prompt.

Most DOS programs, including utilities from Creative Labs, will run fine in the DOS compatibility box. Sometimes though, depending on the version of DOS you're running and the settings used in the Windows INI initialization files, you may have problems. This is especially true of programs that play digital audio or that are dependent on precise timing. Should you encounter problems when running a program in the DOS compatibility box, your best bet is to run that program from the DOS command prompt after quitting Windows.

SOUND BLASTER TOYS

The delightful software toys described here, provided with all models of Sound Blaster and Sound Blaster Pro, offer a fun introduction to your Creative Labs Sound Blaster.

- **The Talking Parrot** plays back digitized audio messages, demonstrating the power of even simple *multimedia,* the integration of sound and animation. It's a guaranteed crowd pleaser that "parrots back" what you say and sometimes speaks its own mind.

- **SBTALKER** illustrates how a computer can read and speak. It pronounces words that you type from the keyboard or that it reads from a file.

- **Dr. Sbaitso,** another text-to-speech conversion program, is your personal, no-hourly-fee therapist, who converses intelligently on a wide range of topics. Be open with the Doctor; he forgets everything when you reboot!

NOTE: *If you encounter terminology that's unfamiliar, please refer to Chapter 1 for background information. The software descriptions that follow apply to the programs first shipped with Sound Blaster 2.0. The software that accompanies the earlier Sound Blaster 1.0 and 1.5 cards is slightly different.*

The Talking Parrot

Packages: SB, SB Deluxe, SB Pro, SB Pro Deluxe

The naughty Talking Parrot, shown in Figure 6-1, demonstrates the excitement generated by digital audio and animation. The Parrot reacts to both speech input and keystrokes. Talk into a microphone, and the Parrot will usually "parrot" you, but it often comes up with its own zany comments. If you don't have a microphone, don't worry. The Parrot isn't shy about speaking to strangers. Just press a few keys and you'll really excite it.

Loading and Setting Up the Parrot

Here are the steps to load the Parrot program and adjust the microphone input.

NOTE: *The Parrot program assumes you have a microphone. Even if you don't have one, you must still do steps 3 and 4 to adjust the microphone input before you can use the Parrot program.*

1. Switch to the Sound Blaster directory.

    SB users: Type **CD \SB** and press ENTER.
    SB Pro users: Type **CD \SBPRO** and press ENTER.

2. Load the Parrot program by typing **parrot** and then press ENTER.

NOTE: *If you have a CGA monitor, you will see the "big" parrot. If you have an EGA or VGA monitor, you see the "little" parrot. Sound Blaster owners can force the display of the "big" parrot on EGA/VGA monitors by adding the /T switch to the command in step 2 (type* **parrot /T***).*

3. Now you need to estimate the background noise level. You see a graph indicating the noise level picked up by your microphone. Press ENTER. Notice the peak height of the noise; it's measured by a number along the vertical axis. In reading this number, don't worry about precision; rounding to the next 10 (to 130 or 140, for instance) is good enough.

4. Enter a number on your screen 10 counts above the measured noise level (the number you estimated in step 3), and press ENTER.

Running the Parrot

There are two ways to communicate with the Parrot—with a microphone or via your keyboard.

If you have a microphone connected to your system, speak into the microphone and listen to the Parrot's response. The Parrot will usually echo

FIGURE 6-1

The Talking Parrot

what you say, but sometimes it gives a random reply, such as "Don't talk nonsense." If you fail to talk to the Parrot, it'll grow impatient and make statements like "I'm a talking parrot."

If you lack a microphone, try pressing various keys on your keyboard and listen to the Parrot's response. For example, when you press any of the letter or number keys, the Parrot will respond with a message such as "Ouch."

You will find most of the Parrot's responses listed in your Creative Labs manual, but there are a number of additional, undocumented replies. Also, some of the "random" messages are actually tied to specific keys. For example, if you press the 3 key (the one at the top of your keyboard, not the function key), you will hear the undocumented reply "Hey buddy."

Giving the Parrot a New Look

To change how your Parrot looks on screen, and even substitute entirely new pictures for the four-cell (four-picture) animation, all you need is a paint program that saves pictures as PCX files, such as the Paintbrush program that comes with Microsoft Windows.

To change the Parrot image, you need to replace or edit the Parrot files that have the filename extensions E0/E1/E2/E3 (for EGA or VGA monitors) or C0/C1/C2/C3 (for a CGA monitor). The following instructions will guide you in modifying the existing image.

Before you edit the image files, it's a good idea to make a copy of them. At the command-line prompt, switch to the Parrot subdirectory (CD \SB\PARROT or CD \SBPRO\PARROT), and type the following:

```
COPY parrot.C? parrotC.C?
COPY parrot.E? parrotE.E?
```

Later, if you want to restore your original Parrot images, delete the revised ones and rename the backups:

```
DEL parrot.C?
REN parrotC.C? parrot.C?
DEL parrot.E?
REN parrotE.E? parrot.E?
```

Now here are the steps to modify your Parrot image files:

1. Run your paint program.

2. Load an image file (found in \SB\PARROT or \SBPRO\PARROT) into the paint program.

Start with PARROT.E0 if you use an EGA or VGA monitor, or
PARROT.C0 if you use a CGA monitor. These files contain images
of the Parrot at rest, before it tries to speak. The files with
extensions E1/E2/E3 and C1/C2/C3 contain the other three
animation cells.

NOTE: *Since the Parrot program has its own color palette, the Parrot's colors in the paint
program will be different from what you see when the Parrot program runs. When you
save the picture file, even if you don't change anything with Paintbrush, the parrot's colors
will change.*

3. Modify the image file as desired. Then save it, replacing the
   original file. When you next run the Parrot program, you see the
   new Parrot.

SBTALKER

Packages: SB, SB Deluxe, SB Pro, SB Pro Deluxe

The Sound Blaster talk program, SBTALKER, is an interesting example
of an uncomplicated program for text-to-speech conversion. You type in
text, and it's converted by the program into speech.

Although SBTALKER is on the surface very simple, text-to-speech conversion is not a simple matter at all. All languages consist of many *phonemes,*
basic units of speech such as /ba/, /bee/, /boo/, and so forth, and a text-to-
speech conversion program must have digital audio recordings of these
phonemes. (The real challenge is to figure out from the spelling of a word
what phonemes must be spoken.)

SBTALKER speaks in American English (actually, with an American
computer accent) when you type in text or have the program read text from
a file. The English language presents a relatively difficult task for text-to-
speech conversion. Because English is such a blend of different languages, it
has many phonemes, a very rich vocabulary, and (an even bigger obstacle)
many exceptions to standard spelling. Text-to-speech conversion is easier in
Spanish, for example, since the written language is more regular than
English.

Some languages contain fewer phonemes than does English, making
text-to-speech conversion easier. For example, Japanese has a very limited
set of phonemes. Japanese text written in its two phonetic alphabets is
straightforward to pronounce. The drawback to a language with few phonemes, however, is that it has many *homonyms* (words that sound the same

but have different meanings, such as *their* and *there*). As a result, speech-to-text conversion is made more difficult because many words can be identified only from context.

Once you finish experimenting with SBTALKER, you'll have a good understanding of the problems involved in text-to-speech conversion—as well as of why speech-to-text conversion machines are only now coming out of the laboratory.

NOTE: *Chapter 7 goes further into the basics of speech technology while describing the Windows software for speech recognition and speech synthesis, a fancy term for text-to-speech conversion.*

Loading and Running SBTALKER

Caution: Before running SBTALKER, you must temporarily disable your computer's memory managers. SBTALKER will conflict with QEMM, 386MAX, and EMM386, as well as with HIMEM.SYS, the Windows memory manager.

To disable your memory managers you need to edit your AUTO-EXEC.BAT or CONFIG.SYS files with an ASCII text editor such as the EDIT program found in your DOS *5.x/6.x* directory. Enter **REM** followed by at least one space at the beginning of the line referencing the memory manager, save the file, and then reboot your machine. Alternatively, you can create a DOS boot disk to be used prior to running these programs. (Review the FORMAT /S command in your DOS manual for instructions on how to create a boot disk.)

Here are the steps for loading and running SBTALKER:

1. Switch to the SBTALKER directory.

   SB users: Type **CD \SB\SBTALKER** and press ENTER.
   SB Deluxe users: Type **CD \SBTALKER** and press ENTER.
   SB Pro users: Type **CD \SBPRO\SBTALKER** and press ENTER.
   SB Pro Deluxe users: Type **CD \SBTALKER** and press ENTER.

2. Type **SBTALK** and press ENTER.

The talk program and its driver will be loaded into memory.

NOTE: *Since SBTALKER is a memory-resident program, remember to type **REMOVE** at the DOS command prompt when you have finished with it. If you don't, there may be insufficient memory for your other programs to load or run properly.*

Using SBTALKER

You can tell SBTALKER to respond to one line only of text that you enter, before returning to the command-line prompt. However, it's easier to use SBTALKER if it's told to respond to every line of text that you type. You can also tell SBTALKER to read an entire file. Here are the procedures for all three modes.

TO HEAR ONLY ONE LINE OF TYPED TEXT   Type **READ** at the command-line prompt, press SPACEBAR, type the text that you want SBTALKER to read, and press ENTER. Here is an example of this command:

READ your wish is my command

TIP: *If you want to hear the same text with shorter, more natural pauses between words, surround the text with double quotes like this: READ "your wish is my command".*

TO HEAR LINE AFTER LINE OF TYPED TEXT   At the command-line prompt, type **READ** and press ENTER. Your cursor will appear on the left edge of the screen, without the command-line prompt. SBTALKER is now ready to read every line you type. To quit and return to the command-line prompt, press CTRL-C (hold down CTRL and press C).

TO HEAR AN ENTIRE FILE OF TEXT   At the command-line prompt, type **READ,** followed by the less-than sign (<) sign, followed by a filename. Press ENTER to issue the command.

For example, to have SBTALKER read the ASCII text file named SBTEST.TXT in the SBTALKER subdirectory, type

READ < SBTEST.TXT

and press ENTER.

To have SBTALKER read a file in a directory other than the current directory, you'll need to specify a full path after the <, such as C:\AUTO-EXEC.BAT to read your AUTOEXEC.BAT configuration file.

To quit before reaching the end of the file, press ESC.

TIP: *Normally, when SBTALKER reads a file, it will pronounce the text without showing it. To have SBTALKER display on the screen the lines of text as they are spoken, use the /W switch with the READ command. For example, type* **READ /W < SBTEST.TXT**.

Mastering SBTALKER

Although SBTALKER has an unlimited vocabulary, it doesn't always guess the correct pronunciation. It can be easily fooled.

For example, feed SBTALKER the word *Chicago*. Notice how it pronounces /ch/ as /sh/. Then try words with a harder /ch/ sound, such as *chunk* or *hitch*. Notice that SBTALKER is either not smart enough to recognize that /ch/ at the end of a word is pronounced slightly differently, or it lacks this phoneme in its speech vocabulary. This example illustrates the challenges of creating natural-sounding speech output, not to mention learning English as a second language.

Also notice that because SBTALKER is programmed with American English phonemes, it butchers words in other languages. For example, type in the Spanish for *good night*, **buenas noches**, and hear what happens.

NOTE: *If you wish to experiment further with text-to-speech conversion, you can do so from within Dr. Sbaitso, discussed in the next section. Dr. Sbaitso uses SBTALKER to communicate with you, and will optionally read from an ASCII file. The advantage of using Dr. Sbaitso is that you can control the volume, pitch, overall tone, and, most importantly, the speech speed.*

Dr. Sbaitso

Packages: SB, SB Deluxe, SB Pro, SB Pro Deluxe

Dr. Sbaitso is your personal consultant on matters of the heart (see Figure 6-2). He reads what you type, ignoring words such as *and* and *the*, while looking for provocative words like *envy*. (To save you the embarrassment of having to ask Dr. Sbaitso such an obvious question, we'll tell you that Sbaitso is an acronym for Sound Blaster Artificial Intelligence Text to Speech Output.)

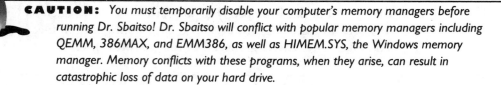

CAUTION: *You must temporarily disable your computer's memory managers before running Dr. Sbaitso! Dr. Sbaitso will conflict with popular memory managers including QEMM, 386MAX, and EMM386, as well as HIMEM.SYS, the Windows memory manager. Memory conflicts with these programs, when they arise, can result in catastrophic loss of data on your hard drive.*

To disable the memory managers you need to edit your AUTOEXEC.BAT or CONFIG.SYS files with an ASCII text editor, such as the EDIT program in your DOS 5.x/6.x directory. Insert **REM** followed by at least one space

FIGURE 6-2

Dr. Sbaitso's

opening screen

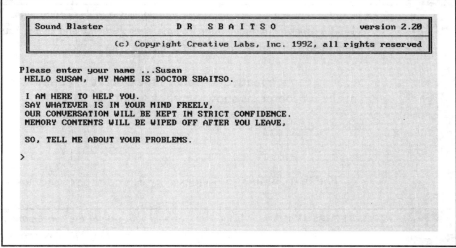

```
┌────────────────────────────────────────────────────────────────────┐
│ Sound Blaster          D R   S B A I T S O          version 2.20    │
│           (c) Copyright Creative Labs, Inc. 1992, all rights reserved│
└────────────────────────────────────────────────────────────────────┘
Please enter your name ...Susan
HELLO SUSAN,  MY NAME IS DOCTOR SBAITSO.

I AM HERE TO HELP YOU.
SAY WHATEVER IS IN YOUR MIND FREELY,
OUR CONVERSATION WILL BE KEPT IN STRICT CONFIDENCE.
MEMORY CONTENTS WILL BE WIPED OFF AFTER YOU LEAVE,

SO, TELL ME ABOUT YOUR PROBLEMS.

>
```

at the beginning of the line referencing the memory manager, save the file, and then reboot your machine. Alternatively, you can create a DOS boot disk to be used prior to running these programs.

Loading Dr. Sbaitso

To load Dr. Sbaitso, switch to your Sound Blaster subdirectory (\SB for Sound Blaster or \SBPRO for Sound Blaster Pro). Then type **SBAITSO2** and press ENTER.

To leave Dr. Sbaitso, type **Quit, Bye,** or **Goodbye.**

NOTE: *If you own a Sound Blaster Pro, you can hear Dr. Sbaitso in stereo, with an echo, by adding the /S switch to the startup command, like this:* **SBAITSO2 /S.**

Using the Doctor

Once Dr. Sbaitso is loaded, he prompts you to enter your name. He then introduces himself, and you can ask any question on your mind. The Doctor displays a > prompt when he's ready for your next question. Follow each question by pressing ENTER.

Dr. Sbaitso emits a lot of initial chatter after you enter your name. To skip over this, enter your name and press ENTER as usual, and then press ESC.

If you are not communicating well with the Doctor, type **help** to get instructions, and then type **m** twice to learn which topics most interest the Doctor.

TIP: *Your Creative Labs Sound Blaster manual lists a table of commands that control the Dr. Sbaitso program, including tone, volume, speech speed, and colors. You can also give a command to have the Doctor read a text file.*

You can ask math questions of the Doctor by entering the keyword **CALC** at the > prompt, as shown in these examples:

CALC 2/3
CALC 1+2

The first command divides 2 by 3, and the second adds 1 and 2.

CAUTION: *Watch your language: Should your side of the conversation be off-color, expect a temperamental reprimand. If you upset the Doctor you will need to type* **.WIDTH 80** *to wrest control of your screen away from the Doctor. This command restores your screen to the normal 80-character display.*

FM INTELLIGENT ORGAN (PACKAGES: ALL)

FM Intelligent Organ lets you create music with the FM Synthesizer. It's so easy and fun to use that even people who hate music will begin to dream of their Carnegie Hall debut. The opening screen for the Organ, with function keys for the main menu on the bottom of the screen, is shown in Figure 6-3.

Loading the Intelligent Organ

Here are the procedures to load the Intelligent Organ:

1. Switch to the Intelligent Organ subdirectory.

   SB users: Type **CD \SB\FMORGAN** and press ENTER.
   SB Pro users: Type **CD \SBPRO\PRO-ORG** and press ENTER.
   SB16 users: Type **CD \SB16\PRO_ORG** and press ENTER.

2. Start the Organ.

SB users: Type **FMORGAN** and press ENTER.

SB Pro users: Type **PRO-ORG** and press ENTER.

SB16 users: Type **PRO-ORG** and press ENTER.

TIP: *If you're encountering difficulties, double-check whether you're typing a hyphen or an underscore following "PRO."*

Using the Intelligent Organ

Suppose you want to do three things with the Intelligent Organ: play a song (automatically stored to memory when you play); replay your song to check your composition; and then save your song to disk. Here are the general steps to do this, beginning from the main menu represented by the function keys shown along the bottom of the screen in Figure 6-3. You'll learn more about the Organ's settings and features throughout this section.

Setting Up the Organ

Your first step is to set up the Organ in the music key you desire, and to adjust other settings that control the Organ's sound.

1. At the main menu, press F5 (default) to display the Default Setting screen (Figure 6-4).

2. Type **O** to restore default values, and then change these as you wish.

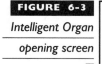

FIGURE 6-3

Intelligent Organ opening screen

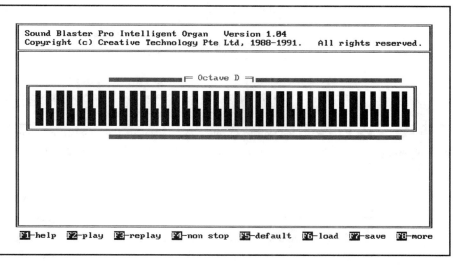

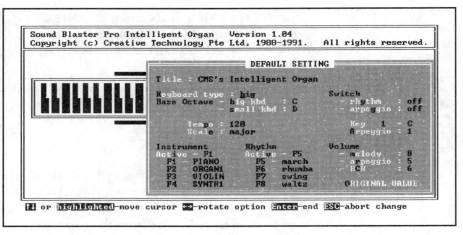

3. When you have finished revising the settings, type **T** (for Title) and enter your song title.

4. Press ENTER until the main menu reappears.

Recording Your Song

1. On the main menu, press F2 (play) to begin recording your song. Don't pause too long before beginning your masterpiece—the Organ assumes your hesitation is an intentional silence at the beginning of the composition and records it as such.

2. Press ESC as soon as you've finished to avoid recording silence at the end of the composition.

Replaying Your Song

When you have finished recording, replay your song by pressing F3 (replay). Your song is stored temporarily in your computer's memory.

CAUTION: *Don't press F2 (play) to replay your song. Doing so erases the song from memory because you haven't yet saved it to disk. Pressing F2 tells the Organ to record a new song.*

Saving Your Song

Once you've recorded and listened to your song, decide if you want to save a permanent copy of it. To save your song, press F7 (save) to store the song on your computer's hard or floppy disk. You will be prompted for your song's filename; type it and press ENTER.

Retrieving (Playing) Your Song from Disk

To retrieve and play the song you just saved to disk with F7:

1. Press F6 (load) to retrieve a song you've previously saved.

2. When the Song Box appears, press PGDN repeatedly to skip to the end of the list of songs (songs are listed in the order they were created, so you must press PGDN several times to go to the end of the list). Use the arrow keys to highlight the song you just recorded.

3. Press ENTER to select and then F3 (replay) to play that song.

Quitting the Intelligent Organ

1. If you haven't already saved your song, do so now by pressing F7.

2. Press F8 (more) to bring up the auxiliary menu, which is a menu with more command options.

3. Press F4 (quit) and then type **Y** to confirm your command.

Deleting Intelligent Organ Files

To delete songs you saved to disk with F7 (save), you must first go to the command-line prompt. Follow these steps:

1. From the Intelligent Organ main menu, select F8 (more) to display the auxiliary menu.

2. Press F3 (shell) to go temporarily ("shell out") to DOS.

3. Delete the song files using the DOS DEL command. Song files have an .ORG filename extension. For example, to delete the file named MYFIRST.ORG, type **DEL MYFIRST.ORG** and press ENTER.

4. When you've finished deleting files, type **Exit** and press ENTER to leave DOS and return to the Intelligent Organ.

Mastering the Intelligent Organ

The following sections introduce you to the Intelligent Organ features that musicians really appreciate. In addition to playing notes and changing instruments, you can adjust volume and tempo, and even have the Organ add harmonious and rhythmic accompaniments to complement what you play.

The Melody: Selecting Notes, Instruments, and Volume

Once you press F2, F3, or F4 from the main menu, the Play menu is displayed. To begin playing the Intelligent Organ, press a key on your computer keyboard to play a note. You are now in PLAY mode and you'll see the Play menu. By pressing keys such as A, S, D, or F, you play the notes that make up the melody. When you play a note, the Organ on the screen will show you which piano key you play by making that key gray in color. Your Creative Labs Sound Blaster manual contains two illustrations that show you which piano keys are played by the various keys on the computer keyboard.

From the Play menu, you can switch to any of 20 instruments by pressing function keys F1 through F4 on the Play screen. The name of the currently selected instrument is displayed in contrasting color to the right of the function key on the Play screen. Press F1 repeatedly to rotate through five different instrument selections, F2 to rotate through another five instruments, and so forth.

Press HOME to increase the melody volume, and END to decrease the volume.

Adding Auto-Bass-Chord Accompaniment

To enliven your music, the Intelligent Organ can add accompaniment that complements your melody, in the form of a bass line, harmonizing chords, or a rhythm section sound. Choose the type of accompaniment you want by pressing function keys F5 through F8 on the Play screen. Each function key rotates through a choice of four accompaniments. The accompaniment is recorded along with your song and can be saved to disk with the song.

Press the SPACEBAR to toggle the accompaniment on and off. Press ENTER to end the accompaniment. To increase the Auto-Bass-Chord volume, press PGUP; to decrease the volume, press PGDN.

Using Auto Arpeggio

In addition to the Auto-Bass-Chord accompaniments, you can use Auto Arpeggio to add a melodious harmony to the main melody that you play. Press either bracket key ([or]) on your computer keyboard to rotate through the various arpeggios available; the number for each arpeggio is displayed, and you can hear the arpeggio as well.

To turn off the arpeggio, press the quotes key (the one that has both an apostrophe and double quotation marks). Press UP ARROW to increase the Auto Arpeggio volume, or DOWN ARROW to decrease the volume.

Adding Artificial Melodies

Instead of using the Auto Arpeggio, you can add four fill-in musical patterns, such as a trill. To do this, press the following keys on the top row of your keyboard: 9, 0, –, or +. The 9 key—the trill—is the most fun. These keys will add character to long notes in a song.

The volume control for these fill-in patterns is the same as for the Auto Arpeggio. Press UPARROW to increase the artificial melody volume, or press the DOWNARROW to decrease the volume.

Controlling Tempo

Two other important keys on the Play menu are the ones that control tempo (the speed of play):

INS	Increases tempo
DEL	Decreases tempo

Features for Advanced Players

Now that you've mastered the fundamentals of the Intelligent Organ, you're ready for more powerful features. This section tells you how to add polish to your performance, using techniques such as transposing to other keys.

Scale Selection

While playing a song, you can select either a major-scale or minor-scale accompaniment from the Play menu by using either of the following:

F9	Produces a major-scale accompaniment
F10	Produces a minor-scale accompaniment

Transposing

You can transpose your music into a higher or lower key from the Play menu by pressing these keys as you play:

+ key	One semitone up
– key	One semitone down
SHIFT and + or =	A perfect fourth
SHIFT and – or _	A perfect fifth

You can then save your transposed song.

Changing Octaves

You can directly address four octaves with the large keyboard, the one that appears by default on your screen. You can switch to another four octaves within the seven octaves accessible to the FM organ by pressing the arrow keys. Press RIGHTARROW to move to a higher octave. Press LEFTARROW to move to a lower one.

Switching to the Small Keyboard

When you begin playing the Intelligent Organ, you get a large keyboard that spans four octaves and plays with the white keys only. If you want to use the black keys, you can switch to a smaller keyboard that allows you this access (but it has only two octaves). Press TAB to toggle between the keyboards. You can tell which keyboard you're playing by examining the width of the Octave bar above the piano keyboard.

TIP: *While playing the large keyboard, you can play accidentals—notes foreign to the key you're playing in—by holding* SHIFT *down while playing.*

Playing with a MIDI Keyboard

You can play the Intelligent Organ with a MIDI keyboard by adding a MIDI adapter cable. These are available from Creative Labs, as described in Appendix F. Refer to your documentation for more information on hooking up a MIDI keyboard and for using MIDI with the Intelligent Organ.

Intelligent Organ Files

The Intelligent Organ files (.ORG) are unique to the program. They cannot be played or edited by a MIDI sequencer program such as Cakewalk Apprentice for Windows or Sequencer Plus Pro, or the Creative Labs utility programs. The ORG files are essentially MIDI files with a special Creative Labs header that defines the instrument patches (instrument assignments) to use.

**PLAY AND
RECORD
UTILITIES
(ALL CARDS)**

his section introduces the following utility programs that play or record digital audio and music files. You're certain to encounter these utilities in your work with Sound Blaster.

- **VPLAY/WPLAY** playback utilities

- **VREC/WREC** recording utilities

VPLAY/WPLAY and VREC/WREC are easy-to-use DOS programs that respectively play and record digital audio files in the Creative Voice/Microsoft Wave (VOC/WAV) format. The files are created by recording your voice through a microphone or from another source, such as line-in or even a CD-ROM if you have a Sound Blaster Pro or Sound Blaster 16. The sound is converted to digital data stored either in memory or on floppy or hard disk. These tools are primarily used to make digital audio recordings that serve as voice-overs for multimedia presentation. The VREC/WREC and VPLAY/WPLAY utilities can also be great fun—like embarrassing your friends by capturing their laugh.

NOTE: *Any serious recording should be done with an editor such as VEDIT2 (SB Pro) or Creative WaveStudio (SB 16). VPLAY/WPLAY and VREC/WREC are for quick-and-dirty handling of voice files.*

- **PLAYCMF** plays Creative Music Files (.CMF) on the sound card's FM synthesizer.

- **PLAYMIDI** plays MIDI music files on either the FM synthesizer or an external MIDI synthesizer, including the SB16 Wave Blaster.
  PLAYCMF and PLAYMIDI are your avenues for converting that boring computer into an exciting Multimedia PC, adding great background music to your presentation.

- **CDPLYR** gives Sound Blaster Pro owners a simple DOS utility for controlling their CD-ROM players. It's ideal for playing audio CDs while working on your computer.

- **READDRV** is a diagnostic utility recently added to the suite of software bundled with Creative Labs sound cards. It will list all of the drivers for your Sound Blaster along with their version numbers.

VPLAY/WPLAY

Packages:

VPLAY	All
WPLAY	SB16

VPLAY is a voice utility that plays VOC (Creative Voice File) format digital audio files such as those created by VREC, VOXKIT (SB only), and VEDIT2 (SB Deluxe, SB Pro, and SB Pro Deluxe only). VPLAY makes it a snap to listen to your audio files.

WPLAY is nearly identical to VPLAY. They differ in that VPLAY plays VOC files while WPLAY plays WAV (Microsoft Wave file) format digital audio files. Wave files are the dominant type of digital audio file in the Microsoft Windows environment. They're created by programs such as Creative Wave Studio and Creative Soundo'LE. (See Chapter 5 for more coverage of Creative Soundo'LE.) Otherwise WPLAY and VPLAY and their optional command switches are identical.

NOTE: *If you have an older version of VPLAY (you bought your sound card package sometime prior to the introduction of the Deluxe packages) you may have a version that doesn't play large audio files—larger than can fit into available memory. If so, you can obtain updated driver software to accomplish this. The Creative Voice Disk driver (CTVDSK.DRV) makes this possible. Look for this file in your \SB\DRV or \SBPRO\DRV directory (all SB16 owners have this new version). If you don't have it, check the Creative Labs bulletin board (BBS) for an updated driver or call the Creative Labs support line. See Appendix D for more help.*

Running VPLAY/WPLAY

As usual, the commands to run VPLAY/WPLAY vary according to which Sound Blaster card you own.

1. Switch to the appropriate subdirectory.

SB users: Type **CD \SB\VOXKIT** and then press ENTER.
SB Deluxe users: Type **CD \SB\VOCUTIL** and then press ENTER.
SB Pro users: Type **CD \SBPRO\VEDIT2** and then press ENTER.
SB Pro Deluxe users: Type **CD \SBPRO\VOCUTIL** and then press ENTER.

SB16 users: Type **CD \SB16\VOCUTIL** and then press ENTER.

2. Type **VPLAY** (or **WPLAY**) followed by a voice filename. For example to use VPLAY:

   SB users: To play TV4.VOC, type **VPLAY TV4.VOC** and press ENTER.

   SB Pro users: To play CNEWS.VOC, type **VPLAY BBCNEWS.VOC** and press ENTER.

   SB16 users: To play FOOTSTEP.VOC in the MMPLAY subdirectory, type **VPLAY \SB16\MMPLAY\FOOTSTEP.VOC** and press ENTER.

NOTE: *To get help with VPLAY (or WPLAY), type the utility name by itself and press* ENTER.

Mastering VPLAY/WPLAY

VPLAY/WPLAY is easy to use. All the command switches are optional. The /T switch (for timer) is the most useful option for most people. VPLAY/WPLAY has a number of optional command switches that allow you to control its actions. These switches include

- /T:*n* specifies the maximum duration for play, in seconds. For example, /T:5 limits playback to a maximum of five seconds.

- /Q, the Quiet option, suppresses the onscreen appearance of messages from VPLAY. This is useful when embedding VPLAY/WPLAY in a batch file.

- /B:*n* specifies the buffer size. This is described in more depth in your Sound Blaster manual.

- /X= runs a DOS program. After recording is started, the DOS command line following the = will be executed. With the proper equipment, this switch can be used to send a command to a serial or parallel port to cause an external device like a CD laser disc player to advance to another image.

NOTE: *You cannot use both the /X= and /T: switches in the same VPLAY command.*

Here is an example of how to play the FROGS.VOC sound file for a maximum of two seconds (and suppressing extraneous status messages from appearing on the screen):

VPLAY FROGS.VOC /T:2 /Q

Sound Blaster 16 owners will find a VOC file, FOOTSTEP.VOC, in their \SB16\MMPLAY subdirectory.

TIP: *The Sound Blaster multimedia toolkit, SBSIM, includes a program called VOICE that also plays VOC files. VOICE has many more features than VPLAY, including the ability to pause and resume audio output. See the SBSIM section near the end of of this chapter for more information on SBSIM.*

Here's an example for SB16 owners for how to play a WAV file for a maximum of 2 seconds (and suppressing extraneous status messages):

WPLAY GLASS.WAV /T:2 /Q

VREC/WREC

Packages:

VREC	All
WREC	SB16

VREC is a voice recording utility that records audio input directly to disk. VREC creates a file in Creative Voice File format (VOC), which you can play with VPLAY.

WREC is similar to VREC. The most significant difference is that WREC creates Microsoft Wave (WAV) files while VREC creates Creative Voice (VOC) files. Most command switches are identical.

Running VREC/WREC

The command to run VREC/WREC varies according to which Sound Blaster version you have.

1. Switch to the appropriate subdirectory.

   SB users: Type **CD \SB\VOXKIT** and then press ENTER.
   SB Pro users: Type **CD \SBPRO\VEDIT2** and then press ENTER.
   SB Deluxe users: Type **CD \SB\VOCUTIL** and then press ENTER.
   SB Pro Deluxe users: Type **CD \SBPRO\VOCUTIL** and then press ENTER.
   SB16 users: Type **CD \SB16\VOCUTIL** and then press ENTER.

2. Specify the voice file you wish to create by typing **VREC** (or **WREC**) followed by at least one space and the filename. For example, to record your voice from the microphone and save it in file MYVOICE.VOC, type **VREC myvoice.voc** and begin talking when you press ENTER.

3. When you have finished, terminate recording by pressing ESC. *Don't forget to do this*—if you forget to terminate recording, VREC will fill your floppy or hard disk with one very long voice file!

NOTE: To get help with VREC, type **VREC** alone and press ENTER.

Mastering VREC

All versions of VREC possess the following optional switches:

■ /B:*kk* controls the buffer size. Omitting this switch results in a default value that usually works well. Don't worry about this switch unless you hear popping sounds when you play your digital audio file. (Popping and pausing are discussed in Chapter 1.) See your manual for more information on possible values for *kk*.

■ /S:*nn* is the recording sample rate where *nn* is a number like 22050 (without a comma). The choice of sample rate depends on which Sound Blaster package you own.

SB & SB Pro: If you have a Sound Blaster your permissible range for *n* stretches from 4,000 Hz up to 15,000 Hz. If you have a Sound Blaster Pro your range extends up to 44,100 Hz (or 22,050 Hz if recording in stereo). Sound Blaster Pro owners should note that selecting stereo recording automatically sets the two-channel (left and right) combined sample rate to 22,050 Hz, and this rate cannot be overridden by the /S switch. The default sample rate, if you don't use this switch, is 8,000 Hz. This rate is fine for both male and female voices.

SB 16: Owners of the 16-bit sound card have both VREC or WREC. The main difference between the two is sample rate range. The VREC sample rate extends from 5,000 Hz to 44,100 Hz. The WREC sample rate is limited to the three standard rates for WAV files in the Microsoft Windows environment: 11,025 Hz, 22,050 Hz, and 44,100 Hz.

See the section on sampling rates in Chapter 1 for more information.

■ /T:*n* sets the timer period, where *n* is from 1 to 65,535 seconds. When the timer expires, recording stops.

■ /Q enables the Quiet mode. This suppresses the display of onscreen status message by VREC.

■ /X= runs a DOS program. After recording is started, the DOS command line that follows the = will be executed. This can be used to send a command to a serial or parallel port, causing an external device to begin play.

NOTE: *You cannot use the /t: switch and the /X= switch in the same VREC command.*

The following example combines three of the switches listed above. This command records to the file PARROT.VOC at a sample rate of 10,000 Hz and for only one second. Quiet mode is selected to suppress all messages other than error messages:

VREC parrot.voc /S:10000 /T:1 /Q

NOTE: *Regardless of the filename extension you suggest, VREC will create a file with the .VOC extension.*

Sound Blaster Pro Enhancements

The Sound Blaster Pro version of VREC has been significantly improved with new switches. It has the following additional command options:

■ /A:*recording source*   Although Sound Blaster's VREC records only from the microphone, Sound Blaster Pro captures sound from the microphone, line-in, CD input or any combination of the three (MIC or line-in only for Sound Blaster 2.0). Use switches /A:MIC for microphone, /A:LINE for line-in, and /A:CD for CD. (The SB16 has an additional choice: FM.) Lacking the /A: switch, the default is microphone (MIC) input.

- **/M:***recording mode*   Use /M:STEREO for stereo recording, or /M:MONO for monaural recording. If you designate STEREO, your sampling rate will be automatically set for 22,050 Hz. The default, if this switch is absent, is MONO.

- **/L:***n* designates the source volume for line-in and CD. This value varies from 0 to 15, where 15 is the maximum and 0 is the minimum. The default is 0, which effectively turns off the source. This has no effect on the microphone volume; all Creative Labs sound cards have automatic gain control that adjusts the microphone level automatically for optimal recording. (The SB16 version of VREC/WREC lacks this switch; volume is set by the mixer software only.)

NOTE: *The VREC /L: switch setting is poorly named; it suggests line-in volume only. This switch actually controls either line-in or CD, whichever source(s) is selected with the /A: switch.*

- **/F:***recording filter*   The filter setting can have two settings: LOW or HIGH. The LOW setting suppresses audio components that exceed 4 kHz; the HIGH setting suppresses components above 8 kHz. The default, if this switch is not used, is LOW. (The SB16 lacks this command option since the recording filter is automatically set by the card's digital audio recording circuitry.)

SB16 Enhancements

The SB16 has additional switch settings reflecting the 16-bit nature and the Advanced Signal Processing capability of the SB16.

- **/A:***recording source*   This is the same as for the Sound Blaster Pro except SB16 owners can combine sources by using the plus sign. For example, /A:LINE+MIC will combine line and microphone input.

- **/R:***xx*   This specifies the number of bits (8 or 16) per recording sample.

- **/C:***type*   This switch specifies the type of compression to use (available only for SB16 cards with the Advanced Signal Processing DSP chip installed). The choices are ALAW (2x compression), MULAW (2x), or CTADPCM (4x). If this switch is used, /R is ignored since the recording is automatically made in 16 bits.

How Compression Influences the Sample Rate

Sound Blaster and Sound Blaster Pro have similar hardware decompression capabilities, but differ in their maximum sampling rate. Be aware that when you're using a digital audio editor program such as VEDIT2 to compress a file, you may need to reduce the sampling rate before doing the compression. This is necessary in order to create a file that doesn't exceed the sound card's playback limitations. For more details, see the section on packing in Chapter 1. There you'll find a table with the maximum sampling rate for each Sound Blaster version.

VREC/WREC Examples

Examples are provided here for how to use VREC with Sound Blaster and Sound Blaster Pro, and how to use WREC (or VREC) with the SB16.

SB EXAMPLE   The following SB command example records from the line-in or microphone source, whichever one (or both) is attached, at the lowest possible sample rate (4,000 Hz) for 5 seconds:

    VREC myvoice.voc /S:4000 /T:5

SB PRO EXAMPLE   The following SB Pro command example records from the line-in source, in stereo, at a reasonable volume:

    VREC opera.voc /A:LINE /M:STEREO /F:HIGH /L:12

NOTE: *You will hear the line-in source as soon as this command is issued, unless you first mute the output with the master volume control. For SB Pro, use SBP-MIX or SBP-SET, which are described in Chapter 3. For SB16, use SB16MIX or SB16SET, which are described in Chapter 4.*

SB16 EXAMPLE   The following SB16 command example records from the line-in and FM synthesizer sources, in stereo with 16 bits per sample, at the lowest possible sample rate (11,025 Hz per channel) for a Microsoft Wave file:

    WREC testrec.wav /M:STEREO /R:16 /S:11025

PLAYCMF

Packages: All

PLAYCMF plays Creative Music File (CMF) format songs on your sound card's FM synthesizer. There's an assortment of these music files in the PLAYCMF subdirectory. Creative Labs, as an early player in the sound card business, pioneered their own file format. These files are called Creative Music Files and have a .CMF filename extension. The CMF files resemble MIDI files, except for an additional Creative Labs header that contains instrument assignments. There's hundreds of CMF files available for the taking on the major bulletin board systems. See Appendix G for more information about this.

NOTE: *Both PLAYCMF and its sister, PLAYMIDI, will convert that boring computer into an exciting multimedia machine, adding great background music to your presentation. While PLAYCMF plays Creative Music Files (CMF), PLAYMIDI plays MIDI music files. PLAYMIDI is discussed in the next section.*

The Sound Blaster multimedia toolkit, SBSIM, which is described at the end of this chapter, includes a program called MUSIC that plays both Creative Music File format CMF files and MIDI files. MUSIC has many more features than PLAYCMF, such as repeat play, pause and continue play, change the tempo, and transpose the music to a higher or lower key.

Loading PLAYCMF

PLAYCMF is easy to use, but you must load the FM synthesizer driver first:

1. To load the Sound Blaster FM driver, first switch to the Sound Blaster directory:

   SB users: Type **CD \SB** and then press ENTER.
   SB Pro users: Type **CD \SBPRO** and then press ENTER.
   SB16 users: Type **CD \SB16** and then press ENTER.

2. Now load SBFMDRV:

   Type **SBFMDRV** and press ENTER.

3. Switch to the PLAYCMF subdirectory:

   Type **CD PLAYCMF** and then press ENTER.

Running PLAYCMF

To use PLAYCMF, simply type **PLAYCMF** followed by the name of the file you wish to hear. For example, to play sample music file JUG.CMF, type

PLAYCMF JUG.CMF and press ENTER. To terminate a song before it has finished, press ESC. To get help with PLAYCMF, type **PLAYCMF** by itself and press ENTER.

When you've finished with PLAYCMF, unload the SBFMDRV driver from memory. To do so, switch to the Sound Blaster directory (one directory level up) by typing **CD..** and then type **SBFMDRV /U** and press ENTER.

NOTE: *PLAYCMF can play audio files too large to fit into available memory. The Creative Voice Disk driver (CTVDSK.DRV) makes this possible. Look for this driver in your \SB\DRV or \SBPRO\DRV directory. If you don't have it, check the Creative Labs bulletin board (BBS) for an update, or call the Creative Labs support line.*

Mastering PLAYCMF

PLAYCMF has two optional switches:

- /Q enables the Quiet mode, which suppresses onscreen displays of PLAYCMF messages.

- /S=*cmdline* starts to play the CMF music file and then executes *cmdline*, a DOS command line. To see this in action, type **PLAYCMF kentucky.cmf /S=DIR**. This will begin play of KENTUCKY.CMF and then do a directory listing while the music is playing.

TIP: *Consider using the /S option to play a background song while displaying a slide show on the computer.*

PLAYMIDI

Packages: SB Deluxe, SB Pro, SB Pro Deluxe, SB16

PLAYMIDI plays MIDI song files with the .MID file extension on either the sound card's FM synthesizer or, if you have an SB Pro or SB16, on an external MIDI synthesizer. The MIDI song file format is used by musicians worldwide. It is part of a specification for a MIDI network of electronic instruments, keyboards, and computer-based sequencing programs that play and record MIDI songs. If you have a compatible MIDI keyboard, you can use the Creative Labs MIDI kit to attach the keyboard to your Sound Blaster card (see Appendix F for details).

Sound Blaster owners will have either \SB\MIDI or \SB\PLAYMIDI on their hard drive that contains MIDI files. Sound Blaster owners prior to the Deluxe package were not provided with PLAYMIDI.EXE.

NOTE: *PLAYMIDI will also play MIDI files recorded with a Sequencer, such as the Cakewalk Apprentice for Windows or Sequencer Plus Pro for DOS. Sequencer Plus Pro was bundled with Sound Blaster Pro at one time and was the DOS MIDI sequencer featured by the Creative Labs' MIDI kit. At this time, Creative Labs includes Cakewalk Apprentice for Windows in the MIDI kits.*

Loading SBMIDI

Before running PLAYMIDI you must load SBMIDI, the Sound Blaster MIDI driver.

1. To load the Sound Blaster MIDI driver, switch to the Sound Blaster directory.

   SB Pro users: Type **CD \SBPRO** and then press ENTER.
   SB16 users: Type **CD** and then press ENTER.

2. Now load the SBMIDI driver:

   Type **SBMIDI** and press ENTER.

OVERRIDING THE DEFAULT SETTINGS   Beginning with the Deluxe software, the default settings for MIDI play—established when your sound card was installed—can be overriden with switches.

Specify the MIDI file format by choosing one of the following three:

- ■ /G for General MIDI (drums on channel 10).

- ■ /E for Extended MIDI (drums on channel 10); this is the default for a multimedia PC and for your sound card in particular.

- ■ /B for Basic MIDI (drums on channel 16).

Determine the MIDI device to play by selecting one of the following:

- ■ /1 for the FM synthesizer chip.

- ■ /2 for an external MIDI device (without MPU401 emulation).

- ■ /3 for an external MIDI device (with MPU401 emulation).

NOTE: *To play the SB16's Wave Blaster, choose either /2 or /3.*

Using PLAYMIDI

1. To use PLAYMIDI, first switch to the PLAYMIDI directory.

   SB Pro users: Type **CD \SBPRO\PLAYMIDI** and then press ENTER.
   SB16 users: Type **CD \SB16\PLAYMIDI** and then press ENTER.

Now to play a song, type **PLAYMIDI** followed by the song name. For example, to play the jazz sample file, type **PLAYMIDI JAZZ.MID** and press ENTER.

To terminate PLAYMIDI before the song has finished playing, press ESC.

Unloading SBMIDI

When you have finished with PLAYMIDI, you should unload the SBMIDI driver from memory.

1. Switch to the Sound Blaster directory.

   Type **CD..** and press ENTER.

2. Now unload the driver by typing **SBMIDI /U** and press ENTER.

NOTE: *To get help with PLAYMIDI, type **PLAYMIDI** and press ENTER.*

Mastering PLAYMIDI

The PLAYMIDI command has four optional switches. The /FMT and /DRUM switches for MIDI are recent additions to the PLAYMIDI command switches.

■ /S=*cmdline* starts to play the MIDI music file and then executes *cmdline*, a DOS command line. To use this switch, follow the /S= with the name of the program you want to run, as in the following example:

   PLAYMIDI jazz.mid /S=DIR

This begins play of JAZZ.MID and then does a directory listing while the music is playing.

TIP: *A real-world use for the /S= option is to execute a program that runs, through your computer's serial port, a slide show.*

- /Q activates Quiet mode, suppressing PLAYMIDI's routine status messages from appearing on the screen. This keeps your screen from becoming cluttered with extraneous messages when you run PLAYMIDI from a batch file.

- /FMT:*type* overrides the SBMIDI default setting for the type of MIDI to expect: BASIC, GENERAL, or EXTENDED.

- /DRUM:*channel* specifies which channel is the drum (percussion) channel. The default is channel 10.

NOTE: *The Sound Blaster Pro toolkit, SBSIM, includes a program called MUSIC that plays both Creative Music File (CMF) files and MIDI files. MUSIC has many more features than PLAYMIDI, such as repeat play, tempo change, and transposing the music to a higher or lower key. See the end of this chapter for more information about MUSIC.*

CDPLYR

Package: SB Pro

The CD Player is an easy-to-use DOS utility program for controlling your CD-ROM drive.

Loading and Running CDPLYR

To load CDPLYR, first switch to the \SBPRO directory; then type **CDPLYR** and press ENTER.

The CD Player is easy to run. Use LEFTARROW and RIGHTARROW, or TAB and SHIFT-TAB to move to a button, and then press ENTER to select it. These buttons (Play/Stop/Pause/Next Track/Previous Track/Fast Forward/Rewind) work just like those on your personal CD player. Your Sound Blaster Pro manual has a full explanation of each button.

To quit CDPLYR, press ESC.

Before you can use your CD-ROM player with CDPLYR, the CD-ROM installation must be complete. You must first install the software drivers provided on the disk that comes with your Creative Labs CD-ROM kit. If the drivers have not been installed yet, and you try to run CDPLYR, you'll see a message stating that MSCDEX has not been loaded.

READDRV

Packages: SB Deluxe, SB Pro Deluxe, SB16

This diagnostic utility lists the Creative Labs software drivers along with their version number and interrupt number or other settings. These software drivers are continuously refined to offer improved performance and compatibility with hardware and software. READDRV is useful for troubleshooting sound card problems. Before you contact Creative Labs to inquire about a compatibility problem, or to see if an improved driver exists, run READDRV to get a listing of what you have.

1. To access READDRV, switch to the voice utilities directory:

   SB Deluxe users: Type **CD \SB\VOCUTIL** and then press ENTER.
   SB Pro Deluxe users: Type **CD \SBPRO\VOCUTIL** and then press ENTER.

   SB16 users: Type **CD \SB16\VOCUTIL** and then press ENTER.

2. Type **READDRV** and press ENTER.

DIGITAL AUDIO EDITORS

This section describes the two digital audio editors, programs that integrate recording, editing, and playback of digital audio files.

- **VEDIT2** (SB Deluxe, SB Pro, SB Pro Deluxe) is a mouse-driven program for creating and revising digital audio files. This editor works with files recorded in the Creative Labs VOC format. It cannot edit Microsoft wave (WAV) files directly.

- **VOXKIT** (SB only) is an elementary digital audio file editor provided with earlier Sound Blaster cards only. This editor works with VOC files only.

VEDIT2

Packages: SB Deluxe, SB Pro, SB Pro Deluxe

Voice Editor II (VEDIT2) is a feature-rich, full-screen program for recording, playing, editing, and enhancing your Creative Labs VOC digital audio files. Just think of VEDIT2 as a recording studio for sound files. You can record from the microphone, line-in, or a CD-ROM (SB Pro and SB Pro Deluxe only). From the VEDIT2 editor you see on your computer screen the actual waveform that you hear when you play your digital audio file. You can mark a piece of this waveform, listen to it, and then delete, move, or enhance that piece. You can, for example, remove words from a speech or change the order of sentences. You can also add special effects, such as fade-ins, stereo panning, and echoes.

NOTE: *If you need an editor that runs in DOS and is more powerful than VEDIT2, you should check out Blaster Master. See the description in Chapter 10.*

Your Creative Labs manual has an extensive array of screen shots and detailed instructions to guide you through VEDIT2. This section is a supplement to your manual. Rather than step-by-step instructions and complete menu descriptions, here you will find information to fill in the "gaps" in your manual—a supplement pointing out interesting features of VEDIT2 and giving you tips on how to get the most out of this editor.

Starting and Quitting

1. To start VEDIT2 first switch to the appropriate subdirectory:

   SB Deluxe users: Type **CD \SB** and then press ENTER.
   SB Pro users: Type **CD \SBPRO** and then press ENTER.
   SB Pro Deluxe users: Type **CD \SBPRO** and then press ENTER.

2. Type **VEDIT2** followed by a voice filename.

You will now see the opening screen, as shown in Figure 6-5. Press any key to advance to the next screen.

To exit from VEDIT2, select File from the main menu, and then select Exit. When prompted, confirm your command by typing **Y**.

Keyboard Fundamentals

You work with VEDIT2 using keyboard commands similar to those of the FM Intelligent Organ. Commands are selected from a menu bar at the top of the screen, by holding down ALT and pressing a letter key. All other

FIGURE 6-5

VEDIT2 opening

screen

■

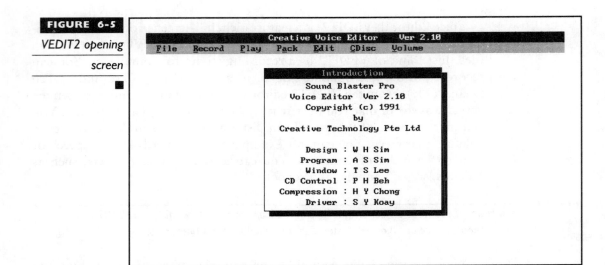

menu and dialog box selections are made by pressing just a single letter or number key.

NOTE: *Because VEDIT2 is a graphically oriented program, you'll probably find that controlling the program with a mouse is more intuitive than with the keyboard. For the sake of brevity, and to ensure that everyone can follow the procedures described here, only keyboard instructions are provided.*

Loading Files

To load a VOC voice file, select Load from the File menu. This displays the File Directory screen that presents a list of VOC files. Once you select a file, the Block Information screen appears, and all the blocks contained within that file are listed. You are now free to delete blocks, move them around, play specific blocks or the entire file, or switch to the Edit menu and modify a block.

NOTE: *Chapter 1 touched upon data and silence blocks, the two most important components of a VOC file. All of the block types are described in the section "Inserting Control Blocks," later in this chapter.*

A typical Block Information screen, with a single voice data block that has been loaded into memory, is shown in Figure 6-6.

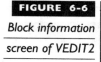

FIGURE 6-6

Block information

screen of VEDIT2

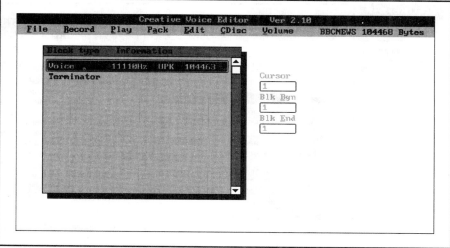

Working with Large Files

Some programs, such as VREC, record audio to disk as a single block that fills the file. More sophisticated programs, such as VEDIT2, record audio to disk as a sequence of smaller, more manageable data blocks. In the case of VEDIT2, the data blocks are 32K in size. To edit a digital audio file, you must select from the Block Information screen a group of blocks that fit in memory. Unfortunately, there are two situations, both of which are very common, in which you cannot load all the blocks at once:

■ *Audio File Consists of One Large Block* In this case, VEDIT2 prompts you to split the block into smaller ones that can be loaded. You can split blocks repeatedly, as described in an upcoming section, until you have a block or group of blocks that will load into memory.

■ *Audio File Consists of a Collection of Blocks Too Large to Load All Together* In this situation, VEDIT2 prompts you to select which block or group of blocks you want to load. You can also split the blocks further, as described in an upcoming section, until you have a block or group of blocks that can be loaded.

SELECTING BLOCKS   If a voice file is too large to fit into conventional memory, VEDIT2 displays the Message screen (Figure 6-7). Here the block selection window on the right provides a numbered list of all the blocks

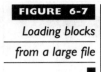

FIGURE 6-7

Loading blocks

from a large file

■

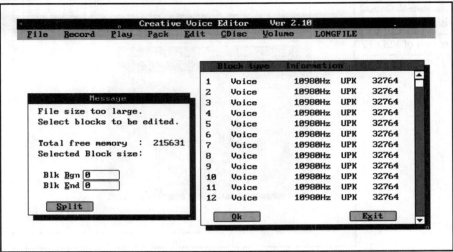

found in this file. The Message dialog box on the left prompts you to select the block or group of blocks you wish to load.

If your file consists of one large block too large to load, you can split that block. Pick that block and then select the Split button.

If your audio file contains too many blocks to load, don't worry. Blocks that you load and then change will be automatically reinserted into the file when you save it to disk. For example, suppose you load the last data block only, and then add a fade-out to soften the music's abrupt ending. When you save your work by selecting File and then Save from the main menu, VEDIT2 will replace the last data block in the disk file with the edited version of this block from memory.

SPLITTING LARGE FILES   If you find you're more comfortable working with smaller files, you can split a long audio file into several pieces. Select a group of blocks and then use the Write command to write them to disk. For example, if you have a file of ten blocks, you can split it into two five-block files. Follow these steps:

1. From the Block Information screen (Figure 6-6) select a group of blocks.

2. Select File and then Write to save these blocks on disk in their own file.

3. Repeat steps 1 and 2 to extract additional sets of blocks, and then save them to disk, each with its own filename.

JOINING SMALL FILES   Unfortunately, VEDIT2 has no provision for inserting a voice file, or blocks within a voice file, into another voice file. If you need to do this, split the file into two or more pieces and then combine them with the JOINTVOC utility, described later in this chapter. You're likely to do this when creating multimedia presentations; otherwise, if you played many small files separately rather than as one combined file, you would hear a pause between sound bites.

Recording with VEDIT2

You can record from any one of the following sources: voice (microphone), CD, or line-in. You can record directly to memory or to a disk file. Before you begin recording, you must set up your recording environment by following these steps, all of which begin at the main menu:

1. Select the Volume menu, and then choose the source you wish to record from. Adjust the volume to a high setting, about 4/5 of the maximum volume level, to ensure a strong input signal.

2. Select the Record menu, and then choose Setting. The Setting window is discussed in the next section.

3. Begin the recording by selecting either To Memory or To Disk from the Record menu. If you are recording from the microphone, begin speaking as soon as possible.

Choosing Recording Settings

Before you begin recording, you must choose Setting on the Record menu to enter the recording parameters on the Setting window (Figure 6-8). Note that once you pick a recording source, such as microphone or CD input, VEDIT2 makes an intelligent guess at what the other settings should be. For example, if you select Stereo and CD, VEDIT2 automatically establishes the 22.05 kHz sampling rate and the No Filter setting.

Unfortunately, VEDIT2 can't ensure that the volume control for the chosen source is set at a reasonable level. You're responsible for setting the volume to a suitably high level, probably 10 or more. Select Volume from the main menu to access the volume controls.

Two important issues—how to select a sample rate, and whether to record to disk or to memory—are discussed next.

NOTE: *Chapter 1 provides additional information to help you understand the recording settings (see the sections on sampling and filters).*

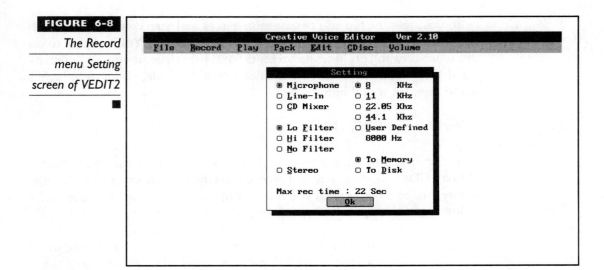

FIGURE 6-8

The Record

menu Setting

screen of VEDIT2

SELECTING THE SAMPLE RATE When selecting the sample rate, keep three issues in mind:

■ If you plan to work in the Windows environment, it's best to select 11, 22, or 44 kHz (or more precisely 11.025, 22.050, or 44.100 kHz—these two-digit numbers are rounded-off forms). These rates are common to both VOC and WAV files, which makes it easier to share sound files between the DOS and Windows multimedia environments.

■ Use a higher sampling rate for music (44 kHz for monaural or 22 kHz for stereo) to accurately record the high-frequency components. Use a lower rate for voice (8 or 11 kHz).

■ Beware of filling up your hard disk with voice files. At the 22 kHz maximum sampling rate for stereo, 44,100 (two channels each at 22.05 kHz) 8-bit (1-byte) samples are taken each second. This means you are consuming disk space at the rate of 44,100 bytes a second, or 2.65 million bytes a minute!

SELECTING THE DESTINATION In the Setting window you must select either the To Memory or the To Disk radio button. Your selection controls which menu item of the same name will be active. When you return to the main menu the item you do not select will appear as a dimmed menu choice. As soon as you choose the menu choice for the desired destination, recording will begin.

■ *Recording to Memory* Select To Memory to record digitized audio in conventional memory. Since digital audio recording generates a lot of data, and very little conventional memory is left after VEDIT2 loads, your recording will be limited to a matter of seconds.

■ *Recording to Disk* Select To Disk to record digitized audio to your floppy or hard disk. VEDIT2 will prompt you for a filename. Enter a new filename and press ENTER, or select an existing file from the file list to overwrite that file. If you type a new filename, you don't need to specify a filename extension; VEDIT2 automatically adds .VOC.

Once you have specified your recording parameters and chosen either To Memory or To Disk, the Setting window will display the maximum recording time at the bottom of the window. Recording will terminate automatically once memory is filled when you're recording To Memory, or when the disk is filled when you're recording To Disk.

Scanning Input

Select Scan Input from the Record menu to view the sound wave from your chosen source before you begin to record. The Scan Input screen is shown in Figure 6-9.

Scan Input ensures that you've selected the correct source in the Setting window and that the volume level is high enough. For a dramatic demonstration of input scanning, set the source to microphone, choose Scan Input,

FIGURE 6-9

Scanning input before recording

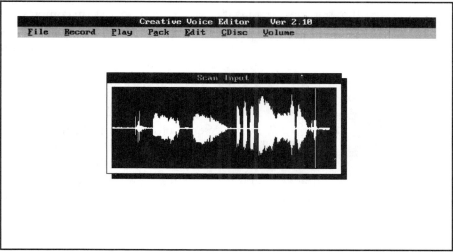

and then speak into the microphone. If you see a flat line, VEDIT2 can't hear anything and you'll need to double-check your settings. Press the ESC key to return to the main menu.

Recording from CD

The CDISK option from the main menu controls your CD player. This menu choice will be dimmed and unavailable if you don't have a CD-ROM player connected.

A very nice feature of VEDIT2 is that it automatically starts the CD player when you begin recording. This makes it easy to start your recording at a precise location on the CD. First, make certain you've selected CD as the recording source in the Setting window. Then, pause at the location where you wish to begin recording. When you give VEDIT2 the command to start recording, by selecting either To Disk or To Memory, VEDIT2 automatically starts CD play from the specified starting point.

Conserving Disk Space

Recording sound files consumes disk space very rapidly. To conserve disk space you can either compress files or delete ones you no longer need. These two alternatives are discussed next.

Compressing Files

By compressing digital audio files, you can conserve disk space. From the main menu, select Pack. Then choose Memory, to compress digital audio temporarily stored in memory, or choose Disk, to compress digital audio stored in a disk file. You will then be given four choices for the packing method.

There are two fundamentally different types of packing available: converting silence in the recording to silence blocks, and compressing data blocks. These are summarized below, but for more detail refer to the section on packing in Chapter 1.

■ *Silence Packing*   Silence block packing replaces stretches of silence or near-silence in your audio data blocks with small silence blocks. The silence control block is essentially a marker with a time period attached. This type of packing is more appropriate for speech than for music, since long pauses are more common in speech. The savings in file size can be impressive; a speech file can often be reduced to half its original size.

■ *Data Packing* You have three choices for performing data compression upon data blocks: 2:1, 3:1, and 4:1 compression. The greater the compression (4:1 is the highest), the more you lose in audio quality. The tightest overall file compression is provided by doing silence packing before data packing. Since silence packing can be quite effective in reducing file size without loss of sound quality, you may not need to do data packing at all.

NOTE: *Silence packing isn't supported by the more recent versions of VEDIT2, so you won't see the silence packing option in the VEDIT2 menu.*

PROTECT YOUR UNPACKED DIGITAL AUDIO   VEDIT2 can pack voice files already loaded in memory (RAM), or voice files on disk. When you pack digital audio recorded directly to memory, you'll overwrite and lose the original raw (unpacked) sound recording. When you pack digital audio recorded to disk, VEDIT2 prompts you for both a source and target filename. The packed audio will be placed in a newly created file, and the original, unpacked sound bytes are preserved. This is preferable over recording to memory, since it minimizes the likelihood that you'll lose a valuable recording by accidentally overwriting it. Always save your digital audio to disk with the File Save command before packing.

PACKED FILES CANNOT BE EDITED   There are drawbacks and limitations to packing audio files. The major drawback is that you cannot further modify your files. This means you won't be able to move blocks around, cut blocks out, or add special effects like echo or panning. In addition, packed files cannot be converted to WAV files that are popular in the Microsoft Windows multimedia environment.

LIMITATIONS ON PACKING   When you attempt to pack, you may get a message that "data cannot be packed." There can be several reasons for this. First, VEDIT2 won't pack voice data with a high sample rate since it knows that the decompression hardware on the Sound Blaster cards won't be able to keep up with the workload. The sound card can't handle too high a sampling rate if it must simultaneously decompress. Another reason you may encounter this message is insufficient memory. VEDIT2 needs a lot of memory to pack, even when it packs a sound file on disk. If you encounter this limitation, you may have to split your file in two, pack the two pieces independently, and then join them together again, as explained earlier.

Deleting Files

You should frequently cleanse your Sound Blaster directory of unneeded VOC files. Unfortunately, there is no command to delete files on disk. You have to quit VEDIT2, return to the DOS command prompt or your file manager, and then use the appropriate command to delete files with a .VOC extension.

TIP: *If you're running out of disk space but don't want to quit VEDIT2 yet, you can free up space by compressing files you no longer need. Select 4:1 compression from the Pack menu to squeeze files as much as possible. You can also prepare for this contingency by creating a tiny (fewer than 1,000 bytes) digital audio file. Load this file into memory and then use the Save As command in the File menu to overwrite larger, no longer needed files.*

Playing Sound Files

To hear your audio files, select Play from the main menu. You have three choices when playing files:

- From Memory lets you hear all of the audio file that you recently recorded to memory or loaded from disk.

- Selected Blocks lets you find the particular word, phrase, or melody you wish to manipulate.

- From Disk lets you listen to a voice file on disk.

NOTE: *Before you play, you should turn off the source (for instance, shut off your microphone) or turn down the source volume by going to the Volume menu. The source is always louder than the digital audio playback, so you must turn down the source volume to avoid drowning out playback of your recording.*

Editing with VEDIT2

VEDIT2 is a powerful voice file editor. You can add control blocks, such as silence markers and ASCII comment blocks. You can also delete, move, and combine data blocks, as well as modify the actual waveform within a data block.

Once a file is loaded or recorded, the Block Information screen is displayed (look again at Figure 6-6). Voice data blocks (and control blocks, if any exist) can be selected from this screen.

From the main menu select Edit to display the editing choices for selected blocks. The choices are organized into the following categories:

- Inserting control blocks
- Rearranging blocks (delete, move, copy, and combine)
- Modifying blocks
- Editing a data block waveform

Inserting Control Blocks

The Edit Insert commands insert various types of control blocks into your voice file. The inserted block is placed immediately above the current block (the block that is highlighted and whose block number appears as the Cursor number). To insert a block below the current block, select the Append button. The types of blocks you can insert and their purposes are explained below.

SILENCE   Select Silence to insert silence blocks into the file. They are also created by silence packing, which compresses your file by replacing a period of silence or near silence with a small silence block. You specify the minimum duration of silence, in milliseconds, for which it's acceptable to replace silence digital audio with a silence block. One thousand milliseconds is equivalent to one second.

The silence block is very useful for conserving disk space, but there is a drawback. The Microsoft wave file format (WAV) and the 16-bit VOC file format (version 1.20) don't support this type of block. When you use VOC2WAV to convert from a VOC to a WAV file format, or VOCO2N to convert from 8-bit to 16-bit VOC, your silence blocks are converted back into "silent" data values, and your file size expands accordingly.

MARKER   Select Marker to insert a marker block into the file. Markers are used by MMPLAY, the Multimedia Player, for synchronizing the display of animation flicks with your sound file. This has no effect upon sound output. For further explanation, see the description of MMPLAY later in this chapter.

ASCII   Select ASCII to add a comment that helps document the sound file blocks that follow. This has no effect upon sound output, and expands the file size only minimally.

REPEAT   Select Repeat to repeatedly play a single data block or a group of data blocks in your file. VEDIT2 will automatically insert both a repeat block and a matching end-repeat block. The repeat block feature is useful for conserving disk space, but there is a drawback. The Microsoft wave file format doesn't support this type of block, so repeated blocks are expanded when converted by VOC2WAV to wave format, and your file will grow significantly in size.

Rearranging Blocks

You can easily and quickly make dramatic changes to the content of your sound file with the following commands. They are accessible by selecting Edit from the main menu:

- Delete
- Move
- Copy
- Combine

NOTE: *The Delete command is always active. The Move, Copy, and Combine commands are available only if one or more blocks have been selected in the Block Information screen.*

The Delete command has a very practical use. It is ideal for removing dead space, or a speech hesitation such as "umm ...", or an accidentally repeated word. When deleting a repeat block, be careful to also delete the matching end-repeat block.

The Delete, Move, and Copy commands offer considerable opportunity for mischief. For example, you can change the order of words, and even completely change the meaning of a sentence by removing the word *not*.

TIP: *Silence packing can assist you in parsing recorded speech into small data blocks, each of which consists of a word, phrase, or sentence.*

The Combine command has a different use. It combines two or more adjacent voice blocks into a single block. This is useful primarily for hard disk housekeeping purposes—for combining several small blocks into a single file. Note that the sample rate must be exactly the same for all blocks you wish to join. You cannot combine silence blocks. Instead, delete one of the blocks and then modify the silence period of the remaining block.

Modifying Blocks

From the main menu, selecting Edit and then Modify (more succinctly expressed as selecting Edit,Modify) displays a rich set of tools for revising your digital audio file. You can add or remove control blocks, perform special effects on voice data blocks, and even edit the waveform within a data block. Note that this set of tools operates only on a single block at a time. Most of the other commands you've used, such as Play from the main menu, manipulate a group of blocks all at once.

CAUTION: *Because the modifications described in this section are generally irreversible, make certain you have a copy of your voice data saved on disk before using Edit,Modify.*

To modify a control block, select that block by using the block begin and block end numbers, and then select Edit,Modify. You'll then see a screen with options relevant to that type of control block. The screens that appear for silence, marker, ASCII, and repeat blocks are identical to those that appear when you create this block type from the Edit,Insert submenu.

To modify a voice data block, position the cursor on that block and select Modify. A new screen, titled Editing Voice Data, appears. Figure 6-8 shows how the current block appears as waveform.

These menu choices are available in the Editing Voice Data screen:

- *Option*   Split the block or change the sample rate.

- *Edit*   Move a piece of the block by cut-and-paste, delete a piece, or create a waveform with the Insert and Fill commands.

- *Effect*   Add special effects like echo, fade in/out, and pan.

The Options submenu is self-explanatory. To take advantage of most of the edit and special-effects commands, you must first select a piece of the voice data block to modify. The paragraphs that follow tell you how to expand and contract the waveform display by using the Zoom control, and then how to mark a piece of the data block. Then you'll read about editing the waveform and entering special effects.

Selecting a Piece of the Block Waveform

Stretching the waveform enables you to see it in more detail. Fortunately this has no effect upon the sound you hear when you select the Play button.

The user interface for VEDIT2's editing of the block waveform (Figure 6-8) is somewhat mysterious; however, the following steps will help you master it quickly.

1. Type **Z** to select the Zoom control.

2. Hold down the LEFTARROW to stretch the waveform.

3. Press ENTER when you have finished zooming.

Notice that once you have stretched the waveform beyond the right edge of the screen by using the zoom control and pressing ENTER, the meaning of the LEFTARROW and RIGHTARROW changes. LEFTARROW now moves you toward the beginning of the waveform (the sound you hear at first), and RIGHTARROW moves you to the end. Notice how the Cursor box displays a number, which is the number of seconds of playing time from the beginning of the block to the cursor location.

The cursor, which is a single vertical line that may be difficult to see (initially it is flush with the left edge of the waveform box), is used to mark a piece of the block to edit. To move the cursor to the right, press TAB. To move the cursor to the left, hold down SHIFT and press TAB. The cursor moves in eight or nine jumps across the screen.

To select the beginning of a piece of the block, move the cursor to the start of the piece and press CTRL-B Then move the cursor to the end of the piece and press CTRL-E The selected piece is shown in inverse color. Note how Block Begin and Block End are automatically filled in with the location of this piece. When you work with the Block Information screen, you specify the beginning and ending block numbers. When you work in the Editing Voice Data screen, you specify the beginning and ending playing time within the current block.

Editing the Voice Data Block Waveform

You can make microscopic changes to the waveform of a digital audio data block. Once you've selected a piece of the block waveform as described just above, you can perform the following operations on this block using the Edit menu choices:

■ *Save*   Save this piece to disk.

■ *Cut*   Remove the highlighted piece. Save it temporarily to the scrap heap (a temporary storage place in your computer). Use this command to copy or move a piece of the waveform.

- *Paste* Insert, at the location of the vertical cursor, the contents of the scrap heap (not available until after you cut).

- *Fill* Fill a piece with a single value.

- *Insert* Insert a new piece that has the same length as the piece currently highlighted.

To move a piece of a block, first select Cut, then move the vertical cursor to where you wish to put the piece, and then select Paste.

Custom waveforms, such as a square wave, can be made with the Fill and Insert commands. Unfortunately, you can paste only once, and you cannot insert a file from disk, so making custom waveforms is very tedious.

Using Special Effects

One of the most powerful features of the VEDIT2 editor is the ability to add special effects to your sound recording. Each of these effects is described in more detail below:

- *Amplify* Select Amplify to amplify the relative amplitude (intensity) of this piece as compared to the rest of your block. The default value of 200% doubles the amplitude; 100% results in no change to the amplitude; and 50% cuts the amplitude in half. If you amplify the voice data too much, it will be clipped (the peaks of the waveform are flattened), causing audible distortion. Once clipping occurs, you have lost information and will have to reload the voice file from disk.

- *Echo* Select Echo to add richness to the sound. This has the most dramatic impact if you insert a stretch of silence just after the place in the voice file where you intend to begin the echo. By doing so the echo will be heard more distinctly as it rolls forward into an otherwise silent stretch of the sound file.

- *Fade In and Fade Out* Select Fade Out to gradually reduce the amplitude, or Fade In to gradually increase the amplitude. Use Fade Out at the end of a song or voice-over to provide a graceful fading of the sound. Use Fade In at the beginning of a song or voice-over to avoid shocking the listener.

- *Pan Left-Right and Right-Left* Select Pan Left-Right when working with stereo voice data, to simultaneously fade out the left channel and fade in the right channel. By repeatedly panning from left to right and right to left, you will add a stereo effect to a monaural recording from the microphone. If this is done well, it will add a dramatic impact to your presentation.

CAUTION: *The special effect commands manipulate the waveform and cause irreversible changes to your sound data. Be certain to have a copy of the voice file saved on disk before trying these special effects.*

Listening to the Block

In Figure 6-10, you see the waveform for CNEWS.VOC. Press P to play the sound file. Changes made to the waveform can be immediately heard. If you enter a nonzero value for Block Begin and Block End, only that block will be played.

VEDIT2 Compatibility with the Windows Environment

VEDIT2 has one major limitation: It can only edit Creative Labs' own VOC format digital audio files. When you work in the Windows multimedia environment, you usually work with Microsoft wave (WAV) digital audio files. Although VEDIT2 cannot edit wave files directly, you can use the WAV2VOC and VOC2WAV utility programs, described in this chapter, to convert your files between the two formats. To work with WAV files in

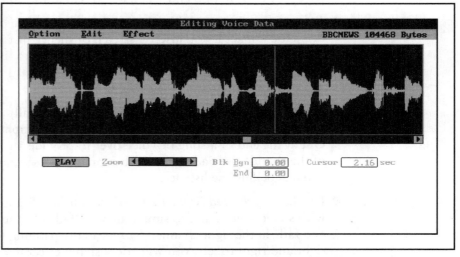

FIGURE 6-10

Editing a voice data waveform

VEDIT2, simply convert the files to VOC files, edit them with VEDIT2, and then convert them back to WAV format. Since both types of digital audio files store audio data in the same way, you can convert between the formats without loss of information.

VOXKIT

Package: SB

The VOXKIT is a very basic voice file editor. It will record and play Creative Labs voice (VOC) digital audio files. VOXKIT can:

- Record from line-in
- Record to memory or to disk
- Play from memory or from disk
- Save from memory to disk
- Load from disk to memory
- Pack voice data in memory or on disk

Loading and Using VOXKIT

To start VOXKIT, switch to the \SB directory. Type **VOXKIT** at the DOS command prompt and then press ENTER. The VOXKIT main menu will appear.

You can advance to a menu item either by pressing UP ARROW or DOWN ARROW, or by holding down ALT and pressing the letter key corresponding to the menu item. Then press ENTER to select the item. The arrow keys work on all menus.

When you first start VOXKIT, it displays "Memory" in the Status Box in the Work Space and stands ready to record to memory or to play voice data stored in memory. At this point, hook up a microphone or, if you have Sound Blaster 2.0, attach a stereo or other sound source to the line-in. Don't try to record from both at the same time.

NOTE: *Voice files are limited to available memory (if recorded to memory) or to available disk space (if recorded to disk). Try to keep your recordings short. You can fill up available memory in about 40 seconds at the default sample rate of 8,000 Hz. At this rate, disk files will grow by 500K (one-half megabyte) for each minute of recording. See the discussion of sampling and sample rates in Chapter 1 for more detail.*

Recording to Memory

To record to memory, follow these steps:

1. *Caution:* Before recording to memory, be sure that the Status Box in the Work Space says Memory or MemMemory. Make sure either the microphone or line-in source is connected, but not both.

2. Select Record Voice.

3. Select Change Sample rate. Note the recording time available at the default sample rate of 8,000 Hz.

4. Press ESC to accept the current sample rate, or enter a new sample rate and press ENTER.

5. Select Record At. You are now recording. Press ESC as soon as you've finished.

NOTE: *If you run out of memory, VOXKIT will stop recording automatically. The "Record to Memory" status indicator will disappear.*

Playing from Memory

Caution: First make sure that the Status Box says Memory or MemMemory. Then select Play Voice. Press ESC to stop playback before the end.

Mastering VOXKIT

The sections below instruct you on how to accomplish the more advanced VOXKIT tasks and give the step-by-step commands for each. In the previous section, you saw how to record and play back sound files to and from memory. This section shows how to save your recordings as sound files on disk. By recording to disk, you can create larger audio files than is possible by recording to memory. Recording to disk will also maintain a permanent copy of the sound file.

Choosing Disk or Memory as the Work Space

Because of a screen display bug in VOXKIT, the Work Space Status Box in your version of VOXKIT may be somewhat confusing to you. The menu item immediately above the Exit option toggles (changes each time you select it) between the Use Memory option and the Use Disk option, changing the work space status message each time. The paragraphs that follow will help you become more comfortable using this menu item.

SELECT DISK   When you select Use Disk, you tell VOXKIT to operate on disk files. The Work Space box shows either Disk or Mem Disk (because of the display bug). This status message indicates that the Record, Play, and Pack commands will operate upon VOC files on disk.

SELECT MEMORY   When you select Use Memory, you tell VOXKIT to operate on voice files in memory only. The Work Space box will show either Memory or MemMemory (because of the display bug). This indicates that Record, Play, and Pack commands will operate upon voice files in memory.

Switching Drives and Directories

When you first select the Save File or Load File command (explained in upcoming paragraphs), VOXKIT will go to the \SB\VOXKIT directory. You may, however, want to store your voice files in another drive and directory. Here's how to do this:

1. *Caution:* Ensure that the Status Box says Memory or MemMemory. If it doesn't, toggle the Use Disk/Use Memory menu item.

2. Select Load File. You will see a box listing sample files.

3. To change the drive, press F1. Enter the new drive letter and press ENTER

4. To change the directory, select .. in the Load File list of files. You now see a list of subdirectories. Move your cursor to the desired subdirectory and press ENTER to select it. (Once you're positioned in the correct directory, press ESC to return to the main menu. When you next select Save File or Load File, you'll be positioned in this directory.)

Saving to Disk

After you have recorded your voice file to memory, you can save it to disk for later use. Here are the steps:

1. *Caution:* Ensure that the Status Box says Memory or MemMemory. If it doesn't, toggle the Use Disk/Use Memory menu item.

2. Select Save File.

3. Enter the filename. You don't need to add .VOC at the end; VOXKIT will do this for you. The file will be saved to the current (VOXKIT) directory.

WARNING: *Be careful when you choose a filename for recording or saving a file to disk. VOXKIT doesn't always warn you if you're about to overwrite an existing file. When you've made a recording that you're satisfied with, it's a good idea to copy the file to a "safe" location.*

Loading from Disk

To load a file from disk, follow these steps:

1. *Caution:* Ensure that the Status Box says Mem or MemMemory. If it doesn't, toggle the Use Disk/Use Memory menu item.

2. Select Load File.

3. Move the cursor to the desired file and press ENTER. Note that the filename is now displayed in the Work Space box.

Playing Files from Disk

When you play from disk, you are not limited to the space available in conventional memory. You can play files of any length.
To play a file from disk:

1. *Caution:* Make sure the Status Box says Disk or Mem Disk. If it doesn't, toggle the Use Disk/Use Memory menu item.

2. Select Play Voice.

3. Move the cursor to the file you wish to play, and press ENTER.

Recording to Disk

When you record to disk, you are not limited to the space available in memory. You can record voice files of any length, up to the maximum space available on your floppy or hard disk. Here are the steps to record to disk:

1. Connect either the microphone or line-in source. Don't try to record from both at the same time.

2. *Caution:* Make sure the Status Box says Disk or Mem Disk. If it doesn't, toggle the Use Disk/Use Memory menu item.

3. Select Record Voice.

4. Select Change Sample rate. Notice the recording time available at a default sample rate of 8,000 Hz. Either press ESC to accept the current sample rate, or enter a new sample rate and press ENTER.

5. Select Record At.

6. Enter the filename that will store your voice data. Press ENTER. You are now recording. Press ESC as soon as you have finished.

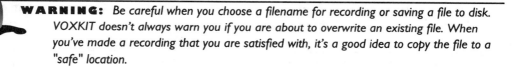

WARNING: *Be careful when you choose a filename for recording or saving a file to disk. VOXKIT doesn't always warn you if you are about to overwrite an existing file. When you've made a recording that you are satisfied with, it's a good idea to copy the file to a "safe" location.*

Deleting Voice Files

There is no menu selection for deleting voice files. The steps to do this are as follows:

1. Select Exit to quit VOXKIT, and confirm your command by pressing Y. You will be returned to the DOS command prompt.

2. Switch to the \SB\VOXKIT subdirectory by typing **CD \SB\VOXKIT** and pressing ENTER. (If you've chosen another directory for storing your VOC files, enter that directory name instead.)

3. Use the DOS Delete command to delete your files; they'll have a VOC filename extension.

CAUTION: *Be careful to not accidentally delete the sample files provided with VOXKIT. These sample files will have a date prior to the date you purchased your sound card.*

About File Size Limitations

Sound Blaster owners should bear in mind that, although VPLAY can play voice files larger than available memory, the VOXKIT voice editor cannot load and subsequently edit files this large. Plan on creating smaller voice files—no more than about 500K (500,000 bytes) each, assuming you have a PC with 640K or more RAM installed.

Sound Blaster Pro owners don't need to be concerned about creating voice files that are too large. Creative Labs provides Sound Blaster Pro owners with VEDIT2, instead of VOXKIT. VEDIT2 can handle files that are too large to fit into memory.

Packing Files

When you select the Data Packing menu item, VOXKIT will compress your sound files, but there are trade-offs to this. Packing reduces the file size by up to 75 percent (4:1 compression), but you will suffer some degradation of audio quality. If you plan to do both data block and silence packing, do the silence packing first. For more information about packing in general, and silence packing in particular, see the section in Chapter 1 that explains packing and compression.

WARNING: *A common accident is to pack a file on disk, accidentally overwriting the uncompressed sound file (the original recording). A similar accident is loading a file into memory, packing it, and then saving it again with the same filename. This type of mistake can be serious, because once a file is packed, it cannot be edited.*

PACKING VOICE FILES IN MEMORY   If you want to pack voice files in memory:

1. *Caution:* Make sure the Status Box says Memory or MemMemory. If it doesn't, toggle the Use Disk/Use Memory menu item.

2. Select Data Packing.

3. Choose the Packing Method. You can do both silence and data packing. With silence packing, you can optionally revise the threshold value and window size.

PACKING VOICE IN A DISK FILE   If you want to pack voice files on a disk:

1. *Caution:* Make sure the Status Box says Disk or Mem Disk. If it doesn't, toggle the Use Disk/Use Memory menu item.

2. Select Data Packing.

3. Move the cursor to the file you wish to pack and press ENTER.

4. Enter the target filename—that is, the name of the new, packed file that will be created—and press ENTER. VOXKIT will not let you overwrite the original, unpacked file.

5. Choose the Packing Method. You can do both silence and data packing. With silence packing, you can optionally revise the threshold value and window size. Unless you have very special needs, the default values should be fine.

DIGITAL AUDIO FILE CONVERSION

This section describes command-line utilities that convert digital audio files from one format to another or perform special tasks like adding a VOC file header to a raw data file.

- JOINTVOC combines small voice files into larger ones. It can insert silence blocks, repeat a sound track, and even insert synchronization markers that trigger the next slide in a multimedia presentation. All cards come with this utility.

- VOC-HDR for the SB and SB Pro, and VOCHDR for the SB16, are special tools for attaching a VOC file header to a raw VOC file.

- WAVE2VOC and VOC2WAVE make it possible to convert digital audio files from the Creative Labs VOC format to Microsoft's WAV format, and vice versa. These two are provided with all sound cards.

- VOCO2N and VOCN2O make it possible to convert from the earlier 8-bit only VOC file format (version 1.10) to the newer 16-bit VOC file format used by the Sound Blaster 16 (version 1.20), and vice versa. These utilities are relevant to the 16-bit sound card only, the SB16.

- VSR, which changes the sample rate, was shipped with Sound Blaster packages that predate Sound Blaster Deluxe.

JOINTVOC

Packages: All

JOINTVOC joins two or more digital audio files, in VOC file format, into a single file. You can add silence blocks between the files, repeat one or more blocks, and add markers that synchronize application programs to the sound tracks (blocks).

1. Switch to the VOCUTIL directory.

   SB users: Type **CD \SB\VOCUTIL** and press ENTER.
   SB Pro users: Type **CD \SBPRO\VOCUTIL** and press ENTER.
   SB16 users: Type **CD \SB16\VOCUTIL** and press ENTER.

2. To join two voice files together into a "target" that combines them, type the JOINTVOC command in this format:

   JOINTVOC /T*targetfilename* file1name file2nameuu

   and then press ENTER.

To get onscreen help with this utility, type **JOINTVOC** and then press ENTER. You can combine voice files with different sample rates, and you can join compressed and uncompressed files. (After combining files, use VPLAY to check your work.) For example, you may want to create a new voice file called MARKER.VOC that begins with one second of silence and then combines the CLP.VOC and MENTS.VOC voice files, inserting a synchronization marker with a value of 99 in between. Assuming all files are in the same directory, the following command line will do this:

    JOINTVOC /Tmarker.voc /S10 voc clp.voc /M99 ments.voc

The command switches used in this command are as follows:

- /T—The target (result of the join) filename
- /S—The silence block time period, in units of 0.1 seconds
- /M—The synchronization marker number (value up to 999) used to synchronize audio and video in multimedia presentations

The Deluxe version software added commands for repeating blocks:

- /R—Repeats the block or group of blocks that follow *xx* times. Enter −1 to indicate endless looping of this block(s). A repeat count of /R9 will cause the block(s) to be heard for a total of nine times.
- /RE—Demarcates the the last block in a group of blocks to be repeated.

NOTE: *Attempting to join version 1.10 and 1.20 version files (the 16-bit format introduced with the SB16 and Deluxe packages) will be unsuccessful and result in an error message.*

VOC-HDR

Packages: SB, SB Deluxe, SB Pro, SB Pro Deluxe

The primary purpose of the VOC-HDR voice header program is to repair voice files that have been rendered unplayable due to damage to their header. The header provides information about the sound file, such as the sample rate and whether it is compressed or not. VOC-HDR can also be used to attach a VOC file header to a raw digital audio file. Adding a header makes it possible to load the file into VEDIT2 (SB Deluxe and SB Pro) or VOXKIT (older SB) and to listen to the file with VPLAY.

Running VOC-HDR

To load VOC-HDR, follow these steps:

1. Switch to the VEDIT2 directory by typing **CD \SBPRO\VEDIT2** and pressing ENTER.

2. At the DOS command prompt, type **VOC-HDR** followed by the filename of the raw audio file and the filename for the VOC file you wish to create, in this format:

   VOC-HDR *raw_audio_filename* VOC_filenameuu

   and then press ENTER. You should see the following response on the screen:

   ```
   Create <VOC file> with data in <raw audio filename>
   File without header
   ```

3. You will now be prompted with a series of questions. VOC-HDR will examine the raw digital audio file, before making any changes, and warn you if that file is already in VOC file format. If so, you will see this message:

   ```
   Voice file already has new header. Change the header?
   ```

To revise the header, type **Y**. (It is highly unlikely you'll need to add a header if one already exists, so don't enter **N** unless you think the utility program is confused.)

NOTE: Don't worry about whether you're guessing correctly on the answers to the questions in step 4. You can easily rerun VOC-HDR and change your responses.

4. You must now tell VOC-HDR the characteristics of this file: the sample rate and whether it is packed. Enter the number between 1 and 5 that corresponds to the type of audio data you believe is contained in the file. You can choose compressed (4-bit, 2.5-bit, or 2-bit); uncompressed monaural (8-bit); or uncompressed stereo (stereo). Type the number corresponding to your choice and then press ENTER Then input the sample rate for this file and press ENTER

NOTE: You may want to refer to the discussions of sample rates and packing in Chapter I for help with step 4. Also, see "Quick Summary of Compression Options" just below.

5. Once everything is correct, press Y. If you wish to change your responses, press N.

Getting Help

To get onscreen help with VOC-HDR, type **VOC-HDR** alone at the DOS command prompt and press ENTER

Quick Summary of Compression Options

VOC-HDR prompts you for the raw audio data type (step 4, above). The choices are 8-bit (uncompressed), 4-bit (2x compression), 2.6-bit (3x compression), or 2-bit (4x compression). If you don't know which to choose, keep in mind that 8-bit is the most likely choice. For more information, see the section on packing in Chapter 1.

NOTE: The medium compression choice (the 2.5-bit, 3x compression) is misnamed in this utility. All other utility programs that handle compression refer to 2.6-bit compression, which is the correct name for this choice.

How to Identify a VOC File

A quick way to check whether a file already possesses a Creative Labs VOC file header is to use the DOS TYPE command to display that file's contents on the screen. Enter **TYPE** followed by the filename, and press ENTER. If this is a VOC file, you will see just "Creative Voice File" on the screen. If not, press CTRL-BREAK to terminate the TYPE command.

Sound Blaster Pro Enhancements

The Sound Blaster Pro version of VOC-HDR has been upgraded to support stereo. Note that the sample rate for stereo is fixed at 22,050 kHz.

VOCHDR

Package: SB16

The VOCHDR voice header program is primarily used to repair voice files that have been rendered unreadable because of damage to their header. It can also be used to attach a VOC file header to a raw digital audio file. Adding a header makes it possible to play the VOC file with the DOS command utility VPLAY. The header provides information about the sound file, such as the sample rate, bits per sample, the type of compression, and whether it is stereo or mono.

Running VOCHDR

To run VOCHDR follow these steps:

1. Switch to the VOCUTIL subdirectory by typing **CD \SB16\VOCUTIL** and pressing ENTER.

2. At the DOS command prompt, type **VOCHDR** followed by the filename of the raw audio file and the filename for the VOC file you wish to create, in this format:

   VOCHDR *raw_audio_filename VOC_filename*

   and then press ENTER. You should see the following response on the screen:

   ```
   VOCHDR: <VOC_filename> DONE.
   ```

The steps just outlined create a VOC file with the following default settings: 22050 Hz sample rate, monaural, 8 bits per sample, no compression, and the newer version 1.20 VOC file format, which supports both 8-bit and 16-bit samples. To create a VOC file with other characteristics, you'll have to add option flags after the two filenames. For example, the following creates a file with a 11025 Hz sample rate, 16-bit samples, with stereo data, and ALAW compression:

> VOCHDR <Raw_audio_filename> <VOC_filename>
> /S:11025 /T:2 /R:16 /C:ALAW

- /S specifies the sample rate. It's a good idea to select a sample rate that's compatible with that of Microsoft Windows wave files: 11025, 22050, or 44100.

- /T: indicates whether the sound bytes in the raw audio file should be interpreted as monaural (/T:1) or stereo (/T:2) data.

- /R: defines the number of bits per sample. This will be either /R:8 or /R:16.

- /C: stipulates that the output file should be compressed. The options are described in the section entitled Quick Summary of Compression Options that follows.

- /O generates version 1.10 VOC files, compatible with the software designed for the 8-bit Sound Blaster, Sound Blaster Deluxe, Sound Blaster Pro, and Sound Blaster Pro Deluxe.

Getting Help

To get onscreen help with VOCHDR, type **VOCHDR** alone at the DOS command prompt and press ENTER.

Quick Summary of Compression Options

You can choose whether to create uncompressed or compressed VOC files. The compression choices differ according to whether you're taking 8-bit or 16-bit samples.

For 8-bit samples, the valid values are 4 (4x compression), 3 (3x), 2 (2x), and 0 for no compression.

For 16-bit samples, the valid values are CTADPCM (4x compression), ALAW (2x), ULAW (2x), and 0 for no compression.

How to Identify a VOC File

A quick way to check whether a file already has the Creative Labs VOC file header is to use the DOS TYPE command to display that file's contents on the screen. Enter **TYPE** followed by the filename, and press ENTER. If this is a VOC file, you will see just "Creative Voice File" on the screen. If not, press CTRL-BREAKto terminate the TYPE command.

WAV2VOC

Packages: SB Deluxe, SB Pro, SB Pro Deluxe, SB16

WAV2VOC is a utility that converts Microsoft WAV files to Creative Labs VOC files. This is useful if you have WAV files you wish to include in a presentation built with MMPLAY, since MMPLAY can play VOC but not WAV files. Also, once they're converted to VOC format, you can also modify these files with the VEDIT2 voice editor.

This utility is very simple, and handles issues such as sample rate conversion automatically. Here are the steps for using WAV2VOC:

1. Switch to the appropriate subdirectory.

   SB Deluxe users: Type **CD \SB\VOCUTIL** and then press ENTER.
   SB Pro users: Type **CD \SBPRO\VEDIT2** and then press ENTER.
   SB Pro Deluxe users: Type **CD \SBPRO\VOCUTIL** and then press ENTER.

   SB16 users: Type **CD \SB16\VOCUTIL** and then press ENTER.

2. To perform the conversion, enter the WAV2VOC command:

   WAV2VOC *wave_filename voc_filename*

   and then press ENTER.

VOC2WAV

Packages: SB Deluxe, SB Pro, SB Pro Deluxe, SB16

VOC2WAV converts Creative Labs VOC files to Microsoft WAV files. This is useful if you work in the Windows environment and have a collection of useful VOC files. This utility is very simple and handles issues such as sample rate conversion automatically. You can optionally override the defaults with command switches. Here are the steps for using VOC2WAV:

1. Switch to the appropriate subdirectory.

   SB Deluxe users: Type **CD \SB\VOCUTIL** and then press ENTER.
   SB Pro users: Type **CD \SBPRO\VEDIT2** and then press ENTER.
   SB Pro Deluxe users: Type **CD \SBPRO\VOCUTIL** and then press ENTER.

   SB16 users: Type **CD \SB16\VOCUTIL** and then press ENTER.

2. To convert a monaural file at the default sampling rate of 11,025 kHz, enter the VOC2WAV command in this format:

   VOC2WAV *wave_filename voc_filename*

   and then press ENTER.

VOC2WAV Switches

- **/R:*nnnnn*** Creative Labs VOC files can have sample rates up to 44,100 kHz, and WAV files can have only one of three rates: 11,025 kHz, 22,050 kHz, or 44,100 kHz (the default is 11,025 kHz). Use the /R switch to select the proper rate for the wave file you are creating. Ideally your VOC and WAV files will have the same sampling rate. If not, VOC2WAV will automatically convert the VOC file (the sample rate is embedded in the file header) to the specified WAV rate without noticeable degradation in audio quality.

- **/S:*OnOrOff*** If your VOC file contains silence blocks, the /S command switch controls whether they are ignored (Off) or converted to "silent" audio data values. The VOC silence blocks provide a way to reduce the size of voice files containing long pauses. The silence block is very compact, typically much smaller than the silent audio it replaces. Unfortunately, the Microsoft wave file format does not support silence blocks, so the silence block is expanded into silence data, causing your file size to expand. Silence blocks are discussed more fully in the section on packing in Chapter 1.

- **/L:*OnOrOff*** If your VOC file contains repeated audio data blocks, the /L command switch controls whether only one copy of the audio data block is included (Off) or whether the audio data block is repeated (On) a specified number of times (this number is embedded in the VOC file; you don't need to specify it). Unfortunately, Microsoft wave file format does not support this, and if the audio data block is replicated, the WAV file will become significantly larger than the equivalent VOC file.

■ */C:n* This selects stereo (/C:2) or monaural recording (/C:1). The default is mono.

NOTE: *The loss of silence and repetition blocks in VOC to WAV file conversion is not as problematic as it may seem. The MMPLAY utility has commands for introducing delays (.DELAY) and repeating digital audio and music files (.REPEAT and .END). This, of course, assumes you've split up your file prior to conversion to wave.*

Example of VOC-to-WAV File Conversion

Here is an example of converting a voice file called BACH.VOC to a wave file called BACH.WAV. Since the voice file was recorded in stereo at 22 kHz, command switches are necessary to override the defaults of 11 kHz and mono. To perform the conversion, you type

VOC2WAV bach.voc bach.wav /C:2 /R:22

and press ENTER.

TIP: *The VEDIT2 voice file editor provided with Sound Blaster Deluxe and Sound Blaster Pro can split up a digital audio file. This way you can extract each digital audio segment and save it to its own file before conversion to wave format.*

VOCO2N

Package: SB16

This utility (*VOC Old 2 New*) converts voice files (VOC) recorded in the the older 8-bit format (version 1.10) to the newer 16-bit format (version 1.20):

1. Switch to the voice utility subdirectory by typing **CD \SB16\VOCUTIL** and pressing ENTER.

2. To convert a file with the name *old_format_filename*, enter the command as shown here:

   VOCO2N *old_format_filename new_format_filename*

   and then press ENTER.

VOCN2O

Package: SB16

This utility (*VOC New 2 Old*) converts voice files (VOC) recorded in the newer 16-bit format (version 1.20) to the older 8-bit format (version 1.10):

1. Switch to the voice utility subdirectory by typing **CD \SB16\VOCUTIL** and pressing ENTER.

2. To convert a file with the name *new_format_filename*, enter the command as shown here:

   VOCN2O2 *new_format_filename old_format_filename*

   and then press ENTER.

VSR

Package: SB

The VSR (Voice Sample Rate) utility revises the sampling rate, and hence the speed at which the file is played, of a VOC format digital audio file. This program has limited usefulness. It can be used for improving the sound of a recording by making subtle changes to the pitch (by changing the playback speed) and for masking a person's voice. Speech played back 20 percent faster or slower can generally be understood, but you won't be able to recognize the speaker.

Sound Blaster Pro, Sound Blaster Pro Deluxe, and Sound Blaster Deluxe owners are not provided with VSR. They can revise the sample rate through the VEDIT2 voice edit utility. Early buyers of Sound Blaster, whose only editor is VOXKIT, will find value in this utility.

To load VSR, switch to the VOXKIT directory by typing **CD \SB\VOXKIT** and pressing ENTER. Then enter the VSR command and press ENTER. Here is the VSR command syntax:

   VSR *source_filename target_filename* /Rnnn

NOTE: *The source file must have the VOC file extension.*

You specify the new sample rate by entering a percentage change from the current rate. For example, for the *nnn* after the /R switch, enter **110** to set the new sample rate at 110 percent of the old rate, which is a 10 percent increase. The target file produced by VSR is identical to the source file, except that the header states a playback speed that's 10 percent higher. When you play the target file, perhaps with VPLAY, the speech or music will have a noticeably higher pitch, and playback will be about 10 percent shorter in duration.

Add the /O command switch to play the target file as it's created. For example, the following command creates a version of the TV4.VOC voice file that's noticeably slower to the human ear even though it's only 2 percent slower (98 percent of the original rate):

VSR TV4.VOC TVNEW.VOC /R98 /O

To get onscreen help, type **VSR** alone at the DOS command prompt and press ENTER.

MULTIMEDIA PROGRAMMING FOR NON-PROGORAMMERS (ALL CARDS)

This section presents a suite of programs for creating multimedia presentations. You're provided with a complete set of tools for combining video, music, and voice-overs.

- **MMPLAY,** the Multimedia Player, integrates other utilities such as VPLAY and VREC (see "Play and Record Utilities") into a tool for playing an eye-catching audio/visual presentation under DOS.

- **SBSIM** is a toolbox that is the foundation for Sound Blaster DOS multimedia environment. It loads and unloads drivers for you automatically, reducing the complexity of selecting the correct drivers.

- **VOICE, MUSIC,** and **SOUNDFX.** Once SBSIM is loaded, you can use SBSIM's sound utilities: VOICE, MUSIC, and SOUNDFX. VOICE is similar to VPLAY but is more powerful. MUSIC is similar to PLAYCMF and PLAYMIDI but has more power and flexibility. SOUNDFX does special effects such as panning and fading. VOICE, MUSIC, and SOUNDFX give you complete mastery over the audio component of your MMPLAY presentations.

NOTE: *This section is designed to supplement your Creative Labs manual. It clarifies areas of confusion, provides missing explanations, offers some hints, and reveals some secrets. This chapter is not intended to serve as a replacement for your manual, and so information that is readily accessible in your Creative Labs manual is not repeated here. Many of the utilities described, such as SOUNDFX, are extensively documented in the manual and need little additional comment.*

MMPLAY

Packages: SB Deluxe, SB Pro, SB Pro Deluxe, SB16

The MMPLAY Multimedia Player is a powerful DOS tool for playing multimedia (audio/video) presentations. You can write a script, using a simple programming language unique to MMPLAY, to combine Autodesk Animator screen animation (FLI/FLC) files or pictures (PCX) files with audio from Creative digitized audio voice files (VOC), Creative Music Files (CMF), MIDI music files (MID), and CD audio tracks.

NOTE: *To play Microsoft wave (WAV) files, use the WAV2VOC utility to first convert them to VOC files.*

To get familiar with script writing for the Multimedia Player, you should start off by writing a simple script. Copy the MMDEMO.ACT sample script that's provided by Creative Labs and found in your MMPLAY subdirectory. Eliminate all but the first few commands from this copy, and begin your experimentation with this script. Use a simple ASCII text file editor, such as the EDIT program found in the DOS 5.*x*/6.*x* directory, to create these scripts.

TIP: *Before doing anything else at this stage, it's a good idea to get a feeling for what MMPLAY can do by running MMDEMO. This sample presentation was copied to your hard disk when you installed your sound card.*

The MMPLAY Commands

The information here supplements what you read about MMPLAY in your Creative Labs manual. Once you're comfortable using MMPLAY with utilities such as PLAYCMF, PLAYMIDI, and VPLAY, you'll want to read the discussion of SBSIM in an upcoming section. The SBSIM utilities add even more power to MMPLAY presentations.

The latest versions of MMPLAY support display of high-resolution PCX images, SVGA animation (FLC), and Creative VideoBlaster video sequences. In addition you can do special audio effects like panning and fading.

NOTE: *When using MMPLAY, always start playing your audio sources before using the .APLAY or .APLAYl commands to show animation.*

ABOUT SYNCHRONIZING ANIMATION WITH SOUND   The .APLAY command "plays" an Autodesk Animator flick (FLI) file containing a slide show of images. As MMPLAY is playing a flick file, it watches for *synchronization markers* that are embedded in audio voice (VOC), MIDI (MID) and Creative Music (CMF) files. A synchronization marker is typically embedded at the end of the voice or sound track. When the marker is reached, the slide show is terminated, and the next command line in the script file is executed. Once .APLAY has been terminated by a synchronization marker, that marker is discarded. A new .SYNC command must be issued to establish the conditions for terminating the next .APLAY animation sequence.

.APLAY   The .APLAY command is best used in conjunction with the .SYNC command. When the synchronization marker specified by .SYNC is detected, .APLAY terminates and the next command in the script is executed.

NOTE: *Don't use .APLAY without an accompanying .SYNC command to repeat an animation sequence until a key is pressed. This technique does not work reliably.*

While testing new scripts, you may need to interrupt the .APLAY command. CTRL-END will stop the command but may cause MMPLAY to misbehave. If your screen display begins to look strange, press CTRL-C to interrupt MMPLAY.

If you find yourself in a screen display mode where the DOS command prompt appears in large letters (or perhaps a blank screen), type **MODE CO80** to switch to normal color, 80-character mode, and press ENTER. MODE is a program that comes with DOS that's found in your DOS directory.

.REPEAT   MMPLAY will repeatedly execute all commands placed between the .REPEAT and .END commands. The .REPEAT command is followed by a number from 1 to 999 that specifies how many times to repeat the command sequence.

.PAUSE   The .PAUSE command causes MMPLAY to pause before executing the next command in the script. This is useful for pausing between FLI animation sequences or PCX images. Music continues to play while

MMPLAY waits for you to press any key. This is similar to the slide presentation technique of pressing a button when you are ready for the next slide.

.WAIT   The .WAIT command is similar to the .PAUSE command; it causes MMPLAY to pause before executing the next command in the script. The .WAIT command is special, however, because it pauses execution until a synchronization marker, specified by an earlier .SYNC command, is encountered in the voice (VOC), Creative Music (CMF), or MIDI (MID) file currently playing.

.SYNC   The .SYNC command posts a synchronization marker value that, when detected, terminates the .APLAY command or triggers the .WAIT command. The .SYNC markers are inserted into a VOC file by using the VEDIT2 editor. The markers can also be inserted into a voice file by JOIN-TVOC, the utility program that combines two or more voice files into one.

.REM   The .REM statement lets you insert a remark into the script file. MMPLAY will ignore this line when it plays, automatically advancing to the next line.

NOTE: *You must follow a .REM with at least one space, or MMPLAY will become confused and report that the command is in error.*

.VOUT

The .VOUT command plays a VOC digital audio file. This usually consists of a short voice-over.

.EXECUTE

As its name suggests, .EXECUTE executes a DOS command line. It's most commonly used to run the sophisticated sound utilities provided in the SBSIM environment. It can also be used to trigger an external device, such as a laser-disc video player, by sending a command to the serial port.

The discussion of the SOUNDFX utility, part of the SBSIM Sound Blaster Standard Programming Tool, illustrates the use of the .EXECUTE command.

NOTE: *SBSIM and its related utilities are ideal companions for MMPLAY. Your MMPLAY script can run the SBSIM utilities through the .EXECUTE command. Once you have become familiar with MMPLAY, try writing MMPLAY scripts taking advantage of SBSIM.*

Multimedia Script Example

To better explain the synchronization of animation graphics with sound, consider the following example that repeatedly plays a new product demonstration.

First, you need to create a voice file called MARKER.VOC containing a synchronization marker of value 99 embedded between two related voice tracks, as illustrated below in pseudo code (*pseudo code* is a representation of programming language instructions not actually adhering to the conventions of any existing languages):

```
"...and now introducing"
silence block
sync marker 99 block
"the new PowerPC"
```

The following extract from a script would begin to play the MARKER.VOC voice-over. Just before the words "the new PowerPC" are spoken, it will display an animation of a PowerPC–based PC appearing from behind a curtain:

```
.rem Previous flick's last screen still appears...
.rem "Introducing the new PowerPC .."
.sync V99
.vout marker.voc
.rem Now show PowerPC computer floating down from space while
.rem announcer says "...what a beauty to behold"
.aplay powerpc.fli
```

You can add markers to voice files by using either JOINTVOC or VEDIT2. (The JOINTVOC discussion in this chapter tells how the file MARKER.VOC was created.) To add markers to MIDI files, use a sequencer program such as Cakewalk Apprentice for Windows or Sequencer Plus Pro. At this writing there is no utility available to add a marker to a Creative CMF music file.

NOTE: *Windows 3.1 includes an application called the Media Player that is documented in its reference manual. Don't confuse the Windows Media Player with the Creative Labs MMPLAY utility. The Windows Media Player plays multimedia files and controls hardware devices, such as a laser videodisc player. Creative Labs' MMPLAY is a DOS utility program that integrates audio and visual files into a presentation. The Windows Media Player is similar in looks to the Creative Labs CDPLYR DOS utility, and similar in function to Creative Labs JukeBox Windows utility. CDPLYR is discussed in this chapter while Creative JukeBox is described in Chapter 5.*

VideoBlaster Support

To include VideoBlaster video in a presentation, you must edit the MMPLAY.CFG configuration file and change the setting for EnableVideoBlaster to ON. To accomplish this use the EDIT program that comes with DOS 5.*x*/6.*x*.

SBSIM

Packages: SB Deluxe, SB Pro, SB Pro Deluxe, SB16

SBSIM (Sound Blaster Simplified Interface Module) is a powerful and easy-to-use environment for experimenting with sound sources and creating the right effects for audio/visual presentations. SBSIM has already proven its value—it was used by Creative Labs for presentations given to the investment community that led to the company's successful initial public offering.

SBSIM makes your life easier by loading and unloading the sound drivers. In addition, it reads a configuration file that remembers settings for buffer allocation, MIDI format, speaker switching, and so forth. SBSIM is the required foundation for using three powerful utility programs discussed in upcoming sections: VOICE, which plays digitized audio (VOC); MUSIC, which plays Creative Music Files (CMF) and MIDI music files (MID); and SOUNDFX. VOICE and MUSIC are much more powerful than their simpler cousins, VPLAY, PLAYCMF, and PLAYMIDI. The SOUNDFX utility adds special effects, such as panning and fading.

SBSIM and its associated utilities are ideal partners for the MMPLAY Multimedia Player. The following batch files will make SBSIM even easier to use. They load both SBSIM and the optional drivers, and then unload them in the correct order.

NOTE: *If the subdirectory location of your drivers does not match that shown below, you'll need to revise these instructions to specify the correct paths. SB Deluxe owners should change \SBPRO to \SB. SB16 owners should change \SBPRO to \SB16.*

```
rem LOAD.BAT
rem Load SBSIM and optional drivers
\sbpro\sbfmdrv
\sbpro\playmidi\sbmidi
\sbpro\sbsim\sbsim
```

```
rem UNLOAD.BAT
rem Unload SBSIM and optional drivers
\sbpro\sbsim /U
\sbpro\playmidi\sbmidi /U
\sbpro\sbfmdrv /U
```

One drawback to SBSIM is that it consumes more conventional memory than just VPLAY or PLAYCMF alone. This is because the drivers are loaded regardless of whether they're really necessary. Your Creative Labs reference manual states that with SBSIM you can load voice files (VOC) into extended memory, conserving scarce conventional memory. This feature is no longer important, however, because recent versions of VPLAY play voice files that are larger than available conventional memory.

To run SBSIM utilities from MMPLAY, you'll use the MMPLAY .EXECUTE command. For example, the following sequence will play the Creative Music File FAIRY.CMF in the \SBPRO\MMPLAY subdirectory, at half speed, and then launch animation flick Z2:

```
.execute \sbpro\sbsim\music /play:fairy /temp:50
.execute \sbpro\sbsim\soundfx start
.aplay1 z2
```

VOICE
....

The VOICE utility, which works in conjunction with SBSIM, is similar to VPLAY, a simpler utility for playing digitized audio (VOC) files. VOICE has additional features, such as the ability to pause and resume play.

Normally, VOICE returns control immediately to the DOS command prompt or to a batch file. If you use the /WAIT command switch, VOICE waits until it has finished playing before returning control. If you use the /WAIT command with a synchronization marker specified, VOICE begins play immediately but does not return control until after the marker is encountered.

Another feature of VOICE is that it can use extended memory, provided by SBSIM, to hold voice files. Although the Creative Labs manual suggests that this feature is important, the ability of VOICE to play voice files directly from disk lessens its significance.

MUSIC
....

The MUSIC utility, which works in conjunction with SBSIM, is similar to PLAYCMF and PLAYMIDI, simpler utilities for playing Creative Music

(CMF) and MIDI (MID) files, respectively. MUSIC has many additional features, such as the ability to pause and resume, and to wait for a synchronization marker or until the end of the song. Other powerful features available for CMF files are the ability to change tempo, transpose into another key, and do endless repetition.

SOUNDFX

SOUNDFX, as its name implies, is a sound-effects utility that works in conjunction with SBSIM to provide panning, fade-in, and fade-out effects to any single source or to the master volume.

SOUNDFX works as described in the manual, but early versions of the manual don't point out one very important fact: nothing happens until you issue the start command! That command is

SOUNDFX start

Refer to your Creative Labs manual for the full list of SOUNDFX commands.

NOTE: *For SB and SB Pro owners: The Creative Labs user manual says that volume levels can range from 0 (no sound) to 255 (maximum sound), though the mixer on your sound card only supports 16 settings for the master volume control. SOUNDFX lets you specify values from 0 to 255, but all the values within a "step" have the same effect. For instance, any values entered from 0 to 15 have the same effect, that is, the effect of step 0, which turns off the sound.*

7

Speech Recognition and Synthesis

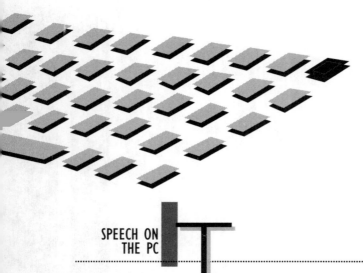

SPEECH ON THE PC

T H E distinction between science fiction and scientific fact for the desktop computer has been irrevocably blurred. It's now completely practical to communicate with your PC through speech. All Sound Blaster cards are accompanied by the Monologue for Windows program that speaks text out loud, called a *text-to-speech synthesizer* or *speech synthesizer*. In addition, the top-of-the-line DigitalEdge CD multimedia upgrade kit includes VoiceAssist speech recognition software that responds to spoken words, such as "file open," as if you were typing at the keyboard. If you don't already own VoiceAssist, you can purchase the VoiceAssist upgrade package from Creative Labs. This inexpensive package includes both the VoiceAssist software and a microphone. See Appendix F for details.

TIP: *It's best to disable screen savers when you're using speech products. If you're not typing, the computer may think you're off on a coffee break and blank the screen prematurely. It's particularly difficult to do data entry by voice when all you can see is flying toasters! More seriously, if you anticipate using Monologue to speak long passages, you should either disable the screen saver or sufficiently delay its onset so that Monologue can finish its oration before the screen saver kicks in.*

This chapter is divided into two major sections: speech recognition and speech synthesis. The speech recognition section walks you through the steps for using VoiceAssist, while the speech synthesis section contains a tutorial that highlights the important features of First Byte's Monologue for Windows (which we'll refer to as just Monologue). We've also included tips and tricks on using these products based on conversations with the engineers at Creative Labs and First Byte, respectively.

CAUTION: *You can't use VoiceAssist and Monologue for Windows, the two Windows speech programs, at the same time. Both programs use the sound card's PCM circuitry to process digital audio, and the circuitry can either record (needed by VoiceAssist) or play back (needed by Monologue), but not both at the same time because Monologue won't share the sound card. You won't do any damage by loading both, but you'll see an error message sooner or later and one or both programs won't work. The new text-to-speech technology by Creative Labs will work correctly with VoiceAssist. See Appendix A for more information on this new technology.*

UNDER-STANDING SPEECH RECOGNITION

Speech recognition is the technology that gives your computer the ability to understand spoken commands. Have you ever wished you could instruct your computer to straighten all its icons? Or ask it to check your e-mail? With speech recognition, you can!

Types of Speech Recognition

Speech recognition technology is available in many forms. You may hear people talk about terms such as isolated-word, speaker-dependent, single-utterance, continuous-speech, and speaker-independent. All of these refer to characteristics of speech recognition systems or speech recognition engines, as they are frequently called.

The most common manifestation of speech recognition today is known as *isolated-word, speaker-dependent.* Isolated word refers to the type of command spoken into the recognition system. This type of recognition system relies on a break in sound between commands. It is also called a *single-utterance* system because short bursts of speech are used, such as single words or phrases. "Exit," "Do it," and "Check my mail," are examples of isolated-word or single-utterance commands. The user says the command and then pauses so that the system can tell that the command has ended.

A speaker-dependent system is trained to recognize the speech patterns of a particular user; so it can only reliably recognize commands spoken by the person who trained it. The benefit of a speaker-dependent system is that, in its extreme case, only the authorized user has control of the system. It could be likened to a voice security device. If your voice doesn't match, the computer ignores you. Most systems, however, are not that demanding and will recognize other users if their voices are similar.

The combination of isolated-word and speaker-dependent technology is the basis of today's command and control applications such as Creative's VoiceAssist. These systems allow the user to control the computer with voice commands in addition to using the keyboard and mouse. By simply saying a word or short phrase, you can make your computer do almost anything you used to do with your keyboard and mouse.

More extravagant, and hence more expensive, systems can recognize continuous speech. This could be likened to the computers in science fiction stories where you can say, "Alright, I want to look at that letter I sent to my boss last Thursday. Can you pull it up for me?" As the user is speaking, the recognition system picks out key words and phrases to determine what is being said. This type of recognition lends itself well to dictation applications. Instead of telling your assistant to take a letter, you can tell your computer to do it and then rattle on for as long as you like.

Finally, speaker-independent systems are being developed so that anyone can talk to the computer. This is the most difficult type of recognition because of the myriad variations between speakers. Someone with a southern accent is quite different from someone with a European accent, for example. Such systems are also very expensive, since they are on the cutting edge of this technology.

How Speech Recognition Works

The actual technique used to detect and compare spoken words is a closely guarded secret in the same way that a magician never reveals how a trick is done. Companies spend years developing and perfecting what they believe to be the most robust and accurate methods for recognizing spoken words. The basic methods behind speech recognition, though, are publicly available.

In an isolated-word system, you first have to know when a command starts and when it ends. This can be accomplished simply by monitoring the microphone input and waiting until the signal exceeds a certain value. This means the command has started. When the signal subsequently drops below that level, the command has ended.

During the period between the detection of the start of the command and the detection of the end of the command, you record the incoming waveform for processing. The type of processing done on the signal is one of the most crucial parts of the technology and a closely guarded secret. Essentially, certain characteristics are extracted from the waveform in order to make up a distinct pattern for the voice command. This extraction method greatly affects the accuracy of the recognition engine.

Once the voice pattern has been attained, the recognition engine can compare it to patterns that have been stored in a user template. Of course, the pattern that is extracted from the spoken command won't exactly match any one in the template. So the engine must calculate the likelihood that the extracted pattern is similar enough to one pattern in the template to warrant a match. This pattern matching ability is also critical in making a robust and accurate recognition engine.

Finally, as in VoiceAssist, once a match has been made, a command is executed. Voilá! You have now achieved speech recognition.

Continuous speech recognition systems are much more complex and are still being perfected. They don't have the benefit of waiting for a command to end before processing, because you continue to speak many words without stopping. As a result, the engine must process what you are saying while you're saying it and figure out when words begin and end. Then the engine must analyze those words to know what you are saying.

In a continuous speech command and control system, the engine must extract key words from your speech and act on them accordingly. This is quite difficult, but it can be managed because many of the words you say to the computer can be left out. For example if you say, "I want to open the file called letter," the computer need only extract "open," and "letter."

In a continuous speech dictation system, however, every word is critical. Since the system is meant to do the typing for you, occasionally dropping words would be unacceptable.

WHAT VOICEASSIST FOR WINDOWS CAN AND CAN'T DO

VoiceAssist is an isolated-word, speaker-dependent recognition system. As such, it has specific abilities and limitations. Below is a short list of its advantages and drawbacks. You can use this for a quick overview of VoiceAssist's capabilities or when comparing it to other systems on the market.

VoiceAssist for Windows Can

- Recognize single words or short phrases less than two seconds in length.

- Recognize a particular user who has trained the system to his/her voice.

- Perform actions such as entering keystrokes, mouse movements, and mouse clicks as if you were doing them yourself.

- Help you work more efficiently by supplementing the use of the keyboard and mouse.

- Work with any Windows-based application program or utility.

- Extract the commands and actions from an application's menus so that you only have to do voice training.

- Be voice trained with only one utterance per command. VoiceAssist does not require the user to repeat the command three or more times as in other systems.

- Average multiple voice trainings to recognize different inflections in a single user's voice or to recognize several different users. Averaging can even make VoiceAssist respond to different words for the same command!

- Support up to 256 users, 30 applications per user, and 1,024 commands per application (992 of which are fully user-definable)!

VoiceAssist for Windows Can't

- Recognize continuous speech such as long phrases or sentences that are more than two seconds in length.

- Recognize many users based on the voice training of one user.

- Take dictation into your word processor so that you don't have to type anymore.

- Totally replace the keyboard and mouse under most circumstances. Don't throw them away yet.

GETTING STARTED WITH VOICEASSIST FOR WINDOWS

As of this writing, VoiceAssist is only available for the Windows platform, although DOS and OS/2 versions are being developed. VoiceAssist is bundled with all of the latest Sound Blaster 16 packages. If you recently bought a Sound Blaster 16 or a Sound Blaster 16 with Advanced Signal Processing, VoiceAssist is already installed on your system. Look for the program group called VoiceAssist. If you have it, skip to the section titled "The Main Window"; you do not need to install VoiceAssist.

TIP: *The disk that accompanies this book contains a demonstration version of VoiceAssist and Appendix G of this book contains installation instructions and a step-by-step keystroke tutorial for using VoiceAssist. The tutorial is valuable for readers with the demonstration version of VoiceAssist as well as for those readers with the unrestricted, regular version of VoiceAssist. If you've never used VoiceAssist, you may want to jump first to Appendix G and go through the step-by-step tutorial before returning to this chapter for a more detailed description of the VoiceAssist screens and features.*

Installing VoiceAssist for Windows

If you bought VoiceAssist as a stand-alone package, you will have to install it first. The following is a brief description of the installation procedure for VoiceAssist. For additional information, also consult the installation guide labeled "Read Me First" that came with VoiceAssist.

1. Start Windows.

2. Insert VoiceAssist Disk #1 into drive A or B.

3. Select Run from the File menu in Program Manager.

4. If you put the VoiceAssist Disk #1 into drive A, type **A:INSTALL** in the Command Line text box. If you put the VoiceAssist Disk #1 into drive B, type **B:INSTALL** in the Command Line text box. Then click OK.

5. The onscreen instructions will guide you through the remainder of the installation.

When the installation is completed, you will have a program group called VoiceAssist containing icons for VoiceAssist, a README file, and a Common Questions and Answers file, appropriately called Q&A.

The Main Window

VoiceAssist's main window, shown in Figure 7-1, is composed of four parts: the Recognition button, the Menu button, the Recognition window, and the Minimize button. By clicking on the Recognition button, you turn VoiceAssist on and off. The picture of the ear indicates the state of VoiceAssist. When an "X" appears over the ear, VoiceAssist is not listening. This is the off state. When the "X" doesn't exist, VoiceAssist is listening. This is the on state.

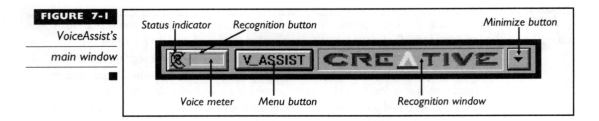

FIGURE 7-1

VoiceAssist's

main window

NOTE: *VoiceAssist can be turned on and off by voice command. Saying the command "Go to sleep" will turn off VoiceAssist until a "Wake up" command is issued. The "X" will not appear on the ear, however, when VoiceAssist is sleeping. If VoiceAssist doesn't seem to respond, try saying "Wake up" first. It may have been sleeping.*

The Recognition Button also contains a Voice Meter to show you the level of sound heard by VoiceAssist. If you have a Sound Blaster 16, check the microphone setting in the mixer utility. When you speak into the microphone, the Voice Meter should come up 60 to 70 percent of the way. If the level goes beyond this, the bar will start turning red, indicating that the level is getting too high. The Sound Blaster and Sound Blaster Pro adjust the microphone level automatically, so you don't have to worry about this.

The Menu button provides access to all of VoiceAssist's training and maintenance functions. The button also displays the name of the currently active application.

The Recognition window displays the Creative logo when VoiceAssist is disabled. When VoiceAssist is enabled, the window will either display the word that it recognized or the phrase "Not Recognized" if it didn't understand what you said.

The Minimize button does just what you'd expect. It minimizes VoiceAssist to an icon. VoiceAssist will continue to operate while minimized, but you won't be able to see what word, if any, it is recognizing or the current state of VoiceAssist. Simply double-clicking on the icon with the mouse will restore it to the normal size.

Commands

VoiceAssist supports up to 1024 commands per application. Each command has three parts: the Command Name, the Voice Pattern, and the

Action. The Command Name is simply the name given to the command. Usually, you'll name the command with the word or phrase that corresponds to what you say to VoiceAssist. For example, if you want to tell your computer to "delete all files," you'd name the command "Delete all files." However, you don't have to do this. You could just as well name the command "Cool demo," to the detriment of an unsuspecting user.

The Voice Pattern is the set of voice characteristics that VoiceAssist extracts when you give a voice command. It cannot be manipulated by the user. The Voice Pattern is generated and stored when you train the command. Then, when you issue a voice command, VoiceAssist generates a Voice Pattern to compare with previously stored patterns for a possible match.

The Action is what VoiceAssist does once it recognizes the voice command. The Action can be as simple as a single keystroke or as complicated as a series of keystrokes, mouse movements, and mouse clicks. Actions are trained in a fashion similar to the way macros are trained in the Windows Macro Recorder utility. Simply begin the training and perform the actions just the way you want VoiceAssist to do them. Once an Action is trained, it can be played back either at the speed at which it was recorded (Recorded Speed) or as fast as the computer can execute it (Fast Playback).

The commands in VoiceAssist are divided into two command sets: the Generic Command Set and the Application-Specific Command Set. The Generic Command Set contains 24 standard Windows commands such as "open," "close," "maximize," and "minimize." The Generic Command Set also includes eight commands for launching applications so that you don't have to go to Program Manager to run commonly used applications. The commands in the Generic Set are available in all applications for easy access.

The other set of commands is the Application-Specific Command Set. This set holds up to 992 user-customizable commands for a particular application.

Templates and User Files

All Command Names, Voice Patterns, and Actions for a particular user are stored in a Speech Recognition Template (SRT) file bearing the user's name. For example, the template for a user named John is stored in JOHN.SRT in the VoiceAssist directory. User templates are also referred to as user files.

By copying your user file to VoiceAssist's directory on another system, you don't have to retrain the system for your commands. Simply select your user file and start working.

USING VOICEASSIST USER FILES

oiceAssist includes two user files: Generic Male and Generic Female. The Generic user files are provided so that most users won't have to perform voice training for every command in the Generic Set and the eight applications in the Generic Set. These templates contain common characteristics of the average male and female. Of course, not everyone talks the same way, so there will be words in the Generic template that don't respond 100 percent of the time.

Creating Your Own User File

VoiceAssist requires that each user have a user file for storing action and voice training. You create, copy, rename, and delete user files via the User & Application Files dialog box, shown in Figure 7-2. To open the User & Application Files dialog box, click on the Menu button and select User from the top of the menu.

If you want to start out with a brand-new user file, you can create one by clicking on the New button and entering your name. The user name must be eight characters or less. When you create a new user file, the Generic

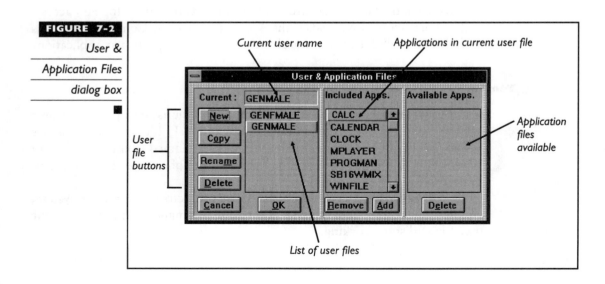

FIGURE 7-2

User &
Application Files
dialog box

Current user name

Applications in current user file

Application files available

User file buttons

List of user files

Command Set is automatically copied into the user file so that you only have to perform voice training.

However, it is recommended that you copy the appropriate Generic template, Male or Female, to your own user file for customization. The copy command will inherit all the applications that are in the template. This way you won't have to retrain all the actions and words, just the ones that VoiceAssist doesn't understand.

To copy a user file, click on the user file you wish to copy from the User File list. Then click on the Copy button. VoiceAssist will ask for the user name. Type in any name up to eight characters in length. Then click OK.

After you've copied one of the Generic user files to your own, click the OK button to make it the active user file. VoiceAssist will continue to use this template until you select a different one.

Setting Up the Mixer

If you have Sound Blaster Pro or Sound Blaster 16 you must check to make sure the Windows mixer is set correctly before you proceed to use VoiceAssist. If the microphone volume is inadequate, you won't be able to create voice templates for command recognition. Make sure to check the following selections.

■ The microphone must be selected as a recording source. For the SB16 the mixer's recording settings should display a dot by the microphone. For the SB Pro, the source setting should be microphone.

■ The microphone volume levels must be set at the usual or higher than usual settings. The microphone volume slide and the master volume slide should be at least two-thirds the maximum volume.

■ For the SB16 only, set the microphone gain to either 4x or 8x.

Fine-Tuning Your User File

Now you're ready to fine-tune your user file. Click on the Menu button and select "Training" from the menu. The Training window pictured in Figure 7-3 contains all the controls for testing and training VoiceAssist. These are the different parts of this Training window:

■ Headers for Training Status Indicators: Empty dots indicate that the feature is disabled or untrained. A green dot in the "E" column indicates that the command is enabled. A green dot in the "A" column

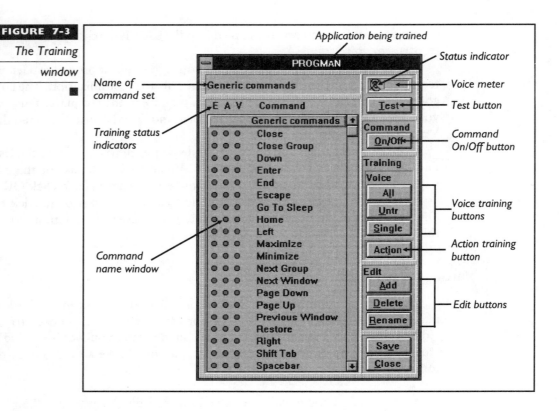

FIGURE 7-3

The Training

window

indicates that the action for the command has been trained. A yellow dot in the "A" column only appears in the Generic Set for the eight application names that you can configure. A green dot in the "V" column indicates that the voice has been trained for the command.

■ Command Names: The name for each command in the template.

■ Test Button: Turns the test mode on and off.

■ Command On/Off Button: Enables and disables a command. The state of the command is indicated in the "E" column next to the command.

■ Voice Training Buttons: "All" voice-trains all the commands. "Untr" voice-trains all commands that haven't yet been trained. "Single" voice-trains the command that is currently highlighted.

■ Action Training Button: Used to record the keystrokes and mouse actions for the command.

- Edit Buttons: "Add" adds new commands. "Delete" removes a command from the template. "Rename" changes the name of the command.

- Save Button: Saves changes to the user file.

- Close Button: Exits the Training window without saving. VoiceAssist will ask for confirmation in case you clicked this button by accident.

A unique feature of VoiceAssist is its ability to test the recognition accuracy of a user file. Since you've copied one of the Generic user files, you can use this feature to see how well your voice matches the generic one.

Click the Test button and try the commands that are displayed in the Command Name window. Each command that VoiceAssist recognizes will be displayed in the window to the left of the ear. If you get a lot of "Not recognized" messages, then you will need to train the commands that aren't correctly recognized by VoiceAssist.

To voice-train a single command, click on the command in the Command window and then click the Single button. The Voice Training dialog box will appear as shown in Figure 7-4. The name of the command is displayed near the top of the window. Below it are options for the number of trainings to perform and for recording a new training or adding to an existing one. Select a single training by clicking on the down arrow and then clicking on New.

NOTE: *For more information on multiple trainings and the use of the Add feature, see the section "Tips and Tricks for VoiceAssist" later in this chapter.*

When you are ready to record the voice pattern, click the OK button. The "X" over the ear will disappear. Say the command into the microphone in a calm and natural manner. If the command is detected without any problems, the Voice Training dialog box will close automatically. If you

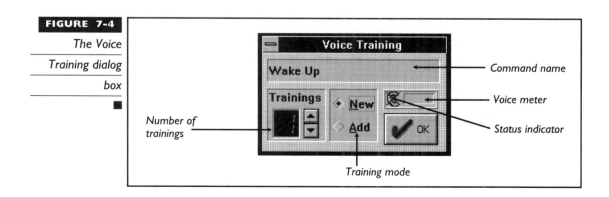

FIGURE 7-4

The Voice Training dialog box

Command name

Voice meter

Status indicator

Number of trainings

Training mode

receive a message that the recording was bad, you may be in an environment that is too noisy or the duration of your command was too long. VoiceAssist can only use commands that are no more than two seconds in length.

NOTE: *Be sure to wait for the "X" to disappear before saying the command into the microphone. VoiceAssist is not listening when the "X" appears over the picture of the ear.*

You can also voice-train all the commands in the Generic Set quite easily by clicking on the "All" button. This will take you to the Voice Training menu again. But this time, when you click OK, the dialog box will not close until you have trained all the words in the set of commands. This makes it much easier to train many commands, because you don't have to do anything except speak each command as it is displayed near the top of the dialog box.

Once you finish voice training, you can go back to test mode to try out your new voice patterns. In case some of the commands don't work well, just use the Single training on them. Finally, click the Save button in the Training window to save your changes.

NOTE: *If the voice pattern for a particular command sounds too similar to one that has already been trained, VoiceAssist is intelligent enough to warn you with an error message which indicates the word that it sounds similar to. If you encounter this, retrain the current command, retrain the command shown in the blank, or rename the command to one that doesn't sound as similar.*

CUSTOMIZING YOUR USER FILE

Now that the basics are done, you're ready to expand your user file by customizing the applications that are listed in the Generic Set and adding new commands and applications.

Remember that VoiceAssist works with any 30 Windows applications that you choose. You can also have up to 992 customized commands per application, so there is a lot of room for making VoiceAssist work for you.

Changing the Generic Set Applications

The Generic Set includes eight application names as command names. These commands are special in that the only action they perform is to launch an application. The benefit of having application names in the Generic Set is that they will be available in the VoiceAssist command set regardless of the application you are using. This means you will be able to launch any of the eight applications you define without going back to Program Manager.

To change the applications defined in the Generic Set, click on the name in the Training window and then click on the "Action" button. The Run Command dialog box will appear:

To change the name of the application, enter it in the Application Name box. Then, enter the complete path and filename of the application to run in the Command Line box. Click OK when you're done and the application will be ready.

NOTE: *Don't forget to voice-train the new command after changing the application in the Generic Set.*

Adding New Applications to VoiceAssist

VoiceAssist automatically tracks the applications that you use and loads the appropriate set of commands for the current application. To add new applications to your user file, all you have to do is run the new application.

VoiceAssist will automatically extract the commands in the application's menus along with the actions needed to access those commands, and then place them in a new Application-Specific Command Set. After you run the new application, open the Training window by selecting Training from the VoiceAssist Main Menu. You will see all of the application's menu commands listed in the Command window.

NOTE: *The Generic Set will always be the first 32 commands in the Command window. To see all the commands for the application, you may have to scroll down the list using the up and down arrow buttons next to the window.*

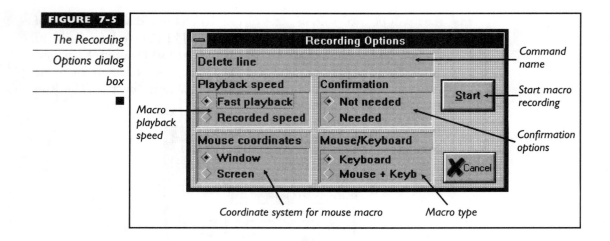

Now all you have to do is voice-train the new commands. To do this, click on the first menu command. This will usually be called "File" since it's normally the first menu in a Windows application. Then, click on the "All" button and proceed as you would when training all the Generic Set commands.

Adding and Deleting Commands in VoiceAssist

To add new commands to VoiceAssist, first run the application for which you want to add new commands and then go to the Training window by selecting Training from the VoiceAssist main menu.

Click on the "Add" button in the Edit box. VoiceAssist will prompt you for the command name. Enter the name into the box and click OK. You have now added a new command for that application.

NOTE: *You cannot add new applications to the Generic Set because its size is fixed at 32 commands. VoiceAssist will alert you if you attempt to add to the Generic Set. You can only add commands to the Application-Specific Command Set.*

To delete a command, select the command in the Command Name window and click on the "Delete" button in the Edit box. The command will be removed from the list. You cannot delete commands from the Generic Set. Clicking on the "Delete" button in the Edit box while a Generic Set command is selected will delete only the voice pattern for the command.

Training VoiceAssist Actions

Once you add a new command to an application, you need to train the action for it. Select the command to train by clicking on the command name in the Command Name window, and then click on the "Action" button. The Recording Options dialog box, shown in Figure 7-5, will appear. The name of the command you chose appears near the top of the box followed by numerous options. Playback speed determines how the action should be performed when you issue the command. Fast playback speed will make VoiceAssist carry out the actions as quickly as it can. This is good for accessing menus and clicking specific areas with the mouse so you don't see everything opening and closing.

Recorded speed tells VoiceAssist to perform the actions at the same speed at which you recorded them. In most circumstances, this is not desirable because you may grow weary of waiting for the actions to finish. It is effective, however, if you want VoiceAssist to demonstrate how to perform a certain task. Recorded speed will also allow the mouse cursor to be seen as it moves, making it perfect for voice-controlled tutorials.

The Confirmation options determine whether or not VoiceAssist asks you if you want to perform the action before it proceeds. If you are training VoiceAssist to perform actions that are potentially destructive if misapplied, you definitely want to turn on confirmation.

The Mouse Coordinates option defines how mouse actions should be tracked. Window coordinates will record the position of the mouse based on where it is in a particular window. This is the best method, since a window could appear anywhere on the screen. Screen coordinates will record the position of the mouse based on where it is on the entire screen. This option is useful only when you're running an application that has a fixed position on the screen at all times or is maximized to occupy the entire screen.

Mouse/Keyboard lets you choose whether you want VoiceAssist to record only the keys you press on your keyboard, or both mouse movements and key presses. Storing mouse movements takes more space in the user file, but it can be a powerful tool. VoiceAssist is unique in its ability to allow you to use the mouse as part of an action.

Once you decide on the options you want to use for the command, click Start. The dialog box will close and VoiceAssist will sit in the background waiting for you to do something. Enter keystrokes on your keyboard or use the mouse as you normally would to perform the action. VoiceAssist will record everything you do as you do it. When you're done, press the PAUSE key on your keyboard to stop the recording. Click the OK button to save the recording or Cancel to ignore it.

NOTE: *The* PAUSE *key is located next to the* PRINT SCREEN *and* SCROLL LOCK *keys on the top row of keyboards with 12 function keys. If your keyboard doesn't have a* PAUSE *key, you can press* CTRL *and* NUMLOCK *to stop recording.*

To retrain the action for an existing command, select the command in the Command Name window and click on the "Action" button. Proceed as described above to record the new action.

TIPS AND TRICKS FOR VOICEASSIST

Now that you've had some exposure to what VoiceAssist can do for you, here are a few tips and tricks to make life even more interesting. Also be sure to check the VoiceAssist manual for other recommendations in getting the best performance from VoiceAssist.

Optimizing Recognition Accuracy

For best results, follow these guidelines when performing voice training.

1. Try to speak in a relaxed, natural manner. To minimize anxiety when training, try speaking the commands into the microphone a few times without actually training the system. Once you feel your speaking style is stable, perform the actual training.

   Talking to your computer is a new experience and may take some time to get used to. Once you feel comfortable talking to your PC, you can always go back and retrain your commands.

2. Train the voice in a quiet environment. If you must train in a noisy environment, try using multiple trainings as discussed below.

3. When using more than one-word commands, such as "Get my mail," avoid long breaks between words. Remember that a pause indicates the end of the command.

4. Don't put the microphone too close or too far away from your mouth. Six to twelve inches is sufficient.

5. For the best possible recognition, you can opt for a unidirectional headset microphone. This type of arrangement provides the maximum amount of audio pickup from your mouth with minimal pickup from the surrounding area.

6. Sound Blaster 16 users should be sure that the AGC option in the Recording Settings dialog box is turned on. Also check the Gain in the Recording Settings dialog box. Gain settings of 4X and 8X are recommended. For more information on changing these settings, consult Chapter 4, or your Sound Blaster 16 User Manual.

Multiple Voice Trainings

In the Voice Training dialog box (Figure 7-4), you can tell VoiceAssist to train a command up to five times. Multiple trainings aren't required but can be useful if you're in a noisy environment. VoiceAssist has operated successfully in a very noisy environment by using two or three trainings per word.

To train a word more than once, click on the up arrow next to the digit in the Voice Training dialog box. The value will change to a maximum of five trainings per word. Select the number of times you want to train a word and then proceed as you normally would for voice training.

The value in the Trainings box will automatically decrement as you train the word so that you know how many more times you have to repeat the command before moving on to the next one.

Averaging Voice Trainings

In the Voice Training dialog box, you have the option to add a voice training into the existing one. Of course, you need to have trained the command at least once in order to add to it. Otherwise the Add function will be grayed out and you won't be able to select it.

Adding to an existing voice training allows VoiceAssist to average the voice patterns for a command. This feature can be used so that VoiceAssist will recognize your voice when you shout as well as when you speak normally. You can try it by setting the number of trainings to one, selecting Add, and clicking OK. Now shout the command. VoiceAssist will recognize both patterns—a useful feature if you're playing a game and get too excited.

An even more amazing capability of the Add feature is the ability to store two different voice trainings for the same command. For example, you could train the Close command with the word "close." Then go back to voice training and select Add. This time say "go away." Now VoiceAssist will be able to recognize "close" and "go away" as the Close command.

In fact, just for fun, the Add feature was tested by training the Close command with "close," "go away," "get lost," "take a hike," "take off," and "beat it." Believe it or not, after adding them all together, all these phrases are recognized as the Close command!

Humanizing Voice Commands

You may want to consider using more human phrases for your voice commands. Instead of simply saying "clock" to run the Clock utility in Windows, use "What time is it?" Instead of saying "WinWord" to run Word for Windows, try "Take a letter." And instead of commanding an application to "close," you could say "I'm done."

You get the general idea. Think of commands that sound like requests that you'd use with humans. It not only makes VoiceAssist more fun, but your friends might start wondering who you're talking to.

THE VOICEASSIST API FOR WINDOWS

Creative Labs provides a Windows Application Programming Interface (API) for third-party developers who want to directly integrate VoiceAssist into their applications. By using the API, you don't have to rely on the standard VoiceAssist user interface but instead can seamlessly incorporate the technology into games, multimedia, and business applications.

If you are thinking about writing an application that uses speech recognition, you will want to consider using the VoiceAssist API. For more information about becoming a registered developer and licensing the VoiceAssist API, contact Creative Labs at (800) 998-5227. For inquiries outside the United States, Canada, and South America, call Creative Technology in Singapore at (65) 870-0433.

TIP: *The OWL library that accompanies Borland's CD-ROM version of C++ contains the VoiceAssist API. If you own this development environment, you have everything you need to add speech recognition to your custom C applications.*

Common Questions and Answers

Question: I moved the VoiceAssist icon to the StartUp window in order to launch VoiceAssist when I enter Microsoft Windows. I start the Windows program, and after hearing the "tada" sound, I get the message "The sound input device is already in use." How can I overcome this?

Answer: To launch VoiceAssist from the StartUp window, you need to disable the Windows Start Sound. To do so, complete the following steps:

1. Switch to the Program Manager. In the Main program group, double-click on the Control Panel icon to display the Control Panel window.

2. In the Control Panel window you'll see the Sound icon. Double-click on this icon to display the Sound window.

3. Select Windows Start in the Event list.

4. Select <none> in the File list.

5. Click on OK.

Question: VoiceAssist's menu extraction capability saves a lot of training time. Why doesn't it work correctly with some applications like Microsoft Word for Windows, PC Tools for Windows, and Norton Desktop?

Answer: VoiceAssist's menu extraction feature works with almost all programs. However, a few applications like Microsoft Word and Norton Desktop handle their menu resources differently than most other applications. Consequently, VoiceAssist can't extract these menu items until their menus have been opened.

If you encounter an application with this problem, try the following work-around. Open VoiceAssist and the Training dialogue window. Run the "problem" application. Manually open each menu. When you have finished, return to VoiceAssist. VoiceAssist will now display the menu items.

Question: I'm a Sound Blaster 16 user and I'm having a problem with VoiceAssist that isn't explained by the other tips or this Q&A. What should I do next?

Answer: Make sure you have an up-to-date Sound Blaster 16 driver. Versions of the SB16SND.DRV driver earlier than 29th April 1993 may not work correctly with the latest applications including VoiceAssist. To get the latest version of this driver contact your local distributor or download the driver from the Creative Labs bulletin board. (The telephone number for the BBS is (405)742-6660.) Look for the update file named SBUPDATE.ZIP.

SPEECH SYNTHESIS

Speech synthesis is not just fun, it's also a great productivity tool. Instead of growing bleary-eyed trying to proof your computer input against the original words or numbers on paper, you can have the computer read out loud to you. All Sound Blaster 16 packages, as well as the Sound Blaster Pro Deluxe and Sound Blaster Deluxe, come with Monologue for Windows, a speech synthesis program that runs in the Microsoft Windows environment. All Sound Blaster packages also come with a DOS-based speech program, called SBTALKER, which is described in Chapter 6.

The Monologue for Windows program was created by First Byte of Torrance, California, and is licensed to Creative Labs. In late October 1993 Creative Labs announced that it had obtained a license to Digital Equipment Corporation's (DEC's) advanced text-to-speech technology called DECtalk speech synthesis. You can expect that Creative Labs' future text-to-speech products will be based on DECtalk. Please see Appendix A to read about this state-of-the-art speech synthesis technology that literally makes your computer sing.

Using Monologue for Windows

Monologue actually consists of two programs: the speech engine that pronounces text and a dictionary manager that maintains the list of word exceptions that override the rules-based speech engine. When Monologue is installed, icons for both programs are placed in the Monologue program group as shown here:

The tutorial in this section will focus on how to read text using Monologue.

Monologue for Windows can read text from either the Windows Clipboard or from Microsoft Excel spreadsheet cells visible on the screen. What's nice about reading from the Clipboard (the temporary storage spot for exchanging information between programs) is that you can use Monologue with virtually any Windows software program. Simply mark a region of text, select Copy from the Edit menu, and it's in the Clipboard ready to be read by Monologue.

Tutorial: Reading a Write Document Out Loud

Because everyone has Write, a simple word processor that comes with Windows, this example illustrates reading text that's visible in a Write document.

1. Launch the Write program.

   Use the Windows Program Manager to launch the Write program from the Accessories group. Next, load a document file that comes with Windows. Select Open from the File menu, navigate to the Windows directory (probably \WINDOWS), and then choose README.WRI from the list. You should see a document with the following (or very similar) title: More Information About Microsoft Windows Version 3.1.

2. Select text to read.

   Select the title and first two paragraphs using either the mouse or keyboard. Now copy this text to the Windows Clipboard by selecting Copy from the Edit menu.

3. Start Monologue.

   If you haven't already started Monologue, switch to the Program Manager and double-click the Monologue icon in the Monologue program group. If you've already started Monologue, switch to the Monologue window by repeatedly pressing ALT-TAB until it appears:

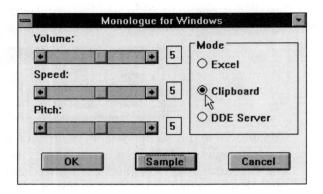

If Monologue's Clipboard mode button hasn't already been selected, click it now. This tells Monologue to read from the Clipboard. Now click OK to save this setting and then click the minimize button at the top right of the Monologue screen to minimize Monologue to an icon at the bottom of your screen. It will initially appear at the bottom-left corner of your screen.

4. Command Monologue to Talk.

Click the right mouse button on top of the Monologue icon to command it to speak. Click the left mouse button on the icon to command it to stop it prematurely, before it has finished reading all the text copied to the Clipboard. Monologue will stop once its speech buffer is emptied, probably within a few sentences.

Monologue for Windows Dictionary

The English language is a challenging one for speech synthesis. English is a blend of many languages, resulting in inconsistent spellings and pronunciations. Because there are so many words in a language, it's not feasible to include the *phonetic value* (the pronunciation) for every word. Monologue economizes by using a *rule-based* system for pronunciation. For example, one hypothetical rule is to pronounce the "y" before a vowel like the *y* in "you" or "yarn," and to pronounce the *y* after a consonant like *i,* as in "by" or "sky."

Because English is so irregular, Monologue also uses an *exception dictionary,* a lookup list of known exceptions, to override the rules. As shown in Figure 7-6, you type the word as it is spelled, then you type your best guess at how it should sound. For example, the word "caveat" is pronounced "cave-at" by Monologue. If you enter "cahviat" (pointed to in the figure by the mouse pointer) as the phonetic value, Monologue will do a much better

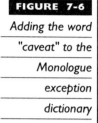

FIGURE 7-6

Adding the word

"caveat" to the

Monologue

exception

dictionary

■

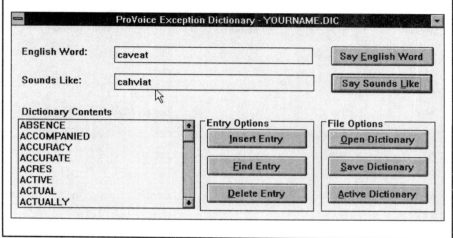

job pronouncing the word when it's next encountered. Monologue doesn't require you to be an expert in speech. Take your best guess, and Monologue will do the rest, translating your guess into a precisely coded set of *phonemes,* the sound building blocks of a spoken language. If you later inspect the phonetic value for "caveat," you'll see the phoneme codes. After you're satisfied with the sound of a word, select the Insert Entry button to insert the word into the current dictionary. When done working with the dictionary, make sure to select the Save Dictionary command to make the additions or changes permanent.

NOTE: *There is one caveat to adding "caveat" to the dictionary. If you're already running Monologue when you update the exception dictionary, Monologue won't know about the new pronunciation. You must close Monologue and restart it. When you restart, Monologue will access the newly updated dictionary.*

Monologue is optimized for the English language; thus it cannot be used for other languages, such as Italian and French, due to their difference in phonemes. Table 7-1 lists the symbols for the phonemes spoken by Monologue. This list, provided to the authors by First Byte, reflects the latest thinking at First Byte about the best way to represent the phonemes. To the right of each symbol is a common English word that illustrates, with the italicized letters in that word, the sound for that phoneme. For example, the first entry in the table is the phoneme whose symbol is AA. This is the phoneme for the "o" sound as in "cot." When working with Monologue's exception dictionary, you must type both the proper spelling of the word as

Vowels		Consonants and Semivowels			
phonetic	as in...	phonetic	as in...	phonetic	as in...
AA	cot	b	bib	v	valve
AE	cat	d	did	z	zoo
AH	cut	DH	this, that	ZH	vision, casual
AW	cow	DX	butter, city	tSH	chin
AX	about, bottom	f	fee	dZH	gin
AY	bite	g	gag	l	light, club
EH	bet	h	he	LX	tile, bulk
ER	bird	k	curse	m	me
EY	bake	KX	skirt, backer	n	no
IH	bit	p	pip	NG	song
IX	rabbit, nation	PX	speak	r	rock, core, car
IY	beet	s	sin	w	we
OW	boat	SH	shin	y	you
OY	boy	t	tin		
UH	book	TH	thin		
UW	boot	TX	stick		

TABLE 7-1   *Monologue Phonetic Codes for English Phonemes* ■

well as instructions on how to say it. Refer to the samples in the phoneme table for ideas on how to spell a word phonetically.

Monologue's biggest problem area is abbreviations (like *"Ave."* for *"avenue"*) and acronyms (words based on initial letters, like *"radar," "ra*dio *de*tection." and *"ra*nging"). Monologue has been educated at the factory to correctly pronounce the most common abbreviations. For example when Monologue encounters "Ave." it'll say "avenue." Unfortunately it doesn't have a clue how to pronounce "CA," the postal code for California, when it's encountered in a letter. Monologue recognizes, due to the capitalization, that CA isn't a regular word so it pronounces it letter by letter, saying the letter "C" followed by "A." Names, especially foreign place names, also prove to be hazards for correct pronunciation. For example Monologue pronounces the name of the Greek philosopher Socrates as "sox-crates." A related problem is foreign place names and words taking their origin from foreign names. There are far too many of these names for all but the very most common to be entered into the dictionary. An example of a non-English word that has been absorbed into English is cologne (perfumed water), which takes its name from a city in the Rhine-Westphalia part of Germany. Cologne should be pronounced like "ko-loan" but Monologue pronounces it as "cala." Perhaps with the next generation of computers, with greater speed and storage capabilities, the exception dictionaries will become more comprehensive.

Tips and Tricks

The Monologue for Windows documentation provided by Creative Labs doesn't sufficiently document the version of Monologue that is shipped by Creative Labs, so we've provided the following sections to explain the discrepancies and work around the irritations.

NOTE: *A commonly asked question about Monologue is how to change the gender of the voice from male to female. Unfortunately, the current version of Monologue can't do this. The license to the female voice is currently held exclusively by Apple Computer. First Byte has stated its intention to provide this feature in the future.*

KEEPING THE MONOLOGUE ICON VISIBLE   The Monologue documentation includes a paragraph on how to resize your Windows to provide access to the Monologue icon, but it's easy to get confused on this point. To make Monologue convenient to use, the icon must appear on the screen at all times. The icon is necessary because you must right-click on it to make Monologue pronounce the text and left-click on it to interrupt the speech. This important step is complicated by the fact that when you bring up a program, such as a word processor, the new window often covers the full screen, hiding the Monologue icon.

To access the Monologue icon, you can use the Windows task-switching keys, ALT-TAB, to make Monologue appear on top. Unfortunately, the next time you select text to read, the icon disappears again. You can solve the problem by reducing the size of your application window so that the Monologue icon is safely tucked away outside the window. You can see in Figure 7-7 how both the Microsoft Word window and the Program Manager window have been reduced slightly in size so that the icon appears outside the Program Manager window. An application program that requires the full screen will not, in this circumstance, cover up the Monologue icon. The Monologue icon initially appears at the bottom-left corner of the screen, an unfortunate choice of position since another icon is likely to be already situated there. The icon can be dragged by the mouse to another position, such as to the bottom right as shown in this figure, to avoid overlaying other icons.

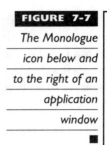

FIGURE 7-7

The Monologue

icon below and

to the right of an

application

window

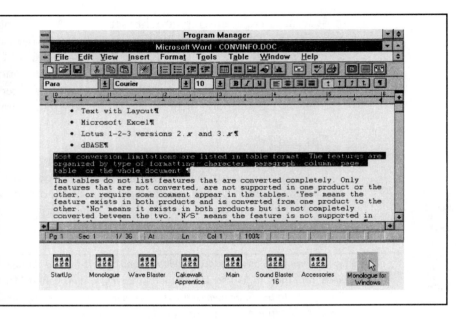

EXCEPTION DICTIONARY   The documentation incorrectly describes the Monologue dictionaries. The master copy of the kernel dictionary (called *kernel* because it's the kernel from which all other dictionaries are built) is FB_DEFLT.DOC, not KERNEL.DIC as stated in the manual (KERNEL.DIC doesn't exist). You create your own personal dictionary by opening FB_DEFLT.DIC and then saving a copy of the dictionary under another name (most likely your own). You then select that dictionary to be your active dictionary. In a nice touch, the Dictionary Manager protects you from yourself by making it impossible for you to accidentally overwrite FB_DEFLT.DIC.

The exception dictionary has codes for special effects such as pitch changes and shortening or lengthening of phonemes. For the most part the effort involved in incorporating these codes isn't matched by the payoff, although in one situation it's worth adding a special code: short words, those with four letters or less, are typically pronounced a little too fast, and you can add the Sn code to slow these down.

MONOLOGUE DLL   Probably only the most techie of the techies tried the DLL speech example provided in the manual. Unfortunately, the SPEECH.DLL file required by the example isn't provided with Monologue. If you want to try Monologue's DLL interface, which gives other Windows programs access to Monologue's speech engine, contact First Byte technical support.

8

Cakewalk Apprentice

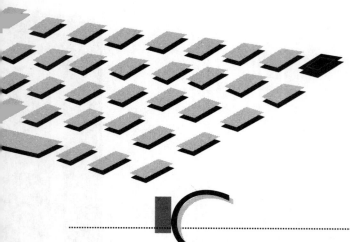

CAKEWALK Apprentice for Windows is a complete MIDI sequencer capable of writing and editing music for all Creative Labs' sound products. If you are reading this chapter, you more than likely have purchased either the Creative Labs Wave Blaster or the Creative Labs MIDI Kit. The version of Cakewalk Apprentice that comes with these two products is a specific version that will only work when used with a Creative Labs product.

This chapter contains some general information on installing and working with Cakewalk Apprentice. The first half of the chapter covers the commands available in the sequencer, followed by a tutorial on Cakewalk's different editing screens using the music file SWINGER.WRK found on the included disk. You will also find some tips that can be used as shortcuts when implementing the sequencer for your music writing and editing needs. If you have already been working with Cakewalk Apprentice, some of the following information might already be familiar to you.

Cakewalk Apprentice for Windows, even though a complete sequencing software package, is in some measure a scaled-down version of Twelve Tone Systems' much acclaimed Cakewalk Professional for Windows. The differences are very slight. Some of the Realtime, Edit, and Settings features as well as three views have been removed. These missing features will not be missed by most people. An explanation of these deletions can be found in the Cakewalk Apprentice for Windows User's Guide. Cakewalk Professional for Windows can be obtained by contacting Twelve Tone Systems directly.

INSTALLATION AND MIDI SETUP

Cakewalk Apprentice for Windows is just that, for Windows. Therefore, you must have Windows 3.1 installed and running before you can begin to install Cakewalk Apprentice. Twelve Tone Systems recommends that you make sure the video drivers you are using are the latest Windows 3.1 drivers from your video card manufacturer. Avoid Windows 3.0 drivers.

It is assumed that you have already installed the sound drivers that came with your sound card. If you haven't yet done so, please refer to Appendix C.

Also, if you are going to be using an external MIDI device, go ahead and connect it now. If you are using a Creative Labs Wave Blaster, it is assumed you have already installed it.

Installation of Cakewalk Apprentice for Windows:

1. Start Windows.

2. Put Cakewalk Apprentice disk 1 in the appropriate drive.

3. From Windows Program Manager, open the File menu and select the Run command.

4. In the dialog box, type **X:SETUP**, and press ENTER. Where **X:** represents which drive the disk is in.

5. Follow all the instructions that appear on the screen.

Now there should be visible in your Program Manager an icon for Cakewalk Apprentice. To start the sequencer, just double-click on the icon.

When you start Cakewalk Apprentice for the first time, you will be prompted to select which MIDI In and MIDI Out devices you will use. The dialog box in Figure 8-1 is the same one that appears when selecting the *MIDI Devices* command in the *Settings* pull-down menu.

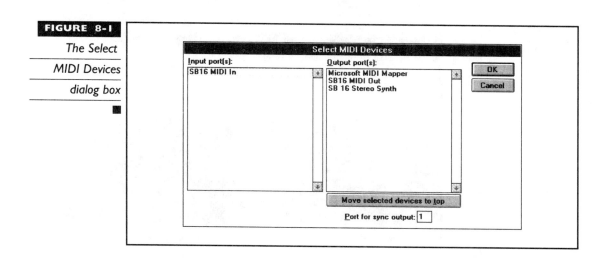

FIGURE 8-1

The Select

MIDI Devices

dialog box

Remember, the version of Cakewalk Apprentice you have received with a Creative Labs product will work only with products manufactured by Creative Labs. However, Cakewalk Apprentice will not limit which MIDI device you connect.

WORKING WITH CAKEWALK APPRENTICE

Now that you have Cakewalk Apprentice running, let's take note of what is visible on the screen (see Figure 8-2). At the top of the Cakewalk Apprentice window are the program name and the current sequence file-name, "Untitled." The filename will be visible at all times.

Below that is a standard Windows pull-down menu bar. Just like the filename, the pull-down menus will always be visible. You will use these menus or their equivalent shortcut keys often when manipulating your work.

Directly under the pull-down menu bar is the Cakewalk Apprentice control bar. The control bar can be relocated to the bottom of your window and is also always visible. It contains information pertinent to your file's timing and the necessary buttons for recording and playback of your music.

FIGURE 8-2

A standard opening screen for Cakewalk Apprentice

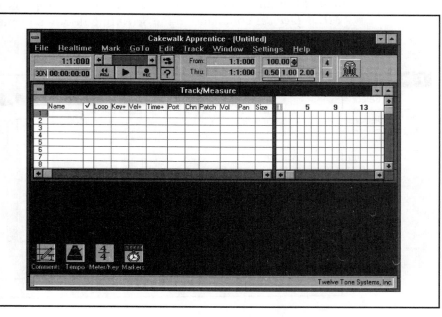

Next, there is the Track/Measure view. This is one of many views that will be discussed later in this chapter. This particular view will default open when you start Cakewalk Apprentice. However, it does not have to always be visible.

At the bottom of the window can be found four icons that are minimized and available to be restored at will. Like the Track/Measure view, these icons default to this location upon startup of Cakewalk Apprentice. Beneath these icons is a message line that will display temporary system messages.

Again, the filename, pull-down menus, control bar, and message line will always be visible for your convenience when you use Cakewalk Apprentice.

Before we take a look at the pull-down menus, it would be a good idea to learn about changing the file default parameters and the different file formats Cakewalk Apprentice uses.

Changing File Default Parameters

If there are specific parameters (tempo, meter, and so on) that you want to use as your default settings, you can create a work template. The name of this template is $DEFAULT.WRK, and it will be loaded whenever you begin a new file. If Cakewalk Apprentice doesn't find $DEFAULT.WRK, the tempo is set to 100, and the meter is set to 4/4. To create your default settings choose the *New* command from the *File* menu. Change the parameters to your liking and choose the *Save As* command in the *File* menu. Name the work file $DEFAULT.WRK, and your settings will always be there for you when you open Cakewalk Apprentice or choose the *New* command.

For example, if you know you will always be writing a piece of music using a specific instrument on a particular track, you can set it as a default. As seen in Figure 8-3, you can set up Cakewalk Apprentice to default with drums and percussion on track 16 using channel 10.

File Format Differences

There are two file formats Cakewalk Apprentice uses: standard MIDI files (MID and MFF) and Cakewalk work files (WRK). The standard MIDI file format was specified by the MMA (MIDI Manufacturers Association). The MIDI file format also consists of two format types, Format 0 and Format 1. Format 0 MIDI files contain all MIDI events in one track. Format 1 MIDI files can have multiple tracks containing MIDI events specific to each track. Cakewalk Apprentice can read and write Format 1 MIDI files but can only read Format 0. Cakewalk work files are similar to Format 1 but also contain temporary track information that cannot be saved in standard MIDI files. This temporary information can be seen in the Track/Measure view: Key

FIGURE 8-3

Saving the

default to include

drums on

track 16

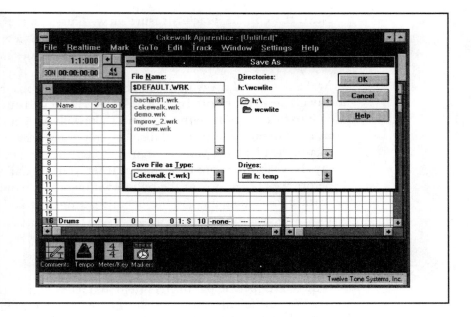

transposition, velocity transposition, forced channel, starting patch, starting volume, and starting pan parameters.

If you have saved a file with temporary track information as a standard MIDI file and load it again, the temporary track information will not appear in the Track/Measure view. However, the music will sound the same, since Cakewalk Apprentice made these changes directly to the events in each track when the file was saved.

CAUTION: *Be sure to un-mute all tracks you want when saving your work as a standard MIDI file. Cakewalk Apprentice will not write empty or muted tracks to a standard MIDI file.*

PULL-DOWN MENU BAR

Cakewalk Apprentice for Windows has nine pull-down menus. These menus provide commands for manipulating your music while working in a variety of views and windows. The commands in the pull-down menus can be accessed by holding down the ALT key and the underlined letter that represents the menu you would like to use. For example, ALT-F will open the *File* menu of commands. Or you can just point and click with a mouse.

TIP: *Take note of the shortcut keys available in each of the pull-down menus. The shortcut keys will help in reducing the amount of keystrokes or mouse clicks required to choose the command you want to use.*

File

The File menu contains commands that allow you to open and save files, extract and merge portions of work, and exit Cakewalk Apprentice.

New

Closes and clears the open file from memory while beginning a new one. If the open file has been altered and not saved, you will be asked if you would like to save it.

Open (CTRL-O)

Opens an existing WRK, MID, or MFF file. If the open file has been altered and not saved, you will be asked if you would like to save it.

Save (CTRL-S)

Saves your current work to the filename and location it was loaded from, without prompting you to assign it a filename. However, if the current work does not already have a filename, you will be asked to name it.

Save As

You can use the *Save As* command to create more than one version of your work. If the current file has already been named, the current filename will be displayed and can be changed. You can also change the type (WRK, MID, and MFF) and location for this version of your work.

Merge

Opens a dialog box prompting you for a filename to merge into the Cakewalk Scrap buffer. This buffer is similar to the Windows Clipboard. A dialog box will prompt you for the file to be merged to the Scrap buffer. You can then use the *Edit/Paste* command to paste the Scrap buffer into your current work.

NOTE: *This command cannot be used for converting Cakewalk DOS release 1.x files. To convert such a file, use the Open and Save As commands previously mentioned.*

Extract

This command works in conjunction with the *Edit/Copy* and *Edit/Cut* commands. *Extract* will open a dialog box prompting you for a filename. The information in the Scrap buffer will then be saved to that filename. This command is similar to the *Save* command except it uses the Scrap buffer instead of the Main buffer.

NOTE: *The Scrap buffer only contains the most recently copied or cut information.*

Exit (ALT-F4)

Ends your session of Cakewalk Apprentice. If the open file has been altered and not saved, you will be asked if you would like to save it.

RealTime

The commands listed in this menu are related to recording and playback of the current file. All of these commands are more readily available on the control bar.

Play (SPACEBAR, or Play button)

Plays the file from the current position. When the sequencer is already playing, this command stops playback.

Record (R, or Record button)

Records MIDI data from the current position. When you are ready to stop recording, this command stops recording. SPACEBAR will also stop the recording process. You will then be asked if you would like to keep the data you have recorded.

NOTE: *There is a one-measure count-off that can be changed using the Settings/Metronome command mentioned later in this chapter.*

CAUTION: *If you record over existing data, the new recording will be blended into what already exists. It will not replace it.*

Rewind (Rewind button)

Sets the current position to the beginning of your work. There is no need to stop the playback or recording process to use this command.

Step Record (SHIFT-F3, or Footprint button)

This command can only be used in conjunction with a MIDI keyboard. Primarily for those who are not particularly proficient at playing a keyboard, the *Step Record* command allows you to record notes or chords one step at a time. Figure 8-4 displays the Step recording dialog box that will always be present in this mode of recording.

- *Step size* Denotes how far apart each note or chord will be. This can be changed during the step recording process. Dotted will add half the value already checked to the *Step size*. If you select another *Step size* the dotted option is turned off automatically.

- *Duration* Establishes how long the note or chord will last. This can be changed during the step recording process. *Follow step size* will set the duration to the *Step size*.

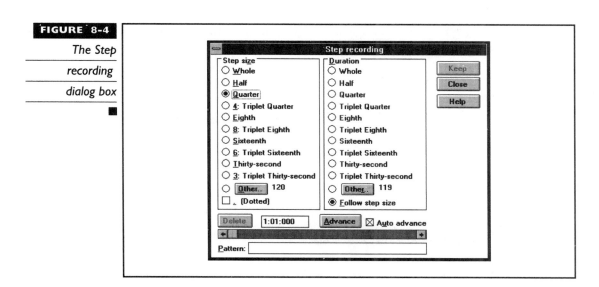

FIGURE 8-4

The Step recording dialog box

- *Delete* Deletes the current step if a mistake has been made.

- *Advance* Clicking this button will advance your current position by one step without playing any notes.

- *Auto Advance* Allows automatic advancing to the next step when the keys of the keyboard are released. This option is on as a default. If this option is turned off, you will have to advance to the next step manually.

- *Pattern* A rhythmic pattern with rests can be defined to make the step recording process more efficient. For example, if you know you only want to record on the second and third beats of a measure, the pattern "R23R" will place rests on the first and fourth beats. You have 64 steps available to a pattern.

NOTE: *You can use* SPACEBAR, R, *or* "." *when you would like a rest placed in your pattern. Any other key will represent where you would like a note.*

Mark

The commands in this menu will be used to select sections of your work for editing purposes. However, using the shortcut keys will more than likely be the way you use these commands. The From and Thru markers will select the range you want to work with.

From Value (From box on the control bar)

Sets the From marker to a position you specify in the Measure:Beat:Tick format.

Thru Value (Thru box on the control bar)

Sets the Thru marker to a position you specify in the Measure:Beat:Tick format.

From=Now (F9)

Sets the From marker to the Now marker position.

Thru=Now (F10)

Sets the Thru Marker to the Now Marker position.

From=<u>S</u>tart (CTRL-F9)

Sets the From Marker to the beginning of the current work.

Thru=<u>E</u>nd (CTRL-F10)

Sets the Thru Marker to the end of the current work.

Select <u>A</u>ll (CTRL-5 on the numeric keypad)

Selects all tracks from the beginning to the end of the current work.

<u>U</u>n-select All (5 on the numeric keypad)

Resets the From and Thru Markers to the Now Marker position.

GoTo

This list of commands will move the Now Marker to a specified position. However, using the shortcut keys will more than likely be the way you use these commands.

<u>T</u>ime (F5)

Opens a dialog box prompting you for a location in the Measure:Beat:Tick format. The Beat and Tick values are optional. When a Beat or Tick value is not used, the time is set to the first Beat or Tick, respectively. For example, entering 3:2 will set the Now marker to the 3:2:000 time location.

NOTE: *When entering the time location, a space can be used instead of a colon.*

<u>F</u>rom (F7)

Go to and set the Now Marker to the current From value.

Thr<u>u</u> (F8)

Go to and set the Now Marker to the current Thru value.

Beginning (CTRL-HOME)

Go to and set the Now Marker to the beginning of the work.

End (CTRL-END)

Go to and set the Now Marker to the end of the work.

Previous Measure (CTRL-PGUP, or scroll bar on the control bar)

Go to the beginning of the current or previous measure.

Next Measure (CTRL-PGDN, or scroll bar on the control bar)

Go to the beginning of the next measure.

Search

Find and go to one or more specified MIDI events. When this command is chosen, the Event Filter dialog box prompts you for the specific search criteria.

Event Filter

Although the Event Filter looks rather complicated, once you know its layout, it can serve as a very powerful device. The Event Filter dialog box can be seen in Figure 8-5.

THE LAYOUT   The Event Filter has a row for each MIDI event type that can be selected as criteria. There are six MIDI event types used:

> Note
> Key After-touch
> Controller
> Patch
> Channel After-touch
> Pitch Wheel

The Include check box in the first column is the way to select which MIDI event type will be used as criteria. All other columns determine the data ranges for the corresponding MIDI event type.

FIGURE 8-5

The Event Filter

Event Filter - Search				
Include	Not Min.........Max	Not Min......Max	Not Min.............Max	
⊠ Note	Key:☐ C 0	G 10	Vel:☐ 0	127	Dur:☐ 0	546:015
⊠ KeyAft	Key:☐ C 0	G 10	Val:☐ 0	127		
⊠ Control	Num:☐ 0	127	Val:☐ 0	127	
⊠ Patch	Num:☐ 0	127		
⊠ ChanAft	Amt:☐ 0	127	Everything	
⊠ Wheel	Val:☐ -8192	8191	Nothing	

Any kind of event — Min........ Max — Chan: 1 / 16 — Beat: 1 / 99 — Tick: 0 / 1919 — OK — Cancel — Help

Keep in mind that MIDI events use different kinds of data parameters. For example, the *Note* event contains a key (pitch), a velocity (volume), and a duration (time), whereas the *Patch* event contains one data parameter, the patch number (instrument).

Each MIDI event has a box associated with it labeled **Not**. When this box is checked the search will include events that are not within the range you have specified.

There is also a set of three rows at the bottom-right corner of the Event Filter dialog box used for all MIDI event types. All MIDI events have a *Channel* associated with them and are located at a particular point in time (*Beat* and *Tick*) in a measure. Knowing this, you will find this part of the dialog box most useful when you want to search a specific location in time.

The *Everything* and *Nothing* buttons allow you to include all MIDI events or clear all boxes so you can select specifically what you want to search for.

ENTERING RANGES   Entering the ranges in the Event Filter is done primarily with the keyboard and mouse just like any other dialog box. Use the TAB key to go from one option to the next or just click on what you want to change.

TIP: *If you have a MIDI keyboard connected and want to specify a pitch parameter, you can simply depress a key on the keyboard and it will be reflected on the screen. When you have found the pitch you want, just hit TAB or use the mouse to go to the next parameter you want to alter.*

TIP: *When selecting a pitch you can use a wildcard in place of the octave. By placing a question mark where the octave number belongs, the pitch criteria will span all octaves for that particular pitch.*

Search Next (ALT-F5)

Find and go to the next MIDI event specified by the criteria in the Event Filter.

Edit

Commands in this menu allow you to manipulate your work in one or more tracks. Most of these commands will have an option to use the Event Filter in order to alter specific events within a certain region. The region is defined by the From and Thru Markers.

Undo (CTRL-Z)

Undo the results of the last *Edit* menu command executed.

TIP: *If you Undo an edit and want to hear the edit again, the Undo command can be undone. It is now called Redo. You can repeat this process over and over again to make comparisons.*

NOTE: *Undo cannot be used with the Copy command. Similarly, Redo cannot be used with the Cut command.*

CAUTION: *If you don't have enough memory to store the work before the edit is initiated, Cakewalk Apprentice will inform you. If there is not enough memory, the Undo command will not function after the edit has been executed. If this is the case, save your work before trying the edit.*

Copy (CTRL-C)

Copies a selected region to the Scrap buffer leaving the work unchanged.

CAUTION: *Copy destroys whatever is already in the Scrap buffer. If you want to save the data located in the Scrap buffer, use the Extract command in the File menu.*

Cut (CTRL-X)

Deletes the selected region and replaces it with silence. If you don't want to replace the region with silence, check the *Delete Hole* box. This will move the remaining material to the left, thus filling the hole.

CAUTION: *Cut destroys whatever is already in the Scrap buffer. If you want to save the data located in the Scrap buffer, use the Extract command in the File menu.*

Paste (CTRL-V)

Inserts the contents of the Scrap buffer into your work. The default insertion point is where the Now Marker is positioned. Using the *To Time* box, you can select exactly where the insertion point is to be located. Enter the time in the Measure:Beat:Tick format. You can also choose how many times you would like the data being pasted to be repeated by using the *Repetitions* box. There are three methods of insertion.

- *Blend old and new material* combines the contents of the Scrap buffer with the existing track information.

- *Replace old material with new* deletes the existing track information where the Scrap buffer information is being inserted.

- *Slide over existing material to make room* moves the existing track information to the right and then inserts the Scrap buffer information.

There are three kinds of objects for pasting.

- *Track events*   If disabled, then no track events are in the Scrap buffer.

- *Tempo changes*   If disabled, then no track events are in the Scrap buffer.

- *Meter/key changes*   If disabled, then no track events are in the Scrap buffer, or the Starting time is not on a measure boundary.

NOTE: *Meter/key signatures are only located on measure boundaries.*

Paste to One track (CTRL-SHIFT-V)

Inserts the contents of the Scrap buffer into any single track. This command can also be used to merge a number of tracks into a single track. Refer to Figure 8-6.

The dialog box that appears when choosing this command has the same options as the *Paste* command dialog box. However, there is an extra box used for identifying which track the information will be pasted to.

Quantize

With the *Quantize* dialog box, shown in Figure 8-7, you can round off MIDI event starting and duration values.

FIGURE 8-6

The Paste to One

track dialog box

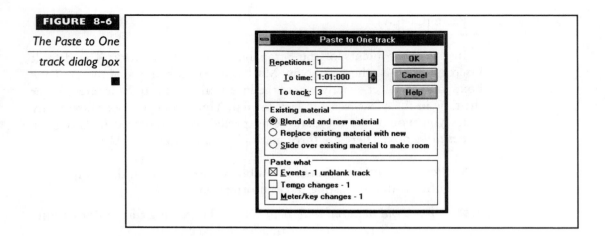

If there are slight timing mistakes in your work, *Quantize* allows you to adjust any and all note events. The adjustment is based on even multiples of ticks, known as *Resolution*.

The range of *Resolution* is from whole notes to 1/32-note triplets. There are two aspects of a MIDI event that can be quantized, *Starting times* and *Durations*. For example, if the *Resolution* is set to 1/4 notes and the *Starting times* and the *Durations* boxes are checked, all MIDI events selected by the *From* and *Thru Markers* will be adjusted to begin on the closest 1/4 note. They will also last for one tick less then a 1/4 note.

Most people would argue that quantizing makes everything sound too exact or mechanical. True, but if you use the *Percent strength* option at something like 75, the region quantized will only be adjusted 75 percent of the way to perfect timing. This option has a range of 1 to 100—100 percent is perfect alignment.

FIGURE 8-7

The Quantize

dialog box

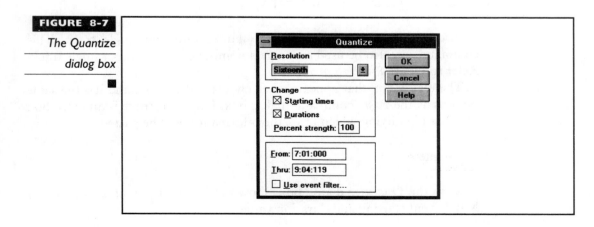

The *Use event filter* is also available for quantizing a more specific series of events.

Length

Alters the *Starting times* and/or *Durations* of notes in a selected region.

By selecting the *Starting times* and/or *Durations* box, each note in the selected region will be expanded or reduced in time. The amount of expansion or reduction depends on the *Percent* box. For example, if a series of 1/4 notes have been selected to have *Starting times* expanded by *Percent 200*, the time between each note will be doubled. With *Durations* checked at *Percent 50*, the note duration is reduced to half its original length.

As usual, the *From* and *Thru* boxes define the region to be altered. Again, the Event Filter can be used to select specific events.

 NOTE: *Percent can only be set to whole numbers (1, 50, 175, and so on), not fractions (such as 1.5, 50.7, 175.25, and so on).*

Slide

Adjusts the start position of a selected region by sliding it forward or backward in time. The *Amount* of time, positive or negative, can be specified in *Measures* or *Ticks*.

Again, the *From* and *Thru* boxes define the region to be altered. In addition, the Event Filter can be used to select specific events.

 TIP: *After this command has been executed, the From and Thru Markers no longer point to the region you moved. They still point to the location the data was in previously.*

Transpose

Allows for the transposition of pitches in a selected region up or down a specified number of steps. The *Amount* of the transposition is chromatic (F, F#, G, G#, and so on) unless *Diatonic math* is checked.

Diatonic math will assure that the transposition remains within a major of the current key. For example, the note F in the key of C transposed +1 will be changed to a G.

The *From*, *Thru*, and *Use Event Filter* boxes are present as usual.

NOTE: *If the Event Filter is used, notes events will be the only events altered and all non-note events will be ignored.*

Controller fill

Similar to the Controller view, described later in this chapter, the *Controller* fill can be used to define a gradual change of a controller event. A specific *MIDI Channel* must be determined, as well as the Value range of the event over the selected region. The *Begin* and *End* ranges from 0 to 127.

Track

The *Track* commands affect the selected track parameters. Most of the commands in this menu can be managed directly from the Track/Measure view.

Name (Double-click in the Track/Measure view)

Allows the labeling of a specified track using up to 15 characters.

Status (Double-click in the Track/Measure view)

Toggles between playing (check mark) and muting (m) the entire track. While being muted, Cakewalk Apprentice continues to process the track information. This processing allows the muting to be toggled during playback.

Archive

The processing of many muted tracks can hinder the sequencer performance. The *Archive* command, a severe muting, tells Cakewalk Apprentice to stop processing the track, thus reducing the amount of processing by the sequencer. In turn, the archived track cannot be toggled on and off during playback.

TIP: *If you encounter any timing problems, Archive the muted tracks you won't be using during playback.*

Loop (Double-click in the Track/Measure view)

Repeats the track a specified number of times:

I	Play once
2–9998	Play the specified number of times
9999	Play until all nonlooped tracks finish

NOTE: *The repeats take place on measure boundaries. Therefore, if the last note of your track is on beat 3 of a 4/4 measure, there will be 1 beat of silence before the loop.*

TIP: *If you want to add a measure of silence to the end of your loop, just place a silent event in that measure. Cakewalk Apprentice will then play through that measure in order to execute that silent event.*

Key+ (Double-click in the Track/Measure view)

Transposes the entire track up or down in pitch with a value of –127 to 127. The value represents the number of half steps the track is to be adjusted.

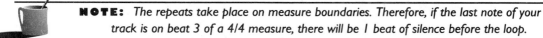
NOTE: *This is not a permanent alteration to the music. You will have to use the Edit/Transpose command for permanency.*

Vel+ (Double-click in the Track/Measure view)

High-end MIDI devices, like the Wave Blaster, are Velocity sensitive. The velocity of a note refers to how hard a note has been attacked. Thus, a note with a high velocity will sound as though it were played fast and hard, whereas a note with a low velocity will sound soft and quiet.

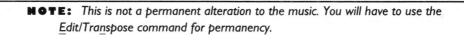
NOTE: *This command is not permanent. You will have to use the Piano Roll view or the Event List view for permanency.*

Time+ (Double-click in the Track/Measure view)

Similar to the *Edit/Slide* command, *Time+* allows the temporary shifting of a track to a later position in time. The amount of the shift is specified in the Measure:Beat:Tick format. For example, if you want to begin a track 5 ticks later than another, you would have to enter 1:1:005 in the *Time+* box.

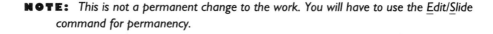
NOTE: *This is not a permanent change to the work. You will have to use the Edit/Slide command for permanency.*

Port (Double-click in the Track/Measure view)

Assigns the selected track to a particular MIDI Out port. The port number corresponds to one of the MIDI Out devices that have been set up in the *Settings/MIDI Devices* dialog box.

Channel (Double-click in the Track/Measure view)

Forces a track to be played through any one of 16 MIDI channels.

NOTE: *If Channel is set to 0, the track will be played through the channel it was originally recorded on.*

Patch (Double-click in the Track/Measure view)

Forces a starting patch to a track. A patch refers to the instrument sound.

NOTE: *Patch change messages later in the track will still take effect.*

Volume (Double-click in the Track/Measure view)

Forces a starting volume to a track.

NOTE: *Volume change messages later in the track will still take effect.*

Pan (Double-click in the Track/Measure view)

Forces a starting pan position to a track. A pan value of 127 pans the track to full right, whereas a pan value of 0 pans the track to full left. Thus, a pan value of 63 is center. If you would like to turn pan off, –1 can be used.

NOTE: *Pan parameter change messages later in the track will still take effect.*

Solo (/)

Mutes all tracks except the one being assigned a solo status.

Un-solo (\)

Returns all tracks to their original status, before a track solo was initiated.

Clone

Completely copies all track events and/or parameters to another track of your choice.

Kill

Eliminates all events and parameters from the selected tracks.

CAUTION: *Undo will not work with this command.*

Wipe

Removes all events in the selected tracks while leaving the track parameters.

CAUTION: *Undo will not work with this command.*

Window

This pull-down menu, shown in Figure 8-8, is divided into three sections for controlling which views are open and how they are organized.

- The top third has two commands *New* and *Options*.

- The middle third contains the standard Windows manipulation commands.

- The bottom third is designated for opening the minimized icons at the bottom of the Cakewalk Apprentice screen.

FIGURE 8-8
The Window
pull-down menu
■

New
Options

Tile in rows
Tile in columns
Cascade
Arrange Icons
Close all

√ 1 Track/Measure
2 Comments
3 Tempo
4 Meter/Key
5 Markers

New

Opens one of the four views listed:

Piano-Roll
Event List
Controllers
Staff

These views will be discussed later in this chapter.

TIP: *By holding down the right mouse button anywhere in Cakewalk Apprentice, the New menu of views will be displayed. Just select the view you would like to open.*

Options

Contains three functions for setting the Cakewalk Apprentice preferences.

■ *Auto-activate* provides the unusual feature of automatically activating a window where the pointer is located. Usually in Windows, you must click in a window for it to become active.

■ *Control Bar at Bottom* will place the control bar at the bottom of the screen instead of the top.

■ *DOS F6 View Keys* assists those familiar with Cakewalk for DOS. This function allows the same F6 commands used in Cakewalk for DOS to open and close views:

F6	Close an active Piano-Roll or Event List view and open the Track/Measure view.
CTRL-F6	Open the Event list view.
ALT-F6	Open the Piano-roll view.

Settings

This list of commands allows for the setting of the MIDI environment.

Metronome

The *Metronome* dialog box, seen in Figure 8-9, allows for adjusting the qualities of the metronome.

The metronome can be heard during playback, recording, or both, by selecting the appropriate box or boxes. The *Accent first beat* box will give

FIGURE 8-9

The Metronome

dialog box

■

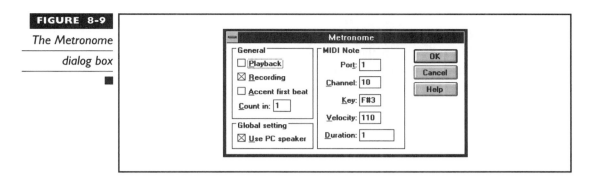

a heavier accent to the first beat of every measure. There is also an option that will allow you to state how many measures should be heard as a *Count in* before recording begins.

The metronome can be heard through the PC speaker and/or your MIDI device. You can turn off the PC speaker by selecting the *Use PC speaker* box. The metronome sound you hear through your MIDI device is defined in the MIDI note section of the dialog box. To disable the MIDI metronome, set velocity to "0".

MIDI Devices

This command brings up the same dialog box that was seen during installation of Cakewalk Apprentice (Figure 8-1). If you change the MIDI device being used, a new driver will have to be selected using this command.

Patch names

Configures a port and channel to have a specific MIDI patch list associated with it. As seen in Figure 8-10, this dialog box contains two lists.

FIGURE 8-10

The Configure

patch name lists

dialog box

■

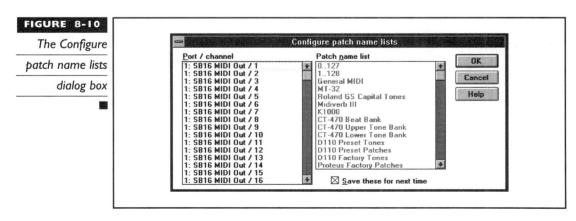

The left side is a list of all ports and channels that are currently available. On the right are the available MIDI patch presets. For one of the Sound Blaster series or the Wave Blaster, you will want to choose the General MIDI patch set for each channel.

MIDI Thru

The *MIDI Thru* command controls how MIDI signals are directed from the master MIDI device. Cakewalk Apprentice has three MIDI Thru modes available (see Figure 8-11):

None	Disables MIDI Thru.
Manual	Enables MIDI Thru, allowing you to control the mapping options.
Auto	Enables MIDI Thru and automatically controls the mapping options by following the parameters of the current track.

Here is a list of the four mapping parameters that are enabled when in the Manual mode.

Port	Destination port.
Channel	Channel to follow. "0" means the channel is not mapped.
Key	Desired note transposition.
Velocity	Desired velocity transposition.

When the Local On Port box is checked, sound will be heard from the synthesizer connected when it is played. If Local Control is off, the synthesizer will only be heard when MIDI data is received by the MIDI In port.

NOTE: *Unless you have a MIDI synthesizer connected that does not have Local Control Off capabilities, set the Local On Port value to zero.*

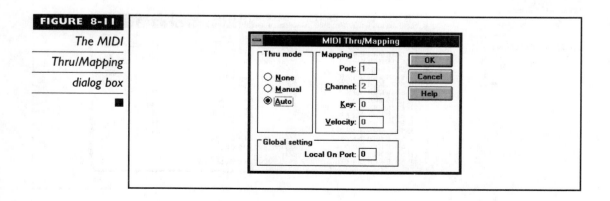

FIGURE 8-11

The MIDI Thru/Mapping dialog box ■

MIDI Out

Controls what is sent to the MIDI Out port.

TRANSMIT MIDI START/CONTINUE/STOP/CLOCK   This option sends MIDI sync information, allowing devices to sync with Cakewalk Apprentice.

TIP: *If this box is not checked, performance should show improvement. However, some synchronization may occur.*

USE START, NEVER CONTINUE   When this option is checked, Cakewalk Apprentice will always begin playback at the start of the work, even if you pause in the middle or place the Now Marker at a specific location.

SEND MIDI SPP   This option is for MIDI devices that can receive MIDI Song Position Pointers (SPP). The SPP number determines where playback should begin. *Locate delay for SPP recipient* gives receiving MIDI devices time to respond to the SPP message. The delay is specified in eighteenths of a second. For example, by placing a "3" in the box there will be a 3/18-second delay.

ZERO CONTINUOUS CONTROLLERS   If this box is checked, Cakewalk Apprentice will reset the pitch wheel, pedals, modulation wheel, and all other continuous controllers on all 16 MIDI channels when playback stops.

TIP: *If you experience "stuck notes" after playback ends, the sustain pedal controller might still be on. If this box is checked, all such events are turned off after playback.*

PATCH/WHEEL/CONTROLLER SEARCH-BACK   If starting playback in a position other than the beginning of your work, checking this box will have Cakewalk Apprentice search backward to locate the most recent settings for the patch, wheel, and other controller events. The time this will take depends on how far back from the Now Marker Cakewalk Apprentice has to search.

TIP: *If you have not altered any of these events during your work, there is no need to check this box.*

Time Format

Allows for the setting of a SMPTE/MTC time format and starting offset as seen in Figure 8-12.

The SMPTE/MTC time format is used when synchronizing sound and video or film. This dialog box displays four possible frame rates to choose from. You also have the ability to select the amount of delay to ensure proper synchronization by using the offset box.

FIGURE 8-12

The Time format

dialog box

■

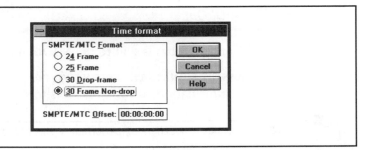

NOTE: *If you intend to work with sound and video synchronization, it is assumed you have knowledge of SMPTE.*

Help

Cakewalk Apprentice has an extensive online help system that can be accessed via this pull-down menu.

CONTROL BAR

art of Cakewalk Apprentice's main window, the Control Bar gives you quick access to many of the pull-down menu commands that have been previously discussed. Refer to Figure 8-13.

NOTE: *The default position of the Control Bar is at the top of the screen. This can be changed to the bottom of the screen by using the Window/Options/Control bar at bottom command.*

Now Marker and SMPTE/MTC Time

The time box in the upper-left corner of the Control Bar allows for setting the Now Marker in the Measure:Beat:Tick format. This time can also be set by using the *Goto/Time* command or F5.

FIGURE 8-13

The Control Bar

■

Below the Now Marker time is the same time in the SMPTE/MTC format (Hour:Minutes:Seconds:Frames). To the left of the SMPTE time is a box for choosing the number of frames per second. By default, it is set to 30-frame Non-drop. This box accesses the *Settings/Time format* command.

Now Marker Scroll Bar

Just to the right of the Now Marker time is the Now Marker scroll bar. This scroll bar can be used to quickly move to the previous or next beat or measure.

Rewind, Play, and Record Buttons

Directly below the Now Marker scroll bar can be found three buttons for Rewind, Play, and Record.

The Rewind button is a shortcut for the *Realtime/Rewind* command. It stops playback or record and moves the Now Marker to the beginning of the work.

The Play button is a shortcut for the *Realtime/Play* command. It starts and stops playback from the current position. Another shortcut is SPACEBAR.

The Record button is a shortcut for the *Realtime/Record* command. It starts and stops the recording process.

For more information, refer to the previously discussed *Realtime/Record* command.

Step Record Button

The button with the footprints is the Step record button. This is the shortcut for selecting the *Realtime/Step record* command.

For more information, refer to the previously discussed *Realtime/Step record* command.

Help Button

The "?" button beneath the Step record button is for easy access to the help file.

From and Thru

These boxes show the From and Thru time of the currently selected region. These are shortcuts for the *Mark/From* and *Mark/Thru* commands. For more information, refer to corresponding menu commands previously discussed.

Tempo

To the right of the From box you can change the tempo to your liking. Click either the arrow buttons or the tempo itself. Default is set to 100 beats per minute.

Tempo Ratios

These three boxes and buttons provide you with the ability to multiply the tempo by the chosen amount. For example, if you want to listen to your work at twice the speed, click on the button beneath the "2.00" box. If you want to specify a different multiple, just click on the value you want to change.

NOTE: *The default ratios have been chosen as slow, normal, and fast-forward playback rates.*

Meter

The default setting for the meter is 4/4 (four quarter notes per measure). If you change this value, the entire work will take on the new meter.

NOTE: *If you want to change an individual measure or section of measures, refer to the Meter/Key view discussed later in this chapter.*

Panic Button

The Panic button stops playback and sends note-off commands to all notes, channels, ports, and controllers. You might need to use this if you experience MIDI feedback loops or stuck notes.

VIEWS

n this final section of the chapter we will be using the file SWINGER.WRK that came with the book. This will be somewhat like a tutorial but will contain important information about all the views Cakewalk Apprentice offers for your writing and editing needs. After discussing the five main views, we will take a look at the four icons at the bottom of the screen.

From the main view let's open SWINGER.WRK by using CTRL-Q

NOTE: *It is assumed you have set every channel in port 1 to be a General MIDI patch by using the Settings/Patch names command. If you haven't, do so now by referring to the Settings/Patch names command previously discussed.*

Track/Measure View

Now take a look at the Track/Measure view in Figure 8-14.

The Track/Measure view is divided into two sections. On the left is the Track pane, which allows you to manipulate different parameters for all 256 available tracks. On the right, the Measure pane displays which measures of each track contain events.

Track Pane

All of the available parameters have been covered in detail during the discussion of the *Track* pull-down menu earlier in this chapter. The parameters can all be accessed by double-clicking in the corresponding field.

PORT, CHN, OR PATCH FIELD   The dialog box that appears when double-clicking in the Port, Chn, or Patch field is different from the ones that appeared when using the menu commands. See Figure 8-15.

As you can see, here you can change the Port, Channel, Patch, Key+, Vel+, Pan, and Volume settings. For more details on these parameters, refer to the *Track* pull-down menu commands discussed earlier in this chapter.

TIP: *You can use this method of manipulation to preview what a track will sound like with a different instrument during playback.*

FIGURE 8-14
The
Track/Measure
view ■

	Name	✓	Loop	Key+	Vel+	Time+	Port	Chn	Patch	Vol	Pan	Size		5	9	13
1	Drums	✓	1	0	0	0	1: S	10	-none-	---	---					
2	Toms	✓	1	0	0	0	1: S	10	-none-	---	---					
3	Cymbals	✓	1	0	0	0	1: S	10	-none-	---	---	2				
4	Bass	✓	1	0	0	0	1: S	2	Electri	---	---	1				
5	Brass	✓	1	0	0	0	1: S	1	Brass	90	---	1				
6	Brass 2	✓	1	0	0	0	1: S	1	Brass	90	---	1				
7	Hammond	✓	1	0	0	0	1: S	3	Hamm	---	---					
8	WAV files	✓	1	0	0	0	1: S	--	-none-	---	---					
9																
10																

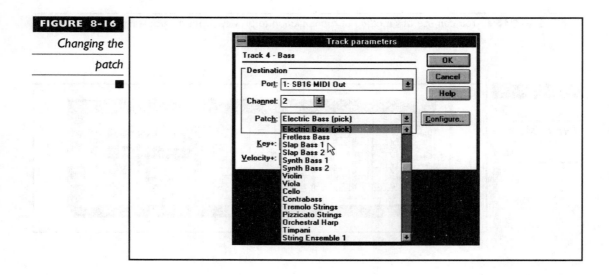

FIGURE 8-15

Track

parameters

dialog box

Let's try it:

1. Click on the Play button.

2. Double-click in the Patch field on track 4.

3. Click on the highlighted *Patch* box.

4. In this pull-down menu click on Slap Bass 1, as in Figure 8-16.

Hear the difference?

PARAMETER COLUMNS   In the Track pane you can place parameter columns in any order you like. Just click and hold the parameter column name you want to move, drag it to the location where you want to place it, and drop.

FIGURE 8-16

Changing the

patch

There is also a parameter column we have never discussed. Size displays the number of events in that particular track. This number will change whenever you add or delete an event from its corresponding track.

For editing or viewing in other multitrack windows (Staff and Event-list), you can click on the track number to the far left of each track you want to work with. These are called "sticky" tracks. You can clear a "sticky" track selection by clicking on the track number again. If you will be using many tracks, you can click and drag down the column to make other tracks the same, either "sticky" or clear. A "sticky" track is identified by reverse video over the track number.

NOTE: *Double-clicking on a "sticky" track number will clear all "sticky" tracks. Double-clicking on a clear track will make all nonblank tracks "sticky."*

Measure Pane

Each track is represented by a row of cells. A cell is a measure and can be in one of three states:

Nothing	Blank track.
Dash	Empty measure.
Circle	Measure containing at least one MIDI event.

From this view you can see the structure of your work and do some block editing.

NOW MARKER   The Now Marker can be changed by clicking on the desired measure.

FROM AND THRU MARKERS   The From and Thru Markers can be set to select a sequence of measures with a click and drag across the track. The selected measures are shown in reverse video.

If you choose to extend what you have already selected, hold the SHIFT key and point to the measure you want to extend to.

If you want to clear the From and Thru selection, just click anywhere in the selection.

CAUTION: *Be careful not to drag the selection to another location when clearing the From and Thru selection.*

BLOCK EDITING   You can drag selected blocks of measures to new locations by using the mouse.

To move a selected block:

1. Point anywhere within the selected block.

2. Hold the left mouse button down.

3. Wait for the cursor to change shape.

4. Drag the new cursor to where you want the block to start (even a different track if you like).

5. Release the mouse button.

To copy a selected block, follow the above procedure while holding down the CTRL key.

Dropped blocks of measures replace existing material and don't leave a hole where they have come from. If you change your mind while using this feature, you can press the ESC key, drag the block outside of the Measure pane, or use the *Edit/Undo* (CTRL-Z) command.

This can be useful for doubling selected blocks with a different instrument. In Figure 8-17 you can see where the Hammond Organ section has been copied to Track 9 and a Choir has been used to double the part.

NOTE: *If you don't want to replace existing material, then you should use the command in the *Edit* pull-down menu previously mentioned in this chapter.*

OPENING OTHER VIEWS   You can quickly access four other editing views by using the right mouse button. These views are the Piano-roll, Event-list, Controllers, and Staff.

Right-click anywhere in the Track pane, select the view you want, and that view will open where the Now Marker is pointing to.

Right-click on a particular measure cell in the Measure pane, select the view you want, and that view will open at the measure you clicked on.

FIGURE 8-17

Using block

editing

techniques to

double an

instrumental track

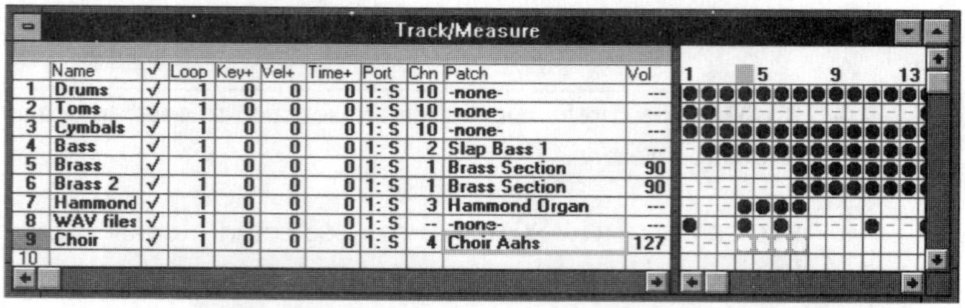

	Name	√	Loop	Key+	Vel+	Time+	Port	Chn	Patch	Vol
1	Drums	√	1	0	0	0	1: S	10	-none-	---
2	Toms	√	1	0	0	0	1: S	10	-none-	---
3	Cymbals	√	1	0	0	0	1: S	10	-none-	---
4	Bass	√	1	0	0	0	1: S	2	Slap Bass 1	---
5	Brass	√	1	0	0	0	1: S	1	Brass Section	90
6	Brass 2	√	1	0	0	0	1: S	1	Brass Section	90
7	Hammond	√	1	0	0	0	1: S	3	Hammond Organ	---
8	WAV files	√	1	0	0	0	1: S	--	-none-	---
9	Choir	√	1	0	0	0	1: S	4	Choir Aahs	127
10										

Track/Measure

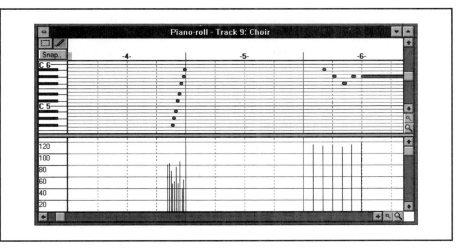

Piano-Roll View

The Piano-roll view can only display one track at a time. Pitch is displayed vertically, and time is displayed horizontally.

Like the Track/Measure view, the Piano-roll view has two panes. When opened, the Piano-roll view shows the Note pane only. The other pane available in this view is the Velocity pane. When you pass the cursor over the gray bar above the bottom scroll bar, you can see the cursor change to up/down arrows. Click, hold, and drag the gray bar up to expose the Velocity pane (see Figure 8-18).

You will also notice the magnifying glass icons in the lower-right corner. There are two sets. The set on the bottom scroll bar will increase or decrease the number of measures visible in the two panes. The set on the right scroll bar will enlarge or reduce the thickness of the notes in the Note pane.

Note Pane

There are three buttons in the upper-left corner of the Note pane: Select, Draw, and Snap.

SELECT   Allows you to set the From and Thru Markers by dragging the mouse. The selected area will appear in reverse video.

DRAW   Allows you to insert, change, and audition notes:

■ To insert a note, just hold down the CTRL key and click with the left mouse button. You now have a note placed. For as long as you hold the mouse button, you may move the note to any position you desire. If you hold the CTRL key and click on an existing note, the note will be copied and you can place it wherever you like. If you have already dragged or deleted a note and you hold down the CTRL key while clicking, the previous note is copied and available for placement.

■ To delete a note, click and hold the left mouse button on the note to be deleted. Now press the DEL key.

■ The part of the note you click on—left, middle, or right—will determine how you can alter an existing note:

Left   This changes the position of a note. By clicking on the left third of a note, the cursor will turn into a left-right arrow. This, in turn, allows you to drag the note to a new place in time without changing the pitch.

Middle   This changes the pitch of a note. By clicking on the middle third of a note, the cursor will turn into an up-down arrow. In turn, this allows you to drag the note to a new pitch without changing the position in time. In this mode the note will also sound.

Right   This changes the duration of a note. By clicking on the right third of a note, the cursor will turn into a left-right arrow. In turn, this allows you to stretch or shrink the note to a new length of duration without changing the position of pitch.

SNAP   The Snap button allows you to round off start times and the duration of notes.

NOTE PARAMETERS   Click on a note with the right mouse button, and a dialog box appears allowing you to alter the note parameters. See Figure 8-19. Some of the parameters aren't even displayed by the Piano-roll view.

AUDITIONING (SCRUBBING)   If you click on any blank location in time and hold the mouse button down, a vertical line will appear, as in Figure 8-20.

FIGURE 8-19

Note parameters

dialog box

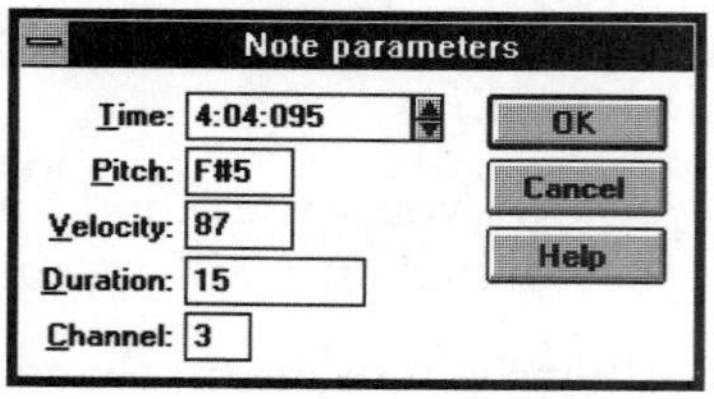

Note parameters

Time: 4:04:095
Pitch: F#5
Velocity: 87
Duration: 15
Channel: 3

OK
Cancel
Help

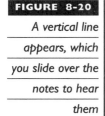

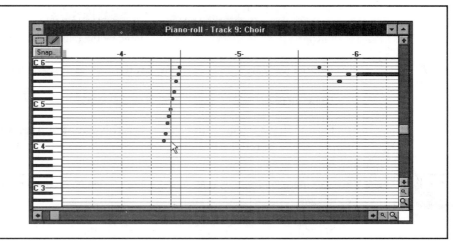

While keeping the mouse button depressed, you can drag the line from side to side and hear the notes it passes over.

TIP: *This can be quite useful for finding bad notes or checking how chords sound.*

Velocity Pane

This pane is always in Draw mode and contains the velocity of each note. You can increase or decrease the velocity by adjusting the height of its velocity mark. Gradual increases or decreases can be achieved by drawing an upward or a downward curve over a specified region.

NOTE: *Velocity is not a separate event type. It is an attribute of a note event, like pitch or duration.*

Event-List View

This view displays all MIDI events in a list from top to bottom. Each event has its own line, which includes the track, location in time, channel, type of event, and values for that event. You can even view more than one track at a time in chronological order from the Event-list view.

The highlight represents the Now Marker and will scroll during playback to show the current position. The following is a list of the available events and the values associated with them.

NOTE   A MIDI note with three value parameters:

Pitch	Represented by the MIDI key number as a note and octave.
Velocity (0–127)	How fast the key was pressed, thus defining the volume of the note.
Duration (Beat:Tick)	How long the note lasts.

PATCH   There is only one value for this event. Either the number or the name of the patch.

NOTE: *For more information, refer to the earlier discussion on the Settings/Patch names command.*

CONTROL   Two value parameters are available for MIDI controller events.

- Controller number (0–127)
- Controller value (0–127)

WHEEL   There is one value for the pitch wheel event. Wheel position from −8192 through 8192, where 0 is center.

KEYAFT   There are two values for the "key after touch" event.

- A pitch that represents the MIDI key number where the key after touch is being applied.
- The pressure amount (0–127).

CHANAFT   The one value available for the "channel after touch" event is pressure amount (0–127).

SYSX   This event is not supported by Cakewalk Apprentice.
The MIDI System Exclusive event is only displayed for file compatibility with Cakewalk Professional for Windows.

MCICMD   This event has one parameter, the text of the Media Control Interface (MCI) command. These commands allow you to control other multimedia devices during playback of your work.
For more information on MCI commands, you can refer to the *Multimedia Programmer's Reference*, published by Microsoft Press.

WAVE   The wave event has one parameter, the wave audio data itself. Information about the wave length and format is displayed. If you move to

FIGURE 8-21

The event list for track 8 of SWINGER.WRK

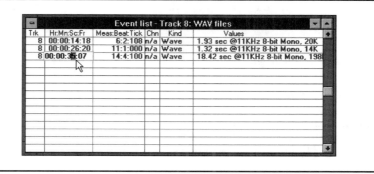

track 8 in SWINGER.WRK and open the Event-list view as previously described, you will see the list of wave files used, as shown in Figure 8-21.

Here we will make a change to the last wave file by starting it two seconds earlier and save a wave from SWINGER.WRK to a file. It is easy to change the location in time of an event—just double-click on the time associated with the event and type in a new time, as above in Figure 8-21.

To save a wave to a file from Cakewalk Apprentice, it is necessary to double-click on the duration of the wave in the Values column. This will bring up the dialog box shown in Figure 8-22.

Choose Save wave to a file, and a "save as" dialog box will appear. Select a filename and press ENTER. The wave file is now saved to your disk.

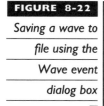

WARNING: This feature will only work if you have correctly installed the wave audio driver that came with your sound card.

TEXT   There is only one value parameter for this event: text. This is a simple vehicle for inserting text into a track at a specified place in time. After a text

FIGURE 8-22

Saving a wave to file using the Wave event dialog box

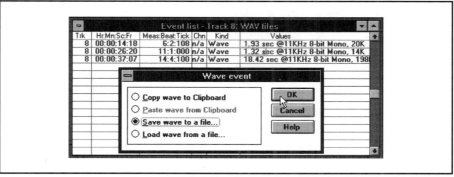

event has been placed, you can type approximately 80 characters in the Values field.

TIP: *You might find a situation where you want a track to repeat after four measures but you only have three measures of events. Adding a text event into the fourth measure would not create any sound and would extend the track length.*

TIP: *You can use this feature to position lyrics for your work. As the work plays the highlight will scroll down like a "bouncing ball" prompter.*

Changing an Event

To change a parameter of a specific event, just double-click in the field that you wish to change. If you are changing the kind of event, a dialog box will appear with the event types available to you, as described earlier.

Inserting an Event

To insert an event in the Event-list view, just click in the list where you want the event to occur. Pressing the INSERT key will copy the event you are currently pointing to. After the event has been copied, you can change the parameters to whatever you desire.

Deleting an Event

To delete an event in the Event-list view, just click in the list where you want the deletion to occur. Pressing the DEL key will remove the event.

NOTE: *Use the Edit/Cut command to delete more than one event at a time.*

Step-Playing Events

While in the Event-list view, there are two ways of auditioning single events.

- With the keyboard, all you have to do is hold down the SHIFT and SPACEBAR keys simultaneously. The event you are currently on will play. If the event is a note or wave event, when the SPACEBAR is released the sound will stop.

■ With the mouse, hold down the SHIFT key and click on the event you want to audition. If the event is a note or wave event, when the SHIFT key is released the sound will stop.

Controllers View

The Controllers view is a graphical representation of MIDI controller events for a single track. The vertical axis represents the value of the controller event, whereas the horizontal axis represents where in time the event is located.

Controller Types

Each track can contain many different types of controller events. However, you will only be able to view one controller type at a time.

If you wish to view and edit a different type of controller, just click on the drop-down list as in Figure 8-23.

Some of the 120 controller types have not been assigned. These can be used by MIDI manufacturers.

You can also select a different MIDI channel by using the above method with the appropriate drop-down list.

NOTE: *Don't forget that a track can contain more than one MIDI channel, and a MIDI channel can contain more than one controller type.*

Controller Edit Modes

The three buttons in the upper-left corner of the Controller view are for choosing the desired edit mode.

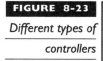

FIGURE 8-23

Different types of controllers

■

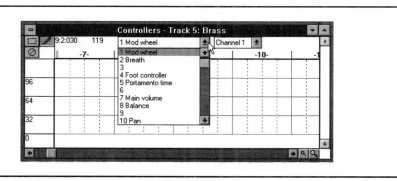

SELECT MODE   The button with the dashed rectangle enables the select mode. When enabled, just click, hold, and drag to the right. This sets the From and Thru Markers. The selected region appears in reverse video.

DRAW MODE   Draw mode is enabled by clicking on the button with the pencil on it. This will allow you to draw the controller changes with your mouse. After you have selected the controller type and channel you want to draw, hold down the left mouse button and draw the shape you want. When you release the mouse button, the view will be updated to represent the new controller event values.

Let's change the volume of the brass section so that it will peak at measure 14.

1. Open the Controllers view on Track 5 at measure 7.

2. Choose "main volume" as your controller type.

3. Click on the Draw mode button.

4. Use the magnifying glass to view from measure 7 through measure 15.

5. Draw the events as in Figure 8-24.

When you release your mouse button you should see something similar to Figure 8-25. (If you make a mistake, just use the Erase mode, described next.) Now play the work. The horns should get louder toward the end.

ERASE MODE   The remaining button with the octagon on it enables the Erase mode. If you make a mistake while drawing your controllers, just enable this mode, click, and drag. The region you drag over will turn red. The controller events in this region will be deleted.

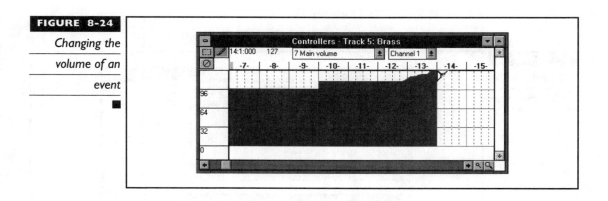

FIGURE 8-24

Changing the volume of an event

FIGURE 8-25

Results of the

volume change

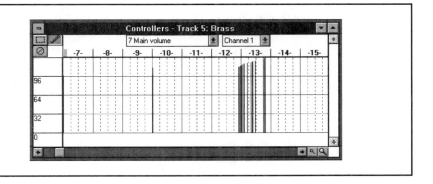

Staff View

The Staff view allows for sequencer data to be viewed as staff notation. There are some basic editing capabilities associated with this view.

The Layout

The Staff view can display up to ten staves at once. If you want to view ten tracks, they must all use only one staff each.

Cakewalk Apprentice will automatically select the appropriate clef (bass or treble) for the track you are viewing. This is done by checking the range of pitches used in the track.

If you choose to change which clef is used, simply click on the Layout button. The Staff View Layout dialog box will appear listing track names and their appropriate clefs. See Figure 8-26.

If you choose Treble/Bass, the track is split into two staves. This uses up two of the available ten staves when viewing. Using the Treble/Bass selection will also give you the option of where to place the split point. The split point is the lowest note that should be included in the treble clef.

FIGURE 8-26

Staff View Layout

dialog box

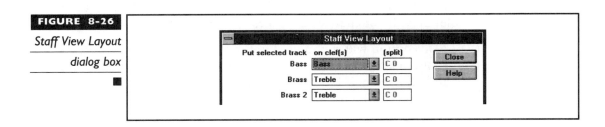

Editing Notes

The Staff view is similar to the Piano-roll view when it comes to manipulation of notes. Therefore, you should refer to the section on the Piano-roll view with regard to inserting notes, copying notes, deleting notes, and changing note parameters.

MOVING AN EXISTING NOTE   Click on the note and drag it to the desired pitch and/or location.

- *Snap-to time*   This check box determines whether the note you are moving is snapped in time based on its duration. For example, if you want to insert an eighth note and Snap-to time is checked, the note will be snapped to the closest eighth-note boundary. This is very useful when entering a series of notes. However, if you want to adjust an eighth note back in time by a sixteenth note, you will have to disable the Snap-to feature. This is also true for inserting notes over measure bar lines.

- *Snap-to key signature*   There is no check box for this feature. It is an automatic feature that can be tricky to disable.

When moving a note to a different pitch, it is automatically snapped to the pitches in the current key signature (diatonically). To drag a note in half steps (chromatically), it is necessary to tap the right mouse button while holding the left button down and dragging the note. This is a toggle switch only for that particular note. The next time you drag a note the diatonic mode is reset.

Other Options

Three other options remain: Resolution, Fill, and Trim.

RESOLUTION   Just for Staff view display purposes, this option is similar to the *Edit/Quantize* command, but does not alter the timing of the notes. Resolution will not change how notes appear in any other view.

FILL   This option will round up durations to the next beat or note, whichever comes first. For example, if a performer was supposed to play a quarter note and released a 1/32 note before the duration should have ended, Fill would extend the duration to the full quarter-note value.

TRIM   The opposite of Fill, Trim will cut off the durations that extend slightly into other notes.

THE FOUR ICON VIEWS

here are just four items left to be covered: the four icon views at the bottom of the main window.

Comments

This view is basically a notepad for jotting down your comments about your work. When the work is saved, so are your comments. The editing commands allow you to work with the Windows Clipboard, enabling you to move text from the Comments view to other Windows applications. The lines will automatically wrap when you reach the right side of the window, so only press ENTER when you desire a new paragraph.

You can have your comments appear automatically when the work is opened by placing the @ character in the upper-left corner. This feature can be quite useful when sharing files with other people. You may even decide to place a copyright notice in your work this way.

Tempo

The Tempo view is a graphical representation of any tempo changes in your work. Just like the Controllers view, you plot the tempo values by drawing with the mouse.

Time is displayed in the horizontal axis, whereas beats per minute (BPM) is shown in the vertical axis. Both the horizontal and vertical scroll bars have a set of magnifying glasses for zooming in and out.

The Tempo view, like the Controllers view, has three modes for editing: Select, Draw, and Erase. Please refer to the Controllers view section previously described for the details.

Meter/Key View

This view will allow you to define meter and key changes on measure boundaries. When first opened, the Meter/Key view will have one entry, the default entry, 4/4 in the key of C.

Click on the Add button if you would like to add a new meter or key. You will be prompted by a dialog box for the location, meter, and key for the new entry.

Click on the Change button if you wish to change an existing entry. Be sure to click on the entry you wish to change before selecting the Change button. You will be able to change either the meter or key, but not the location.

If you decide to change the location of an entry, select it and click on Add. Change the information in the dialog box to reflect the location of your choice, and then delete the original entry.

To delete an entry, just click on the unwanted entry and then click on Delete. If you would like to delete a series of entries, drag the mouse over the unwanted entries to select them, then click on Delete.

CAUTION: *Adding or deleting entries will alter the measures that follow.*

Meter changes will affect Cakewalk Apprentice in the following ways:

- Metronome accents
- How Measure:Beat:Tick times are calculated and displayed
- How the Staff view is drawn

Key changes will affect how Cakewalk Apprentice displays pitches. An E$^\flat$ will still sound like an E$^\flat$.

Markers View

Markers are primarily used for indicating "hit points" when scoring film or video. However, you can use markers for other things as well. Markers are very useful as section indicators for large pieces of music. Markers use both musical and SMPTE time formats.

Markers are always listed in chronological order within the Markers view. You may have more than one marker for a specific time.

To add a new marker, simply click on the Add button and a dialog box appears. Complete the dialog box by naming the marker and locking it to SMPTE (if you choose), and set the location where you want the marker placed.

To change a marker, select it and click on Change. Again, complete the dialog box to your liking. If you have changed the location of the marker, it will automatically be placed in its designated position in the list.

To delete a marker, select it and click on Delete. The *Edit/Undo* command will not replace a deleted marker.

CAKEWALK PROFESSIONAL FOR WINDOWS

A

s mentioned at the beginning of this chapter, Cakewalk Apprentice for Windows is a complete sequencing software package. However, it is also a scaled-down version of Twelve Tone Systems' Cakewalk Professional for Windows. Appendix A of the Cakewalk Apprentice for Windows User's Guide outlines the features that are only available in the professional package.

If you find the need for the few features that have been removed, you can obtain Cakewalk Professional for Windows by contacting Twelve Tone Systems directly. You will find contact information in your Cakewalk Apprentice for Windows User's Guide.

9

Sequencer Plus Pro

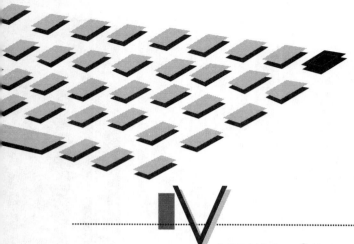

V O Y E T R A ' S Sequencer Plus Pro (Sp Pro) is an introductory DOS-based MIDI sequencing and editing program that comes bundled with the Sound Blaster Pro and the Sound Blaster MIDI Kit. This MIDI kit can be purchased for the Sound Blaster, Sound Blaster Pro Basic, and the Sound Blaster MCV versions. Sp Pro is nearly identical to Voyetra's entry-level sequencing software, the Sequencer Plus Junior.

In this chapter you will find some tips and advice on using Sp Pro. The information included here was selected according to three criteria: some facts are already presented in the Sp Pro manual, but not adequately emphasized. Some information wasn't available when the Sp Pro manual or disk was produced. And some of the information is new, based on feedback from the Voyetra technical support staff.

The following topics are covered:

- Installation issues, particularly everything you ever wanted to know about TAPI drivers.

- What actually happens when you load Sp Pro?

- Demystification of how the File Load command works.

- How to add stereo effects with the stereo panning feature.

- How to lay down drum parts.

- Installing and running Sp Pro under Windows 3.1.

- Miscellaneous hardware tips, including getting your MIDI keyboard to talk to Sp Pro and selecting your monitor's display mode.

If you haven't already worked through the Tutorial of the Sp Pro manual, this is a good time to do so. There you will find all the basic program commands; we are assuming you already have a familiarity with operating

Sp Pro, such as how to start and stop song play (by pressing the SPACEBAR) and how to delete all the tracks (by the Delete All command).

CONNECTING MIDI INSTRUMENTS TO THE SOUND BLASTER

This section provides extensive background on the TAPI drivers and Creative Labs sound board versions. The Sp Pro software will misbehave if the correct driver is not loaded, and the information presented here may save you time in diagnosing a problem. This information supplements the installation instructions provided in your Sp Pro manual.

NOTE: *The illustrations and figures in this section display the 25-row screens of a CGA or monochrome/Hercules graphics monitor. If you have a high-resolution EGA or VGA monitor, your screens will look different from those illustrated here. Sp Pro takes advantage of your higher-resolution monitor to display more tracks or other information. In this book we have used the 25-row screen shots because they are easier to see on the printed page.*

All the Sound Blaster cards have a MIDI (Musical Instrument Digital Interface) port built in. The MIDI international standard defines how synthesizers, musical keyboards, and computers should communicate. By means of this standard, all electronic instruments can communicate regardless of their origin or of the make of computer.

MIDI data is in digital form and consists of a variety of messages. The most commonly used are Note On (when to play a note), Note Off (when to stop playing a note), Velocity (how loudly to play the note), and Instrument Number (what instrument should play the note).

Two pins on the Sound Blaster's joystick connector are used to receive MIDI data (MIDI In) and send MIDI data (MIDI Out). If you own a Sound Blaster Pro, the interface cable necessary for MIDI connections is included. If you own a Sound Blaster 1.*x*/2.0 or a Sound Blaster Pro Basic, you can purchase the MIDI Kit from Creative Labs, Inc.

The MIDI interface cable connects to the joystick port on the Sound Blaster card. On one end of the cable is a 15-pin male connector that plugs into the joystick port. On the other end is a female 15-pin connector and two 5-pin DIN-type connectors (the round ones). The female 15-pin connector is for your joystick, so that you don't lose the functionality of the joystick connector on the Sound Blaster card. The two 5-pin DINs are the MIDI In and MIDI Out connectors and are labeled as such.

When connecting a MIDI instrument such as a keyboard, the Out cable from the Sound Blaster MIDI interface connects to the In port on the back of the keyboard; and the In cable of the Sound Blaster MIDI interface connects to the Out port of the keyboard. This may sound backward to you at first; to make it easier to understand, just remember that the data that comes *out* of the Sound Blaster goes *into* to the keyboard, and the data that comes *out* of the keyboard goes *into* the Sound Blaster.

Some keyboards and synthesizer modules also have a MIDI Thru connector. This connection simply duplicates any data that comes into the In port. By connecting a cable from the Thru port to another synthesizer's In port, the computer or keyboard can control two MIDI instruments. Then, if the second MIDI instrument also has a Thru port, it can be connected to the In port of another MIDI instrument.

CAUTION: *Hooking up more than a few synthesizers by means of MIDI Thru ports can affect the timing of music playback. The Thru port incurs a very short delay when copying the information from the In port. Thus, after several copies, a note can be noticeably delayed.*

Once you have made the proper connections, anything you play on the keyboard can be recorded by the computer. Likewise, any data in the computer can be played back on the keyboard. Of course, you need software to accomplish the recording and playback; this software is called a *sequencer*. Voyetra's Sequencer Plus that comes with your Pro card (or MIDI Kit if you bought it separately) is just the software you need to record, edit, and play back your musical compositions.

Understanding the TAPI Driver

Sp Pro uses a special driver called the TAPI driver. (TAPI is an acronym for Tertiary Application Program Interface; "tertiary" because TAPI complements Voyetra's SAPI and VAPI drivers.) The TAPI driver allows the Sp Pro software to talk to the Creative Labs Sound Blaster sound cards. Because Sp Pro uses this software driver, a single version of the program can work with all versions of Sound Blaster and Sound Blaster Pro.

The TAPI driver is a terminate-and-stay-resident program (TSR) that, once loaded, remains in memory. In order for Sp Pro to work, you must first load the correct TAPI driver. When you are done with Sp Pro, the TAPI driver is removed to free memory for other applications. The SP.BAT batch file that you use to start SP Pro, automatically loads the TAPI driver before it runs SPPro. After you quit SP Pro, the batch file automatically removes TAPI before it returns control to you at the DOS prompt.

There are two different TAPI drivers for the Sound Blaster: TAPISB and TAPISB3. TAPISB is used with the Sound Blaster 1.*x*/2.0 cards and the two-operator Sound Blaster Pro card. TAPISB3 is used with the newer four-operator Sound Blaster Pro 2 (CT-1600 is stenciled clearly on the Pro 2 circuit board; look for it close to the top edge). The installation program for Sp Pro examines the SET BLASTER= string in your AUTOEXEC.BAT file to determine the correct TAPI driver to install. The installation program also modifies the SP.BAT file to ensure that the correct driver is loaded for Sp Pro.

Checking for the Correct TAPI Driver

When you install your Sound Blaster software, the installation program detects the card model and modifies your AUTOEXEC.BAT file to identify the characteristics of the card. Your AUTOEXEC.BAT contains an environment variable called BLASTER that indicates the DMA, IRQ, I/O address, and card version number (the T number). Based on the value assigned to T, the Voyetra/Creative Labs Sp Pro installation program installs the correct driver.

Early versions of the Sound Blaster installation program didn't always set the BLASTER variable correctly. Accordingly, the Voyetra/Creative Labs installation program for Sp Pro is sometimes given incorrect information about which card is installed. As a result, it is possible that you have a TAPISB driver installed when you should have TAPISB3 installed. This should have little or no effect upon the performance of your Sound Blaster, but we recommend you contact Voyetra to receive instructions on how to install the correct driver.

There are two methods to find out which TAPI driver is loaded by Sp Pro:

■ Use the DOS Type command on the SP.BAT file in the \VOYETRA (or \SBPRO) directory, and look to see if it says TAPISB or TAPISB3.

■ While working with Sp Pro, you can display the Hardware Configuration screen by pressing F3 from the main screen and then typing **H.** If you see a name under Auxiliary Sound Drivers such as Voyetra OPL3 FM Driver for Sound Blaster Pro, or something similar that references OPL3, you have the TAPISB3 driver running.

Figure 9-1 shows the configuration screen for a Sound Blaster Pro that has the wrong driver installed (TAPISB instead of TAPISB3). Note that this driver is the first version that supports General MIDI; this is indicated by the *GM*.

General MIDI TAPI Drivers

Newer versions of Sp Pro include TAPI drivers that provide Sound Blaster with a General MIDI implementation. Prior to establishment of the General MIDI standard, there was no single standard for the assignment of instrument sounds (*patches*) to channels. An even greater problem was that the *patch layout (*the assignment of numbers to patches) differed from synthesizer to synthesizer. As a result, a MIDI song might play different instruments on different synthesizers.

A General MIDI driver is one that conforms to the Standard MIDI File Specification, and uses the patch map and drum note map specified by the General MIDI standard. This means your MIDI song will automatically play the correct instrument on the FM synthesizer of your sound card. Without a General MIDI driver, you might have to use a MIDI mapper, such as the MIDI Mapper utility that comes with Windows 3.1, to make the correct assignments. In particular, the driver expects that channel 16 will be used for the drum parts of a base-level synthesizer. This assignment conflicts with the earlier Roland standard, but ensures compatibility with Microsoft Windows 3.1 multimedia extensions.

FIGURE 9-1

Sp Pro Hardware Configuration screen

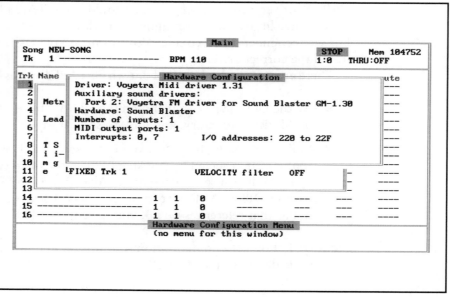

```
                                        Main
   Song NEW-SONG                                      STOP      Mem 104752
   Tk  1 -------------------- BPM 110                 1:0   THRU:OFF
   Trk Name              Hardware Configuration                      ute
    1    │    Driver: Voyetra Midi driver 1.31                       ----
    2    │    Auxiliary sound drivers:                               ----
    3  Metr │    Port 2: Voyetra FM driver for Sound Blaster GM-1.30 ----
    4    │    Hardware: Sound Blaster                                ----
    5  Lead │  Number of inputs: 1                                   ----
    6    │    MIDI output ports: 1                                   ----
    7    │    Interrupts: 0, 7        I/O addresses: 220 to 22F      ----
    8  T S │                                                         ----
    9  i i-│                                                         ----
   10  n g │                                                         ----
   11  e   └FIXED Trk 1              VELOCITY filter    OFF        │- ----
   12                                                              │- ----
   13                                                              │- ----
   14  --------------------  1  1   0    ------    ----    ----    ----
   15  --------------------  1  1   0    ------    ----    ----    ----
   16  --------------------  1  1   0    ------    ----    ----    ----
                         Hardware Configuration Menu
                         (no menu for this window)
```

The new General MIDI-compliant TAPI drivers are identified by a version number of 1.30 or higher and a *GM* prefix in front of the version number. The version number is displayed when the driver loads. When you use the SP.BAT batch file to load the driver, you won't have time to see the driver version number. You can load the driver without loading Sp Pro by running the DRIVER.BAT batch file. Switch to the directory where your Sequencer is located by typing **CD\VOYETRA** (or **CD\SBPRO**) and then press ENTER. To load the driver alone, type **DRIVER** and press ENTER. Once you've checked the driver version, type **DRIVER /REM** to remove the driver from memory.

Almost all commercial MIDI files available today (including Voyetra's MusiClips library) are mapped for General MIDI. The main benefit of the new General MIDI TAPI drivers is that they allow you to play these files and use them with Sp Pro without having to remap them. The major changes to General MIDI TAPI drivers are as follows:

- The TAPI driver's default patch map and drum note map fully comply with General MIDI and are considerably different from the older TAPIs.

- Your Sound Blaster will now use channel 16 as its drum channel. Older versions of the TAPI drivers used channel 10.

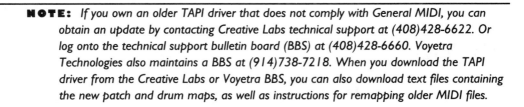

NOTE: *If you own an older TAPI driver that does not comply with General MIDI, you can obtain an update by contacting Creative Labs technical support at (408)428-6622. Or log onto the technical support bulletin board (BBS) at (408)428-6660. Voyetra Technologies also maintains a BBS at (914)738-7218. When you download the TAPI driver from the Creative Labs or Voyetra BBS, you can also download text files containing the new patch and drum maps, as well as instructions for remapping older MIDI files.*

STARTING SP PRO AND LOADING SOUND FILES

NOTE: *There are several versions of the installation program for the Sequencer Plus Pro. This chapter assumes your installation program has placed the Sp Pro software in a directory called VOYETRA. If your Sp Pro is in directory SPPRO instead, substitute SPPRO for VOYETRA in all the instructions throughout this chapter.*

This section describes how to load and run Sp Pro on a DOS-based computer. From the DOS prompt, you will run the SP batch file (SP.BAT), which loads the TAPI driver, runs Sp Pro, and then automatically unloads the TAPI driver when you quit.

To start Sp Pro, type **SP** and press ENTER. You will see the Voyetra sign-on screen. Press any key to advance to the Main screen (Figure 9-2), or wait a few seconds for the Main screen to appear.

NOTE: *If you type SPPRO instead of SP to start Sp Pro, you will receive an error message, "TAPI Driver Not Installed." Press any key to begin Sp Pro in demonstration mode. Then type **Q** twice to return to the DOS prompt and start again.*

Loading Sound Files to Play with Sp Pro

In this section you will find instructions for loading files to play in Sp Pro, including the two favorite types of sound files: Sequencer Plus song files (SNG) and MIDI files (MID). These procedures are a bit confusing in the Sp Pro manual.

TIP: *If your Sound Blaster or Sound Blaster Pro works fine with other software packages that came with your sound card, but won't work with the Sp Pro, you probably have a DMA conflict. Refer to Appendix B for instructions on resolving this conflict.*

FIGURE 9-2

Sp Pro Main

screen

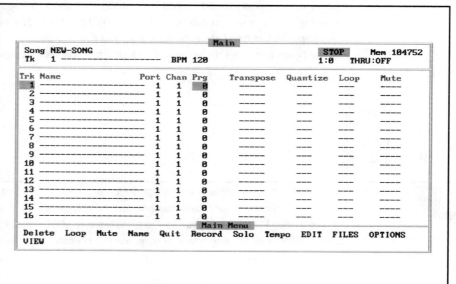

You can load and play three different types of files with Sp Pro:

- Sequencer Plus song files (SNG)

- Standard MIDI files (MID)

- AdLib song files (ROL)

Sp Pro comes bundled with a number of SNG song files and standard MIDI files to get you started. Both the MIDI files and the SNG files are located in the \VOYETRA\SONGS subdirectory. As with most programs, you must "navigate" to the drive and directory where the desired file is located in order to load it.

Switching Among the Files Display Modes

Sp Pro's Files screen has several different display modes. In Song Files mode, you see a list of files with the .SNG extension; MIDI Files mode lists files with the .MID extension; and ROL Files mode lists files with the .ROL extension. To load a file, the Files screen must be in the mode listing the desired file type.

To access the Files screen and access the various display modes, follow these steps:

1. From the Main screen, type **F** to access the Files screen. The Files screen always comes up in Song Files mode, as indicated by the "Ext.SNG" in the top-left corner of the screen.

2. To change from Song Files mode to MIDI Files mode, type **M** (for Mode). You'll see the indicator in the top-left corner change to "Ext.MID". To change to ROL Files mode, type **M** again. As you repeatedly type **M**, the Files screen cycles among the three modes.

3. After you've seen all the mode displays, press ESC to return to the Main screen.

Loading a Song (.SNG) File

Here are the steps to load a song (SNG) file from the Files screen:

1. From the Main screen, type **F** to access the Files screen. The Files screen always comes up in Song Files mode, as indicated by the "Ext.SNG" in the top-left corner of the screen.

2. Using the arrow keys, highlight one of the listed files, type **L**, and then press ENTER to load the file.

Once the file loads, Sp Pro returns to the Main screen.

Loading a MIDI (MID) File

When you load a MIDI file, its tracks are appended to other tracks.

1. If you're in the Main screen, which shows the track assignments, and want to clear out the existing tracks first before loading the file, type **D** and then **A** to delete all tracks.

2. From the Main screen, type **F** to access the Files screen. To switch to MIDI Files mode, type **M** until you see "Ext.MID" in the top-left corner of the screen.

3. Using the arrow keys, navigate to the \VOYETRA\SONGS directory by highlighting SONGS (see Figure 9-3). Press ENTER to move into this directory.

4. Highlight one of the listed MID files, type **L**, and press ENTER.

5. On the bottom-left corner of your screen, you will see the word

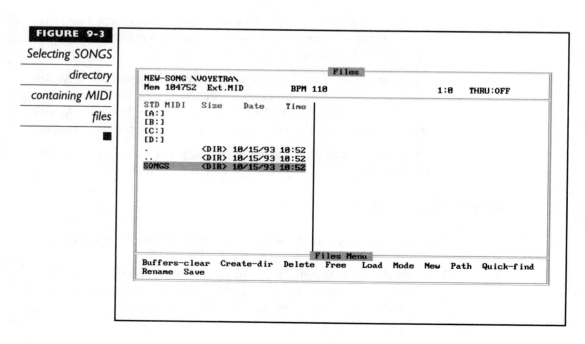

FIGURE 9-3

Selecting SONGS directory containing MIDI files

"Meters" highlighted. The message "Accept timesig" will appear below "Meters." Press ENTER again.

6. The file now loads. Sp Pro returns to the Main screen, and you will see track names, as well as port, channel, and program assignments.

SOME SPECIAL TECHNIQUES IN SP PRO

This section shows you how to take full advantage of the stereo capability of your Sound Blaster Pro by adding pan messages that give a stereo effect to your MIDI music. Another special technique described here is the procedure for quickly laying down a drum part using the QWERTY synthesizer. You'll also see how to do "one-finger" playing with the TAB key.

Stereo Panning

Sp Pro lets you control the left/right/center channel positioning of the Sound Blaster's on-board FM synthesizer, by using a type of MIDI message called a MIDI Pan message. *Panning* enables you to assign individual tracks in Sp Pro to the left, right, or center channel of a stereo sound system. By using panning, you can often make a song sound fuller and more interesting. Also, changing the pan positioning as the song plays (that is, changing it dynamically) lets you add some unique and novel effects.

The various Sound Blaster models interpret MIDI Pan messages differently. Sound Blaster 1.*x*/2.0 and the older Sound Blaster Pro are capable of continuous panning. In other words, their notes can be placed left, center, right, or anywhere in between. The Sound Blaster Pro 2, on the other hand, can do "hard" panning only. This means its notes can be placed at either full left, center, or full right.

NOTE: *Before experimenting with panning, make sure your Sound Blaster card is connected to a stereo sound system, and that the left and right audio channels are assigned correctly to your left and right stereo speakers.*

Adding Stereo Effects to a Song File

To add stereo effects to a MIDI song file,

1. Load a song file and select a track to which you want to add panning effects.

2. Type **E** (for Edit) to bring up the Edit screen. Then type **M** to get the MIDI Edit screen. Examine Figure 9-4 to see what this screen looks like (on a VGA/EGA monitor it will look different).

3. The Class field is now highlighted. Press the + key on your numeric keypad to step through the MIDI event classes until you reach Controller.

4. Press DOWN ARROW to highlight the Type field. Enter the number **10** to select the pan positive controller, and press ENTER. The field now says "10 Pan Position."

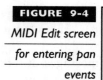

NOTE: *The next step is to enter the pan value. This step requires that you know which version of Sound Blaster Pro you have. If you don't know this, refer to the previous section, "Checking for the Correct TAPI Driver," earlier in this chapter.*

5. Type **V** to input the pan position value

■ *For Sound Blaster 1.x/2.0 and the two-operator Sound Blaster Pro,* enter a value between 0 and 127 (full left is 0, center is 64, and full right is 127). You can also enter values in between these;

FIGURE 9-4

MIDI Edit screen

for entering pan

events

■

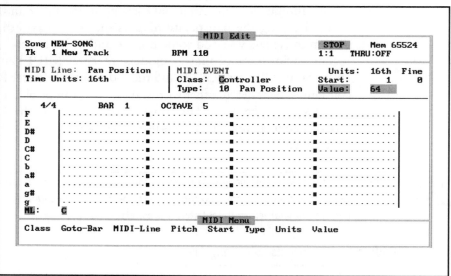

for example, 32 will position the notes halfway between left and center. This is called *continuous panning.*

■ *For Sound Blaster Pro 2,* enter a value between 0 and 127 (full left is 0–31, center is 32–95, and full right is 96–127). Sound Blaster Pro 2 does *hard panning* only. Thus any value within these ranges will give the same result: a full left, center, or full right panning.

6. After entering a pan position value, press ENTER. This takes the highlight bar to the MIDI event line ("ML" at the bottom of the screen, above the menu selections).

7. To enter a pan event on the selected track, use the LEFT ARROW and RIGHT ARROW keys to move the cursor to the point (the note) on the MIDI line where you want to insert the pan event. Then press the INS key, and you will see the letter C (for Controller) appear. You can enter additional pan events by repeating steps 5 through 7.

TIP: *Once you've entered all the pan events you want, you can quickly move between them by pressing the TAB and SHIFT-TAB keys.*

8. From the MIDI Edit screen or the Main screen, press the SPACEBAR to play back the song and hear your results.

NOTE: *From the MIDI Edit screen, the play will resume from the first measure visible in the screen. From the Main screen, play will resume from the beginning of the song.*

Using the QWERTY Synthesizer to Lay Down Drum Parts

Sp Pro's QWERTY (PC keyboard) Synthesizer is perfect for creating simple drum parts with your Sound Blaster card, especially if you don't feel like setting up your MIDI keyboard, or entering the notes manually from the Edit screen. So when you need to lay down a dance-type drum part that doesn't require much spontaneity, try using the QWERTY synthesizer.

Here are the steps to follow for laying down a drum part:

1. From the Main screen, choose an empty track and assign it to port 2, channel 16. Use the RIGHT ARROW key to move to these fields, type in the value, and press ENTER.

2. Set the tempo to about 110 beats per minute (BPM). Type **T** (for Tempo), enter **110**, and then press ENTER. Enable the Metronome by pressing F2.

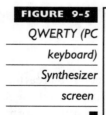

NOTE: *Nothing on your screen will confirm that the Metronome is turned on after you press F2—trust that it works.*

3. Type **R** to put Sp Pro into Record mode.

4. Press SHIFT-F1 to access the QWERTY Synthesizer. You will see a screen similar to Figure 9-5 (on a VGA/EGA monitor it will look different).

5. Use the + and – keys on the numeric keypad to set the Octave to 4.

6. Try using the Z key for bass drum and the X key for snare drum. You can even play the X and C keys with two fingers to do snare drum rolls.

7. Press the SPACEBAR to start recording your drum part. Press the SPACEBAR again when you're done.

Troubleshooting the QWERTY Synthesizer

If, while following the steps above, you don't hear anything, or if you

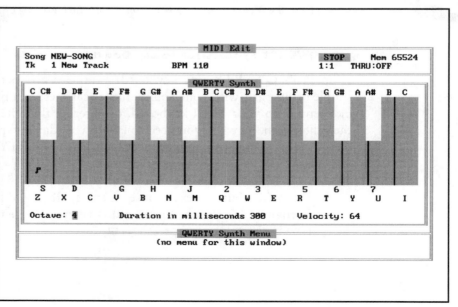

FIGURE 9-5

QWERTY (PC keyboard) Synthesizer screen

heard an instrument other than the drum from channel 16, you may have an older, non-General MIDI TAPI driver installed. If this is the case, first make certain you did select Octave 4 in step 5 above. The instrument mappings vary according to the octave, so selecting Octave 4 is essential.

If this doesn't solve your problem, check to see that the correct version of the TAPI driver is loaded. Display the Hardware Configuration screen by pressing F3 from the main screen, and then type **H**. At the top of the screen, in the Driver field, you should see something like "Voyetra Midi Driver 1.*XX*" where *XX* is a version number. If the version shown is earlier than 1.30, the TAPI driver supports the Roland MT-32 channel assignments. The Roland uses channel 10 for drums. If the version is 1.30 or later, the TAPI driver supports the general MIDI standard, with drums assigned to channel 16.

One-Finger Playing with the TAB Key

While in the Edit or Note Edit screens, you can advance from one note to the next using one finger, with the TAB key. This is sometimes useful for checking out a new melody, to find that one bad note in a track so you can edit it, or even just to have fun. Press SHIFT-TAB to go backward one note at a time.

USING SP PRO IN WINDOWS 3.1

Y ou can run Sp Pro in the DOS compatibility box (the DOS prompt icon) within Microsoft Windows 3.1 environment, but special steps must be taken to do this. Although Windows 3.1 has drivers for the MIDI interface and FM synthesis, Sp Pro must use its own TAPI driver. In addition, Sp Pro and other DOS-based MIDI software cannot be loaded by Windows in 386 Enhanced mode (the default Windows mode on 386/486 computers). The TAPI driver must be loaded at the DOS prompt *before* you start Windows. Then Windows must be run in Standard mode; enter the command **WIN /S** at the DOS prompt.

Installing Sp Pro in the Windows 3.1 Environment

Before running a DOS application, such as Sp Pro, in Windows 3.1, you need to set up a Windows Program Item. You can put the Sp Pro icon in any Program Manager group you want.

How to Create an Sp Pro Icon

Follow the steps below to create an Sp Pro icon:

1. From the Windows Program Manager, double-click to activate the program group where you want to locate the Sp Pro icon. For example, you may want to put Sp Pro in the Accessories group.

2. From the File menu, choose New.

3. From the New Program Object dialog box, select Program Item and then choose OK.

4. From the Program Item Properties dialog box, enter **Sp Pro** in the Description line.

5. For Command Line, type in the complete path and program file name of Sp Pro. In most cases, you will enter **C:\VOYETRA\SPPRO.EXE**.

6. From the Program Item Properties dialog box, click OK.

A new icon labeled "Sp Pro" will now be visible within the group that you selected.

If you have any trouble with the above instructions, or you wish to choose a different icon, refer to your Windows user's guide for further instructions on how to set up a Program Item for a DOS application.

Running Sp Pro in the Windows 3.1 Environment

Once you've designated the Sp Pro program icon, you can start it and run it exactly as if you loaded it from the DOS prompt. There is one major advantage of running Sp Pro from Windows, however: you don't need to load the SBP-MIX pop-up mixer program before running your Sp Pro program. While using Sp Pro in Windows, you can switch back to the desktop and use the Windows version of the Sound Blaster Pro Mixer program to control your sound card's mixer. See Chapter 6 for details on the mixer and mixer software.

Once you've created an icon for Sp Pro, it's very easy to run the program. (You might consider using a batch file to automatically load the TAPI driver and then start up Windows.) The steps for running Sp Pro under Windows 3.1 are as follows:

1. If you're still running Windows, exit to DOS.

2. Switch to the \VOYETRA directory by typing **CD \VOYETRA** at the DOS prompt and then press ENTER.

3. Load the TAPI driver by typing **TAPISB** or **TAPISB3**, and press ENTER.

NOTE: *If you're not certain which driver to load, review the section,"Checking for the Correct TAPI Driver, earlier in this chapter."*

4. Start Windows in Standard mode by typing **WIN /s**.

5. From the Program Manager, double-click on the Sp Pro icon.

If you have problems running Sp Pro from Windows 3.1—dropping MIDI notes, timing errors, or Windows error messages, for example—check to make sure you're running Windows in Standard mode, not 386 Enhanced mode. To find out what mode you're running in, choose About Program Manager... from the Program Manager's Help menu.

TIP: *If you have a modem, you can download an icon file for Sp Pro from the Voyetra Technologies Bulletin Board at (914)738-7218.*

SOME TIPS ABOUT SP PRO HARDWARE

The following hardware tips were provided by the technical support staff at Voyetra. These answer some of the most frequently asked questions.

MIDI Keyboard Problem: Beware of Cables Installed Backward

Many first-time users of Sp Pro have trouble recording or playing with their external MIDI keyboard. Frequently this is because the MIDI cables connecting your Sound Blaster card and your keyboard are plugged in backward. The ends of the Sound Blaster's MIDI cables are marked IN and OUT. The IN cable should be connected to your keyboard's OUT plug, because what your keyboard puts *out* is what the sound card takes *in*, and vice versa.

Controlling the Screen Display

NOTE: *If you have a Monochrome/Hercules or CGA monitor, this tip does not apply to your system. It concerns only computers with an EGA, VGA, or SuperVGA monitor.*

If you have an EGA or VGA monitor, Sp Pro can take advantage of the monitor's high resolution to display up to 41 tracks (on a VGA monitor) and 3 octaves in the Edit screen. (If you have a monochrome or CGA monitor, Sp Pro will display only 16 tracks at most.) When you run Sp Pro's installation program, it tries to correctly detect your computer's monitor type. In the earlier installation programs, the /ega switch was added to SP.BAT to force EGA/VGA monitors into 25-line mode (only 16 tracks). In later installation programs, the /ega switch was not added, so your program automatically appears with 41 tracks.

Here is a tip for controlling your screen display:

■ If your Edit screen has 41 tracks, but you'd prefer 16 larger, easier-to-read tracks instead, type the following command to start SP.BAT (or edit the SP.BAT file to include this):

SP/EGA

■ If your Edit screen has 16 tracks, and you want more, edit your SP.BAT file to remove the /ega command option.

NOTE: *To learn more about editing SP.BAT, refer to Chapter 2 for information on editing ASCII files.*

Upgrading to Sp Classic or Sp Gold

All registered owners of Sp Pro are eligible for upgrades to Voyetra's intermediate and professional sequencing packages, Sp Classic and Sp Gold.

These programs offer a host of additional, advanced features. Most importantly, they offer Transforms functions. Transforms are preset editing commands that allow you a greater degree of flexibility in modifying and customizing your songs. Sp Gold even includes an editor for the original two-operator Sound Blaster driver, a full-featured MIDI data analyzer, and a Universal Librarian that supports more than 130 different MIDI instruments.

For upgrade information, contact Voyetra Technologies at (800)233-9377.

IV

Hardware and Software Enhancements

10

Third-Party Software

S O U N D , or the lack of it, traditionally has been one of the few weak areas of the DOS PC. With a SB sound card, PC users can get great music and sound effects from their software. In fact, almost all contemporary PC game software supports the SB sound cards.

Because Creative Labs provides Windows drivers for the SB, all multimedia Windows applications can automatically take advantage of the SB. The popularity and acceptance of the Windows environment has brought about a shift in software development. As Windows becomes the dominant desktop interface on PCs and new multimedia titles are developed, sound becomes an increasingly important addition to the PC status quo.

Following is a selected list (it is by no means a comprehensive one) of some of the best tools, applications, utilities, and games available to help you maximize your investment in your SB sound card. Some of the software programs described below are just plain fun, some are educational, while others are serious professional programs with matching professional price tags.

We start off with disk-based software, divided into functional categories. We cover some outstanding games first, followed by discussions of MIDI music software, educational software, some utility software, and then some programming tools. After that, you'll find a CD–ROM section, which features some of the best multimedia software currently available for a personal computer. Finally, we provide the addresses and phone numbers of the publishers whose products are featured, so you can contact them directly for more information.

Think of this chapter as a mini buyer's guide. A few of the software programs mentioned in this chapter may be included with your Sound Blaster sound card. Remember to use the special offer coupons included in this book for exclusive, special savings from some of the software publishers represented in this chapter.

NOTE: *Just because we didn't include a certain program in this chapter doesn't mean it is not good. The ones we do write about represent some of the best titles we've personally encountered. With the multitude of software available, it would be no surprise if we missed some.*

Remember, you don't have to pay retail prices for software. You will find that software is regularly discounted from 10 to 50 percent. Purchase software from a store that has a money-back guarantee when possible. That way, you won't be stuck with software that doesn't have the features you're looking for. Also check to make sure you've got the latest version—software updates occur so frequently that many stores may still have older versions of the software on the shelf. Call the software publisher to find out about later versions.

Happy hunting.

GAMES GALORE

Not surprisingly, some of the most sophisticated uses of sound cards and multimedia technology can be found in games. Besides CAD (Computer Aided Design), few applications require more computing power than games. Just look at a typical modern flight simulator like Falcon 3.0 as an example. At any given moment, the computer has to track where your aircraft is in a 3-dimensional environment; update all the instruments on the instrument panel; update the outside view; keep track of other airplanes, ground vehicles, and missiles; play appropriate sounds such as the engine or radio communications; update the radar system; read the input from your keyboard, joystick, and/or mouse; and countless other details. A spreadsheet or word processor couldn't keep a computer this busy.

Since there is a seemingly unending number of games, we've tried to narrow the list down to those that make exceptional use of your Sound Blaster sound card and those on the cutting edge. The section is divided into various game categories. We do not go into very much detail on the individual games themselves due to length considerations.

We have played many, many games ourselves, and the games that we mention here have left an indelible impression in our minds and have entertained us for many hours.

NOTE: *Retail prices are not included in our survey of games. However, retail prices for these games pretty much fall into the $50 to $90 range.*

Simulations

Simulators are programs or games that attempt to model aircrafts, automobiles, or vehicles realistically on the PC. They allow a PC user to experience the thrill of actually being in the cockpit of an airplane or the driver's seat of a formula-one race car.

Simulations—flight simulators in particular—are probably some of the most sophisticated software ever written for a PC. This area shows a lot of maturity, as some software programs are in their fourth or fifth incarnations. In fact, a whole cottage industry, providing sophisticated aircraft controls and the like, has emerged from the enthusiasm of this group of gamers.

If your preference leans toward the days of old, when you saw the whites of your opponents' eyes as you shot them down, look no further than Red Baron, by Dynamix. Red Baron accurately portrays the flight characteristics of World War I aircraft, with vivid engine and machine gun sounds. Dynamix continues to establish a tradition of excellence with the follow-up to Red Baron, Aces of the Pacific. This simulator recreates the American and Japanese aircraft flown in the Pacific Theater in World War II. One of the highlights is the distinctive engine sounds for each aircraft—the drone of the twin-engine P-38 Lightning is louder and certainly different than the drone from a P-51 Mustang.

Modern-day jet simulators sport some stunning sound effects, including speech. Spectrum Holobyte's Falcon 3.0 (Figure 10-1) is a perennial favorite and best-seller (with over 100,000 registered copies) for good reason. The flight characteristics are accurate and can be set to various levels of difficulty. Not only do you get all the regular sounds, such as missile lock tone, your wingman actually responds and talks to you. The MiG-29 add-on even has copilots complete with Russian accents. An expansive mission generator rounds out this standard, to which every jet combat simulator is compared.

Microprose's F-15 Strike Eagle III has a great introduction. The programmers paid close attention to programming the sound effects, and this attention to detail shows: Explosions that are closer are louder, and the engine becomes louder when you zoom in on the external view. The various radar modes can be bewildering, just like the real thing. The sky is absolutely gorgeous, but it is devoid of wingmen, a notable omission.

Origin's Strike Commander arguably has the best external view of any flight simulator. Every plane is rendered in camouflage paint and is shaded— a level of detail unheard of on PCs before Strike Commander. Also, each

FIGURE 10-1

Falcon 3.0

by Spectrum

Holobyte

wingman has a distinctive voice (with the optional Speech Pack) over the radio, and you do get to listen to your mortal enemies scream as your missile destroys their airplanes. However, these lavish details have a negative effect on Strike Commander, as it runs at a snail's pace on anything other than a 486/66 MHz computer. You can lower the detail level, which will improve the speed somewhat, but which will also detract from the game's beautiful scenery.

Microsoft Flight Simulator 5.0 (Figure 10-2) is relatively boring compared to the combat-oriented flight simulators we've discussed earlier. However, the fact remains that it is probably the most accurate of all flight simulators, and the graphics are the best of its genre. It is the only game that runs in high-resolution mode with 256 colors and uses actual satellite photos, providing the sharpest and most realistic views ever seen on the PC. You also can't do better than sounds taken from recordings of actual aircraft. This game should be on everybody's computer, whether you're a flight enthusiast or not. Flying around San Francisco at dusk turned our mouths into Venus flytraps as we gaped at the stunning scenery displayed before us on the screen.

Another simulation that makes great use of sound is Nova Logic's Comanche: Maximum Overkill. This futuristic helicopter simulation has stereo sound effects as well as different sounds for its many weapons. The graphics are excellent, and because it's based on a future helicopter design, the simulator is very easy to control, compared to traditional helicopters both in real life and on the computer.

FIGURE 10-2

*Microsoft Flight
Simulator 5.0*

While not strictly a realistic simulator, X-Wing from LucasArts allows you to enter the *Star Wars* world. You join the Rebellion forces and pilot a variety of spacecraft—the A-Wing, X-Wing, and Y-Wing—in several dozen missions. It is amazing how much the sound effects are exactly like those in the *Star Wars* movies. You can even hear the whistles and beeps of your very own R2 unit. Be forewarned: even if you are just a minor *Star Wars* fan, X-Wing will have you staying up late, shooting at Darth Vader's fleet of TIE Fighters to get to the Death Star trench.

Action

Action games abound in the world of Nintendo and Sega game machines. In the PC world, fewer such games exist. However, the quality of action games on the PC easily surpasses most of what is offered on the dedicated game machines. Among them is Interplay's Out Of This World and SSI's Flashback. Both games, programmed by the same French company, make extensive use of digital sound effects on your Sound Blaster sound card.

Id Software's Wolfenstein 3-D is a highly successful, well-executed action game that features smooth scrolling graphics and good sound to accompany the carnage. You can hear Nazi soldiers yelling at you, machine guns rattling, dogs barking, and sliding metal doors, along with numerous other sounds.

Brøderbund's Prince of Persia 2 features speech-enhanced animated scenes with great graphics and sound effects. The smooth animation is accurately synchronized with the sound, adding a great deal to the game.

You can hear opening and closing gates, the clashing of swords, and the screams of the "Don King heads" (monsters).

Adventure

Adventure games are a very popular game category. The current games in this genre usually feature a full soundtrack that plays throughout the game in addition to numerous sound effects. Probably the most prestigious game of this kind is the King's Quest series from Sierra On-Line. King's Quest VI continues to break new ground in this category with a lip-synching technology that synchronizes the voice with the movement of the character's mouth. King's Quest VI is also designed to be extremely flexible, allowing the beginner to complete the game by solving only 40 percent of the problems presented in the game.

The Monkey Island series from LucasArts is not only funny and thoroughly enjoyable, but the music soundtrack is some of the best Caribbean/reggae music this side of the computer screen. Both Monkey Island 2 and Indiana Jones: Fate of Atlantis (Figure 10-3) feature their innovative iMuse sound system, which provides smooth transitions between different tunes as well as distinctive tunes for each character in the game. The graphics for both games are wonderfully done, and the stories are top-notch (in fact, Fate of Atlantis would make an excellent Indiana Jones movie).

Alone in the Dark from I-Motion is a European import that successfully blends an interesting storyline with some innovative camera angles. You explore a haunted house full of ghosts and monsters. The animation is smooth, and the sound is just plain spooky. You hear sounds of creaking floorboards, a shotgun being fired and recocked, eerie moans and groans, and the clashing of swords.

Sports

LinksPro 386 (Figure 10-4) from Access Software is a standout product in the sports category. This is the best looking golf game available for the PC, bar none. Not only are the graphics eye-popping (the foliage is digitized from the actual course), the whole course is meticulously recreated with the help of video footage, photographs, actual playing time, and course architect plans and designs. During your rounds at a variety of golf courses, you hear birds chirping right before the swoosh of your golf club as you swing. Short commentary, such as "Looks like you hit the tree, Jim," do little for your nerves as you prepare for your next shot. You can select either a male or female golfer and you can customize the shirt color. The comments are also made with the appropriate male or female voice.

FIGURE 10-3

Indiana Jones:

The Fate of

Atlantis

by LucasArts

Front Page Sports: Football Pro from Dynamix is about the best blend of action and statistics you'll find in a PC football game. Dynamix has a license to use the names of actual NFL players with their corresponding statistics, so you can place some of your favorite players into action. You get to hear the snap count and audible calls from the quarterback ("red forty-

FIGURE 10-4

LinksPro 386 by

Access Software

twooo...red forty-twooo...hut-hut"), as well as the cheering (or booing) crowd and the crunch of players colliding.

The unmistakable voice and style of Al Michaels can be heard in Hardball III from Accolade, as he provides running commentary for the baseball game in progress. Though the spoken sentences are sometimes choppy, the crack of the bat and the cheer of the crowd as you hit one out of the ball park gets your adrenaline flowing. The game even starts with the traditional national anthem.

Strategy

While admittedly we're not strategy game players, we couldn't resist Buzz Aldrin's Race Into Space (Figure 10-5) from Interplay. This game pits you against either the Russians or Americans as you try to build your space program beginning in 1957. The goal is to be first to put an astronaut on the moon and bring him back safely. You have to manage your R & D (research and development) dollars, select and train astronauts, and purchase equipment. During the missions, you see actual footage from various rocket launches while listening to actual recordings of communications between astronauts and ground control. You'll be watching with great anticipation as a Titan rocket blasts off, waiting to see if it makes it into

FIGURE 10-5

Buzz Aldrin's

Race Into Space

by Interplay

CAPE KENNEDY   SPRING 1968   CASH: 173 MB

orbit or explodes after launch due to a malfunction. You can honestly say you know what it feels like to watch the real thing in Mission Control.

MUSIC AND MIDI MAGIC

Computers are commonly called upon to supplement and perfect the modern musician's art. The software programs used by professionals to control their MIDI systems are now readily available to everyone. Simpler systems are also available, allowing the uninitiated to enter the MIDI music world and explore their musical inclinations.

TIP: *Refer to Chapters 1 and 8 for detailed discussions of MIDI technology.*

Since the Sound Blaster sound card behaves like a MIDI component, all the software programs described in this section can work correctly with the Sound Blaster sound card. To take full advantage of all the capabilities of MIDI software, you really should have a professional musical keyboard or sound module, and not just the FM synthesizer found in your Sound Blaster sound card. If you're one of the lucky ones to have purchased a Wave Blaster to accompany your Sound Blaster 16, you should hear some stunning music from these software programs.

The following is a sampling of some professional-grade MIDI software as well as easier, less-sophisticated incarnations for the beginners among us. You'll find various MIDI sequencers that allow you to compose or edit music. We also include a couple of auto-accompaniment programs for those of you who may know how to play one instrument but not others; these auto-accompaniment programs play the other instruments for you while you play the instrument of your choice. Several notation programs allow you to compose music using standard music notation.

SuperJAM! by Blue Ribbon SoundWorks (Retail: $129)

SuperJAM! (Figure 10-6) is one of the few programs that helps any nonmusician create original music. You simply select a style of music from the 30 styles included, then choose a key and tempo, and click on the Play button. You're on your way to creating your own musical masterpiece.

You can purchase additional styles from Blue Ribbon apart from the standard repertoire, which includes rock, pop, jazz, dance, classical, and samba. You may choose to create your own style as well. These styles include complex musical instructions that help you create dynamic original music.

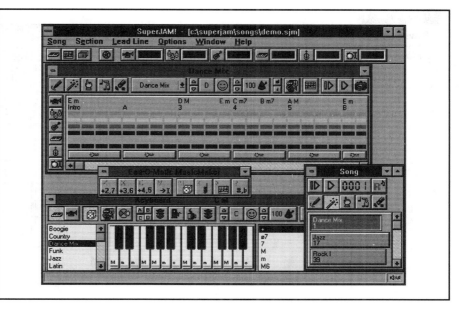

Each one contains special musical embellishments like intros, fills, breaks, and ends, to provide you with different means of expression when composing. To top it off, each style includes four distinctive rhythmic grooves that can help you fill your composition with an ever-changing, lifelike sound.

An onscreen keyboard is controlled with a mouse or your computer keyboard, allowing you to make changes to your composition quite easily. Strike up the band with up to six other instruments (which you can select individually) that follow your lead.

When you feel more ambitious, you can use the editing and recording features of SuperJAM! to change drum mappings, edit notes, control velocity, and perform real-time recordings. Your work can be saved in a standard MIDI file, allowing you to share your compositions with friends and enemies alike.

Power Chords by Howling Dog Systems (Retail: $84.95)

Power Chords (Figure 10-7) is an innovative sequencing program that differentiates itself from other sequencers by using an onscreen guitar (or other stringed instrument) to build chords that are then used to create songs. Other portions of the music, such as the drum and bass parts, can also be created and easily plugged into the song framework.

Power Chords actually allows you to use the mouse to "play" the guitar. Guitarists and string players can even draw chords right on the screen. Power

FIGURE 10-7

Power Chords

by Howling Dog

Systems

■

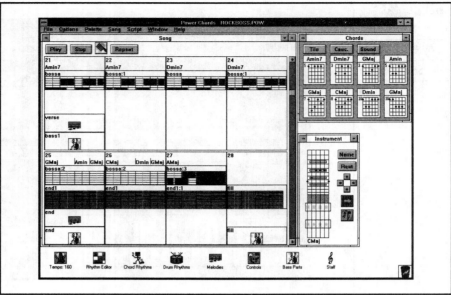

Chords also lets you pluck, strum, and do "string bends" and "hammer-ons" too. The onscreen instrument can have up to 12 strings and 24 frets and can be tuned any way you want. You'll find it simple to recreate the sounds of instruments, such as guitars, banjos, and ukuleles, or to create new, fantasy instruments.

Because of its unique interface, you don't have to know how to read score sheets or music notation. There is even a chord request feature: You can request almost any chord, and Power Chords provides a number of different variations on it no matter how many strings the instrument has or how it is tuned.

Writing music with Power Chords is easy. You first create a chord progression and then build a plucking or strumming pattern. This chord progression repeats until another pattern is encountered. Drum and bass parts are created similarly and are also automatically repeating.

Power Chord's comprehensive scripting capability is best demonstrated by the interactive tutorial and demo (which were written entirely using Power Chord). Lesson and presentation scripts can be created with relative ease. If you are a musician, the recording capability allows you to simply play and record your performance with a MIDI instrument. Any mistakes can be corrected using the built-in editor. Power Chords also imports and exports files in standard MIDI format.

Boom Box by Dr. T's Music Software (Retail: $59.95)

Are you ready to jam? Boom Box (Figure 10-8) is an exciting interactive program that allows you to get in the groove by triggering music samples using a keyboard, mouse, or joystick.

Boom Box draws heavily from the metaphor of popular rap and hip-hop styles. Dr. T's Music Software recruited the assistance of musical engineers from New York City's acclaimed Unique Recording Studios to create a number of the featured musical grooves. A lot of the grooves were developed by the same people who create some of the tunes you hear on the Billboard Top 100.

Boom Box's Remix screen allows you to completely rearrange the songs, mix the different instruments and effects, trigger outrageous samples, and even record your virtuoso performances to disk.

This is a party machine. You will love it and your friends won't leave it alone. Your Sound Blaster sound card with Boom Box will transform you from a computer nerd to the coolest guy with a computer. Break it down; check it out!

QuickScore Plus by Dr. T's Music Software (Retail: $149)

This DOS-based combination sequencer and notation program allows you to simply "draw in" notes with a mouse or record a MIDI keyboard

FIGURE 10-8

Boom Box by Dr. T's Music Software

performance in real time using an icon interface. You can immediately see and play back your score, up to 16 tracks simultaneously.

With the Sound Blaster sound card, a MIDI keyboard is not required for recording, editing, and/or playback in QuickScore Plus. The program allows you to enter any time or key signature and add any tempo changes at any point in the score. You can also enter lyrics in a composition; but QuickScore Plus, or any other notation program for that matter, has yet to gain the ability to sing the lyrics.

Studio for Windows by Midisoft Corporation (Retail: $249.95)

This Windows-based program is a MIDI music composition and playback control program that allows music and multimedia enthusiasts to compose, record, edit, and print music with their Sound Blaster sound card–equipped PC. Studio for Windows (Figure 10-9) displays standard music notation in real time—a capability that, together with its Windows interface, provides an intuitive and spontaneous environment for creating music. Heading the list of powerful editing features that contribute to the program's versatility are Punch, Loop, Splice Cut/Paste, and Step Play.

With Punch, you can record a new part, and Studio automatically inserts it quickly and accurately into a predetermined place within an existing track. This technique is often easier than editing the track manually. Loop is a convenient feature to use when a phrase or section needs to be repeated. For

FIGURE 10-9

Midisoft Studio for Windows

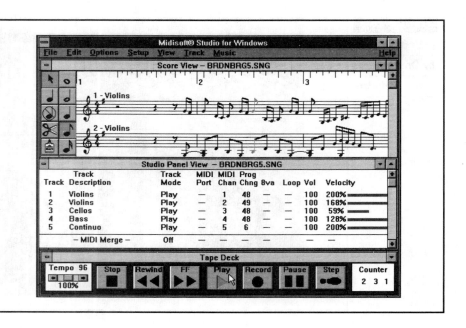

example, it allows you to record one or more measures, select them, and choose the number of repetitions.

Splice Cut removes a selected passage from a track and shifts all subsequent measures earlier in time to fill the empty space. Splice Paste takes a selection from the clipboard and places it into a target area on a track. Subsequent measures are shifted later in time to make room for the pasted music. Step Play is a mode that steps through music one event at a time. This feature is useful for a dense passage of music that you want to isolate and hear each note or phrase.

Studio for Windows is the only notation-based MIDI sequencer that provides a score–printing capability. You can select the tracks you wish to print, including text for header and footer information, page numbers, track numbers, and measure numbers.

The program is tightly integrated with Windows 3.1. It supports the MIDI Mapper feature, which lets users conveniently specify different mapping schemes to coordinate their sound devices, using either General MIDI standards or Microsoft's Authoring Guidelines for MIDI files. With the multi-MIDI port feature, you have access to more than 16 MIDI channels and can easily assign different tracks to specific MIDI devices.

MusicTime by Passport Designs (Retail: $249)

Passport Designs has been long established in the Apple Macintosh market as one of the premier providers of MIDI and music software. With the MusicTime Windows software, which echos its Mac siblings in capabilities, Passport offers some of the best MIDI software around for the PC.

Watch your music and songs come to life in standard music notation with MusicTime (Figure 10-10). This program lets you place notes on an electronic staff paper with a mouse. Simply click and drag notes with a mouse from the toolbox onto your musical score. Any musical symbol—notes, sharps, flats, and others—can be used. You can even play each note through the SB while you're composing. You can notate up to six staff systems with up to four voices.

One of the best features of MusicTime is its ability to record a live performance onto a score (if you have a MIDI keyboard hooked up to your Sound Blaster sound card). MusicTime transcribes what you play into standard music notation. Score sheets can also be automatically produced from a standard MIDI file.

With MusicTime, note-aligned lyrics and text can be added to your composition. Add guitar chord notation to the score and justify the music as well. Of course, you can transpose notes and change the key of your music

FIGURE 10-10

MusicTime

by Passport

Designs

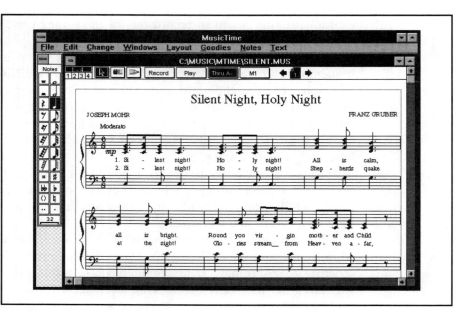

too. When your masterpiece is printed on a laser printer, you have professionally published–quality sheet music.

The program is very useful for music teachers, band directors, and choir directors. You can easily enter a score by recording a performance, then, using MusicTime's transpose function, switch it to another key or transpose the score for another instrument. Finally, you can reprint the edited score for other performers or members of the group.

If you're a professional composer, the additional capabilities of Encore, MusicTime's paradigm and elder brother, may prove to be more suitable.

Encore by Passport Designs (Retail: $595)

Encore is a full-featured music notation software. Priced for the professional musician, it has all the features of MusicTime, plus a few other advanced features.

While MusicTime only allows six staffs, Encore allows up to 64. This comes in handy if you're composing for an orchestra (those of you who aspire to be like John Williams, please take note). Encore also performs multiple–part extraction for those complicated scores.

A header and footer capability helps you keep your pages organized. You can have more than one score open at any time. Using cut and paste, you can easily transfer, or duplicate, sections of one score to another.

Master Tracks Pro by Passport Designs (Retail: $395)

Master Tracks Pro (Figure 10-11) is a professional MIDI sequencing software. It features the capability to record up to 64 tracks, step-time input, and graphic and event list editing. The dizzying array of buttons and menu options on the screen may confuse the uninitiated, but Master Tracks Pro promises to deliver its powerful features with fast and intuitive operation for those so inclined.

Clearly aimed at the high end, Master Tracks Pro provides esoteric features, such as the ability to "sync-lock" your music to SMPTE (Society of Motion Picture and Television Engineers) time standards via MIDI Time Code with MIDI/SMPTE interface (which allows you to synchronize your music to film, video, or tape), automatically chase MIDI controllers and program changes for automation control, fit time to SMPTE values, and control the music's feel by sliding regions forward or backward in time.

The track sheet in Master Tracks combines song and track information into one area. Adjustments to the volume fader can be recorded, which allows you to perform live mixing with immediate graphic feedback.

If you're a performing musician, you'll like the Song Play List feature. It allows you to cue up several files for automatic playback in any order. You can use a variety of ways to stop and start playback, including using a pedal hooked up to your MIDI keyboard.

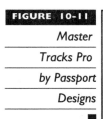

FIGURE 10-11

Master Tracks Pro by Passport Designs

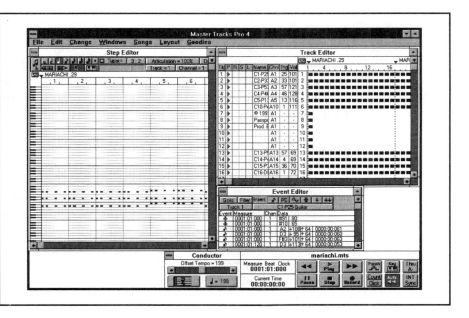

Also of interest to those of you who perform live, Master Tracks Pro has a Preset Palette feature, which allows you to automatically select different sets of sounds for different keyboards. You can also edit this list and add banks of presets (groups of preprogrammed instrument sounds) from synthesizers that are not included with factory-supplied sounds.

Other Master Tracks Pro highlights include editing and recording features too numerous to list that should prove to be more than adequate even for the most demanding professional musicians. The program has a consistent interface and is easy to learn. Like other sequencer software, Master Tracks Pro really shines when you hook up a professional MIDI keyboard to the Sound Blaster sound card.

Trax by Passport Designs (Retail: $99)

Trax is a MIDI sequencer based on Master Tracks Pro. Both siblings share a similar interface. This scaled-down version omits some of the esoteric functions and features (which may be a requirement for professional applications) found in Master Tracks Pro.

At a bargain basement price of $99 for sequencing software, Trax is a steal. Moreover, you can progress to Master Tracks Pro very easily when your requirements outgrow Trax.

NOTE: *Creative Labs includes a special version of Trax and MusicTime, called Trax with Notation, with the Sound BlasterStudio 16XL.*

Band-in-a-Box Pro by PG Music (Retail: $88)

Band-in-a-Box Pro (Figure 10-12) is an amazing auto-accompaniment program that is truly unique in its function. One of the challenges for any musician or composer is to create the various accompaniments, or instrument parts, to any music. Adding these parts and producing good music requires that you know how to play the main instrument as well as the accompanying instruments. Band-in-a-Box Pro allows you to just concentrate on your lead part while it takes care of the drums, bass, piano, guitar, and string parts.

Creating a song with backup instruments is a cinch with Band-in-a-Box Pro. Here's all that you're required to do: First, specify the chord progressions of any song in simple chord notation (for example, C or Fm7). Second, select a musical style from jazz swing to waltz to new age; 75 styles are included with the program, and an additional 25 styles are available in a separate set priced at $29. Third, select a tempo, start the metronome, and off you go.

FIGURE 10-12

Band-in-a-Box

by PG Music

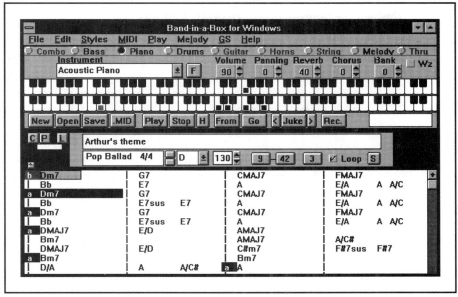

The results can be very satisfying, and often you can hear interesting, professional-sounding material emanating from your Sound Blaster sound card or MIDI instruments. Don't worry if you have no idea where to start composing; Band-in-a-Box Pro includes some tunes in the package to get you started. Another 100 prebuilt songs can be purchased for $29.

Elementary sequencer capabilities, such as editing and saving to MIDI format files, are built into Band-in-a-Box Pro. You can save a file with or without the melody (which can be a recording of your performance). These files can then be edited in other more capable sequencers.

You owe it to yourself to listen to some of what Band-in-a-Box Pro comes up with, given a certain song and style. It is both educational and fun to just vary the style and listen to the different musical results from the program. Selecting different instruments (Fender Bass versus Upright Bass, for example) can also dramatically alter a song.

The Band-in-a-Box Pro package includes both DOS and Windows versions and works with the Sound Blaster sound card FM synthesizer or MIDI port. Files created with either version are completely compatible and interchangeable with each other. A Band-in-a-Box Pro Standard Edition with 24 styles is available at a reduced cost of $59.

If you're like us and you lack one or more of the instrument skills necessary for becoming a one-person showcase, Band-in-a-Box Pro is the perfect solution and is certainly a most capable addition to your repertoire. It is the next best thing to having a live band at your disposal.

WinSong by Softronics (Retail: $79.95)

WinSong (Figure 10-13) is the Swiss army knife equivalent of MIDI music software. Softronics has combined a music composer, sequencer, and juke-box into an attractively priced Windows-compatible product.

With the WinSong Composer, you can write music with musical notes and symbols by dragging them (with a mouse) from the toolbar onto a music staff. Notes can also be placed on the staff by simply playing on a MIDI keyboard attached to your Sound Blaster sound card. The staff scrolls by as it is played, providing instant visual feedback to the notes being played. Lyrics can be added to the composition and printed out as sheet music.

The WinSong Sequencer allows up to 64 tracks to record separately and mix together for a full performance. It converts any standard MIDI file into standard notation for editing with the Composer. You can also loop, move, transpose, and adjust the volume of entire tracks. WinSong's Sequencer supports complex time signatures as well as user-defined nonstandard key signatures. As with most sequencing software, you can quantize, cut, copy, paste, transpose, and change volume, length, and pitch for each MIDI channel.

To listen to your compositions, use WinSong's Jukebox to queue up any number of MIDI files. You can create sets of music to suit your changing moods. Use it to play background music as you work.

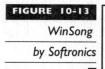

FIGURE 10-13

WinSong

by Softronics

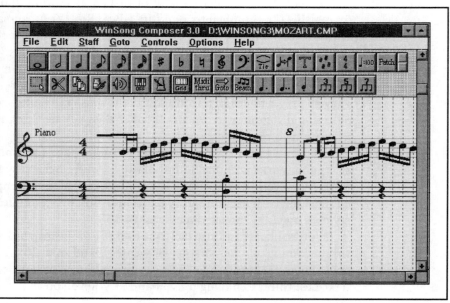

Cakewalk Professional by Twelve Tone Systems (Retail: $349)

Cakewalk Pro (Figure 10-14) is a MIDI sequencer with an easy interface and a potent set of features. Having already taken a commanding share of the DOS sequencer market, Cakewalk's Windows version should set a few standards for other software publishers to match.

Cakewalk Pro's greatest asset is that it can have multiple views and editing windows on the screen at once. Changes made in one window are instantly reflected in all other windows, and they all update during playback. These windows include a track/measure view, a piano-roll grid, and a staff view that can display up to ten staves at once. An event list can also be displayed along the separate graphical controller and fader windows.

Other professional-level features found in Cakewalk Pro include fractional tempos (for example, 120.34 beats per minute); pitch and velocity transpositions; a built-in application language for creating, among other things, your very own chord generators and drum maps; and support for all four SMPTE and MTC (MIDI Time Code) synchronization formats. And though most sequencers record only up to 64 tracks, Cakewalk Pro allows you to record and edit up to 256 tracks. A SysEx (System Exclusive) Librarian has 256 banks to store SysEx information from most keyboard synthesizers.

Cakewalk Pro supports MCI (Media Control Interface) commands in tracks. This allows you to control and synchronize equipment such as CD

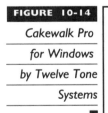

FIGURE 10-14

Cakewalk Pro

for Windows

by Twelve Tone

Systems

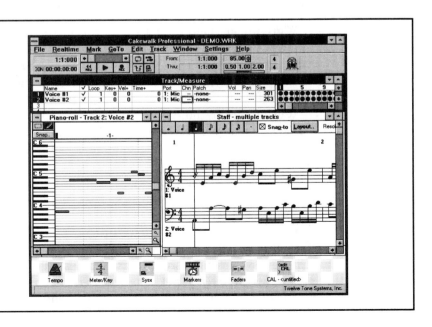

players and VCRs to MIDI sequencers. Digital audio data in a Wave (.WAV) file can be embedded into a sequence as well.

Cakewalk Pro has about every feature a professional could ask for. The program lacks a score-sheet printing capability, but it lets you store your sequence in standard MIDI format so that you can use a notation program such as Passport's MusicTime to print the score. Cakewalk Pro is arguably the best-executed MIDI sequencer on the market.

Sequencer Plus series by Voyetra Technologies (Retail: $69.95-$299.95)

The Sequencer Plus series is made up of the big brothers to Sp Pro, Voyetra's line of DOS-based MIDI sequencers/editors. The series includes Sp Jr, Sp Classic, and Sp Gold. These sequencers are capable of addressing the Sound Blaster sound card's internal FM sounds while simultaneously triggering external MIDI instruments.

The Voyetra DOS sequencers are more difficult and confusing than Windows-based products. This is an inherent problem with most DOS text-based software when compared with their Windows counterparts. However, the Sequencer Plus series of products do work as advertised, and should be seriously considered if you're looking for a sophisticated DOS-based MIDI sequencer.

WinJammer by WinJammer Software Limited (Shareware: $50)

WinJammer (Figure 10-15) is a full-featured MIDI sequencer for Windows. It plays and records standard MIDI files. WinJammer may not be a match for other professional MIDI sequencers in terms of the sheer number of editing and performance features, but sometimes less is more. In this case, the payoff is an uncluttered and simple interface.

WinJammer is the only sequencer we ran across that reads ROL files. (Refer to Chapter 4 for more information on ROL files.) This one feature clearly reveals the primary target audience for WinJammer—the beginning or amateur MIDI-ite as well as those who do not have a MIDI keyboard to accompany their Sound Blaster sound card but would like to start creating music with the FM synthesizer on their sound card.

You won't find WinJammer lacking too much in important features. You can create up to 64 tracks and use up to 256 MIDI channels. Editing is carried out in a traditional piano-roll notation window. WinJammer can send real-time system-exclusive events (synthesizer-specific data) as well.

The WinJammer package includes a companion program called WinJammer Player, which is used to play MIDI song files in the background while

FIGURE 10-15

WinJammer
■

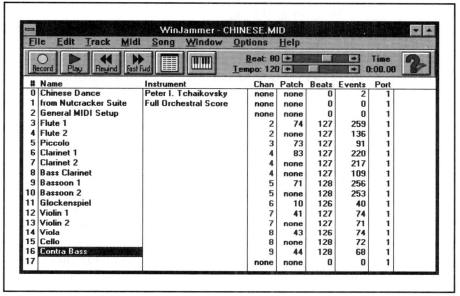

you're working in Windows. The repeat mode and shuffle play options are two unique features of this program.

For those who want a taste of MIDI without spending money up front, this shareware program might just be the ticket. It should be available on many bulletin boards and can be found on CompuServe.

EDUCATIONAL EXCELLENCE

Computers are excellent tools for the school classroom or the home. With the addition of sound and speech capability of the Sound Blaster sound card, educational software takes on a whole new dimension. Software can literally direct or talk to the user verbally, which makes the computer easier to use. Many educational software programs are disguised as games to make learning more fun and attractive for both children and adults alike. We'll look at some notable educational titles in this section.

NotePlay by Ibis Software (Retail: $49.95)

Ibis Software has created a series of educational music titles that has been adopted by various school districts, grade schools, high schools, and colleges around the country. The wide acceptance of its software as an appropriate teaching and learning tool at these varied levels is a testimony to the well thought out, flexible, and mostly fun software.

As amateur guitarists and drummers, we found Noteplay (available for both DOS and Windows) and all the following Ibis software to be extremely easy to use and very valuable in helping to develop and improve our musical skills. These are indispensable tools for any music teacher or student.

Designed primarily for people who want to learn to play music or who want to improve their current playing abilities, NotePlay can be used to teach how to read notes on a staff and play them correctly from a keyboard. Using either the computer keyboard (which has been mapped to replicate an electronic keyboard) or an actual MIDI keyboard, you select and play back the correct notes as displayed on a staff. In this game format, points are awarded for speed and accuracy. If you beat the timer, bonus points are given.

There are 36 drill levels to select from, with new musical phrases introduced with every session. You can choose from three different play modes (slow, normal, and automatic), tailoring the program to your level. Advanced-level drills include two-handed exercises dealing with counterpoint, intervals, and chords. You can choose to practice a certain level as often as you like.

NotePlay for Windows (Figure 10-16) has been designed to be easy enough for beginners, yet powerful enough to satisfy advanced musicians. NotePlay's multilevel approach and different play modes make the program appropriate for users at all levels—beginner, hobbyist, student, or serious musician.

The program can also be used in an exploratory mode by disabling the game. Here you can randomly play notes and see them appear on the Grand Staff in their correct locations and with their correct names. The attractive graphical interface and ease of use make the program as fun as it is instructional.

Play It By Ear by Ibis Software (Retail: $99.95)

Play It By Ear (Figure 10-17) provides a variety of self-paced ear-training exercises, featuring an onscreen piano keyboard and guitar fret board. The program's strength lies in its instant response to your actions, helping you to quickly identify and improve upon your weaknesses.

Play It By Ear offers a variety of interactive melodic and harmonic exercises. Topics include note, chord, and interval recognition; chord and interval naming; pitches; scales; modes; and much more.

FIGURE 10-16

NotePlay

for Windows

by Ibis Software

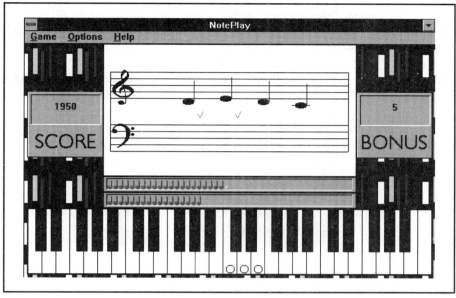

In each exercise, you are asked to play back or identify specific notes, melodies, intervals, or chords. The program immediately indicates whether each answer is correct or incorrect. If you are stumped, ask Play It By Ear

FIGURE 10-17

Play It By Ear

by Ibis Software

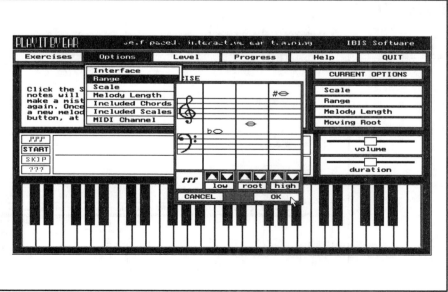

to highlight the correct location of the note, chord, or interval on the onscreen keyboard or fret board. The program then asks again for the correct answer. A scorekeeper tracks your progress and displays it in a progress graph, postexercise summary, or an exercise report.

A suite of options gives you complete control over the content and difficulty of each exercise. For example, you can increase or reduce the range of the keyboard or fret board covered by each exercise. Play It By Ear plays back melodies of 2 to 16 notes, and also allows you to vary the speed at which notes are played back. In all, the program offers six levels of challenge.

You can use a mouse to play the onscreen piano keyboard or guitar fret board, or you can choose to apply the exercises directly to a MIDI-equipped keyboard or guitar.

Play It By Ear does not help the tone deaf, but it does help the budding musician or singer to develop a keener sense of pitch and an improved ability to recognize notes, chords, and melodies.

RhythmAce by Ibis Software (Retail: $99.95)

RhythmAce (Figure 10-18) is an interactive music education program featuring onscreen rhythmic notation. Offering a variety of different exercise modes, RhythmAce provides enough flexibility to tailor the presentation of drills to suit individual needs. Topics such as tempo, measures per drill, time

FIGURE 10-18

RhythmAce by Ibis Software

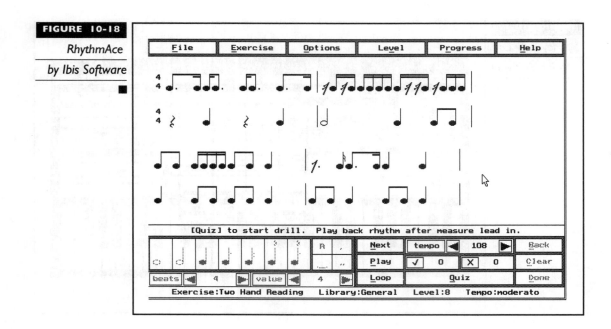

signatures, notation values, and mixed meters provide for a complete rhythm training regimen.

In a typical exercise, you hear a metronome ticking and are required to play back the rhythmic notation shown on the screen using a mouse, the PC keyboard, or a MIDI keyboard. In another exercise, the program plays a rhythmic phrase and you are asked to reproduce the notation utilizing onscreen notation buttons. Drills are selected from a single-user library, including a classical style, which follows traditional notation rules closely, and a jazz style, which reflects a more relaxed notation. The program even includes the option of single- or two-handed rhythms.

RhythmAce provides comprehensive feedback concerning correctness, accuracy, and improvement over time. In the notation area, a red "X" indicates a note or rest played incorrectly. Under this area, two timing diagrams display the expected response and the actual response, letting you know if notes and rests were held the correct length of time. Once the rhythm has been played correctly, the program calculates an accuracy figure based on what it expected and what was actually played. At the end of a block of exercises, you can print a summary of the exercise just performed.

RhythmPlay by Ibis Software (Retail: $49.95)

RhythmPlay (Figure 10-19) is a simpler version, or subset, of RhythmAce, presented in a game format. Special features include an audio and visual metronome; 24 types of drills; sustain and timing accuracy; timing diagram; high score table; slow, normal, and automatic modes; and one- and two-handed exercises. This is an excellent program for beginners to get a feel for rhythm. Experienced musicians can use RhythmPlay to hone their sense of timing. RhythmPlay isolates one of the skills of successful sight-reading, rhythm reading, to help the user concentrate on just this skill.

The 24 types of drills are grouped into six skill levels to provide a progressive introduction to reading and playing rhythms. You begin with simple rhythmic phrases using quarter and half notes in 4/4 time. As you progress in the drills, you are introduced to rests, eighth and sixteenth notes, dots and ties, changing meters, and two-handed phrases.

Typical applications for RhythmPlay may include rhythm training for church choir members or training drummers to read rhythms from a score.

Soloist by Ibis Software (Retail: $59.95)

Soloist (Figure 10-20) is another innovative program from Ibis Software. Basically, this program allows you to hone your skills as a musician or singer by measuring your accuracy. This is done by attaching a microphone to your

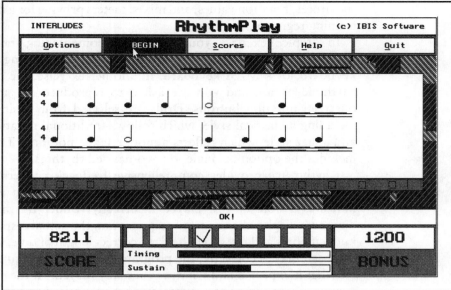

Sound Blaster sound card and playing the instruments while following the notes that are displayed on the screen. Soloist provides several measures of music for you to follow with any instrument that you care to use: piano, guitar, violin, trumpet, saxophone, or even your voice.

Soloist presents these practice sessions in levels. Once you've successfully played a given number of notes, you advance to a higher level where the

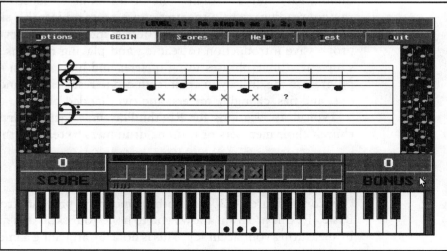

sequence of notes becomes harder and you have to deal with tempo changes as well. The program is designed to provide the budding musician with practice in sight-reading and playing. Using Soloist to check the accuracy of your singing voice is especially fun.

The only drawback to soloist is that it does not recognize chords. Since it's targeted at solo instruments and beginning musicians, this is not a big loss. As a bonus, the program can be used to tune your instrument. The manual also contains a succinct section on music theory. Soloist is an excellent program for beginning and improving musicians.

Music Mentor for Windows by Midisoft Corporation (Retail: $149.95)

Music Mentor offers an entertaining music tutorial and utilizes a notation-based MIDI sequencer that makes music concepts spring to life, even for beginners. The product features lively text, graphics, animation, and MIDI-generated sounds.

For those just getting started in music, Music Mentor offers an introduction to basic music reading skills and explains the essential elements of all musical composition—rhythm, melody, harmony, timbre, texture, and form. The tutorial includes demonstrations of the ways in which famous composers have used musical elements in the different musical periods.

Because Music Mentor stores information in standard MIDI file format, you can access and manipulate all musical examples in the program. After listening to various pieces and learning about their components, you can then alter sounds, tempos, and other aspects of the music however you please. Even newcomers to music will find concepts like pitch reading and rhythm notation easier to grasp with Music Mentor's multimedia approach.

Music Mentor includes a notation-based MIDI recording and editing utility called Midisoft Recording Session for Windows (Figure 10-21). Music Mentor and Recording Session interface in such a way that you can listen to an example in the tutorial session, and with a single command open Recording Session to edit or play along with the piece. You can also create original music in Recording Session, or import MIDI files from other sources.

An important benefit of Recording Session is that it displays music in standard notation during both recording and playback like its upscale counterpart, Midisoft Studio for Windows. This capability sets it apart from common sequencer-style MIDI event lists and graphic editors, which tend to be less intuitive for users.

FIGURE 10-21

Midisoft

Recording Session

■

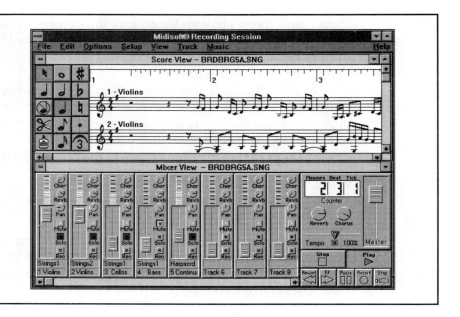

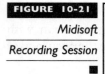

USEFUL UTILITIES

This section describes various utilities to help you use your Sound Blaster sound card to the best of its abilities. You'll find utilities that are simply fun additions to your computer, some software that allows you to experiment with generating sounds, as well as sophisticated sound editing tools. Most of these software programs are Windows applications, while a few are geared for those of you who still work in DOS.

Whoop It Up! by Advanced Support Group (Retail: $79.95)

Whoop It Up! attaches sound, both Wave and MIDI files, to Windows events, such as Application Start and Shutdown, Move, Minimize, Maximize, and many others. It can also attach sounds to message boxes such as the Exclamation box and Question box icons. Each application can have its own custom set of sounds assigned to it. There is even a random feature that selects a random sound every time you use the program.

Whoop It Up! includes over 2.5 megabytes of Wave and MIDI files. Additionally, the four following utilities are all part of this collection:

- Yakkity Clock is a talking clock that features both preset and custom alarms, voice announcement of the time at various intervals, and both a male and female voice. It can be configured to display time maximized or as icon text when minimized.

- Yakkity Monitor is a talking system monitor. It continuously monitors system resources and disk space and literally tells you when they fall below the preset levels. The program can be set to "stay on top" so that you can visually monitor Windows' current use of resources.

- Wave Editor is a 16-bit stereo Wave file editor that boasts as wide a range of features as any professional sound editor. Besides basic functions such as recording and cut and paste, Wave Editor provides routines for fades, transforms, filters, and echoes.

- Yakkity Savers is a collection of fourteen screen savers that include sound and animation sequences. With Yakkity Savers loaded, you can have fun with animated mice on pogo sticks and rollerblades, skiing fruit, and various kaleidoscope-like savers that you see on your screen. These savers work with the standard Windows 3.1 screen saver program.

Wired for Sound Pro by Aristosoft (Retail $79.95)

The granddaddy of this type of utility, Wired for Sound Pro enhances Windows by allowing you to attach sounds to Windows events. Over 100 sound effects in Wired for Sound Pro provide ear candy for most mundane Windows events such as moving or resizing windows. A talking system monitor, a talking clock, and a Wave sound editor round out this collection.

After Dark by Berkeley Systems (Retail $49.95)

After Dark is one of the largest selling Windows utility software programs. It was first made available on the Apple Macintosh but has gathered quite a following in the Windows arena. This is the program that started the screen saver craze. Most modern VGA color monitors actually do not have problems of the older CGA and monochrome monitors with phosphor burn-in. Software programs like these are more fun than functional and are great entertainment.

After Dark is a screen saver for Windows that includes the famous flying toasters and the ever-popular fish aquarium. The different modules sport different sounds including "blub-blub" sounds to accompany the air bubbles from the aquarium module. There are howling coyotes and screen-munching worms among the 40 or so modules. Our favorite is the Swan Lake module, in which beautifully rendered swans and their cygnets float and swim gracefully across the screen. More After Dark is an add-on module that adds over 20 fun modules to After Dark.

Another version of After Dark is tailored for Star Trek afficionados, aptly called Star Trek: The Screen Saver. This version contains digitized pictures of the actual crew from the TV series. It also features actual sound effects, music, and dialogue from the original series. Go ahead, reminisce, as Captain Kirk says, "Scotty, get us out of here!" Star Trek: The Screen Saver is, as Mr. Spock would say, "fascinating."

Blaster Master by Gary Maddox (Shareware: $29.95)

Blaster Master is a DOS-based program for working with Sound Blaster VOC, WAV, and SND format files. It requires EGA/VGA graphics, a mouse, a hard disk, and preferably a fast PC such as a 386 or 486. Blaster Master is available as shareware. The unregistered version only processes a sound file of up to 25 seconds, while there is no limit on the registered version.

The program is completely mouse driven. Features include conversion among the different supported formats and sampling rates. You can add effects such as echoes and fades. The mousedriven interface is easy to learn and use.

EZSound FX by Future Trends Software (Retail: $69.95)

EZSound FX is a multipurpose sound utility for Windows. Six different programs are included with EZSound FX, each one with specific capabilities.

- Digital FX (Figure 10-22) and Synth FX allow you to attach any sound or music to such mundane events as resizing a window or deleting a file. These are separate software that can be run simultaneously; for instance, you can have Digital FX play a digitized gunshot when you close a window, while Synth FX plays the beginning of Beethoven's 5th whenever you resize a window.

- Music FX plays music files (CMF and ROL formats) in the background while you're working on other more important matters. Over 100 such files, from classical to new age, are included.

- CD FX is a CD player program included for those who also have a CD drive connected to their Sound Blaster sound card. While it is a very basic program without any fancy displays or database features,

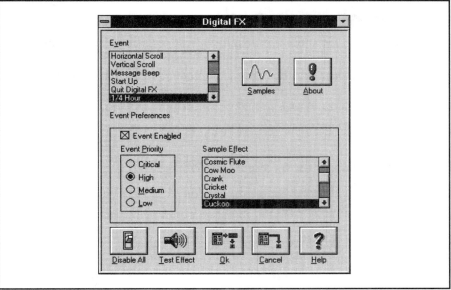

CD FX works well and is an adequate enhancement to the Windows Media Player when you want to listen to a CD.

■ Master FX is a versatile sound editor that fully supports stereo recording, editing, and playback on the Sound Blaster sound card. It imports and converts sound files from various formats, even those from Macintosh, Amiga, NeXT, and Sun. You can start experimenting with the over 100 included digital sound effects. Master FX supports sampling rates from 5,000Hz to 44,100Hz, but lacks the ability to support 16-bit recording. That aside, it is very easy to use and the variable view magnification and resizable window are a big improvement over the standard Windows Recorder.

■ Panel FX is a custom control panel for controlling the volume level of the Sound Blaster sound card. Additionally, you can use it to adjust and assign the Windows system error sound.

EZSound FX easily qualifies as the bargain of the bunch of Windows sound utilities for your Sound Blaster sound card. The program interface is simple and intuitive. If your budget is tight (whose isn't nowadays?), this is the one to get.

SoundSculptor by Ibis Software (Retail: $39.95)

SoundSculptor allows you to edit the FM sounds of the Sound Blaster sound card in a graphical format. You can create your own sounds or edit some of the sounds included with the program. Sounds created using SoundSculptor can then be used in other Ibis software such as RhythmPlay. Since the sounds can be saved in the standard BNK or INS format, other software can also use these customized sounds.

Mr. Sound FX by Prosonus (Retail: $24.95)

Remember the movie *Police Academy* and its long line of sequels? Michael Winslow played a zany cadet and, later in the sequels, a police officer who made many sound effects using only his voice. Mr. Sound FX includes over 150 sounds, about half of which are recordings of Mr. Winslow's vocal antics. Added to Winslow's selections are short music cuts including riffs, fanfares, and "blats" and other assorted sound effects.

With an incredible display of vocal gymnastics, Mr. Winslow's repertoire in this package includes such notable feats as car crashes and brakes squealing, jet flybys, bird tweets, a UFO flyby, a tennis ball, and the sound of breaking glass. You can integrate them into your own multimedia presentations.

Mr. Sound FX is similar to a limited Whoop It Up! or Wired For Sound Pro, in that you can assign sounds to events such as program launch, moving, or minimizing and maximizing windows. The software also works with Norton's Desktop for Windows and many other Windows applications, including After Dark from Berkeley Systems, Screen Craze from Gold Disk, the Cathy calendar from Amaze, Inc., and others.

AudioView by Voyetra Technologies (Retail: $129.95)

AudioView (Figure 10-23) is a professional-quality graphical digital audio editor for Windows 3.1. It allows you to record, modify, edit, and play back Wave (.WAV) and Voice (.VOC) files with your Sound Blaster sound card. You can also enhance these files with special effects such as compression, echo, reverb, sample rate conversion, and more. It features an easy-to-use tapedeck-style transport.

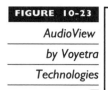

FIGURE 10-23

AudioView

by Voyetra

Technologies

Multimedia Toolkit by Voyetra Technologies (Retail: $499.95)

Multimedia Toolkit features a special selection of DOS and Windows software and utilities for your Sound Blaster sound card, including the following:

■ WinDAT is an entry-level digital audio editor for Windows.

■ Windows Jukebox allows you to arrange MIDI files, digital audio files, and CD tracks into custom playlists.

■ SoundScript is a multimedia scripting language for DOS that allows you to create multimedia presentations combining sound and animation.

■ Command Line File players allow you to play MIDI and digital audio from the DOS command line or from batch files.

Multimedia Toolkit includes 10 MIDI files and 10 digital audio files from Voyetra's extensive MusiClips library.

PatchView FM by Voyetra Technologies (Retail: $99.95)

PatchView FM (Figure 10-24) is a Windows-based patch editor and bank arranger for your Sound Blaster sound card's FM synthesizer. With PatchView FM, you can graphically create new FM voices and sound effects and arrange voices into custom banks.

PatchView FM also includes Voyetra's enhanced Sound Blaster sound card drivers for Windows. New patches can be utilized with the Sequencer Plus series and any Sound Blaster sound card–compatible Windows application.

PROGRAMMING TOOLS

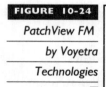

Whether you're preparing a multimedia presentation or programming an application that uses the Sound Blaster sound card, you may want to obtain some programming tools to help you in your endeavor. This section covers some of the many products available to help the professional accomplish tasks faster, and to help the amateur sound like a professional.

FIGURE 10-24

PatchView FM

by Voyetra

Technologies

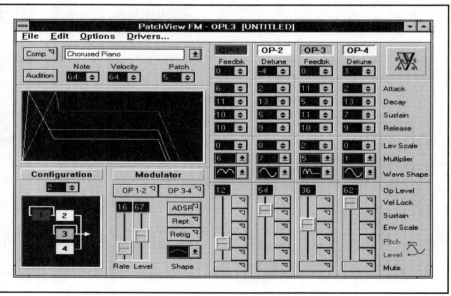

DigPak and MidPak by THE Audio Solution
(License fees vary from $69.95 to $5,000)

If you're a professional developer or programmer—or even if you're just a budding amateur—and you want to take full advantage of the Sound Blaster sound card, then these are the APIs (Application Program Interfaces) you're looking for. DigPak is a set of TSRs that provides a simple API, through a user interrupt vector, to play 8-bit digitized sounds. C procedures for inclusion with your program are provided, as well as software for compression and decompression of sound files.

MidPak, on the other hand, provides support for FM synthesis and MIDI music. The MidPak TSR works alone or in conjunction with the DigPak drivers to provide the developer with the complete sound solution. MidPak is a derivative of John Miles's Audio Interface Library, which is used in many games, including Interplay's Buzz Aldrin's Race Into Space, and Origin's Ultima Underworld and Strike Commander.

DigPak and MidPak are widely used in the PC game industry. Well-known game publishers like Strategic Simulations, Frontier, Software Toolworks, Electronic Arts, and Spectrum Holobyte, among many others, have embraced these APIs.

DigPak and MidPak are the premier solution for developers requiring music and sound effects in their applications, whether the output medium is the Sound Blaster sound card or other sound cards on the market.

Multimedia Music Library by Midisoft Corporation
(Retail: $79.95)

Multimedia Music Library is a compilation of over 100 MIDI format files on floppy disks. The tracks in this collection mainly comprise pop and orchestral music. The 14 main themes, 28 variations, and a wide assortment of snips and backgrounds are all original compositions and can be distributed royalty free. Since the files are in standard MIDI format, they can be modified with any MIDI sequencer.

A simple interface, MIDIBase (Figure 10-25), facilitates access to these individual files. It stores information about the style and length of each piece. You can review descriptions and then listen to a selection while in MIDIBase. The music is organized into categories consisting of assorted related musical cues grouped around main themes.

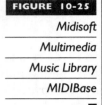

FIGURE 10-25

Midisoft

Multimedia

Music Library

MIDIBase

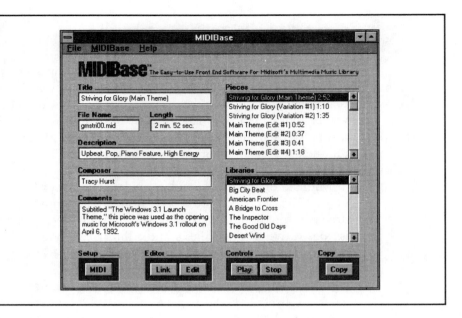

MusicBytes by Prosonus (Retail: $99.95)

MusicBytes (Figure 10-26) contains dozens of original tunes ranging from rock to classical and from industrial to novelty, all kept handily organized by a feature called the Music Librarian. The music and sound effects are designed for use by multimedia software developers and those producing multimedia presentations.

In addition to their varying lengths, each tune is presented in various formats including 11KHz and 22KHz Wave files, 44.1KHz standard Red Book audio, and MIDI sequences. Red Book audio is CD audio; it can be accessed by any standard CD player. Each music clip is available pre-edited in 60-, 30-, 15-, and 5-second versions. The various file formats and lengths are provided to accommodate all PC users, from novice to power user. The Wave format files permit you to edit the music clips to any length, loop a section, or combine other music clips with a Wave format editor such as the Windows Recorder.

Also included in MusicBytes is the Media Librarian, an easy to use software front-end, designed to audition, catalog, customize, and search for files on the CD-ROM. The Librarian allows you to scroll through the files on the CD-ROM and select the desired music or sound effects files. The desired file can then be auditioned without quitting the program. The Librarian also allows you to rename, catalog, and make notes about the files

FIGURE 10-26

MusicBytes

by Prosonus

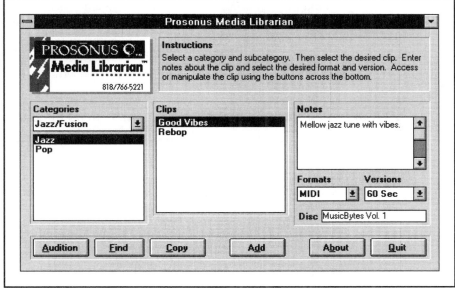

as you wish. In addition, the Librarian features a Find File mechanism that allows you to easily search for a specific file or category of files.

The MusicBytes CD-ROM features performances by numerous world-renowned artists, including Scott Page (Pink Floyd, Supertramp), Jeff Porcaro (Toto, Paul McCartney), Steve Lukather (Toto, Michael Jackson), Neil Stubenhaus (Quincy Jones, Michael Bolton), Jeff "Skunk" Baxter (Doobie Brothers, Steely Dan), and Michael Lang (Barbra Streisand, Lee Ritenour, Neil Diamond).

Music and sound effects on MusicBytes can be used license-free. There are no extra copyright or licensing fees attached to MusicBytes for commercial applications. The tunes and effects on this CD are of consistently high quality and varied selection, and can be highly recommended.

Sound Factory by Voyetra Technologies (Retail: $199.95)

Sound Factory is a complete sound development toolkit that provides DOS applications with a similar level of sound functionality as Windows.

Sound Factory is built around the high-level Voyetra Multimedia Player (VMP) and a set of low-level APIs. This approach allows the programmer to create device-independent applications that support not only the Sound Blaster sound card but nearly every major sound card.

Sound Factory contains nearly 100 different functions for MIDI, synthesis, digital audio, audio CD, mixer control, SMPTE synch, timer services, and more. Sound Factory includes extensive documentation with complete function call specifications, programming support files, sample code, digital audio editor, and a function call test utility, as well as sample MIDI and digital audio files.

MusiClips by Voyetra Technologies (Retail: $69.95 and Up)

MusiClips is Voyetra's huge library of MIDI files for multimedia productions. Eight packages are available:

- Signatures Edition (three different packages) features styles characterizing different eras in pop music.
- Classics Edition (two different packages) includes symphonies, operas, piano concertos, Joplin rags, and much more.
- Collectors Edition (three different packages) contains popular favorites including ethnic, holiday, patriotic, original production music, and more.

All MusiClips files are specially designed to work with your Sound Blaster sound card, and they comply with Microsoft's Multimedia Authoring Guidelines for MIDI files.

COMPELLING CD-ROM TITLES

CD-ROM software contains some of the most exciting multimedia experiences you can have on a PC. The gargantuan capacity of the CD-ROM media allows software designers to cram lots of information onto the disk and enhance them with animation, video clips, and sound. The CD-ROM software programs we describe here were chosen specifically for their applicability to the Sound Blaster sound cards. Many other excellent reference titles are not presented in multimedia format but may also be indispensable additions to your CD-ROM library.

Games

There is little question that games are the most prevalent examples of multimedia applications. This format is most beneficial to adventure games, where dramatic interaction and dialogue with other characters in the gaming environment is the norm.

Recently, one game has been hailed as the mother of all CD-ROM titles. This game is called The 7th Guest from TriloByte. Combining some of the most stunning graphics and animation you'll see on any computer, the game requires you to solve the mystery of a haunted house by solving numerous classical puzzles found in various rooms. The musical score is hauntingly well done and adds much atmosphere to the game. Ghostly apparitions are actually live actors who have been videotaped and digitally manipulated. All the dialogue is also recorded during the actual performance by the actors. The 7th Guest was one of the few games that our noncomputer/nongamer friends wanted to play after seeing the introduction. We bet that this game will sell a lot of CD-ROM drives.

LucasArts has produced some noteworthy disk-based adventure games, but their CD-ROM versions of Day of the Tentacle (Figure 10-27) and Indiana Jones: The Fate of Atlantis are particularly outstanding. The dialogue in both these CD-ROMs is done entirely by a cast of professional voice actors. Richard Sanders, who played Les Nessman in the TV series *WKRP in Cincinnati,* as Bernard in Day of the Tentacle is one of the more recognizable talents used. The music and voices add a very tangible atmosphere and give each character a very distinct and recognizable personality, which is missing in the disk versions of the same games. You don't want to miss either one of these titles.

FIGURE 10-27

Day of the

Tentacle

by LucasArts

Sierra On-Line is not about to be outdone in the CD-ROM arena, and both the CD-ROM versions of King's Quest VI and Space Quest IV are excellent, featuring numerous enhancements to the disk-based versions. Sierra also used an established talent to play Alexander in King's Quest VI— Robby Benson, the voice of the Beast in the Walt Disney animated feature *Beauty and the Beast*. If you play King's Quest VI in Windows, you get enhanced high-resolution close-ups of the characters when they are talking. Also, the lip-synching technology used here must be seen to be believed. As a bonus, a video for Windows on the making of King's Quest VI is included.

Reference

Plain text can be plain boring—few of us would choose to read a dictionary rather than an illustrated encyclopedia. With a CD-ROM drive and a Sound Blaster sound card, you can make any seemingly boring subject come alive with animation, video, and sound. Some reference CD-ROMs are devoid of multimedia enhancements, as they're geared toward professional applications. The ones that are multimedia-enabled are fun to explore, and you may even learn something without realizing it.

Microsoft is a strong supporter of the multimedia concept. They also produce a variety of great multimedia CD-ROM reference titles. One of these is Cinemania (Figure 10-28), a companion for movie buffs. Cinemania contains 19,000 capsule reviews and 750 detailed reviews of movies taken from *Leonard Maltin's Movie and Video Guide*. While you don't get to see movie clips, you do get photographs and sound clips from some of the featured movies. Multimedia Beethoven: The Ninth Symphony is a must for classical music buffs. It is a guide to the composer himself and the Ninth Symphony, of course. Professor Robert Winter, a world-renowned expert on Beethoven, serves as our guide as the symphony is dissected. This CD-ROM helps you learn to appreciate classical music at a new level.

Microsoft Bookshelf Multimedia Edition is a collection of several reference works that includes an encyclopedia, a dictionary, a thesaurus, an atlas, an almanac, and two quotation dictionaries. Here's an example of how learning can be fun. In the atlas, you simply click a country to display its flag and play its national anthem. You even get to hear the names of cities and countries pronounced correctly by simply clicking the name.

Space Shuttle from Software Toolworks is another fine example of a highly entertaining yet informative reference. This reference includes descriptions of the first 53 Space Shuttle missions, plus actual NASA video footage from these missions. You start at the Johnson Space Center, where you learn the history of the Space Shuttle complete with narration, photographs, schematic diagrams, and full motion video. Explore the equipment and gear used

Cinemania

by Microsoft

for Space Shuttle missions and discover what it takes to work and live in space. In case you're wondering: yes, the footage of the Challenger disaster is included.

Educational

The sound capabilities of your Sound Blaster sound card open a whole new world of opportunities for nonreaders. Prereaders can be given these software programs to explore on their own without fear of their getting lost. Most of these educational programs are presented in a game format to hold a child's interest a little longer.

Brøderbund is the premier publisher of interactive books on CD-ROM. Just Grandma and Me is Brøderbund's first foray into what they call Living Books. Just Grandma and Me is an adaptation of a Mercer Mayer storybook. Almost anywhere you click on the screen invokes some animation and sound, making it ideal even for preschoolers. But the idea is to teach—to help the child read and speak the words on each of the ten pages of the story. The program can read in English, Spanish, or Japanese. Arthur's Teacher Trouble is the follow-up to Just Grandma and Me, and it attempts to teach reading skills in the same vein. Both programs have superb graphics and crystal-clear sound.

Mixed Up Mother Goose from Sierra On-Line is the granddaddy of CD-ROM multimedia entertainment titles. It is an animated adventure where you have to wander around Mother Goose land in the hopes of getting

18 nursery rhyme characters their appropriate missing objects. Once you match the object and the character, they recite and perform a rhyme in either English, French, German, Japanese, or Spanish.

THE SOFTWARE PUBLISHERS

Below is the list of software publishers whose products we've described in this chapter. We didn't include the overwhelming number of software publishers for games, because you're likely to find those in nearly any software or computer store.

Advanced Support Group
11900 Grant Place
Des Peres, MO 63131
Orders Only: (800) 767-9611
Information: (314) 965-5630
CompuServe ID: 70304,3642

Aristosoft
7041 Koll Center Parkway, Suite 160
Pleasanton, CA 94566
(800) 338-2629 (outside California)
(800) 426-8288 (within California)

Berkeley Systems
2095 Rose Street
Berkeley, CA 94709
(510) 540-5535

Blaster Master
Gary Maddox
1901 Spring Creek #315
Plano, TX 75023
CompuServe ID: 76711,547

Blue Ribbon SoundWorks, Ltd.
Venture Center
1605 Chantilly Drive, Suite 200

Atlanta, GA 30324
(800) 226-0212 or (404) 315-0212

Dr.T's Music Software, Inc.
124 Crescent Road, Suite 3
Needham, MA 02194
(800) 989-6434 or (617) 455-1454

Future Trends Software
1508 Osprey Drive, #103
DeSoto, TX 75115
(214) 224-3288

Howling Dogs Systems
Box 80405
Burnaby, BC
Canada V5H 3X6
(604) 436-0420
CompuServe ID: 70044,2736

Ibis Software
140 Second Street, Suite 603
San Francisco, CA 94105
(415) 546-1917

Midisoft Corporation
P.O. Box 1000
Bellevue, WA 98009
(800) 776-6434 or (206) 881-7176

Passport Designs, Inc.
100 Stone Pine Road
Half Moon Bay, CA 94019
(800) 443-3210 or (415) 726-0280

PG Music, Inc.
266 Elmwood Avenue, Suite #111
Buffalo, NY 14222
(800) 268-6272 or (416) 528-2368
CompuServe ID: 75300,2750

Prosonus
11126 Weddington Street
North Hollywood, CA 91601
(800) 999-6191 or (818) 766-5221

Softronics
5085 List Drive
Colorado Springs, CO 80919
(800) 225-8590 or (719) 593-9540

THE Audio Solution
P.O. Box 11688
Clayton, MO 63105
(314) 567-0267

Twelve Tone Systems
P.O. Box 760
Watertown, MA 02272
(800) 234-1171 or (617) 926-2480

Voyetra Technologies
5 Odell Plaza
Yonkers, NY 10701-1406
(914) 966-0600
CompuServe ID: 71052,2416

WinJammer Software Limited
Dan McKee
69 Rancliffe Road
Oakville, Ontario
Canada L6H 1B1
CompuServe ID: 70742,2052

Software Excitement! (Attn: Registrations)
6475 Crater Lake Highway
Central Point, OR 97502
(800) 444-5457

11

A CD-ROM Compendium

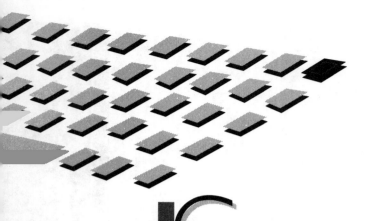

C D - R O M (compact disc read-only memory) technology can be daunting in many respects. We could spend a whole book discussing the theory and application of digital audio and storage, error-correction formulas and methods, signal timing and—well, you get the idea. Instead, this chapter simply explains why you'd want to purchase a CD-ROM drive. You learn what to look for when shopping for a CD-ROM drive—what's important and what's not. Then we have a section highlighting some of the best CD-ROM drives we could get hold of.

For those of you who will be purchasing a CD-ROM drive, or who are looking for CD-ROM accessories, we've listed some vendors who provide great prices for CD-ROM–related products. The section following the vendor listings is the installation section, which provides some hints on connecting any CD-ROM drive to your Sound Blaster sound card and loading the correct driver software.

TIP: *If you've already purchased a CD-ROM drive and intend to install it yourself, jump straight to the CD-ROM drive installation section further along in this chapter for valuable information and guidance. You can then come back and read the earlier part of the chapter.*

Finally, don't forget to check out some of the outstanding CD-ROM software described in a special section in Chapter 10. You'll find some exciting, groundbreaking products described there, including a few that you may want to purchase just to show off your new CD-ROM drive.

WHY DO YOU WANT A CD-ROM DRIVE?

Not so long ago, the invasion of the audio CD (compact disc) into our living rooms, cars—our everyday lives—began in earnest. Today, virtually everyone has been exposed to the marvelous and seemingly magical little silvery plastic discs. In recent years, sales of CDs have long surpassed those of vinyl record albums, and the dollar volume has surpassed that of the analog cassette. The convenience and sound quality of CDs have been widely accepted as the standard by which both old and new music mediums are judged. Close cousin to the CD is the CD-ROM, which is poised to extend CD popularity to the PC storage arena. Recent software developments, the establishment of new standards, and falling prices are the driving forces behind the widespread acceptance of the CD-ROM as a common storage medium on personal computers.

Software developers are beginning to exploit the capabilities of the medium. Some of them, including Microsoft, Lotus, and Corel Systems, already distribute enhanced versions of popular floppy disk–based products on CD-ROM. Many software publishers are now including their manuals on CD-ROM as well. This not only saves printing costs and materials, but it also allows you to find a topic much faster than by flipping through a printed manual.

The razzle-dazzle of multimedia, with its enormous appetite for storage, is another driving force behind this new trend. In fact, many new educational and entertainment titles are appearing on CD-ROM only—they are just too big to fit onto floppies. Voluminous reference materials can now be cheaply stored on CD-ROM. These materials, such as encyclopedias, are being transferred to electronic text format and enhanced with pictures, sound, and video clips. All this is made possible by the advent of CD-ROM technology and your Sound Blaster sound card.

A Brief History Lesson

CD technology was first explored in 1974 by both Sony Corporation of Japan and Philips of the Netherlands. By 1976, most other major Japanese electronics companies, including Pioneer, Mitsubishi, and Matsushita, submitted proposals for a digital audio format. The audio CD, as we know it today, was born in 1979 when Sony and Philips collaborated on a standard; the standard was accepted in 1980 by a committee of 35 worldwide manufacturers. The commercial introduction of the CD was stalled until *semiconductor lasers,* used for reading the CD, and *large-scale integrated (LSI) circuits,* for processing the digital audio data, were ready. So it wasn't until 1982 that the first CD player was released in Japan and Europe and became widely available shortly thereafter in North America.

NOTE: *Although popularly known simply as "CD," audio CDs were officially named "Compact Disc-Digital Audio." Somewhere on the cover, insert, or disc itself, you'll find a stamp or logo with this official name. However, like most everybody else, we refer to these audio discs simply as CDs, or audio CDs.*

The PC industry quickly realized the positive implications of being able to store hundreds of megabytes of information on a cheap plastic disc. The CD-ROM quickly followed the audio CD. *CD-ROM* describes the computer function of a CD—compact disc read-only memory. Unlike a hard disk, data cannot be written on or erased from a CD-ROM by the average consumer. Instead, the data is encoded on the CD-ROM during the manufacturing process, as seen in Figure 11-1. The only exception to this rule is the new recordable CD, known as *CD-R* or *CD-WO* (compact disc-write once),

FIGURE 11-1

CD-ROM manufacturing process

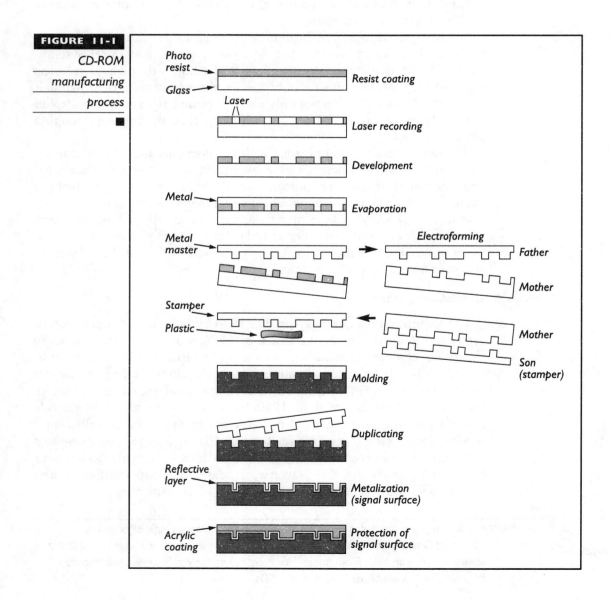

which permits an appropriate recorder to write data—one time only—to a blank CD. The resulting CD can then be read by any CD-ROM drive.

NOTE: *CD-ROM, a read-only storage medium, cannot be infected by a virus. Your computer is also extremely unlikely to contract a virus from a CD-ROM because the manufacturing process uses stringent quality assurance tests.*

CD-ROM Storage Capacity

A CD-ROM possesses a lot of storage space. To give you an idea: the average hard disk is only 120MB in size; a CD-ROM's capacity is approximately 680MB, which is equivalent to 450 high-density 3 1/2-inch floppy disks—that's 450 of the same type of disk that came with this book! (See Figure 11-2.) More than 270,000 pages of uncompressed text can be stored on a CD-ROM. Since the CD-ROM is removable, like a floppy disk, a CD-ROM drive has an unlimited capacity, which is a clear advantage over a hard disk.

Keep in mind that both audio CDs and CD-ROMs refer to identical mediums that store different information for separate applications. All varieties of CDs, except the new recordable CDs, can be produced with the same equipment at the same factories. Despite the myriad of standards in existence, the basic operations involved in producing and reading data from the silvery discs remain the same. The material required to make a CD-ROM is quite cheap, so that CD-ROMs are a much cheaper storage medium than the floppy or hard disk. The cost of manufacturing a CD can be as little as

FIGURE 11-2

CD-ROM storage

capacity

■

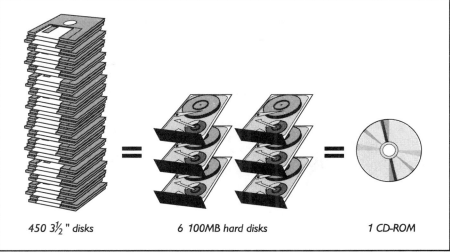

450 3½" disks   *6 100MB hard disks*   *1 CD-ROM*

CD: Perfect Sound and Data Forever?

It has often been said that CDs last forever. Forever is a long time, but a CD that's properly cared for will more than likely outlive us. Some of you may have heard the dreaded "CD rot" story, in which some older CDs actually became unplayable due to the deterioration of the reflective aluminum layer. Thankfully, this phenomenon has only occurred in some of the very first batches of CDs.

Advancements in equipment and quality assurance have since been made in this process and such complaints are now mostly nonexistent. However, no process is perfect, and there are a very few defective CDs that escape quality assurance and make it to the retail shelf, though this is highly unlikely.

Will a stable and perfected manufacturing process for CD-ROMs mean perfect data forever? Well, it really doesn't matter, since the information on most CD-ROMs, unlike that on audio CDs, becomes obsolete within a few years anyway. If data needs to be stored for all posterity, there still isn't a medium that can approach the life span, speed, and convenience of a CD-ROM at anywhere close to its cost.

$1. Since programs are only getting larger, and floppy disks can cost up to $1 each, you can quickly see why CDs may eventually replace floppy disks as a distribution medium for software.

NOTE: While a CD-ROM costs very little to make, the information and programs contained on it cost far more to create. The information is what you're paying for when you buy a CD-ROM, not the physical disc itself.

So whether you're looking for the best electronic reference data, innovative educational software, or the snazziest games, you'll find the best of them available exclusively on CD-ROM. CD-ROM is the ideal medium to distribute increasingly sophisticated software. It is only a matter of time before CD-ROM drives become as commonplace as floppy and hard drives on personal computers—the trend has already begun.

TIP: Unlike floppy disks, CD-ROMs are impervious to magnetic fields. You can place them safely next to your monitor or speakers.

KNOW BEFORE YOU BUY

A smart shopper should always have a proper understanding of the goods before purchasing. Knowing what to look for and understanding some of the terms used to describe CD-ROM drives and CD-ROM technology are equally important, especially when you're trying to wade through the ever-changing deluge of products. Besides your budget, due consideration must be given to the following areas whenever you decide to shop for a CD-ROM drive: speed, compatibility, and reliability.

How Fast Is It?

Speed is probably the single most important factor in selecting a CD-ROM drive. The overall performance of any storage device is based on a combination of two measurements: average access time and transfer rate.

Average access time is the more important measurement if you intend to use your CD-ROM drive primarily to access reference material such as magazine article databases or census information. It is less important if your primary CD-ROM applications involve transferring or reading large megabyte-sized files (multimedia CD-ROMs fall into this latter category). In these instances the transfer rate, rather than the access time, is the more important criteria.

TIP: *For help in improving the speed of any CD-ROM drive, refer to "Caching CD-ROM" at the end of this chapter for a preview of software that will accomplish this.*

Average Access Time

Average access time, or *average seek time,* is a measurement of how fast a drive positions its reading assembly, reads the data of any part of the disc, and returns the data to the computer. Average access time is measured in thousandths of a second, or *milliseconds* (ms). The assembly takes slightly longer to move from the outermost to the innermost edge of the disc but is a little quicker at moving just to an adjacent section of the disc. A CD-ROM drive has to brake and accelerate frequently as data is read from different parts of the disc, just like a car needs time to accelerate to a faster speed or brake to slow down. Any motor requires time to stabilize at any given speed. This speed adjustment, in combination with the comparatively bulky reading assembly, accounts for the slow access times of CD-ROM drives.

All measurements are relative; that is to say, you should only compare seek times among CD-ROM drives. Anything faster than 250ms is currently state of the art. Also bear in mind that you will have an impossible time telling the difference between an average access time of 280ms versus one of 265ms. You're more likely to tell the difference between 350ms and 200ms. First-generation CD-ROM drives had access times of over one second

(1,000ms). In comparison, when the hard disk drive was first introduced on a PC, it had an average seek time of about 90ms. The fastest CD-ROM drive at the time of this writing is the Toshiba 3401 series, with an average access time of 200ms. This is leaps and bounds better than the first-generation CD-ROM drives but is still a slowpoke compared to today's sub-16ms hard disks.

CD-ROM drives are abysmally slow compared to hard disk drives. However, this disadvantage is easily offset by the CD-ROM's larger and much cheaper storage capacity. Fortunately, CD-ROM drives are faster than floppy disk drives.

Transfer Rate

Transfer rate is perhaps the most important measurement for multimedia compatibility of a CD-ROM drive, including most, if not all, educational and entertainment CD-ROM programs. Unlike searching for many snippets of information that may reside on different areas of a disc, multimedia applications usually involve transferring large amounts of text, audio, and video data to the computer at any one time. The faster this process, the higher the number of frames that can be transferred and displayed within a second. Fast throughput can be used to transfer better quality audio and also translates into smoother video, more detailed images, more colors, and more realistic animation.

The *transfer rate* measures the speed at which the CD-ROM drive reads data off the disc and transfers it to the computer once the laser assembly has positioned itself onto the desired track. Transfer rate is not affected by average access time, as transfer rate occurs after the seek has occurred. Transfer rate is measured as the number of kilobytes that can be transferred in a second, or *K/sec (kilobytes per second)*.

At a minimum, all CD-ROM drives are supposed to transfer data at 150K/sec. Since this is a standard, we would assume that all CD-ROM drives adhere to this minimum transfer rate; unfortunately, such is not the case. Initially, a variety of software and hardware bottlenecks prevented the drive from actually transferring data to the computer's memory at that rate. The solution came in the form of some software changes and a RAM (random access memory) buffer built into the CD-ROM drive itself. With these changes, data could be read into the *RAM buffer*—which acts as a temporary holding place for the data—while other data is being transferred to the computer. This process is somewhat similar to airplanes waiting on the apron prior to takeoff on the runway.

It is pretty common for today's CD-ROM drives to use a buffer to smooth and speed up data transfer. Buffer sizes typically range from 32K to as much as 256K. Keep in mind that the buffer size alone doesn't mean too much—a drive with a 64K buffer and a 300K/sec transfer rate is still faster than one with a 256K buffer and a 150K/sec transfer rate.

Double-Speed Drives

A relatively simply technical innovation was developed to improve the transfer rate of CD-ROM drives. Manufacturers and software programmers quickly recognized that a 150K/sec transfer rate is completely inadequate to meet the minimum requirement for the Multimedia PC (MPC) Level 1 standard, which specifies displaying digital high-resolution color video at 30 frames per second (fps). In the so-called double-speed drives, the disc's rotational speed is doubled. Increasing the rotational speed of the disc increases the transfer rate. When the computer is accessing data, the drive spins the CD-ROM anywhere from 400 to 1,060 rpm (revolutions per minute). Since the disc is spinning two times faster than normal, twice the number of sectors containing data pass over or under the reading assembly at any given time. This increased rotational speed effectively doubles the transfer rate of the drive from 150K/sec to 300K/sec.

Double-speed drives technically conflicted with the audio CD standard, which called for a 150K/sec transfer rate. Therefore, all faster CD-ROM drives automatically slow down to normal speed when playing a regular audio CD to maintain compatibility with the standard audio CD DAC (digital-to-analog converter), which only accepts data at 150K/sec. In contrast, data such as video, pictures, and text bypasses the CD-ROM DAC and audio circuitry and is transferred directly to the CD-ROM drive's RAM buffer, then on to the computer (see Figure 11-3).

NOTE: *Some drive manufacturers are trying even harder to speed up their CD-ROM drives beyond double-speed. Toshiba and Texel increased the rotational speed of their drives to 2.2 times normal for a transfer rate of 330K/sec and 335K/sec, respectively. Pioneer pushed the envelope further by speeding up the rotational speed of its 604X CD-ROM Changer by four times, thus increasing the transfer rate to a speedy 612K/sec! This technology, dubbed Quadraspin by Pioneer, is no doubt the next frontier for other CD-ROM drive manufacturers.*

You should seriously consider purchasing at least a double-speed CD-ROM drive if you plan to use any multimedia software in the foreseeable future. While such drives may cost more than a standard-speed drive, you'll more than recoup the difference in price in the long run. Double-speed drives are already reasonably priced. And the prices will erode even further as

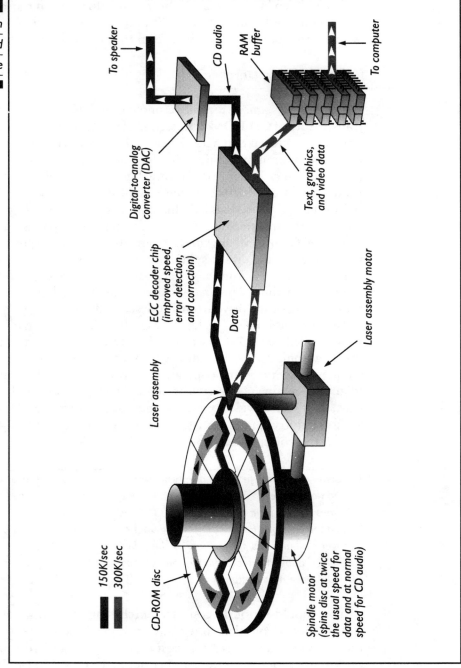

To speaker

CD audio

RAM buffer

To computer

Digital-to-analog converter (DAC)

Text, graphics, and video data

ECC decoder chip (improved speed, error detection, and correction)

Data

Laser assembly motor

Laser assembly

150K/sec
300K/sec

CD-ROM disc

Spindle motor (spins disc at twice the usual speed for data and at normal speed for CD audio)

manufacturers prepare for the next salvo—the triple and quadruple-speed CD-ROM drive.

How Compatible Is It?

The first compatibility issue you should concern yourself with is whether the CD-ROM drive is compatible with your Sound Blaster CD-ROM interface. Second, software compatibility has become increasingly important as the proliferation of CD standards continues at a brisk pace. Fortunately, there are only a few software standards you must keep in mind when selecting a CD-ROM drive. These standards usually mandate a variety of minimum hardware performance requirements. Most newer CD-ROM drives already adhere to or surpass these standards—the ones in our survey do. The two standards you may not want to do without are the MPC (Multimedia Personal Computer) certification and Kodak Photo CD compatibility on your CD-ROM drive.

NOTE: *Adherence to any standard is important only if you are going to use CD-ROMs that require that particular capability. Currently, the most popular standard for the PC is the MPC standard. Even if your current applications do not require MPC compliance, it is likely that a future upgrade will.*

Sound Blaster CD-ROM Interface Compatibility

When you're shopping for a CD-ROM drive, you should be on the lookout for one you can hook up directly to your Sound Blaster card. Unless you own a regular SB 1.*x*, SB 2.0, SB MCV, or the SBP MCV, you will find a CD-ROM interface on your sound card. Check the following table to see which CD-ROM will work with your sound card.

Sound Card	Interface	Compatible CD-ROM Drive
SB 1.*x*	None	Any CD-ROM drive with an additional PC interface card
SB 2.0	None	Any CD-ROM drive with an additional PC interface card
SB MCV	None	Any CD-ROM drive with an additional PC interface card
SBP Basic	Panasonic	Creative Labs or Panasonic CR-52*x* and CR-56*x* series

Sound Card	Interface	Compatible CD-ROM Drive
SBP	Panasonic	Creative Labs or Panasonic CR-52x and CR-56x series
SBP 2	Panasonic	Creative Labs or Panasonic CR-52x and CR-56x series
SBP MCV	None	Any CD-ROM drive with an additional PC interface card
SB16	Panasonic	Creative Labs or Panasonic CR-52x and CR-56x series
SB16 ASP	Panasonic	Creative Labs or Panasonic CR-52x and CR-56x series
SB16 Multi-CD	Panasonic/Sony/Mitsumi	Creative Labs or Panasonic CR-52x and CR-56s series, Sony CDU-31A, Mitsumi CRMC-FX001, CRMC-LU005
SB16 SCSI-2	SCSI	Almost any SCSI-1 or SCSI-2 CD-ROM drive

The CD-ROM interface found on most Sound Blaster cards is proprietary—you can only use CD-ROM drives specifically designed for the Sound Blaster cards. This interface is also referred to by many as the Panasonic interface. The only peripherals you can connect to this interface are CD-ROM drives sold by Creative Labs, or their identical twins from Panasonic. Panasonic's parent company, Matsushita, is the manufacturer of the proprietary CD-ROM drives sold by Creative Labs.

 TIP: *Be sure to check with Creative Labs for the latest list of CD-ROM drives that are compatible with your Sound Blaster card before making a purchase.*

Two new versions of the Sound Blaster 16 were introduced in October 1993. The first was Sound Blaster SCSI-2, which as its name implies, contains an industry-standard interface known as SCSI (Small Computer Systems Interface). The SB16 SCSI-2 contains a chip manufactured by Adaptec, considered by many to be the industry leader in SCSI technology. SCSI is considered the best CD-ROM interface, as the latest technology is usually first implemented in SCSI versions of CD-ROM drives and you can find a variety of such drives on the market. A CD-ROM drive is only one of the many SCSI-compatible devices you can connect to the SB16 SCSI-2 card. Refer to Chapter 4 for a discussion of SCSI and EZ-SCSI, a software package that allows you to connect hard drives, tape drives, and more to the SB16 SCSI-2 port. Below is a list of SCSI CD-ROM drives supported by the SB16 SCSI-2 card. As usual, check with Creative Labs for the latest list if a new SCSI CD-ROM drive is not in this one.

Manufacturer	CD-ROM Drives
CD-Technology	CD Porta-Drive T-3301, CD Porta Drive T-3401
Chinon	CDX-431,CDS-431, CDS-435, CDS-535
DEC	CDU-541, RRD-42
Denon	DRD-253, DRD-551, DRD-553, DRD-555
Hitachi	CDR-1650S, CDR-1750S, CDR-3650, CDR-3750
IBM	XM 3301-TA, 3510-002, 7210-001, 800, 845 CD-ROM I, CD-ROM II
LMSI	CM-212, CM-214, CM-231-232
NEC	BFV35 CDR-36, CDR-37, CDR-38, CDR-55, CDR-72, CDR-73, CDR-74, CDR-74-1, CDR-75, CDR-77, CDR-80, CDR-82, CDR-83, CDR-84, CDR-84-1
Panasonic	LK-MC501S, CR501B, CDR532, CDR533
Philips	CDD521
Pioneer	DRM-600, DRM-604X
Sony	CDU 541-01, CDU-561, CDU-561-31, CDU-6111, CDU-6211, CDU-7211
Teac	CD-50
Texel	DM-3021, DM-3024, DM-3121, DM-5020, DM-5024, DM-5121
Toshiba	XM-2200A, XM-3101BMB, XM-3201A1, XM-3201B, XM-3301B, XM-3301TA, TX-3401TA, TM-3301E, TXM-3201, TXM-3301,TXM-3401

The second of the SB16s introduced was the Sound Blaster 16 MultiCD, which actually incorporates three types of CD-ROM interfaces—the Panasonic, Sony, and Mitsumi proprietary interfaces. If you already own one of the compatible CD-ROM drives listed in the previous table, you can save some money and free up a slot in your computer by purchasing the SB16 MultiCD.

MPC Standards Level 1 and Level 2

The Multimedia Personal Computer (MPC) standard was created by the MPC Marketing Council. The council was formed by a number of hardware and software vendors, including Microsoft and Creative Labs, to establish and license a standard that specifies the minimum requirements for a PC to be considered multimedia-ready. The standard includes specifications for a PC, a sound card, a CD-ROM drive, speakers, and Microsoft Windows.

NOTE: *All of the CD-ROM drives sold by Creative Labs are MPC compatible. Do check for MPC compliance if you're purchasing a third-party CD-ROM drive.*

The MPC logo is licensed only to hardware companies that provide complete upgrade kits, and to software companies whose software requires an MPC-compliant computer to run on. It is unlikely that you'll see the MPC logo if you're purchasing a CD-ROM drive separate from the other components, like a sound card. However, a CD-ROM drive does have to meet certain minimum criteria to qualify as an MPC-compliant drive.

There are currently two levels or standards that have been established by the council: MPC Level 1 and MPC Level 2. Figure 11-4 shows the CD-ROM drive requirements for both levels. The main difference between the two is performance—the Level 2 specifications require faster and better hardware than Level 1. You should also note that when Level 1 was first adopted, the standard specified a minimum of an 80286/12-MHz computer. The council, upon realizing that the hardware platform was inadequate, later upped the minimum requirement to an 80386SX/16-MHz computer.

MPC Level 2 was introduced in May 1993 to keep up with the growth in hardware capabilities. This specification for the next generation of multimedia PCs was designed to allow for the playback of a video clip in a 320-by-240-pixel window at 15 fps (frames per second). The key difference as far as the CD-ROM drive is concerned is that Level 1 required a sustained transfer rate of 150K/sec, while Level 2 requires at least a double-speed drive with a sustained transfer rate of 300K/sec. MPC Level 2 is fully backward compatible with MPC Level 1, meaning Level 2–compatible equipment works properly with CD-ROMs designed for Level 1 systems.

NOTE: *You should be aware that, until recently, the MPC Council did not actually test products before certifying them—the certification was strictly based on the manufacturers' specifications and their ability to pay a fixed fee for the logo usage. This all changed in May 1993 when the Level 2 specification was approved. Now, all members have to submit their products to the council for testing. The MPC standard has become a stamp of certification, which makes it more valuable than before.*

Kodak Photo CD

The Kodak Photo CD standard is gaining in popularity and momentum— you may want to make sure the CD-ROM drive you purchase has the capability to use discs of this format. Photo CDs can be filled up with photographs in one pass, thus making them *single-session photo CDs*. You can also append photographs to a photo CD that is not full. This creates a *multisession photo CD*.

NOTE: *The MPC Level 2 specifications require Kodak Multisession Photo CD compatibility.*

Since the new standard was not clearly defined at first, the early CD-ROM players to claim Kodak Photo CD compatibility could only play back a single-session photo CD. Adapting older drives that were not compatible with Kodak Photo CD for single-session compatibility typically just involved

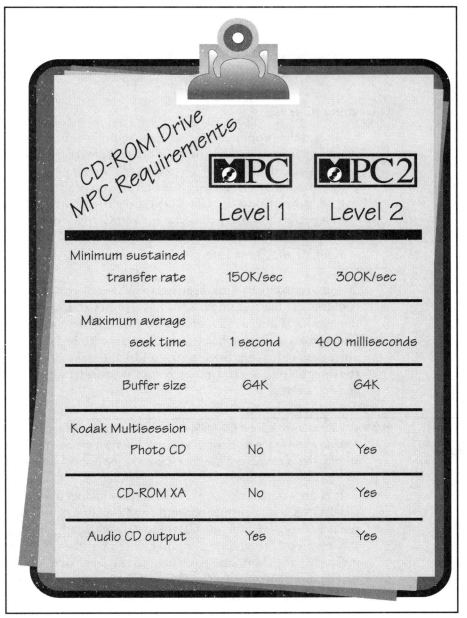

CD-ROM Drive MPC Requirements	MPC Level 1	MPC2 Level 2
Minimum sustained transfer rate	150K/sec	300K/sec
Maximum average seek time	1 second	400 milliseconds
Buffer size	64K	64K
Kodak Multisession Photo CD	No	Yes
CD-ROM XA	No	Yes
Audio CD output	Yes	Yes

a software driver update. However, this is not the case for multisession compatibility. At the least, a firmware change—replacing some chips in the drive—and a software driver update is required. Some manufacturers offer a trade-in program for customers who need multisession capability. This trade-in involves returning the old drive and paying an additional fee in exchange for a new model.

Most if not all of the newly introduced CD-ROM drives now include Kodak Multisession Photo CD compatibility as a standard feature. It never hurts to check, though, before plunking down your hard-earned cash for a CD-ROM drive.

How Reliable Is It?

The early proponents of CD technology argued that this technology would guarantee perfect sound (or data) forever. Reality has proven otherwise, as usual—CDs can be rendered unreadable or unreliable without proper maintenance and care. Certain aspects of the reliability of the medium can be attributed to the CD-ROM drive itself. After all, you can't possibly read a perfectly healthy disc in a broken CD-ROM drive.

Keeping the Data Safe

Many consumers have been led to believe by early CD zealots that the CD is indestructible and immune to fingerprints and scratches. This is far from the truth. While a CD or CD-ROM is less susceptible to damage by fingerprints and scratches, a very dirty or scratched disc can become unreadable. Less-damaging fingerprints and light scratches can force the drive to re-read the disc several times before it successfully reconstructs the data, causing delays.

NOTE: It is okay to leave a CD-ROM in the drive when you're not using it. The disc may become warm to the touch when you remove it from the drive after an extended period of time. This is normal and does not jeopardize the disc in any way.

It is no wonder, then, that instructions included with nearly all CDs and CD-ROMs advise proper handling and cleaning of the disc to keep its shiny surface clean. Handle all CDs and CD-ROMs by their edges to prevent leaving an oily fingerprint. If you have to put the disc down for a moment, make sure the shiny side faces up and the label side is down.

The disc caddy (or CD caddy) and the dust door are two devices designed by CD-ROM drive manufacturers to counter the dust and fingerprint problems.

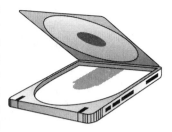

DISC CADDY   Regular audio single-CD players use a tray or top-loading mechanism to "cradle" or load the CD (multidisc players may use a different mechanism). The disc caddy, shown here, is the more popular method among CD-ROM drives. Most of the CD-ROM drives in our informal survey later in this chapter use the CD caddy. It looks like the plastic storage case that most CDs come in, except it has a metal gate on the bottom that opens up when inserted into the drive so that the laser in the reader assembly can read the shiny disc surface. First developed and used by Sony, these plastic caddies serve the primary function of protecting the disc from dust, fingerprints, and scratches by isolating them from direct handling. You first load the CD-ROM into a CD caddy, then load the caddy containing the disc into the drive.

One of the drawbacks to the CD caddy is that changing discs in it is inconvenient and awkward. The simple solution to this problem is to purchase additional caddies for every CD-ROM you own. This may seem expensive (at $7 to $15 per caddy), but it is the best solution if you change discs frequently. Tray- or top-loading drives are easier in this respect, but they expose your discs to dust and fingerprints.

All of the high-end and most of the midrange drives use the CD caddy. Only a handful of drives use an alternative method to load a disc. The multidisc Pioneer DRM-604X in our survey uses a unique disc magazine to hold up to six CD-ROMs in the drive at once. There are advantages and disadvantages to using either method. The choice is one of personal preference.

DUST DOORS AND LENS CLEANERS   Many CD-ROM drives incorporate dust doors to supplement the caddy in keeping grime and dust away from the CD. These dust doors remain closed whether or not a disc is in the drive. They are extremely important, especially if the drive is to be used in a dusty environment, such as a workshop, a basement recording studio, or an automobile repair garage. NEC actually included two dust doors on the CDR-74 and CDR-84 drives to further improve its immunity to dust.

Some drives also include an automatic lens cleaner that cleans the lens (through which the laser beam is projected) on the laser assembly whenever a disc is ejected. Since the laser beam must pass through this focusing lens, it must be clear of dust or other contamination. Otherwise, the drive has a hard time reading the data off the disc, much like dust and fingerprints on a camera lens would blur or obscure the subject in a photograph.

Many early CD-ROM drives that didn't have these doors or an automatic lens cleaner became unreliable without constant cleaning. Both a dust door and an automatic lens cleaner are useful features.

DRIVE FAILURES   Even the best mechanical devices are bound to fail eventually. CD-ROM drives are sophisticated mechanical devices that can be costly to repair. Manufacturers attempt to give you an idea of the reliability of their drives by providing an MTBF (mean time between failure) specification. They also provide varying warranty periods and various levels of technical support for their CD-ROM drives.

MTBF   *MTBF* is a measurement that indicates approximately how long a CD-ROM drive operates before it fails. Although MTBF is a measurement that is emphasized by manufacturers, it can be generally ignored. The measurement would be useful if an independent certification lab faithfully compared drives and rated their MTBF, but unfortunately, each manufacturer uses its own standards instead. Therefore, comparing MTBF claims by different companies is like comparing apples and oranges.

WARRANTIES   A good warranty period, on the other hand, is important. A one-year warranty is the industry standard, but some manufacturers, notably NEC, offer two-year warranties on their CD-ROM drives. Since CD-ROM drives are expensive to replace (unlike a floppy disk drive) and are generally more sensitive to damage than hard disks, a longer warranty ensures that costly repairs will be covered by the manufacturer.

TECHNICAL SUPPORT AND UPGRADES   The quality of technical support is also important, especially if you run into difficulties with your CD-ROM drive either during or after installation. Upgrade policies are another important consideration. Some companies will upgrade an older drive to give it new capabilities. Others have liberal and reasonable policies regarding upgrades to future products with added capabilities. This type of policy proved invaluable to those who took advantage of the offer from some manufacturers to upgrade their drives from single-session compatibility to Kodak Multisession Photo CD compatibility.

MAKING A PURCHASE DECISION

To many of you, cost is the primary consideration. Buy the best and fastest drive you need for your application. If you're planning to use mainly textual reference material such as a dictionary or phone directory, the cheapest drive in the survey below will suffice. However, if you want to run some of the hottest multimedia titles (like most educational and entertainment programs) and even better ones to be introduced in the future, you'll want to get the fastest drive possible. Hold off if your budget doesn't permit at least an MPC Level 2–compatible CD-ROM drive; prices will only drop, and buying a slow drive is like throwing money out the window if the drive will not run the type of programs you want. It is a good idea to test any intended application with the drive before purchasing it, just as you would test a prospective CD player by bringing and playing your favorite CD at the store. Or you can purchase the drive from a store with a money-back guarantee.

If you haven't purchased either a sound card or a CD-ROM drive, consider purchasing a Creative Labs multimedia upgrade kit. The multimedia upgrade kit is usually more cost effective and is a better value because it contains all the necessary cables, connectors, software drivers, and instructions required to hook up the drive to the Sound Blaster card. The kit also includes a number of CD-ROM programs to get you started with your CD-ROM collection. These items, when purchased separately, certainly cost much more than the price of the kit.

Purchasing a Creative Labs multimedia upgrade kit is not a viable option if you've decided on a CD-ROM drive that is not currently being bundled with the kits. In that case, you may want to look at a third-party bundle that includes a Sound Blaster card.

If you already have one of the many Sound Blaster cards with the proprietary Panasonic CD-ROM interface, you are limited in what drives you can purchase. Creative Labs' Omni CD package is a good option in this case. The kit contains a double-speed drive that is fully compatible with your existing card. The Omni CD does include an interface card (although you don't have to use it if you already have the Panasonic interface on your Sound Blaster card) for those of you with an older SB 1.*x* or 2.0.

As you can see, there are many ways to go about getting the combination you're after. As a general rule, if you do not already own a sound card, decide which CD-ROM drive you want first, then go shopping for a multimedia bundle that includes the Sound Blaster sound card as well. Refer to "Finding the Bargains" later in this chapter for vendors.

Internal or External?

You have to decide whether to get an internal or external CD-ROM drive. An external drive requires a separate case and power supply, as well as an empty slot on the back of your computer. The empty slot is taken up by a special adapter from Creative Labs, which makes the Sound Blaster's internal CD-ROM interface accessible from outside the computer.

An external drive also means extra cables hanging off the back of the computer and an extra power cable that needs to be plugged into an AC outlet. However, the installation for an external drive can be much simpler than for an internal drive. An external installation also provides an opportunity to place the drive within easy reach; this is especially useful if your computer is hidden away underneath the table, or out of arm's reach. External drives typically cost more—$50 to $200—than their internal counterpart because it costs more to provide the required extra case and power supply. External CD-ROM drives can be more flexible and can provide you with more expansion choices in the long run, though you may have to sacrifice some desktop real estate to house them.

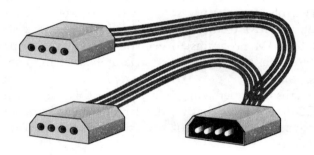

An internal drive requires at least a half-height 5 1/4-inch drive bay and a free disk drive power connector inside your computer. The installation is a little bit more involved, as you may have to temporarily remove other drives from your computer to install the CD-ROM drive. If you don't have any extra power connectors, you also need to get a power connector splitter, like the internal Y-splitter shown here, from a local dealer. An internal CD-ROM drive does cost less than an identical external one.

Finding the Right Cables and Drives

Check the following tables for items that you need for a complete CD-ROM drive installation. An item you cannot do without is the CD-ROM audio cable, which is available directly from Creative Labs. The following table lists the audio cables you may need if you didn't purchase a CD-ROM drive from Creative Labs.

Drive manufacturer	Part Number
Chinon	0411610040
Goldstar	0411610050
Matsushita (Panasonic)	0411610020
NEC	0411610070
Sony	0411610010
Toshiba	0411610030

Because there is no standard for audio connectors on the back of CD-ROM drives, making a single internal CD audio cable for the Sound Blaster sound cards isn't possible. You must buy one from either Creative Labs or a dealer.

A Selection of CD-ROM Drives

While the range of CD-ROM drives for a regular Sound Blaster Panasonic interface is small, there are myriad drives available with a SCSI interface. SCSI is the most common interface for a CD-ROM drive, so you'll find a wide variety of them to choose from. This one reason alone may convince many of you to purchase the SB16 SCSI-2 over any other Sound Blaster cards.

Below is a select compilation of some of the most readily available and best-performing CD-ROM drives currently on the market. Any of them can be easily attached to the appropriate Sound Blaster cards and is supported by the free CD-ROM driver software provided by Creative Labs. The prices, except for the NEC, are suggested list prices (the street price should be somewhat lower). We'll start with a Creative Labs drive and continue with some fast SCSI drives. These drives are listed in alphabetical order by manufacturer.

NOTE: *We did not use an extensive lab, or elaborate equipment and procedures, to test the CD-ROM drives. We offer only a subjective view of our experience with the drives. Use this as a guide to, not a review of, a few of the many drives available on the market.*

Creative Labs Omni CD

Creative Labs, Inc.
1901 McCarthy Blvd.
Milpitas, CA 95035
(800) 998-5227
Suggested list price: $395

The Omni CD from Creative Labs (see Figure 11-5) is a double-speed drive with a transfer rate of 300K/sec and is MPC Level 2 compatible. This drive is made by Panasonic and uses a tray-loading mechanism (instead of a CD caddy), much like a regular CD player. It is the only drive in our survey that is compatible with the prevalent Panasonic CD-ROM interface found on most Sound Blaster cards.

It has just about everything you'd look for in a CD-ROM drive, including Kodak Multisession Photo CD compatibility. An additional feature is the

FIGURE 11-5

The Omni CD

from Creative

Labs

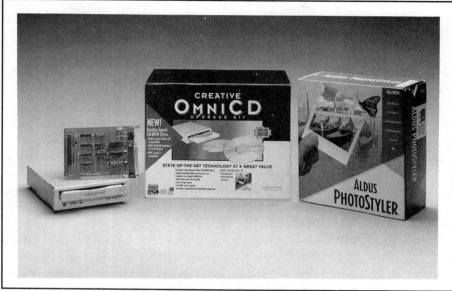

ability to chain up to four Omni CD drives on the Panasonic interface. One of the four drives can even be a Creative Labs CR-*52x* drive. It's the easiest way to add double-speed technology to your old Creative Labs CD-ROM drive.

Having the right cables and connectors and clear instructions are always helpful. In this area, the Omni CD excels. Since the drive was specifically designed for the Sound Blaster Panasonic CD-ROM interface, hooking it up was a cinch and the installation went flawlessly. An interface card is included as well, just in case you have one of the Sound Blaster cards that do not have a Panasonic CD-ROM interface on board.

While the drive worked flawlessly, we couldn't help but notice the slightly slower access time of 350ms compared with the faster SCSI drives that zip along at 300ms or less. However, this speed sacrifice is offset by the drive's attractive low price. For a trouble-free and quick installation, the Omni CD is an unbeatable bargain. For cutting-edge—or bleeding edge—performance, albeit at higher prices, read on.

NEC MultiSpin 38, 74, and 84 Series

NEC Technologies, Inc.
1414 Massachusetts Ave.
Boxborough, MA 01719
(800) NEC-INFO or (800) 632-4636

Estimated street price (we couldn't obtain list prices for the drives): MultiSpin 38, $465; MultiSpin 84, $515; MultiSpin 84, $615.

NEC was the first to introduce a double-speed CD-ROM drive in 1992. The MultiSpin series (see Figure 11-6) is the latest offering from the pioneer of double-spin technology.

The MultiSpin 38 is the entry-level drive. With an average access time of 400ms and a transfer rate of 300K/sec, this drive is unique in that it can operate on an optional battery pack. This makes it ideal for portable-computer users. It has a 64K buffer and is Kodak Multisession Photo CD compatible, making it an affordable MPC Level 2–compatible drive.

The MultiSpin 74 is the external version of the internal MultiSpin 84. Both feature an average access time of 280ms and a transfer rate of 300K/sec. These NEC drives feature an attractive two-year warranty. They also are MPC Level 2 compatible, meaning they feature about everything you'd look for in a CD-ROM drive including Kodak Multisession Photo CD, a 256K RAM buffer, and SB16 SCSI-2 compatibility.

NEC tech support doesn't have a good reputation. The quality of support was spotty, and the company's technicians were sometimes hard to reach. It does, however, have an excellent automatic-fax service, through which you can receive all kinds of information regarding the installation of their drives.

FIGURE 11-6

The NEC MultiSpin series CD-ROM drive

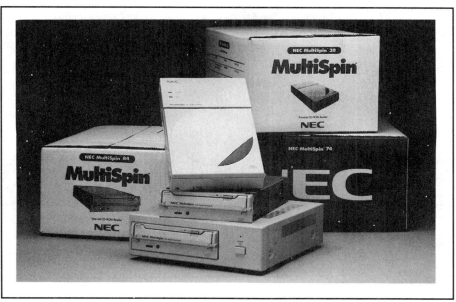

CAUTION: *There have been some reports that many NEC drives do not read standard CD-ROMs created with the new Sony and Philips CD-WO drives. If you plan on using discs made on these write-once drives, make sure you test for compatibility before committing to a NEC drive.*

Pioneer DRM-604X

Pioneer Communications of America
3255-1 Scott Blvd., Suite 103
Santa Clara, CA 95054
(800) 527-3766
Suggested list price: $1,845

Pioneer is the only CD-ROM drive manufacturer that offers a multidisc CD-ROM changer. The DRM-604X (as seen in Figure 11-7) automatically switches among six CD-ROMs that can be loaded at once. The discs are loaded in a multidisc magazine, similar to those used in Pioneer multidisc CD players for cars and home stereos. The drive is expensive, but it's well worth the price, especially if you're a heavy user of CD-ROM titles in a commercial or educational setting.

FIGURE 11-7

The unique, quadruple-speed multidisc Pioneer DRM-604X

Once installed, the drive appears as six DOS drive letters—each CD in the 604X is assigned a drive letter. The discs are switched automatically depending on which drive letter you access. Amazingly, it takes a mere five seconds for the drive to swap to the appropriate disc. It can certainly switch discs as fast or faster than you can manually with a regular CD-ROM drive. Disc swapping is not only quick, it is also fairly quiet. The drive does not, however, automatically search through all six discs for the appropriate one—you have to tell the computer which drive letter you want. You can simulate an automatic search by including all six drive letters in the PATH statement in your AUTOEXEC.BAT file.

The drawback to the multidisc changer is that you almost always have to load the same disc into the same spot in the changer. Many programs, such as Compton's Encyclopedia, expect to find the appropriate disc as a certain drive letter. For example, if Compton's Encyclopedia was originally installed from drive G:, it expects to always find the Compton's CD-ROM in drive G:. One way to solve this is to buy additional disc magazines whenever you fill one up to the six-disc maximum—that way, all your drive letters stay the same because you're not constantly loading and unloading discs from one magazine. For example, you could have a disc magazine that contains only reference-type CD-ROMs, one with just games, and yet another with just Windows applications.

The 604X is currently the only drive that spins the disc at four times normal speed. It boasts an outrageous 612K/sec transfer rate, the highest of any drive in our survey. This speed is especially evident when playing back animation from a CD-ROM. Multimedia film clips with simultaneous sound play back very smoothly without the slightest pause; the busy light on the drive barely stays lit even when the drive is working hard on retrieving the film and sound. Loading a big program like Corel Draw! from the CD was noticeably quicker than with other CD-ROM drives. Seek time is a somewhat more down-to-earth 300ms, although it's no slouch in that area either. The drive operates silently during seeks, and it switched discs without a hitch during its stay on our system.

You would think that the 604X, being cutting-edge technology, would be a lot harder to install. The good news is that it isn't. And Pioneer has made sure that tech support is nothing short of first-class. Of all the drives we played with, this was the one we wanted to keep most. It is very expensive, but the convenience for those who need the changer capability may easily justify the cost. The DRM-604X is only available in an external model.

Sony CDU-31A and CDU-561

Sony Computer Peripheral Products Division
655 River Oaks Parkway
San Jose, CA 95134
(408) 432-0190
(800) 352-7669
Suggested list price: CDU-31A, $499; CDU-561, $649

Sony is a well-known giant in the world of consumer electronics. Sony products are widely available at competitive prices; they are also among the most popular and are renowned for their excellent quality.

The CDU-31A is Sony's low-end MPC Level 1–compliant drive that is capable of Multisession Photo CD. This is a tray-loading drive that does not require a disc caddy. The CDU-31A is the slowest drive in our survey—it musters a mere 150K/sec transfer rate but is also one of the cheapest.

The Sony CDU-561 (Figure 11-8) is an internal double-speed CD-ROM drive that boosts performance to levels similar to other drives such as the NEC CDR-74. With an average access time of 295ms, it can transfer data at 300K/sec and boasts SB16 SCSI-2 compatibility. This is Sony's premier CD-ROM drive, and it also features a double dust door, similar to the ones on the NECs. Its external sibling—the CDU-7811—became available in the fall of 1993.

FIGURE 11-8

The Sony CDU-561 is a capable performer

Texel DM-3024 and DM-5024

Texel America Inc.
1605 Wyatt Drive
Santa Clara, CA 95054
(408) 980-1838
(408) 980-1840 (fax)
Suggested list price: DM-3024, $499; DM-5024, $599

For many years, Texel has inconspicuously supplied CD-ROM drives to various manufacturers who resold these drives under their own labels. The Japanese company decided to go after the CD-ROM–drive market directly and has established a subsidiary in California to pursue these efforts. It has succeeded in establishing itself as one of the premier suppliers of quality CD-ROM drives—in the same vein as the larger companies such as NEC, Sony, and Toshiba.

The DM-xx24 series (see Figure 11-9), which consists of the internal DM-3024 and external DM-5024, are state of the art, MPC Level 2–compliant offerings. They sport a speedy 265ms access time, second only to the Toshiba, and a transfer rate of 300K/sec. This is a result of its double-speed capability and also a generous 64K buffer. The external case is graced with a clean and elegant modern design. Standard features include a dust-resistant

FIGURE 11-9

The Texel CD-ROM drives are excellent values

door and a self-cleaning laser assembly.

The drive lacks nothing in terms of compatibility, featuring SB16 SCSI-2 compliance, Kodak Photo CD Multisession compatibility, and CD-ROM XA compliance. This was the quietest drive in the group we tested; we had to look at the drive light to see when the drive was being accessed.

Texel has been known for its excellent technical support, and we were not disappointed. We got quick, patient responses from Texel every time we called. Overall, Texel drives have the best price/performance ratio of any drive we tested.

NOTE: *As we go to press, Texel has introduced a couple of new CD-ROM drives—the DM-3028 and DM-5028 are successors to the DM-3024 and DM-5024, respectively. The new DM-xx28 series bear an identical exterior appearance to their older cousins, but internal improvements speed up the drive to a faster 240ms average seek time and a 335K/sec transfer rate. The best news is that the prices for the improved drives remain the same as the older drives.*

Toshiba XM-3401B and TXM-3401E

Toshiba America Information Systems, Inc.
9740 Irvine Boulevard
Irvine, CA 92718
(714) 583-3000
Suggested list price: XM-3401B, $695; TXM-3401E, $895

Currently, the title for the fastest random access seek time belongs solely to the Toshiba XM-3401 series of drives (see Figure 11-10). The record-setting 200ms average seek time is achieved by a unique (patent pending) mechanism. The increased rotational speed of the drive, exactly 2.2 times normal, also contributes to this achievement. While other manufacturers have doubled the rotational speed and derived a transfer rate of 300K/sec, Toshiba squeezed in an extra 10 percent in rotational speed, which results in a 10 percent improvement in transfer rate, to 330K/sec. The transfer rate of the XM-3401 is second only to the quadruple-speed Pioneer DRM-604X.

The XM-3401 is a good choice for multimedia applications. Some programs taxed the slower drives and pushed them to their limits. This was especially evident when playing back a sample music video from a CD. On drives with transfer rates of 150K/sec, the bus light would stay lit while the five-minute music video ran. The Toshiba's busy light, on the other hand, only flashed about every half-second to one second.

FIGURE 11-10

FIGURE 11-10

The popular

Toshiba 3401

series drive

Other notable features include the sealed, contamination-free enclosure and an automatic lens cleaner. This drive should work well even in dusty environments. The XM-3401B is the internal model; the TXM-3401E is the external version.

FINDING THE BARGAINS

All right, so you're all set to purchase the latest and greatest CD-ROM drive. Here's a brief look at some of the vendors that offer a great variety of CD-ROM drives, multimedia upgrade kits, and CD-ROM accessories.

NOTE: *We have tried our best to provide a list of vendors who we feel are reputable. However, we cannot, and do not, specifically endorse any one of them. Use a credit card for your purchases whenever possible. This gives you better recourse should any company fail to deliver on its promise. It may also be useful to check with the Better Business Bureau of the city in which the business operates for any complaints against the company.*

Several mail-order companies repackage the Toshiba XM-3401 series CD-ROM drive and sell it at a lower price. Relax Technology at (510)

471-6112 markets it as the Vista II; Procomm Technology at (800) 800-8600 sells it as both the MCD-DS External and the SiCD-DS Internal drives; and Consan Storage Solutions at (800) 229-3475 sells it as the 3401XT. The drives used in these offerings should be identical to the ones that Toshiba uses in the XM-3401 series. You should not have any compatibility problems if you use the same software drivers as the real McCoy.

The same is true of Texel drives, which are repackaged by other companies. One is the prominent mail-order firm Insight Computers at (800) 359-0633. Insight has several CD-ROM drive OEMs (which gives the company license to sell other manufacturers' brands under its name) for its Talon line of drives; make sure you specify one with a Texel drive.

A multimedia one-stop shopper's delight is TigerSoftware. It has various CD-ROM drive bundles. They usually include thousands of dollars' worth of CD-ROM titles for seemingly measly prices. They can be reached at (800) 888-4437. Make sure you ask for a free copy of the company's colorful catalog. Other popular mail-order giants are MicroWarehouse at (800) 367-7080 and PC Connection at (800) 800-0003. Both have big catalogs with lots of goodies, including CD-ROM drives, software toys, and more.

Don't neglect the most obvious source for a CD-ROM drive—your local EggHead, Software Etc., CompUSA, BizMart, and other software and computer superstores. They may not always offer the best price or the brand you're looking for, but they're local, they have excellent return policies, and sometimes they offer good service too. Also note that these companies often sell third-party CD-ROM drives with the Panasonic interface at bargain prices. This may be the most economical way to add a CD-ROM drive to any Sound Blaster card with the Panasonic CD-ROM interface.

TIP: *One of the best places to purchase CD-ROM titles is your local software store. Remember, the best deals on CD-ROM software are at the time you purchase the drive—you can obtain a drive with loads of bundled CD-ROM titles at a fraction of their actual costs if purchased separately.*

Two places to get CD-ROM software and CD-ROM caddies at great prices (under $5 per caddy) is SofTec Plus at (800) 779-1991, and Walnut Creek CDROM at (800) 786-9907. Interestingly, SofTec not only includes 1 free caddy for every 10 caddies (or 4 free for every 25 caddies), but also a free caddy with some titles! That is one feature everyone should get in the habit of offering. When we last checked, SofTec sells Japanese caddies, while Walnut Creek sells U.S. caddies.

Walnut Creek CDROM offers other services—it's especially helpful if you want to make your own one-copy CD-ROM. The company also has valuable, up-to-date collections of shareware software on custom-made but affordable CD-ROMs. Call for more information. A well-known giant can also produce CD-ROMs for you—call IBM Software Manufacturing Company at (800) 926-0364.

There are hundreds, if not thousands, of companies in addition to the ones above, that are starving for your business. Keep in mind that it's a buyer's market, and arm yourself with the proper information. Be skeptical of wild claims or promises; shop wisely, and good luck.

TIPS ON INSTALLING A CD-ROM DRIVE WITH YOUR SOUND BLASTER CARD

The Sound Blaster Getting Started guide contains very clear illustrated instructions on installing your new CD-ROM drive. Here are several tips to supplement the manual.

A Sound Installation

Installing anything in your computer can turn out to be a frustrating and even destructive experience. Arming yourself with the right tools, information, and instructions can greatly reduce the likelihood of any unpleasantness. A Sound Blaster card may be the first card you'll install on your computer. Fortunately, the Creative Labs Getting Started manuals are clearly illustrated. Read through the installation completely before actually doing the installation. Below are a few additional tips to help you along the way.

Tools and Work Tips

The first thing you'll want to do is make sure you've got the right tools. Although your computer may be slightly different than others, all PCs share many common elements. A #2 Phillips screwdriver and/or a 1/4-inch nut driver is required to remove the screws that hold the computer cover and slot covers. On most Compaq computers, you'll need a Torx wrench to remove the screws. Tweezers are helpful for when you inadvertently drop the screws onto the motherboard, between two add-on cards.

Before you perform surgery on a computer, make sure that you've discharged any static electricity that has built-up on your body by grounding yourself. Computer chips don't react well to static electricity—you can easily ruin your day by shocking yourself and destroying a $250 sound board all at the same time. Keep the sound card in its protective antistatic bag till you're ready to plug it into the slot. Figure out what internal connections need to be made before inserting the board into its resting place.

CAUTION: *Contrary to popular advice, leave your computer plugged into the wall whenever possible. This will ground the computer while you're working on it. Ground yourself, to remove built-up static electricity, by touching the metal case of the power supply before handling any circuit boards or chips. Please be sure that the computer is turned off before opening it up. Imagine what a deadly situation it would be for a surgeon and the patient, if the latter was not under anesthesia when the surgeon worked inside the body!*

It's very important to make correct cable connections. Take note of the orientation of all cables before disconnecting or attaching them. An inverted connection can destroy a circuit card or the computer itself. When using flat-ribbon cables, the colored stripe (usually red) on one side denotes pin 1. As far as connectors are concerned, pin 1 is usually marked with a small triangle or the number 1. Be careful not to bend any pins when inserting a connector—align all the pins with the holes before applying pressure on the connector. Double-check to ensure that all connections are tight. When you replace the cover, be careful not to dislodge a connector by accidentally catching the cable when you slide the cover back on.

Make sure that the card is completely seated in its slot. You may want to examine the card's gold "fingers" that are still just visible after the card is seated in the bus. Check that the top of the fingers all protrude the same amount to ensure that the card has been inserted without tilting. It's also important that you replace the screw that holds the card down. It is very easy to unseat a loose card when plugging cables, such as the joystick cable, into the external connectors. If you turn the computer on with a card loose in its slot, you'll probably blow up at least your pocketbook!

You may want to leave the cover unscrewed till you're sure you've solved all hardware conflicts. Replacing the cover with six screws and then finding out you have to change a jumper setting on the card is a very trying experience—especially it this occurs more than once.

The Hardware

The first thing to do when you open the CD-ROM–drive package is to find the packing list and make sure all the standard items (like cables and a CD caddy) are in the box.

Refer to your Sound Blaster Getting Started guide for step-by-step instructions on installing your CD-ROM drive and the appropriate cable kit. Basically, you need to make three connections using the data cable, power cable, and CD audio cable. The data cable is a flat-ribbon cable for an internal drive, and a regular cable for an external drive. The power cable is either an internal connector or a regular AC cable for an external drive.

Be careful when attaching the internal cable; make sure that the red stripe on the cable corresponds with pin one on the connectors. This means the red stripe is up (at the top) on the Sound Blaster CD-ROM connector. The same applies for the external CD-ROM bracket adapter. If you're hooking up an internal CD-ROM, check the drive for pin 1 orientation and make sure that the red stripe is the side connected to this pin. Most drives have pin 1 next to the power-supply connector, but check your drive's manual. Alternatively, look for a triangular mark on the drive's printed circuit board into which the connector is soldered. An inverted connection means that your drive won't work at all. It could also potentially damage the drive or the Sound Blaster card.

The internal audio connection is pretty straightforward, but if you connect the audio cable upside down, you reverse the left and right channels. The same happens if you make an upside-down connection from the audio connection to the external CD-ROM adapter bracket. If you use an internal audio cable that is not matched to the brand of drive you're installing, you probably won't get any sound at all. Oh, by the way, make sure you've got the right audio cable for the right drive.

TIP: *Correct cables for the appropriate CD-ROM drives can be obtained from Creative Labs or your dealer. The part numbers are listed in the section "Finding the Right Cables and Drives" earlier in this chapter.*

Last, if you've purchased a CD-ROM drive separately, don't forget to check the CD-ROM drive's installation manual for additional information when installing the drive. Be aware that some of the instructions in the drive manufacturer's manual may conflict with those in your Sound Blaster manuals. In such cases, always follow the instructions in the Sound Blaster manual.

The CD-ROM Driver Software

The automatic install on the installation disk copies the appropriate files to a new directory on your boot drive. The directory name changes depending on which Sound Blaster card you've purchased; refer to your Sound Blaster Getting Started manual to find out what this directory name is. It also makes some changes to your CONFIG.SYS and AUTOEXEC.BAT files.

A line is added to CONFIG.SYS to load the CD-ROM driver. Here is an example (the name of your driver may differ slightly):

```
DEVICE=C:\SBCD\SBCD.SYS /D:MSCD001 /P:220 /S:D0 /A
```

Another driver is added to AUTOEXEC.BAT to enable DOS and Windows to recognize the CD-ROM drive as a drive letter:

```
C:\SBCD\MSCDEX /D:MSCD001 /L:E
```

CAUTION: *Both the driver in CONFIG.SYS and MSCDEX.EXE must be loaded into your computer's memory before any program can use the CD-ROM drive. Loading one without the other renders the drive unusable. Both these drivers, or programs, should be loaded automatically when you first start your computer.*

Your system needs to be booted, or restarted, before these changes take effect; restart by turning off your computer and turning it back on, or press CTRL-ALT-DELsimultaneously. When your computer restarts, it will load the drivers into memory and display a message like the following:

```
MSCDEX Version 2.22
Copyright (C) Microsoft Corp. 1986-1993. All rights reserved.
      Drive E: = Driver MVCD001 unit 0
1616    bytes free memory
0       bytes expanded memory
12978   bytes CODE
2112    bytes static DATA
22948   bytes dynamic DATA
38304   bytes used
```

If you see this startup message, congratulations—you've completed a successful installation of the CD-ROM drive. If you don't get the message, turn off the computer and check to make sure that all your connections have been made properly. If that doesn't work, double-check CONFIG.SYS and

AUTOEXEC.BAT to ensure that the proper commands have been added by the installation program.

TIP: *A new CD-ROM drive is treated like a floppy disk except that you cannot write to the drive. During the installation, the CD-ROM drive is usually given the next free drive letter after your hard disk. If you have hard disks C and D, the CD-ROM is usually assigned the E drive; if you only have a single hard disk C, the CD-ROM drive becomes drive D. You can change the letter assigned to your CD-ROM drive by changing a parameter in AUTOEXEC.BAT. See the "MSCDEX.EXE Parameters" section in this chapter for more detail.*

Once you boot up successfully, you can test the CD-ROM drive by requesting a directory listing from any data CD-ROM you have. Assuming your CD-ROM drive is drive D, insert a CD-ROM in the drive and type **DIR D:** at the C:\ prompt. A directory listing of the CD-ROM should appear on your screen. A CD-ROM drive is a removable storage device, like a floppy drive, so if you do not have a CD-ROM in the drive and you try to access it or view a directory, you get the following message (note that the drive letter may vary on your setup):

```
CDR101: Not ready reading drive e
Abort, Retry, Fail?
```

If this happens, just press A to abort, insert the appropriate CD-ROM, and try again. You see the following message if you've tried to copy a file (in this case, CONFIG.SYS) to the CD-ROM drive:

```
Access denied  - E:CONFIG.SYS
        0 file(s) copied
```

You may encounter other error messages, depending on the application, when trying to add or modify information on a CD-ROM. Remember, you cannot write data to a CD-ROM drive!

TIP: *A good way to check that the CD-ROM hardware, software, and connections have all been installed correctly is to play a regular CD in the CD-ROM drive—you should hear music through the speakers connected to your Sound Blaster card. You can do this by inserting a regular CD (you do have one of these lying around somewhere, right?) into the CD-ROM drive and using a CD player such as the CDPLYR program to play the CD.*

The CD-ROM drivers can consume a lot of conventional (base) memory. You can free up this base memory, and thus give some breathing space to large DOS programs, by loading both SBCD.SYS (for example) and

MSCDEX.EXE into high memory. To load into high memory, you have to use a memory manager like DOS's EMM386.EXE. Your system files may look something like the following.

Sample entries in CONFIG.SYS:

```
DEVICE=C:\EMM386.EXE RAM
DOS=HIGH,UMB
DEVICEHIGH=C:\SBCD\SBCD.SYS /D:MSCD001 /P:220 /S:D0 /A
```

Sample entry in AUTOEXEC.BAT:

```
LOADHIGH C:\SBCD\MSCDEX /D:MSCD001 /L:E
```

If you do not have enough high memory to load both these drivers, load the biggest one that fits. Note that the current version of MSCDEX.EXE, version 2.22, is easier to load in high memory than prior versions.

 TIP: *If you're using DOS 6, run MEMMAKER after installing your CD-ROM software to automatically optimize your memory configuration. QEMM users can run an equivalent program called OPTIMIZE.*

The automatic installation should suffice most of the time. If you want to tweak or optimize your system, be ready to dust off your CONFIG.SYS and AUTOEXEC.BAT editing skills. In an upcoming section, we describe the different parameters you can use with MSCDEX.EXE to fine-tune your setup.

Mixer Settings

Depending on which connection you made for the audio cable, you may have to use either the CD input or LIN (Line In) input levels to control the volume of a regular audio CD. Not all music or sounds from a CD are controlled by these settings, though—sounds can actually originate from the FM synthesizer or PCM circuit on the Sound Blaster card, which are controlled by other settings instead. Most of the time, CD-ROM software programs use digitized audio and MIDI data files to generate sound on the Sound Blaster card.

There is much confusion, especially with CD-ROM games, as to which audio source is being used, and therefore which levels need to be adjusted in the mixer. Very few games use regular audio CD for the accompanying music or sound effects; most use sounds generated from the Sound Blaster FM synthesizer or PCM circuit. Two notable exceptions of games that use audio CD extensively for music and speech are LucasArt's CD-ROM versions of Loom and Monkey Island.

One way to check if a game (or any program) is using audio CD for its music or sounds is to plug a set of headphones into the 1/8-inch headphone sockets at the front of most CD-ROM drives. If the sound is heard through the headphones, then the program is using audio CD. If the sound comes only from the speakers connected to your Sound Blaster sound card, then the sound is generated by the FM synthesizer or PCM circuitry on the Sound Blaster card. After determining the source, you can adjust your mixer settings appropriately.

Refer to your Sound Blaster User Reference Manual for more detailed explanations of the mixer settings.

MSCDEX.EXE Parameters

MSCDEX.EXE acts like a translator for all software that wants to access the CD-ROM drive. It receives instructions from various programs, deciphers them, and then passes the request to the Sound Blaster CD-ROM driver (loaded in CONFIG.SYS) for processing. This driver is run in AUTO-EXEC.BAT. The current version of MSCDEX.EXE is 2.22, and it occupies 35,570 bytes of memory by default. The entry in the AUTOEXEC.BAT is as follows:

[*path*]\MSCDEX /D:[*device name*] [/L:[*drive letter*] /V /M[*n*] /E /K]

The parameters are as follows:

[*path*]	Specifies the DOS path to the driver.
[*device name*]	Specifies the name of the device, which should be identical to the entry for the Sound Blaster CD-ROM driver loaded in CONFIG.SYS. Example: MSCD001, CDROM01, or NECCDR74.
/L:[*drive letter*]	Specifies the drive letter to be assigned to the CD-ROM drive. Example: /L:E. If this parameter is omitted, MSCDEX.EXE assigns the next available drive letter. If more than one CD-ROM drive is attached, the drive letters are sequentially assigned starting with [*drive letter*].
/V	Provides a verbose (detailed) listing of MSCDEX.EXE memory usage. This is useful to determine exactly how much memory MSCDEX.EXE uses.

/M:[*n*]	Specifies the number of buffers to use for caching CD-ROM information. By default, MSCDEX uses 10 buffers. Each buffer requires an additional 2,048 bytes in memory. 10 to about 20 are ideal. Reduce this amount to between 3 and 8 when using a CD-ROM software cache program.
/E	Tells MSCDEX.EXE to load all its data buffers into EMS (Expanded Memory Specification) memory. If you are using a memory manager, this saves you about 16K of main memory.
/K	Used only when the CD-ROM directory is written in Kanji (Japanese).

For example, the following entry installs MSCDEX as the drive with the name MSCD001, assigns drive letter E: to the CD-ROM drive, assigns 20 buffers to cache data, loads the buffers into EMS, and displays a verbose listing of memory being consumed by MSCDEX.

```
MSCDEX /D:MSCD001 /L:E /M:20 /E /V
```

Making a List and Checking It Twice

That concludes our brief notes about installing a CD-ROM drive with your Sound Blaster card. If you installed your Sound Blaster card and it is working correctly, the CD-ROM installation should be a breeze. You should be enjoying your fully operational CD-ROM drive by now. If not, go through the Sound Blaster Getting Started manual again to make sure you haven't missed something. The installation program (usually INSTALL) provided with your Sound Blaster card should automatically copy all the appropriate files to your hard disk and make the necessary changes in your startup files. Remember, you may need to run an additional setup program in Windows (usually WINSETUP) to properly install your Sound Blaster card for operation in Windows.

If you own the SB16 SCSI-2, don't let the seemingly daunting Adaptec EZ-SCSI manual scare you—you only need to read parts of it to install the appropriate CD-ROM drivers correctly. Pay special attention to Chapter 2 of that manual, since it contains the installation instructions for the CD-ROM software drivers. The last couple of pages in Chapter 3 of the same manual have some instructions on running the included audio CD player program. You can skip the rest of that manual. Thankfully, the Adaptec installation program is fairly automatic. You can get the shorthand version of the SCSI CD-ROM installation in Chapter 3 of the SB16 SCSI-2 Getting Started manual if you prefer.

IMPROVING PERFORMANCE WITH A SOFTWARE CACHE

ne of the ways to speed up any storage device, such as a CD-ROM drive, is to hold some of the data in a temporary holding place in main memory using a software cache. Access to main memory is almost instantaneous, so a computer can read data from a cache faster than from the hard disk or CD-ROM. Of course, this is only true if the data the computer is looking for is already residing in the cache. When data is read, a copy is placed in this cache. The data in this cache is temporary and is replaced by the most recently accessed data—as the cache fills up, data in the cache changes in FIFO (first in, first out) order. Examples of some popular hard disk software caches that you may be familiar with include Microsoft's SmartDrive, included with DOS 5, DOS 6, and Windows 3.1; Norton's NCache; PC-Kwik's Super PC-Kwik; Hyperware's Hyperdisk; and Future Systems' Speed Cache+.

Not all software caches can handle the special requirements for caching CD-ROMs. The versions of SmartDrive that come with MS-DOS 5.0 and 6.0 are examples of hard disk software caches that do not cache CD-ROMs. If you also want to cache a CD-ROM drive, you have to purchase a separate cache program or use the version of SmartDrive included in MS-DOS 6.2.

NOTE: *A software cache should not be confused with a hardware cache, such as the RAM buffer built into most CD-ROM drives. The RAM buffer—even at 256K—is too small to cache any data file or program. Also confusing is the CPU cache, often quoted as part of the computer's specifications in sales literature and advertisements. For example, a computer ad may read "Intel 486DX/50 with 8K internal cache and 64K cache." The 8K and 64K caches are both dedicated to the CPU (central processing unit) and are used for caching CPU instructions—they are not used for caching data from a hard disk, CD-ROM, or any other storage device.*

Caching CD-ROM

A handful of companies have designed programs that specifically cache a CD-ROM drive. The most visible is probably CD Speedway from Bloc Publishing. Another recently introduced CD-ROM cache is Lightning CD from Lucid Corporation. Caching a CD-ROM is a completely different

NEC's MultiSpin Series

N EC has recently introduced the next salvo in CD-ROM–drives—the NEC MultiSpin 3X and 4X series. The 3Xi internal ($500) CD-ROM drives boast triple-speed motors, which translates to access times of 195ms and transfer rates of 450K/sec. The portable 3Xp ($455) will run on an optional battery pack and shares the same transfer speed, albeit with a slower—but still respectable—access time of 250ms. The 4X Pro ($995) is targeted at professionals requiring quadruple-speed CD-ROM drives; it boasts a transfer rate of 600K/sec, the fastest of the lot. Check with Creative Labs to see whether its Sound Blaster 16 SCSI-2 CD-ROM drivers support these drives.

process than caching a hard drive. CD Speedway allows CD-ROM data to be cached only to the hard disk (instead of RAM), while Lightning CD can cache to either RAM or a hard disk.

CD Speedway only caches data from CD-ROMs, so you still must use a cache like SmartDrive for your hard disks. Lightning CD, on the other hand, caches hard drives as well as CD-ROMs. Either program eats up significant amounts of memory, preventing some DOS programs from running. Unless you set up a fairly large cache or access the same information over and over again, the drawbacks of both products overwhelm their advantages. Multimedia titles, because of their inherently large data files, do not benefit greatly from these products.

The most successful program we encountered for caching CD-ROM drives was Norton's SpeedCache Plus. Its caching technique is different than CD Speedway or Lightning CD. A multipurpose cache, SpeedCache also caches hard disks and floppy disks. The program uses a reasonable amount of memory, considering its functionality, and it is much smaller than CD Speedway or Lightning CD (it's about half the size of Lightning CD).

Unless you can afford to sacrifice some memory, you have a lot of free hard disk space, or you access many reference-type CD-ROMs frequently, the $80 or so you'd spend on a CD-ROM software cache program is better spent on a faster CD-ROM drive. If you already have a CD-ROM drive and are looking to improve performance, Norton's SpeedCache Plus is the best of the lot.

You can obtain more information from the following companies:

CD Speedway
Bloc Publishing
800 SW 37th Avenue, Suite 765
Coral Gables, FL 33134
(800) 888-2562
List: $72.99

Lightning CD
Lucid Corporation
101 W. Renner Road, Suite 450
Richardson, TX 75082
(214) 994-8100
List: $99.99

Norton's SpeedCache Plus
Symantec Corporation
10201 Torre Avenue
Cupertino, CA 95014
(408) 253-9600
List: $89.99

V

Sound Blaster Programming

12

Programming the Sound Blaster Family

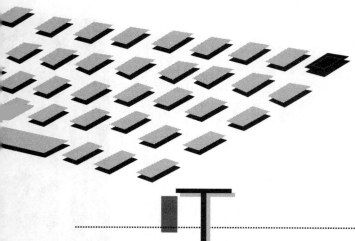

THIS chapter presents a though description of how to utilize the capabilities of your sound card via the Sound Blaster Standard Interface Module (SBSIM). For those of you who don't program, the source code in C, Pascal, and Basic are included on the disk that accompanies this book.

For adapt programmers who would like to skip the high-level stuff and write code that will access the Creative Labs drivers directly, the text file on the disk named DRIVERS.TXT, contains pseudo-code and function definitions.

If you are a bit twiddler and do not wish to have any code between you and the hardware, then you should contact Creative Labs Customer Service and purchase the Sound Blaster DOS Developers Kit.

PROGRAMMING THE SOUND BLASTER STANDARD INTERFACE MODULE (SBSIM)

THE Sound Blaster Standard Interface Module (SBSIM) is a terminate-and-stay-resident (TSR) program that combines and simplifies the interfaces to the Sound Blaster drivers. It loads the Sound Blaster drivers at startup, relieving the application program of this task. A configuration file is used to specify which drivers will load and how much memory should be reserved for each driver's buffer.

SBSIM supports playback of digital recordings (VOC files) from conventional memory, from extended memory, or from disk and playback of music files (CMF or MID) from disk. It also provides control functions for source selection and volume if you have a Sound Blaster Pro or Sound Blaster 16.

SBSIM utilizes Creative's CT-VOICE driver for digitized voice playback from memory, CTVDSK for voice playback from disk, SBFMDRV for CMF music file playback, SBMIDI for MID music playback, and AUXDRV for mixer control. SBFMDRV and SBMIDI are TSRs that must be loaded before SBSIM if music is desired.

Configuration File

A *configuration file* defines which drivers are to be loaded and which parameters are to be passed to the drivers. The configuration file is read when SBSIM loads into memory. After SBSIM has been loaded, changes to the configuration file will have no effect until SBSIM is reinstalled.

The format of SBSIM's configuration file is based on the Windows INI file format. A tag identifying the driver to be loaded is surrounded by brackets and followed by a set of parameters. This format is as follows:

```
[  <DriverTag> ]
<parm>=value                    ; parameters requiring values
    :
<parm>=ON                       ; switch parameters
<parm>=OFF                      ;
    :
    :
```

Comments are also supported and are marked using a semicolon. Everything after the semicolon on a line is ignored.

A Sample Configuration File for SBSIM

The following is an example of an SBSIM configuration file:

```
; Load the FM driver
;
[FM]
BufferSize=32

; Load the VMEM driver
;     and use Extended memory
[MemVoice]
ExtendedMemory=on
SBSIMhandles=5
```

If a driver is not specified in the configuration file, it will not be loaded into memory.

Supported Drivers and Their Parameters

The supported drivers and their associated parameters are as follows:

[FM]	Loads SBFMDRV.COM (CMF files)
BufferSize:<nn>	Size of buffer in K (2..32)(32)
[DskVoice]	Loads CTVDSK.DRV (VOC files from disk)
BufferSize:<nn>	Size of buffer in K (2..32)(32)
DMABufferSize:<nn>	Size of buffer in K (2..32)(8)
[MemVoice]	Loads CT-VOICE.DRV (VOC files from memory)
ExtendedMemory:<OFF/ON>	Indicates if extended memory is to be used (OFF)
XMShandles:<nn>	Maximum No. of SBSIM handles, if XMS is specified. Refer to (4) below (10)
DMABufferSize:<nn>	Size of buffer in K (2..32)(8)
[Auxiliary]	Loads AUXDRV.DRV (Volume controls)
CDswitchSpeakers: <OFF/ON>	Switch specifying if CD-ROM output to the speakers should be swapped (OFF)
[MIDI]	Loads SBMIDI.EXE (MID Files)
BufferSize:<nn>	Size of buffer in K (2..32)(32)
MidiMap:<nn>	MIDI mapper format to use 0 => GENERAL MIDI 1 => BASIC MIDI 2 => EXTENDED MIDI

Calling an Interrupt

All of SBSIM's functions are called by filling specified registers with their pertinent values and invoking the interrupt assigned to SBSIM. As is the case with most programming languages, there are several ways to accomplish a desired function. The C language is no exception. The simplest way to call an interrupt is to use C's *int86()* function. *int86()* will call an 80x86 interrupt passing registers to it via a pointer to a C union defined as REGS. Data is also returned with another REGS union. Below is the *GetSndStat()* function, which demonstrates this concept.

```
unsigned GetSndStat(DRIVER driver)
{
    union REGS inregs, outregs;
    inregs.h.bh = driver + 1;
```

```
        inregs.h.bl = 5                         // get sound status function
        inregs.x.cx = 0;
        int86(SIMint, &inregs, &outregs);
        return(outregs.x.ax);                   // return status
}
```

Locating SBSIM

The *SBSIM functions* are invoked by calling the interrupt that was defined when the TSR was loaded. When loading, SBSIM will scan interrupts between 80h and BFh, choosing the first interrupt that is unused (0000:0000). SBSIM can be identified by searching for the signature string "SBSIM" located at offset 103h from the interrupt vector's segment (ISEG:0103h). The *FindDvr()* C function listed below demonstrates how to locate the SBSIM driver.

```
/**************************************************************************
*
*
*
* FUNCTION: FINDDVR - Searches for the requested driver's interrupt number
*              by looking for IDStr (in this case it will be
*              SBSIM) in the interrupt vector table memory at the
*              offset (as in SEGMENT:OFFSET) location passed to
*              this function.
*
* Inputs:      IDStr - driver ID string (for example, "SBSIM").
*              IDOff - driver's ID offset.
*
* Output:      interrupt number or 0 (error condition) if not found.
*
**************************************************************************/
unsigned FindDvr(char *IDStr, unsigned int IDOff)
{
    unsigned dvrInt,
    intFound = FALSE;
    char far *far *dvrVec;
    /*--------- Search each interrupt looking for the driver signature ----------*/
    for(dvrInt = 0x80; (dvrInt < 0x0C0) && (intFound == FALSE); ++ dvrInt)
    {
        /*-------- Create a pointer that points to the interrupt's vector ---------*/
        dvrVec = MK_FP(0, dvrInt * 4);
```

```
        /*---- Use the interrupt's segment and the requested ----*/
        /*---- offset to find signature and test it ---*/
        if(!_fstrncmp((char far *)MK_FP(FP_SEG(*dvrVec), IDOff), IDStr,
        strlen(IDStr)))
    {
    intFound = TRUE;
    /*------- Return the interrupt's number if successful -------*/
    if(intFound == TRUE)
          return(--dvrInt);
    /*-------Error! return a zero -------*/
    return(0);
    }
}
```

Playing a Digitized Voice File from Conventional Memory

Files loaded into conventional memory may be played if SBSIM has successfully loaded the CT-VOICE driver. The *StartSnd()* function, for conventional memory playback, requires a pointer to a data block within the VOC file. This means that you should skip the VOC file header at the beginning of the file. Files loaded into conventional memory may be played if SBSIM has successfully loaded the CT-VOICE driver. The *StartSnd()* function for conventional memory playback requires that a pointer to a data buffer be passed to it. The size of the buffer allocated is determined by the file size, and then the file is loaded into the buffer. The pointer to the buffer passed to *StartSnd()* must skip over the file's header block and point directly to the first data block, which is where the audio data begins. Before another file can be played using SBSIM, either the file currently playing must finish or the *StopSnd()* function must be called. You can determine if the file has finished playing by calling the *GetSndStat()* function.

The PLAYVOC.C program works only with files smaller than 64K. If you need to play larger files, use PLAYVOCD.C or PLAYVOCX.C.

```
/**************************************************************************
 *
 *   PROGRAM NAME: PLAYVOCM.C
 *
 *   COMPILER:     Borland/Turbo C/C++
 *
 *   DESCRIPTION: Plays a VOC file from the conventional memory using
 *                            the CT-VOICE.DRV driver (accessed from
 *                            SBSIM).  To run the program, type the
 *                            following at the command line:
```

```
*
*                           PLAYVOCM FILENAME
*
*                           Where FILENAME is the drive/path/filename
*                           of the VOC file to play.
*
*  NOTE:          SBSIM driver must be loaded before running this program.
*
*  WARNING:       This program does NOT support files larger than 64KB!
*
*******************************************************************************/
#define HEADER_OFFSET   0x1A
#define VOC_MEM_DRIVER  0x04
#include <ctype.h>
#include <conio.h>
#include <fcntl.h>
#include <stdio.h>
#include <io.h>
#include "drvrfunc.c"
#include "drvrfunc.h"


/******************************************************************************/
void main(int argc, char **argv)
{
  char    *Buffer,
      Command,
      UserQuit;
  long    Filesize;
  int     FileHandle;
  SIMERR RetValue;
  if (argc != 2)  // argc = no. of parameters entered on command line
  {
    puts("Command line must contain EXACTLY ONE filename parameter!");
    return;  // Terminate program
  }

  /*--- SEE IF SBSIM DRIVER HAS LOADED ------------*/
  SIMint = FindDvr("SBSIM", 0x0103);  // Get SBSIM's interrupt no.
  if (SIMint == 0)
  {
    puts("SBSIM driver not loaded!");
    return;  // Terminate program
```

```
}
/*--- SEE IF CT-VOICE.DRV DRIVER HAS LOADED -------*/
if (!(GetDrvrs() & VOC_MEM_DRIVER))
{
  puts("CT-VOICE.DRV not loaded!");
  return;  // Terminate program
}


/*--- OPEN FILE SPECIFIED ON COMMAND LINE (STORED IN argv[1] ------*/
if ((FileHandle = _open(argv[1], O_BINARY | O_RDONLY)) == -1)
{
  printf("FILE: %s not successfully opened!\n", argv[1]);
  return;  // Terminate program
}
/*--- GET THE FILE SIZE ------------------------*/
Filesize = filelength(FileHandle);
if (Filesize > 65535)
{
  puts("File size > 64KB not supported!");
  return;  // Terminate program
}


/*--- ALLOCATE BUFFER AND LOAD IT FROM FILE -----------*/
if ((Buffer = (char *) malloc((size_t) Filesize)) == NULL)
{
  puts("Memory buffer not allocated!");
  _close(FileHandle);
  return;  // Terminate program
}
_read(FileHandle, (void *) Buffer, (unsigned) Filesize);
_close(FileHandle);  // Done with the file, close it!

/*--- StartSnd() INITIALIZES THE CT-VOICE DRIVER -----------*/
RetValue = StartSnd(MemVoice, (void far *) (Buffer + HEADER_OFFSET), 0,
            0);
if (RetValue != SIMerr_NoErr)
{
  printf("ERROR CALLING SBSIM: %s\n", errorMsg[RetValue]);
  free(Buffer);  // Deallocate memory allocated by malloc()
  return;  // Terminate program
}
/*--- StartSnd() BEGINS PLAYING OF THE FILE ----------*/
```

```
      RetValue = PlaySnd(MemVoice);
      if (RetValue != SIMerr_NoErr)
      {
        printf("ERROR CALLING SBSIM: %s\n", errorMsg[RetValue]);
        free(Buffer);  // Deallocate memory allocated by malloc()
        return;  // Terminate program
      }

      clrscr();  // Clear screen
      printf("\n\n\n\n\n      SELECT ONE OF THE FOLLOWING OR WAIT UNTIL DONE:\n\n");
      printf("                          (P)ause\n");
      printf("                          (R)esume\n");
      printf("                          (Q)uit\n");
      UserQuit = FALSE;
      /*--- PROCESS USER INTERACTION OR WAIT FOR SOUND TO STOP -----------*/
      do
      {
        if (kbhit())  // Was a key pressed?
        {
          Command = toupper(getch()); // Get char typed & convert to upper case
          if (Command == 'P')
        PauseSnd(MemVoice);
          else if (Command == 'R')
        ResumeSnd(MemVoice);
          else if (Command == 'Q')
        UserQuit = TRUE;
        }
        // Exit do-while loop if file is done playing or user typed 'Q'
      } while (GetSndStat(MemVoice) != 0 && UserQuit == FALSE);

      /*--- IF SOUND IS STILL PLAYING AND USER HIT 'Q', STOP THE SOUND ---*/
      if (GetSndStat(MemVoice) != 0 && UserQuit == TRUE)
        StopSnd(MemVoice);
      free(Buffer);  // Deallocate memory allocated by malloc()
      return;
    }
```

Playing a Digitized Voice File from Extended Memory

When using the CT-VOICE driver, SBSIM allows an application to make use of extended memory. Before this program can run, you must set the *ExtendedMemory* switch statement in SBSIM.CFG to ON and HIMEM.SYS must be loaded properly by CONFIG.SYS at boot-up time. Before another file can be played using SBSIM, either the currently playing file must finish or the *StopSnd()* function must be called. You can determine whether the file has finished playing by calling the *GetSndStat()* function.

SBSIM makes use of extended memory by using its own internal handles called SBSIM handles. SBSIM handles are used instead of memory pointers or filenames when accessing a VOC file in extended memory. By default there are ten SBSIM handles, but this may be modified by changing the *XMSHandles* parameter in the SBSIM.CFG file.

To obtain an SBSIM handle for a VOC file, load the file into extended memory and call the *LoadExtMem()* function, passing it a far pointer to a string containing the filename. The SBSIM handle will be returned by *LoadExtMem()*. This SBSIM handle will be used for calling other extended memory functions that require an SBSIM handle. Now, instead of using the filename for these function calls, use the SBSIM handle. For example, after playing the file loaded into extended memory, PLAYVOCX.C calls *FreeExtMem()*, with the SBSIM handle passed to it. *FreeExtMem()* will free the memory occupied by the file associated with that SBSIM handle.

```
/******************************************************************
 *
 *    PROGRAM NAME: PLAYVOCX.C
 *
 *    COMPILER:     Borland/Turbo C/C++
 *
 *    DESCRIPTION: Plays a VOC file from extended memory using the
 *                 CT-VOICE.DRV driver (accessed from SBSIM).  To run
 *                 the program, type the following at the command line:
 *
 *                 PLAYVOCX FILENAME
 *
 *                 Where FILENAME is the drive/path/filename of the VOC
 *                 file to play.
 *
 *    NOTE: SBSIM driver must be loaded before running this program.
 *
 ******************************************************************/
#define VOC_MEM_DRIVER  0x04
#include <ctype.h>
#include <conio.h>
```

```
#include <fcntl.h>
#include <io.h>
#include <stdio.h>
#include "drvrfunc.c"
#include "drvrfunc.h"

/**********************************************************************/
void main(int argc, char **argv)
{
  char    Command,
      UserQuit;
  int     FileHandle,
          SBSIMHandle;
  SIMERR RetValue;
  if (argc != 2)  // argc = no. of parameters entered on command line
  {
    puts("Command line must contain EXACTLY ONE filename parameter!");
    return;  // Terminate program
  }

  /*--- SEE IF SBSIM DRIVER HAS LOADED ------------*/
  SIMint = FindDvr("SBSIM", 0x0103);  // Get SBSIM's interrupt no.
  if (SIMint == 0)
  {
    puts("SBSIM driver not loaded!");
    return;  // Terminate program
  }
  /*--- SEE IF CT-VOICE.DRV DRIVER HAS LOADED -------*/
  if (!(GetDrvrs() & VOC_MEM_DRIVER))
  {
    puts("CT-VOICE.DRV not loaded!");
    return;  // Terminate program
  }

  /*--- OPEN THE FILE SPECIFIED ON COMMAND LINE (stored in argv[1])
----*/
  if ((FileHandle = _open(argv[1], O_BINARY | O_RDONLY)) == -1)
  {
    printf("FILE: %s not successfully opened!\n", argv[1]);
```

```
  return;  // Terminate program
  }
 /*--- LOAD THE FILE INTO EXTENDED MEMORY ----------*/
 SBSIMHandle = LoadExtMem((void far *) argv[1]);
 _close(FileHandle);  // Done with the file, close it!

 /*--- StartSnd() INITIALIZES CT-VOICE DRIVER ------*/
 RetValue = StartSnd(MemVoice, (void far *) 0, EXTENDED_MEM_VOC,
             SBSIMHandle);
 if (RetValue != SIMerr_NoErr)
 {
   printf("ERROR CALLING SBSIM: %s\n", errorMsg[RetValue]);
   return;  // Terminate program
 }
 /*--- PlaySnd() BEGINS PLAYING THE FILE ------------*/
 RetValue = PlaySnd(MemVoice);
 if (RetValue != SIMerr_NoErr)
 {
   printf("ERROR CALLING SBSIM: %s\n", errorMsg[RetValue]);
   if(FreeExtMem(SBSIMHandle) != 0)
   {
     puts("ERROR: Error freeing extended memory");
     return;
   }
   return;  // Terminate program
 }
 clrscr();  // Clear screen
 printf("\n\n    SELECT ONE OF THE FOLLOWING OR WAIT UNTIL DONE:\n\n");
 printf("                    (P)ause\n");
 printf("                    (R)esume\n");
 printf("                    (Q)uit\n");
 UserQuit = FALSE;
 /*--- PROCESS USER INTERACTION OR WAIT FOR SOUND TO STOP -----------*/
 do
 {
   if (kbhit())  // Was a key pressed?
   {
     Command = toupper(getch()); // Get char typed and convert to upper
                               // case
     if (Command == 'P')
```

```
  PauseSnd(MemVoice);
    else if (Command == 'R')
  ResumeSnd(MemVoice);
    else if (Command == 'Q')
  UserQuit = TRUE;
  }
  // Exit do-while loop if file is done playing or user typed 'Q'
} while (GetSndStat(MemVoice) != 0 && UserQuit == FALSE);

/*--- IF SOUND IS STILL PLAYING AND USER HIT 'Q', STOP THE SOUND ---*/
if (GetSndStat(MemVoice) != 0 && UserQuit == TRUE)
  StopSnd(MemVoice);

/*--- FREE UP THE EXTENDED MEMORY THAT WAS OCCUPIED BY THE FILE ----*/
if(FreeExtMem(SBSIMHandle) != 0)
{
  puts("ERROR: Error freeing extended memory");
  return;
}
return;
}
```

Playing Digitized Voice File from Disk

The *StartSnd()* function for the PLAYVOCD.C program below requires that a far pointer to a string containing the filename be passed to it. Before another file can be played using SBSIM, either the file currently playing must finish, or the *StopSnd()* function must be called. You can determine if the file has finished playing by calling the *GetSndStat()* function.

```
/******************************************************************
*
*  PROGRAM NAME: PLAYVOCD.C
*
*  COMPILER:     Borland/Turbo C/C++
*
*  DESCRIPTION:  Plays a VOC file from the disk using the CTVDSK.DRV
*                       double buffering driver (accessed from
*                       SBSIM).  To run the program, type the
*                       following at the command line:
*
*                                                                *
```

```
 *                          PLAYVOCD FILENAME
 *
 *                          Where FILENAME is the drive/path/filename
 *                          of the VOC file to play.
 *
 *
 *  NOTE: SBSIM driver must be loaded before running this program.
 *
 ************************************************************************/
#define  VOC_DSK_DRIVER  0x02
#include <ctype.h>
#include <conio.h>
#include <fcntl.h>
#include <io.h>
#include <stdio.h>
#include "drvrfunc.c"
#include "drvrfunc.h"

/************************************************************************/
void main(int argc, char **argv)
{
  char Command,
       UserQuit;
  int    FileHandle;
  SIMERR RetValue;
  if (argc != 2)  // argc = no. of parameters entered on command line
  {
    puts("Command line must contain EXACTLY ONE filename parameter!");
    return;  // Terminate program
  }

  /*--- SEE IF SBSIM DRIVER HAS LOADED ------------*/
  SIMint = FindDvr("SBSIM", 0x0103);  // Get SBSIM's interrupt no.
  if (SIMint == 0)
  {
    puts("SBSIM driver not loaded!");
    return;  // Terminate program
  }
  /*--- SEE IF CTVDSK.DRV DRIVER HAS LOADED -------*/
  if (!(GetDrvrs() & VOC_DSK_DRIVER))
```

```c
{
  puts("CTVDSK.DRV not loaded!");
  return;  // Terminate program
}


/*--- LOAD THE FILE SPECIFIED ON COMMAND LINE (stored in argv[1]) ----*/
if ((FileHandle = _open(argv[1], O_BINARY | O_RDONLY)) == -1)
{
  printf("FILE: %s not successfully opened!\n", argv[1]);
  return;  // Terminate program
}


/*--- StartSnd() LOADS THE FILE AND INITIALIZES THE CTVDSK.DRV DRIVER. ---*/
RetValue = StartSnd(DskVoice, (void far *) argv[1], NULL, NULL);
if (RetValue != SIMerr_NoErr)
{
  printf("ERROR CALLING SBSIM: %s\n", errorMsg[RetValue]);
  _close(FileHandle);
  return;  // Terminate program
}
/*--- BEGIN PLAYING OF THE FILE -----------------------------------*/
RetValue = PlaySnd(DskVoice);
if (RetValue != SIMerr_NoErr)
{
  printf("ERROR CALLING SBSIM: %s\n", errorMsg[RetValue]);
  _close(FileHandle);
  return;  // Terminate program
}
clrscr();  // Clear screen
printf("\n\n\n\n\n    SELECT ONE OF THE FOLLOWING OR WAIT UNTIL DONE:\n\n");
printf("                    (P)ause\n");
printf("                    (R)esume\n");
printf("                    (Q)uit\n");
UserQuit = FALSE;


/*--- PROCESS USER INTERACTION OR WAIT FOR SOUND TO STOP -----------*/
do
{
  if (kbhit())  // Was a key pressed?
  {
```

```
    Command = toupper(getch());  // Get char typed and convert to uppercase
      if (Command == 'P')
    PauseSnd(DskVoice);
      else if (Command == 'R')
    ResumeSnd(DskVoice);
      else if (Command == 'Q')
    UserQuit = TRUE;
    }
    // Exit do-while loop if file is done playing or user typed 'Q'
  } while (GetSndStat(DskVoice) != 0 && UserQuit == FALSE);

  /*--- IF SOUND IS STILL PLAYING AND USER HIT 'Q', STOP THE SOUND ---*/
  if (GetSndStat(DskVoice) != 0 && UserQuit == TRUE)
    StopSnd(DskVoice);
  return;
}
```

Playing a CMF File

SBSIM can play CMF (FM) files if SBFMDRV.COM is loaded before
running SBSIM. The *[FM]* section must also be included in the SBSIM.CFG
configuration file. The *StartSnd()* function in PLAYCMF.C must be passed
a far pointer to a string containing the filename you wish to play. Before
another file can be played using SBSIM, the file currently playing must finish,
or the *StopSnd()* function must be called. You can determine if the file has
finished playing by calling the *GetSndStat()* function.

```
/****************************************************************************
*
*   PROGRAM NAME: PLAYCMF.C
*
*   COMPILER: Borland/Turbo C/C++
*
*   DESCRIPTION: Plays a CMF FM file from the disk using the FMDRV
*                                driver (accessed from SBSIM).To run the program,
*                                 type the following at the command line:
*
*                                PLAYCMF FILENAME
*
*                                Where FILENAME is the drive/path/filename of
*                                the .CMF file to play.
*
```

```c
*   NOTE: SBSIM driver must be loaded before running this program.
*
*********************************************************************/
#define FM_DRIVER 0x01
#include <ctype.h>
#include <conio.h>
#include <fcntl.h>
#include <io.h>
#include <stdio.h>
#include "drvrfunc.c"
#include "drvrfunc.h"


/*********************************************************************/
void main(int argc, char **argv)
{
  char Command,
          UserQuit;
  int    FileHandle;
  SIMERR RetValue;
  if (argc != 2)  // argc = no. of parameters entered on command line
  {
    puts("Command line must contain EXACTLY ONE filename parameter!");
    return;  // Terminate program
  }

  /*--- SEE IF SBSIM DRIVER HAS LOADED -------*/
  SIMint = FindDvr("SBSIM", 0x0103);  // Get SBSIM's interrupt no.
  if (SIMint == 0)
  {
    puts("SBSIM driver not loaded!");
    return;  // Terminate program
  }
  /*--- SEE IF FMDRV DRIVER HAS LOADED -------*/
  if (!(GetDrvrs() & FM_DRIVER))
  {
    puts("FMDRV not loaded!");
    return;  // Terminate program
  }

  /*--- LOAD THE FILE ENTERED ON COMMAND LINE (stored in argv[1]) ----*/
  if ((FileHandle = _open(argv[1], O_BINARY | O_RDONLY)) == -1)
  {
```

```
      printf("FILE: %s not successfully opened!\n", argv[1]);
      return;  // Terminate program
    }


/*--- StartSnd() LOADS THE FILE AND INITIALIZES THE DRIVER ---------*/
RetValue = StartSnd(FM, (void far *) argv[1], NULL, NULL);
if (RetValue != SIMerr_NoErr)
{
  printf("ERROR CALLING SBSIM: %s\n", errorMsg[RetValue]);
  _close(FileHandle);
  return;  // Terminate program
}
/* PlaySnd() BEGINS PLAYING THE FILE -------------------------------*/
RetValue = PlaySnd(FM);
if (RetValue != SIMerr_NoErr)
{
  printf("ERROR CALLING SBSIM: %s\n", errorMsg[RetValue]);
  _close(FileHandle);
  return;  // Terminate program
}

clrscr();  // Clear screen
printf("\n\n\n\n\n    SELECT ONE OF THE FOLLOWING OR WAIT UNTIL DONE:\n\n");
printf("                   (P)ause\n");
printf("                   (R)esume\n");
printf("                   (Q)uit\n");
UserQuit = FALSE;
/*--- PROCESS USER INTERACTION OR WAIT FOR SOUND TO STOP -----------*/
do
{
  if (kbhit())  // Was a key pressed?
  {
    Command = toupper(getch());  // Get char typed and convert to uppercase
    if (Command == 'P')
  PauseSnd(FM);
    else if (Command == 'R')
  ResumeSnd(FM);
    else if (Command == 'Q')
  UserQuit = TRUE;
  }
  // Exit do-while loop if file is done playing or user typed 'Q'
} while (GetSndStat(FM) != 0 && UserQuit == FALSE);
```

```
/*--- IF SOUND IS STILL PLAYING AND USER HIT 'Q', STOP THE SOUND ---*/
if (GetSndStat(FM) != 0 && UserQuit == TRUE)
  StopSnd(FM);
return;
}
```

Playing a MID File

SBSIM can play MIDI files if SBSIM.EXE is loaded before running SBSIM. The *[MIDI]* section must also be included in the SBSIM configuration file. The *StartSnd()* function in PLAYMIDI.C must be passed a far pointer to a string containing the filename you wish to play. Before another file can be played using SBSIM, the file currently playing must finish or the *StopSnd()* function must be called. You can determine if the file has finished playing by calling the *GetSndStat()* function.

```
/****************************************************************************
 *
 *   PROGRAM NAME: PLAYMIDI.C
 *
 *   COMPILER:      Borland/Turbo C/C++
 *
 *   DESCRIPTION: Plays a .MID MIDI file from the disk using the SBMIDI
 *                            driver (accessed from SBSIM). To run the program,
 *                            type the following at the command line:
 *
 *                            PLAYMIDI FILENAME
 *
 *                            Where FILENAME is the drive/path/filename
 *                            of the MID file to play.
 *
 *   NOTE: SBSIM driver must be loaded before running this program.
 *
 ****************************************************************************/
#define  MIDI_DRIVER  0x10
#include <fcntl.h>
#include <ctype.h>
#include <conio.h>
#include <io.h>
#include <stdio.h>
#include "drvrfunc.c"
```

```c
#include "drvrfunc.h"

/***********************************************************************/
void main(int argc, char **argv)
{
  char Command,
       UserQuit;
  int   FileHandle;
  SIMERR RetValue;
  if (argc != 2)  // argc = no. of parameters entered on command line
  {
    puts("Command line must contain EXACTLY ONE filename parameter!");
    return;  // Terminate program
  }

  /*--- SEE IF SBSIM DRIVER HAS LOADED --*/
  SIMint = FindDvr("SBSIM", 0x0103);  // Get SBSIM's interrupt no.
  if (SIMint == 0)
  {
    puts("SBSIM driver not loaded!");
    return;  // Terminate program
  }
  /*--- SEE IF MIDI DRIVER HAS LOADED ---*/
  if (!(GetDrvrs() & MIDI_DRIVER))
  {
    puts("SBMIDI not loaded!");
    return;  // Terminate program
  }

  /*--- LOAD THE FILE -------------------*/
  if ((FileHandle = _open(argv[1], O_BINARY | O_RDONLY)) == -1)
  {
    printf("FILE: %s not successfully opened!\n", argv[1]);
    return;  // Terminate program
  }

  /*--- StartSnd() LOADS THE FILE AND INITIALIZES THE SBMIDI DRIVER ---*/
  RetValue = StartSnd(Midi, (void far *) argv[1], NULL, NULL);
  if (RetValue != SIMerr_NoErr)
  {
    printf("ERROR CALLING SBSIM: %s\n", errorMsg[RetValue]);
    _close(FileHandle);
```

```
    return;  // Terminate program
  }
  /*--- PlaySnd() BEGINS PLAYING THE FILE -------------*/
  RetValue = PlaySnd(Midi);
  if (RetValue != SIMerr_NoErr)
  {
    printf("ERROR CALLING SBSIM: %s\n", errorMsg[RetValue]);
    _close(FileHandle);
    return;  // Terminate program
  }
  clrscr();  // Clear screen
  printf("\n\n\n\n\n    SELECT ONE OF THE FOLLOWING OR WAIT UNTIL DONE:\n\n");
  printf("                    (P)ause\n");
  printf("                    (R)esume\n");
  printf("                    (Q)uit\n");
  UserQuit = FALSE;
  /*--- PROCESS USER INTERACTION OR WAIT FOR SOUND TO STOP -----------*/
  do
  {
    if (kbhit())  // Was a key pressed?
    {
      Command = toupper(getch());  // Get char that's in buffer
      if (Command == 'P')
    PauseSnd(Midi);
      else if (Command == 'R')
    ResumeSnd(Midi);
      else if (Command == 'Q')
    UserQuit = TRUE;
    }
    // Exit do-while loop if file is done playing or user typed 'Q'
  } while (GetSndStat(Midi) != 0 && UserQuit == FALSE);

  /*--- IF SOUND IS STILL PLAYING AND USER HIT 'Q', STOP THE SOUND ---*/
  if (GetSndStat(Midi) != 0 && UserQuit == TRUE)
    StopSnd(Midi);
  return;
}
```

Controlling the Mixer (SB Pro and SB16 only)

SBSIM utilizes the AUXDRV driver to control the volume levels of the
digital voice channel, the FM music or the Wave Blaster channel (SB16 only),

the microphone, the line-in source, or the CD player. Additionally, if you own an SB16, you can also control the gain level as well as the bass and treble tone controls.

```
If SBSIM's entry interrupt is located
{
    Call the Query Drivers function
    If the AUXDRV driver is found (bit 3 is set)
    {
        Call Get Source Volume
        Call Set Source Volume
        Call Get Gain function (SB16 only)
        Call Set Gain function (SB16 only)
        Call Get Tone function (SB16 only)
        Call Set Tone function (SB16 only)
    }
}
```

SBSIM Function Definitions

Below are the definitions for the functions offered by SBSIM. Where applicable, functions defined in the *DRVRFUNC.C* file that utilize these calls have been listed.

SBSIM Control Functions

The *SBSIM control functions* perform processes specific to the SBSIM program itself. These functions are independent of the individual drivers that the interface controls and are denoted by register BH = 0.

GET SBSIM VERSION NUMBER (FUNCTION 0)   This function returns the version number of the SBSIM program.

The C function calling *Get SBSIM Version Number* is *Version()*.

- **Entry** Upon entry to the driver, the registers should be set as follows:

  BH = 0 — SBSIM control function
  BL = 0 — sub-function number (Get *SBSIM version number*)

- **Exit** Upon exit from the driver, the following values will be returned in the registers listed:

AH = Major version number
AL = Minor version number

■ **Possible Errors** No error codes are returned by this function.

QUERY DRIVERS (FUNCTION 1)   This function returns a *bit mask* indicating which drivers were loaded when the SBSIM program was executed. A bit mask is an integer where each bit represents a driver. A one indicates that the driver was loaded when SBSIM was run, and a zero indicates that the driver failed to load.

The C function calling *Query Drivers* is *GetDrvrs()*.

■ **Entry** Upon entry to the driver, the registers should be set as follows:

BH = 0 — SBSIM control function
BL = 1 — sub-function number (*Query Drivers*)

■ **Exit** Upon exit from the driver, the following values will be returned in the registers listed:

AX = bit mask indicating which drivers were loaded
  bit 0 = SBFMDRV — driver for playing CMF files
  bit 1 = CTVDSK — driver for playing VOC files direct from disk
  bit 2 = CT-VOICE — driver for playing VOC files from conventional or Expanded memory
  bit 3 = AUXDRV — driver for controlling the mixer functions
  bit 4 = SBMIDI — driver for playing MID files

■ **Possible Errors** No error codes are returned by this function.

LOAD FILE INTO EXTENDED MEMORY (16)   This function loads a file into extended memory (XMS). Currently, only VOC files are supported. The VOC file's header is removed by the function so you don't have to remove it as you do with conventional memory playback. An SBSIM handle must be related to the file and is specified in the CX register. A handle is nothing more than a number assigned to represent the file that's loaded into memory. This handle should be used when calling any functions operating on the file. If the CX register is set to zero, then the function will assign the next available handle to the file. This is generally how this function would be called.

The C function calling *Load File Into Extended Memory* is *LoadExtMem()*.

- **Entry**   Upon entry to the driver, the registers should be set as follows:

  BH = 0 — SBSIM control function
  BL = 16 — sub-function number (*Load File* to XMS)
  AX = file type (0 = VOC file)
  DS:DX = far pointer to filename
  CX = SBSIM handle number to use (0 to use next available handle)

- **Exit**   Upon exit from the driver, the following values will be returned in the registers listed:

  AX = SBSIM handle assigned by the driver. This handle should be used when calling all other functions pertaining to the file loaded in this memory block.

- **Possible Errors**   SIMerr_NoXMS, SIMerr_BadFileType, SIMerr_NoSIMFree, SIMerr_BadFile.

FREE EXTENDED MEMORY (19)   This function frees an extended memory block and its associated SBSIM handle. This function should be called when you exit your application or if you need to free some extended memory for use by another file.

The C function calling *Free Extended Memory* is *FreeExtMem()*.

- **Entry**   Upon entry to the driver, the registers should be set as follows:

  BH = 0 — SBSIM control function
  BL = 19 — sub-function number *(Free Extended memory)*
  AX = SBSIM handle

- **Exit**   Upon exit from the driver, the following values will be returned in the registers listed:

  AX = 0 — if there is no error

- **Possible Errors**   SIMerr_NoXMS, SIMerr_BadSIMHandle, SIMerr_BadFreeXMS

Source Playback Functions

These functions pertain to the individual drivers themselves. They offer the simplest interface to the CTVDSK, CT-VOICE, SBFMDRV, and SBMIDI drivers.

BH = 1 => *SBFMDRV* FM driver
BH = 2 => *CTVDSK* digital voice from disk driver
BH = 3 => *CT-VOICE* digital voice from memory driver
BH = 5 => *SBMIDI* MIDI driver

NOTE: *In the previous section we used the value BH = 0 to denote an SBSIM control function. Values for BH given in this section are listed in the table above. You should use the value pertaining to the file type you are working with.*

START SOUND SOURCE (FUNCTION 0)   This function prepares the specified driver for subsequent sound output. For the SBFMDRV driver, the specified CMF file is loaded into a buffer and the driver is initialized for FM playback. For the CTVDSK digital voice driver, the specified VOC file is opened for input and the driver is initialized for playback. For the CT-VOICE digital voice driver, you should load your sample into memory before calling the *Start Sound Source* function. The function is only responsible for initializing the driver for playback. For the SBMIDI driver, the specified MID file is loaded into a buffer and the driver is initialized for MIDI playback.

This function should be called whenever you wish to play back a sound unless the sound is the same as the last sound played. This function will not play the sound, but it will perform the initialization of the driver necessary to play back the sample. The sample can only be played by invoking the *Play Sound* command.

It should also be noted that music playback will only occur if the buffer sizes specified in the *[FM] Buffersize* and the *[MIDI] Buffersize* parameters in the configuration file are larger than the file size of the file that you wish to play.

The C function calling *Start Sound Source* is *StartSnd()*.

■ **Entry** Upon entry to the driver, the registers should be set as follows:

BH = Driver number (see "Source Playback Functions")

BL = 0 — sub-function number (*Start Sound Source*)

CX= 0 (if playing a CMF file, a MID file, or a VOC file directly from disk)

AX = near pointer to filename (if playing a VOC file from conventional memory)

DX:AX = far pointer to the data block of the VOC file (if playing a VOC file from extended memory)

AX = SBSIM handle

- **Exit** Upon exit from the driver, the following values will be returned in the registers listed:

  AX = 0 — if there is no error

- **Possible Errors** SIMerr_BadBuffer, SIMerr_BadFile, SIMerr_VDSKnoStart, SIMerr_VMEMnoStart

PLAY SOUND (FUNCTION 1) This function starts the actual sound output. The C function calling *Play Sound* is *PlaySnd()*.

- **Entry** Upon entry to the driver, the registers should be set as follows:

  BH = Driver number (see "Source Playback Functions")
  BL = 1 — sub-function number (*Play Sound*)
  CX= 0

- **Exit** Upon exit from the driver, the following values will be returned in the registers listed:

  AX = 0 — if there is no error

- **Possible Errors** SIMerr_BadFileHandle, SIMerr_VDSKnoStart, SIMerr_VMEMnoStart

STOP SOUND (FUNCTION 2) This function stops the sound output. The C function calling *Stop Sound* is *StopSnd()*.

- **Entry** Upon entry to the driver, the registers should be set as follows:

  BH = Driver number (see "Source Playback Functions")
  BL = 2 — sub-function number (*Stop Sound*)
  CX= 0

- **Exit** No values are returned by the drivers upon exit.
- **Possible Errors** No error codes are returned by this function.

PAUSE SOUND (FUNCTION 3) This function pauses the current sound output. The C function calling *Pause Sound* is *PauseSnd()*.

- **Entry** Upon entry to the driver, the registers should be set as follows:

  BH = Driver number (see "Source Playback Functions")
  BL = 3 — sub-function number (*Pause Sound*)
  CX= 0

- **Exit** No values are returned by the drivers upon exit.
- **Possible Errors** No error codes are returned by this function.

RESUME SOUND (FUNCTION 4) This function resumes a previously paused sound output.
The C function calling *Resume Sound* is *ResumeSnd()*.

- **Entry** Upon entry to the driver, the registers should be set as follows:

  BH = Driver number (see "Source Playback Functions")
  BL = 4 — sub-function number (*Resume Sound*)
  CX= 0

- **Exit** No values are returned by the drivers upon exit.
- **Possible Errors** No error codes are returned by this function.

READ SOUND STATUS (FUNCTION 5) This function returns the current sound's status.
The C function calling *Read Sound Status* is *ReadSndStat()*.

- **Entry** Upon entry to the driver, the registers should be set as follows:

  BH = Driver number (see "Source Playback Functions")
  BL = 5 — sub-function number (*Read Sound Status*)
  CX= 0

- **Exit** Upon exit from the driver, the following values will be returned in the registers listed:

AX = Sound status word
    0000h = sound stopped
    FFFFh = playing (—1 *signed decimal*)
Other values are marker values (see VOC file format's block type 4)

■ **Possible Errors**   No error codes are returned by this function.

Mixer Functions

The following definitions pertain to the mixer functions made available by the Auxiliary driver. The mixer functions are denoted by register BH = 4. The source and volume definitions are the same for all the mixer functions.

SOURCES   These are the sources that SBSIM's auxiliary functions can control. A source is given in the AX register when calling the *Get Source Volume* and the *Set Source Volume* functions.

    0 = Master volume
    1 = Voice volume
    2 = FM / Wave Blaster (SB16 only) volume
    3 = CD volume
    4 = Line-in volume
    5 = Microphone volume
    6 = PC speaker volume (SB16 only)

VOLUME VALUES   Volumes for all the sources are is represented by values from 0 to 255. This means that if you are controlling a Sound Blaster Pro (the Pro has eight volume steps for all sources except the microphone) and you wish to change the volume by one step, you must change the driver's level by 32 (256 / 8 = 32). Since the SB16 has 32 levels, you need only change the driver's level by 8 (256 / 32 = 8).

Volume levels are always represented as a word. The lower byte defines the right channel and the higher byte defines the left channel. If a mono source is selected, then the high byte should be set to zero.

    Left channel—high byte = 0 to 255
    Right channel—low byte = 0 to 255

GAIN VALUES (SB16 ONLY)   The gain values range from 0 to 3. Each setting represents a doubling of the sound's level. Zero represents the original signal's volume, and 3 represents 8 times the original level (Volume = Volume * (2 raised to the "gain" power)).

Gain values are also represented as a word. As in the volume settings, the lower byte defines the right channel and the higher byte defines the left channel.

TONE VALUES (SB16 ONLY)   Tone values range from 0 to 255. Since the SB16 has 16 settings, you need to change the driver's value by 16 (256 / 16 = 16) to change the tone by one step.

Tone values are also represented as a word. The lower byte defines the right channel, and the higher byte defines the left channel.

GET SOURCE VOLUME (FUNCTION 0)   This function returns the current volume of the specified source.

The C function calling *Get Source Volume* is *GetVolume()*.

- **Entry**   The registers should be set as follows for entry to the driver:

    BH = 4 — mixer function
    BL = 0 — sub-function number (*Get Source Volume*)
    AX = source (see "Mixer Functions")

- **Exit**   Upon exit from the driver, the following values will be returned in the registers listed:

    AX = Volume (AH = left channel, AL = right channel)

- **Possible Errors**   SIMerr_AuxBadSource.

SET SOURCE VOLUME (FUNCTION 1)   This function sets the volume level of a specified source.

The C function calling *Set Source Volume* is *SetVolume()*.

- **Entry**   The registers should be set as follows for entry to the driver:

    BH = 4 — mixer function
    BL = 1 — sub-function number (*Set Source Volume*)
    AX = source (see "Mixer Functions")
    DX = volume level (see "Mixer Functions")

- **Exit**   Upon exit from the driver, the following values will be returned in the registers listed:

    AX = 0 if there is no error

- **Possible Errors**   SIMerr_AuxBadSource, SIMerr_BadVolSet.

GET GAIN (FUNCTION 2) (SB16 ONLY)   This function returns the current gain setting.

The C function calling *Get Gain* is *GetGain()*.

- **Entry**   The registers should be set as follows for entry to the driver:

    BH = 4 — mixer function
    BL = 2 — sub-function number (*Get Gain*)
    AX = 1 — Get output gain

- **Exit**   Upon exit from the driver, the following values will be returned in the registers listed:

    AX = Gain value (AH = left channel, AL = right channel)

- **Possible Errors**   SIMerr_AuxBadSource

SET GAIN (FUNCTION 3) (SB16 ONLY)   This function sets the gain value.

The C function calling *Set Gain* is *SetGain()*.

- **Entry**   The registers should be set as follows for entry to the driver:

    BH = 4 — mixer function
    BL = 3 — sub-function number (*Set Gain*)
    AX = 1 — Set output gain
    DX = gain value (see "Mixer Functions")

- **Exit**   Upon exit from the driver, the following values will be returned in the registers listed:

    AX = 0 if there is no error

- **Possible Errors**   SIMerr_AuxBadSource.

GET TONE (FUNCTION 4) (SB16 ONLY)   This function returns the current tone level.

The C function calling *Get Tone* is *GetTone()*.

- **Entry**   The registers should be set as follows for entry to the driver:

    BH = 4 — mixer function
    BL = 4 — sub-function number (*Get Tone*)
    AX = Treble — 0, Bass — 1

■ **Exit** Upon exit from the driver, the following values will be returned in the registers listed:

AX = Tone level (AH = left channel, AL = right channel)

■ **Possible Errors** SIMerr_AuxBadSource.

SET TONE (FUNCTION 5) (SB16 ONLY) This function sets the treble and bass levels.

The C function calling *Set Tone* is *SetTone()*.

■ **Entry** The registers should be set as follows for entry to the driver:

BH = 4 — mixer function
BL = 5 — sub-function number (*Set Tone*)
AX = Treble — 0, Bass — 1
DX = tone level (see "Mixer Functions")

■ **Exit** Upon exit from the driver, the following values will be returned in the registers listed:

AX = 0 if there is no error

■ **Possible Errors** SIMerr_AuxBadSource.

Error Codes Returned by SBSIM's Functions

Upon exit from an SBSIM function, the carry flag will indicate the success or failure of the requested operation. If the carry flag is set, then one of the following errors can be found in the AX register.

Code #	Error Name	Description
1	SIMerr_IsBusy	SBSIM is currently busy and unable to process requested command.
2	SIMerr_BadDriver	An invalid driver number was requested.
3	SIMerr_BadFunction	An invalid function number was specified.
4	SIMerr_VoiceActive	Digitized voice playback is already in progress.
5	SIMerr_VMEMnoStart	CT-VOICE process was unable to initialize.
6	SIMerr_VDSKnoStart	CTVDSK process was unable to initialize.
7	SIMerr_BadSIMHandle	A bad SBSIM handle was given.
8	SIMerr_BadBuffer	No buffer available for process.
9	SIMerr_BadFile	A bad file/filename was given.

Code #	Error Name	Description
10	SIMerr_BadFileHandle	A bad file handle was given.
11	SIMerr_NotInited	*Play Sound* was attempted without first calling *Start Sound Source.*
12	SIMerr_NoXMS	XMS driver not installed (HIMEM.SYS).
13	SIMerr_NoSIMFree	No free SBSIM handles available.
14	SIMerr_BadFileType	Bad file type specified.
15	SIMerr_BadFreeXMS	Unable to free XMS block and SBSIM handle.
16	SIMerr_AuxBadSource	Invalid source specified.
17	Reserved	
18	Reserved	
19	SIMerr_BadVolSet	Set volume function failed because other process in progress.

SOUND FILE FORMATS

Most popular sound files are recorded as 8-bit Pulse Code Modulated (PCM) data. This produces one 8-bit byte of data for each sample of sound data. Stereo sound files contain two 8-bit bytes of data for each sample, one for each channel (left and right).

Some files, such as Sound Blaster 16 VOC files, use a 16-bit file format that uses two data bytes per sample but gives a finer resolution and higher-quality sound at the cost of additional disk space to store the file.

The total number of bytes in the file depends on the recording frequency and the total length of the recording. The recording frequency, also called the *sample rate,* is the number of times a sound is sampled within one second. In 8-bit PCM format, each sample yields a single byte. Using higher frequencies, or sample rates, produces higher-quality recordings but requires an appropriately faster machine to drive the Sound Blaster in Direct mode to be able to play back the recording at the proper speed. Again, the price of a higher-quality recording is still more disk space.

In order to make higher-quality recordings without using so much disk space, many compressed file formats have been developed. These techniques often incorporate a method of encoding a long series of repeated bytes, such as silence, into a short sequence of 2 or 3 bytes. Many different compression algorithms are in use, which compress 8-bit PCM data down to 5-, 3-, 2-, and even 1-bit Adaptive Differential Pulse Code Modulation (ADPCM). The trade-off here is that once a file has been compressed (to save disk space), it can no longer be edited or modified in any manner.

Creative Voice File Format (VOC)

The *VOC file format* consists of a header block and a data block. Within the data block, a number of different block types may exist. These different block types provide an elegant means of programming pauses, loops, and markers into the sound file, for synchronizing audio with video animations. Simpler applications probably will contain only a single block type (voice data).

When using the Creative Labs CT-VOICE driver, it is up to the application program to read the sound file and pass only the data block to the driver. If you are writing your own driver, the driver must read the data block and handle the processing of the embedded block types appropriately.

Recording a VOC file using the normal 8-bit PCM format will allow the file to be played on any internal or external sound device from another manufacturer, and will even permit the file to be transported to computers other than PCs.

If you decide to compress the VOC file to save disk space, it is recommended that you first back up the original sound file on disk. This will ensure that you still have the options of editing the file at a future date or transporting the file to another sound device or computer type. The following tables give you the byte-by-byte details for the header block, the data block, and the associated block types.

VOC Header Block

The VOC header block is divided into subblocks of data as follows:

Byte	Description
0–13h	File type description "Creative Voice File",1Ah
14–15h	Offset of data block from start of voice file (usually 1Ah)
16–17h	Voice file format version number ("0A, 01" = 1.10)
18–19h	Voice file identification code complement of file format version number + 1234h (for 1.10 = 1129h)

VOC Data Block

The VOC data block is divided into subblocks of data as follows:

Byte	Description
0	Block type
1–3	Block length following this byte
4-end	Block data

BLOCK TYPE 0 — TERMINATOR   Terminates the entire data block. It indicates that there is no other subblock after it.

Byte	Description
0	"00" End of block

BLOCK TYPE 1—VOICE DATA   Indicates that this subblock is a new set of voice data. It may use a different sampling rate or packing method.

Byte	Description
0	"01"
1–3	Block length
4	Time constant (256 – 1000000 / sampling rate)
5	Pack type: 0 = 8-bit unpacked 1 = 4-bit packed 2 = 2.6-bit packed 3 = 2-bit packed
6–end	Voice data (length = block length – 2)

BLOCK TYPE 2—VOICE CONTINUATION   Defines a continuation of the voice data from the last voice data subblock.

Byte	Description
0	"02"
1–3	Block length
4–end	Voice data

BLOCK TYPE 3 - SILENCE   Defines a silence period in the voice data.

Byte	Description
0	"03"

Byte	Description
1–3	Block length (always 3)
4–5	Pause period in sampling cycles
6	Time constant

BLOCK TYPE 4—MARKER This is a special subblock that specifies a marker in the voice data. Both the CT-VOICE and CTVDSK drivers update the status word with the contents of the marker value. Your program may check the status word for the desired marker value to perform synchronization with the voice output process.

The marker value can be inserted into the Voice file using the Sound Blaster Voice Editor, VEDIT2 or JOINTVOC.

Byte	Description
0	"04"
1–3	Block length
4–5	Marker value

BLOCK TYPE 5 —ASCII TEXT This specifies a null-terminated ASCII string in the voice data file.

Byte	Description
0	"05"
1–3	Block length
4–end	ASCII data
end	"00" null byte

BLOCK TYPE 6—REPEAT LOOP Specifies the beginning of a repeat loop. The data subblocks between this block and the next end repeat loop subblock are repeated by the driver for Count +1 times.

Byte	Description
0	"06"
1–3	Block length (always 2)
4–5	Count (1 to FFFEh, FFFFh = endless loop)

BLOCK TYPE 7—END REPEAT LOOP Specifies the end of a repeat loop.

Byte	Description
0	"07"
1–3	Block length (always 0)

BLOCK TYPE 8—EXTENDED BLOCK

Byte	Description
0	"08"
1–3	Block length (always 4)
4–5	Time constant Mono: 65536 - (256,000,000 / sampling rate) Stereo: 65536 - (256,000,000 / (2 * sampling rate))
6	Pack
7	Mode 0 = mono 1 = stereo

Block Type 8 must always precede Block Type 1. It carries voice attributes of the following voice data subblock, such as sampling rate, packing, and voice mode. It usually precedes stereo or high-speed voice data. When this block is present, the voice attributes in the next Block Type 1 are ignored.

BLOCK TYPE 9   Block Type 9 is a new sound data block that replaces the old Block Type 1 and Block Type 8. This block type supports 16-bit audio as well as 8-bit audio, and also supports ADPCM and CCITT compressed audio.

Byte	Description
0	"09"
1–3	Block length (length of digitized data in bytes plus 12)
4–7	Samples per second (actual sampling frequency, not a time constant)
8	Bits per sample (bits per sample after compression, if any)
9	Channels (1 for mono, 2 for stereo)
10-11	Format tag: 0x0000— 8–bit unsigned PCM 0x0001 — Creative 8-bit to 4-bit ADPCM 0x0002 — Creative 8-bit to 3-bit ADPCM 0x0003 — Creative 8-bit to 2-bit ADPCM 0x0004 — 16–bit signed PCM 0x0006 — CCITT a-Law 0x0007 — CCITT u-Law 0x0200 —Creative 16-bit to 4-bit ADPCM
12-15	Reserved (fill with zero)

NOTE: *This is a new Block Type introduced on VOC files with a version number 1.20 or higher.*

NOTE: *Block Type 9 superscedes Block Type 1 and Block Type 8. All new drivers will produce files with Block Type 9.*

Microsoft Waveform Audio File Format (WAV)

This is an overview of the *Waveform audio file format* (WAV). For more detailed information, refer to the Multimedia Specification available from Microsoft Corporation.

The Waveform audio file is organized in the RIFF (Resource Interchange File Format) structure. This structure was developed for multimedia resource files.

RIFF File Format

The basic building block of a RIFF file is called a chunk, which is formatted as follows:

<rID> <rLen> <rData(rLen)>

where

- *<rID>* "RIFF" identifies the representation of the chunk data (4 bytes).

- *<rLen>* is the length of data in the chunk that follows (4 bytes).

- *<rData>* is the RIFF Data Chunk (rLen bytes long).

Within this block, many different RIFF forms are supported, but only the WAV format will be discussed here.

WAV Format Definition

The WAV format of a RIFF Data Chunk is further divided into chunks. It must always contain a Format Chunk, followed by a Data Chunk.

<rData> = <wID> <Format Chunk> <Data Chunk>

where

- *<wID>* "WAVE" identifies the data as WAV format audio data (4 bytes).

WAVE Format Chunk

The Format Chunk contains data that specifies the format of the data contained in the Data Chunk. The syntax of the Format Chunk is as follows:

<Format Chunk> = *<ChunkId> <fLen> <wFormatTag> <nChannels> <nSamplesPerSec> <nAvgBytesPerSec> <nBlockAlign> <FormatSpecific>*

where

- *<fId>* "fmt" identifies the block as a Format Chunk (4 bytes).

- *<fLen>* is the length of data in the Format Chunk that follows (4 bytes).

- *<wFormatTag>* indicates the Wave format category of the file (2 bytes). For example:

  Pulse Code Modulation (PCM) format = 01

- *<nChannels>* indicates the number of channels for output (2 bytes). For example:

  1 = mono, 2 = stereo

- *<nSamplesPerSec>* indicates sampling rate (in samples per second) at which each channel should be played back (2 bytes).

- *<nAvgBytesPerSec>* indicates the average number of bytes per second that the data should be transferred at (2 bytes).

  *<nAvgBytesPerSec>=n*Channels**n*SamplesPerSec* (*n*BitsPerSample ÷ 8)

- *<nBlockAlign>* indicates the block alignment (in bytes) of the data in the Data Chunk. Playback software needs to process a multiple of *<nBlockAlign>* bytes of data at a time, so that the value of *<nBlockAlign>* can be used for buffer alignment (2 bytes).

  <nBlockAlign> = *n*Channels * (*n*BitsPerSample ÷ 8)

- *<FormatSpecific>* This field consists of zero or more bytes of parameters (2 bytes).

WAV Data Chunk

The Data Chunk contains the actual WAV audio data. The format of the data depends on the *<wFormatTag>* value stored in the Format Chunk.

<Data Chunk> = <dId> <dLen> <dData(dLen)>

where

- *<dId>* "data" identifies the block as a Data Chunk (4 bytes).

- *<dLen>* indicates the length of data in the Data Chunk that follows (4 bytes).

- *<dData>* is the actual waveform data (*dLen bytes long*).

Creative Music File Format (CMF)

The CMF file format consists of three different block structures including a header block, an instrument block, and a music block.

CMF Header Block

Offset	Description
00–03h	File ID "CTMF"
04–05h	File format version (current version is 1.10) MSB = major version LSB = minor version
06–07h	Offset of instrument block from start of file
08–09h	Offset of music block from start of file
0A–0Bh	Ticks per quarter note (one beat) [default = 120]
0C–0Dh	Clock ticks per second [default = 96]
0E–0Fh	Offset of music title from start of file (0 = none)
10–11h	Offset of composer name (0 = none)
12–13h	Offset of remarks (0 = none)
14–23h	Channel-in-use table (16 bytes long)
24–25h	Number of instruments used
26–27h	Basic tempo
28h	Title, composer, and/or remarks are stored here

CMF Instrument Block

The instrument block contains one 16-byte record for each of the instruments referred to in the music block. Each record is a 16-byte image of the register sets of the FM music chip. The format of the record is the same as those at offset 24-33h in the Sound Blaster Instrument (SBI) file format, which is described in the section "Sound Blaster Instrument File Format (SBI)" later in this chapter.

Offset	Description
00h	Modulator Sound Characteristic
01h	Carrier Sound Characteristic
02h	Modulator Scaling/Output Level
03h	Carrier Scaling/Output Level
04h	Modulator Attack/Decay
05h	Carrier Attack/Decay
06h	Modulator Sustain Level/Release Rate
07h	Carrier Sustain Level/Release Rate
08h	Modulator Wave Select
09h	Carrier Wave Select
0Ah	Feedback/Connection
0B–0Fh	Reserved for future use

CMF Music Block

The music block adheres to the Standard MIDI Format (SMF). It is single-track, multichannel, and polyphonic, with the maximum number of channels from 1 to 16.

The Standard MIDI File format specification defines three types of events: MIDI, System-exclusive, and Meta events. The CMF file format uses only the MIDI events at the current time.

Delta time values are variable-length fields, as defined by the Standard MIDI format.

The Music Block data appears in the following format:

<Music Block> = <delta time> <MIDI event> <delta time> <MIDI event> ...

where

- *<delta time>* is the amount of time before the following event. Delta time is stored as a variable-length quantity.

- *<MIDI event>* is any MIDI channel message.

CMF defines the following MIDI Control Change events:

Control Number	Control Data
66h	1 - 127 Used as markers in the music
67h	0 Melody mode 1 Rhythm mode used to select the melody or rhythm mode of the FM chips

In Rhythm mode, the last five channels are allocated as follows:

Channel	Rhythm
12	Bass Drum
13	Snare Drum
14	Tom-Tom
15	Top Cymbal
16	High-Hat Cymbal

Control Number	Control Data
68h	0 – 127 —Changes the pitch of all following notes upward by the specified number of 1/128 semitones. Control data of 0 cancels the pitch change.
69h	0 – 127 —Changes the pitch of all following notes downward by the specified number of 1/128 semitones. Control data of 0 cancels the pitch change.

Sound Blaster Instrument File Format (SBI)

Instrument files contain the data necessary to program the FM chip registers to synthesize a single instrument. The format of the SBI file is as follows:

Offset	Description
00–03h	File ID, ASCII string "SBI",1Ah
04–23h	Instrument Name, Null-terminated ASCII string
24h	Modulator Sound Characteristic

Offset	Description
25h	Carrier Sound Characteristic bit 7 Pitch Vibrato (AM) bit 6 Amplitude Vibrato (VIB) bit 5 Sustaining Sound (EGTYP) bit 4 Envelope Scaling (KSR) bit 3–0 Frequency Multiplier (MULTIPLE)
26h	Modulator Scaling/Output Level
27h	Carrier Scaling/Output Level bit 7–6 Level Scaling (KSL) bit 5–0 Output Level (TL)
28h	Modulator Attack/Decay
29h	Carrier Attack/Decay bit 7–4 Attack Rate (AR) bit 3–0 Decay Rate (DR)
2Ah	Modulator Sustain Level/Release Rate
2Bh	Carrier Sustain Level/Release Rate bit 7–4 Sustain Level (SL) bit 3–0 Release Rate (RR)
2Ch	Modulator Wave Select
2Dh	Carrier Wave Select bit 7–2 all bits clear bit 1–0 Wave Select (WS)
2Eh	Feedback/Connection bit 7–4 all bits clear bit 3–1 Modulator Feedback (FB) bit 0 Connection
2F–33h	Reserved for future use

Sound Blaster Instrument Bank File Format (IBK)

A Bank file is a group of up to 128 instruments, combined into a single file in the following format:

Offset	Description
00–03	File ID, ASCII string "IBK",1Ah
04–803h	Instrument parameters, 128 instruments, 16 bytes each; same as bytes 24-33h of the .SBI file
804–C83h	Instrument names, 128 instruments, 9 bytes each; each Instrument name must be null-terminated

Musical Instrument Digital Interface File Format (MID)

This is an overview of the *MIDI file format*. For more detailed information, refer to the Standard MIDI Files (SMF) 1.0 specification available from the International MIDI Association.

MIDI files are made up of chunks. Each chunk has a 4-character type and a 32-bit length, which is the number of bytes in the chunk. Two types of chunks are currently defined: Header Chunks and Track Chunks.

A MIDI file always starts with a Header Chunk, and is followed by one or more Track Chunks.

"MThd" *<length of header data> <header data>*

"MTrk" *<length of track data> <track data>*

"MTrk" *<length of track data> <track data>*

MIDI Header Chunk

A Header Chunk provides a minimal amount of information pertaining to the entire MIDI file. The syntax of the Header Chunk is as follows:

<Header Chunk> = <chunk type> <length> <format> <ntrks> <division>

where

- *<chunk type>* is the four ASCII characters "MThd".

- *<length>* is a 32-bit number of the bytes in the rest of the chunk.

- *<format>* specifies the overall organization or contents of the file, where

  0 = single multichannel track
  1 = one or more simultaneous tracks of a sequence
  2 = one or more sequentially independent single-track patterns

- *<ntrks>* is the number of track chunks in the file.

■ *<division>* specifies the meaning of the delta-times. It has two formats: one for metrical time, and one for time-code–based time as shown here:

	0	Ticks per quarter-note	
bit:	15	14 ←——————→ 0	

	1	Negative SMPTE format	Ticks per frame
bit:	15	14 ←——————→ 8	7 ←——————→ 0

MIDI Track Chunk

The Track Chunk is where the actual song data is stored. Each Track Chunk is simply a sequential stream of MIDI events, preceded by delta-time values. It may contain information for up to 16 MIDI channels. The concepts of multiple tracks, multiple MIDI outputs, patterns, sequences, and songs may all be implemented using several Track Chunks. The syntax of the track chunk is as follows:

<Track Chunk> = <chunk type> <length> <MTrk event> <MTrk event> ...

where

■ *<chunk type>* is the four ASCII characters "MTrk".

■ *<length>* is a 32-bit number of the bytes in the rest of the chunk.

<MTrk event> = <delta time> <event>

where

■ *<delta time>* is the amount of time before the following event stored as a variable-length quantity

<event> = <MIDI event> | <sysex event> | <meta event>

where

■ *<MIDI event>* is any MIDI channel message.

■ *<sysex event>* is a MIDI System–exclusive message as follows:

F0 *<length> <data string>*
or
F7 *<length> <data string>*

where

- *<length>* is stored as a variable-length quantity.

- *<meta event>* specifies non–MIDI information for the sequencer as follows:

    FF *<type> <length> <data string>*

where

- *<type>* is a single byte 0–127.

- *<length>* is variable–length.

Meta events defined by the specification are as follows:

FF 00 02 ssss	Sequence Number
FF 01 *<len> <text>*	text Event
FF 02 *<len> <text>*	Copyright Notice
FF 03 *<len> <text>*	Sequence/Track Name
FF 04 *<len> <text>*	Instrument Name
FF 05 *<len> <text>*	Lyric
FF 06 *<len> <text>*	Marker
FF 07 *<len> <text>*	Cue Point
FF 20 01 cc	MIDI Channel Prefix
FF 2F 00	End of Track
FF 51 03 tttttt	Set Tempo
FF 54 05 hr mn se fr ff	SMPTE Offset
FF 58 04 nn dd cc bb	Time Signature
FF 59 02 sf mi	Key Signature
FF 7F *<len> <data>*	Sequencer-Specific Meta-Event

Some numbers in MIDI files are represented as variable-length fields. These numbers use from one to four bytes, where each byte uses the least significant seven bits to represent a value. All bytes except the last byte have the highest bit (bit 7) set. The last byte has bit 7 cleared.

Here are some examples of numbers represented as variable-length fields:

Number (hex)	Representation (hex)
00000000	00
00000040	40
0000007F	7F
00000080	81 00
00002000	C0 00
00003FFF	FF 7F
00004000	81 80 00
00100000	C0 80 00
001FFFFF	FF FF 7F
00200000	81 80 80 00
08000000	C0 80 80 00
0FFFFFFF	FF FF FF 7F

THE DEVELOPER KIT FOR SOUND BLASTER SERIES

For those of you who feel that you need more information than this chapter provides, the Developer Kit for Sound Blaster Series, Second Edition, is now available for $99. The package includes three manuals with all the software and hardware information you need to develop programs and drivers in both high- and low-level (x86 assembly) languages.

Hardware Programming Reference

- Block diagrams for the entire Sound Blaster family
- Introduction to programming the Digital Sound Processor
- Digitized sound programming

- Programming the mixer chip

- Programming the MIDI ports, including the MPU-401

- DSP command listing

- I/O address maps for the entire Sound Blaster family

Programming Guide

- Step-by-step turotials on how to interface with the drivers supplied with all the Sound Blaster sound cards.

Library Reference

- Descriptions of all the library functions supplied on the included disk:

  High-level digitized sound drivers
  Mixer drivers
  Low-level digitized sound
  Low-level auxiliary services
  Low-level signal processing services
  MIDI driver functions
  CD-ROM audio interface

- Creative VOC file format

- Creative ADPCM wave format

The Developer Kit also includes a disk with library functions for the following languages:

- Microsoft C/C++ 6.0, 7.0

- Microsoft Visual C++ 1.0

- Turbo C 2.0

- Turbo C++ 1.0

- Borland C++ 2.0, 3.0, 3.1

- Microsoft Basic PDS 7.1

- Microsoft Visual Basic for DOS 1.0
- Microsoft Quick Basic 4.5
- Turbo Pascal 6.0, 7.0 (TPU only)

To order the Developer Kit for Sound Blaster Series, Second Edition, call Creative Labs at (800) 998-5227.

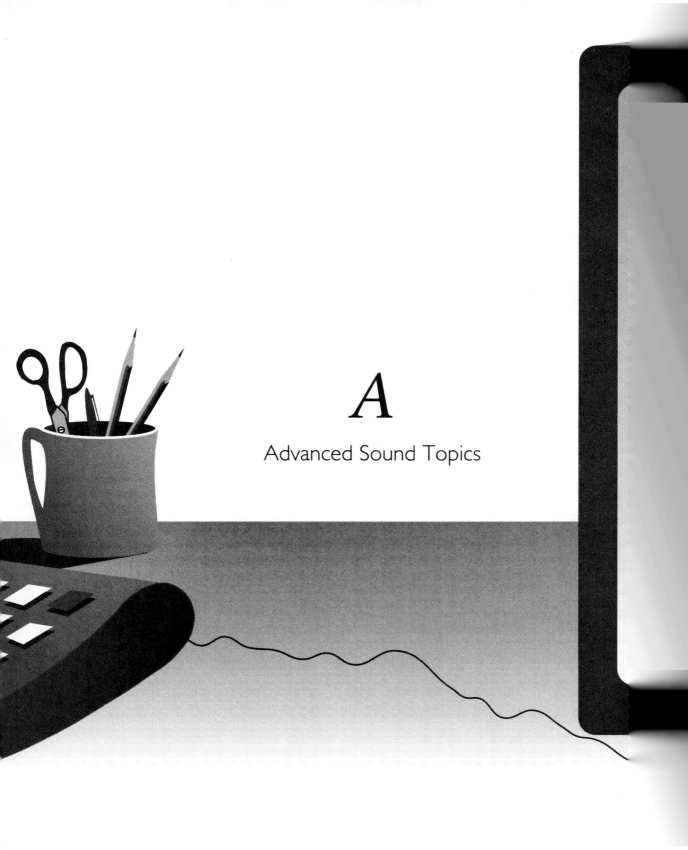

A

Advanced Sound Topics

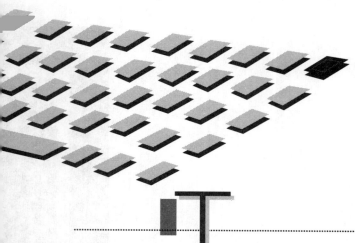

THE purpose of this appendix is to build upon and go beyond the audio essentials presented in Chapter 1. This appendix navigates through a number of the more esoteric and technical subjects, which will prove fascinating once you've mastered the basics. We'll discuss complex waveforms, the mechanics of FM synthesis, digital audio sampling and aliasing, and audio compression technology featuring Adaptive Differential Pulse Code Modulation (ADPCM). The background discussion on digital signal processing leads into descriptions of the leading edge audio technologies that Creative Labs is planning to bring to the market. These will include the EMU8000 audio DSP chip that's slated to become the foundation of Creative Labs' next generation of high-end sound cards. The appendix culminates with an in-depth view into the breakthrough DECtalk™ speech engine, which is slated to become the core of the TextAssist family of speech synthesis (text-to-speech synthesis) products.

TIP: *If you encounter unfamiliar terminology while reading this appendix, please review Chapter 1 for an overview of the basic principles of sound.*

COMPLEX WAVEFORMS

This section takes up the challenge of describing complex waveforms, the foundation of music and speech. You'll understand a complex waveform, and you'll see how to reduce wonderful sounds to simple components that are easily manipulated by the computer.

Musical Instruments

Both repetition and complexity are essential elements of music. To the musician humming a musical score, repetition relates to rhythm, melody, phrasing, and revisiting previous musical experiences. To the physicist watching sound waves pulsing across the oscilloscope screen, repetition means a waveform that repeats itself hundreds or thousands of times, long enough to give our ears the sensation of a tone.

An essential feature of musical sound is its complexity. Music that is described as rich in texture or timbre has a complex waveform. Figure A-1 illustrates the complex waveform that might be associated with a real instrument.

Speech

It's been said that of all musical instruments, the human voice is the most versatile and expressive, with the richest timbre. You witness this every time you recognize a friend's laugh over the telephone or the voice of a favorite singer on the radio. The repetitive quality of speech is evident in the phonetic building blocks of speech. These building blocks are a relatively small set of the many possible sounds humans are capable of uttering. More detail on these fundamental building blocks and on the characteristics of speech are provided in Chapter 7, and "DECtalk Speech Technology," which is found later in this appendix.

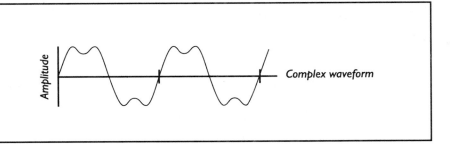

FIGURE A-1

Complex waveform created by a musical instrument

The Male Opera Singing Voice

Scientific research in the area of speech over the last several decades is now having a practical impact in audio technology. Many of the secrets of the singing voice have been unlocked by science. Normal male speech finds its greatest strength at about 450 Hz, which happens to be the same frequency at which an orchestra reaches its peak of strength. Having the same peak frequency makes it difficult for the male voice to be heard above the orchestra. The very interesting characteristic of the male opera voice is that the peak strength of the voice has been pushed upward by the singer, into the 2500 Hz to 3000 Hz range. Remarkably, the singer accomplishes this higher peak without having to exert himself beyond the effort required for normal speech. This higher frequency peak is ideal for voice projection because it's strong in the frequency band where the orchestra is weak, soaring above the orchestra music. At the same time, this peak falls comfortably within the range where the singer can exert good control. Inheriting the right genes is definitely beneficial. A man with a larynx that resonates (naturally reverberates) in this range has an innate advantage over other men in developing an operatic voice.

Reducing Complex Waveforms to Simple Components: Fourier Analysis

The intriguing fact about complex waveforms, whether their source is a musical instrument, a human voice, or the vibration of a machine, is that they are actually composed of simpler waves. According to Fourier's (pronounced "fo-yea") theorem, every complex periodic wave is actually a series (family) of simple sine waves and includes many harmonics. The term *Harmonics* describes the relationships between waves, shown in Figure A-2, where the waves have frequencies that are multiples of the so-called *fundamental frequency,* the dominant (strongest amplitude) wave. The second harmonic wave has twice the frequency of the fundamental wave, and the third harmonic has three times the frequency of the fundamental.

NOTE: As an aside, the topmost waveform in Figure A-2 depicts the sound of concert A, the note used by orchestras for tuning. This has a frequency of 440 Hz in the United States, but is 442 Hz or higher in Europe.

Fourier's theorem predicts that a complex wave can be reduced to a series of simple waves. The opposite is just as true, that a series of simple waves can be combined to create a complex wave, as illustrated by Figure A-3. Add the heights of the two simple sine waves, at every point of time, and the result is the complex waveform first seen in Figure A-1.

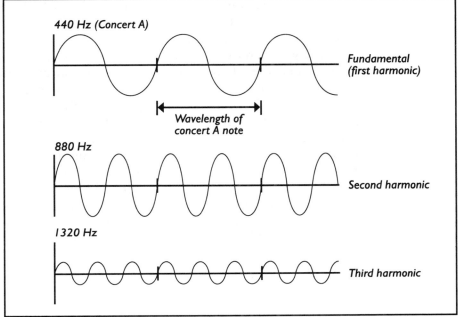

FIGURE A-2

Fundamental frequency (concert A) and two harmonics ∎

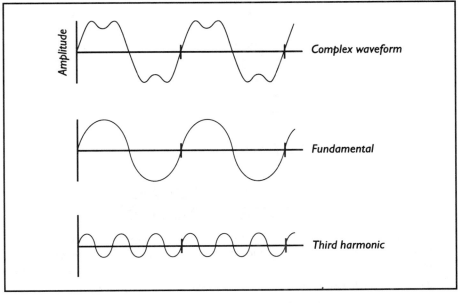

FIGURE A-3

Complex waveform consisting of two simple sine waves: a fundamental frequency and its third harmonic ∎

Here's the practical payoff of Fourier's theorem. There are special audio effects that can only be performed by manipulating the sound that falls into a narrow range of frequencies. For example, a cheap microphone may excessively boost the signal at 10 kHz but otherwise perform reasonably well with a flat bandwidth. By a technique called *equalization,* the shaping of the frequency response of a signal, the frequency components around 10 kHz can be reduced in strength, creating a signal that sounds like it has been recorded with a much better, flatter bandwidth microphone. This shaping can be done by a digital computer such as your PC, using a computer *algorithm* (a simple set of computer instructions) known as the *fast Fourier transform* (FFT). This particular example of equalization can also be done with inexpensive analog audio circuitry costing only a few dollars. More complex equalizations, however, and special effects like changing the playback speed of a voice without changing the person's pitch, can't be easily accomplished with analog circuitry. FFT technology is also the foundation for most speech-recognition software and a host of commercial and military applications.

THE TECHNOLOGY OF FM SYNTHESIS

All Creative Labs sound cards produce music using a built-in FM synthesizer. Chapter 1 gives a brief introduction to the FM synthesizer and the chips used to implement it on the sound card. This section provides more background and technical detail on the sound card's FM synthesizer.

The FM synthesizer produces a wide range of sounds, both music and special effects, using a simple approach invented by John Chowning of Stanford University in 1971. Prior to the discovery of FM audio synthesis, electronic music was created by complicated, expensive equipment. Chowning discovered that a wealth of musical sounds could be created by varying

The Rainbow

If your eyes began to glaze over when you read "wave theory," "Fourier's theorem," and "algorithm," feel free to forget about everything you've just read, relax for a moment, and visualize a rainbow. Here's an example of Nature taking a complex waveform— sunlight—and with the assistance of tiny rain drops separating the white light into its constituent simple waves: the pure rainbow colors you see.

the frequency of one sine wave with a second sine wave (simple) sound source to create a third, frequency-modulated (FM) output (complex) sound. This process can be done with very inexpensive equipment and, in recent years, has been reduced to a single integrated circuit smaller than a fingernail.

This section provides an introduction to the theory behind FM synthesis, with a specific explanation of two-operator versus four-operator sound synthesis, and information about your sound card's FM synthesizer.

The Theory of FM Synthesis

The terms *FM* and *AM* will be familiar to anyone who listens to the radio. The technique underlying FM-synthesized music is exactly the same method used to produce FM radio broadcast signals: low-frequency (audible to the human ear) speech and music is used to vary the frequency of a pure, very high frequency electro-magnetic wave to create a more complex signal, an FM-modulated electro-magnetic wave. This signal is called a *radio signal* because of its very high frequency The role of your FM radio is to capture this signal and extract the low-frequency—audible to humans—component. After your FM radio selects and amplifies this signal, the incoming radio signal is combined with one produced locally by the radio that has the same high frequency used by the radio station—for example, 99.7 MHz (mega-hertz). When the broadcast signal and the local signal are combined, one of the results is a wave that is the exact difference between the signals, the audible component of the radio signal. If your radio is precisely tuned, you will hear the speech and music that was sent piggy-back on the very high frequency radio wave that propagates through the air.

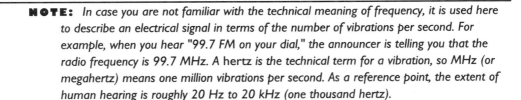

NOTE: *In case you are not familiar with the technical meaning of frequency, it is used here to describe an electrical signal in terms of the number of vibrations per second. For example, when you hear "99.7 FM on your dial," the announcer is telling you that the radio frequency is 99.7 MHz. A hertz is the technical term for a vibration, so MHz (or megahertz) means one million vibrations per second. As a reference point, the extent of human hearing is roughly 20 Hz to 20 kHz (one thousand hertz).*

FM audio synthesis is done by modulating two pure, low-frequency waves of similar frequency, resulting in the creation of additional waves. The resulting sound is very complex, as it contains components of both the two original frequencies and many harmonics. Since FM audio synthesis provides a technique for modulating signals in a very controlled fashion that also produces rich harmonics, it is capable of creating a wide range of musical sounds.

Two-Operator FM Synthesis

Sound Blaster 1.*x*/2.0 and Sound Blaster Pro cards prior to Pro 2 use the Yamaha 3812 OPL2 integrated circuit (chip) that produces FM-synthesized sound by two-operator synthesis. The 3812 chip has 12 *operator cells* that can be combined into 6 pairs for creating 6 FM-synthesized sounds. In addition, the chip has special programming for simulating 5 percussion instruments: snare drum, bass drum, tom tom, top cymbals, and high hat. In total, the 3812 can create 11 simultaneous voices (instrument sounds). The Sound Blaster Pro 2 was built with the latest Yamaha chip, the YMF262 OPL3, which is capable of both two-operator and four-operator synthesis. The Sound Blaster 16 also contains this OPL3 chip. In four-operator synthesis, four operators are used for the synthesis of a single instrument.

The timbre of a sound is only partly a function of the frequency of the operator cells. A wide range of parameters for these operators can be controlled, creating sound of very rich texture. Each of the following operator cell parameters can be controlled in the Yamaha chip to create a unique sound:

- Frequency
- Envelope type (percussive or nonpercussive)
- Envelope amplitude
- Attack/decay/sustain/release (ADSR) rates
- Key scaling rate
- Waveform selection (sine or non-sine)
- Vibrato depth
- Tremolo depth

Two of the operator cell parameters, envelope type and ADSR rates, have a major influence on the timbre. These two parameters can be easily understood through pictures, and in this way will give you a good idea of what's involved in programming an FM chip—not recommended for anyone but the most hard-core music programmers!

The Yamaha chip supports two envelope types. The envelope with diminishing sound simulates a percussion instrument; the one with continuing sound better simulates a nonpercussion instrument such as a violin or horn (see Figure A-4).

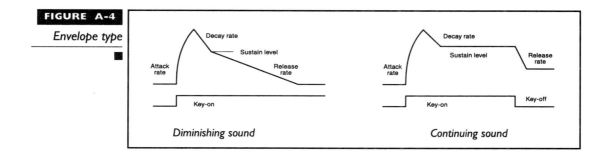

FIGURE A-4

Envelope type

The attack/decay/sustain/release (ADSR) parameters control the relative extent of these four phases in the lifetime of a note. Note that "Key-on" in Figure A-5 indicates the interval of time during which a note is held down.

Stereo Sound

The Sound Blaster Pro card (prior to Pro 2) has two 3812 chips. As a result, it can produce as many as 11 stereo voices or 22 monaural voices. Of the 11 stereo voices, 6 are instruments and 5 are percussion. The YMF262 used on the Pro 2 is *almost* downward-compatible with the earlier 3812. As anyone who has worked with computers knows, "almost" compatible is never compatible enough. Though the 3812 has 11 voices, and the early stereo Sound Blaster Pro has two 3812 chips for 22 voices, the newer Sound

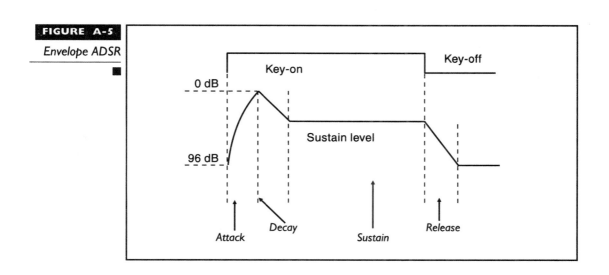

FIGURE A-5

Envelope ADSR

Blaster Pro 2 with the YMF262 chip has only 20 voices, of which 15 are melody instruments and 5 are percussion. The 20-voice limitation doesn't have much practical impact, as 20 monaural voices or 10 stereo voices are usually quite sufficient—few people need to compose music for more than 10 instruments at once!

NOTE: *When playing the FM synthesizer with MIDI data a maximum of 16 monaural voices can be played at once because MIDI supports a maximum of 16 channels.*

Four-Operator FM Synthesis

The Sound Blaster Pro 2, with the newer Yamaha chip, can do either two-operator or four-operator FM synthesis. The advantage of two-operator synthesis is that it ensures compatibility with existing drivers and supports up to 12 synthesized voices. The advantage of four-operator FM synthesis is that the FM synthesizer can create very rich sounds by utilizing twice the number of operators. The drawback is that the Pro 2 is limited to 6 synthesized voices, because two operator pairs are used for each voice instead of one pair.

The Windows 3.1 drivers for Creative Labs sound cards originally supported four-operator FM synthesis only, and the DOS drivers supported only two-operator synthesis. The most recent Windows drivers optimize use of the operator cells, combining four-operator and two-operator voices. If you're playing four-operator voices and run out of operator cells, the driver will steal two operators from a four-operator voice rather than steal all four operators and drop that voice completely.

TIP: *If you have an older version of Sp Pro Sequencer from Voyetra that uses their two-operator DOS driver, you can obtain the newer, four-operator driver directly from Voyetra. If you'd like the newer Windows 3.1 drivers, contact Creative Labs technical support line or dial into their support BBS. See Appendix D for more details on contacting Creative Labs.*

Creative Labs Developer's Kit

If you're interested in experimenting with the FM synthesizer, you can obtain a third-party utility for programming it. If you are a software developer, or interested in prospecting the depths of your Creative Labs sound card, purchase the nominally priced ($99) Creative Labs Sound Blaster Software Developer's Toolkit (SDK) package.

MASTERING
DIGITAL
AUDIO
SAMPLING

reative Labs' latest digital audio recording software shields you from the sound card's filter. This software automatically selects the proper input and output filter setting for your choice of sampling rate, preventing you from making an error. Even though you can't select the filter settings during recording, an understanding of the purpose of these filters is important for gaining a complete understanding of digital audio. This discussion assumes you're already familiar with the basics of digital audio presented in Chapter 1.

The situation regarding access to the input and output filter varies from card to card in the Sound Blaster family. The Sound Blaster Pro is unique in that the SBP-MIX and SBP-SET mixer programs do offer you the opportunity to enable or disable the input and output filter. The Sound Blaster 1.*x*/2.0 filters have fixed settings. Sound Blaster 16's filter settings are variable but are automatically controlled by the sound card circuitry. The SB 16's filter settings can't be overriden, even by programs based on Creative Labs Software Developer's Toolkit. This is beneficial because selecting the wrong filter will result in degradation of sound quality.

The Input Filter

As mentioned in Chapter 1 the Sound Blaster contains both an input and an output filter. The input filter (sometimes called a *recording filter*) is essential for successful operation of the PCM circuitry that records digital audio. The input filter is a low-pass digital filter that freely passes signals below a certain frequency while blocking signals above that frequency. The input filter is set internally, by the sound card circuitry, to the correct *roll-off frequency*, the frequency above which the signal is reduced in strength. This roll-off frequency is just below the Nyquist limit. Nyquist's theorem states that the maximum frequency that can be accurately sampled is one-half the sampling rate used for recording. For example, if the sample rate is 44.1 kHz, the Nyquist limit is 22.05 kHz, and the roll-off frequency would be a little below this, at about 20 kHz. Since it's impossible to create a perfect filter, one that passes all frequencies below the roll-off frequency but stops all frequencies above, engineers are forced to select a roll-off frequency below the Nyquist limit. Failure to filter properly introduces a type of signal distortion called *aliasing*.

Aliasing

The correct setting for the input filter prevents *aliasing*, a type of signal distortion where low-frequency *false* sounds, sounds that never existed, show up in your recording. Aliasing occurs if the sampling rate is too low to accurately sample the higher frequency components of the sound you're recording. For example, suppose you select the sample rate of 11.025 kHz to record speech. According to the Nyquist theorem, this rate is adequate for recording sound as long as the highest frequency you're recording doesn't exceed about 5.5 kHz (safe bet for a deep-voiced adult, but not so safe for recording a young child's voice). If there's a frequency component in excess of the Nyquist limiting frequency—perhaps a toddler screaming—a false sound with a frequency that's the difference between the two will be created by the PCM circuitry that does digital audio sampling.

AUDIO COMPRESSION

In this book we've mentioned several times that digital audio sound files will rapidly take up a lot of real estate on your hard disk—as much as 10.5MB per minute. Fortunately, sophisticated compression schemes exist

A Cinema Example of Aliasing

Since a false sound is a pretty strange concept, here's a way you can visualize what happens if Nyquist's theorem is violated. You've seen a false image due to aliasing if you've ever watched a vintage Ben Hur flick at the movie house. During the scene showing two horse-drawn chariots with spoked (and spiked) wheels racing across the plains, you may have been surprised to see the chariot wheels appearing to slowly rotate backwards. What happened is that the movie camera's sampling rate of 24 frames per second wasn't fast enough to accurately capture the image of the spinning wheel. Recalling Nyquist's theorem, the sampling rate must be twice the highest frequency component you're trying to record. In the case of the spinning chariot wheel, the spokes are passing by a given compass position at a rate slightly faster than 12 times per second. For example, if the spokes pass a given point at 17 times a second, the wheel will appear to be rotating backward at the difference, 5 rotations per second.

that reduce the audio file to a more manageable size, to as little as one-half to one-quarter of the original size. This means that a compressed 44.1 kHz stereo file will take up the same amount of space as an uncompressed 22.05 kHz mono file.

Audio Compression Requirements

Audio files are fundamentally different from the other data files you work with, and they consequently require a different style of compression. For example, spreadsheet, word processing, and other files consisting of text and numbers contain lots of repeating characters such as spaces and lines. You can compress these files, using a general-purpose file-compression tool such as PKZIP or LHA, to as little as one-fifth of their original size. This type of compression program doesn't do a good job of compressing audio, since by its nature audio (as well as video) continually changes. Even so-called "silent" periods are rarely devoid of sound. Consequently, a more sophisticated method of compression is necessary, one designed to take advantage of the characteristics of sound.

NOTE: *The VOC file format has the concept of silence blocks, in which an extended period of near silence in the audio file is replaced with a small marker and a time-duration value. You may notice this when playing games that feature digital audio. This scheme works relatively well, but it's not supported by most sound file formats. In particular, Microsoft's Wave format doesn't support silence blocks.*

Linear Pulse Code Modulation

Chapter 1 describes how sound is converted by pulse-code modulation circuitry from analog to digital and back to analog. Each sample is assigned an 8-bit or 16-bit value that's proportional—linear—to its height, and this process is called linear PCM (LPCM). The digital audio stored on your audio CD is 16-bit LPCM digital audio. When using a Creative Labs sound card and recording digital audio to disk, unless you've selected a compression method, you're saving the audio as LPCM digital audio.

Adaptive Differential Pulse-Code Modulation

A sophisticated variation of PCM, called adaptive differential pulse-code modulation (ADPCM), stores sound with fewer bits per sample than LPCM and is commonly used for audio compression. ADPCM tightly squeezes digital audio while retaining fidelity of sound following decompression.

Figure A-6 compares LPCM and ADPCM samples. The left half of Figure A-6 shows that with LPCM the audio is captured by recording the amplitude of the waveform at each point of time. With 8-bit samples, the amplitude can be recorded to an accuracy of 1 part in 256. With 16-bit samples, preferred for high-fidelity recordings, the amplitude can be recorded to an accuracy of 1 part in 65,536.

The trick behind ADPCM is to capture the difference from one sample to the next, rather than the actual value of each sample. You can reconstruct the waveform by starting from an initial point and plotting each change. This technique resembles the recording of a chess game, in which you note only the change (next move) and not the appearance of the entire board. You don't need to record what the board looks like before each move, since the record of moves allows you to reconstruct the game by playing out, in a step-by-step fashion, the list of moves made by the chess pieces.

The right half of Figure A-6 illustrates how a complex waveform is recorded by taking just 4-bit samples with ADPCM. It's surprising but true that just 4 bits, which means just 16 different values, can do a decent job in replicating a complex waveform. The ADPCM technique accomplishes this by assigning a 4-bit value that is a scale factor for that sample. The value is *not* the amplitude of the waveform at that point of time, it is the *scaling factor*, the amount the previous sample should be multiplied by to arrive at the amplitude for the current sample. Figure A-7 shows the relative amplitude of two adjacent samples, illustrating the effect of just eight scale factors. With 4-bit ADPCM there will be 16 scale factors, giving finer control over the curvature of the waveform, and with 8-bit ADPCM there can be up to 256 scale factors, clearly more than enough.

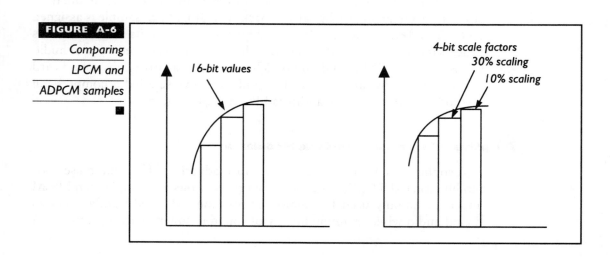

FIGURE A-6

Comparing LPCM and ADPCM samples

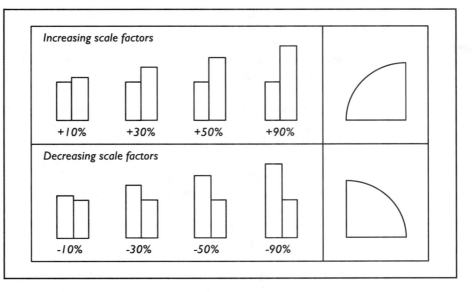

FIGURE A-7

Scaling a digital audio sample by eight different scaling factors

Creative ADPCM

There are actually two variants of ADPCM used by Creative Labs, both of which are referred to as CT-ADPCM (Creative Technology ADPCM). The Sound Blaster 1.*x*/2.0 and Sound Blaster Pro 8-bit cards, as well as the Sound Blaster 16 when it handles 8-bit digital audio, use the Creative ADPCM algorithm pioneered for the original Sound Blaster 1.*x*. This ADPCM algorithm offers a choice of 4:1, 3:1, or 2:1 compression. The 16-bit Sound Blaster 16 card uses a different variant of ADPCM that features 4:1 and 2:1 compression only. The 3:1 compression choice is absent with the Sound Blaster 16 in favor of two 2:1 compression schemes, A-law, and Ω-law, which are described in the next section.

Alternative 16-bit Compression Techniques

The Soundo'LE and WREC programs (which run under Microsoft Windows and DOS, respectively) that are provided with the Sound Blaster 16 offer a choice of three compression techniques for 16-bit samples: ADPCM, A-law, and Ω-law. Both A-law and Ω-law are CCITT standard algorithms for compression of speech. A–law is used primarily in Europe, while Ω–law is more popular in the United States and Japan. A-law and Ω-law differ only in the details of their implementation. While Creative Labs' ADPCM is available for compressing either 8-bit or 16-bit digital audio samples, A-law and Ω-law are available for 16-bit samples only.

NOTE: *CCITT is the International Consultative Committee for Telegraphy and Telephony; it reports to the United Nation's International Telecommunications Union (ITU) and recommends standards for communications equipment, such as the V.32, V.42, and V.42bis MODEM data transmission and compression standards.*

A-law and Ω–law are close cousins to linear PCM. With LPCM, the amplitude of the waveform is recorded by measuring against a linear ruler, like a yard stick, where distance is measured by uniformly placed marks. Something twice as long is assigned a number twice as large. While watching sound waves displayed on an oscilloscope, you'd see that this type of ruler isn't so appropriate for speech and music. This is most noticeable in orchestral music. The music is played at a relatively low volume punctuated occasionally by a surge of energy. A linear ruler won't do justice to either the quiet period featuring a woodwind solo nor the sudden jolt from the crash of cymbals and drums. A logarithmic ruler, which is also a good match for the ear's response to music (as discussed in Chapter 1), is better suited than a linear ruler recording the dynamic range of sound. For this reason it was selected as the basis for A-law and Ω–law.

The net effect of A-law and Ω–law is that, in theory, 8-bit digital audio circuitry that utilizes one of these algorithms can achieve a signal-to-noise (s/n) ratio and dynamic range equivalent to that of 12-bit LPCM circuitry. The Sound Blaster 16 card uses the A-law and Ω-law in a different fashion. Rather than improve the fidelity of sound, given a fixed 8-bit or 16-bit sample size, it compresses the sound to fewer bits—from 16 bits to 8 bits—but does so with relatively good fidelity, certainly better fidelity than equivalent 2:1 compression with ADPCM. Sound Blaster 16 owners should try recording music with all three compression techniques and hear the difference for themselves.

VOC File–Compression Techniques

When Creative Labs shipped their first Sound Blaster 1.*x* card, the cost per byte of hard disk space was considerably more than it is today. With this in mind, Creative Labs engineers put considerable thought into the design of the Voice (VOC) digital audio file.

A VOC file consists of a file header that identifies the file as a VOC file followed by a train of data blocks. Each block contains a specific type of information or a marker. Two techniques for *packing* (which is file compression specific to Creative Labs' VOC digital audio files) are provided for Voice files: replacement of silence periods with silence blocks, and compression of data stored in data blocks. With these packing techniques, files can be reduced to just one-quarter of their original, unpacked size. However there are trade-offs involved:

- There is some degradation in audio quality.

TIP: *It's easy to find out how data packing changes your recording's audio quality. Use a digital audio edit program such as Sound Blaster Deluxe and Sound Blaster Pro VEDIT2, Creative WaveStudio, or the earlier Sound Blaster VOXKIT program. Repeatedly load a sample digital audio file, pack it, and then listen to the results.*

- Packed files cannot be converted to another format, such as Microsoft wave (WAV).
- Digital audio editors such as Creative WaveStudio (Windows) and Sound Blaster Pro's VEDIT2 (DOS) cannot revise compressed files.
- Packing of VOC files cannot be done on voice files recorded at a high sampling rate (relevant to Sound Blaster 1.*x*/2.0 and Sound Blaster Pro cards only). Before you attempt to pack, you must first use a software program like VEDIT2 to reduce the sample rate.

Silence Block Packing

Silence blocks are markers that contain a time duration value that represents a stretch of silence or near silence. *Silence packing* removes silent periods, perhaps from the pause between words or sentences, replacing them with silence blocks. When your sound software encounters a silence block while playing a VOC file, it will suspend digital audio output for the duration specified by the silence block. Note the stretch of silence in waveform depicted in Figure A-8; this will be replaced by a silence block.

The shaded region illustrates the silence window, which is superimposed upon the wavefront. A silence block will be created if a stretch of silence is uncovered that's at least as long in duration as this silence window. "Silence" is defined as waveform amplitude that doesn't extend beyond the confines of this silence window. A stretch of silence that's shorter than this silence window is deemed to be too short to merit conversion into a silence block.

Silence blocks are part of the Creative Labs VOC file format, but they don't exist in most other file formats. In particular, Microsoft WAV file format doesn't contain silence blocks.

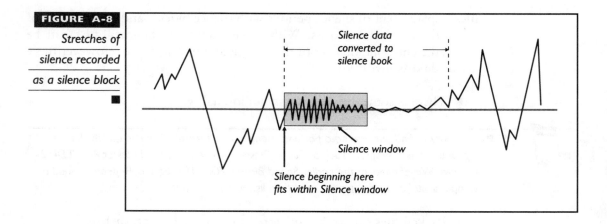

FIGURE A-8

Stretches of silence recorded as a silence block

Silence data converted to silence book

Silence window

Silence beginning here fits within Silence window

Data Block Packing

Data blocks represent the bulk of a file, the bytes of actual digital audio sound. *Data packing* uses ADPCM compression to squeeze the data blocks to as little as one quarter of their original, uncompressed size. When the file is decompressed, the sound bytes are restored and can be played by the sound card's digital audio circuitry, although there is some loss of fidelity.

An important element of the data packing scheme is that the file header isn't compressed. A packed VOC file and an unpacked VOC file share the same superficial characteristic: the .VOC file extension. Your software must examine the file header to validate that the file is a VOC file and to see whether it has been compressed. Information in the file header also indicates whether it's an 8-bit or 16-bit VOC file and provides instructions for how to play the file, including information such as the sample rate and whether the file is stereo or monaural.

Data packing is a two-step process. First, the VOC digital audio file is compressed. Second, the file is decompressed when played. The compression is done by software, after the sound file has been recorded; both VEDIT2 and earlier Sound Blaster 1.*x*/2.0 VOXKIT editor perform this compression for you. Decompression is done by the Sound Blaster card's hardware during playback, by means of dedicated circuitry.

While the compression technique used for quick decompression is simple and fast and results in a considerable economy in storage, it also results in some information loss and consequent loss in sound fidelity. The amount of loss is dependent on the degree the file was compressed. The greatest loss of fidelity occurs with the most extreme compression, 4:1, because it's difficult to preserve a significant amount of information when squeezing 8-bit samples into 2 bits, or 16-bit samples into 4 bits.

Although you can do data packing with as much as 4:1 compression, you must take several factors into consideration before selecting the amount of compression. Extreme compression, such as 4:1, will cause too much distortion to be practical for music and even speech. This amount of compression is suitable for sound effects only. The 3:1 compression choice (available for 8-bit samples only) is appropriate for speech while 2:1 compression is preferable if disk space isn't too tight. Compression is not recommended for recorded music.

NOTE: *For the best overall compression, silence packing is done before data packing (once you've done data packing it is too late to perform silence packing). The data blocks—which are probably now separated by silence blocks—are individually compressed. Creative Labs ADPCM compression technique is fast and simple—a necessity if speech and music are to be compressed on the fly (as the sound is heard).*

Decompression Hardware

The 8-bit sound cards, the Sound Blaster 1.*x*/2.0 and the Sound Blaster Pro, include a special controller chip that aids in ADPCM decompression (compression is done without the aid of a dedicated chip—it's done *in software*, which means it's done by the PC's CPU). Although the chip is labeled with "DSP," it's not a digital signal processing chip and the name was an unfortunate choice. Creative Labs now refers to this chip as the digital *sound* processing chip. While a digital signal processing chip is programmable for many tasks (see the section that follows on DSP technology) this digital sound processing chip only serves to aid decompression and handle a few other minor tasks. The benefit of this chip is that a Sound Blaster card is capable of playing compressed digital audio files even on a relatively slow computer, such as the original IBM-PC with an 8088 CPU, since the decompression work is handled by the sound card. When the Sound Blaster 16 was introduced, a bona fide DSP chip was designed into the Sound Blaster 16 sound card that's capable of performing compression, decompression, Q-Sound processing (see Chapter 4 for more details), and any other task that is programmed into it. An SB16 without the Advanced Signal Processing DSP chip can perform compression and decompression, but robs your PC of vitality since the SB16 must use your computer's CPU chip for these tasks.

Technical Limitations on Compression

There are two limiting factors in working with compressed files: loss of fidelity and the lack of computing horsepower to perform the compression or decompression fast enough to maintain the normal flow of sound. This section addresses the latter, a limitation based on the speed of the sound card's PCM circuitry and your computer's own CPU and disk access times.

Voice File — Compression Limitations

If you have an 8-bit Sound Blaster or Sound Blaster Pro card, and you're planning to store your sound data in a data packed 8-bit VOC file, you'll want to avoid exceeding the maximum allowable sample rate (the 16-bit SB16 handles 44 kHz without straining). Decompressing a file places an additional burden on your sound card's circuitry. As a result, the sound card cannot play back packed voice files as quickly as unpacked ones. The recommended maximum sample rate varies according to the compression selected (see the following table). If the sample rate exceeds the maximum shown below, your sound card will play back the sound file but the output will sound "slow."

Choices for 8-bit Data Compression	Maximum Sampling Rate
Uncompressed	44.1 kHz (Sound Blaster Pro and Pro MCV)
	15 kHz (Sound Blaster 2.0)
	13 kHz (Sound Blaster 1.5 and MCV)
2:1 (4-bit) compression	12 kHz
3:1 (2.6-bit) compression	13 kHz
4:1 (2-bit) compression	11 kHz

NOTE: *The minimum sample rate is 4 kHz. The Sound Blaster MCV is the PS/2 microchannel version of Sound Blaster. For more details on the MCV see Appendix B.*

Sound Blaster Pro's VEDIT2 can compress 8-bit digital audio, but only after it has been captured in an uncompressed form to memory (held in your computer's RAM, not written to the hard disk). When you're ready to save to disk, you can select either 4:1 compression (8 bits are saved as 2 bits), or 3:1 compression (8 bits are saved as approximately 2.6 bits, or 2:1 compression (8 bits are saved as 4 bits). This compression is feasible because VEDIT2 saves to disk at its own pace, which seems fast to us but is leisurely compared to keeping up with sound as it comes in over the microphone, line-in, or CD-ROM audio output.

Wave File—Compression Limitations

Creative Soundo'LE is a Microsoft Windows–compatible recording and editing program shipped with today's Sound Blaster cards. Creative Soundo'LE can compress and decompress 16-bit ADPCM, A-law, and Ω-law digital audio files in real–time—but only when run on the powerful Sound Blaster 16. The 8-bit Sound Blaster 1.*x*/2.0 and Sound Blaster Pro cards are shipped with Soundo'LE, but their version of Soundo'LE isn't capable of compression. Sound Blaster Pro's VEDIT2 can do compression, but not in real–time. It is capable of compressing files when it saves from memory to a disk file. WaveStudio, a digital audio editor that accompanies Creative Soundo'LE, is incapable of compression or decompression, even when run on the Sound Blaster 16.

The Sound Blaster 16 with Advanced Signal Processing uses its digital signal processing chip to perform sound compression. If you have a Sound Blaster 16 without this chip, your sound card and software combination performs 16-bit audio compression in software. This is computer lingo for saying that your computer's general-purpose CPU will have to do the compression work, since there isn't another chip, either on the sound card or on your computer's motherboard, that's available to do the job.

There are two reasons why Creative Labs' cards—with the exception of the Sound Blaster 16 with Advanced Signal Processing—are severely limited in their ability to do real-time compression. The first reason is that without a chip dedicated to compression (such as the Advanced Signal Processing chip), many PCs don't have the computer horsepower to handle real-time compression at the highest sample rates. For example, a Sound Blaster 16 with Advanced Signal Processor to handle compression still needs at least a 386DX/33MHz or 486SX/25MHz CPU chip to push the digital audio samples through the PC fast enough. A Sound Blaster 16 without the DSP utilizes your computer's CPU for compression, so more horsepower is necessary. You'll probably need at least a 386DX/40MHz or 486SX/33MHz CPU chip. The reason you can record or play back raw (uncompressed) digital audio at the top 44.1 kHz rate (Sound Blaster Pro and Sound Blaster 16) is that the sound card has dedicated PCM circuitry that handles the work load.

NOTE: *Most personal computers sold today have sub–30-millisecond hard disk access times, more than adequate for the transfer of digital audio.*

The second reason for not doing real-time compression in software is that the sound card industry still lacks a single standard for audio compression. While the ADPCM technique is broadly accepted, the implementations of it vary, so a sound file compressed by one software package is unlikely to be readable by a package sold by another company.

Dangers of Repeated Compression and Decompression

Compression schemes can be either lossless or lossy. With *lossless compression* techniques (like that done by PKZIP or LHA), you can compress your audio or video or other type of file, for storage or for phone line transmission, and then later expand and use it without any degradation in quality. Since audio files lack redundancy, there's little savings in file size when they are compressed with lossless techniques. As a result, audio files are typically compressed with the ADPCM or similar type *lossy compression* technique.

Avoid repeatedly compressing and decompressing audio files because every time the audio file is compressed or decompressed, a little bit more of the information is lost. This degradation occurs in the following fashion. *Quantization errors* occur when a sample value must be rounded. For example, if a waveform has a height of 8.53 units, but it can only have a whole value between 1 and 10, then it must be rounded up to 9. In this case, the quantization error is about five percent. Successive compressions and decompressions, with errors like this, can quickly ruin the quality of the sound.

DIGITAL SIGNAL PROCESSING: THE LEADING EDGE OF TECHNOLOGY

All Creative Labs sound cards record and play back LPCM (uncompressed) digital audio. Once sound is stored in a digital form, as numbers in the computer, it can be easily processed (transformed). A fancy name for working with audio and video while they are in a digital form is *digital signal processing*. Audio special effects traditionally performed by analog hardware, such as using an echo unit to add an echo, are often accomplished on a restricted basis by software and are limited because they use the PC's CPU. Examples of software programs that do a limited amount of digital signal processing, using the CPU, are Creative WaveStudio, Sound Blaster Pro's VEDIT2, and Sound Recorder, a Microsoft Windows accessory.

The Sound Blaster 16 Advanced Signal Processing, the Creative Labs top-of-the-line card, has a digital signal processing (DSP) chip built into the sound card. With a digital signal processing chip, the Sound Blaster 16 is capable of faster and better signal processing than are the 8-bit sound cards because there's a chip dedicated to the task. This chip is a special type of microprocessor chip designed specifically for the operations most basic to digital signal processing: addition, multiplication, and delay.

There are many audio applications for digital signal processing, such as Q-Sound sound processing, compression and decompression, sample rate conversion, equalization (changing the relative strength of the frequency components), mixing, error concealment (masking flaws), frequency decomposition (FFT for speech recognition), and music effects. At this time, the only processing done by the DSP is compression, decompression, and Q-Sound.

The beauty of using a DSP instead of your computer's CPU for digital signal processing is that the DSP takes over the mundane yet very computationally intensive work of digital signal processing. Your computer's CPU will then be better able to interact with you and handle other tasks. The relationship between the CPU and the DSP is the same as the relationship between your computer's CPU and its math coprocessor. In addition, since the DSP has been optimized for digital signal processing, it tackles this task at a furious pace, faster than a general-purpose processor like an 80386 or 80486 and at least comparable to a Pentium.

Audiophiles will appreciate the music effects, such as reverberation (the slight echo you hear within a music hall or building) and the chorus effect (slight delays in initiation of the instrument sound that cause the sound of a single synthesized instrument voice to resemble that of a group of identical instruments playing togther), and can do it in real-time so you can process sound as you're recording or performing.

DSP chips are still too expensive for widespread use on sound cards. For this reason Creative Labs offers both Sound Blaster 16 and the more expensive Sound Blaster 16 Advanced Signal Processing sound card. Once DSP costs come down, DSPs will make their appearance on all sound cards, and audio applications will blossom with new power and flexibility. The next section in this appendix, "EMU8000: Next Generation Audio DSP," describes the new generation of audio technology from Creative Labs— products that capture the previously elusive combination of low cost and comprehensive audio capabilities.

TIP: *If you bought the Sound Blaster 16, you can upgrade it to the Sound Blaster 16 Advanced Signal Processing by purchasing the DSP chip for $69. See Appendix F for details.*

EMU8000: NEXT GENERATION AUDIO DSP

Visitors to the November 1993 Comdex computer show in Las Vegas were given a glimpse into the next generation of audio technology: the EMU8000 integrated audio digital signal processing chip from E-Mu Systems, Inc. (E-Mu). E-Mu, founded in 1972 and now a wholly owned subsidiary of Creative Labs, is a leading manufacturer of digital sample-based musical instruments. E-Mu is regarded as a leader in the recording, musical instrument, and file/video post-production industries. On the basis of their extensive experience with professional equipment, they have created a high-quality, low-cost DSP that combines the most important functions for sound cards: 16-bit digital audio, wave-sample synthesis, full MIDI

DSP Technology in the Macintosh

Be careful when talking to your Macintosh friends about multimedia PCs and DSPs—they may have just bought one of the new AV (audio visual) Macs. The IBM-compatible world has made rapid advances in sound and multimedia, yet Apple keeps raising the ante. In August 1993, Apple rolled out their Quadra 840AV and Centris 660AV machines. These machines put motion video, stereo sound, and DSP technology into a powerful multimedia platform that doesn't require any add-in cards.

The Centris 660AV was introduced with a base price of just $2,489. Both machines use the powerful 32-bit AT&T 3210 DSP chips to complement the 68040 CPU in the Macintosh.

The list of software applications bundled with these computers will give you a good idea of the breadth of applications that digital signal processing can tackle. The software includes Apple's PlainTalk speech synthesizer and their Casper voice-recognition technology.

These Macs also come with ApplePhone, literally a telephone on the screen with which you can make and receive phone calls as well as send and receive voicemail messages. Other bundled software includes ExperVision, Inc.'s ExperFAX, which translates fax data to text, Video Fusion Ltd.'s Fusion-Recorder, which captures digital video, QuickKeys' OSA Component, which permits you to create speech-activated macros to automate running programs, and a video conferencing program by The Electronic Studio.

support, audio mixing, 32-voice polyphony, built-in audio filtering, and digital effects such as reverberation, chorus, digital equalization, panning, sample rate conversion and pitch change (without changing the playback speed).

The EMU8000 chip isn't the first or only DSP chip to surface in the audio world (IBM is pushing their powerful M-Wave DSP), but it's special in being part of a complete audio subsystem with just the right set of features for becoming an industry standard. E-mu will soon provide an integrated hardware and software audio solution that's ready for incorporation in Creative Labs sound cards, computer motherboards, professional audio equipment, and even embedded applications (perhaps a clothes dryer that plays a funeral dirge when it realizes that it accidentally cooked your polyester shirts). The package includes the EMU8000 Integrated Audio Digital Signal Processor, EMU8100 SoundFont Library, and EMU8200 DSP control software. The EMU8100 sound file library is a comprehensive collection of digitally sampled musical instrument and sound effects, everything you'd expect in a synthesizer and more. The EMU8200 control software is a software application interface (API) that hides the nasty programming inherent in controlling a DSP chip. It's a high-level interface, capable of translating industry-standard MIDI music commands into the low-level hardware commands that play music on the EMU8000 DSP. With this API, software engineers should be able to get EMU8000-based products into the marketplace at a much lower cost and months faster than possible with competing DSP chips. Hardware without software is like a car without gas; Creative Labs and E-mu have put together a winning combination of technology that's ready to fly off the starting line.

DECTALK SPEECH TECHNOLOGY

Creative Labs made a quantum jump in speech synthesis (text-to-speech conversion) technology by acquiring an exclusive license to Digital Equipment Corporation's (DEC) DECtalk *speech engine,* a tightly written software module that's been optimized for speech synthesis. In the speech industry, the DECtalk engine is regarded as the most natural sounding text-to-speech engine created to date. Most text-to-speech software is intelligible but limited. Typically you hear a single voice with a mechanical ring to it, fine for 1970's vintage science-fiction movies, but not terribly satisfying as the genie in your PC that talks to you on a daily basis.

Creative Labs has fashioned new speech synthesis software, called TextAssist, built around the DECtalk engine. Creative has rewritten the DECtalk engine so it'll run on the Sound Blaster 16 Advanced Signal Processing chip. TextAssist not only sounds more natural than Monologue for Windows, but it also offers many additional features, including nine pre-defined voices, male and female, child and adult, all with excellent voice quality. You'll be able to add your own voices to match your personal tastes by adjusting parameters such as the pitch, phoneme duration, speed and volume settings as well as the physical characteristics of the voices.

TextAssist Family

TextAssist is actually a family of Windows applications built on the DECtalk engine. These include a Text Reader with a Dictionary Editor, similar in purpose to the exception dictionary provided with the Monologue for Windows. Creative Talking Scheduler will be revamped to take advantage of TextAssist. Text OLE, an OLE speech server, will be available for embedding TextAssist speech capability into all OLE-compliant software programs. You can also expect upcoming releases of today's most prominent business software applications to support TextAssist right out of the box. You'll be amazed when your favorite word processor, spelling checker, database software, spreadsheet, contact manager, or communications package starts to talk to you. Soon after the introduction of TextAssist for American English, it'll be available in many other languages.

NOTE: *An application programming interface (API) to Creative TextAssist will be available for registered software developers. See Chapter 12 for details.*

Invention of DECtalk Synthesis

DECtalk speech synthesis was invented by Dennis Klatt, a senior research scientist at MIT and a consultant to DEC until he passed away in 1988. Klatt, with a background in electrical engineering and an interest in perceptual psychology, was regarded as one of the foremost speech scientists in the world. His life work was the creation of a computer "model" of the human vocal tract. His capstone achievement was the creation of a working speech synthesizer that was carefully honed for the American English accent. This technology first appeared in 1983 as the software component of a custom-built item of hardware the size of a briefcase. DECtalk PC was first available in an affordable form in 1991 as an EISA/ISA PC card with a retail price of $1195. This same technology has been converted to run on the Sound Blaster 16's Advanced Signal Processing DSP.

Principles Underlying DECtalk PC

The most common approach to speech synthesis is through a phoneme or diphoneme (half of phoneme) synthesizer. Phonemes are briefly defined in Chapter 7, but a more in-depth look is merited here in view of the treatment of speech technology that follows in this section. *Phonemes* are the most important speech sounds making up the building blocks of language. In American English, for example, there are over 40 phonemes (see the table of phoneme codes for Monologue in Chapter 7). Phonemes are the sounds that when substituted cause the meaning of the word to change. For example, /b/ and /k/ are clearly different phonemes because substituting /b/ for /k/ in the word "cat" (/k/ /a/ /t/)changes the word to "bat" (/b/ /a/ /t/). There are clearly many more than 40 *sounds* in English. In an example taken from the Cambridge Encyclopedia of Science, the "el" sound in "leaf" differs from that in "pool," yet these sounds (called *allophones*) can be substituted without changing the meaning of either word, although you'd detect an accent in the pronunciation. In Russian, though, these two allophones are phonemes, since their substitution changes the word meaning. As an aside, English is very rich in phonemes, as shown by the ease in creating nonsensical new words: dat, gat, jat, lat and so forth.

NOTE: *If you're fascinated by speech technology or the variety, history, structure, or theory of language, you owe yourself a special treat. David Crystal's "Cambridge Encyclopedia of Language" (Cambridge University Press) has been universally acclaimed as the most exciting, readable, and comprehensive book on language ever written. Overflowing with pictures, maps, and illustrations and with over 400 pages of text and a cornucopia of references, it's available in an inexpensive (under $30) softcover edition.*

Phoneme Synthesizers

With the notable exception of DECtalk PC, the technology underlying text-to-speech synthesis on the PC is currently based on phoneme synthesis. Monologue for Windows, shipped with hundreds of thousands of Creative Labs sound cards, is an example of a phoneme synthesizer. For the purpose of enhancing the quality of speech synthesis, each phoneme can be divided into two halves, each of which is called a *diphone*. For instance the word "cat" can be viewed as four diphones:

Diphone	Sound
1	Silence + 1st half of the "c"
2	2nd half of "c" + first half of the "a"
3	2nd half of the "a" + first half of the "t"
4	2nd half of the "t" + silence

NOTE: *Monologue for Windows, which synthesizes speech by analyzing words as phonemes rather than diphones, views "cat" as three phonemes: /k/ /AE/ /t/ where /AE/ is Monologue's phonetic code for the "a" sound in "cat."*

A phoneme synthesizer contains prerecorded samples for each phoneme or diphone. For each voice (such as an adult female or adolescent female), all samples must come from the same native speaker. During speech production (see Figure A-9), incoming text is converted into a string of phonemes, and in the case of speech synthesizers based on diphones, the sounds are further reduced to diphones. Based on rules and dictionaries—the proprietary part of phoneme speech synthesis—the diphone string (collection of diphone codes) is then optimized for the creation of natural sounding speech by the addition of special markers into the phoneme or diphone string for intonation (loudness), rate (speed), and pitch. The resultant command string is dispatched to the speech hardware for creation of the sound waveform.

Formant Synthesizers

Formant synthesis (a *formant* is a burst of acoustic energy, a burst of sound, that's characteristic of many phonemes) is an approach to speech synthesis that's radically different from phoneme synthesis. Rather than glue together a string of recorded voice samples, the approach taken by phoneme synthesizers, a formant synthesizer uses a mathematical model of the human

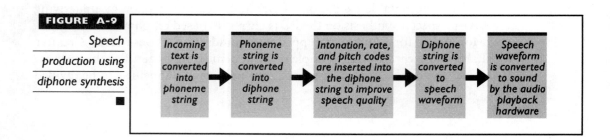

FIGURE A-9

Speech production using diphone synthesis

vocal tract implemented as computer software. The vocal tract can be modeled by familiar physical constructs such as a pipe (for the throat) and a taut string (for the vocal cords—physicists have mathematical models that describe their vibratory behavior). A formant synthesizer, such as the Klatt formant synthesizer (developed by Dennis Klatt) that's contained in DECtalk PC, creates natural-sounding speech by using a mathematical model that contains parameters for varying the pitch, amplitude, duration, and other factors that contribute to speech production. Phoneme synthesizers and formant synthesizers, like the DECtalk engine within Creative TextAssist, share the same first and last steps (see Figures A-9 and A-10) but differ in how the phoneme string is handled.

Using rules and dictionaries, the DECtalk engine converts the phoneme string into synthesizer control values that are sent to the vocal tract computer model (see Figure A-10) for creation of the speech waveform. Voices are easily changed. For example, a deeper voice is created by changing the parameters for the size of the larynx and the thickness of the vocal chords.

ADVANTAGES OF FORMANT SYNTHESIZER   Formant synthesizers, which don't rely on prerecorded sounds for each voice, are much more flexible and extensible than phoneme synthesizers. For a phoneme synthesizer, creation of a new voice requires laborious recordings and a signficant amount of storage space—350K to 750K, depending on the sample size and sample rate. Spontaneous creation of new voices is out of the question. In contrast, with a formant synthesizer, new voices can be created or tweaked (like changing from a spoken voice to a singing voice) as needed by simply passing new parameter values to the speech engine. Since each voice requires a small set of parameters comprising in total a mere 56 bytes, it's possible for you to customize the voices in your computer (such as the Talking Scheduler voice).

With the creation of novel software, your own voice characteristics could be extracted and mimicked. Few of us could tolerate listening to a computer waxing in our own voice, but it might become standard etiquette in the office of the 21st century to attach your "voice print" to electronic messages that

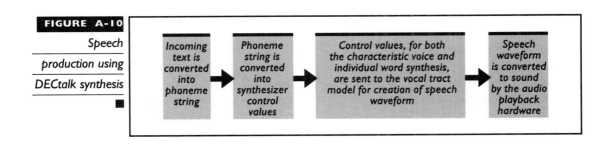

FIGURE A-10

Speech production using DECtalk synthesis ∎

| Incoming text is converted into phoneme string | Phoneme string is converted into synthesizer control values | Control values, for both the characteristic voice and individual word synthesis, are sent to the vocal tract model for creation of speech waveform | Speech waveform is converted to sound by the audio playback hardware |

you transmit. Since voice characteristics can be concisely defined, it's conceivable that an interactive multimedia novel designed for Creative Labs' TextAssist would contain hundreds if not thousands of unique voices, most created dynamically in response to twists in the plot, such as your decision whether to ask directions from the shopkeeper, tourist, or policeman in a bustling Tunisian bazaar.

Voices aren't limited to humans. The DECtalk speech engine has the potential to create a dog's bark, cat's meow, and any other animal sound that's based on a vocal tract reasonably similar to that of the human. The same speech engine, by the addition of text-to-phoneme string parsers for another language, can speak that tongue. Perhaps this is a case of technology running amok, but with future versions of TextAssist you should be able to create a computer voice that sings in your choice of language and accent.

B

Earlier Members of the Sound Blaster Family

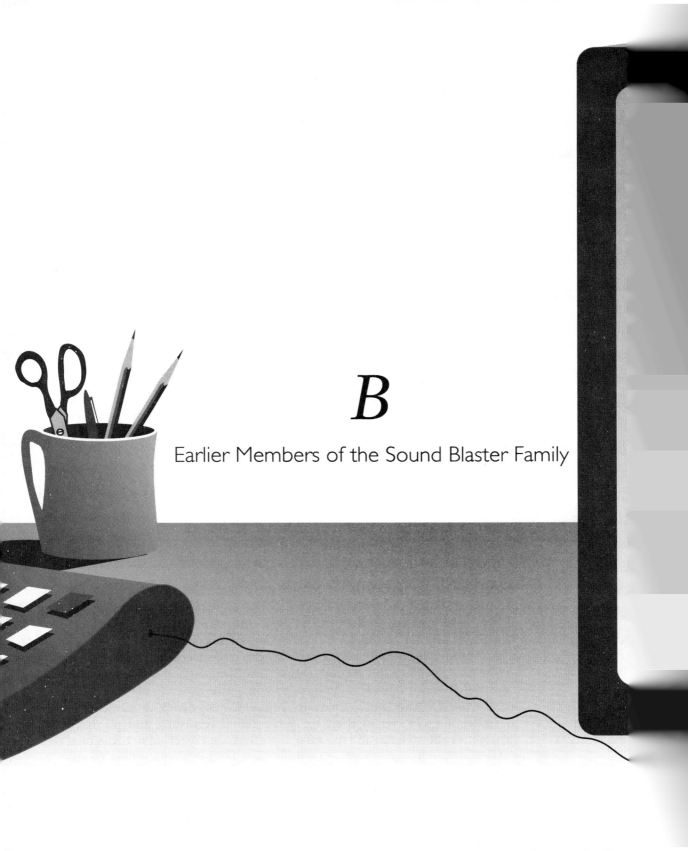

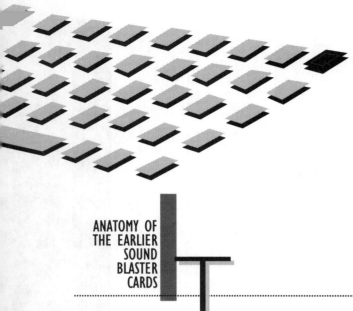

ANATOMY OF THE EARLIER SOUND BLASTER CARDS

The Sound Blaster cards covered in this appendix are no longer sold in the retail channel. Nevertheless, we didn't want to leave them out because most of you still have your original Sound Blasters.

This appendix serves as the Sound Blaster encyclopedia, a sort of time capsule of the history of the Sound Blaster family. In it you will find descriptions of the chips, connectors, and jumpers on the Sound Blaster 1.0 and 1.5, the Sound Blaster Micro Channel Version (MCV), and the Sound Blaster Pro MCV.

THE SOUND BLASTER 1.0 AND 1.5

Before the Sound Blaster 2.0, Creative Labs released two versions of the original Sound Blaster, model numbers 1.0 and 1.5. These Sound Blaster cards can be used on an IBM PC XT, AT, 386, 486, PS/2 (models 25 and 30), Tandy (except 1000 EX/HX), and compatible computers.

The original Sound Blaster is an 8-bit card that incorporates 11-channel FM synthesis, 8-bit digital sound recording and playback, and a joystick/MIDI port. What this means to you is that you can play up to 11 musical instruments simultaneously, bringing new depth to games and presentations. On top of that, the 8-bit digital recording and playback capabilities allow you to add special sound effects and speech. For occasional gamers as well as serious game enthusiasts, a built-in joystick port means you don't have to buy another card to use joysticks; you just plug in the Sound Blaster. And for those who want to explore music, a MIDI (Musical

Instrument Digital Interface) port is included as well, so that MIDI-compatible keyboards and synthesizers can be easily connected to your computer without the expense of additional MIDI cards.

The Sound Blaster 1.0 and 1.5, shown in Figure B-1, are essentially the same card, except that the 1.5 card does not include the Creative Music System upgrade (CMS chips). This upgrade was originally offered by Creative Labs to provide backward compatibility with the older Game Blaster (discussed above). The CMS chips are not as good as the newer FM technology that has subsequently been incorporated into Sound Blaster.

Support for the Game Blaster, and thus the CMS chips, has gradually fallen off and is almost nonexistent today, although you can still obtain the CMS chips and add them to your Sound Blaster. However, given the lack of support for them, there would be very little you could gain by adding them.

The Chips for Sound Blaster 1.0/1.5

The chips on the Sound Blaster are what bring all of its extraordinary features to life. These chips include the FM synthesizer, the Digital Sound Processor, and the bus interface.

Digital Sound Processor Chip

The most versatile chip on the Sound Blaster is the Digital Sound Processor (DSP) chip; it processes all the commands that come from an application. The DSP chip must also instruct all the other sound chips on your Sound Blaster in order to produce the sounds you hear.

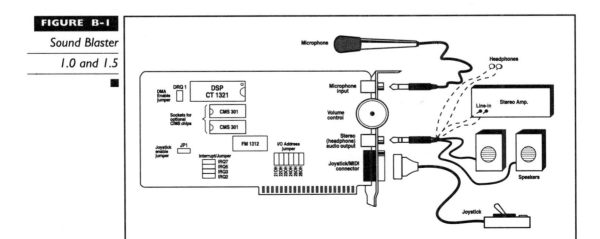

FIGURE B-1

Sound Blaster 1.0 and 1.5

As shown in Figure B-1, the DSP chip is numbered CT 1321 on the 1.0/1.5 card and is the largest chip on the card. When a presentation program wants to play notes through the FM synthesizer, the DSP must accept the data from the computer and instruct the FM chip on how to play the music. When a game wants to surprise you with a digitally recorded explosion, the DSP accepts the sound data from the computer and converts it from digital to analog form so that you can hear the sound.

The DSP is responsible for sending and receiving the MIDI data used by electronic keyboards and synthesizers. The DSP also performs the analog-to-digital and digital-to-analog functions that allow you to do digital recording and playback of music, sound effects, and speech.

Some digital sound files are stored in compressed format to save disk space and must be decompressed. The DSP can play these sound files by decompressing the data as it arrives from the computer. By performing the decompression in the chip, your computer can spend its time doing more important things, such as keeping track of your game opponents on the screen.

You may be interested or surprised to know that some versions of Sound Blaster 1.5 come with version 2.00 of the DSP chip. DSP 2.00 is faster than the 1.05 version and is Windows 3.1 compatible. Version 1.05 was the latest technology when Windows 3.1 was published, but Windows 3.1 requires more sound processing power than the 1.05 version could provide. As a result, a DSP 2.00 is offered by Creative Labs as an upgrade to the Sound Blaster's original DSP, to conform with Windows 3.1 requirements for sound processing power.

NOTE: *If you are running Windows 3.1 without the DSP upgrade from 1.05 to 2.00, you will find that digital sound playback in Windows can waver and stumble. You may also find that some games, such as Wing Commander II, may lock up your system unexpectedly. Both of these problems are caused by the inability of DSP 1.05 to process sound fast enough. If you currently have a Sound Blaster 1.0 or 1.5 with the 1.05 DSP, you can upgrade to a 2.00 DSP by calling Creative Labs. At this writing, the cost of the DSP 2.00 is $30 plus shipping and handling and any applicable sales tax. You may instead want to simply upgrade from Sound Blaster 1.x to the faster DSP and extra features of Sound Blaster 2.0, or even to Sound Blaster Pro or Sound Blaster 16; these newer cards are better suited to the requirements of today's software.*

The FM Synthesizer Chip

The FM synthesizer chip is the same on both versions of the Sound Blaster card, as shown in Figure B-1. The FM chip is responsible for synthesizing the sounds of musical instruments. This chip, numbered FM 1312 (and also known as the Yamaha 3812 OPL2), can play up to 11 instruments simultaneously. It does this by manipulating sine waves to approximate the waveforms created by real instruments.

Other Chips on Your Sound Blaster

The rest of the chips on the Sound Blaster card are support chips, including gates, buffers, and amplifiers that help the main chips communicate with your speakers, microphone, joystick, and computer.

The Connectors for Sound Blaster 1.0/1.5

Figure B-1 points out the various connectors on the Sound Blaster 1.0 and 1.5 cards. These connectors provide a means for passing sound from the card to speakers, stereos, and headphones, and for receiving sound from a microphone, tape player, or stereo. There are three connectors on the 1.*x* cards.

- The microphone jack is the first connector on the 1.*x* cards (look at the top-right corner of the card in Figure B-1). It is a 1/8-inch monaural minijack.

- The connector just below the volume knob, as shown in Figure B-1, is the speaker output. It is a 1/8-inch stereo minijack. The speaker-out connector has a built-in amplifier that can output up to four watts of power per channel, so be sure to turn down the volume before connecting anything to it. Also, do not connect a mono 1/8-inch miniplug to the speaker output, as this can short-circuit and damage the amplifier.

- The last connector is a 15-pin, D-sub connector used for joystick input and MIDI input/output. This connector is shown in Figure B-1 and is the same on both cards. The joystick/MIDI port can support one or two joysticks. Using two requires a Y-adapter available from Creative Labs; generic Y-adapters from other vendors may not work properly. Two pins on the joystick/MIDI connector (pins 12 and 15) are used for MIDI Out and MIDI In, respectively. This allows you to connect MIDI keyboards and synthesizers to the Sound Blaster with the optional MIDI cable.

The Jumpers for Sound Blaster 1.0 and 1.5

Jumpers are used to configure the card so that it doesn't conflict with other cards in your computer. These jumpers set the card's configuration when you install your sound card. Their labels and locations can be seen in Figure B-1.

- Jumper JP1 on the Sound Blaster 1.*x* allows you to turn the built-in joystick on or off. The only time you will need to remove the jumper is if you have another joystick port in your computer. Many combination I/O cards have a joystick port that is turned on by default. If you have such a card, check the documentation for the card to see if the joystick is enabled. If it is, disable the port on either the I/O card or the Sound Blaster, but not on both.

- The DRQ1 jumper enables the DMA (direct memory access) channel on the sound card for digital sound recording and playback. Do not remove this jumper, as the sound card cannot perform digital sound functions correctly without it.

- The IRQ jumpers select the hardware interrupt number of the card, which is also known as its IRQ. These interrupts are compatible with XTs, ATs, and later machines. The interrupts are used for digital sound recording and playback, as well as MIDI input.

- Jumpers 210 through 260, shown in Figure B-1, select the base I/O address of the 1.0 and 1.5 cards. The I/O address is the location of the communications channel that the computer uses to send and receive data from the Sound Blaster.

SOUND BLASTER MCV

The Sound Blaster MCV (Micro Channel Version), shown in Figure B-2, incorporates 11-channel FM synthesis, 8-bit digital sound recording and playback, and a joystick/MIDI port. The Micro Channel is simply the connector on the motherboard used to interface with peripheral cards. A regular AT card will not plug into a Microchannel machine because the connectors are different.

The name Micro Channel Version refers to proprietary architecture developed by IBM to eliminate competition from clone manufacturers. The Sound Blaster Micro Channel Version was developed to support this Micro Channel architecture.

The Sound Blaster MCV card can be used only on the IBM PS/2 model 50 or higher, or computers that are 100-percent compatible with the IBM PS/2 with Micro Channel bus architecture. The Sound Blaster MCV cannot

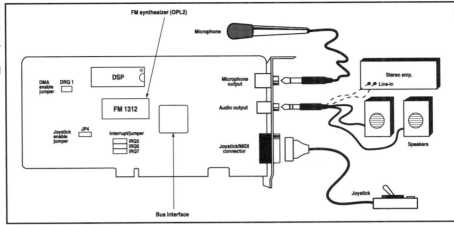

FIGURE B-2

Sound Blaster

MCV

be used on PS/2 models below 50 because they do not use the Micro Channel architecture.

The Chips for Sound Blaster MCV

The Sound Blaster MCV's chips are identical to those in the newer Sound Blaster 2.0. Figure B-2 shows where each chip is located.

The Connectors for Sound Blaster MCV

The Sound Blaster MCV connectors are exactly the same as those on the Sound Blaster 1.0 and 1.5. Refer to Figure B-2 for the location of the connectors.

NOTE: *Sound Blaster MCV does not have a powered audio output like the Sound Blaster 1.x and 2.0 or Sound Blaster Pro. As a result, the Sound Blaster MCV requires the use of powered speakers, a portable stereo, or a home stereo system with a line-in connector.*

The Jumpers for Sound Blaster MCV

The jumpers are used to configure the card. Their locations and labels are shown in Figure B-2.

■ JP4 allows you to turn the built-in joystick on or off. The only time you will need to remove the jumper is when you have another joystick port in your computer. Many combination I/O cards have a joystick port that is turned on by default. If you have such a card, check the documentation for the card to see if the joystick is enabled. If it is, disable the port on either the I/O card or the Sound Blaster, but not on both.

■ Jumper DRQ1 enables the DMA channel on the sound card. Do not remove this jumper, as the sound card cannot perform digital sound functions correctly without it.

■ The IRQ jumpers select the hardware interrupt numbers for the card. The interrupts are used for digital sound recording and playback, as well as MIDI input.

SOUND BLASTER PRO MCV

The Sound Blaster Pro MCV, shown in Figure B-3, has 20-channel stereo FM music, stereo digital sound recording and playback, a built-in joystick/MIDI port, and a digitally controlled mixer.

The Sound Blaster Pro MCV card can be used only on the IBM PS/2 model 50 or higher, or computers that are 100-percent compatible with IBM PS/2 computers with Micro Channel bus architecture. The Sound Blaster MCV cannot be used on PS/2 models earlier than model 50 because they do not use the Micro Channel architecture.

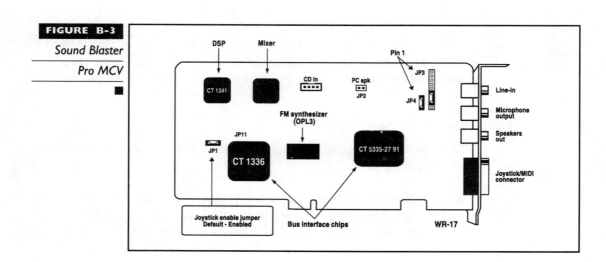

FIGURE B-3

Sound Blaster Pro MCV

Pin	Signal
I	+5V
2	SPK

TABLE B-I   PC Speaker Connector (JP2) ■

The Chips for Sound Blaster Pro MCV

The Sound Blaster Pro MCV uses the same chips as the Sound Blaster Pro 2, including the OPL3 FM synthesizer. The major difference is the addition of the CT 5335 bus interface chip in the Pro MCV, for communicating with the Micro Channel bus. See Figure B-3 for the location of the CT 5335 bus interface chip and other chips on this card. Also, refer to the previous discussions about Sound Blaster Pro 2 for more information on the functions of each chip.

The Connectors for Sound Blaster Pro MCV

The Sound Blaster Pro MCV has the same connectors as the Sound Blaster Pro 2, except the Pro MCV does not have a connector for the CD-ROM data cable. See Figure B-3 for the specific location of the connectors. Tables B-1 and B-2 show the pin configurations for JP2 and J1.

The Jumpers for Sound Blaster Pro MCV

The jumpers are used to configure the hardware on the board. Their locations and labels can be seen in Figure B-3.

Jumper JP1 allows you to turn the built-in joystick on or off. The only time you will need to remove the jumper is when you have another joystick

Pin	Signal	I/O
I	Ground	IN
2	CD left channel	IN
3	Ground	IN
4	CD right channel	IN

TABLE B-2   CD IN Connector (J1) ■

Pin	Description
1	MICR (microphone input, right channel) Input range 0.004 to 0.7 volt rms
2	MICGEN (microphone input ground)
3	MICL (microphone input, left channel)
4	SPKGND (speaker output ground)
5	SPKR (speaker output, right channel) Maximum output voltage 3 volt rms at 4 ohms
6	SPKL (speaker output, left channel) Maximum output voltage 3 volt rms at 4 ohms
7	SPKRL (speaker output return signal, left channel)
8	SPKRR (speaker output return signal, right channel)

TABLE B-3 *Connector JP3 Pin Configuration* ■

port in your computer. Check the manuals that came with your system to see if you already have a joystick port in your machine.

Jumpers JP3 and JP4 are different from all the other jumpers on the board; they don't change the configuration of the board. Instead, JP3 and JP4 are extensions to the audio connectors on the board. Their pin configurations are shown in Tables B-3 and B-4. Notice that there is a jumper on pins 6 and 7 of JP3 and on pins 1 and 2 of JP4. Removing these jumpers will prevent sound from coming out of the Speaker Out connector on the board.

WARNING: *Do not experiment with the Audio Extension jumpers unless you are experienced with audio electronics. A mistake in making connections here can render the sound card useless.*

Pin	Description
1	SPKR (speaker output, right channel) Maximum output voltage 3 volt rms at 4 ohms
2	SPKRR (speaker output return signal, right channel)

TABLE B-4 *Connector JP4 Pin Configuration* ■

C

Installing Your Sound Blaster

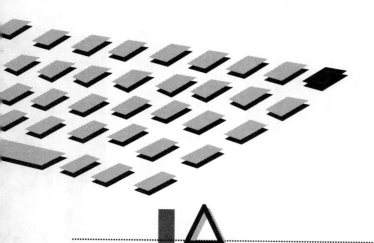

A correctly installed Sound Blaster card will provide you with countless hours of fun and enjoyment. An incorrectly installed Sound Blaster will most likely give you countless hours of frustration and disappointment.

If you have any problems at all with your Sound Blaster, it is usually because of an improper installation. For some people, installation is a breeze. They just plug the board into an available expansion slot, attach a pair of speakers, and away they go. But for others, this may not be the case. After installing the board, they might find that the Sound Blaster will not function, or that some other part of the computer no longer works correctly.

This chapter will help you overcome many of the common (and not so common) difficulties associated with installation of the Sound Blaster family of sound boards. If you've already installed your board and are having problems, or are having trouble doing the installation, we suggest you give this chapter at least a good browse. And of course, you'll want to read it thoroughly if you've just purchased your card and want to install it.

The chapter begins with some general information about the various Sound Blaster cards and about important tasks to perform before you begin an installation. The installation procedures themselves are divided into several sections, each one dedicated to a specific card in the Sound Blaster family. As you step through the instructions, you will be installing the DOS drivers and utilities that are included on the disks that came with your card. If you are running Windows, there is also a section on installing the Windows drivers. In addition to installation and testing instructions for each card, you will find lots of important information and many helpful tips. You will also want to check out Appendix D, which contains answers to the questions most often asked of the technical support folks at Creative Labs.

NOTE: *If you get confused about some of the topics discussed in this chapter—such as hardware conflicts, joystick ports, or what to do with jumpers—don't despair. The troubleshooting topics you find in Appendix D will help you with that, too.*

DETERMINING THE SOUND BLASTER VERSION

The Sound Blaster family has many members. The easiest way to determine which Sound Blaster you have, in case you threw away the box, is to check the model number. It consists of the letters CT followed by four digits. Hold the board so that the volume knob is in your right hand and the chips are facing you. The model number is located at the top-left corner of the board. Some boards have the model number in the bottom-left corner. Below is a list of model numbers with corresponding card names.

Model #	Card Name
CT 1320	Sound Blaster 1.x
CT 1330	Sound Blaster Pro
CT 1350	Sound Blaster 2.0
CT 1600	Sound Blaster Pro 2
CT 1740	Sound Blaster 16
CT 1750	Sound Blaster 16 MCD
CT 1770	Sound Blaster 16 SCSI-2
CT 5320	Sound Blaster MCV
CT 5330	Sound Blaster Pro MCV

In case you already plugged your card into your computer and put in all the screws, the Sound Blaster version can also be determined by the version of the Digital Sound Processor (DSP). To find the DSP version number, you have to run the test program for your card. Since you don't know which card you have, you won't know the exact name of the test program. Have no fear! The test program filename always begins with the letters TEST and is located on the first installation disk. Insert Installation Disk #1 and look for a file that starts with TEST and ends with the .EXE extension.

When you run the test program, you will be confronted with one or more message screens and then a main menu. At the top of the screen is a status line that indicates the card's settings as well as the DSP version number. Compare the version number you see with the list below.

DSP Version	Card Name
1.xx	Sound Blaster 1.x or Sound Blaster MCV
2.00	Sound Blaster 1.5 with DSP upgrade
2.01	Sound Blaster 2.0
3.xx	Sound Blaster Pro or Pro 2 or Pro MCV
4.xx	Sound Blaster 16 (including MCD and SCSI-2)

As you can see, finding out which card you have is not as straightforward using the DSP version rather than the model number. Nevertheless, it will point out the level of technology that's installed in the machine.

If the test program says you have a DSP version 1.*xx* or 3.*xx* remember that only a Microchannel-type computer, such as the IBM PS/2 series, can use the MCV version of the Sound Blaster and Sound Blaster Pro. If your PC is not a Microchannel, you don't have an MCV card installed.

BEFORE INSTALLING THE SOUND BLASTER

Before installing your Sound Blaster hardware and software, make backups of all the disks included with the Sound Blaster card. Put away the originals in a safe place, and use the copies for the installation process. Turn off the power to the computer and remove the cover. (See your computer's manual for details on removing the cover.)

CAUTION: *Read the following sections carefully—before you begin your installation—to prevent potential problems with ports used for all versions of Sound Blaster, IRQ/interrupt conflicts, and other hardware conflicts.*

Preventing Conflicts with Joystick (Game) Ports

The Sound Blaster comes equipped with a built-in joystick port (also called a game port). If your computer already has a joystick port, it will conflict with the joystick port on the Sound Blaster. To avoid this conflict you'll have to disable one of the ports. See the Sound Blaster manual for jumper locations.

- To disable the joystick port on the Sound Blaster 1.*x* card, remove jumper JP1; on Sound Blaster 2.0, remove jumper JP8.

- To disable the joystick port on Sound Plaster Pro, Pro 2, or Pro Basic, remove jumper JP4.

- To disable the joystick port on Sound Blaster MCV, remove jumper JP4; on Sound Blaster Pro MCV, remove jumper JP1.

- To disable the joystick port on all versions of the Sound Blaster 16, remove jumper JYEN.

Resolving IRQ/Interrupt Conflicts

Before you install your Sound Blaster card, check your computer manual and the manuals of all peripheral cards in your system for possible conflicts with the default Sound Blaster card settings for I/O Address, IRQ, and DMA. Conflicts typically occur with handheld scanner cards (DMA 1), and on primary printer ports when used with laser printers (IRQ 7).

The default card settings and choices for changing them on each version of Sound Blaster are covered in the following sections that describe installation procedures for the various cards.

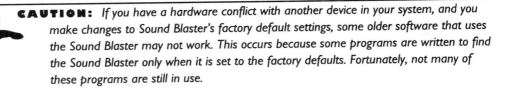

CAUTION: *If you have a hardware conflict with another device in your system, and you make changes to Sound Blaster's factory default settings, some older software that uses the Sound Blaster may not work. This occurs because some programs are written to find the Sound Blaster only when it is set to the factory defaults. Fortunately, not many of these programs are still in use.*

Important Facts About Interrupt 7

Earlier Sound Blaster cards were factory set to use interrupt 7 (IRQ 7). Unfortunately, some people encountered intermittent problems and occasional computer lockups at this setting. There are two reasons why problems occur with the IRQ 7 setting.

- The hardware for the first parallel printer port (LPT1) in the computer uses IRQ 7. The printer port hardware on some computers doesn't allow this interrupt to be shared with other devices, such as your Sound Blaster. This results in a hardware conflict and, hence, problems with the printer, Sound Blaster, or both.

- The interrupt controller, the chip that handles all the interrupt requests in most PCs, is designed to treat noise on the interrupt lines in a special manner. If there is an interrupt at any IRQ number that doesn't conform to the timing specification for a valid interrupt, the controller assumes that it's noise. It then redirects this false interrupt to IRQ 7. Bingo! Big problems.

  If the Sound Blaster is on IRQ 7, any software that is using the Sound Blaster will think that the Sound Blaster requested the interrupt. Since the Sound Blaster didn't request it, the program locks up. This situation occurs because most applications weren't written to correctly handle a false interrupt, not because the interrupt controller is faulty.

So, the moral to the story is not to set the Sound Blaster to IRQ 7 unless you have an older program that can work only with the Sound Blaster at IRQ 7. Creative Labs changed the factory setting of new cards to IRQ 5 in order to avoid these problems.

THE SOUND BLASTER 1.x /2.0 AND DELUXE

This section tells you how to install versions 1.0, 1.5, and 2.0 of the Sound Blaster. Before you begin the installation, be sure you have read the previous section, "Before Installing the Sound Blaster." Also note that the Sound Blaster 2.0 and Sound Blaster Deluxe packages use the same Sound Blaster 2.0 model CT 1350.

See Figure C-1 for an illustration of the Sound Blaster 1.x and Figure C-2 for an illustration of the Sound Blaster 2.0 card.

FIGURE C-1

The Sound

Blaster 1.0/1.5

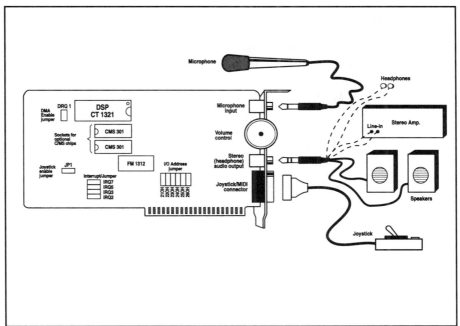

FIGURE C-2

The Sound

Blaster 2.0

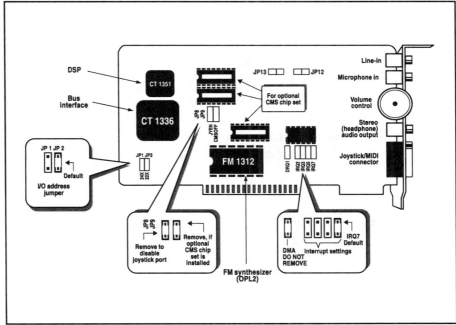

Changing the Sound Blaster 2.0 Default Settings

Your Sound Blaster 2.0 card comes from the factory with the following default settings: I/O Port Address 220H, IRQ 5, and DMA channel 1.

- If another device in your system uses I/O Port Address 220H, you can change the Sound Blaster I/O Port Address by moving the I/O Address jumper to a value not used in your system. On the Sound Blaster 1.*x*, you can choose from 230H, 240H, 250H, and 260H. On the Sound Blaster 2.0, your only alternative is port 240H.

- If another device in your system uses Interrupt 5, you can change the Sound Blaster interrupt by moving the IRQ jumper to a value not used in your system. Choose IRQ 2, 3, 5, or 7, but bear in mind the following: IRQ 3 is used for the second serial port (COM2). IRQ 5 is sometimes used on bus mouse interface cards, as well as for hard disk controller cards on XT computers. The Tandy 1000 uses IRQ 7 internally and will not allow the Sound Blaster to use it.

- If another device on your system uses DMA channel 1, you will have to change the setting on that device, because the Sound Blaster can only use DMA channel 1. Consult the manual for the device in question to see how to select a different DMA channel. *Do not remove the DMA jumper on the Sound Blaster card.* The card will not work correctly without this jumper installed.

Installing the Sound Blaster Hardware

Before you start the installation, be sure you know what version of Sound Blaster you have, and have handled possible port problems and card setting conflicts, as explained in the earlier section "Before Installing the Sound Blaster." Then you can start your installation.

Follow these steps to install the Sound Blaster card:

1. Plug the card into any free 8-bit or 16-bit slot.

NOTE: *Other cards in your system may have an impact on the quality of recording and playback of the Sound Blaster. If possible, install the Sound Blaster away from other cards in your system. The most troublesome cards are usually disk controllers, video cards, and fax/modem boards.*

2. Connect headphones, stereo speakers, or your home stereo system to the Sound Blaster speaker output connector. The connector

requires a 1/8-inch stereo miniplug, like that used on portable
audio tape player headphones. See Figure C-1 for the location of
the connectors.

3. Adjust the volume knob on the Sound Blaster card; put it halfway
   between the maximum and minimum limits.

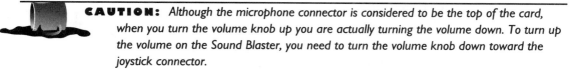

CAUTION: *Although the microphone connector is considered to be the top of the card,
when you turn the volume knob up you are actually turning the volume down. To turn up
the volume on the Sound Blaster, you need to turn the volume knob down toward the
joystick connector.*

WARNING: *When turned up to the maximum volume, the built-in amplifier on the Sound
Blaster puts out 4 watts of power per channel into 4-ohm speakers, and 2 watts per
channel into 8-ohm speakers. Do NOT turn the volume up to maximum if your speakers
are not rated for this much power. If you are connecting the Sound Blaster output to
the line-level inputs of a stereo system, we recommend that you keep the volume about
3/4 of the way up. Turning the volume up higher can generate distortion or noise in
the output signal. You may have to adjust the volume knob from this position for
minimum distortion.*

Testing the Sound Blaster Hardware

Once you've installed the Sound Blaster card, you need to test it. Follow
these steps to make sure that your installation has been successful:

1. Insert the Sound Blaster Disk 1 into drive A or B. Type
   A:TEST-SBC or **B:TEST-SBC**, and press ENTER. The test program
   will inform you of each test that is being performed and any
   conflicts that arise. Also, write down the DSP version number that
   is reported at the top of the test program, for future reference.

2. If the program reports a conflict in I/O Address, Interrupt, or
   DMA settings, turn off the computer and pull out the Sound
   Blaster card. Select a different I/O Address, Interrupt, or DMA
   setting, following guidelines in the earlier section about changing
   the default settings on the card. Also, double-check your
   computer's manual for guidance about conflicts in these settings.
   All conflicts must be resolved before the Sound Blaster card will

work properly. After making the necessary changes, reinstall the card and run the test program again.

3. Once the test program has determined there are no conflicts in the settings, it displays a menu with selections for testing the FM (music) and DAC (voice) output from your card. Highlight the FM test, and press ENTER.

4. As the music plays, turn up the volume knob on the Sound Blaster until you hear the music. (Remember: to turn the volume down, turn the volume knob up toward the microphone connector. To turn the volume up, turn the volume knob down toward the joystick connector.)

5. When the FM test stops, highlight the Voice test and press ENTER. You should hear a voice saying several times, "Hello there."

If you do not hear output from either of these tests, even after turning the volume knob to both extremes, you may have a bad card. Contact Creative Labs Technical Support or your nearest dealer to resolve the problem.

Installing the Sound Blaster Software

The software installation for the Sound Blaster changes periodically. As a result, you will have to consult your manual for the exact instructions needed to correctly install the software on your version of the installation disks. After the software installation is complete, continue reading this section for additional installation notes.

When the installation program finishes, you will have a new directory named \SB, containing a number of subdirectories for the drivers, utilities, and other software.

WARNING: *There is a subdirectory under \SB called DRV that contains all the drivers for the Sound Blaster card. Do NOT rename the DRV subdirectory. In order for programs to find the necessary drivers, this subdirectory must exist exactly as the installation program creates it. You can rename the \SB directory but not the DRV subdirectory.*

The statement SET SOUND=C:\SB (assuming you installed on drive C) is added to the AUTOEXEC.BAT file. If you change the \SB directory name to something else, you must also change the SET SOUND= statement in the AUTOEXEC.BAT file so that programs will know where to find any necessary drivers.

The AUTOEXEC.BAT file will also contain the statement SET BLAS-TER=A220 I5 D1 T3 (the T3 parameter will be T1 if you have a Sound Blaster 1.*x*). Here are the parameters and their functions:

- A*n*   Specifies the base I/O Address. The *n* value is either 220 or 240 (also 210, 230, 250, or 260 for Sound Blaster 1.*x*).

- I*n*   Specifies the Interrupt setting. The *n* value is 2, 3, 5, or 7.

- D*n*   Specifies the DMA channel. The *n* value is always 1.

- T*n*   Specifies the card type. The *n* value is 1 for the Sound Blaster 1.*x* and 3 for the Sound Blaster 2.0.

If this SET BLASTER= statement does not exist in your AUTOEXEC.BAT, use a text editor and add the line, based on the parameters described above. If you changed the hardware settings on your card from the factory defaults, you have to update the SET BLASTER= statement. You can change it manually by editing the AUTOEXEC.BAT file, or you can run the SET-ENV utility (it's in the \SB directory).

NOTE: *If some of your programs cannot find the Sound Blaster card or drivers, move the SET SOUND= and SET BLASTER= statements to the beginning of your AUTOEXEC.BAT file. If you still have problems and you are running DOS 4.01 or an earlier version, look for an @ symbol at the beginning of the SET SOUND= and SET BLASTER= statements. If the @ exists, delete it.*

THE SOUND BLASTER PRO, PRO 2, PRO BASIC, AND PRO DELUXE

This section tells you how to install the Sound Blaster Pro, Pro 2, and Pro Basic cards. Before you begin the installation, be sure you have read the earlier section, "Before Installing the Sound Blaster." Also note that the Sound Blaster Pro Basic and Sound Blaster Pro Deluxe packages use the Sound Blaster Pro 2 model CT 1600.

Figures C-3 and C-4 show pictures of the Sound Blaster Pro and Pro 2 cards.

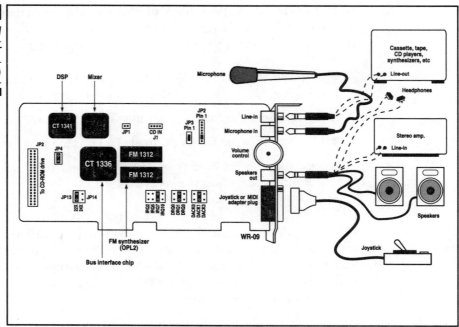

FIGURE C-3

The Sound Blaster Pro (CT 1330)

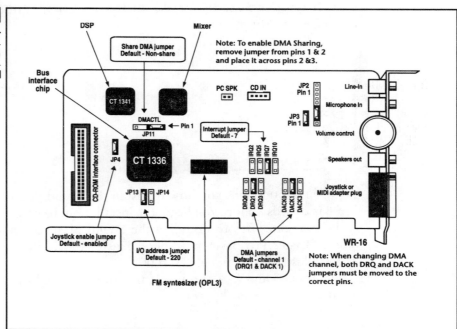

FIGURE C-4

Sound Blaster Pro 2 (CT 1660)

Changing the Sound Blaster Pro Default Settings

The Sound Blaster Pro cards come from the factory with the following default settings: I/O Port Address 220H, IRQ 5, and DMA Channel 1.

- If another device uses I/O Port Address 220H, you can change the Sound Blaster Pro I/O Port Address by moving the I/O Address jumper to a value not used in your system. You have a choice of two I/O Addresses: 220H or 240H (jumpers JP14 and JP13, respectively).

- If another device uses Interrupt 5, you can change the Sound Blaster Pro Interrupt by moving the IRQ jumper to a value not used in your system. Choose from IRQ 2, 5, 7, and 10 (jumpers JP21, JP20, JP19, and JP18, respectively), but bear in mind the following: IRQ 3 is used for the second serial port (COM2). IRQ 5 is sometimes used on bus mouse interface cards and for hard disk controller cards on XT computers. The Tandy 1000 uses IRQ 7 internally and will not allow the Sound Blaster Pro to use it.

- If another device uses DMA channel 1, you can change the setting on the Sound Blaster Pro by moving the DRQ and DACK jumpers. Choose from DMA 0, 1, and 3. The DRQ jumper value must match the DACK jumper value. In other words, for DMA 0, a jumper must be on JP5 and JP15 so that DRQ0 and DACK0 are selected. For DMA 1, a jumper must be on JP6 and JP16 so that DRQ1 and DACK1 are selected. For DMA 3, a jumper must be on JP7 and JP17 so that DRQ3 and DACK3 are selected.

Installing the Sound Blaster Pro Hardware

Before you start the installation, be sure you know what version of Sound Blaster Pro you have, and have handled possible port problems and card setting conflicts, as explained in the earlier section "Before Installing the Sound Blaster." Then you can start your installation. Follow these steps:

1. Plug the Sound Blaster Pro card into any free 16-bit slot in the computer. Sound Blaster Pro will also work in an 8-bit slot, but this will not allow access to IRQ 10 or DMA 0.

2. Connect headphones, stereo speakers, or your home stereo system to the Sound Blaster Pro speaker output connector. The connector

requires a 1/8-inch stereo miniplug, like those used on portable audio tape player headphones.

3. The Sound Blaster Pro cards have a jumper labeled PC SPK. By connecting a cable from the speaker jumper on your computer's motherboard to PC SPK, the Pro will be able to amplify the computer's beeps. Most people do not use this feature because the amplified beeps are VERY loud. If you choose to hook your PC speaker up to the Sound Blaster Pro, turn the volume down until you can judge the proper setting after you hear the system beep.

CAUTION: *If you connect the PC SPK jumper to your motherboard, be prepared for the resulting loud volume level of the computer's beeps. The PC SPK input is NOT connected to the Sound Blaster Pro MCV's mixer and can be very loud!*

4. Adjust the volume knob on the Sound Blaster Pro card so it is between the maximum and minimum limits.

CAUTION: *Although the microphone connector is considered to be the top of the card, when you turn the volume knob up you are actually turning the volume down. To turn up the volume on the Sound Blaster Pro, you need to turn the volume knob down toward the joystick connector.*

WARNING: *When turned up to the maximum volume, the built-in amplifier on the Sound Blaster outputs 4 watts of power per channel into 4-ohm speakers, and 2 watts per channel into 8-ohm speakers. Do NOT turn the volume up to maximum if your speakers are not rated for this much power. If you are connecting the Sound Blaster output to the line-level inputs of a stereo system, we recommend that you keep the volume about 3/4 of the way up. Turning the volume up higher can generate distortion or noise in the output signal. You may have to adjust the volume knob from this position for minimum distortion.*

Testing the Sound Blaster Pro Hardware

Once you've installed the Sound Blaster Pro card, you need to test it. Follow these steps to make sure that your installation is successful:

1. Insert the Sound Blaster Pro Disk 1 into drive A or B. Type **A:TEST-SBP** or **B:TEST-SBP**, and press ENTER. The test program will inform you of each test that is being performed and any

conflicts that arise. Also, write down the DSP version number that is reported at the top of the test program for future reference.

2. If the program reports a conflict in I/O Address, Interrupt, or DMA settings, turn off the computer and pull out the Sound Blaster Pro card. Select a different I/O Address, Interrupt, or DMA setting. Also, double-check your computer's manual for guidance about conflicts in these settings. All conflicts must be resolved before the Sound Blaster card will work properly. After making the necessary changes, reinstall the card and run the test program again.

3. Once the test program has determined there are no conflicts in the settings, it displays a menu with selections for testing the FM (music) and DAC (voice) output from your card. Highlight the FM Music test, and press ENTER.

4. As the music plays, turn up the volume knob on the Sound Blaster until you hear the music. (Remember: To turn the volume down, turn the volume knob up toward the microphone connector. To turn the volume up, turn the volume knob down toward the joystick connector.)

5. After the FM test stops, highlight the Voice test and press ENTER. You should hear water sounds moving from the left speaker to the right speaker. (On fast computers, the water can sound like noise, so don't be alarmed.)

If you do not hear output from either of these tests even after turning the volume knob to both extremes, you may have to adjust the on-board mixer. (See the upcoming section "Installing the Sound Blaster Pro Files" for instructions on installing the drivers and utilities, including the mixer program.) If you still have trouble even after turning up the mixer settings, contact Creative Labs Technical Support or your nearest dealer to resolve the problem.

Installing the Sound Blaster Pro Software

The software installation for the Sound Blaster Pro changes periodically. As a result, you will have to consult your manual for the exact instructions needed to correctly install the software on your version of the installation disks. After the software installation is complete, continue reading this section for additional installation notes.

When the installation program finishes, you will have a new directory named \SBPRO, containing a number of subdirectories for the drivers, utilities, and other software.

WARNING: *There is a subdirectory under \SBPRO called DRV that contains all the drivers for the Sound Blaster Pro card. Do NOT rename the DRV subdirectory. In order for programs to find the necessary drivers, this subdirectory must exist exactly as the installation program creates it. You can rename the \SBPRO directory, but not the DRV subdirectory.*

For the Sound Blaster Pro cards, the statement SET SOUND=C:\SBPRO (assuming you installed on drive C) is added to the AUTOEXEC.BAT file. If you change the \SBPRO directory name to something else, you must also change the SET SOUND= statement in the AUTOEXEC.BAT file so that programs will know where to find any necessary drivers.

The AUTOEXEC.BAT file will also contain the statement SET BLAS-TER=A220 I5 D1 T2. (The T2 parameter will be T4 if you have a Sound Blaster Pro 2, Pro Basic, or Pro Deluxe). Here are the parameters and their functions:

- An Specifies the base I/O Address. The n value is either 220 or 240 for Pro 2; 230, 250, or 260 for Pro.

- In Specifies the Interrupt setting. The n value is 2, 5, 7, or 10.

- Dn Specifies the DMA channel. The n value is 0, 1, or 3.

- Tn Specifies the card type. The n value is 2 for Sound Blaster Pro, and 4 for Sound Blaster Pro 2, Pro Basic, or Pro Deluxe.

If this SET BLASTER= statement does not exist in your AUTOEXEC.BAT, use a text editor and add the line, based on the parameters described above. If you changed the hardware settings on your card from the factory defaults, you have to update the SET BLASTER= statement. You can change it manually by editing the AUTOEXEC.BAT file, or you can run the SET-ENV utility (it's in the \SBPRO directory). There is no need to make any changes to the driver files themselves. Changes to the driver files were required only on earlier versions of the Sound Blaster 1.x.

NOTE: *If some of your programs cannot find the Sound Blaster card or drivers, move the SET SOUND= and SET BLASTER= statements to the beginning of your AUTOEXEC.BAT file. If you still have problems and you are running DOS 4.01 or an earlier version, look* *for an @ symbol at the beginning of the SET SOUND= and SET BLASTER= statements. If the @ exists, delete it.*

THE SOUND BLASTER MCV

This section tells you how to install Sound Blaster MCV. Before you begin the installation, be sure you have read the earlier section, "Before Installing the Sound Blaster."

Figure C-5 shows a picture of the Sound Blaster MCV card.

Installing the Sound Blaster MCV Hardware

Follow these steps to install a Sound Blaster MCV card:

1. If you have not yet done so, make a backup copy of your PS/2 Reference Disk. (And don't forget to make the usual backups of all the Sound Blaster disks.)

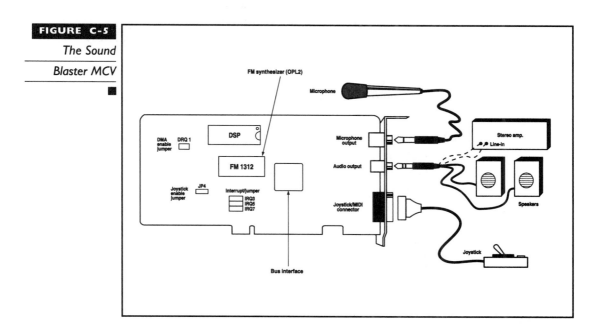

FIGURE C-5

The Sound Blaster MCV

2. Copy the file @5084.ADF from the Sound Blaster MCV Disk 1 to the backup copy of the PS/2 Reference Disk.

3. Turn off the power to the computer and remove the cover.

4. Disable the joystick port, if necessary, as described in "Before Installing the Sound Blaster" earlier in the chapter.

5. Plug the Sound Blaster MCV card into any free slot in the computer.

6. Insert the backup PS/2 Reference Disk into drive A and turn on the computer. The computer will report error 165, indicating that a change has been made to the adapter configuration. Select automatic setup and follow the onscreen instructions to configure your computer.

7. After the computer finishes its automatic configuration, it restarts. Leave the PS/2 Reference Disk in the drive. If you do not get an adapter configuration error at this point, skip to step 9.

8. Wait for the configuration software to come up. Select Set Configuration and then Change Configuration to view the adapter card configuration screen. A conflicting adapter card will be listed with an asterisk beside it. Make any necessary changes to the conflicting devices as outlined by the onscreen instructions. Refer to your system manual for details on using the PS/2 configuration software.

9. Exit from the configuration software. Your computer now restarts. Remove the PS/2 Reference Disk, and boot the computer from the hard drive or with a DOS disk.

10. Connect powered stereo speakers or your home stereo system to the Sound Blaster MCV speaker output connector. The connector requires a 1/8-inch stereo miniplug, like that used on portable audio tape player headphones.

NOTE: *Sound Blaster MCV does not have a powered audio output like the Sound Blaster 1.x/2.0 or Sound Blaster Pro cards. As a result, Sound Blaster MCV requires the use of powered speakers, a portable stereo, or a home stereo system.*

Testing the Sound Blaster MCV Hardware

Once you've installed the Sound Blaster MCV card, you need to test it. Follow these steps to make sure that your installation has been successful:

1. Insert the Sound Blaster MCV Disk 1 into drive A or B. Type **A:TEST-SBC** or **B:TEST-SBC** and press ENTER. The test program will inform you of each test that is being performed and of any conflicts that arise.

2. If the program reports a conflict in I/O Address or DMA settings, repeat steps 6 through 9 of the hardware installation procedure (in the foregoing section) to select a different I/O Address or DMA setting. If there is an interrupt conflict, turn off the computer, pull out the card, and change the interrupt jumper setting. See the Sound Blaster MCV manual for jumper locations. You must resolve all system conflicts before the Sound Blaster card will work properly. After making the necessary changes, run the test program again.

3. Once the test program has determined there are no conflicts in the settings, it displays a menu with selections for testing the FM (music) and DAC (voice) output from your card. Highlight the FM Music test, and press ENTER.

4. When the FM test stops, highlight the Voice test and press ENTER. You should hear a voice saying several times, "Hello there."

If you do not hear output from either of these tests, even after turning the volume up on your speakers, you may have a bad card.

Installing the Sound Blaster MCV Software

The software installation for the Sound Blaster MCV has changed periodically. As a result, you will have to consult your manual for the exact instructions needed to correctly install the software on your version of the installation disks. Also refer to the notes given in the section on installing the Sound Blaster 1.x/2.0.

THE SOUND BLASTER PRO MCV

This section tells you how to install Sound Blaster Pro MCV. Before you begin the installation, be sure you have read the earlier section, "Before Installing the Sound Blaster."

Figure C-6 shows a picture of the Sound Blaster Pro MCV card.

Installing the Sound Blaster Pro MCV Hardware

Follow these steps to install a Sound Blaster Pro MCV card:

1. If you have not yet done so, make a backup copy of your PS/2 Reference Disk. (And don't forget to make the usual backups of all the Sound Blaster Pro MCV disks.)

2. Copy the file @5103.ADF from the Sound Blaster Pro MCV Disk 1 to the backup copy of the PS/2 Reference Disk.

3. Turn off the power to the computer and remove the cover.

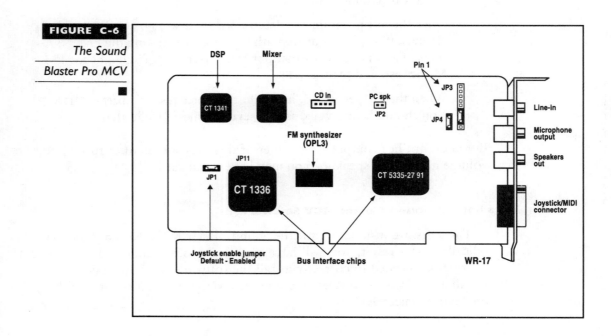

FIGURE C-6

The Sound Blaster Pro MCV

4. Disable the joystick port, if necessary, as described in "Before Installing the Sound Blaster" earlier in the chapter.

5. Plug the Sound Blaster Pro MCV card into any free slot in the computer.

6. Insert the backup PS/2 Reference Disk into drive A and turn on the computer. The computer will report error 165, indicating that a change has been made to the adapter configuration. Select automatic setup and follow the onscreen instructions to configure your computer.

7. After the computer finishes the automatic configuration, it restarts. Leave the PS/2 Reference Disk in the drive. If you do not get an adapter configuration error at this point, skip to step 9.

8. Wait for the configuration software to come up. Select Set Configuration and then Change Configuration to view the adapter card configuration screen. A conflicting adapter card will be listed with an asterisk beside it. Make any necessary changes to the conflicting devices as outlined by the onscreen instructions. Refer to your system manual for details on using the PS/2 configuration software.

9. Exit from the configuration software. Your computer will now restart. Remove the PS/2 Reference Disk, and boot the computer from the hard drive or with a DOS disk.

10. Connect headphones, powered stereo speakers, or your home stereo system to the Sound Blaster Pro MCV speaker output connector. The connector requires a 1/8-inch stereo miniplug, like that used on portable audio tape player headphones.

WARNING: *When turned up to the maximum volume, the built-in amplifier on the Sound Blaster Pro MCV outputs 1/2 watt of power per channel into 4-ohm speakers. Do NOT turn the volume up to maximum if your speakers are not rated for this much power. If you are connecting the Sound Blaster Pro MCV output to the line-level inputs of a stereo system, we recommend that you keep the volume about 3/4 of the way up. Turning the volume up higher can generate distortion or noise in the output signal. You may have to adjust the volume from this position for minimum distortion.*

The Sound Blaster Pro MCV card has a jumper labeled PC SPK. By connecting a cable from the speaker jumper on your computer's motherboard to PC SPK, the Pro MCV will be able to amplify the computer's beeps.

Most people do not use this feature because the amplified beeps are VERY loud.

CAUTION: *If you connect the PC SPK jumper to your motherboard, be prepared for the resulting loud volume level of the computer's beeps. The PC SPK input is NOT connected to the Sound Blaster Pro MCV's mixer and can be very loud!*

Testing the Sound Blaster Pro MCV Hardware

Once you've installed the Sound Blaster Pro MCV card, you need to test it. Follow these steps to make sure that your installation has been successful:

1. Insert the Sound Blaster Pro MCV Disk 1 into drive A or B. Type **A:TESTPMCV** or **B:TESTPMCV** and press ENTER. The test program will inform you of each test that is being performed and any conflicts that arise.

2. If the program reports a conflict in I/O Address, Interrupts, or DMA settings, repeat steps 6 through 9 of the procedure for installing the Pro MCV card (in the section just above) to select a different I/O Address, Interrupt, or DMA setting. All conflicts must be resolved before the Sound Blaster Pro MCV card will work properly. After making the necessary changes, run the test program again.

3. Once the test program has determined there are no conflicts in the settings, it displays a menu with selections for testing the FM (music) and DAC (voice) output from your card. Highlight the two-operator FM test, and press ENTER.Then highlight the four-operator FM test and press ENTER.

4. When the FM test stops, highlight the Voice test and press ENTER. You should hear water sounds moving from the left speaker to the right speaker. (On fast computers, the water can sound like noise, so don't be alarmed.)

If you do not hear output from either of these tests, you may have to adjust the onboard mixer. (See "Installing the Sound Blaster Pro MCV Software" for instructions on installing the drivers and utilities, including the mixer program.) If you still have trouble even after turning up the mixer settings, contact Creative Labs Technical Support or your nearest dealer to resolve the problem.

Installing the Sound Blaster Pro MCV Software

The software installation for the Sound Blaster MCV has changed periodically. As a result, you will have to consult your manual for the exact instructions needed to correctly install the software on your version of the installation disks. Also refer to the notes given in the section on installing the Sound Blaster Pro.

When the installation program finishes, you will have a new directory named \SBPRO, containing a number of subdirectories for the drivers, utilities, and other software.

WARNING: *There is a subdirectory under \SBPRO called DRV that contains all the drivers for the Sound Blaster Pro MCV card. Do NOT rename the DRV subdirectory. In order for programs to find the necessary drivers, this subdirectory must exist exactly as the installation program creates it. You can rename the \SBPRO directory, but not the DRV subdirectory.*

For the Sound Blaster Pro MCV cards, the statement SET SOUND=C:\SBPRO (assuming you installed on drive C) is added to the AUTOEXEC.BAT. If you change the \SBPRO directory name to something else, you must also change the SET SOUND= statement in the AUTOEXEC.BAT file so that programs will know where to find any necessary drivers.

The AUTOEXEC.BAT file will also contain the statement SET BLASTER=A220 I7 D1 T5. Here are the parameters and their functions:

- An Specifies the base I/O Address. The n value is 220 or 240.
- In Specifies the Interrupt setting. The n value is 3, 5, or 7.
- Dn Specifies the DMA channel. The n value is 0, 1, or 3.
- Tn Specifies the card type. The n value is always 5 for Pro MCV.

If this SET BLASTER= statement does not exist in your AUTOEXEC.BAT, use a text editor and add the line, based on the parameters described above. If you changed the hardware settings on your card from the factory defaults, you will have to update the BLASTER statement. You can change it manually by editing the AUTOEXEC.BAT file or by running the SET-ENV utility in the \SBPRO directory.

NOTE: *If some of your programs cannot find the Sound Blaster card or drivers, move the SET SOUND= and SET BLASTER= statements to the beginning of your AUTOEXEC.BAT file. If you still have problems and you are running DOS 4.01 or an earlier version, look for an @ symbol at the beginning of the SET SOUND= and SET BLASTER= statements. If the @ exists, delete it.*

THE SOUND BLASTER 16, BASIC, MCD, AND SCSI-2

This section tells you how to install the Sound Blaster 16, Basic, MCD and SCSI-2 cards. Before you begin the installation, be sure you have read the ealier section, "Before Installing the Sound Blaster."

Figures C-7, C-8, and C-9 show pictures of the Sound Blaster 16, SCSI-2 and MCD cards, respectively.

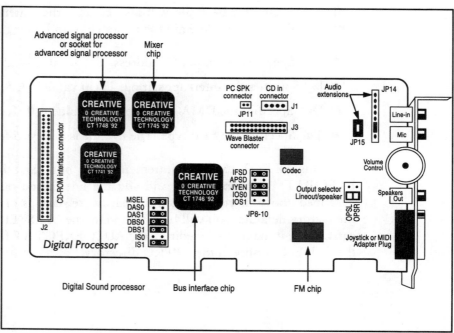

FIGURE C-7

Sound Blaster 16 (CT 1740) connector and jumper locations

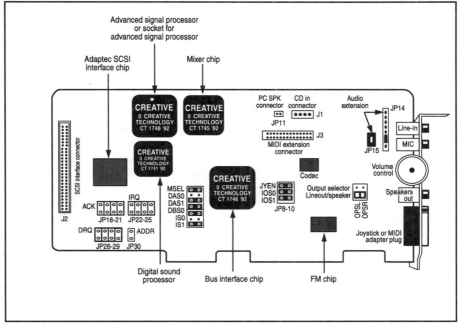

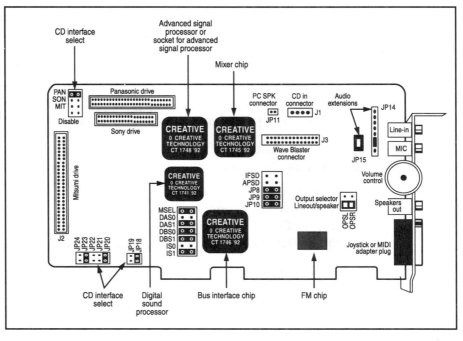

Changing the Sound Blaster 16 Default Settings

The Sound Blaster 16 cards come from the factory with the following default settings: I/O Port Address 220H, IRQ 5, DMA Channel 1, HDMA Channel 5 and MIDI Port Address 330H.

- If another device uses I/O Port Address 220H, you can change the Sound Blaster 16 I/O Port Address by changing the I/O Address jumpers IOS0 and IOS1 to a value not used in your system. You have a choice of four I/O Addresses: 220H, 240H, 260H, and 280H (see Chapter 4 for jumper configurations).

- If another device uses Interrupt 5, you can change the Sound Blaster 16 interrupt by changing the IRQ jumpers ISO and IS1 to a value not used in your system. Choose from IRQ 2, 5, 7, and 10 (see Chapter 4 for jumper configurations), but bear in mind the following: IRQ 3 is used for the second serial port (COM2) and IRQ 5 is sometimes used on bus mouse interface cards.

- If another device uses DMA channel 1, you can change the setting on the Sound Blaster 16 by changing the DAS0 and DAS1 jumpers. Choose from DMA 0, 1, and 3 (see Chapter 4 for jumper configurations).

- If another device uses HDMA channel 5, you can change the setting on the Sound Blaster 16 by changing the DBS0 and DBS1 jumpers. Choose from DMA 5, 6, and 7 (see Chapter 4 for jumper configurations).

- If another device uses MIDI port 330H, you can change the setting on the Sound Blaster 16 by changing the MSEL jumper. Choose from 300H and 330H (see Chapter 4 for jumper configurations).

Installing the Sound Blaster 16 Hardware

Before you start the installation, be sure you know what version of Sound Blaster 16 you have and have handled possible port problems and card setting conflicts, as explained in the earlier section "Before Installing the Sound Blaster." Then you can start your installation. Follow these steps:

1. Plug the Sound Blaster 16 card into any free 16-bit slot in the computer.

2. Connect headphones, stereo speakers, or your home stereo system to the Sound Blaster 16 speaker output connector. The connector requires a 1/8-inch stereo miniplug, like those used on portable audio tape player headphones.

3. The Sound Blaster 16 cards have a jumper labeled PC SPK. By connecting a cable from the speaker jumper on your computer's motherboard to PC SPK, the 16 will be able to amplify the computer's beeps. Unlike the Sound Blaster Pro, the SB16 can control the volume of the PC speaker through the mixer utilities.

4. Adjust the volume knob on the Sound Blaster 16 card so it is between the maximum and minimum limits.

TIP: *Although the microphone connector is considered to be the top of the card, when you turn the volume knob up you are actually turning the volume down. To turn up the volume on the Sound Blaster Pro, you need to turn the volume knob down toward the joystick connector.*

WARNING: *When turned up to the maximum volume, the built-in amplifier on the Sound Blaster 16 outputs 4 watts of power per channel into 4-ohm speakers, and 2 watts per channel into 8-ohm speakers. Do NOT turn the volume up to maximum if your speakers are not rated for this much power. If you are connecting the Sound Blaster output to the line-level inputs of a stereo system, we recommend that you change the Sound Blaster 16 output to line-level (see Chapter 4 for jumper configurations).*

Testing the Sound Blaster 16 Hardware

Once you've installed the Sound Blaster 16 card, you need to test it. Follow these steps to make sure that your installation is successful:

1. Insert the Sound Blaster 16 Disk 1 into drive A or B. Type **A:TESTSB16** or **B:TESTSB16**, and press ENTER. The test program will inform you of each test that is being performed and any conflicts that arise. Also, write down the DSP version number that is reported at the top of the test program for future reference.

2. If the program reports a conflict in I/O Address, Interrupt, DMA, or HDMA settings, turn off the computer and pull out the Sound Blaster 16 card. Select a different I/O Address, Interrupt, DMA, or

HDMA setting. Also, double-check your computer's manual for guidance about conflicts in these settings. All conflicts must be resolved before the Sound Blaster card will work properly. After making the necessary changes, reinstall the card and run the test program again.

NOTE: *If the computer locks up when testing the 16-bit DMA (also known as the HDMA) channel, and you are sure there are no device conflicts, the DMA controller on your motherboard is faulty. Some earlier versions of DMA controller chips by OPTi and UMC do not handle 16-bit DMA correctly and will cause memory parity errors and system lockups.*

3. Once the test program has determined there are no conflicts in the settings, it displays a menu with selections for testing the 2-operator FM (music), 4-operator FM, 8-bit digital audio and 16-bit digital audio output from your card. Highlight the 2-operator FM Music test, and press ENTER.

4. As the music plays, turn up the volume knob on the Sound Blaster 16 until you hear the music. (Remember: To turn the volume down, turn the volume knob up toward the microphone connector. To turn the volume up, turn the volume knob down toward the joystick connector.)

5. Repeat with the 4-operator FM music test. After the FM test stops, highlight the 8-bit digitized audio test and press ENTER. You can select whether to play from the left speaker, right speaker, or both. Try them all to ensure that your speakers are oriented correctly.

6. Repeat with the 16-bit test.

If you do not hear output from any of these tests even after turning the volume knob to both extremes, you may have to adjust the onboard mixer. The installation program sets the volume a little low so try turning it up. An output gain of 2 with the volume controls at 80% should do it. If you still have trouble even after turning up the mixer settings, contact Creative Labs Technical Support or your nearest dealer to resolve the problem.

Installing the Sound Blaster 16 Software

The software installation for the Sound Blaster 16 changes periodically. As a result, you will have to consult your manual for the exact instructions needed to correctly install the software on your version of the installation disks. After the software installation is complete, continue reading this section for additional installation notes.

When the installation program finishes, you will have a new directory named \SB16, containing a number of subdirectories for the drivers, utilities, and other software.

WARNING: *There are several subdirectories installed under \SB16. They should not be moved or renamed since both DOS and Windows programs will look for the drivers and software to be in those directories. In order for programs to find the necessary drivers, these subdirectories must exist exactly as the installation program creates them. Don't rename the \SB16 directory either.*

For the Sound Blaster 16 cards, the statement SET SOUND=C:\SB16 (assuming you installed on drive C) is added to the AUTOEXEC.BAT file.

The AUTOEXEC.BAT file will also contain the statement SET BLASTER=A220 I5 D1 H5 T6 P330. Here are the parameters and their functions:

- A*n*   Specifies the base I/O Address. The *n* value is either 220, 240, 260, or 280.

- I*n*   Specifies the Interrupt setting. The *n* value is 2, 5, 7, or 10.

- D*n*   Specifies the DMA channel. The *n* value is 0, 1, or 3.

- H*n*   Specifies the 16-bit HDMA channel. The *n* value is 5, 6, or 7.

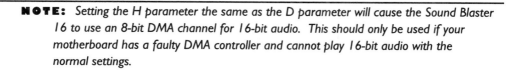

NOTE: *Setting the H parameter the same as the D parameter will cause the Sound Blaster 16 to use an 8-bit DMA channel for 16-bit audio. This should only be used if your motherboard has a faulty DMA controller and cannot play 16-bit audio with the normal settings.*

- T*n*   Specifies the card type. The *n* value is 6 for the Sound Blaster 16.

If this SET BLASTER= statement does not exist in your AUTOEXEC.BAT, use a text editor and add the line, based on the parameters described above. If you changed the hardware settings on your card from the factory defaults, you have to update the SET BLASTER= statement. You can change it manually by editing the AUTOEXEC.BAT file, or you can run the SBCONFIG utility (it's in the \SB16 directory).

NOTE: *If some of your programs cannot find the Sound Blaster card or drivers, move the SET SOUND= and SET BLASTER= statements to the beginning of your AUTOEXEC.BAT file. If you still have problems and you are running DOS 4.01 or an earlier version, look for an @ symbol at the beginning of the SET SOUND= and SET BLASTER= statements. If the @ exists, delete it.*

INSTALLING A CREATIVE LABS CD-ROM DRIVE

If you have purchased the Creative Labs CD-ROM drive model CR-52*x* or CR-563, either separately or with the Multimedia Upgrade Kit, follow these steps to install it. The CD-ROM drive can only be connected to the Sound Blaster Pro/Pro 2, Sound Blaster 16, or Sound Blaster 16 MCD. It will not attach to the Sound Blaster 1.*x*/2.0, Sound Blaster MCV, Sound Blaster Pro MCV, or Sound Blaster 16 SCSI-2.

NOTE: *The Sound Blaster 16 SCSI-2 uses a SCSI interface for CD-ROM drives, hard disks, and other SCSI-compatible devices. You cannot connect a Creative CR-52x or CR-563 CD-ROM drive to it.*

1. Turn off the power to the computer and remove the cover. See your computer's manual for details on removing the cover.

2. Locate an empty, half-height, 5 1/4-inch drive bay. Remove the blank plate that covers the bay.

3. If your computer case requires plastic runners on floppy drives and hard drives, use the four screws included with the kit to attach the runners to the CD-ROM drive.

4. Connect the flat ribbon cable to the drive, making sure that the edge with the colored stripe is closest to the audio connector. Also connect the small audio cable to the drive (it only goes in one way).

5. Carefully pull the audio and ribbon cables through the empty drive bay, and slide the CD-ROM drive into place.

6. Secure the drive with the mounting hardware that came with your computer. If you do not have the appropriate hardware to secure the drive, contact your computer system dealer.

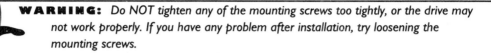

WARNING: *Do NOT tighten any of the mounting screws too tightly, or the drive may not work properly. If you have any problem after installation, try loosening the mounting screws.*

7. Attach the flat ribbon cable to the large data cable connector on the Sound Blaster Pro card. Make sure that the colored stripe on the cable is toward the top of the Pro card. Also attach the audio cable to the CD IN connector on the Pro card (it will only go in one way).

8. Replace the cover on your computer and turn it on.

9. Insert the CD-ROM installation disk into drive A or B. Type **A:** or **B:**, depending on which drive contains the disk, and press ENTER.

10. To install the drivers on drive C, type **INST-HD C:** or just **INSTALL** on newer installation disks, and press ENTER. If you want to install them on a different drive, enter the letter of that drive instead of the **C:**. It is recommended that you install on the same drive used to install the Sound Blaster Pro drivers.

NOTE: *The installation program copies the drivers SBPCD.SYS, or SBCD.SYS on newer installation disks, and MSCDEX.EXE into the \SBPRO\DRV directory on your hard disk. It also adds this line to your CONFIG.SYS file: DEVICE=C:\SBPRO\SBPCD.SYS /D:MSCD001 /P:220, or DEVICE=C:\SBPRO\SBCD.SYS /D:MSCD001 /P:220 on newer installation disks. If your Sound Blaster Pro is set to I/O Address 240H, change the /P:220 parameter to /P:240. If you have another CD-ROM drive in your system that uses the name MSCD001, change the /D:MSCD001 parameter to /D:MSCD002.*

11. Restart the computer to enable the CD-ROM driver.

TROUBLE-
SHOOTING
YOUR
SOUND
BLASTER
INSTALL-
ATION

though we have made every attempt in this appendix to anticipate all possible installation pitfalls, installing Sound Blaster can be a complicated matter. Follow the above instructions as closely as possible, paying attention to the various notes and tips, cautions, warnings, and so forth. If you do encounter problems, see the questions and answers in Appendix D, from the tech support department at Creative Labs. Or you can call Creative Labs Technical Support directly at (405) 742-6622.

D

Technical Support from Creative Labs

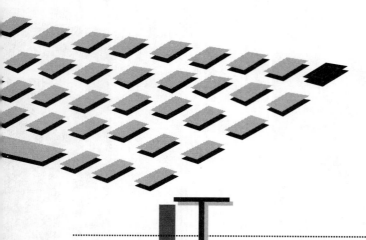

T H I S appendix contains answers to many questions frequently asked about the Creative Labs sound cards. You'll find suggestions on how to solve a number of problems commonly encountered while installing or using the Sound Blaster, Sound Blaster Pro, and Sound Blaster 16 cards. Before calling Creative Labs' technical support line for assistance, read through these sections to see if your problem is answered; chances are it can be solved quickly and easily. Since Creative Labs' technical support staff is a toll call, the information here may save you time and money.

 NOTE: *If you encounter a problem that's not mentioned here, the problem may be due to an incorrect installation. You may be able to eliminate the difficulty by reinstalling your sound card and software, using the instructions provided in Appendix C, and the Getting Started manual that came with your card.*

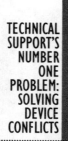

TECHNICAL SUPPORT'S NUMBER ONE PROBLEM: SOLVING DEVICE CONFLICTS

ere is the question most commonly asked of the staff at Creative Labs:

PROBLEM: *I think I installed my Sound Blaster correctly, but when a game tries to play music or sound effects, the computer freezes or the sound doesn't play. What's wrong?*

SOLUTION: Your problem is likely due to one of two things: Either the software program that's running incorrectly isn't configured properly for your Sound Blaster, or the card itself has a conflict with another peripheral in your computer. Before going any further, check to make sure that your software is configured properly to run with your version of the Sound Blaster. If it is, and setup does not appear to be the problem, read on.

Solving Conflicts with Other Peripheral Devices

When installing Sound Blaster in the typical PC or PC-compatible computer, there is a significant chance that you will encounter a problem called a *hardware conflict*. Such conflicts will generally occur between two or more installed devices in your computer. These devices might include a network interface card, the parallel printer port, a modem, your mouse, a scanner, or even a hard disk or tape drive.

Conflicts come in three types: a conflict over an interrupt, a port address, or the DMA channel assignment. These conflicts result when two devices in your computer accidentally share the same setting for any of these three elements. If your computer tries to talk to a device, such as your sound card, and another device thinks it is being addressed, the computer's messages may be captured by that other device, causing your sound card to either sit idle or lose pieces of information.

Although a conflict is most likely to occur when you first install your Sound Blaster, it can just as easily occur when you install another device in your computer, if that new equipment is configured to use the same port, interrupt, or channel as your sound card. The more equipment you have installed in your computer, the more likely you are to encounter a conflict.

NOTE: *As mentioned earlier, a conflict with the sound card frequently occurs on a typical PC that has the Industry Standard Architecture (ISA) bus. If you are installing the Sound Blaster MCV, which is the Sound Blaster for the PS/2, you are much less likely to have a conflict because the PS/2s use a more sophisticated bus, the Micro Channel bus, which was designed to avoid these conflicts.*

Parallel Printer Conflict

PROBLEM: *I just purchased a Sound Blaster, and I notice that the IRQ (interrupt request) is set to a default setting of 7. I've been told that my parallel printer port also uses that IRQ setting. Do I need to change the Sound Blaster's interrupt setting?*

SOLUTION: Since the Sound Blaster family uses IRQs for digitized voices and MIDI IN, a conflict will occur only if you attempt to print while playing digitized voices or recording MIDI data through your sound card.

This conflict can become a factor, however, when multitasking with software such as Microsoft Windows or DESQview, in which printing occurs in the background. Also, some printer cards do not share their IRQ, especially if you're connected to a laser printer. If you have a problem, consider selecting another IRQ setting for your Sound Blaster. (Refer to Appendix A for more information about changing IRQ settings.)

Important Facts About Interrupt 7

Earlier Sound Blaster cards were factory set to use interrupt 7 (IRQ 7). Unfortunately, some people encountered intermittent problems and occasional computer lockups at this setting. There are two reasons why problems occur with the IRQ 7 setting.

- The hardware for the first parallel printer port (LPT1) in the computer uses IRQ 7. The printer port hardware on some computers doesn't allow this interrupt to be shared with other devices, such as your Sound Blaster. This results in a hardware conflict and, hence, problems with the printer, Sound Blaster, or both.

- The interrupt controller, the chip that handles all the interrupt requests, is designed in most PCs to treat noise on the interrupt lines in a special manner. If there is an interrupt at any IRQ number that doesn't conform to the timing specification for a valid interrupt, the controller assumes that it's noise. It then redirects this false interrupt to IRQ 7. Bingo! Big problems.

  If the Sound Blaster is on IRQ 7, any software that is using the Sound Blaster will think that the Sound Blaster requested the interrupt. Since the Sound Blaster didn't request it, the program locks up. This situation occurs because most applications weren't written to correctly handle a false interrupt, not because the interrupt controller is faulty.

So, the moral to the story is not to set the Sound Blaster to IRQ 7 unless you have an older program that can work only with the Sound Blaster at IRQ 7. Creative Labs even changed the factory setting of new cards to IRQ 5 in order to avoid these problems.

Solving Installation Difficulties

The next paragraphs provide instructions for isolating and solving general installation problems. Although the process of isolating conflicts is not difficult, it is tedious and requires a methodical plan of attack.

TIP: *Keep a list of the pieces of equipment installed in your computer and their settings. Using this list, you can avoid conflicts between devices when you next upgrade your machine. Your list should include each device's name and settings, such as port address (for example, COM1), memory address, interrupt request (IRQ), and DMA channel.*

The following may be of help in isolating your particular type of installation problem.

YOUR SOUND CARD IS NEW TO YOUR MACHINE In this scenario, your computer was working fine until you installed your card. Now that you've installed a sound card, your computer doesn't work. The solution is to change the settings on your sound card and try the installation again.

YOUR SOUND CARD WORKED FINE UNTIL YOU ADDED ANOTHER DEVICE In this scenario, Sound Blaster was working fine until you added another card (device) to your computer. Now either Sound Blaster or the new device, or both, won't work. Your solution in this case is to remove the new device and confirm that your Sound Blaster works without the other device installed. If it does, change the settings on the other device and try again.

Use Diagnostics to Isolate Your Problem

Once you've encountered a conflict, try to identify exactly what is conflicting by running the diagnostic/testing program for your Sound Blaster or Sound Blaster Pro. This program is provided on your Sound Blaster program disk, and it diagnoses hardware conflicts. It is called TEST-SBC (for Sound Blaster cards), TEST-SBP (for Sound Blaster Pro cards) or TESTSB16 (for Sound Blaster 16 cards). The test program can probably identify whether the conflict occurs on an IRQ, memory address, or DMA setting. Once a conflict is identified (possibly by the test program stopping), you can quickly zero in on fixing the problem.

For example, if you have an IRQ conflict, you can try each of the IRQ settings one at a time. If you have a DMA conflict, you will have to change the DMA setting on the other device, since your sound card is set to use one DMA channel only. Try to avoid changing DMA settings until you have ruled out IRQ and memory address conflicts.

NOTE: *Sound Blaster 16 owners should be aware that some motherboards have faulty DMA controllers and will not handle 16-bit audio correctly. If your motherboard has a faulty DMA controller, it will either lock up when playing 16-bit audio or generate parity errors. To work around this problem, run SBCONFIG.EXE in the \SB16 directory to set your SB16 to use 8-bit DMA only for 16-bit sound.*

If your computer is still under warranty, definitely get a new motherboard. This problem could affect other cards that use 16-bit DMA such as SCSI controllers and network interface cards.

If All Else Fails

So you've tried everything, but you still can't seem to isolate the conflict?

Start by removing as many of the other cards from your computer as possible and then reinstalling them one by one. This means you need to pull out all the cards—except the video display card and the hard disk/floppy disk controller card if these functions aren't built into the motherboard. If you have an expanded-memory card, you can leave it in, too, since it won't cause a conflict.

Now add the Sound Blaster card and confirm that it works. Next, add the other cards one by one (turn the computer off, insert a card, turn it on, and test), verifying that they all still work. For example, you should be able to listen to digital audio and do a directory listing on your hard drive at the same time, as well as use your mouse while playing the FM Intelligent Organ. As soon as you add a card and a problem occurs, you can change the settings on that card to avoid the conflict.

The Last Resort for Solving Conflicts

The absolutely last-resort steps in problem resolution are as follows:

1. The Sound Blaster test program, like all diagnostic tests, can be fooled. If the test program doesn't help, or you don't trust its results, then you must follow a methodical procedure. You must examine every card in your computer and, in conjunction with the manuals for that card, document the settings to ensure there are no conflicts.

2. If Sound Blaster still doesn't work properly, even though you've removed all other nonessential cards from your computer, contact Creative Labs. Your sound card may be defective.

3. The very last step you should take, after you know your Sound Blaster will work correctly only if other devices aren't installed in the PC, is to change the settings of these other devices. Be very careful to document their settings *before* making changes, in case you need to restore the original settings to get the devices to work again. The fundamental rule for car mechanics also holds true for reconfiguring devices in your computer: "If it ain't broke, don't fix it."

MISCELLANEOUS PROBLEMS AND SOLUTIONS

The following problems and solutions for the Sound Blaster and Sound Blaster Pro cards are supplied by the Creative Labs technical support department. We have categorized the information to make it easier for you to find the answers you need.

REMEMBER: *Unless otherwise noted, the terms* Sound Blaster *and* sound card *refer to all Sound Blaster cards.*

Joystick Problems

PROBLEM: *I've plugged a joystick into the game port on my sound card and loaded my game, but the joystick doesn't work.*

SOLUTION: There is a jumper on the sound card that enables the joystick port on the sound card. When the jumper is removed, the joystick port is disabled. Check that this jumper is in place. If the jumper is installed, then you probably already have another game (joystick) port active in your system. Only one can be active at a time, so your computer can't see the one on the sound card.

To determine if another game port exists, examine the back of your sound card to familiarize yourself with what a game port looks like. If you see another connector on the back of your PC with the same 15 pins as the game port on your Sound Blaster, you've probably found the offending game port.

NOTE: *A game port is likely to be found on a combination I/O card that combines serial, parallel, and joystick ports on a single card. Usually, but not always, such a combination card will include a jumper for disabling the game port.*

PROBLEM: *I've purchased a Y-cable adapter so that I can connect two joysticks to my Sound Blaster joystick port. Everything works fine except for the two buttons on the second joystick, which don't do anything.*

SOLUTION: The sound card MIDI/joystick port isn't 100 percent compatible with the standard game port, because it has been modified. Two pins, which provide power to the second joystick only, have been redefined to become the MIDI In and Out pins. As a result, many Y-cable adapters that expect a standard game-port pin assignment won't work correctly with your Sound Blaster.

There are several fixes to this problem. If you have the Creative Labs MIDI Kit, you have a game port extension cable whose connector is IBM standard. Simply plug the Y-adapter into this MIDI adapter cable, and plug the MIDI adapter cable into the sound card. If you don't have the MIDI Kit, you can order a special Y-cable adapter designed for dual joysticks from Creative Labs.

PROBLEM: *I have a 25-MHz 386 (or faster) machine, and I have my joystick plugged into the Sound Blaster joystick port. Some games work correctly with my joystick, but some don't. Most of the games won't let me center the joystick.*

SOLUTION: Many games were designed for much slower computers than those now available. In the past, game software developers made assumptions about the computer's speed, which in turn influenced how the joystick position was measured. As computer speed has increased, the joystick position can no longer be measured accurately by these games.

If your computer has a "turbo" mode, you should first see if cranking down the computer's speed will make the joystick work correctly. Another solution is to forgo the use of the sound card game port and replace it with a "speed-aware" (sometimes called 386-aware) game port card that solves the game software problem with new game-port hardware. CH Products and Advanced Gravis sell the most popular speed-aware game ports. (If you install one of these special ports, be sure to disable your Creative Labs sound card port.)

If nothing else works, contact the game's manufacturer to see if it has an update that works correctly on the faster machines.

Sound Blaster Doesn't Work

PROBLEM: *I've just added an IDE hard disk drive to my system for the first time (or added a Sound Blaster card to a system with an IDE disk drive), and now my Sound Blaster card doesn't work.*

SOLUTION: An IDE controller card (the card your IDE hard drive plugs into) can conflict with the Sound Blaster. Problems have been encountered with some of the cheaper controllers, which are incorrectly set to use DMA channel 1, and which cannot be altered. Since the Sound Blaster 1.*x*/2.0 also uses DMA channel 1 for digitized audio, a conflict occurs between your sound card and your controller.

You can buy another controller for a nominal price, but be careful to select one that doesn't use DMA channel 1. If you encounter this problem with the Sound Blaster Pro or Sound Blaster 16, each of which offers a choice of DMA channels, you can resolve things by changing the DMA setting on the Sound Blaster Pro or Sound Blaster 16.

Volume Too Low on Sound Blaster Pro

PROBLEM: *I've installed my Sound Blaster Pro correctly, but something must be wrong. The volume is always too low.*

SOLUTION: This is the most common complaint about the Sound Blaster Pro, Pro 2, Pro MCV, and SB16. The problem usually results from the fact that the Sound Blaster Pro's mixer control is factory-set to a medium level. The Sound Blaster 1.*x*/2.0 versions do not have a mixer.

Solve this problem by adding the utility SBP-SET (for SBPro) or SB16SET (for SB16) to your AUTOEXEC.BAT file. SBP-SET and SB16SET set the master and source volume levels. A setting of 70 percent or 80 percent will ensure that your sound card is audible.

Sound Blaster Line-In Source Doesn't Work

PROBLEM: *I have a CD-ROM drive hooked up to the line-in input on my Sound Blaster, but I can't hear anything.*

SOLUTION: You can't hear anything because the Sound Blaster doesn't have a built-in mixer that allows you to combine the regular Sound Blaster sounds, such as the internal FM synthesizer music or the microphone input, with the line-in sound from your CD-ROM. The line-in on the Sound Blaster is used for recording only; the sound is not passed on to the speaker and headphone output. The solution is to upgrade to a Sound Blaster Pro or Sound Blaster 16, both of which include a built-in mixer that allows you to simultaneously mix line-in, dedicated CD-ROM input, internal FM synthesizer sound, and microphone input.

Diagnostic Test Results Are Confusing

PROBLEM: *When I run the test program (TEST-SBC for Sound Blaster and TEST-SBP for Sound Blaster Pro), I get digitized speech; however, I hear nothing when I run the FM test.*

SOLUTION: This problem usually occurs on 486 machines with speeds of 50 MHz or higher. The solution is to either slow the machine down (don't run it at turbo speed) or obtain an updated version of the test program from Creative Labs. This same problem will occur if you try to run the FM Intelligent Organ. You can get a software update that will fix both the TEST program and the FM Intelligent Organ problems by dialing into the Creative Labs BBS and downloading file 486-50MH.ZIP.

If you have Sound Blaster Pro 2 and you're still having problems with the FM, your motherboard may not be delivering a good timing signal. Contact Creative Labs for a software *patch* (a fix) to compensate for this motherboard problem.

Difficulties with Games

PROBLEM: *I have a 486 computer, and when I run Sierra On-Line games I get the message "Unable to initialize sound hardware." What's wrong and what can I do about it?*

SOLUTION: There are two solutions for this. The first is to contact Creative Labs for a software update (the 486SBDRV.EXE driver) that solves the problem. A more immediate fix is to turn off the turbo button on your machine if there is one and wait until the music starts for the game. When the music starts, turn the turbo button back on. This problem stems from a bug in the sound driver that's embedded in Sierra's older games; in Sierra's newest games the bug has been fixed.

PROBLEM: *I am playing the game Lemmings that came with my Sound Blaster and either I am not getting any music or the music selection isn't available (the F3 selection does not show the music feature, a score note, when in the Main Menu).*

SOLUTION: The base memory in the system is below 465K. Use a memory manager, such as QEMM or DOS 6's MEMMAKER, to acquire more memory. Another solution is to remove any unneeded TSRs from your AUTOEXEC.BAT and CONFIG.SYS.

PROBLEM: *I have the game "The Seventh Guest" and the SBCD.SYS device driver for the Creative Labs CD-ROM drives. When digitized speech is played, it sounds "jerky"—like it is stuttering. How can I fix this problem?*

SOLUTION: The fix for this problem is the SBCD.SYS driver version 4.10.0 or later. You can download it from the Creative Labs BBS.

Windows Problems

PROBLEM: *I have Windows 3.1, and when I run the Jukebox program everything seems fine until I quit Windows. When I go to exit, it locks up my system.*

SOLUTION: The version of Jukebox you're using is most likely an earlier version meant for Windows 3.0 only. An update for Jukebox that supports Windows 3.1 is available from Creative Labs.

PROBLEM: *I have the updated Jukebox from Creative Labs. When I attempt to play the MIDI files that are included with my Sound Blaster, I get a dialog box that tells me this file will not play correctly with the default MIDI map setup. How can I fix this?*

SOLUTION: In this case, the file does not contain a signature, which signifies that it conforms to Microsoft's specifications for MIDI channels, program numbers, and such. While the file may play, it may not play correctly. To resolve this problem select the Basic FM map in the MIDI Mapper. If you still don't hear music, try EXT FM or ALL FM.

PROBLEM: *I am using Soundo'LE in Windows, and when I try to either record or playback a WAV file with compression, the following error message appears:*

```
"Not enough memory to run this application...close
applications and try again."
```

How can I fix this problem?

SOLUTION: This error only occurs when you have the Microsoft Audio Compression Manager driver installed on your system. The easist remedy to this problem is to obtain a new version of Soundo'LE from the Creative Labs BBS.

PROBLEM: *Why is there a Voyetra/Sound Blaster SuperSAPI driver and not the old Sound Blaster Pro or 16 MIDI Synthesizer in the Windows Control Panel?*

SOLUTION: When the Sound Blaster Pro was repackaged as the Sound Blaster Pro Deluxe, Creative Labs chose to use a driver that better utilizes the Yamaha OPL3 FM chip. This new driver, which comes with the Sound Blaster Pro Deluxe and all Sound Blaster 16 cards, will make all MIDI music sound truer to the real instruments.

Other Hardware Questions

PROBLEM: *What is the default IRQ for the Sound Blaster cards?*

SOLUTION: With the new Deluxe package, the default IRQ setting has been changed from IRQ 7 to IRQ 5 for both the Sound Blaster Deluxe and the Sound Blaster Pro Deluxe. The main reason for this is to eliminate any possible hardware conflict between the sound card and the parallel port (LPT1), which is almost always set to IRQ 7.

The Sound Blaster 16 family of cards has always shipped with a default of IRQ 5.

PROBLEM: *I seem to be picking up strange noises from my Sound Blaster card. These noises occur with hard drive accesses, with CD-ROM accesses, and even when I move my mouse. Is there something I can do to eliminate these noises?*

SOLUTION: These noises are caused by a number of things. Some are due to a noisy bus on the motherboard, a bad or noisy power supply, or a combination of both. The best thing to try is to place the sound card as far away from the power supply as possible. If this doesn't solve the problem, then replacing the power supply or ultimately the motherboard may help. One other possibility is something called a Ground Loop Isolator. This can be found at Radio Shack, *although it is not guaranteed to work.*

PROBLEM: *I have a Sound Blaster 16 and I'm hooking up a MIDI device (such as a Roland MT-32 or Sound Canvas) to the MIDI port on the card. When I choose to use a MIDI device for music in my games, it hangs the system. Is there a fix for this problem?*

SOLUTION: There is a program available on the Creative Labs BBS that will correct the problem. The name of the file is SBMPU401.EXE. This file is self-extracting.

PROBLEM: *I installed my Sound Blaster 16 in my computer, which has an Adaptec 1542B/1542C SCSI controller card and now the hard drive won't boot. What can I do?*

SOLUTION: The reason this is occurring is that the Adaptec uses I/O address 330h and DMA channel 5 for its default settings, and the Sound Blaster 16 also uses these settings for the MIDI port address and the high DMA (HDMA, 16-bit DMA) channel. The preferred fix for this is to change the base address and 16-bit DMA channel settings on the Adaptec.

Changing the SB16 configuration is easier, but some programs will only find the MPU-401 port at 330H becuase that is the default for the original Roland MPU-401. Also, some older games don't know what to do with the HDMA and won't work properly if the HDMA is not set to 5.

If you must change the Sound Blaster 16's settings, change the MIDI Port address from 330h to 300h and the high DMA channel (HDMA) from 5 to either 6 or 7.

Choosing a Microphone

PROBLEM: *I want to buy a microphone for my Sound Blaster. I don't know what kind to get.*

SOLUTION: Any microphone will suffice for simple recordings, as long as it is rated at 600 ohms. If you are using VoiceAssist or any other speech recognition package, be sure that the microphone is also unidirectional. In other words, it should pick up sound from only one direction, the direction you point it.

GETTING MORE HELP

If, after reading this appendix and trying its suggestions you still have an unresolved problem with your Sound Blaster card, call Creative Labs Technical Support (405) 742-6622, or consult your local Sound Blaster dealer.

Updates to drivers and other programs are available for downloading from the Creative Labs BBS. The phone number is (405) 742-6660. Set your modem to 8 data bits, 1 stop bit, and no parity. The BBS supports transmission speeds up to 14,400 bps.

E

Reference to Online Services

NEARLY four million U.S. households now dial into online services to read news reports, get stock quotes, send and receive e-mail (electronic mail), do computer-based shopping, get technical help from vendors and experts, and download (electronically fetch over the phone line) software. Online services are crammed with interesting software, both sound programs and sound data files, for owners of one of the Sound Blaster family of cards. The software that's available includes shareware (a nominal payment is expected if you like the program) and freeware (yours to enjoy at no expense) software. There are demonstration versions of new sound programs and games. Music and sound utility programs like MIDI sequencers, digital audio editors, MOD music players, and sound conversion utilities are also found in the file libraries of online services. In addition, you'll find hundreds if not thousands of music files, both MIDI (MID) and Creative Music (CMF), as well as Voice (VOC) and Wave (WAV) digital audio sound files. Whatever your tastes, a virtually unlimited assortment of "goodies" is available for the asking on the online services. All you need, in addition to the computer, is a modem, communications software, and an account with an online service.

Whether you're just now considering joining an online service or you're already a member, this appendix is full of valuable information. Four of the most popular online services are described: CompuServe, America Online, GEnie, and the Internet. This appendix will steer you to the most relevant information resources on these online services, from the standpoint of a sound card owner. If you're new to online services, this appendix may help you to decide whether to join one. Be sure to check the end of the appendix for answers to many of the most burning questions about accessing online services. Please note that this appendix is oriented toward online services from the perspective of a sound card owner. For a broader treatment of online communications, there are plenty of fine books on the subject. For information on the Creative Labs bulletin board system (BBS), please refer to Appendix D.

This appendix focuses on four of the major online services. There are many more popular services, such as Delphi, Prodigy, and BIX, which have hundreds of thousands of satisfied customers but can't be covered within the scope of this appendix. We've picked four online services with which the authors are most familiar and which we believe have the most to offer owners of a Creative Labs Sound Blaster card.

NOTE: *The distinction between a bulletin board service (BBS) and an online service is that the latter is typically a commercial service accessible on a fee basis only, while the former is generally open to all comers at no cost or at a very low cost. While a BBS is usually limited to e-mail and file exchange, a typical online service offers a plethora of services such as electronic shopping, stock quotes, and a communications gateway for communicating with other online services and networks (such as a gateway to the Internet).*

RELATED RESOURCES

In addition to the online services described in this appendix, there are two other excellent resources: sound CD-ROM discs and local BBSs.

Sound CD-ROM

For a modest cost, probably $12 to $20 each, you can buy a CD-ROM disc stuffed with upwards of 630 million bytes' worth of sound goodies. That's equivalent to about 180 hours of nonstop downloading at 9600 bps (bits per second)! If the disc says "shareware," you're essentially paying for the effort someone else put into scrounging the bulletin boards for you. You can be a lot more discriminating about what you download—and probably save big bucks—by sampling the contents of a shareware disc or two before dialing into an online service.

A good CD-ROM to start with is the Mega series by Profit Press. The MegaDemo CD contains over 350MB of graphics, sound files, MOD files, and shareware and freeware applications for DOS, Windows, and OS/2. Several other CDs are topic-specific: MegaCD-ROM (PC shareware programs); MegaWinOS/2 (Windows & OS/2 shareware programs); MegaA/V (Audio/Visual software and files for the PC).

Profit Press
2956 N. Campbell Ave.
Tucson, AZ 85719
(602) 577-9696 (information)
(602) 577-9624 (fax orders)

Local Bulletin Boards

The big advantage of a local BBS is that you won't be paying a connect fee or long-distance charge. Some of these BBSs offer thousands of files, many of which are shareware that was downloaded from online services. Be aware that sharing is expected—if you download a lot of files you're expected to occasionally contribute too. If you're in a major metropolitan area, you can find the phone number for local BBSs in local computer magazines or by contacting local PC user groups.

TIP: *Local BBSs are essential for obtaining digital audio files (like VOC or WAV files), which are often very large—and consequently very expensive to download if you're paying connect charges.*

A PEEK AT AN ONLINE SERVICE: COMPUSERVE

This section will show extracts from CompuServe so you can see what sort of information can be delivered to your desktop via a modem, phone line and online service.

CompuServe Message Threads

CompuServe and other online services feature gathering places called forums (on CompuServe) or round tables (America Online) or a similar catchy name. This is where messages and files on a topic are grouped for easy reference. For example, CompuServe's Multimedia Vendor Forum is a good source for current information and technical help on sound cards in general and Creative Labs products in particular. An extract showing the first 14 message threads is shown here. You can browse through the message threads to quickly gain a bird's-eye view of what's hot and what's not.

```
Subject (# msgs)
Section 1 - General Information
 1 1-time CDROM PLAY?!  (2)
 2 PAS 16 Spectrum Upgrade  (2)
 3 SB Drivers  (2)
 4 Pro Graphics 1280  (3)
 5 Where is Creative Labs?  (14)
 6 video capture  (4)
 7 Execuvoice + .WAV Files  (3)
 8 SoundBlaster w/ Windows  (10)
 9 Using MV BBS  (1)
10 SoundBlaster Pro Prob  (2)
11 Wrong DOS Version...!!!  (4)
12 Creative forum  (1)
13 Soundblaster  (1)
14 cd-rom problems  (2)
```

List of Uploads

When you enter a CompuServe forum, you're likely to encounter a list of new uploads. The following extract was taken from the MIDI/Music Forum:

```
News Flash:

Recent uploads to Library 1 (New Uploads) as of Sunday, 17-Oct-93

 MF2T.ZIP     88K MIDI File to/from ASCII Text Conversion
 SCHROE.BMP  151K Peanuts Wallpaper - Schroeder at Piano
 SONGS.ZIP    61K Index: MIDI/Music Forum song files (GEN/MFF/SEQ)
 CHORDZ.ZIP  192K CHORDMASTER V2.05 - Sequencing SW for  guitarists.
 WAVS16.ZIP  110K WaveS16: Professional Sound Editor For Windows!
 LIB220.ZIP   96K Roland U220 SYX Librarian for Windows 3.1
 WAVMAN.ZIP  882K Wave Manager/Player w/ADPCM<>PCM converter
 W2S4WI.ZIP   26K WAV2SDS (Windows version) converts WAV to SDS fmt
 GLYPH.TXT     3K Glyph Technologies Press Release-SCSI Storage
```

What's nice is that the *system operator* (or *sysop*, pronounced SIS-op), a volunteer who logs countless hours each week keeping the forum running, has arranged to display a list of introductory material that shouldn't be missed when you join this forum:

```
Are you new to MIDI? Check out the following information files
in Library 2 (Basics & Product Guide):

IBMSW.TXT    5K List of IBM sequencers and notation programs
INTERF.ACE  12K Text file describing IBM/compat MIDI Interfaces
MMQUST.TXT   9K That Infernal MIDI Mapper - Help File
MACFIL.TXT   4K Mac TYPE and CREATOR Information for MIDI Files
MACIF.TXT    8K Macintosh MIDI Events and Interfaces Description
MACSW.TXT    3K Macintosh Sequencer & Notation Software Listing
STSW.TXT     3K List of MIDI software for Atari ST
NUMIDI.TXT  10K Discussion: What does MIDI do? (for beginners)
GLOS21.ZIP  17K A Glossary of MIDI-computing Terms
GENMID.TXT  13K General MIDI Description - patch and percussion
```

Note how most of these files are plain text files (TXT) which can be read by an editor like the DOS EDIT or most word processors. One file, GLOS21.ZIP, has been compressed and will require PKWARE's PKUnzip or a similar file-compression program (discussed later in this chapter) to make the file accessible.

File Description

Once you've seen an interesting one-line file description you can get more detailed information before you go to the hassle and expense of downloading the file. For example, the following description was culled from the Multimedia Forum, Section 2, where there's a lively discussion about sound and music:

```
[70353,3401]
WAVLST.TXT/Asc  Bytes:  12572, Count: 2949, 09-Aug-92(25-Sep-93)

  Title   : Test file list of WAV files in Multimedia Libs
  Keywords: WAV WAVE SOUND EFFECT FILES LIB LIBRARY WIN WINDOWS

A listing of WAV files in the Multimedia Libraries.

Updated 9-25-93.
```

This ASCII file with the name WAVLST.TXT is 12,572 bytes long and has been downloaded almost 3,000 times so far. It was last updated on September 25, 1993.

COMPUSERVE

The CompuServe Information Service (CIS), better known as CompuServe, is the largest of the commercial online services. Its strength is also its weakness: It can be overwhelming, with hundreds of forums, each of which has its own membership, sysops, message threads, libraries, conferencing, and personality. Of all the online services, this is the one with the most vendor support, both in terms of vendor-supported forums and the number of experts that dial in. In addition, there are probably more sound-related programs on this online service than on any other.

Forums to Visit

In this section you'll read a short description of the "must visit" locations on CompuServe for owners of a Creative Labs sound card. Be aware that online users flow from forum to forum; some forums are suspended when there's little activity or they are split when they get too large—and established forums are constantly spawning new ones.

Game Forums

See the free Game Publishers Forums (GAMPUB) to find out what's available in the other Game forums. The Game Publishers Forums comprise dozens of game publishers that provide hints for playing their games as well as patches (software fixes) to ensure that their software works correctly on various computers and sound cards. An exciting new Section 6 (on Multimedia games) was just created in the GAMERS Forum. The latest game news is found in GAMECON.

MIDI Vendor Forums

MIDI Vendors are accessible through the MIDI Vendor Forums. You'll find exhaustive coverage of MIDI in these forums.

Multimedia Forums

The Multimedia Forum features a lot of Sound Blaster activity. In particular, check out Section 2, where you'll find all sorts of utilities and sound files. There are several Multimedia Vendor Forums that are worth examining if you're interested in the broader multimedia area. The file MMLIB.ZIP contains a list of all the files in the Multimedia Libraries.

Sight and Sound

The Sight and Sound Forum is loaded with WAV files.

Windows Fun Forum

The Windows Fun Forum (WINFUN), Section 5 (Sounds/Utils), is a good place to go if you're only interested in Windows (not DOS) sound programs and files. There's a spirited discussion of Sound Blaster topics here.

Official Creative Labs Forums

Although Creative Labs (U.S.) doesn't yet support a forum on CompuServe, there's a Sound Blaster area in the Pacific Vendor (PACVEN) forum, intended for New Zealand, Australia, and users thereabouts, that's supported by a Creative Labs Pacific Rim distributor. So far, this has been a good source for downloading the latest drivers and software fixes.

A message posted on CompuServe on October 6, 1993, indicated that as of October 5 an official Creative Labs forum on CompuServe was created. Creative Technology (Singapore) acquired Westpoint Creative, formerly their distributor in the United Kingdom. Their forum (WESTPOINT) is currently situated in the UK Computing area, but it will be moving to a general area and will be renamed in the coming months.

Joining CompuServe

You can obtain a sign-up kit by contacting member sales at (800) 848-8199. The most popular pricing plan, the standard pricing plan, includes unlimited connect time (at up to 14,400 bps) to a set of core services such as e-mail, stock quotes, shopping, encyclopedias, and entertainment/game areas. Gaining access to forums, which are the heart and soul of CompuServe, and other "extended" services is a pay-as-you-go proposition. At 1,200 and 2,400 bps, this costs $8 per hour; at 9,600 and 14,400 bps the cost is $16 per hour. If you have a fast modem, it's best to browse at 2,400 bps and then download at your top speed of 9,600 or 14,400.

CompuServe can provide you with either a DOS or a Windows software program called the CompuServe Information Manager (CIM), which isolates you from the cryptic CompuServe commands. The DOS version of CIM is loaded with features but is quite clunky. If you run Microsoft Windows you should obtain CompuServe's Windows version of CompuServe Information Manager (WinCIM) or order a third-party CIM. To obtain WinCIM go to the WinCIM forum (type **GO WINCIM**) and download the program. To obtain a third-party CIM look for advertisements in the *CompuServe* magazine (a glossy *paper* magazine) that's automatically mailed to CompuServe members.

AMERICA ONLINE

America Online is the third biggest online service (CompuServe and Prodigy occupying the number 1 and 2 spots, respectively) and reportedly the fastest growing, having added more than 100,000 customers in the last six months of 1993. When you join America Online you're provided at no charge with a nicely crafted software program, possibly the most nimble among the major online services, for navigating your way around their service. You'll find plenty of files to download (30,000 public domain software programs) and lots of computing advise from experts, including more than 100 hardware and software makers.

You'll find plenty of music and Sound Blaster–related files on America Online. You can start your search in the PC Music and Sound Forum (keyword PMU or PCMUSIC). The Music and Sound Utilities section is loaded with demonstration, shareware, and freeware programs for sound cards in the Sound Blaster family. Check out the Music & Sound section for files to download. The MIDI area has over 1100 entries including the always-popular Monster Mash (MNSTRMSH.MID). The Sound Blaster section is stuffed with music files, primarily CMF files, but there are over 400 VOC files too. After CompuServe, this is probably your best source for shareware and freeware Sound Blaster programs. The other part of the Music & Sound section has over 1200 files, most of which are MOD files. Before downloading check whether your MOD player uses the standard four-channel MOD music or the 669-format files. There are lots of Apple Macintosh music files as well.

Also note that the PC Music and Sound Forum has a message area where you can post your sound hardware/software questions and read what others are doing with their Sound Blasters. Through the message area, you can make friends with Sound Blaster users all around the world as well as get help from industry experts and even some of the authors of this book.

The Windows Music and Sound area has over 2500 WAV digital audio files. Check out the Windows Shareware 500 library, a library of WAV digital audio files that is also available from a book of the same title.

The major drawback to America Online at this time is the relatively slow 2400-bps access. America Online claims it'll have 9600-bps access by the time this book rolls off the press.

TIP: *America Online provides a Chat area where you can type back and forth with other users while online. If you have problems doing something on the system or can't find what you're looking for, go to the Chat area and look for any user with the word "Guide" in their name (for example, GuidePR). Such users can provide invaluable help and are very friendly.*

Joining America Online

You can order a free membership kit, which includes ten free hours online to check out America Online, by calling (800) 827-6364. You'll receive a disk with a program that automatically dials into America Online and sets up an account for you. Once it finishes its preparations (which take about 15 to 20 minutes of downloading), you can jump right into America Online. After the first month, you'll be billed $9.95 per month, which includes five free hours each month. Additional connect time is $3.50 per hour.

GENIE

GEnie is the online service provided by the General Electric Information Services division, which caters to home users with entertainment, online game, and hobby interests. Over 150,000 files are available for downloading. GEnie is organized by round tables (RTs) on a topic. The most relevant RTs for Sound Blaster card owners are the Games & Entertainment section of the IBM PC Software RT (go to page M615) and the MIDI & Computer Musicians RT (go to page M430), found in the Leisure area.

The Games & Entertainment area of the IBM PC RT is the place to go on GEnie. It has the usual assortment of sound files, sound utilities, games, and other goodies for Sound Blaster owners. This is the place to be for seeking help on getting your games to work correctly with your Sound Blaster card. There are also programs of interest in the ASP (Association of Shareware Professionals) Shareware section of the IBM PC Software RT.

The MIDI RT, like the MIDI forums on other online services and BBSs, is oriented toward serious MIDI musicians. It organizes MIDI files into Top

40, classical, and similar categories. This round table also marks MIDI files by the hardware type, such as EMU, for which the files were composed. Another potentially interesting area is the Multimedia Desktop Video and VR RT (Virtual Reality RT). The software library in this RT contains dazzling animations, graphics, and sounds, along with a broad selection of utilities for converting all types of multimedia files to the format required by your PC.

An interesting facet of GEnie is its Internet support. There's an Internet RT in the Computing area that provides access to many Internet resources, such as Internet utility programs and documentation on how to use the Internet. While GEnie doesn't provide a full gateway to the Internet at this time, you can send a *subscribe* message to an Internet news group. The subscribe message will register you with a news group, ensuring that you automatically receive Internet news just as if you had a regular Internet account. This access to Internet news provides much of the benefit of the Internet at no additional cost to you (unless reading the 100 news groups messages a day causes you to exceed the four hours of free connect time allowed each month!).

Joining GEnie

Call (800) 638-9636 to listen to a recording explaining how to sign up with GEnie. The monthly fee of $8.95 includes four hours of connect time at 2400 bps each month. Additional connect time costs $3 per hour. There is a surcharge of $9.50 per hour for prime time access (8 A.M. to 6 P.M. Monday through Friday). There is also a surcharge of $6 per hour for 9600-bps access. If dialing into an online service is a toll call for you because you're outside of a metropolitan area, you're in luck. GEnie has a free 800 number for your use.

Once you join GEnie you should download Aladdin (it takes about 20 minutes at 2400 bps), a freeware DOS program that makes it easy to interact with GEnie. By January 1994 there will be a freeware Windows version as well.

THE INTERNET

I f you're technically inclined or have very esoteric interests, and you feel you've already exhausted the Creative Labs BBS, CompuServe, Genie, and America Online, you're ready to tap into the mother of all networks: the Internet. The Internet isn't the ideal source for downloading sound files or making new BBS friends. Rather, the Internet shines as a truly international source for news and very specific questions on state-of-the-art topics. For sound card owners, this means you read through the message traffic where technical gurus exchange information on how to get their sound cards working in new environments, such as Windows NT and OS/2 2.1, or share details on file formats or even more esoteric topics.

The Internet is fundamentally different from CompuServe, America Online, GEnie and the typical BBS service where the information is essentially stored in one big computer. The Internet is a voluntary association of networks comprising hundreds of thousands of computers. With the Internet, popular files and news messages are copied and forwarded to other Internet nodes throughout the world. News messages fall into any of more than 4,500 news groups to which you can subscribe. When you subscribe to a news group, you'll get a steady flow of news—as many as 50 to 100 messages per day—into your mail box. You'll probably find many of the most frequently requested files on your service provider's computer, but if the one you want isn't there, you can perform a search across the Internet network using special Internet utility programs. Once located, you can do a cost-free file transfer.

The Internet has already become the heralded "information highway," the artery through which "cross-community mail" (an Internet term) flows between different networks. For example, two of the authors have their primary e-mail account on CompuServe yet exchange messages with associates who have mail accounts on America Online and the Microsoft corporate mail system. This cross-community mail flow occurs because both America Online and Microsoft's mail system are connected to the Internet.

The Internet had a much different origin than did the online services. The Internet was started over 20 years ago by the U.S. Department of Defense Advanced Research Projects Agency (ARPA) network that connected military and civilian research centers, both in the United States and overseas. It has proven to be an amazing success story in the crossover of military technology to the civilian sector. The technology was picked up by the U.S. National Science Foundation for connecting a handful of supercomputer centers. Since then the Internet has mushroomed, becoming without question the biggest worldwide computer network.

The Defense Department designed a *peer-to-peer network* (a democratic network in which every computer can talk to every other computer as a peer) to meet the military goal of ensuring survivability in the face of catastrophe. This open architecture in turn has fostered explosive growth. The Internet is now so popular that it's available to most students attending a four-year university or college program in the U.S. In addition, it has already expanded to 137 countries (it's very popular in the former Soviet Union) and has an estimated 17 *million* users (all statistics as of September 1993).

TIP: *A detailed discussion of the Internet can easily fill an entire book. An up-to-date source is The* Internet Complete Reference, *by Harley Hahn and Rick Stout, published by Osborne/McGraw-Hill, 1993.*

Where to Look on the Internet

Here are a few places to check on the Internet. For sound programs and audio files, check the news group for sound files at **alt.binaries.sounds.music** and **alt.binaries.sounds.d**. For discussions of music, check out **comp.music**, and for music composition check **rec.music.compose**. Since the Internet is a truly international forum, you'll find a lot of information about Amiga, Commodore, and other machines that are more popular in Europe than in the United States. For discussions specific to the PC, PC sound cards, programs, and files, check **comp.sys.ibm.pc.soundcard**. Sound Blaster programmers should examine **alt.sb.programmer** news group. It has shown a lot of life recently. A new information resource, with its first release on August 22, 1993, is a FAQ (frequently asked questions) document on music file formats found in **comp.sys.ibm.pc.soundcard**. The author, Harald Zappe, is well on his way to constructing a compendium of valuable information.

NOTE: *In addition, be aware that the Internet is not a secure mail system. E-mail is sent as ASCII files that can potentially pass through many computer systems before arriving at its ultimate destination.*

Joining the Internet

To join the Internet as an individual, you sign up with a service provider that provides dial-in access. Books on Internet contain lists of such providers. A few of the major providers with national reach include The Well (Sausalito, California (415) 332-4335), Portal Communications (Cupertino, California (408) 973-9111), and NetCom Online Communications Services (San Jose, California (408) 554-8649).

NetCom in particular is growing rapidly due to its attractive pricing. For a flat monthly fee of $17.50 a month (plus a $20 startup fee), you have unlimited Internet access. You can dial into NetCom with a local call from approximately 20 metropolitan areas.

If you belong to a university or major corporation, you may already have access through your institution. The online services are edging toward becoming Internet providers and some (see the section on GEnie earlier in this appendix) provide more intimate connectivity with the Internet than others.

IMPORTANT ISSUES FOR ONLINE USERS

f you're new to online services, or you've used them for e-mail but not for downloading files, this section will save you time and money.

Gurus, Sysops, and Tech Support from the Person Next Door

The single most valuable facet of an online service is direct access to two groups of people who can really make a difference: the one expert who can take a good guess at solving anything and the 999 other people who've already struggled with—and found the solution to—the problem you're now pondering. By reading through message *threads,* each a chain of messages on a single topic, you can find out what the problems and issues are *before* you get stuck. You can download new drivers and software patches to correct an existing problem, get technical advice on how to change your software or hardware setup to work around a problem, or at least be reassured that you're not crazy and there really is a complication. If you're so unlucky as to become the first person to encounter a problem, you can achieve temporary folk hero status by being the first to report it online!

A few words of advice on how to get help on the online service. First, you need to locate the appropriate forum. For example, if you're having problems getting your game software to work with your sound card, you should find out if the game software company has a forum on the online service; if not, locate a game forum. Next, before posting your question on the board, scan through the message threads to see if your problem and its solution have already been described. If you're not certain which forum is best for posting your message, feel free to inquire with the system operators (sysops) in charge of the forum. They are happy to guide you to the correct forum and, quite frequently, will provide you with an answer to your question.

Viruses

The commercial online services exert centralized control over the operation of the service including virus checking and posting of new file submissions. As a consequence, you're unlikely to catch a virus by downloading a program file. The situation with local BBSs is quite different. There's no way to know whether the files are checked at all, much less how carefully they're checked, so the adage "better safe than sorry" really rings true for your local BBS. The situation with Internet is somewhat murky. In theory, the system administrators check submissions, but in an environment that's a hacker's heaven, open to millions of users worldwide, you'd better be extra cautious when downloading files from unfamiliar sources.

TIP: *There's virtually no risk in downloading data files, like a MIDI file, or electronic messages, since viruses can only be stashed away in program files—files that when run are given a temporarily life of their own.*

NOTE: *If you're simply calling an online service or BBS to browse, read mail, chat, and use any available services, your computer won't be vulnerable to a virus attack. Viruses are caught by downloading an infected program and running it on your machine.*

9600 Versus 2400

Many sound and music files are quite large, perhaps the better part of a megabyte (1 million bytes) in size, and can seemingly take forever to download at 2400 bps. Check the file size before you initiate a download. Should you elect to download a large file, you'll probably discover that downloading at 9600 bps is worth the extra connect surcharge that many online services charge. You download approximately four times faster at 9600 than you do at 2400 bps. Some services, such as CompuServe, now provide 14,400-bps access too.

Modem Protocol

If you're planning to repeatedly download large files, it's worth the effort to identify the optimal communications protocol (like ZMODEM or Kermit) for your combination of modem communication rate, information provider, and communications software package. For example, when downloading from CompuServe you'll probably get the best overall performance by using CompuServe's own communications protocol. For other services, when downloading at 9600 or higher, it's best to use one of the newer, high-performance protocols such as ZMODEM that provide much faster data throughput (more bytes per minute at a given modem bps rate) than a classic protocol like XMODEM, which dates back to the days of 300- and 1200-bps modems only.

File Decompression

Most files posted on online services are compressed so you can download them more quickly and at less expense. The most popular program for files posted on online service and BBSs is the shareware program PKZIP/PKUNZIP by PKWARE (2.04G was the latest version as this book went to press). You can recognize these files by their .ZIP file extension. The next most popular program, which is frequently used for software installation disks, is the freeware program LHA (formerly LHARC) by Haruyasu Yoshizaki. It's recognized by its .LZH file extension or, as a self-unzipping (self-decompressing) file, by its .EXE file extension. These programs can be downloaded from virtually any online service.

Copyright Issues

If the digital audio recording you've downloaded from an online service contains sound from a popular movie or TV show, be aware that it's probably copyrighted information that's not supposed to be floating around in the public domain. So far, the media owners and online services have winked at this, since it doesn't really damage their business; but as multimedia takes off and these small snippets of recognizable sound grow in commercial value, there may be a crackdown. As long as you limit your use of these sound snippets to personal use, there's no problem. It wouldn't be a good idea to incorporate these sound samples into a business presentation, especially one delivered to Hollywood studio moguls, or to include these snippets with software you distribute within your company or sell. If you do need sounds for business presentations, you can buy sound and music libraries specifically designed for commercial re-use and distribution.

MIDI Files

You need to be aware that most of the MIDI files posted on the online services are intended for high-end MIDI equipment capable of 10 or 16 channels of MIDI music. These music files may not play at all, or may play incorrectly, on the base-level synthesizer (four channels) built in to every card in the Sound Blaster family. However, these MIDI files should play fine on the Sound Blaster 16's Wave Blaster synthesizer.

Apple Macintosh Music Files

The online services and BBSs have tons of Macintosh music files, which may or may not be useful to PC owners. If the files are in Macintosh format, you'll need a utility program like MACSTRIP.ZIP or AOMAC2PC.ZIP (these are the filenames for two utilities on America Online) to strip off the 32-byte file header. The *file header* is an identification at the beginning of a file that's needed by the Macintosh but which isn't needed by the PC. You'll then need to add a file header that your Sound Blaster programs understand. The VOCHDR utility program will attach a VOC file header to raw data, such as a Macintosh file without (or with!) its header. If what you really want is a WAV file, you can then use the WAV2VOC utility to convert from VOC to WAV.

CAUTION: *Be aware that Macintosh files may also be compressed, necessitating use of a Macintosh file-decompression program tool.*

F

Other Creative Labs Products

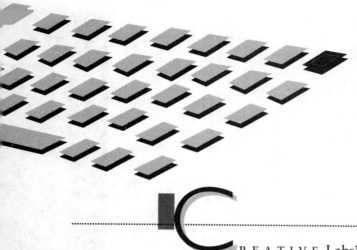

C R E A T I V E Labs' goal is to popularize multimedia by providing multimedia products at affordable prices. Toward that end, Creative Labs designs, produces, and markets not only sound cards for the PC, but also CD-ROM drive upgrade kits for owners of sound cards who are ready to step up to multimedia, and complete multimedia kits that include a sound card, a CD-ROM drive, CD-ROM titles, and speakers. Creative Labs also sells Wave Blaster, a professional-caliber music synthesizer that attaches to Sound Blaster 16. See Chapter 4 for more information on the Wave Blaster and wave-table technology.

Several MIDI kits are offered, some of which provide both hardware and sequencing software for controlling external MIDI equipment. In addition, Creative Labs makes video add-in cards for the PC and Macintosh.

The multimedia kits, Wave Blaster synthesizer, and video add-in cards are described in this appendix. See Chapter 11 for a description of CD-ROM upgrade kits.

Because Creative Labs' product line is growing at a phenomenal rate, this appendix can't be completely up-to-date with respect to the latest offerings. Also be aware that since Creative Labs may freshen the suite of software bundled with its packages, the multimedia titles and other software you receive may be slightly different than that described here. The prices and software bundles described here reflect the Creative Labs October 1993 product list.

MULTIMEDIA KITS

The multimedia kits provide the complete solution for adding multimedia capability to your PC. These kits come with either the 8-bit Sound Blaster Pro or the 16-bit Sound Blaster 16. They include an internally mounted (internal to the PC) Multimedia PC (MPC)–compliant CD-ROM drive, stereo speakers, CD-ROM titles, and the Creative Windows software that's included with the Deluxe cards: Creative WaveStudio, Creative Soundo'LE, Monologue for Windows, Creative Talking Scheduler, Creative Mosaic, and various DOS and Windows sound utilites.

The multimedia kits listed here begin with the entry-level Discovery CD 8 kit and finish with the top-of-the-line DigitalEdge CD multimedia kit. All these kits require an IBM-compatible 386SX or faster computer running Microsoft Windows 3.1, with at least 4MB of system RAM and a super-VGA display card capable of 640×480-pixel resolution with 256 colors.

Discovery CD 8 (Retail Price: $549.95)

This multimedia kit is the economical entry-level solution for educational use. It's based on the industry-standard Sound Blaster Pro Deluxe, which is compatible with all popular game and educational software. Its MPC Level 1–compatible CD-ROM drive (150 kilobytes per second) can play Kodak Photo CDs (only the first session of a multisession Photo CD) using third-party software.

Discovery CD 8 includes four true multimedia titles, not just old-fashioned software shoved onto a CD-ROM. These titles include Brøderbund's Just Grandma and Me, the first in Brøderbund's Living Books collection; the famous Where in the World is Carmen Sandiego? Deluxe Edition, which supplements the original version of Carmen Sandiego with photographic images and traditional folk music from around the world; the Software Toolworks Multimedia Encyclopedia, with motion video, animations, and high-quality audio; and The San Diego Zoo Presents...The Animals, a breakthrough CD-ROM that lets you see and hear more than 200 exotic mammals, birds, and reptiles.

Discovery CD 16 (Retail Price: $649.95)

Discovery CD 16 is a big jump up in capability from Discovery CD 8. It's designed to address the needs of an audience interested in both education and entertainment. You move from the 8-bit Sound Blaster Pro to the 16-bit Sound Blaster 16. The CD-ROM drive is upgraded to an MPC Level 2–compatible double-speed (300 K/sec) drive with a 64K buffer that provides fast access to your CD-ROM discs. This CD-ROM drive is fully CD-ROM XA ready and Kodak Photo CD (multisession) compatible.

This multimedia kit is bundled with the same best-selling educational software provided with Discovery CD 8 plus Aldus PhotoStyler SE, a powerful and versatile Windows program for color image processing. You can have fun or do serious graphic art production with PhotoStyler SE, modifying, enhancing, and adding special effects to color images.

Since this kit is based on the Sound Blaster 16, you can upgrade your MIDI capability by adding the professional-caliber Wave Blaster synthesizer. In addition, the Advanced Signal Processor upgrade boosts overall system performance by providing hardware-based digital audio compression and decompression. These upgrades are described in more detail in their own section later in this appendix.

Edutainment CD 16 (Retail Price: $749.95)

Edutainment CD 16 differs from Discovery CD 16 only in the suite of multimedia titles. This Edutainment kit, true to its name, is stuffed full of both education and entertainment software. It offers, in common with Discovery CD 8, The Software Toolworks Multimedia Encyclopedia and Aldus PhotoStyler. In addition, this kit has the following games: Sherlock Holmes, Consulting Detective, which contains 90 minutes of digitized video; Lemmings, a game of skill. The CD also has three offerings from Lucasfilm Games: Secret Weapons of the Luftwaffe, a World War II air combat simulation from Lucasfilm Games; The Secret of Monkey Island, an adventure game with great audio CD music and graphics; and Indianapolis 500, the Simulation.

DigitalEdge CD (Retail Price: $999.95)

The DigitalEdge CD multimedia kit, shown in Figure F-1, was put together by Creative Labs for anyone who wants a no-compromise MPC Level 2 multimedia upgrade. It includes the same sound card—the Sound Blaster 16—as the Discovery CD 16 and Edutainment CD 16 but with the Advanced Signal Processing upgrade for real-time hardware compression and decompression and QSOUND sound processing. In addition, it includes a microphone and Creative VoiceAssist speech recognition software for controlling your computer with voice commands.

The DigitalEdge CD kit contains a top-of-the-line selection of multimedia production- and business-oriented CD-ROM titles. The multimedia production software includes Macromedia Action!, the industry-standard software for creating stunning presentations and self-running demonstrations that combine animation, video, and sound; the Authorware Star computer-based training (CBT) package for easy creation of training materials; and Aldus PhotoStyler SE.

The business software includes Microsoft Bookshelf, an extensive reference library for Windows including a dictionary, a thesaurus, an encyclope-

FIGURE F-1.

DigitalEdge CD

MPC Level 2

multimedia kit

features the

Sound Blaster 16

Advanced Signal

Processing card,

a double-speed

CD-ROM drive,

microphone,

speakers, and

library of

professional

multimedia

software

dia, an atlas, and a book of quotations. You also receive The Software Toolworks Multimedia Encyclopedia. If there are any gaps in your collection of business productivity software, it'll be filled by Microsoft Works for Windows, a multimedia version of the well-regarded productivity package that combines a word processor, spreadsheet, database, and drawing program.

MIDI HARDWARE AND SOFTWARE

Every Sound Blaster card has a built-in FM synthesizer and software, such as FM Organ, that plays music on this synthesizer. If you're serious about MIDI music, there's a range of accessories you can buy. Foremost is Wave Blaster, a high-end MIDI sound module (synthesizer) that attaches directly to Sound Blaster 16. When you buy Wave Blaster, you also receive Cakewalk Apprentice for Windows MIDI sequencing software. If you need to attach an external keyboard synthesizer or sound module to your PC, you'll need to buy a MIDI upgrade kit to get the necessary cabling or a MIDI Connector box.

MIDI Upgrade Kits

These upgrade kits are designed to connect an external keyboard, synthesizer, sound module, or other MIDI equipment to your PC.

MIDI Adapter (Retail Price: $24.95)

This is the least expensive way to connect MIDI equipment to your PC. It consists of a cable, which plugs into the Joystick/MIDI connector of your sound card. The other end of the cable has one MIDI In connector and one MIDI Out connector that plugs into a keyboard synthesizer or other MIDI device. The MIDI Adapter also has a joystick connector so that you don't lose the functionality of the joystick port. If you already have MIDI sequencing software such as SP Sequencer Pro or Cakewalk Apprentice, and you need to connect a keyboard synthesizer to your PC, this is the kit to buy.

MIDI Adapter with Cakewalk (Retail Price: $79.95)

This kit is identical to the MIDI Adapter kit except for the addition of the Cakewalk Apprentice for Windows MIDI sequencing software. If you have a keyboard synthesizer but haven't yet invested in MIDI sequencing software, you'll want to buy this upgrade kit.

MIDI Box (Retail Price: $79.95)

This kit consists of a MIDI Connector box that plugs into the sound card's Joystick/MIDI connector. The MIDI Connector box has a joystick connector that substitutes for the one taken over by the MIDI Connector box cable. The box also has several MIDI sockets for attaching MIDI equipment. The primary advantage of the MIDI box over the MIDI cable provided in the less expensive MIDI Adapter kit is that you get one MIDI In socket, one MIDI Thru socket, and four MIDI Out sockets for connecting multiple MIDI devices.

MIDI Connector Box with Cakewalk (Retail Price: $129.95)

This kit is identical to the MIDI Box upgrade except for the addition of the Cakewalk Apprentice MIDI sequencing software. If you didn't buy Wave

Blaster (which includes Cakewalk Apprentice), and you don't already have sequencing software with a modern, graphical user interface, this is the upgrade kit to buy.

Wave Blaster MIDI Synthesizer (Retail Price: $249.95)

Wave Blaster, shown in Figure F-2, is the ideal MIDI companion for the Sound Blaster 16 line of 16-bit sound cards. Wave Blaster delivers professional-quality stereo synthesized music, the same as expensive high-end MIDI synthesizers and sound modules, without the high-end price. Wave Blaster is ideal for any situation where you use MIDI, from a multimedia business presentation to a garage jam session.

Following the acquision of E-mu, Creative Labs repackaged E-mu's synthesizer, creating a tiny daughterboard, a small circuit card that's easily mounted on any version of the Sound Blaster 16—you just pop it into place. Wave Blaster is based on E-mu's wave-table synthesis technology, discussed in Chapter 1. You can choose to play 32 simultaneous voices from among 213 CD-quality (44.1-kHz sampling rate) digitally recorded instrument and special-effect sounds. To achieve instant access to these sounds, the Wave Blaster stores the sounds and waveforms in 4MB of read-only memory (ROM).

Wave Blaster is compatible with MIDI music standards for the Multimedia PC as well as General MIDI, the music world's standard for synthesized

FIGURE F-2

Wave Blaster daughterboard adds a General MIDI sampled-wave music synthesizer to the Sound Blaster 16

music. By emulating the MT32 MIDI mapping, you can play, without modification, MIDI songs composed for the popular MT32 synthesizer. The broad repertoire of sounds, including 128 instrument presets (patches), 18 drum kits, and 50 sound effects, is sure to guarantee the right ambience for any music setting, from a jazz lounge to a hard rock concert. The Wave Blaster Control Panel software makes it easy to configure the Wave Blaster with your choice of presets and to store this configuration to disk for quick recall.

Cakewalk Apprentice for Windows

The highly rated Cakewalk Apprentice for Windows, a user-friendly MIDI sequencer, is bundled with Wave Blaster. It's the ideal software for music composition, preparation of multimedia audio tracks, and just having fun. You can view notes on the screen, in the familiar staff notation, as they're played. You examine and edit MIDI notes in your choice of format: staff notation, piano roll, or MIDI event list. You can also use Cakewalk to control an external MIDI synthesizer connected to the Joystick/MIDI connector, as well as record from a MIDI keyboard. Cakewalk also allows you to use wave files for sound effects in your MIDI files.

OTHER SOUND CARD PRODUCTS

The following products are hardware and software upgrades for the Sound Blaster line of sound cards. In addition, Creative Labs sells speakers custom designed for the PC desktop environment.

Hardware Upgrade

Sound Blaster 16 owners who do a lot of work with digital audio and want to give their computer a performance boost would be well served by the Advanced Signal Processor upgrade.

Advanced Signal Processor (Retail Price: $69.95)

The Advanced Signal Processor upgrade kit will enhance the performance of the Sound Blaster 16 to match that of a Sound Blaster 16 Advanced Signal Processing sound card. The kit contains a digital signal processing chip, which is easy to install on your Sound Blaster 16. This chip speeds up your computing by taking on the task of compression and decompression or QSound processing, tasks that would otherwise be handled by your computer's CPU chip.

Software Upgrade

Speech recognition is among the most exciting software developments today, and Creative Labs offers a software and microphone package that works with any card in the Sound Blaster family.

VoiceAssist (Retail Price: $69.95)

VoiceAssist for Windows, shown in Figure F-3, adds speech recognition and speech command and control to your Microsoft Windows environment. The VoiceAssist package includes a dynamic microphone and the VoiceAssist for Windows software. This package is bundled with several of the Sound Blaster 16 sound cards and with the Sound Blaster DigitalEdge CD multimedia kit. If your sound card package or multimedia kit lacks VoiceAssist, this is the upgrade kit to buy. VoiceAssist works with any sound card supported by the Windows environment, including the Sound Blaster, Sound Blaster Pro, and Sound Blaster 16, as well as sound cards made by other companies. You'll need at least a 386SX/25-MHz computer for satisfactory performance.

FIGURE F-3
VoiceAssist speech recognition-package controls Microsoft Windows programs

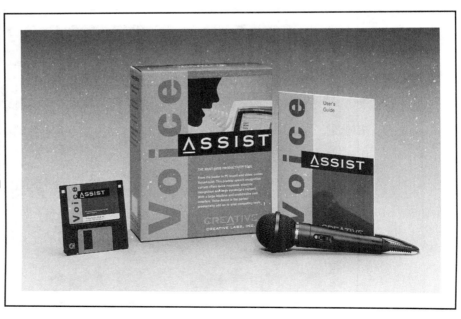

Speakers

Chapter 11 features speakers from a variety of vendors that match any budget. Creative Labs also sells speakers priced in the low- to mid-range.

SBS300 (Retail Price: $149.95)

This high-tech speaker system, shown in Figure F-4, is the latest offering from Creative Labs. These speakers provide high-quality sound reproduction over a wide range of frequencies. The bass response is particularly noteworthy since most desktop speakers are seriously lacking in the low frequencies. The speakers are magnetically shielded so that you can place them next to your monitor or computer without compromising sound quality or disrupting your equipment. Power is provided by the included 14-volt DC power supply so you can really pump up the volume.

CT-38 (Retail Price: $59.95)

These are the same speakers included with the DigitalEdge CD multimedia kit. Their outstanding characteristic is a switch that enables DXBB circuitry for boosting the bass sound. The CT-38 speakers can be used without power amplification, but it's best to power them. They can be powered by either a 6-volt DC external power supply or four standard C-size flashlight batteries.

FIGURE F-4

The new SBS300 speakers with high-tech styling

CDR Speakers (Retail Price: $29.95)

These Labtec powered speakers nicely complement inexpensive Sound Blaster cards. You can optionally buy an external DC power supply or run these on flashlight batteries.

PC VIDEO PRODUCTS

Creative Labs offers two video capture (video-to-VGA) add-in cards and one video output card (VGA-to-video) for PC owners. In addition, Creative Labs offers a video conferencing package for the Apple Macintosh, described near the end of this appendix.

The video capture cards provide everything you need to easily capture and compress digital video from your camcorder, video-cassette recorder, laser disc, cable TV box, or any other NTSC, PAL, or SECAM (VideoSpigot only) source—faster than ever, and using less disk space. You can compress videos on your PC in real time at 30 frames per second (fps) in a 320ö240-pixel window (VideoSpigot) or at 15 fps in a 640ö480-pixel window (Video Blaster).

Video capture cards, such as Video Blaster and VideoSpigot for Windows, are used to produce motion video sequences on your desktop. Video sequences are used for video presentations, interactive training, and still-frame capture for desktop publishing. You can even use object linking and embedding (OLE) to add sizzle to your multimedia presentations, spreadsheets, and documents by embedding an audio/video interlaced (AVI) file. Depending on which add-in card you select, you can capture video at either 15 fps or 30 fps. At 30 fps you're capturing *full-motion* video, the same full-speed video you see on television.

The two video capture cards, Video Blaster and VideoSpigot for Windows, are sufficiently similar to cause confusion between the two. The similarities are that both capture analog video from a variety of sources and save it to disk in a digital form. Once saved, you can edit and play back the video sequence on your PC's VGA monitor using the included Microsoft's Video for Windows software. Video capture requires a fast machine, preferably a 486DX or better, and at least 8 megabytes of system RAM. To play video on a television screen or save it on a video cassette recorder, you'll need a signal decoder box such as the Creative TVCoder, which is described in this appendix.

The next two sections describe Video Blaster and VideoSpigot for Windows and articulate their differences. Both products combine software and hardware (the video add-in card) to capture and process live video. Where they fundamentally differ is that the Video Blaster solution places a greater emphasis on *hardware,* which in general provides higher performance.

Video Blaster (Retail Price: $499.95)

Video Blaster, pictured in Figure F-5, captures video at the standard full-screen VGA resolution of 640×480 pixels at 15 fps and can play back video that's scalable from full-screen to icon size. With powerful capabilities built in to the video card hardware, you can watch a video image as it's captured to disk. You can even watch television in a window onscreen while you work in other windows. Video Blaster can do video overlays, of text and graphics, on top of the video, and has a resizable, movable window. The major drawback to Video Blaster is that it requires a VGA display card with a feature connector (available with ISA cards but not local bus cards). Video Blaster has a built-in audio capability including an audio mixer, but use of Video for Windows software requires that you use a Sound Blaster or similar sound card to provide digital audio playback and recording.

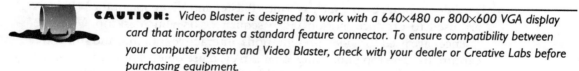

CAUTION: *Video Blaster is designed to work with a 640×480 or 800×600 VGA display card that incorporates a standard feature connector. To ensure compatibility between your computer system and Video Blaster, check with your dealer or Creative Labs before purchasing equipment.*

VideoSpigot for Windows (Retail Price: $399.95)

VideoSpigot for Windows, pictured in Figure F-6, captures video at up to 30 fps (if your system has enough horsepower and memory) and is best suited for digital video production. It has a maximum resolution of 320×240 pixels, so video playback is limited to a window (usually one-quarter of the full size) on the screen. Since VideoSpigot for Windows does not have the video overlay feature of the Video Blaster, you can't watch a television image in a window. As you capture video, you're limited to a preview mode with a low-resolution image. Another disadvantage is that you can't lay graphics and text over the video. The advantages are that you don't need to use a VGA card with a feature connector and you can use as much of your

FIGURE F-5

Video Blaster captures full-screen VGA-resolution video, does graphics and text overlays, and shows live television in a window

computer's RAM as you have to manipulate the video in your software. You do need a Sound Blaster or similar sound card for audio.

FIGURE F-6

VideoSpigot for Windows is the low-cost solution for capturing full-motion video

Creative TVCoder (Retail Price: $199.95)

Creative TVCoder is a VGA-to-Video signal decoder that provides inexpensive color video output. With Creative TVCoder, anything you see on your PC's VGA screen can be simultaneously displayed on a regular TV or recorded on a video-cassette recorder. You can combine and output pictures, text, graphics, and animations, making TVCoder the ideal tool for producing product demonstrations, company profiles presentations, and training materials. By combining Creative TVCoder with the Video Blaster, you have a cost-effective multimedia production system right at your desk.

MACINTOSH VIDEO CONFERENCING PRODUCTS

The video conferencing products, ShareView 300 and ShareView 3000, were developed by ShareVision, now a subsidiary of Creative Technology, Ltd. Although you're undoubtedly an owner of an IBM PC, we'll briefly describe Creative Labs' Macintosh video products in anticipation of Creative Labs introduction of similar products for the PC. At the November 1993 Comdex computer show in Las Vegas, Creative demonstrated a prototype of an upcoming video-conferencing product for the IBM-PC–compatible world. The prototype's capabilities closely resemble those of ShareView 300 described in the section that follows.

NOTE: *The ShareView 300 was formerly called the ShareView, while the ShareView 3000 was previously known as the ShareView Plus.*

When you hear the term *video conferencing,* the images of teleconferencing shown on television, courtesy of the long distance phone companies like AT&T, Sprint, and MCI, probably come to mind. These advertisements depict groups of people surrounding a conference table, fixated on a big-screen television displaying live video of a presenter or another group. Creative Labs' video-conferencing product is a more personal type of product, better described as a *desktop visual communication system.* The idea is for two individuals to sit down in front of their respective Macintosh computers, across town or even across the world, and use ShareView and an ordinary telephone line to collaborate on a project. With ShareView, you chat on the phone while you jointly view and revise documents on the

Macintosh screen. You can use all of your favorite Macintosh software. A shared whiteboard, similar to one in a lecture hall or conference room, makes it easy to communicate your point by drawing and pointing. And although Creative doesn't advertise ShareView as such, it's the ideal product for *telecommuting*—working at home or at a remote site and communicating with your office brethren over the telephone. As this book goes to press, ShareView is the only desktop video-conferencing product that can operate over normal telephone lines; all others products need special high-speed communications connections such as ISDN.

ShareView 300 (Retail Price: $999)

The ShareView 300 system includes everything you need to communicate with another ShareView 300 or ShareView 3000 owner: ShareVision's Onsight software, a hands-free headset, a communications card (not a Sound Blaster family card) with a 14,400-bps fax-modem built in, and cables. An upgrade kit is available so that you can start with ShareView 300 and later upgrade to the capabilities of ShareView 3000.

ShareView 3000 (Retail Price: $3,999)

With the addition of the color video camera and video board included with ShareView 3000, you can add live video images of the video conference participants. The sharing of expressions, gestures, and nonverbal, visual nuances enhances communication and simulates the effect of an in-person meeting. You'll need one NuBus slot for the ShareView 3000 card and a second slot for the accompanying video compression/decompression (CODEC) upgrade card.

TIP: *If you already own a video camera, you should purchase the ShareView 3000 NC, which is identical to the ShareView 3000 except for "no camera." Its retail price is $3,499.*

G

Using the Software Included with the Book

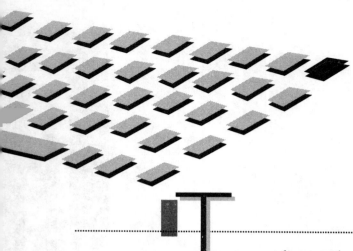

THIS appendix provides installation instructions and helpful information about the software provided on the disk that accompanies this Book. The disk contains a carefully selected suite of software aimed at complimenting the software you received with your sound card. On this disk you'll find software for both DOS and Microsoft Windows.

Each software program is succinctly described in its own section. An exception is the extensive keystroke tutorial provided for VoiceAssist that complements the descriptive introduction to VoiceAssist provided in Chapter 7. For additional help on the Windows programs, see the Windows Help file associated with the particular program. A summary of the disk contents follows.

VOICEASSIST   Speech command and control of the computer is a hot topic now, and you've probably heard of Creative VoiceAssist, described in Chapter 7. With this software and microphone package you can add speech control over any computer that has a Sound Blaster card and runs Microsoft Windows. If you haven't already bought the upgrade package, you're in for a lot of fun experimenting with the working demonstration version included with this book.

DUAL MODULE PLAYER   Dual Module Player (DMP) from Otto Chrons of Finland is rated among the best MOD music file players. Through the use of digitized instrument samples stored along with notes in a MOD music file, DMP plays nice-sounding synthesized music—better in quality than is possible using MIDI JukeBox or another MIDI player program that pipes music through your sound card's FM synthesizer. DMP can be played at the DOS command line or from a DOS session (DOS compatibility box) under Microsoft Windows. Several MOD files, including a famous classical music one called CANON.MOD, are provided.

DUAL MODULE PLAYER COMPANION Dual Module Player Companion (DMPC) is a "front-end" that makes using DMP a snap. DMP is designed to be run by typing a command at the DOS command prompt. DMPC shields you from this, providing easy control over DMP. DMPC includes a file manager for locating and selecting MOD files to play. It'll search through archive files, such as PKZIP ZIP, LHarc LZH, and Robert Jung's ARJ archives, showing you MOD files embedded in these. Should you select an archived file to play, DMPC will automatically decompress it, play the file, and then delete the decompressed copy from the temporary directory.

GOLDWAVE GoldWave is a digital audio editor that runs under Microsoft Windows. Until the Deluxe version of Sound Blaster and Sound Blaster Pro was shipped, Sound Blaster owners lacked a modern, Windows–based digital audio editor. With this in mind, the authors have included GoldWave on the disk that accompanies this book. GoldWave manipulates WAV and many other digital audio file formats and is capable of powerful transformations such as echoes, pans, reversal, and generation of custom waveforms. Many of the capabilities of GoldWave exceed that of Creative WaveStudio, such as the ability to automatically convert sample rate and sample size when copying and pasting across file formats.

PROGRAMMER SOURCE CODE Also included on the disk is a ready-to-run DOS program that plays CMF, MID, and VOC files. This program is intended as a working sample for programmers in Borland C who would like to learn how to program their sound card. Additional ready-to-compile source code examples in C, Turbo Pascal, and Quick Basic are provided in the \SBBOOK\SOURCE directory. Please refer to Chapter 12 for more information.

OTHER GOODIES ON THE DISK The sample Cakewalk Apprentice for Windows music file, SWINGER.WRK (featured in Chapter 8) is found in \SBBOOK\CAKEWALK.

DISK INSTALLATION

You need about 3.5MB (3 1/2 million bytes) of available space on your hard drive to install all of the software from the disk that accompanies this book. The installation process creates a directory called \SBBOOK. It then decompresses files on the disk and copies them to subdirectories under \SBBOOK. If you cannot perform the full installation, see the "Partial Installation" section for details on how to select individual programs to install. The installation process also copies all the files for Chapter 12 to your hard disk.

NOTE: *The installation procedure does not change your AUTOEXEC.BAT or CONFIG.SYS file, so you needn't be concerned about making backup copies of these before you begin the installation of the disk. The final installation of the Windows programs will, under your control, create program icons in your Sound Blaster program group. If you like, you can create a Sound Blaster Book program group for these programs. For more background on how to do this, please consult your Microsoft Windows User's Guide.*

Full Installation

To install all the programs, place the disk into your A (or B) floppy drive. Switch to the DOS prompt for that drive by typing **A:** (or **B:**) and press ENTER.

NOTE: *If you're in Microsoft Windows, go to the Program Manager and select Exit from the File menu to return to DOS.*

Now run the INSTALL batch file on the disk, selecting one of the following options:

- To install to hard drive C, type **INSTALL C:** and then press ENTER.
- To install to hard drive D, type **INSTALL D:** and then press ENTER.

NOTE: *You must include the colon (:) after the drive letter.*

After the installation starts, you'll be prompted several times to press any key to continue.

NOTE: *You can prematurely terminate the installation process by pressing CTRL-C (hold down the CTRL key and press C). Then press Y to confirm that you wish to terminate the batch (installation) file.*

If you run only DOS on your machine, then once the installation batch file finishes, you're done with the installation. If you run Microsoft Windows, your next step is to finish the installation of the Windows programs on the disk. The INSTALL batch file displays information on your screen that tells you how to perform the Windows part of the installation. This information can be captured to your printer with a Print Screen command;

however, for your convenience this information is duplicated in the sections that follow.

Creating a Program Group

You're likely to add program icons for the Windows programs to your Sound Blaster program group, but if you wish to create a program group for the programs in this book, follow these instructions. From your Microsoft Windows Program Manager, follow these steps:

1. Select New from the File menu.

2. Select Program Group, and then click OK.

3. Type **Sound Blaster Book** in the Description field.

4. Click OK.

Creating Program Icons

Select the program group (probably your Sound Blaster program group, but maybe a new Sound Blaster Book group) that will be the home for the Windows programs that accompany Sound Blaster: The Official Book. From your Windows Program Manager, make certain that this program group is the currently selected one, the one that has the highlighted window title. From this program group, create program items for each of the files listed below, following these steps:

1. Select New from the File menu.

2. Click OK (program item is already selected).

3. Select Browse. (If you don't see the Browse button, you're in the File Manager.)

4. Navigate to each filename below, double-click them, then click OK:

   \SBBOOK\GOLDWAVE\GOLDWAVE.EXE
   \SBBOOK\VADEMO\V_ASSIST.EXE

Partial Installation

You can install the software onto the hard disk without running the installation program. A partial installation is necessary if you lack 3.5MB of available space on your hard disk.

The file FILELIST.TXT on the disk lists the software provided with the name of the self-extracting file that contains each program. Suppose you want to make a fresh copy of the VoiceAssist demonstration program. It's provided in the self-extracting file VADEMO.EXE.

Let's say you've put the disk into the A drive and you want to copy the files in VADEMO.EXE to your C drive. Follow these instructions:

1. Type **C:** and then press ENTER.

2. Type **A:VADEMO.EXE** and then press ENTER.

   If the \SBBOOK directory doesn't already exist, it will be created automatically. The directory VADEMO, containing Voice Assist, will be created as subdirectory \SBBOOK\VADEMO.

USING THE SOFTWARE

nce the Windows software is installed on your hard drive, you will see the new icons added to your Sound Blaster or Sound Blaster Book program group (shown here for the SB16), with icons for VoiceAssist and GoldWave.

sdiG.1

DUAL MODULE PLAYER

ual Module Player (DMP) by Otto Crons is one of the most adept MOD-type file players around. Figure G-1 shows DMP playing the song "In the Mix," which is provided as file INTHEMIX.MOD on the disk that accompanies this book. DMP supports MOD, STM, NST, AMF, S3M, 669, and MTM format files and can play up to ten tracks of music each with a different note.

TIP: *You'll probably find everything you need to know about DMP here, but if you have further questions about DMP, or the companion product DMPC, which is described in the next section, use a text editor to read the documentation files in the DMP subdirectory. DMP.FAQ contains frequently asked questions and answers about DMP (.FAQ is an Internet convention for an introductory Q&A file), DOC files, and a REV revision file.*

FIGURE G-1

Dual Module Player (DMP)

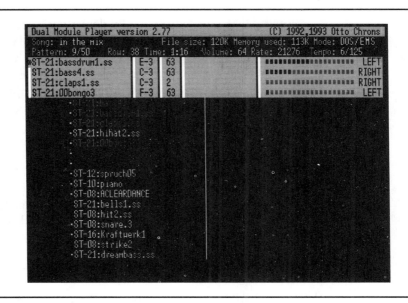

Running DMP

DMP will auto-detect your sound card and its settings by simply running the DMP program followed by the name of the file you want to play. For example,

```
DMP inthemix.mod
```

will play the file INTHEMIX.MOD using default settings. You can also have DMP play several files by using wildcards. For example,

```
DMP *.mod
```

will play all the MOD files in the current directory.

TIP: *If you're listening to the SB16 through unpowered speakers and don't hear much, don't despair. The SB16's default output volume may be too low to easily hear DMP. Use the mixer utilities SB16MIX or SB16SET to turn up the VOC volume. You may also need to crank up the mixer's output gain to 4x or 8x.*

Configuring DMP

Although DMP can automatically detect your sound card's settings, for best results you should configure it for your Sound Blaster. Instead of simply typing the command name followed by the file you want to play, as in the previous examples, you can add parameters to tell DMP the options you want.

Figure G-2 lists the available command-line options for DMP. The following are some examples for various types of Sound Blasters.

```
DMP -c1 -p220 -i5 -d1 -q -l1 inthemix.mod
```

This sets DMP for the Sound Blaster 1.*x*/2.0 (-c1), I/O port 220, interrupt 5, and DMA 1, turns on quality mode, and turns off looping (the repetition of MOD files that were designed to play over and over). Quality mode greatly enhances the clarity of MOD-type files when played on 8-bit cards such as the Sound Blaster 1.*x*/2.0 and Sound Blaster Pro.

```
DMP -c2 -p240 -i7 -d1 -q -s22 inthemix.mod
```

This sets DMP for the Sound Blaster Pro (-c2), I/O port 240, interrupt 7, and DMA 1, turns quality mode on, and sets the playback sampling rate to 22 kHz.

```
DMP -c5 -p220 -i5 -d5 -1 -s44 inthemix.mod
```

This sets DMP for the Sound Blaster 16 (-c5), I/O port 220, interrupt 5, and DMA 5 for 16-bit audio output, turns off looping, and sets the playback sampling rate to 44 kHz.

TIP: *If your machine doesn't play correctly or the sound breaks up, it probably isn't fast enough for the settings you've chosen. Typically, the sampling rate is too high. Use a smaller number for the -s parameter, such as -s11. Also, quality mode requires more CPU computation. Try removing the -q parameter if you still have trouble.*

Instead of typing in these parameters each time, you can also put them into an environment variable by using the SET command in DOS. For the first example above, you'd type

```
SET DMP=-c1 -p220 -i5 -d1 -q -1
```

and press ENTER. Now you can simply type **DMP** followed by the name of the file you want to play and DMP will know what settings to use.

To have this environment variable set every time you start your computer, simply add the line to your AUTOEXEC.BAT file. If you've never done this before, refer to Chapter 1 for instructions on editing DOS files such as AUTOEXEC.BAT.

FIGURE G-2

DMP command-

line options

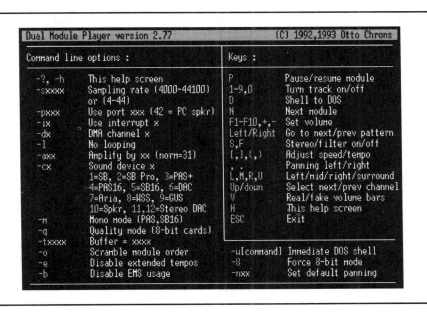

The DMP Screen and Commands

Figure G-1 is a screen shot of DMP. The upper area of the screen is for song information. In addition to the customary program name, version number, and copyright notices, there is the following song-specific information:

- *Song*   The title of the song.

- *File size*   The size of the song file.

- *Memory used*   The actual amount of memory used by the song.

- *Mode*   The environment DMP is running under. This will be DOS or Windows. When running under DOS, the Mode will also show EMS (expanded memory) if DMP is using EMS.

- *Pattern*   MOD-type files are made up of blocks of notes that are referred to as *patterns* in DMP. This shows the current block number over the total number of blocks in the song. The right and left arrow keys go to the next and previous pattern number, respectively.

- *Row*   The beat number within the current block. MOD-type files usually have 64 beats (0 to 3F in hexadecimal) per block.

- *Time*   The elapsed time in minutes and seconds since the current song started playing. Note that the time is not relative to the position in the song file. If you skip around in the song, the time will simply continue counting regardless of where you are in the song.

- *Volume*   This is the master volume control for DMP. The value ranges from 0 to 64. Function keys F1 through F10 pick among 10 predefined volume settings. The "+" and "−" keys change the volume incrementally. Note that doing this does not change the mixer volume on the Sound Blaster Pro and Sound Blaster 16.

- *Rate*   The sampling rate used for playback. This is set with the -s command-line parameter. Higher sampling rates require faster computers but produce cleaner sound.

- *Tempo*   The first number is the playback speed. Decreasing this value speeds up the playback. The second number is the tempo. It is similar to the speed but changes the playback rate in finer steps. Larger tempo values speed up the playback. The opening and closing brackets, [and], increase and decrease the speed, respectively. The opening and closing braces, { and }, decrease and increase the tempo, respectively.

Below the song information is the track status area. This displays all the tracks that are playing in the current song. The MOD variety of MOD-type files has four tracks so you'll see four lines in the track status area. Other file formats can support more than four tracks and you'll see more than four lines when playing those files. For example, an S3M file can contain up to 10 tracks, and DMP will assign a track for each one. The function of the six fields for each track are as follows:

- *Instrument name*   The name of the instrument that is currently playing on the track.

- *Note value*   Displays the note being played. It is made up of the note name, a letter from A to G, possibly a sharp or flat symbol, and the note's octave number.

- *Volume*   This is the volume for the track. Each track can have its own volume level. Do not confuse this with the overall volume shown in the song information area.

- *Command name*   MOD and other file formats support special commands such as vibrato, slide, and portamento. When DMP performs these commands, they are displayed here. Note that not all MOD-type players support these commands, so if you've been using a different player, your files may sound different now that they are being played correctly.

- *VU meter*   Graphically displays the volume of notes played on the track. You can select between real and fake volume display by pressing V (on the keyboard). DMP doesn't show you which mode you're in, but if all the volumes look pretty high, then you're in fake mode.

  The meter will display the word "MUTE" when you press the number key for that particular track. Press the same number key again to turn the track back on. For example, pressing 3 will mute track 3.

- *Pan*   This is the placement of the track within the stereo field. It only applies to the Sound Blaster Pro and Sound Blaster 16, which support stereo. To select a track for the Pan command, use the UP ARROW and DOWN ARROW keys. Pressing L and R will set the track to the left or right speaker, respectively. Pressing M will set the track to the middle. You can also use the comma (,) and period (.) keys to position the track from –60 (left) to 60 (right) in single steps. Pressing U will set the track into surround mode, which simply makes it sound like stereo from both speakers.

The bottom area of the screen lists all the instruments stored in the song file. Many MOD-type song writers use this area to display messages, copyright notices, and so forth rather than the names of the instruments they use.

Beside each instrument name you will see a dot if the instrument has been played at least once since the beginning of the song. Also, when each instrument is played, you will see the track number to the left of the instrument's name.

Other DMP Commands

H	Help.
P	Pause/Resume.
S	Stereo mode on/off.
F	Output filtering on/off.
N	Skips to next module. Only works if you use wildcards in the file specification.
D	Shell to DOS. Enjoy great music while working on your computer! Be aware that MOD files can take up quite a lot of memory. You may not have enough to run your application after shelling out to DOS. Run the MEM command to see how much memory you have free.

NOTE: *If you use DMP to shell to DOS or run DMP in a DOS box under Windows, you may hear the music skip or stutter. This is not a DMP program bug but is rather a consequence of running multiple applications at the same time. You don't normally notice this with other applications because they spend much of their time idle. DMP, on the other hand, plays music, and your brain can be very sensitive to disruptions in the rhythm.*

The DMP Initialization File

DMP has an initialization file named DMP.INI that contains default sound card configuration information as well as screen color parameters that you can customize to your taste. The file can be edited with a text editor, and instructions for the settings are detailed inside the file.

DSMI Developer Kit

If you're as impressed as we are with the performance and sound quality of DMP and would like to have this capability in your own programs, you'll want to check out the Digital Sound and Music Interface (DSMI), also by Otto Crons. DSMI is a library of sound routines for C and Turbo Pascal.

These are the same routines used to make DMP and its protected mode cousin PMP.

DMP far exceeds all other other module players because it's based on the DMSI Developer's Kit. This kit supports play of up to 32 channels at once, including the simultaneous play of music tracks and sound effects (and in stereo on cards that support stereo sound)! The kit is available for $70 (U.S. dollars) and includes full documentation (printed), object files and libraries for the C version, TPUs for Turbo Pascal, and also most of the source code so you can modify the behavior of DSMI.

Write to

> Otto Chrons
> Pyydyspolku 5
> SF-36200 Kangasala
> FINLAND

Or via Internet:

`c142092@cc.tut.fi`

DMP COMPANION

The DMP Companion (DMPC) by Brad Meier is an extension to DMP and makes playing MOD-type files much easier. The DMPC logo screen, which flashes before your eyes for a split-second only, is shown in Figure G-3. With DMPC, you can tag files from a list and play them in any sequence, including random order.

Running DMPC

Simply type **DMPC** at the DOS prompt and press ENTER. You will see the file scroll window, as shown in Figure G-4. DMPC lists the filename, song name, and size of all the MOD-type files in the directory and the names of subdirectories, if any. If you have any MOD-type files in ZIP, LZH, or ARJ format archives, DMPC will display the files contained in the archives as well. Now you can compress all those huge song files into archives and still play them! A great space saver.

FIGURE G-3

DMP Companion

logo screen

■

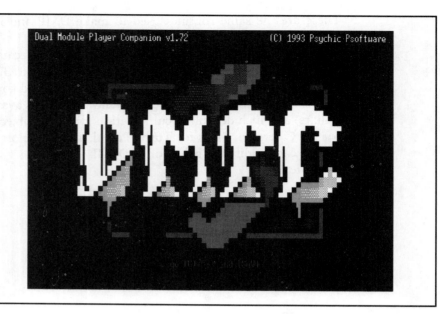

DMPC Commands

H	Help.
UP/DOWN ARROWS	Moves the highlight up and down.
ENTER *	When a directory is highlighted, pressing the ENTER key will change to that directory. When a file is highlighted, pressing ENTER will play the file.
C	Change to a different drive.
SPACEBAR	Tag/untag a file for playback. You can tag as many files as exist in the directory in any order you wish. DMPC will place a number next to the file showing the file's placement in the playback queue.
T/U	Tag/Untag all files.
S/L	Save/Load list of tagged files.
P	Play tagged files.
R	Play tagged files in random order.
D	Delete the highlighted file. Handy for killing those occasionally garbled files from bulletin boards.
Number keys	Select a sound card configuration. DMPC supports up to ten different sound card configurations. See the next section for a list of the included configurations.

* Pressing ENTER with the highlight on the ".." directory name will take you to the parent directory, i.e., the directory one level higher than the current one. The "." directory is the current directory. Pressing ENTER on this one won't do anything.

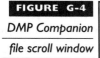

FIGURE G-4

DMP Companion

file scroll window

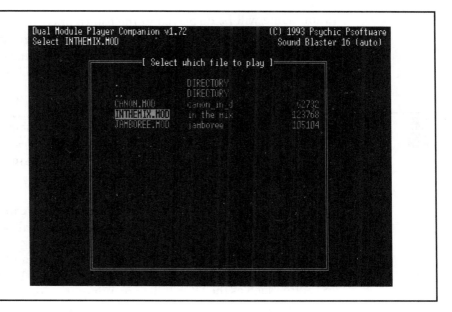

DMPC Configuration File

DMPC comes with a configuration file, DMPC.CFG, that holds configuration options for up to ten different sound card setups and multiple player programs. The DMPC.CFG file included on this disk has the following configurations for your convenience.

Configuration Number	Settings
1 Sound Blaster (auto)	SB 1.*x*/2.0 auto detect
2 Sound Blaster Pro (auto)	SB Pro auto detect
3 Sound Blaster 16 (auto)	SB16 auto detect
4 SB (P220, I5, D1)	SB 1.*x*/2.0 at I/O port 220, IRQ 5, DMA 1, quality mode on
5 SB Pro (P220, I5, D1)	SB Pro at I/O port 220, IRQ 5, DMA 1, quality mode on
6 SB 16 (P220, I5, D5)	SB16 at I/O port 220, IRQ 5, DMA 5 for 16-bit audio
7 SB (P220, I7, D1)	SB 1.*x*/2.0 at I/O port 220, IRQ 7, DMA 1, quality mode on
8 SB Pro (P220, I7, D1)	SB Pro at I/O port 220, IRQ 7, DMA 1, quality mode on
9 SB (auto, no q)	SB 1.*x*/2.0 auto detect, quality mode off
0 SB Pro (auto, no q)	SB Pro auto detect, quality mode off

Select the configuration that's most appropriate for your sound card by pressing the number key that corresponds to it. Once selected, the configuration name will be displayed in the top-right corner of the DMPC screen. The first configuration above is the default configuration when you run DMPC. This is also the configuration likely to produce music on all Sound Blaster cards, although it may not be the optimal choice for your specific card.

NOTE: *If you select an incorrect configuration, you'll probably hear nothing and your computer may lock up, requiring that you reboot and try another configuration choice. Before rebooting, make certain that the volume control dial on your sound card is set for maximum volume.*

Configurations 9 and 0 are provided so that you can compare the sound difference between having quality mode off and quality mode on (configurations 1, 2, 4, 5, 7, 8).

If your sound card is set to a different I/O port address, IRQ, or DMA than the ones listed above, you will need to edit the DMPC.CFG file. Use a text editor such as the DOS Editor or Windows Notepad to accomplish this. Below is a sample of a configuration entry in DMPC.CFG.

```
SB (P220, I5, D1)
-p220 -i5 -d1 -1 -c1 -q -8
MSF3N6
DMP.EXE
```

The first line is the configuration name that is displayed on the DMPC screen. The second line contains the parameters that are passed to DMP. The third line lists the file formats supported by this version of DMPC and DMP. The fourth line lists the player program to be used—DMP in this case.

If you changed your sound card to I/O port 240 and IRQ 3, you'd change the second line to

```
-p240 -i3 -d1 -1 -c1 -q -8
```

NOTE: *The parameters for DMP are described in the section "Dual Module Player" earlier in this appendix.*

Updating the Configuration File

If you forget to specificy a configuration, DMPC will default to the first entry in the configuration file, choice #1, the Sound Blaster (auto) choice.

Once you've identified the best configuration for your sound card, you should move that configuraton to the beginning of the DMPC configuration file. That way, the correct configuration will become the default and you won't have to be bothered in the future by specifying the correct entry.

VOICEASSIST DEMO

The keystroke tutorial provided here is equally applicable to both the unrestricted retail version of VoiceAssist and the demonstration version provided on the disk that accompanies this Book. You'll find additional tips and an explanation of VoiceAssist in Chapter 7. Among these are tips for how to best handle the microphone and explanations for each element of the VoiceAssist window and dialog boxes. This tutorial will skip much of this detail and focus on moving you through the product as quickly as possible. For further clarification or to see screens depicting VoiceAssist, refer to "Understanding Speech Recognition" in Chapter 7.

TIP: *At the end of the speech recognition section of Chapter 7 are troubleshooting hints relevant to the VoiceAssist demonstration program.*

Limitations of the Demonstration Package

The demonstration package is a scaled-down but capable version of the full VoiceAssist package. The limitations are outlined in Table G-1

Version	Demonstration	Retail
Number of users	1	256
Number of applications	2	30
Commands per application	20	992
Number of commands at one time	52	1024
User-defined commands	Yes	Yes
Automatic extraction of menu commands	Up to 18	Yes

TABLE G-1 *Comparison of the unrestricted retail package with the demonstration version.* ■

As you can see from the table, the chief limitations are that you can have only one user file at a time; this file can contain commands for two applications (perhaps Creative Talking Scheduler and Lotus 1-2-3 for Windows) and there can be up to 20 commands of your choice for each of these two applications. For example, you can have 20 commands for Talking Scheduler, including "what's happening," which selects Appointments,Review from Talking Scheduler's menu.

NOTE: *You're probably more interested in the capabilities of the unrestricted retail version of VoiceAssist, so we'll refer to these in the discussion of VoiceAssist that follows. On occasion, as you're running through the tutorial, the limitations of the demonstration product will be mentioned so you won't be surprised if you bump into these restrictions while experimenting.*

Installing the VoiceAssist Demonstration Program

1. Start Windows.

2. While in the Program Manager, switch to the Sound Blaster, Sound Blaster Pro, or Sound Blaster 16 program group. If you don't have one of these groups, or you'd like to place the VoiceAssist icon in another program group such as Accessories, switch to that group.

NOTE: *If you recently bought the SB16 that includes VoiceAssist, you can use it instead of the demo version. The icon for VoiceAssist will already be in your Sound Blaster 16 program group.*

3. From the Program Manager, select File,New.

4. In the New Program Object dialog box, select Program Item and then click OK.

5. In the Program Item Properties dialog box, enter **VoiceAssist Demo** in the Description box. Then enter **C:\SBBOOK\VADEMO\V_ASSIST.EXE** in the Command Line box.

NOTE: *If you installed the Sound Blaster disk onto a driver other than C, substitute that drive letter in the Command Line box. For example, if you installed the disk onto drive D, the Command Line box should contain the following: D:\SBBOOK\VADEMO\V_ASSIST.EXE.*

6. Click the OK button.

When the installation is completed, an icon for VoiceAssist will appear in the program group you selected.

Setting Up the Mixer

If you have a Sound Blaster Pro or Sound Blaster 16, you must check that the Windows mixer is set correctly before you proceed to use VoiceAssist. If the microphone volume is inadequate, you won't be able to create accurate voice templates for command recognition. Check the following:

■ Microphone must be selected as a recording source. For the SB16 the mixer's recording settings should display a dot by the microphone. For the SB Pro, the source setting should be microphone.

■ Microphone volume levels must be set at the usual or higher than usual settings. The microphone volume slide and the master volume slide should be at least two-thirds maximum volume.

■ For the SB16 only, set the microphone gain to either 4x or 8x. Also, make sure that you don't have music coming into the MIDI, CD, or line inputs. VoiceAssist will think that they are part of the voice commands.

Run VoiceAssist

The first step is to run VoiceAssist and ensure that its setup is correct for this tutorial. When VoiceAssist is running, you'll see the main window shown in Figure G-5.

TIP: *If you find the VoiceAssist main window to be in the way, put it elsewhere by dragging with your mouse.*

1. Double-click on the VoiceAssist icon. You'll see a pester box that reminds you of the limitations of this demonstration product. Click OK to move on to the next step.

   The VoiceAssist main window—which looks like a bar running across the top of the screen—should appear. The menu button, which provides access to VoiceAssist menu options, indicates which window is currently active. Since you just launched VoiceAssist, the button says "V_ASSIST."

2. You'll now double-check that VoiceAssist is set up to stay on top of the other windows. Click the menu button and select Options.

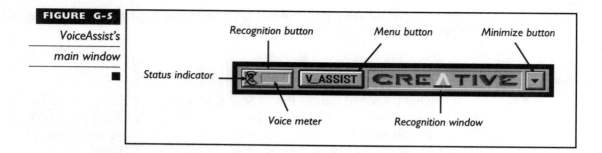

In the Options dialog box ensure that there's a check mark before Always on Top. If not, click there and then click OK to close the Options dialog box.

OnLine Help

Both versions of VoiceAssist share the same on-line help screens. Press F1 or select Help from VoiceAssist's main menu. Users of the demonstration version must keep in mind that some of the capabilities described in the help screens don't apply to their version of VoiceAssist.

Adding a User

VoiceAssist is customizable for individual users, so before you can do anything else you must create a user file. All the voice patterns and command instructions will be stored in this user file. With the retail version of VoiceAssist, up to 256 users can have their own user file. With the demonstration version, there can be only one user file. The following steps create a new user:

1. Click the menu button and select User. The User & Application Files window appears.

2. Click the New button. Enter your name (up to 8 characters) or initials and then click OK.

3. Click the New button to create a new user.

4. Click Close to close the User & Application Files dialog box.

TIP: *If you have the retail version of VoiceAssist, you can save time and effort by copying one of the previously prepared Generic user templates. People with relatively high-pitched voices, including most children, are advised to use GENFMALE. People with deeper voices*

should use GENMALE. For the purposes of this tutorial, you'll be better able to follow this tutorial by sticking to the instructions provided here for creating a new template.

Rerunning the Tutorial

If you're running the demonstration version and you'd like to start from scratch, you'll need to delete the current user file.

1. Click the menu button. Then select User.

2. Click the Delete button (there are two Delete buttons; click the one on the far left) and confirm the deletion.

3. Click the New button to create a new user.

4. Click the Close button to close the User & Application Files dialog box.

Train the Generic Command Set

VoiceAssist comes out of the box with 32 generic commands. These include keystroke commands such as TAB, ESC, and ENTER; Window navigation commands such as Next Window, Close, and Task List; and Window menu commands such as Maximize and Restore. These commands can be used for basic control of all applications, not just the applications added to the user file. In addition, at the end of the generic command list you'll see eight generic command "slots" that contain the names of applications that you launch by saying their names. When you create a new user you'll see commands for Clock, Calculator, Calendar, File Manager, and four other familiar applications that come with every copy of Microsoft Windows.

VoiceAssist already knows how to execute the generic commands like Down and Close, so you don't need to show it how to execute these actions. Later on in this tutorial, in the section "Adding Custom Commands," you'll add new commands. VoiceAssist was programmed in the software factory to execute the generic commands, but you'll have to tell it how to execute these custom commands. You'll show VoiceAssist what to do in a process called *macro recording*.

Although VoiceAssist knows how to execute these 32 generic commands, it must be trained to recognize your voice before they can be used. This will take only one or two minutes, since VoiceAssist can be trained with just a single utterance for each command.

1. Click the menu button. Then select Training. The Training dialog box appears.

2. Click the Generic Commands item at the top of the list to ensure that you'll begin to train from the top of the list. Click All to display the Voice Training dialog box, which prompts you word by word. The option titled "New" should have an arrow by it; if not, click it.

3. Click OK to begin training. Soon—after you've read the note below—you'll say each word that's displayed until you've finished the generic command list. The last command that you need to train is "Win Write." If VoiceAssist prompts you with yet another command (probably File, the first menu item for Program Manager and many other programs), click Cancel to cease training.

NOTE: *Before you begin training by clicking the OK button, you should see an ear above the button with a red X. When you click the button, the ear is replaced with a color bar volume meter that shows the strength of your voice when you speak. This should momentarily fill with green (and possibly some red) when you speak. If you don't see a prominent flash of color when you speak, you won't be successful in recording the voice templates. See the suggestions in "Optimizing Recognition Accuracy" in Chapter 7 and the notes in "Setting Up the Mixer" earlier in this appendix. SB Pro and SB16 owners must have their mixer set for recording from the microphone with a strong gain setting.*

4. Click Save to save the voice template recordings to your user file.

CAUTION: *You could click Close and then confirm that you wish to save but this isn't the recommended procedure. There are circumstances where VoiceAssist doesn't prompt you to save.*

5. Click Close to close the VoiceAssist training dialog box.

Test Recognition Accuracy

With VoiceAssist you can easily test the robustness of your voice templates and, if necessary, rerecord selected commands. In this exercise you will test two commands: Clock and Close.

1. Click the menu button. Then select Training. The Training dialog box appears.

2. Click Test and repeatedly say "Close" and "Clock" with a short pause between words. VoiceAssist will either recognize the command, displaying the command name, or state "Not

recognized." You can experiment by saying the commands faster or slower and with a higher or lower pitch to see how readily VoiceAssist would recognize your command if your voice changed due to a sore throat or the excitement of an action game.

TIP: *For successful command recognition, it's important to hold the microphone in the same position that you used for training and to speak with approximately the same volume. Also, be sure that the red X doesn't appear over the ear when saying a word.*

3. When you've finished testing, click the Disable button. Now click Close to close the training dialog box.

Retrain Selected Words

In this exercise you'll rerecord two commands, Clock and Close, to ensure the highest accuracy possible. Although VoiceAssist does an excellent job with a single utterance, you'll make multiple utterances per command to create a superior quality voice template.

1. Click the menu button. Then select Training. The Training dialog box appears.

2. Click the Close command, the topmost of the generic commands. Now click the Single button.

3. When the Training dialog box appears, click the UPARROW twice to increase the number of training prompts to three. Now click OK and say the word "Close" three times with a short pause between repetitions.

4. Repeat steps 2 and 3, this time for the command "Clock."

5. Click the Test button to test for successful recognition of Clock and Close. You should discover that VoiceAssist, armed with additional samples of your voice, has become more skillful in recognizing these commands. Click Disable when you have finished testing.

6. Click Save and then Close to close the Training dialog box.

Test Command and Control

Now you're ready to take over control of your PC by voice command. You'll display the Clock and then close it.

1. Activate VoiceAssist by clicking the Recognition button. Upon selection, a colored-bar voice meter will appear as you speak.

2. Say the word "Clock." The Clock application, from the Accessories group, should appear. Note how the title bar of the active window on your desktop—the Clock—is highlighted. The VoiceAssist menu button also says "CLOCK," another indicator for which window is the currently active window. All VoiceAssist commands are directed toward the active window, so if you issue a command like "File Open," this is the window that will be affected.

3. Now close the active window (the Clock) by saying "Close."

4. Try several other commands that you trained. For example, "Task List" shows all the programs currently running. If you don't remember which commands are available, select the VoiceAssist menu button and select Training to see the list. Training an Application's Menu Commands

You can train up to 30 applications (2 in the VoiceAssist demonstration program) with up to 992 commands for each (up to 20 for the demo). When VoiceAssist loads an application (like Clock or Program Manager), VoiceAssist automatically extracts the list of menu commands from the application, tacking them onto the end of the command list in the training window. The commands for the first 30 applications (2 for the demo) that are trained will become part of your user file. You can train these commands, add additional commands to this set of menu commands, and record new actions for either set of commands.

This exercise will feature the Clock application to demonstrate the automatic extraction of commands and their training:

NOTE: *If you select the Clock's No Title menu option, you'll lose control over the clock. You can restore the title bar and access to the menus by double-clicking anywhere on the Clock window.*

1. Examine the clock menu commands. Activate VoiceAssist by clicking the Recognition button. Now say "Clock" to bring up the Clock application. Click the menu button (which now says "Clock"), select Training, and scroll down to the end. You'll see the "CLOCK commands" header followed by the list of Clock menu commands. You'll see "Settings," the only entry in the Clock

main menu, followed by an indented set of menu items, the menu items that fall under Settings. Click on the Clock title bar and then select the Settings main menu choice. Compare the menu choices that you see here with the list shown in VoiceAssist.

2. Train the clock menu commands. Click Untr (which stands for "untrained") in the Training dialog window and run through the Clock menu commands. If you've already trained all the generic commands, the only commands still untrained are the Clock ones.

3. When you have finished training, click Save and Close.

TIP: *When you click the Save button, VoiceAssist will save in your user file the updated voice templates for the Clock menu. If you're running the demonstration version of VoiceAssist, this application becomes one of only two that you can maintain in your user file. Fortunately, the generic commands, such as Close and Enter, are trained and available for all applications. To see for yourself that Clock has been assigned to your user file, click the VoiceAssist menu button and then select User to see the list of Included Apps. Click Close to move on to step 4.*

4. Try out your ability to control the Clock application by going through the menus step by step. If the menu button doesn't currently show "CLOCK" say "clock" to launch the Clock or, if it's already running, to switch to the Clock window. Then say "Settings" to display the Clock Settings menu. Now toggle the Clock display between digital and analog. If the Settings menu displays a check by Digital, say "Analog." If the Settings menu displays a check by Analog, say "Digital." If you're having recognition difficulty, retrain these commands.

5. Directly execute a low-level menu command. In step 4 you gave the commands Settings,Digital (or Settings,Analog). As a shortcut, VoiceAssist is capable of proceeding through a series of menu commands when you utter just the lowest level one. For example, if you say "Digital" VoiceAssist will match your utterance against "digital" in the command list, and then give the Settings menu command followed by the Digital menu command. This eliminates the need for recording most menu command sequences, such as was done in step 4.

TIP: *You may want to rename the low-level menu command and give it a more meaningful name. For example, you could rename "Analog" to be "Show Analog" and train this*

*command to respond to the utterance "show analog." The action, which is
Settings, Analog, is unaffected by this change.*

Deleting an Application

If you're running the demonstration version and can't click the Save
button in the Training window, that's because you've already reached the
limit of two applications that can be trained and saved. To add another
application, you'll have to delete the VoiceAssist commands for one of these
applications from your user file. To delete an application's commands:

1. Click the menu button and select User to view the User &
   Application Files dialog box.

2. Click the application you wish to remove (perhaps Program
   Manager was inadvertantly added).

3. Click the Remove button.

Add Custom Commands

You can add custom commands to your applications that complement
the menu commands that VoiceAssist automatically adds when you're
running a program. Custom commands are added by recording a series of
steps, either keystrokes or mouse movements or a combination of both, as
you execute the steps. If you've ever used the Windows macro recorder or
created a Lotus 1-2-3 or other spreadsheet macro, you're already familiar
with how this works.

In this example, you'll toggle the Clock display between the normal
display with the date and seconds flashing to a simpler display that features
time only:

1. Launch Clock if you haven't already done so. Change the clock
   display to digital by saying "Digital."

2. Click the menu button and then select Training. Click the Add
   button. A dialog box appears. Type **Toggle Digital** and click OK.
   The dialog box disappears. At the bottom of the command list, at
   the end of the CLOCK commands, you'll see this new entry.

3. Train the Toggle Digital command. Click Toggle Digital to
   highlight it and then click Single to train just this one command.

4. Now begin the macro recording sequence that executes the Toggle Digital command. Toggle Digital should still be highlighted. Click the Action button. The Recording Options dialog box appears. Leave the default settings as they are, and click the Start button to begin macro recording. You'll now see the VoiceAssist icon with the flashing message "Press Pause," which reminds you to press the PAUSE key (the same key is also labeled with BREAK) when you've finished recording.

5. Record the Clock menu actions. Using the keyboard only (VoiceAssist's Recording Options were set for keyboard recording only), press ALT to activate the menus and then press S twice (for Settings,Seconds). Now press ALT again and then press S followed by T (for Settings,Date). Press the PAUSE key. A "Stop Recording" dialog box appears. Click OK to save this action. The Toggle Digital command is now trained. In the Training window, select Save followed by Close.

6. Test your new command. Go to the Clock application and manually change the display by selecting Settings,Analog. Now say "Toggle digital" and watch the Clock display change.

Change the Launch Applications

The generic command list includes the names of eight applications, including Clock, that can be launched by saying their name. You can change these commands to launch applications of your choice. In this exercise you'll customize VoiceAssist to launch the Creative MIDI Jukebox instead of the infrequently accessed Cardfile application that's found in the Accessories group.

NOTE: *There's no necessary connection between the applications you train (up to 30 for the retail product; up to 2 for the demo product) and the eight applications that can be launched by generic commands. However, it's likely that you'll choose to launch by voice applications for which you have voice commands.*

1. Click the menu button. Then select Training. The Training dialog box appears.

2. Change from Cardfile to MIDI JukeBox. Go to the bottom of the generic command list. Click the Cardfile command to highlight it, and then click Action. The Run Command dialog box appears.

Type **MIDI JukeBox** into the Application Name field. Type the full path to the Jukebox into the Command line field:

Sound Blaster Version	Path to MIDI JukeBox Program
SB 1.x/2.0	C:\SB\WINAPPL\MMJBOX.EXE
SB Pro	C:\SBPRO\WINAPPL\MMJBOX.EXE
SB16	C:\SB16\WINAPPL\MMJBOX.EXE

NOTE: *Be careful to add the correct drive letter, path, and filename. VoiceAssist doesn't check whether you entered correct information into the Command line field. If you make a mistake, you'll discover only later, when you give the spoken command, that you made some type of error in the command line. You'll see a message box stating "File Error" or "Cannnot run application" or both if VoiceAssist can't find the program you specified.*

3. Click OK to save this action. You'll be returned to the Training dialog box.

4. Train the MIDI JukeBox command to recognize your voice. Click Single, train it, and then click Save and Close to close the User & Application Files window.

5. Try out your new application launch command. Click the Recognition button to enable VoiceAssist and then launch the MIDI JukeBox by saying "MIDI JukeBox."

6. Either close the MIDI JukeBox by saying "Close" or minimize it to an icon (so it'll still be running on the desktop) by saying "Minimize." If you choose to minimize rather than close, the Clock will appear more quickly the next time you invoke its name since it's already running on the desktop.

TIP: *You can use any spoken utterance up to 2 seconds long for each VoiceAssist command. You can even add commands in other languages. For example, you could rename a generic command that launches MIDI JukeBox to be "ongaku," the Japanese word for music, and train this VoiceAssist command to launch the MIDI JukeBox when you say "ongaku."*

Put VoiceAssist to Sleep

Sometimes you'd like to temporarily disable VoiceAssist, perhaps to talk on the phone without having to worry about VoiceAssist making a mess of your work when you say "Please close the door and help me update the task list...."

1. Say "Go to sleep" to deactivate VoiceAssist. VoiceAssist will now show "Go to sleep" as the last command. The volume meter in the Recognition button will continue to register and you'll see "Sleeping..." as the last command every time you speak. However no action will be taken. You might notice, especially while word processing on a slower machine, that your other programs respond more quickly. This is because VoiceAssist drains only a minimal amount of your computer's computational power while it's sleeping. While sleeping, VoiceAssist has the luxury of checking incoming sounds against just one voice template—"Wake up"—a much less taxing job than checking incoming sounds against up to 991 other commands that are potentially operative at any one time.

2. Say "Wake up" to activate VoiceAssist. Once you see "Wake up," VoiceAssist will be attentive to your other commands.

NOTE: *If VoiceAssist refuses to respond to wake up, you need to first turn it on by clicking the Recognition button.*

Quitting VoiceAssist

Click the menu button and select Exit.

NOTE: *If you're running the demonstration version of VoiceAssist, you've probably already witnessed the irritating pester screen that tells you that "This demo version only allows you to save 2 applications." Fortunately, you'll see this only when you're training VoiceAssist.*

GOLDWAVE

GoldWave turns any PC running Microsoft Windows into a digital audio workstation (see Figure G-6). GoldWave is packed with great features, such as

- Multiple windows, each containing a digital waveform
- Full 16-bit stereo editing

- Individual left and right channel editing (for the stereo SB Pro and SB16 only)

- A zoom to magnify digital sample detail for precise editing

- A Detachable "Scope and Control" window that consolidates the most important controls like play, record, and volume

- Powerful effects such as echo, pan, volume, and reversal

- The ability to automatically convert sampling rates, bit sample size, and channels when copying and pasting

- Built-in support for a wide range of digital audio file types including WAV, VOC, IFF, AU, and SND, as well as raw digital audio

- An Expression evaluator for real-time creation of sounds

The last three features most clearly distinguish GoldWave from the Creative WaveStudio that's bundled with the SB16, SB Pro Deluxe, and SB Deluxe. Only GoldWave has these features. If you need to mix and match different types of sound file formats, GoldWave is the ideal product for you. Its main deficiency, from the perspective of a Sound Blaster owner, is that it doesn't yet support the 16-bit VOC file format.

FIGURE G-6

GoldWave

playing a wave

file

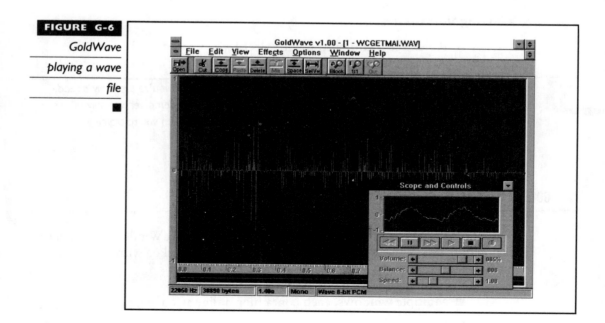

Learning GoldWave

GoldWave is accompanied by an extensive user manual that's provided as a Windows Write document. Look for the file GOLDWAVE.WRI in your \SBBOOK\GOLDWAVE directory. To read GOLDWAVE.WRI, navigate to this file with File Manager and double-click on GOLDWAVE.WRI to run the Windows Write application and open GOLDWAVE.WRI in a single step. You can then print this manual in the usual fashion for documents in Microsoft Windows.

The GoldWave manual is a professional-caliber effort, complete with a table of contents, troubleshooting tips, samples, and a lot of interesting technical explanations. For additional help, you can access GoldWave's extensive set of online help screens.

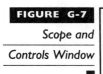

TIP: *For an introduction to the chief features of a digital audio editor, read "Creative WaveStudio" in Chapter 5.*

The GoldWave Screens

To give you a feeling for GoldWave the main screens are shown here. In Figure G-6 you see a waveform that's been loaded into GoldWave (this is a digital audio file provided with WinCIM, the Windows version of the Compuserve Information Manager, that tells you whether there's any mail in your mail box when you dial into CompuServe). This wave file is currently playing, and you can see in the oscilloscope of the Scope and Controls window the part of the waveform that is currently playing. The Scope and Controls window is shown in an expanded view in Figure G-7.

FIGURE G-7

Scope and Controls Window

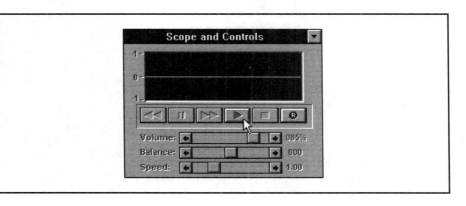

The most important controls are readily accessible. The row of buttons feature the familiar international symbols for play (the button pointed to by the mouse cursor), pause, stop, record, and so forth. The horizontal sliders make it easy to adjust the playback speed, volume, and balance.

In Figure G-8 you see that the Scope and Controls window has been minimized to provide a better view of the waveform. Although only one waveform window is shown, and it has been maximized to fill the screen, you can have many windows open at the same, each with their own waveform. In Figure G-8 you can also see the Effects menu, which provides access to special effects such as echo, fade out, waveform inversion, playback rate change, addition of silence, and waveform amplitude (volume) change.

The last Effects menu item shown in Figure G-8 leads to a feature of GoldWave that's certain to fascinate the technophiles: custom waveforms. Select Expression evaluator to open the Expression Evaluator dialog box, which resembles a calculator loaded with special function buttons, as shown in Figure G-9.

By creating mathematical expressions, you can manipulate an existing sound file as it plays or generate novel ones in real time. The GoldWave user manual provides examples of how to create a square wave, saw tooth (triangular) wave, an exponential decay, a pure tone, and other waveforms.

FIGURE G-8

GoldWave

special effects

menu pulled

down

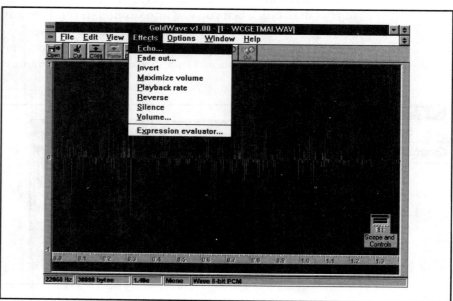

FIGURE G-9

GoldWave

Expression

Evaluator dialog

box

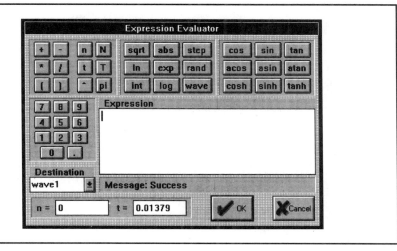

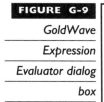

THE SOFTWARE PUBLISHERS

isted in this section are the addresses and phone numbers of the publishers whose products are described in this appendix. Some of the software on this disk is shareware, which means that the publishers ask you to provide a small monetary contribution if you like the product or if you'd like to receive a version that is richer in features. If you've found that a software program has become part of your computer routine, please register the software program. Two of the programs are "cardware"—the authors would be pleased to receive just a postcard.

TIP: *Check the README files in the directories for registration information on these products. Also check the back of the book for money-saving coupons on products from these publishers.*

Otto Chrons (Dual Module Player)
Pyydyspolku 5
SF-36200 Kangasala
FINLAND
Internet: c142902@cc.tut.fi

This is cardware. If you like DMP please send Otto a postcard.

Psychic Psoftware (Dual Module Player Companion)
Brad Meier
8 Jasmay Place
Nahoon Valley
East London
5241
South Africa
Internet: cslm@alpha.ru.ac.za

This is cardware, so, if you enjoy DMPC, the author requests a postcard (or a letter with a picture) of your hometown.

Chris Crain (GoldWave)
P.O. Box 51
St. John's, NF
CANADA A1C 5H5
Internet: chris3@garfield.cs.mun.ca

Standard registration fee is $30 to remove registration messages and unlock future versions.
Deluxe registration fee is $59 to receive the next version, when available, and to receive the password for unlocking future versions.

INDEX

U

V